"This book will become *the* volume that Christian communication scholars pull from their shelves to anchor, reset, and inspire their writing and research for decades to come. Drawing upon the finest thought from legacy thinkers and smartly written by fresh faces and senior scholars alike, readers will find new insight into what it means to apply the mind of Christ to a polarized society in need of peace."

—**L. Ripley Smith**, PhD, Professor of Media Communication, Department Chair, Bethel University

"This beautiful collection of essays is a response to evangelical anti-intellectualism echoed in the Academy. The writers encourage those committed to reshaping the narrative by offering practical, thoughtful ways to engage in Christian scholarship. The voices of prominent Christian intellectuals within these pages are inspiring and convicting, showing us how faith-integrated work can challenge, renew, and even transform the people and institutions that resist it."

—**Diane M. Badzinski**, PhD, Chair and Professor of Communication, Colorado Christian University

"Creative guru Michael Michalko suggests when facing a problem, we should create a Board of Directors whose writings help us think through an issue and overcome challenges. The question raised in this exceptional edited volume is how can our modern universities be saved from a deterioration marked by close-mindedness to and demonization of alternative views? Building off the seminal work of Mark Noll and George Marsden, the editors have assembled a Board of Directors consisting of leading scholars who don't merely critique the Academy but offer unique and hopeful solutions. It is an invaluable resource for anyone concerned about the future of higher education."

—**Tim Muehlhoff**, PhD, Senior Director of Biola University Winsome Conviction Project; author, *End the Stalemate: Move Past Cancel Culture to Meaningful Conversations*

"This book springs from the question of Christian scholarship's place in the Academy and sings with the complex and lovely harmonic participation of a multiplicity of voices in dialogue. Broadly contextualized and brimming with interaction, the essays provide a veritable feast of ideas. The bounty begins with rich contributions from Mark Noll, George Marsden, Richard Mouw, Paul Soukup, Quentin Schultze, Calvin Troup, and Clifford G. Christians, to name just a few. It continues with additional entries that take the form of prayer, poetry, story, and lively discussion. This weighty volume engages the reader on multiple levels, encouraging religious scholars to apprehend faithful scholarly attendance to our Christian heritage, while respecting the gifts and challenges of the great intellectual tradition.

—**Stephanie Bennett**, PhD, Professor of Communication and Media Ecology, Palm Beach Atlantic University

From the
Outrageous
to the
Scandalous

Re-imagining Christian Thinking
and Scholarship in an Age of
Tribalism & Ideological Resentment

From the
Outrageous
to the
Scandalous

Re-imagining Christian Thinking
and Scholarship in an Age of
Tribalism & Ideological Resentment

Edited by
Robert H. Woods Jr. and Mark Allan Steiner

Integratio Press
Pasco, Washington

FROM THE OUTRAGEOUS TO THE SCANDALOUS: Re-imagining Christian Thinking and Scholarship in an Age of Tribalism and Ideological Resentment

This is a publication of Academe, a Division of Integratio Press.

integratiopress.com

Integratio Press is an Imprint of the Christianity and Communication Studies Network.
11503 Easton Dr.
Pasco, WA 99301

www.theccsn.com

Cover design: Carol O'Callaghan
Interior design: Carol O'Callaghan

Cover image: Depositphotos composite

paperback isbn: 978-1-959685-33-3
ebook isbn: 978-1-959685-34-0

Library of Congress Control Number available from the publisher.

For Legacy Scholars—Past, Present, and Future

Opening Unconference Prayer

PAUL D. PATTON

DEAR GOD, with your words you brought light into existence. May we shed a tiny bit of light with our words! You made us in your image, giving us the unique ability within your creation to offer words to redemptively guide, inform, even command and confront. May we be wise in the use of our words.

Lord God, you gave Adam the creative ability to name the animals, a creative process requiring intellectual analysis of comparing and contrasting, thus creating concepts and categories. May we rejoice with vigor in this intellectual process!

May you be honored and glorified in this holy process.

In the name of Jesus of Nazareth, your holy son!

Amen!

A Liturgy for the Knowledge Seekers

Donna M. Elkins

O Father of all knowledge,
We gather in schools and universities,
In offices and classrooms and libraries,
Seeking for truth and to add virtue to our character
Through the intellectual and practical daily work
Done in speaking and writing and reading
And thinking of higher things.

At times the tasks feel heavy and the critiques sting,
And we still seek a way forward,
Not arriving at a Christian worldview,
But striving to be Christian world viewing,
Ever seeking to understand and explain to others,
What we can know and discover about
This fantastical world You have created.

Called to this life of the mind,
Is at times a form of diaspora and lonely toil,
But we know that others have taken similar serious vows,
Commitments to creative teaching and scholarship—
Fellow seekers who both celebrate and critique
The faith handed down to us from
The beginning of time and place.

As we seek, O Father, let us not grow weary,
As we labor, let us not grow disillusioned,
As we write, give us right and uplifting words,
As we read, open our eyes to grace-filled facts,
As we assist others on the knowledge journey,
Let us build virtue alongside them,
Joyed by new ideas and building courage together.

Even in times of weariness or distress,
Grant us to remember that learning is a manifestation
Of Your common grace and participation in Your kingdom
So we do not lose hope in the present or the future,
So we learn well both in our own scholarship search
And through the attempts of our students and colleagues
To open new doors of seeing.

Above all, Father, grant us continued and fueled desire
To see our words on pages that reach others,
To hear Your voice in the way we speak and teach,
To hold to highest standards of truth and character,
No matter what others around us may be lacking,
And give us fire to keep seeking, continually seeking,
Always led forward by Your glorious creation.

Amen

Table of Contents

PART I:
LEGACY SCHOLAR PRESENTATIONS

PART II:
RESPONSES TO OUR LEGACY SCHOLARS

SECTION ONE: FOUNDATIONS
AND HISTORICAL ROOTS

SECTION TWO: REIMAGINING THE UNIVERSITY
AND CHRISTIAN HIGHER EDUCATION

SECTION THREE: COMMUNICATION, PEDAGOGY,
AND INTELLECTUAL FORMATION

TABLE OF CONTENTS

Acknowledgements

GOOD THINKING ABOUT how to practice Christian faith and scholarship in the Academy is a profoundly communal and not individual effort. As such, we are thankful for those who participated in the November 2024 Christianity and Communication Studies (CCSN) unconference out of which this volume has arisen—for their attendance, thoughts, insights, and questions. And, most of all, for the engaging intellectual and spiritual fellowship that they helped to build during and after our gathering. We are also thankful for all the additional voices that joined the "conversation" begun by the November 2024 gathering—for their initiative, creativity, insight, and patience with the process of putting this volume together and giving it a meaningful coherence.

We recognize that our own individual efforts and growth as faith-informed academics were created and sustained by friends and mentors who came alongside and blessed us with their friendship and wise counsel. These friends and mentors include (but are not limited to) Martin Medhurst, Calvin L. Troup, Nate Baxter, Clifford G. Christians, Quentin Schultze, Terry Lindvall, Benson Fraser, William J. Brown, and John Pauley. We owe additional thanks to Mark Noll and George Marsden, the two scholars around which the conversations of this volume are structured. Noll's *Scandal of the Evangelical Mind* and Marsden's *The Outrageous Idea of Christian Scholarship* were (and still are) important guideposts for honest and nuanced thinking about both the function and consequences of the relationships among faith, scholarship, and intellection. But for us, they were lifelines for graduate students struggling to make sense of how to see the "Kingdom value" of research and scholarship in the academic world.

We are glad that those of us who desire to bring the Christian faith fully to bear on our academic work benefit not only from the wise counsel of friends and mentors, but also from those seasoned scholars who have a proven track record of public witness of doing this kind of work. We have not only Noll and Marsden to thank for this, but also the other "legacy" scholars (featured in the unconference and in this volume) who have been faithful over the years (in alphabetical order): Clifford G. Christians, Mark Fackler, Robert S. Fortner, Terry Lindvall, Richard J. Mouw, Quentin Schultze, Fr. Paul A. Soukup, SJ, Greg Spencer, Calvin L. Troup, and Nicholas Wolterstorff. We are also pleased to have the contributions of two additional veteran scholars: J. Matthew Melton, who wrote the Foreword, and Kenneth R. Chase who wrote the Afterword.

We are particularly thankful for the community of teachers and scholars that has invested their labors and their hearts in the work of the CCSN, including but not limited to Geraldine E. Forsberg, Joshua D. Hill, A. Chase Mitchell, Lance Croy, Elaine V. Fung, Brandon Knight, Janie Marie Harden Fritz, Diane M. Badzinski, Mark A. E. Williams, John Hatch, Ken Waters, John R. Katsion, Paul D. Patton, David Enns, and Mark Gring. These fine and gracious scholars and teachers have reminded us continually that doing faithful "Kingdom" work in the academic world is not just a collection of good ideas to be contemplated, but also sustained and mundane labor to be done in community and, often, anonymity.

Finally, we could not have managed to have this volume ready for display at our 2025 unconference in Denver without the commitment of Integratio Press's superb editorial team. A very special thanks to Carol O'Callaghan, Heidi Livingston, and Jessica McFarland for their record-breaking turnaround at every phase of production. Your attention to detail and quality blesses us all.

Foreword

IN MY DOCTORAL PROGRAM under the tutelage of such luminaries as Terry Lindvall and Michael Graves, I signed up for an intensive seminar conducted by Clifford G. Christians, one of the Legacy Scholars identified in this book. My academic mentors had strongly encouraged my participation, so I wasted no time in signing up, given Dr. Christians's outstanding reputation.

It would not be overstating things to say that I felt almost immediately ambushed by the material in the class, and by Dr. Christians himself. The seminar was on Communication and Technology, but Dr. Christians kept talking about things like "distributive justice," a term that got under my skin; and a few of us in the room, after hearing him go on for a while, finally gathered the pluck to ask him if he was using the term in a Marxist sense. He paused, and then said thoughtfully, "In a Christian Marxist sense, maybe."

It was as though a bolt of lightning almost knocked me out of my chair. My formal education before graduate school had consisted largely of the milestones of evangelical "anti-intellectualism" identified by Mark Noll in *The Scandal of the Evangelical Mind*, featured throughout this book.[1] I had grown up in an isolationist, authoritarian evangelical sect in rural Virginia, as a student in a tiny, one-room school subsisting on a steady diet of intensely fundamentalist and nationalist curricula. Outside reading included classics like the spine-chilling *None Dare Call it Treason*, a book from the 1960s that claimed to expose the betrayal of America by socialist atheists.[2] I had then attended a fundamentalist (unaccredited) Bible college in Texas that continued the same pattern, requiring us to wear red, white, and blue six days a week. I was a member of the Creation Research Society, a disciple of Bill Gothard's Institute in Basic Life Principles, and an avid subscriber to the monthly newsletter of the Chalcedon Foundation dedicated to the notion that Christians are called to set up a theocracy in the United States. In other words, like Paul's boast to the Philippians that he was a Hebrew of Hebrews, my street cred among the fringe elements of evangelicalism was second to none.

Staring at Dr. Christians that day, I tried to conjure all the Satanic images that had been fed into my brain about "those people" who seemed to think Marxism was not a "devil term." But I could not. He was soft spoken, gentle, caring, and immensely patient. He explained himself exhaustively in response to my belligerent questioning. I thought I had him cornered when I quoted a facile free-market mantra, that when new technologies put people out of work in one sector, other jobs are created in another. But he just looked at me with the saddest expression of pity that anyone had ever directed my way, and I could not for the life of me understand why he would feel sorry for me. He eviscerated my final paper on Edison's "beneficial" technological innovations, wondering why I had entirely ignored the unjust working conditions in Edison's factories and labs.

In that classroom, Dr. Christians and I were jousting along Martin Buber's uncertain, dialogic "narrow ridge," a dialogic space where uncertainties merge into a meeting with something previously undisclosed.[3] In this case, a young acolyte of entrenched, recycled religiosities along the lines of those described in Mark Noll's book was confronted by a living practitioner of the hopes expressed in George Marsden's *The Outrageous Idea of Christian Scholarship*.[4] Something new did in fact emerge from that meeting.

The happy ending is that Dr. Christians, with the help of readings by Walter Ong, Ivan Illich, and the others that he assigned for the seminar, along with his consistently ethical and humane approach, planted seeds in my scandalized ("trapped" in the Greek sense of the word) mind that bore fruit swiftly. I had, in truth, already broken with much of my misinformed past. But Christians's persistent grace constructed a substantial portion of the foundation upon which much of my own sense of faithfulness in higher education—and beyond—would come to rest. I am deeply grateful to him for his patient endurance.

While I was regrettably not part of the unconference that led directly to the formation of this book, I have been a part of the larger conversation for many years. I count as friends many of those represented in this text. Others are known to me from shared events, conference panels, and restaurant tables, or from presentations, articles, or books. All of us are part of a larger interaction that, like Mortimer Adler's Great Conversation, has been going on for quite some time.[5] Across a great many accumulated discussions and symposia and other academic interchanges, we have learned many truly wonderful things from one another. We have not always agreed. But the dialectic among us has created rich veins of inquiry.

In September 2006, at the very dawn of Facebook, YouTube, and Twitter and more than a decade before Tiktok and ChatGPT, before the threat of toxic misinformation assailing us these days, I gave a talk to a large auditorium full of undergraduates and faculty at a Christian university. It was entitled, "The Medium is the Master: Barbarians of the New Dark Ages" (an unconscious nod to philosopher Alasdair MacIntyre's *After Virtue*).[6] While I do not consider myself a prophet, these words proved to be eerily predictive:

> Every person jacked into the Internet, with or without wires, is now a stockholder in the welfare of the world, a newly empowered member of the kind of community Marshall McLuhan could only dream of. And it is a dream, but to its underbelly clings a nightmare that no one anticipated. Who would have thought that the exponential proliferation of information would have the opposite effect from what was intended? Rather than sharing the rewards of accelerated enlightenment, the glut of knowledge unleashed on the world has turned what was once *important* knowledge into mostly *irrelevant* knowledge. Ideas that were once as precious as gold are now like the little ketchup packets that we collect in desk drawers and minifridges. Worthy ideas that once merited lengthy deliberation and studious contemplation are swallowed whole, digitized, and reconstituted as cute little quotes laid over pastel backgrounds.

> We are awash in a sea of trivia. But far from being a calm sea, the face of the trivial world confronts us every day with newer and more tempestuous manipulations created for our endless amusement by trillion-dollar information conglomerates. The worst of it is that the canon of Civilization, including Homer and Cicero, Aristotle and Augustine, Buddha and Lao Tse, even the Bible, has not been

destroyed as it was in the good old Dark Ages; they haven't been burned with the libraries that housed them. No, they have simply been stored among countless other bytes of data that includes everything from where to get an airline ticket to how to self-treat an ingrown toenail. So rather than dealing with a deep darkness upon which we might shine a light, our problem is more like that of Indiana Jones in the scene from *The Temple of Doom* where a priceless diamond is kicked onto a floor covered with hundreds of pieces of ice. Which is the ice and which the diamond? The Internet unfortunately doesn't come with a pop-up guru to help us discern the gems from the garbage. The Internet is simply there, like a riverbed is there. And where oh where is the digital guide who will help us pan through the gigabytes to find the gold?[7]

In *Orthodoxy*, G. K. Chesterton compared the good in the world to things that have been divinely saved from a cosmic wreck.[8] As Robert H. Woods Jr. and Mark Allan Steiner mention in the Introduction, our discursive sea has become highly toxic. This book performs precisely the salvaging function that is so very needed at this Kairos moment in time. It offers a treasury of sorts, a mosaic in an almost Byzantine iconic sense.

I believe the authors in this text share a common thread of *caritas*, that empathetic love that Saint Augustine argues is the essential ground for the Christian interlocutor in *De Doctrina Cristiana*. Wolterstorff might add to this his terrific conception of *shalom*. This empathetic communal element embraces the Other, sometimes even like Saint Francis embraced the leper, and it guards against a forbidding hermetic tribalism that defines itself by excluding and even driving away.

The question of just how the work and life of Christian scholars can re-imagine and reform a particular part of the world, the world of higher learning, is not given to simple, straightforward answers. The essays in this book embrace the inevitable complexity inherent in the question and provide ample justice to its breadth. The spectrum of contributors is as impressive as it is varied. One would expect a significant showing of thinking practitioners from the fine record of intellectual excellence in the reformed tradition of Abraham Kuyper, and this volume does not disappoint in that regard, but other voices from other intellectual Christian traditions are present as far more than mere tokens. The fine Jesuit tradition of Paul Soukop and the always welcome holy laughter of Terry Lindvall join the conversation. The writers have labored in both public and private institutions, and in each case, they have found ways to remain true to their sense of mission while speaking the truth in love. In every way, what you hold in your hands is a unique collection, almost as much an uncouncil as it is an unconference.

In *After Virtue*, MacIntyre writes, "What matters at this point is the construction of local forms of community within which civility and the intellectual and moral life can be sustained through the new dark ages."[9] Amidst the toxic noise of exploding data and unhinged polarization where lifelong friends are going their separate ways and family members are disowning one another, this collection welcomes the reader to a community of *shalom* and meaningful conversation. We hope you join the dialog.

J. Matthew Melton
Decatur, Georgia

List of Contributors

Abram J. Book (PhD, Regent University) is an Assistant Professor in the Communication Studies and Modern Languages Department at Southeast Missouri State University. He has published articles in *The Journal of Communication & Religion*, *Artifact Analysis*, and the *Kentucky Journal of Communication*. He currently serves on the executive council of the Kentucky Communication Association and is a charter member of the editorial board of *Artifact Analysis*. He lives in Scott City, Missouri, with his wife and three children.

William J. Brown (PhD, University of Southern California) is a Professor and Research Fellow in the School of Communication and the Arts at Regent University in Virginia Beach, Virginia. In addition to his doctorate, he received a BS in Environmental Science from Purdue University, an MA in Communication Management, and an MA in Communication also at the University of Southern California in Los Angeles. His academic research interests include international media, development, and the use of entertainment for social change. Dr. Brown has published extensively in academic journals and books in the field of communication during the past 30 years and has served as a Fulbright Senior Specialist in the Netherlands and Norway. He also is a partner of Brown, Fraser & Associates, an international media research and consulting company that has conducted more than 250 media studies in North America, Central and South America, the Caribbean, Europe, Asia, Africa, and the Middle East. Dr. Brown especially enjoys giving workshops and seminars to media professionals on how to use entertainment media as a catalyst for social change, drawing on more than 40 years of international research and teaching experience.

Dennis D. Cali (PhD, Louisiana State University) is a Professor of Communication at the University of Texas at Tyler. He is the recipient of the Louis Forsdale Award for Outstanding Educator in the Field of Media Ecology; the President's Scholarly Achievement Award at the University of Texas at Tyler; and the Media Ecology Association's Top Paper Award for his essay on "The Sacramental View of Marshall McLuhan, Walter Ong, and James Carey," which appears in the *Explorations in Media Ecology* journal. In 2018 he was named Distinguished Professor of Arts and Sciences. He is also the author of *Mapping Media Ecology: Introduction to the Field* (Peter Lang, 2017), two other books, and numerous scholarly articles in communication journals as well as book chapters in edited volumes and two other books in progress. He teaches in the areas of media ecology, interpersonal communication, rhetorical criticism, political communication, and religious communication. His primary research interest areas are in media ecology and in religious and sacramental communication.

Thomas J. Carmody (PhD, Regent University) currently serves as a Professor of Communication in the Communication Department of the Patty Arvielo School of Business and Management at Vanguard University where he has taught for over 35 years. His research focus ranges from nineteenth-century American sermonic rhetoric, comic books, and graphic novels to Anglican Studies. He is an ordained Anglican priest in the Anglican Church in North American and serves both the diocese of Churches for the Sake of Others (C4SO) and the local parish.

Kenneth R. Chase (PhD, University of Illinois at Urbana-Champaign) is an Associate Professor of Communication at Wheaton College in Illinois. His teaching and research focus on the ethics and theology of rhetoric. He formerly served as Chair of the Communication Department and Vice Chair of the Faculty at Wheaton. He also has served as Director of the Center for Applied Christian Ethics (Wheaton), President of the Religious Communication Association, and Chair of the Communication Ethics Division of the National Communication Association.

Clifford G. Christians (PhD, University of Illinois at Urbana-Champaign) is the past Director of the Institute of Communications Research and Chair of the doctoral program in communications. He has been a visiting scholar in philosophical ethics at Princeton University, a research fellow in social ethics and a visiting scholar at the University of Chicago, and a PEW fellow in ethics at Oxford University. He has a Doctor of Letters Honoris Causa degree from Marquette University and an honorary Doctor of Humane Letters degree from Emerson College. He was a Charles H. Sandage Distinguished Professor, has won six teaching awards, and is a faculty member in the Fulbright Specialist Program. His research is in the philosophy of technology, communication theory, and media ethics. A Festschrift Ethics and Evil in the Public Sphere has been published in his honor. He is a founding member of the International Ethics Roundtables with venues in Stellenbosch, Dubai, Delhi, and Beijing. He has lectured or given papers or taught classes in 35 countries. He is listed in Who's Who in America, Who's Who in the World, International Who's Who in Education, and Outstanding Scholars of the Twenty-first Century: Communication Ethics. The Carl Couch Center for Social and Internet Research offers annually the Clifford G. Christians Ethics Research Award. He has been given academic awards such as these: Ethics Scholar Award (Lambda Pi Eta Honor Society, Duquesne University); the AEJMC Presidential Award for distinguished service and AEJMCs Paul J. Deutschmann Award for Excellence in Research; James A. Jaksa Ethics Scholar in Residence; Ralph Crossman and FIRST Scholar awards (University of Colorado); Fellow at the University of Stellenbosch Institute for Advanced Study; Honor Medal for Distinguished Service in Journalism (University of Missouri); Best Edited Book of the Year (with Lee Wilkins, *Handbook for Media Ethics*); Kappa Tau Alpha Award for Normative Theories of the Media; Distinguished Scholar Award from the National Communication Association; James W. Carey Media Research Award; First Place Faculty Research Paper award (with Stephen Ward, from Media Ethics Division, AEJMC); Louis Forsdale Award as Outstanding Educator in the Field of Media Ecology; Charles Colson Award for Outstanding Contribution to Ethics, Media and Culture; and the Guido H. Stempel III Award for Journalism and Mass Communication Research.

Terri Lynn Cornwell (PhD, University of Maryland) has more than 40 years of experience teaching in public and private schools and universities. She is an administrator at Virginia

University of Lynchburg and served as Legislative Director for the Congressional Arts Caucus in Washington, D.C., and Director of Communications for Cleveland State University's urban college. She is the author of *Democracy and the Arts: The Role of Participation* and a variety of book chapters and articles on communication and the arts and Christianity and communication. She is an ordained Presbyterian (USA) pastor, as well as a Compassion Consortium Animal Chaplain. She and her husband live in Forest, Virginia, with their rescued Ragdoll cat.

Lance Croy (PhD, Southeastern University) is a SAG/AFTRA member who has performed in and produced theatrical, commercial, and industrial film projects. He presented at the University of Michigan's Arts, Sciences, and Letters Conference, the Association for Theatre in Higher Education Symposium, and Regent University's Leadership Roundtable. His peer-reviewed publication on Charles Spurgeon and Followership is in the *Theology of Leadership Journal*. Currently, he is a Scholar in Residence with the CCSN, where he has edited plays for Integratio Press, facilitated workshops for educators, and participated in strategic planning and leadership development initiatives. Lance is married to Tara and has a son, Zayvier.

David Dockery (PhD, Texas A & M University) is an Assistant Professor of Mass Communication at William Carey University in Hattiesburg, Mississippi. His main areas of interest are media ethics, game studies, and narratology. His research studies how media, especially video games, can serve as equipment for religious and philosophical reflection. His dissertation, *Mythic Games: Narrative Design for Exercising the Moral Imagination*, explores how games integrate narratives of reality into their game design. Related interests include semiotics, spatial rhetoric, philosophy of communication, and media ethics.

Desiree C. Duff (PhD, Michigan State University) is a retired Professor of Communication, having spent the majority of her career at Cornerstone University. Her scholarship and professional experience reflect her interests in health communication, intercultural communication, and vocational calling. Desiree and her husband John, a retired professor of theology, call Cary, North Carolina, their home when not satisfying their wanderlust or enjoying their five children, their spouses, and eight grandchildren who live across the U.S. Throughout her adventures, Desiree is passionate about reflecting the light of Christ to those around her.

Kathleen M. Edelmayer (PhD, Wayne State University) is a Professor of Communication and Department Chair at Madonna University in Livonia, Michigan. She teaches a variety of communication courses including Public Speaking, Interpersonal Communication, Argumentation and Persuasion, and Rhetorical Theory and Criticism. Her primary areas of research address Catholic rhetoric, political rhetoric, and communication pedagogy. She previously taught and coached debate and speech at public universities, a Lutheran college, and a college in the "Methodist tradition." Edelmayer is a life member of the Central States Communication Association and the Religious Communication Association and has served as a board member and president of the Religious Communication Association.

David Enns (ABD, Liberty University) is the Executive Pastor of Worship & Creative Arts at GateWay Bible Church in Santa Cruz, California, where he blends two decades of ministry leadership with a passion for creative communication. Currently completing a PhD in Communication, he researches how everyday "Christianese" shapes public perception and cross-cultural dialogue. His ministry and academic work are enriched by his stage persona "Dave the Horn Guy," a comedic musician featured on *America's Got Talent* and *The Tonight Show*. Whether designing worship experiences, producing media, or writing on religious rhetoric, David aims to foster clear, compelling, and spiritually grounded communication for the church and the wider world.

Donna M. Elkins (PhD, University of Kentucky) serves as the Associate Vice President for Institutional Effectiveness and a Professor of Mass Communication at Campbellsville University in Kentucky. In addition to her doctoral, she holds an MA in Political Science from the University of Louisville, and a MA in Mass Communication from Morehead State University. She is currently pursuing a MA in Biblical Studies at Kentucky Christian University. Previously, she was the Dean of Online Education and a Professor of Communication at Spalding University as well as Dean of Academic Affairs and Professor of Communication at Jefferson Community and Technical College. She has publications on leadership, virtual training, onboarding new employees, and cancer recovery and support in the workplace. Dr. Elkins recently published a Bible study based on the book of Acts titled *Redeeming Failure*.

Gillette Elvgren (PhD, Florida State University) created and led the MFA programs in directing at the University of Pittsburgh and Regent University in Virginia Beach. While in Pittsburgh he served as staff director for the professional Three Rivers Shakespeare Festival, as well as full-time tenured faculty member at the University. He co-founded Saltworks Theatre Company, a professional faith-based theatre group that tours in the Tri-State area, as well as directing for the New City Theatre. Several of his productions in both Pittsburgh and Virginia Beach were heralded as "Best of the Year" in the *Pittsburgh Post Gazette* and *Portfolio Magazine* in Virginia Beach. He is also a playwright with over 8,000 performances of his plays performed in the United States and Canada. His publications include articles in *Children's Theatre Review, Educational Theatre Journal, Modern Drama, Dictionary of Literary Biography, Steel/City* (with Attilio Favorini), *Image Journal*, and *Christianity and Theatre*. Several of his scripts have been published by Blue Moon Plays and Christians in Theatre Arts.

Mark Fackler (PhD, University of Illinois at Urbana-Champaign) is a respected scholar in media ethics and international communication whose academic career includes long-standing appointments at Calvin University and Wheaton College. He earned his PhD from the University of Illinois at Urbana-Champaign, where formative collaborations helped shape his interdisciplinary approach to communication studies. Fackler's teaching and research span journalism, democratization, peace studies, and ethical theory. He has taught internationally at Addis Ababa University in Ethiopia and Daystar University in Kenya and continues to mentor students through Calvin's prison education initiative at Handlon Correctional Facility. He is co-author and editor of several foundational texts in media ethics, including *Media Ethics: Cases and Moral Reasoning* and *The Handbook of Global Communication and Media Ethics*, both co-written with Clifford G. Christians. His work reflects a deep commitment to ethical inquiry and cultural engagement, often drawing on theological models such as Niebuhr's "Christ transforming culture." Fackler's scholarship is marked by a belief in communication as a symbol-making vocation rooted in the *imago Dei*, aiming to foster responsible culture and reflect the mission of God from Genesis to Revelation.

Geraldine E. Forsberg (PhD, New York University) has been a full-time and affiliate staff member with Campus Crusade for Christ (CRU) since 1975. Currently, she is a Faculty Fellow with Faculty Commons, the faculty ministry of CRU. She earned her doctorate in Media Ecology from New York University in 1991 and a Master of Arts in Christian Ministry in 1987. She taught at Trinity Western University in Langley, British Columbia, while also speaking across university campuses throughout North America. She currently serves as a Senior Instructor in the English Department at Western Washington University, and she has provided leadership to the Western Christian Faculty Forum for over 20 years. Additionally, she is co-president of the International Jacques Ellul Society and serves on the board of the Christianity and Communication Studies Network (CCSN). Her most recent writings include: "Being Human in a Technological Society: A Theological Perspective," which will be published in *Questioning Twenty-first Century Technology with Jacques Ellul*; "Informationally Lost with No Sense of Place," published in Quentin Schultze's *Habits of the High-Tech Heart: Living Virtuously in the Information Age*; and "Transformation in the Public University," published in *Professing Christ: Christian Tradition and Faith-Learning Integration in Public Universities*. She is actively involved in her evangelical Anglican church, where she leads a weekly life group. She is married to Paul Madison, and they have one married son who lives with his wife, Honoka, in Tokyo.

Robert S. Fortner (PhD, University of Illinois at Urbana-Champaign) is a distinguished scholar in Communication and Media Studies whose academic career spans institutions including Calvin University, Palm Beach Atlantic University, Northwestern University, and Hope College. In addition to his doctorate, he earned a bachelor's degree from Otterbein College and a master's degree from Indiana University. Fortner's research focuses on international communication, media ethics, and the political economy of new technologies. He has taught globally, including at the University of Addis Ababa and the American University in Bulgaria, and has advised organizations such as the BBC and the International Center for Media Studies. He is the author or editor of several influential books, including *Communication, Media, and Identity: A Christian Theory of Communication*, *The Handbook of Media and Mass Communication Theory*, and *International Communication: History, Theory and Practice*. His work bridges academic rigor with practical insight, especially in post-conflict and cross-cultural contexts.

Janie Marie Harden Fritz (PhD, University of Wisconsin, Madison) is Professor and Chair of the Department of Communication & Rhetorical Studies at Duquesne University. She is the author of *Professional Civility: Communicative Virtue at Work*, co-editor (with S. Alyssa Groom) of *Communication Ethics and Crisis: Negotiating Differences in Public and Private Spheres* (Fairleigh Dickinson University Press), co-editor (with Becky L. Omdahl) of *Problematic Relationships in the Workplace* (Peter Lang) and *Problematic Relationships in the Workplace, Volume 2* (Peter Lang), and co-author (with Leeanne Bell McManus and Michael R. Kearney) of *Communication Ethics Literacy: Dialogue and Difference* (3rd ed.) (Kendall Hunt). She has published multiple journal articles and book chapters and is editor-in-chief of *Listening: Journal of Communication Ethics, Religion, and Culture*. Her work focuses on organizational and interpersonal communication and relationships, communication ethics, religious communication, and environmental phenomenology.

Elaine V. Fung (ABD, Regent University) is working to complete her dissertation at Regent University. Her research interests include organizational and interpersonal communication. She is also a Graduate Fellow with the CCSN and coordinates our summer workshops and conferences in communication and supports our social media and content creation outreaches.

Joshua D. Hill (PhD, Duquesne University) has earned graduate degrees in both Communication and English, has taught for over 20 years, and has practiced the craft of copyediting all along the way. Currently an Associate Professor and department head at Pennsylvania College of Technology, Hill helps lead his institution in Writing Across the Curriculum while also maintaining his own writing and research in rhetoric and hermeneutics, especially in the context of evangelicalism. His dissertation on Augustine and evangelical hermeneutics won the Religious Communication Association's 2017 Dissertation of the Year Award, and he has published chapters on divine communication, Paul Ricoeur, Information Literacy in the digital age, Kenneth Burke's eloquence, and C. S. Lewis's rhetoric of fiction. Whether writing, advising writers, or editing, his joy is to find the words fitly spoken that channel grace to the audience in its situation.

Elizabeth B. Jones (PhD, The Ohio State University) is Associate Professor and Director of Graduate Studies at Asbury University in the School of Communication Arts. Her research occurs at the intersection of communication technology, interpersonal communication, and health communication. She is particularly interested in how communication and media narratives may function to either cultivate or curtail flourishing for older persons.

John R. Katsion (PhD, Regent University) has dedicated himself to teaching communication studies for over 30 years, and his extensive academic background speaks to his passion for the field. He received his BS in Bible and Speech from Pillsbury Baptist Bible College, followed by an MA in Speech Communication from Minnesota State University, and his PhD from Regent University. John has primarily taught in Christian higher education institutions throughout his career but has been teaching at Northwest Missouri State University in Maryville, MO, for the last 10 years. His teaching has been the cornerstone of his academic life, and he has published many of his pedagogical activities in academic journals and books over the years. In addition to his teaching, he has dedicated much of his academic focus to rhetorical studies, with a particular interest in visual rhetoric and the rhetoric of religious music. His work has been published in various academic journals and book chapters, covering a range of visual and sacred music texts. Administratively, John has held various leadership roles in national communication associations, including chairing the Visual Communication Division of the National Communication Association twice and serving in the Senate of the National Communication Association. Outside of his academic pursuits, he spends his summers practicing the craft of preaching. He preaches in churches in Missouri and Iowa and speaks to 4th–6th graders at camps across the country. John is happily married to Peggy, and the couple has three children: Jacob, Lincoln, and Elijah.

Douglas Kelley (PhD, University of Arizona) is Professor Emeritus of Communication at Arizona State University. His research and teaching focus on how relational partners can treat one another humanely as they pursue intimacy and love and negotiate their responses to hurt and struggle. Professor Kelley is recipient of NCA's 2017 Bernard Brommel Award for Family Communication and has authored seven books, including *Just Relationships: Living Out Social Justice as Mentor, Family, Friend, and Lover, Intimate Spaces: A Conversation about Discovery and Connection*, and *A Communicative Approach to Conflict, Forgiveness, and Reconciliation*, and *Reimagining Our Relationships*. He continues to teach, write, pursue reconciliation, and offer spiritual direction in his local community (www.groundedinsanity.com).

Brandon Knight (PhD, University of Southern Mississippi) is Assistant Professor of Speech Communication and Director of Forensics at William Carey University. He also earned an MDiv with an emphasis in Biblical Studies from New Orleans Baptist Theological Seminary. Prior to teaching in the Academy, he served as a youth pastor for five years at two locations in the local Hub City area and, more recently, served as an interim at Leaf River Baptist Church in Collins, Mississippi. His research is featured in the *Journal of Communication and Religion, Management Communication Quarterly*, the *Journal of Christian Teaching Practice (in Communication Studies)*, the *Interdisciplinary Journal of Research on Religion*, and, most recently, the *Journal of the Evangelical Homiletics Society*.

Isaiah Lin (PhD, Syracuse University) is Associate Professor of Philosophy at Providence Christian College in Pasadena, California. His wide-ranging academic interests include metaphysics, philosophy of language, and philosophy of art, but his real passion is participating with students in engaging the life of the mind in pursuit of the good life. Outside of academic work, Dr. Lin enjoys practicing jiu-jitsu, arguing about movies, and traveling in pursuit of gustatory pleasure. He serves as an elder at The Chapel at Pasadena and is married to Aubree, with whom they have two sons, Levi and Lukas.

Terry Lindvall (PhD, University of Southern California) occupies the C. S. Lewis Chair of Communication and Christian Thought at Virginia Wesleyan University. He has taught on Communication, Theology, and Laughter (and Film) at Duke University Divinity School, Regent University, and was the Mason Fellow at the College of William and Mary. He has published 14 books including award-winning *Sanctuary Cinema* (NYU Press, 2007), *God Mocks* (NYU Press, 2015), *Divine Film Comedies* (Routledge, 2016), and *Animated Parables* (Lexington Press, 2023). He just produced the documentary feature film, *Hollywood, Teach us to Pray* (2023), based on his book, *God on the Big Screen* (NYU Press, 2019). He once pretended for over four years to be a University President at Regent University.

Michael A. Longinow (PhD, University of Kentucky), grew up in the Chicago area, attended Wheaton College, and earned a less than stellar grade in Mark Noll's history class there. But at Wheaton, he felt God's call on his life to take the message of Christ into newsrooms. He worked for daily newspapers near Chicago and Atlanta. After graduate studies in journalism at the University of Illinois and a doctorate from the University of Kentucky, he began a journey in Christian academia that provided nationwide attention for his Christian worldview involving student media advising, innovations in journalism pedagogy, and research into the history of evangelicals, journalism and media in the United States. Longinow has made media ethics, trauma, ethnicity, media literacy, excellence in writing and investigative reporting his pedagogical specialties. He currently serves as Professor of Communication at Biola University.

George Marsden (PhD, Yale University) is the Francis A. McAnaney Professor of History Emeritus at the University of Notre Dame. His best-known books include *The Soul of the American University: From Protestant Establishment to Established Nonbelief* (1994); *The Outrageous Idea of Christian Scholarship* (1997); *Fundamentalism and American Culture* (1980), and *Jonathan Edwards: A Life* (2003).

Craig Mattson (PhD, Regent University) is an organizational researcher who serves as a Professor of Communication at Calvin University, where he holds the Arthur H. DeKruyter Chair in Faith and Communication. He has written several books and numerous essays, often exploring the communicational complexities of organizational life. But when he is not writing and reading and podcasting, he is enjoying the natural world, hiking, biking, and playing pickleball. He lives with his wife Rhoda in Grand Rapids, Michigan, and their four adult children live and study and work across the Midwest.

Brian D. Mattson (PhD, Regent University) is Assistant Professor of Communication at Lee University, where he brings together expertise in theology, media ecology, and rhetorical studies. In addition to his doctorate, he holds advanced theological training from Grand Rapids Theological Seminary. Dr. Mattson's research focuses on the intersection of theology, media, and culture, with particular interest in how communication shapes both social and ecclesial transformation. His work engages topics such as digital religion, preaching in a digital age, and theological aesthetics. A frequent conference presenter and contributor to volumes on religious rhetoric and civic engagement, Dr. Mattson offers a distinct voice at the crossroads of faith, persuasion, and mediated communication.

J. Matthew Melton (PhD, Regent University) is a past President of the Religious Communication Association. In 1995, he joined the Communication faculty at Lee University in southeast Tennessee. Over the succeeding 28 years, Melton served as Director of Speech Forensics, Student Media, the honors program, as Department Chair, and as Dean of the College of Arts and Sciences. He taught media, speech, journalism, film, and classical humanities. He has authored (or edited) newspaper columns, magazine articles, chapters, and textbook materials for communication courses and the freshman collegiate experience. Since 2023, he has worked with the Southern Association of Colleges and Schools Commission on Colleges in Atlanta, Georgia.

A. Chase Mitchell (PhD, Texas Tech University) is Associate Professor of Media & Communication at East Tennessee State University, where he teaches undergraduate and graduate courses in multimedia production, strategic communication, and media ecology, among others, and directs the Technical & Professional Writing Program. His popular and scholarly work has appeared in venues such as *Christian Scholar's Review*, *FaithTech*, and *Christ & Pop Culture*. He contributes a monthly online column, "Image to Image," for the Christianity & Communication Studies Network. He lives in Bristol, Tennessee, with his wife Mott and their two dogs, Bigfoot and Fuzzle. He enjoys baseball, books, and British comedy.

Julie Morgan (EdD, Nova Southeastern University) is a full-time professor and Department Chair for Communication at Eastern University in St. Davids, Pennsylvania, and can be often found at school with her emotional therapy dog Duke at her side. She is a seasoned communication training and education specialist with over 25 years of experience and has collaborated with CEOs to enhance their communication and leadership skills, fostering more cohesive and productive teams. As a published author and tenured professor, Dr. Morgan is dedicated to improving the quality of relationships through better communication. She is mom to her son Will, a support to her students, a committed Orangetheory Fitness member, and a loving aunt to many.

Richard J. Mouw (PhD, University of Chicago) grew up straddling two spiritual worlds—his mother steeped in liturgical tradition, and his father a converted hillbilly musician who embraced revivalist evangelicalism. This dual heritage shaped Mouw's lifelong commitment to both theological depth and public dialogue. After earning degrees from Houghton College, Western Theological Seminary, the University of Alberta, and a PhD in philosophy from the University of Chicago, Mouw spent 17 formative years as a Professor of Philosophy at Calvin College. There, he joined a legendary faculty cohort that included George Marsden, Alvin Plantinga, and Nicholas Wolterstorff, helping to define a golden age of Reformed scholarship. In 1985, Mouw joined Fuller Theological Seminary as Professor of Christian Philosophy and Ethics. He became Provost in 1989 and then served as President from 1993 to 2013. His tenure was marked by a deep commitment to "convicted civility"—a phrase he popularized to describe the balance between firm theological convictions and respectful public discourse. His leadership at Fuller was distinguished by interfaith engagement, including dialogues with Catholics, Mormons, and Jewish communities. Mouw authored over 19 books, including *Uncommon Decency, Calvinism in the Las Vegas Airport*, and *Talking with Mormons*. His writing reflects a consistent theme: the pursuit of grace in cultural engagement. In 2007, Princeton Theological Seminary awarded him the Abraham Kuyper Prize for Excellence in Reformed Theology and Public Life, honoring his role as a leading voice in public theology. Even after retiring from Fuller, Mouw continued to teach and write, returning to Calvin University as a senior research fellow. His legacy lives on through the Mouw Institute at Fuller, which promotes faithful Christian engagement in public life.

Mark A. Noll (PhD, Vanderbilt University) is retired after serving as a historian at Wheaton College and the University of Notre Dame. His books charting the relationship of believing communities to their wider contexts include *America's God: From Jonathan Edwards* *to Abraham Lincoln*, *The Civil War as a Theological Crisis*, and two books on the history of the Bible in America (2016, 2022). He has also published studies on American evangelicals including *The Scandal of the Evangelical Mind*. Mark and his wife Maggie are long time members of Immanuel Presbyterian Church in Warrenville, Illinois.

Kim Okesson (PhD, Regent University) is Assistant Professor of Communication in the School of Communication Arts at Asbury University. She is also the Director of Asbury University's Cross-Cultural Engagement program. Prior to coming to Asbury, Professor Okesson lived and worked for 13 years in three countries outside of her passport country: Kenya, Tanzania, and England. Her areas of research include identity formation, immigration, intercultural communication, and international communication. How students engage with cultural differences and equipping students to work in a globalized world are of particular concern to her. Dr. Okesson is also a co-editor for the Kentucky Communication Association Journal. Her doctoral dissertation focused on intercultural communication issues on Christian college campuses.

Rick Olsen (PhD, Regent University) is a Professor and Department Chair at The University of North Carolina Wilmington. He has enjoyed finding ways that his faith could inform his teaching, research, service and leadership. His scholarship often focuses on the intersection of rhetoric and popular culture as well as communication and leadership. He has also found that playing music and basketball have provided great points of connection with students and faculty across campus.

Paul D. Patton (PhD, Regent University) is Professor Emeritus of Communication and Theater at Spring Arbor University in Michigan. It was while pastoring at Trinity Church in Livonia, Michigan, that he founded Trinity House Theater in 1981. He is the author of over 30 produced stage plays, radio plays, and performance essays. He is contributing author to the books, *Understanding Evangelical Media* (IVP), *Evangelical Christians and Popular Culture* (Praeger), and *Prophetic Critique and Popular Culture* (Peter Lang), and co-author of *Prophetically (In)Correct: A Christian Introduction to Media Criticism* (Brazos Press), and the newly published, *Everyday Sabbath: How to Lead Your Dance with Media and Technology in Mindful and Sacred Ways* (Cascade Books).

John R. Peck is a British theologian and cultural thinker known for his work in integrating biblical wisdom with contemporary social analysis. He co-authored *Uncommon Sense: God's Wisdom for Our Complex and Changing World*, a volume that explores Christian discernment in the face of modern complexity. Peck has been active in educational and community initiatives such as College House in Cambridge and the Greenbelt Arts Festival, where he has contributed to conversations on faith, justice, and cultural renewal. His writing reflects a commitment to theological depth, practical engagement, and the cultivation of Christian imagination in public life.

Stephen D. Perry (PhD, University of Alabama) is Chair and Professor in the Department of Journalism and Communication Studies at Regent University. He is an editor of three academic books including *Pro Football and the Proliferation of Protest: Anthem Posture in a*

Divided America and Communication Theories for Everyday Life. He also authored *A Consolidated History of Media*. He has authored over 35 peer-reviewed journal articles and over 15 book chapters. He is an experienced journal editor (*Mass Communication and Society*, *Artifact Analysis*, and *Communication Research Replication*) and has chaired the research committee for the Broadcast Education Association. Perry has served on the Board of Trustees for Eastern Nazarene College and as an elected member of the School Board for Bloomington, IL, public schools. Together with his wife he has planted two churches and has served as a church worship leader for most of the last 40 years.

Jonathan Pettigrew (PhD, Penn State) is Associate Professor in the Hugh Downs School of Human Communication at Arizona State University. His scholarship is dedicated to promoting healthy relationships for youth, families, and society. His work has an international scope, interdisciplinary bent, and aims for social impact. Projects involve designing, delivering, and evaluating interventions through partnerships with communities. His publications advance understanding of parent-child drug talks, social processes that impact intervention effects, and real-world program dissemination and implementation. Pettigrew is co-author of *Family Communication and the Christian Faith: An Introduction and Exploration* and co-editor of *Professing Christ: Christian Tradition and Faith Learning Integration in Public Universities*.

Nick Pertler (PhD, Duquesne University) is Associate Provost for Academic Studies at Point Loma Nazarene University, where he serves faculty and academic leaders developing and supporting high-quality academic programs. Dr. Pertler oversees the Office of Instructional Design, academic policy, and student appeals processes. After earning a BA in Communication from California State University, San Marcos and MA in Speech Communication from California State University, Fullerton, he completed a PhD in Rhetoric from Duquesne University. He has well over a decade of higher education leadership and administrative experience and previously served on the faculties of Duquesne University, Baker College, and MiraCosta College, teaching a wide range of communication courses. Additionally, Dr. Pertler directs and teaches in the Strategic Communication BA program at PLNU. His research agenda focuses on C. S. Lewis, philosophy of education, the premodern rhetorical tradition, and media ecology. He is a published author, has presented his work at regional, national, and international conferences, and is currently writing a manuscript for publication with Integratio Press. Dr. Pertler and his wife Alison have five children.

Robert Stephen Reid (PhD, University of Washington) is an Emeritus Professor of Communication at University of Dubuque, Iowa. He directed the MA in Organizational Communication and Leadership 2001–2017 and served as Communication Department Head 2000–2014. He is author of *The Four Voices of Preaching, Preaching Mark*, co-author of *The Six Deadly Sins of Preaching: Becoming Responsible for the Faith We Proclaim*, and *Connecting with the Congregation: Rhetoric and the Art of Preaching*. He is co-author of a textbook, *Connecting with Your Audience: Making Public Speaking Matter* that is distinguished by its use of Supreme Court opinions for student values-in-dispute speeches, current legislative proposals for policy-in-dispute speeches, and personal experience for the basic informative speech design. He lives near Seattle, Washington, with his spouse, the Rev. Dr. Barbara Reid.

Adam Sonstroem (Doctoral Candidate, Fuller Theological Seminary) has taught history and communication at the high school and college levels for over 20 years. He earned his MA in Teaching from Wheaton College, an MA in US History from Pace University, and an MA in Communication from Spring Arbor University. He is a PhD student at Fuller Theological Seminary studying theology and film. Adam taught at Arizona Christian University for 15 years and currently serves as a visiting Assistant Professor of Communication at Taylor University. Adam and his wife, Erin, live with their daughter in Phoenix, Arizona.

Fr. Paul Soukup, SJ (PhD, University of Texas at Austin) teaches courses in technology and communication at Santa Clara University and conducts research on religious communication. He has authored or edited numerous books and collaborates with both the US Conference of Catholic Bishops and the American Bible Society on communication issues. Since 1982, Fr. Soukup has explored the connections between communication and theology. His publications include *Communication and Theology*; *Christian Communication: A Bibliographical Survey*; *Media, Culture, and Catholicism*; *Mass Media and the Moral Imagination* (with Philip J. Rossi); *Fidelity and Translation: Communicating the Bible in New Media* (with Robert Hodgson); *Out of Eden: 7 Ways God Restores Blocked Communication*; and *Of Ong & Media Ecology: Essays in Communication, Composition, and Literary Studies*. He and Thomas J. Farrell also edited four volumes of Walter J. Ong's collected works, *Faith and Contexts*, which led him to examine how orality-literacy studies contribute to understanding theological expression. Fr. Soukup currently serves on the Board of Trustees of the American Bible Society and recently served on the Board of Trustees at Loyola University of New Orleans.

R. Tyler Spradley (PhD, Texas A & M University) is a Professor at Stephen F. Austin State University in Nacogdoches, Texas. He is an organizational communication scholar whose research focuses on crisis and risk communication. He is the current editor for the *International Crisis and Risk Communication Reports*. Recent projects employ his degree from Southwestern Baptist Theological Seminary and his experience as a pastor and elder writing on church leadership. He and his wife, Elizabeth, have four boys and enjoy the outdoors.

Mark Allan Steiner (PhD, Indiana University) is Associate Professor of Communication at Christopher Newport University in Newport News, Virginia, and is a past President of the Religious Communication Association. His areas of expertise include rhetorical theory and criticism, religious rhetoric, public/political discourse, and the relationship between mediation and religious identity. He is the author of *The Rhetoric of Operation Rescue: Projecting the Christian Pro-Life Message* (2006) and "Reconceptualizing Christian Public Engagement: 'Faithful Witness' and the American Evangelical Tradition" (2009) and has published a range of articles and book chapters on evangelical Christian rhetoric, media and religion, undergraduate communication pedagogy, and rhetoric education at the primary and secondary school levels. He lives in Suffolk, Virginia with his wife and four children.

Quentin Schultze (PhD, University of Illinois at Urbana-Champaign) is Professor of Communication Emeritus at Calvin University and the author of many books, including *Communicating for Life*; *Christianity and the Mass Media in America*; *Habits of the High-Tech*

Heart; *Communicating with Grace & Virtue*; *Servant Teaching*; *An Essential Guide to Public Speaking*; *An Essential Guide to Interpersonal Communication*; *Communicate Like a True Leader*; *You'll Shoot Your Eye Out! Life Lessons from the Movie A Christmas Story*; and *Gutenberg, God, and the Devil's Plug-In*. He mentors, speaks widely, conducts faculty-development workshops, and blogs at www.quentinschultze.com.

Kevin Schut (PhD, University of Iowa) is a Game Studies scholar, Chair of Game Development, Professor and Dean of the School of the Arts, Media + Culture at Trinity Western University in British Columbia, Canada. He received a BA in Communication Arts & Sciences, History, and French from Calvin College and an MA and PhD in Communication Studies from the University of Iowa. His research explores the intersection of communication, culture, media, technology, and faith, primarily by discussing computer and video games. He authored the book *Of Games & God: A Christian Exploration of Video Games* and has published articles or chapters on fantasy-role-playing computer games and masculinity, on computer games and myth, on the presentation of history in computer games, and on evangelicals and games. He is currently researching moral and ethical decisions in video games and teaches a range of courses on media and culture. Hailing from Edmonton, Alberta, he still cheers for the Oilers. After graduating from Calvin College, he married and taught overseas in schools for missionary kids in the Cote d'Ivoire and Hungary for three and a half years. He has three daughters who love playing board games, adventure games, Mario Kart, and Vive Virtual Reality with him. His favorite game series is Sid Meier's Civilization.

Deanna D. Sellnow (PhD, University of North Dakota) is Professor and Chair of the Department of Communication at Clemson University. Dr. Sellnow's research focuses on instructional communication in multiple contexts ranging from traditional classroom environments to health, risk, and crisis situations. Her work with instructional communication in risk and crisis contexts is widely published in interdisciplinary and international journals. She has conducted funded research for such agencies as the United States Geological Survey, the United States Departments of Agriculture, the Department of Homeland Security, and the Centers for Disease Control and Prevention. She is the author and co-author of six books focused on instructional communication. Two recent titles are, *The Rhetorical Power of Popular Culture: Considering Mediated Texts* and *The Challenge of Effective Speaking in a Digital Age*.

Timothy L. Sellnow (PhD, Wayne State University) is Professor of Communication at Clemson University. Dr. Sellnow's research focuses on risk and crisis communication. He has conducted funded research for the Department of Homeland Security, the United States Department of Agriculture, the Centers for Disease Control and Prevention, the Environmental Protection Agency, the United States Geological Survey, and the World Health Organization. He has also served in an advisory role for the National Academy of Sciences, the Federal Emergency Management Agency, and the Food and Drug Administration. He has published many refereed journal articles and co-authored six books on risk and crisis communication. Dr. Sellnow's most recent book, co-authored with Deanna D. Sellnow, is *Before Crisis: The Practice of Effective Risk Communication*.

Gregory Spencer (PhD, University of Oregon) taught about words, perception, narrative, and the importance of questions for 35 years at Westmont College. He is now Professor Emeritus. He has published two novels, *The Welkening* and *Guardian of the Veil*, and is currently working on a third, *Boomer Boy*. He has also published three works of nonfiction, *A Heart for Truth*, *Awakening the Quieter Virtues*, and *Reframing the Soul: How Words Transform Our Faith*, as well as dozens of articles, poems, and op-ed pieces. He lives in Santa Barbara, CA, with his wife of over 40 years. They have three married daughters and eight grandchildren, six of whom live too far away. He enjoys gardening, tennis, hiking, and asking involved dinner questions.

John R. Terrill (PhD, Seattle Pacific University) is the Executive Director of The Stephen & Laurel Brown Foundation, serving the UW-Madison community through its Upper House and Dottie's Ranch facilities by leading Christian thought and formation to shape today's pluralistic university. He previously served as Director for the Center for Faithful Business at Seattle Pacific University and as National Director for InterVarsity Christian Fellowship's Professional Schools Ministries. Prior to InterVarsity, he served in the business sector. Dr. Terrill recently completed a nine-year board term with Religion News Service and Religion News Foundation and currently serves as a board member for Science for the Church and the Theology of Work Project. He and his family live in Middleton, Wisconsin.

Calvin L. Troup (PhD, Pennsylvania State University) is the twentieth president of Geneva College. Prior to assuming his current role, Dr. Troup served on the faculties of Penn State, University Park, Pennsylvania; Indiana University, Bloomington, Indiana; and Duquesne University, Pittsburgh, Pennsylvania, where he directed the university's nationally ranked Rhetoric PhD program. Dr. Troup's scholarly interest is the rhetoric and philosophy of St. Augustine, and the rhetoric of technology. His books include *Temporality, Eternity, and Wisdom: The Rhetoric of Augustine's Confessions* (Univ. of South Carolina Press, 1999); *Augustine for the Philosophers: The Rhetor of Hippo, the Confessions* (Baylor University Press, 2014); and *The Spoken Word: A Public Speaking Handbook* (Geneva College, 2021). Dr. Troup has edited the *Journal of Communication and Religion* and is a past President of the Religious Communication Association. He is the editor-elect of *Explorations in Media Ecology*, the international journal of the Media Ecology Association.

Reid Vance (PhD, Azusa Pacific University) is Professor and Chair of Communication at Mississippi College. In addition to his doctorate, he holds a BS and MS in Communication from Mississippi College, and an MA in Christian Education from New Orleans Baptist Theological Seminary. He teaches courses in communication, journalism, sports media, and in higher education research, and serves as a professor in Mississippi College's Honors College. He also serves as the broadcast Voice of the Choctaws for Mississippi College athletics. Reid has further professional experience in college student affairs, campus ministry, church leadership, and Christian camp ministry. A native of Canton, Mississippi, Reid and his wife, Cheli, live in Clinton and are leaders in the young single adult ministry at First Baptist Church of Jackson, Mississippi.

James W. Vining (PhD, University of Wisconsin-Milwaukee) is an Associate Professor of Communication Studies at Governors State University, a regional state university in the Chicago Southland. His research interests include the roles of religion and theology in political and social movement communication, and theological insights into human communication and education. With undergraduate and graduate degrees in Bible, Religion, Culture, and Religious Education, he spent 15 years in pastoral ministry in various contexts before earning his PhD and entering the Academy. He actively serves in his church and community, as well as in various roles at his university and in academic associations, most notably as a member of the Executive Council and Vice President of the Religious Communication Association.

Ben Voth (PhD, University of Kansas) is Professor of Rhetoric and Director of Debate and Speech at Southern Methodist University in Dallas, Texas. He published seven academic books since 2014. Voth is editor of *Argumentation and Advocacy* and the *Lexington Political Communication* book series. His professional consultations include: The *United States Holocaust Memorial Museum* in Washington D.C., the *U.S. State Debate Department* in Rwanda, the *Ronald Reagan Presidential Foundation*, the *George W. Bush Institute*, and the *Calvin Coolidge Presidential Foundation*. He has coached and directed more than a dozen world and national champions in speech and debate.

Annalee R. Ward (PhD, Regent University) is Director of the Wendt Center for Character Education and Professor of Communication Emerita, and she explores the intersection of communication, character, and Christianity in both scholarly and popular publications. Her research and writing have also opened opportunities to preach and to teach preaching. In addition, her service on various non-profit boards provides grounded, practical contexts for observing and reflecting on how these three areas of interest inform one another in everyday life. She served as editor of *Character And . . .* , a faculty journal exploring various issues related to character and is the author of *Mouse Morality: A Rhetoric of Disney Animated Films*.

Ken Waters (PhD, University of Southern California) is an Emeritus Professor of Journalism at Pepperdine University. His 32-year teaching career included a variety of writing courses, intercultural communication, communication ethics, and an occasional public relations class. Waters also served a seven-year stint as Divisional Dean for Communication at the university. In that role, he managed 30 faculty and planned classes for nearly 400 majors. His overseas teaching assignments have taken him to London, Lausanne, and Florence. He has also written a dozen journal articles, primarily on the intersection of religious publications and culture. He recently published *Words that Shape Us: How America's Most Influential Magazines Craft the Narrative of Christian Culture*. Waters received a BA in Journalism and History from Pepperdine, and he served as editor of the award-winning student newspaper, The Graphic. In addition to his doctorate, he also holds an MA in Religion from Pepperdine. He and his wife, Julie, are parents to two adult daughters, Katie and Alison. Waters is a life-long resident of Southern California.

Mark A. E. Williams (PhD, Louisiana State University) is a past President of the Religious Communication Association and a Professor Emeritus of Rhetoric in the Communication Studies Department of California State University, Sacramento, where he taught both graduate and undergraduate courses in communication and religion, rhetorical criticism, and the history of rhetoric with an emphasis on the premodern era. He received a research fellowship at Oxford University and the École Biblique et Archéologique de Jérusalem. He is an adult convert to Catholicism and was confirmed in the Church of the Holy Sepulcher toward the end of the last century while working on his dissertation in Jerusalem. His writings include "St. Socrates, Pray for Us: Rhetoric and the Physics of Being Human" in *Rhetoric in the Twenty-first Century: An Interactive Oxford Symposium*, "From Here to Eternity: The Cost of Misreading Plato's Religion" in *The Global Landscape of Faith*, "Anselm of Canterbury: Solemnity and Humility Beyond All Words" in *Words and Witnesses: Communication Studies in Christian Thought from Athanasius to Desmond Tutu*, "Substantive Discourse: Love, Justice, and Hierarchy as the Basis for Civility" in *Humility and Hospitality*, and "Integrating Secular Faith and Navel Gazing" in *Professing Christ*. His books include *Well-behaved Words* (an introductory text on public speaking), *Essential Latin Vocabulary* (an introductory study guide for students of Latin), and *Just Words: Lessons of Ancient Education, Classical Rhetoric, and Pagan Religion for a Post-Christian World*, a consideration of the connections between education, rhetoric, religion, and justice in ancient Athens. Left to his own devices, he will indulge his Tolkien addiction, bind books by hand, write just for fun, and think about things. He is married to a scientist who keeps him grounded. They have two adult children.

Nicholas Wolterstorff (PhD, Harvard University) is Noah Porter Professor Emeritus of Philosophical Theology at Yale University and Senior Research Fellow of the Institute for Advanced Studies in Culture, University of Virginia. He graduated from Calvin College in 1953 and received his PhD in philosophy from Harvard University in 1956. After teaching philosophy for two years at Yale, he joined the Philosophy Department of his alma mater in 1959. He returned to Yale in 1989, where he was on the faculty of the Divinity School and associate member of the Philosophy Department and the Religious Studies Department. He retired from Yale at the end of 2001. He taught, during leaves of absence, at Haverford College, the University of Michigan, the University of Texas, The University of Notre Dame, Princeton University, and the Free University of Amsterdam. He is the author of over 30 books, including *Justice: Rights and Wrongs, Hearing the Call, Justice in Love, The Mighty and the Almighty, Understanding Liberal Democracy, Journey toward Justice, Art Rethought, Acting Liturgically, In This World of Wonders*, and *Religion in the University*. He has been President of the American Philosophical Association (Central Division) and President of the Society of Christian Philosophers. He is a fellow of the American Academy of Arts and Sciences. Among the named lecture series he has delivered are the Wilde Lectures at Oxford University, the Gifford Lectures at St Andrews University, the Taylor Lectures at Yale University, and the Stone Lectures at Princeton Seminary.

Robert H. Woods Jr. (PhD, Regent University) served as Professor of Communication and Media at Spring Arbor University for 20 years. He currently serves as the Executive Director of the Christianity and Communication Studies Network (CCSN) (www.theccsn. com), a nonprofit network providing resources and training on faith-learning integration in the field of communication studies. He is the editor-in-chief of the CCSN's imprint, Integratio Press. Dr. Woods has served as the President of the Religious Communication Association (RCA) and was named Scholar of the Year by RCA. He is the recipient of multiple research and scholarship awards and the editor/author of over a dozen books. Most recently, Dr. Woods is the co-author with Paul D. Patton on *Everyday Sabbath: How to Lead Your Dance with Media and Technology in Mindful and Sacred Ways* and *Professing Christ: Christian Tradition and Faith-learning Integration in Public Universities*. His book co-authored with Kevin Healey (University of New Hampshire), titled *Ethics and Religion in the Age of Social Media: Digital Proverbs for Responsible Citizens* received the Book of the Year Award from RCA.

Franklin Nii Amankwah Yartey (PhD, Bowling Green State University) is Professor of Communication at the University of Dubuque in Dubuque, Iowa. Yartey received an undergraduate degree from Northwestern College and a master's degree from Indiana State University. His research focuses on Digital Media and Globalization/Social Media, with a secondary focus on Intercultural Communication. Other research interests include online microfinance, health communication, media ethics, and globalization. He received the University of Dubuque's John Knox Coit Prize and was inducted into the Faculty Hall of Fame in 2021, in recognition of his exemplary commitment as a dedicated teacher and advisor to students. In 2014, he received the Iowa Communication Association (ICA) Outstanding New Teacher Award. Yartey enjoys running, ping-pong, chess, and content creation.

Introduction

ROBERT H. WOODS JR. AND MARK ALLAN STEINER

YOUR EDITORS WERE part of a small group of professors and students who gathered for dinner in downtown Baltimore, Maryland, ready to debrief after attending all day meetings that were part of the National Communication Association (NCA) annual conference. NCA is the oldest and largest nonprofit scholarly society dedicated to advancing communication research, teaching, and practice, especially in public speaking. NCA's annual convention typically attracts around 4,500 attendees.[1]

All of us at dinner were also associated with the Christianity and Communication Studies Network (CCSN). The CCSN is a nonprofit organization whose mission it is to equip and train Christian faculty, administrators, students, and others in public and private higher education to integrate and extend a Christian worldview in their research, teaching, and leadership (theccsn.com).

Shortly after being seated, we ordered drinks, appetizers, exchanged pleasantries, and asked each other about our experiences at the day's meetings. Several common themes emerged as we reflected on the highs and lows of our day, what was being emphasized, and what was missing from the conversations.

It was clear to us not too far into the discussion—and probably not surprising to many of you reading this now—that the Academy, much like American public and political culture, is fractured and toxic. Individualism and consumerism dominate communal values and lifestyles. The embrace of self-righteous and resentment-fueled victimhood all too often justifies individual and tribal interests. Recent books point out the one-sided political leanings of most public universities and the demonization of certain voices—including Christian voices—that challenge the ideological status quo.[2] The biblical foundations of our public universities that once provided spiritual, moral, civil, and social protection, have long been deteriorating. Generations of students have been indoctrinated with worldviews that abandon capital-T truth, skew logic, and threaten freedom of thought and expression. All of this was on full display at NCA.

Rather than simply add to the critique, we wanted our dinner talk to embrace the Kingdom opportunities that our current cultural crises presented and offer viable pathways forward. Sources and places of common ground are scarce and endangered for Christians in the Academy. Christian scholars committed to a sustained engagement in this environment need encouragement and supportive spaces and communities, and we wanted to offer that to others moving forward. Ever the dreamer, one of your editors (Robert) asked if we should have our own pre-conference at next year's NCA. Others chimed in with a hearty "yes," and your other editor (Mark) came up with the theme around which our first-ever NCA pre-conference was organized. We were off and running. What follows in the remainder of this brief introduction is the context and description of the eventual CCSN pre-conference (what we called an "unconference") at NCA in New Orleans, Louisiana, the following year, 2024.

An Outrageous and Scandalous Unconference

The title we settled on for the gathering was "From the Outrageous to the Scandalous: Reimagining Christian Thinking and Scholarship in an Age of Tribalism and Resentment." It was devoted to exploring the contemporary relevance and impact of two seminal books from the 1990s related to the intellectual life and practices of American evangelical Christians: Mark Noll's *The Scandal of the Evangelical Mind* and George Marsden's *The Outrageous Idea of Christian Scholarship*, each celebrating their thirtieth anniversary.[3]

In *The Outrageous Idea of Christian Scholarship*, Marsden addresses the relevance and the unique heuristic value of scholarship done from an explicitly faith-informed perspective, making the case that Christians can and should let their faith commitments animate their research and scholarship, and that doing so will be beneficial to the Academy and to society as a whole. In *The Scandal of the Evangelical Mind*, Noll traces the historical development and contemporary consequences of anti-intellectualism, pressing the claim that faithfulness in religious practice and cultural engagement requires a much more serious collective commitment to intellectual and theological work.

The 2024 CCSN Unconference at NCA was an invitation for Christians to dialogue on the legacy and contemporary relevance of these two books in the current state of the Academy and beyond. What kind of impact have Marsden's and Noll's ideas had on the church and on researchers and scholars who engage and extend their work and life from a Christian perspective? In what ways are Marsden's and Noll's calls still needed and how might they be applied today given the multitude and complexity of social and political challenges we face? Additionally, how might the work and life of Christian scholars help re-imagine and reform the current state of higher education? In short, what are the challenges and opportunities of being a faithful and hopeful Christian scholar in today's educational arena? However re-imagined and applied, Marsden's and Noll's ideas are an important wellspring for this type of faithfulness in the world of ideas and the world of culture.

We called it an *unconference* because it was structured to prioritize conversation and intellectual collaboration, as opposed to the presentation of completed scholarship. An unconference tries to capture the kinds of conversations that occur between formal larger conferences—the hallway talks, coffee shop conversations, the impromptu, spontaneous interactions that occur as we move from one organized session to another. So, by design, there are few, if any, formal presentations during the face-to-face gathering. We invited people who were passionate about the theme of the event and were willing to do some pre-work so we could hit the ground running during our short time together and focus on small group discussion. After identifying such individuals, we simply put them in the same room together, divided them into small groups, and let things progress organically. We offered several topics for discussion, but participants were encouraged to change the topics if necessary or move among groups as their interests evolved. All participants came together on occasion for intermittent debriefs before returning to small group discussion.

Participants could either stay with the group they had been with prior to the debrief, find another one to join, or even start a new group based on a theme or themes not yet explored.

In attendance were 43 faculty and administrators and a half-dozen students, both graduate and undergraduate, from over 30 different institutions of higher education. About half of all who attended were from private Christian colleges and universities and the other half were individuals serving in public university settings. In keeping with the CCSN's mission, there were a wide array of theological, denominational, cultural, and political perspectives represented.

As mentioned earlier, participants were asked to do some pre-work prior to arriving at the unconference. They were asked to read George Marsden's and Mark Noll's seminal books and watch short video presentations from our Legacy Scholars. Legacy Scholars included George Marsden (University of Notre Dame); Mark Noll (University of Notre Dame); Clifford G. Christians (University of Illinois at Urbana-Champaign); Quentin Schultze (Calvin University); Terry Lindvall (Virginia Wesleyan University); Fr. Paul A. Soukup, SJ (Santa Clara University); Richard J. Mouw (Fuller Theological Seminary); Nicholas Wolterstorff (Yale University); Greg Spencer (Westmont College); Mark Fackler (Calvin University); Robert S. Fortner (University of Illinois at Urbana-Champaign), and Calvin L. Troup (Geneva College). The Legacy Scholar presentations were later transcribed and shared with those in attendance. These 11 Legacy Scholar presentations comprise Part One of this book.

We are aware that the description of "legacy" to describe these scholars can all too easily connote a sense of reactionary elitism that is insensitive to the range and diversity of individuals who are working earnestly and faithfully to engage in this type of important academic work.

Our final list of 11 in this volume is not intended to be exhaustive or even representative of the full spectrum of voices available on the subject. Our initial wish list of presenters included another dozen or more names of individuals from disciplines outside of communication who were unavailable to participate for several legitimate reasons. And at some point, there is only so much time to prepare and pre-work to assign and we were already pushing those limits.

We are also quite aware that all the Legacy Scholars featured in this volume are White men, and we understand the unspoken message that can be sent and heard by this. At the time when the Legacy Scholars featured in this book were prominent, the Academy offered limited opportunities for women and people of color to participate in theological scholarship—particularly in the institutions and traditions that shaped this particular legacy. The absence of marginalized voices in this volume is not a reflection of their value or potential, but rather a recognition of the historical realities that shaped who was teaching, publishing, and leading in these academic spaces at the time. Our hope is that someone reading this book will be encouraged to address these limitations and offer future works that highlight such important, and often overlooked, voices.

That said, our goal in this collection is to draw upon the work and insight of several faithful Legacy Scholars over the past generations who have a long record of teaching, scholarship, and mentoring, particularly in the subject of what it means to be a Christian in the (non-Christian) Academy. Our Legacy Scholars have served in the Academy for many decades and have been among the primary, leading contributors to the corpus of what we now define as "Christian scholarship." And because of these decades of long service, they are in a unique position not only to bring novel and heuristic insights to the subject, but also to be retrospective about longer-term developments of their own work. Our Legacy Scholars have a lengthy track record of helping new generations of students and younger scholars grapple more productively and faithfully with faith-learning integration.

And while some of these Legacy Scholars—most notably Mark Noll and George Marsden—have published truly seminal works, the rest of our Legacy Scholars have contributed significantly to their respective fields and subfields in ways that have extended beyond the bounds of their own fields or disciplines. For these reasons, we believe that their ideas and reflections work particularly well to establish a framework and a set of questions and issues to guide the conversations that unfolded at our unconference and now appear in this volume.

Finally, given our culture's penchant for what C. S. Lewis coined as "chronological snobbery,"[4] we think that there is value in honoring the kind of thinking of our Legacy Scholars that has stood a longer test of time. This sort of respect and honor is humorously captured by a cartoon by Jack Harkema, a distinguished professor at Michigan State University, which caricatures the four Beatles of faith-informed intellectual activity in the Academy for the past 50 years—three of whom are part of our group of Legacy Scholars who comprise this volume.

Used with permission by the artist, Jack R. Harkema.

How to Read This Book

With all of this in mind, we encourage you to immerse yourself in the conversation as it unfolds in this edited volume. There are 11 short chapters that reproduce the contributions of the Legacy Scholars from the unconference, and then there are smaller contributions that feature others who responded to our Legacy Scholars to further the conversation. Contributions include long and short form essays, book reviews, case studies, think pieces, devotionals, prayers, and short meditations. We also invited a handful of individuals to contribute who were not in attendance at the unconference but who had special interest in or connection with one or more of the Legacy Scholars. Therefore, what provides unity across the collection is not the form of response but the attention to the unconference theme and responses to the Legacy Scholars' reflections on the key questions introduced above.

Our goal is for this volume to function as a heuristic that encourages and inspires readers and gives them a front-row seat to our exchanges. It is intended to be read as a conversation, not as a polished or uniform academic anthology. The spontaneity, diversity of format, and occasional informality are intentional—they reflect the dynamic, face-to-face nature of the unconference itself. Rather than smoothing out the edges for horizontal consistency, we chose to preserve the immediacy and authenticity of the moment.

In Part One, we begin with the Legacy Scholar presentations by Mark Noll and George Marsden since they were spotlighted in our unconference. The remaining Legacy Scholar contributions in Part One are ordered based on the flow of ideas that seemed to unfold during the editing process. The same goes for the responses to the Legacy Scholars offered by unconference attendees and others in Part Two. Rather than group the responses around a particular Legacy Scholar, we present them in a way that seems to capture the spirit of the exchanges and big ideas that emerged during our seven-plus hours of conversations. Four key themes seemed to capture the big ideas as we worked our way through the collection so we ended up grouping them accordingly: (1) Section One: Foundations and Historical Roots; (2) Section Two: Reimagining the University and Christian Higher Education; (3) Section Three: Communication, Pedagogy, and Intellectual Formation; (4) Section Four: Personal and Vocational Reflections; and (5) Section Five: The Church, Public Witness, and Evangelical Identity. You should expect some overlap among sections, but the five sections help break up a lengthy list of responses for the interested reader. Our hope is that readers will feel as though they are sitting among us, listening in, and even forming their own responses as the dialogue unfolds.

Our prayer is that your mind and heart will be rejuvenated by listening to the conversations about the relevance and value of distinctively Christian thinking and scholarship in our contemporary cultural moment, and that you will eventually join this important conversation yourself. In so doing, you will be joining a community of intellectuals, scholars, and theologians that go all the way back to second-century figures like Justin Martyr and Origen. May our thinking and our work show the same faithfulness as theirs to the glory of God.

Part I:
Legacy Scholar Presentations

Chapter 1

The Scandal of the Evangelical Mind: Then and Now

MARK A. NOLL

*[This chapter is a revised transcript of the author's
unconference video presentation.]*

Chapter Summary: This Legacy Scholar chapter assesses the current state of Christian scholarship in American universities, building on the author's earlier work in *The Scandal of the Evangelical Mind* first published in 1994. Noll highlights four key points: (1) The academic landscape for Christian scholars has improved, with a growing number of Christian voices across multiple disciplines, and more Christian organizations—like the CCSN—supporting faith-integration work; (2) However, challenges persist, particularly with economic pressures, ideological divides, and the decline of the humanities, which make the academic environment increasingly hostile for Christians; (3) There is a disconnect between the academic world and church communities, limiting the impact of scholarly work; and (4) Despite these obstacles, opportunities for Christian scholars to contribute to both academic and religious life are more abundant than ever. The author concludes by stressing the importance of combining intellectual clarity with charitable action.

THANK YOU FOR this invitation to address the Christianity and Communication Studies Network (CCSN). It's a special privilege for me to talk with this group. After I read your book that was published a few years ago, *Professing Christ: Christian Tradition and Faith-learning Integration in Public Universities*, I came away very impressed with the range of believers, the range of strategies, and the range of conceptions you presented concerning how to exist as faithful believers in a university setting.[1]

The assignment that I've been given is to attempt an assessment, now more than a generation after the publication of *The Scandal of the Evangelical Mind*,[2] about how I look upon the current situation for Christian learning and Christian activity in the American academic world. I was certainly no more than one of many voices at the time appealing for a healthy combination of, on the one side, rooted, stable, serious Christian faith, but also on the other side, open, dedicated, and discerning commitment to intellectual pursuits.

For today, I have a simple outline of two sets of two observations, so there are four points, none of them radical or dramatic. All of them are things that I'm sure you have talked about. First, the picture is brighter than it was. But second, the landscape is treacherous. Third, there are real problems in the Christian world. But fourth, there exist many ways forward.

The Picture is Brighter than it Was

So first, the picture is brighter than it was. When I was recently asked to prepare a new preface and afterward for a reprinting of *The Scandal of the Evangelical Mind*, I pointed out that compared to the situation 30 or 40 years ago, there are now many Christian voices actively publishing, actively contributing in many of our main academic disciplines. The book contains quite a few examples. Among the publications, I have been most impressed by works in serious Christian theology and Christian apologetics produced by philosophers—most of that work coming from university presses, especially Oxford University Press and Cornell University Press. Then there are the discipline-specific groups like the CCSN that, like the Christian philosophers, have provided viable organizations to promote academic and extra-academic encouragement for believers.

It is also noteworthy that the 180 or so members of the Council for Christian Colleges and Universities include many institutions that are trying to do more than just protect their students from the outside world but are also trying to engage that world with Christian values and Christian thinking. On another front, the Veritas Forum has enlisted a stellar lineup of outstanding scholars willing to be identified as believers and is coordinating a major new initiative to bring training and mentorship in Christian learning to new generations of younger scholars.

I'm also struck by the Christian studies centers that have been established on many pluralistic campuses and with the national organization that now links these centers. It has been my privilege to visit or at least know something about such centers at the University of Florida, University of Wisconsin, Cornell University, University of North Carolina, University of Chicago, University of Illinois, University of Minnesota, University of Virginia, and Duke University. They are usually funded and supported by local church groups but are doing a relatively new thing in maintaining an understated but genuine Christian presence on the campuses of pluralistic universities. Having such an organization sometimes reveals how much Christian activity is present in the academic realm of the institutions where they exist. I recently read a publication from Anselm House, which is the Christian Study Center at the University of Minnesota, that pointed out a striking fact about that university—which is that there are probably more Christian faculty and certainly more Christian students at the University of Minnesota than at almost any of the self-identified Christian colleges or universities. Of course, they are dispersed throughout a major university, but it was especially encouraging to recognize that reality.

In sum, it is certainly not the case that we are living in a golden age of Christian learning. It is also certain that Christian scholars do not dominate either the intellectual realm or loom especially large in the public sphere. But it is a reasonable judgment to say that there is now more scholarship by individuals willing to be identified as believers, more scholarship with observable Christian meaning disseminated in pluralistic venues, more intentional Christian thinking about pedagogy, and more American academics regarding their work as a calling from God than ever before in the nation's history.

The Landscape is Treacherous

But second, the landscape is treacherous. There is little need to expand on this matter since all of you have experienced the way university-age students, and even more their parents, seem to be focused on economic self-interest with an overriding concern to find their first money-producing job.

For the humanities, which are the areas that traditionally have invited the most direct Christian thinking, declining enrollments mean declining job opportunities for aspiring scholars. We also live in a world in which experts on social media—those who really know how to use the Internet, those who make video presentations attractive—dominate public discourse, and with a very large influence in the academic sphere as well. And this is not to speak of the ideological factors that are common knowledge. Political partisanship affects almost all academic domains. Cancel culture and politically driven interventions in public education make the academic life, which many people got into because it promised space and relaxation, precarious. Identity politics, the United States's fraught racial history, the fact that most college and university environments favor progressive certainties concerning families, sexuality, race, and economic inequality—all of these realities can make it very difficult for religious believers who question the certainties that seem to dominate the university world of our day.

These difficulties are widespread in pluralistic academic settings, but sometimes also in institutions identified as Christian. Examples of slights, bullying, and discrimination against those who wish to express their faith even in appropriate ways are not uncommon. These difficulties are real. Thus, alongside what might be called, from some perspectives, the best of times for Christian intellectual life, we can also talk about the worst of times for the academic environment.

Real Problems in the Christian World

Third, there are real problems in the Christian world. For the life of the mind, I would identify the most serious problem as the disconnect between the academic world and the churches. Paul Miller is a well-regarded political theorist at Georgetown University who has published several well-received university press books. Recently he brought out *The Religion of American Greatness: What Is Wrong with Christian Nationalism?* from Inter-Varsity Press, with this sobering judgment: "We do not lack for good academic political theology [he lists several books from Christian and university presses], but that theology is not getting to the pews because pastors are not transmitting it."[3] The books he listed do not necessarily agree, but all show how to be a serious-minded Christian studying political life and the values that are influencing America's political culture. Yet the solid Christian reasoning of that kind is not reaching the pews because pastors are not transmitting it. I would amend Miller's conclusion only to say that this is a weakness lying at the feet of professors as well as pastors.

We do live in a world where the masters of social media tend to be partisan, populist, conspiracy mongers for whom scholarship, particularly disinterested scholarship, is a dirty word. My sense when working on *The Scandal of the Evangelical Mind* and still today is that that most academics want to do the kind of good quality work that will be recognized by their peers. It is not that they think other people are unimportant or that non-academic venues are unimportant. But if you've committed to mastery of one particular realm of scholarship, and you are teaching or writing or trying to organize projects in that area, you are most concerned about speaking to those who have that same level of interest in and commitment to your subject. But the churches mostly exist in a world where attitudes, outlooks, impressions, presuppositions, are dominated by what comes through social media and popular communications. It has taken me quite a while to realize that the American context constrains what academics can accomplish among academics, but even more in the world at large. There may be good quality thinking in the churches and by Christians in the Academy. But that good quality work will not have the kind of impact it could have if there is not also attention to the means of propagation, the means of publicity, the means of presentation of solid work in the world. Although there are some healthy signs, it seems to me that Christian academics, along with scholars in general, have been slow to realize how important it is to think about communicating in the broader realm.

A historical footnote: for some time, it has struck me as significant that at the dawn of the television age, a medium that would have an immense impact on all aspects of life in the Western world, there were very few Christian analysis of television. One small book by E. J. Carnell of Fuller Theological Seminary is the only one that I know of that attempted an analysis.[4] Such lack of attention is indicative of the need for those interested in Christian learning and committed to the life of the mind as believers, to be considering the broader landscape in which ideas, arguments, and important discussions take place. The churches have not been a particularly welcoming place for that kind of broader dissemination to occur.

Many Ways Forward

But fourth, there do exist many ways forward. I come back to being heartened by the really good work that is going on in many academic domains and many kinds of scholarship with many different approaches—all striving for clearer thinking and more charitable thinking about how the world works. I am also encouraged when Christian academics take their place in local Christian congregations. After I published *The Scandal of the Evangelical Mind*, I heard from quite a few people who said in one way or another, "I feel that in my academic life, I can't tell people that I'm a serious church member. I feel at church that I can't tell people I'm committed to the academic life." That situation is still with us, but there are now more opportunities in more different Christian churches for those who have a calling as academics to share that calling with the church, even as they are being strengthened in their personal Christian lives in the church.

Let me refer again to the book that your organization produced not long ago, *Professing Christ, Christian Tradition and Faith-learning Integration in Public Universities*, where I was so greatly impressed with the number of practical strategies that the contributors described for how they had gone about living out a Christian vocation, almost always in pluralistic, secular environments. I was really impressed with the way in which authors wrote about attention to pedagogy, about viewing pedagogy in relationship to scholarship, and about bringing together scholarship, pedagogy, and life in general. Here are a few of the phrases that I found to be helpful for suggesting a path forward for scholars and teachers in other fields: worldview critique, sacramental vision, a Daniel perspective, faith integration, an epistemology of love, compassionate invitational pedagogy, a relationship perspective, servant leadership, discussing authenticity, and probing presuppositions. Showing how the teaching behind these phrases worked out in practice pointed ways forward that includes building Christian character and strengthening Christian congregants alongside improving Christian intellectual life. And that combination of character, congregation, and intellectual life makes me hopeful, even though the general academic landscape is indifferent or opposed to many of the things that Christian believers, who are scholars, would like to accomplish.

Going further toward the goals of Christian learning is possible. And it's appropriate at the end of this brief presentation, to repeat what seems to me to be the goals of all who are involved in the enterprise of Christian learning. One goal is clarity, seeing more clearly what God has made possible for those who are concerned about the world. But then another goal is charity, acting always with the understanding that all humans are made in the image of God, and all are called to redemption in Christ.

Chapter 2

Mere Christian Scholarship

GEORGE MARSDEN

[Note: This essay is based on a video interview that Quentin Schultze conducted with George Marsden for the unconference which Schultze later edited for print.]

Chapter Summary: Legacy Scholar George Marsden reflects on the evolution of Christian scholarship, drawing from his own experience and his now classic book *The Outrageous Idea of Christian Scholarship* first published in 1997. Marsden reaffirms that Christian scholars must reflect seriously how their faith shapes their academic pursuits, engaging with the broader academic community while maintaining distinct faith-driven perspectives. Marsden highlights the importance of humility in scholarship, emphasizing that Christian scholars must embrace a diversity of viewpoints, including within their own faith traditions. He also discusses the current challenges facing Christians in today's Academy, including the increasing difficulty of securing academic positions and the polarization within academia. Despite these obstacles, Marsden highlights Christian scholarship as both a calling and a rewarding pursuit, urging scholars to act with integrity, engage respectfully, and contribute thoughtfully to academic discourse.

I'M GRATEFUL FOR the rich conversations that my book, *The Outrageous Idea of Christian Scholarship*, has generated over the years.[1] The word "outrageous" in the title might have helped generate interest among both supporters and detractors of the idea of "Christian scholarship." As best I can remember, I made it up, based partly on a comment I received from a mainstream scholar who said "Christian scholarship" was a loony idea. It occurred to me that "outrageous" would be good to use in the title of my book. I don't come up with many great book titles, but that one worked very well with Christians and non-Christians alike.

I think that the basic aspects of Christian scholarship are pretty much the same today as they were when I started 60 years ago. A scholar who is also a Christian ought to be thinking about how their faith shapes their scholarly agenda. Why are you doing this scholarship in the first place? Whom are you trying to serve? What good are you trying to do? They are all pretty obvious investigative and ethical questions that have to do with the purpose and nature of our work.

Also, the Christian scholar today, as before, can enter existing conversations in a discipline, especially addressing the "secular" ideas that might merit critique. Entering contemporary academic discourse does not have to be combative or even negative. We Christians use the same types of reason, evidence, and questioning that other scholars might employ—although our underlying assumptions and questions might be different and our conclusions different because of our own, faith-shaped examination of the issues and disagreements addressed.

For instance, we might ask: "What does it mean that we live in a created universe?" "What does it mean that there is a right and wrong, or some sort of moral order that's not simply arbitrary or humanly concocted?" What does it mean for our scholarship if we generally agree with Blaise Pascal (a seventeenth-century French mathematician and physicist who wrote *Pensées*) that human beings are both the crown of creation and the scum of the earth? What about our faith-based assumption that we want to honor and love our neighbors even though they, like us, are flawed? It seems to me that the Fall from Grace guarantees our scholarship, even as Christians, will be imperfect and that we need to learn from others. These are the kinds of helpful, enduring Christian questions and perspectives that we can bring into academic situations. In other words, we seek to identify root truth, faith-based wisdom, in tune with Scripture but also proven by history and empirical investigation, that gives us a basis for entering scholarship in fresh, interesting, and sometimes even compelling ways.

Of course, since Christian scholarship is, like all other scholarship, imperfect, we are always feeling our way through the work—perhaps even testing out our ideas with students and colleagues. We humbly invite others to critique our efforts.

Along the way, some of our efforts emerge that really work for a lot of people. Our work gains traction among Christians and perhaps even among mainstream scholars. The "truth" within our work begins to speak for itself.

Still, we face a confounding situation both within and beyond the Christian Academy—the existence of many different paradigms, perspectives, and methodologies. This is why we should beware of saying that there is only one, right, and fully accurate "Christian perspective." In fact, different Christian theological and biblical traditions often bring their own strengths to the general goal of Christian scholarship. We Christians must engage with and sometimes negotiate with other Christian scholars in our disciplines, and in the overarching, perspectival disciplines such as philosophy and theology. We ought not to silo our efforts. In this sense, there is an inherently multi-disciplinary aspect of Christian scholarship.

Since I started doing scholarship some 50 years ago, there is much more variety in perspectives. It used to be that there were only a few competing theories and perspectives in most disciplines. Today, partly because of postmodern challenges to traditional, reason-based scholarship, most disciplines, even in the natural sciences, have vibrant, competing models, theories, and methods.

I believe that there is a positive side to this twenty-first century plethora of ideas. There is much more recognition today of the legitimacy of diversity of points of view. So the mainstream, largely empirical argument that there ought not to be Christian perspectives has faded. Some people had the old idea that scientific thinking would always progress, and that religious thinking was based on non-empirical principles and so was outdated. The scholarly idea from the 1960s and 1970s called the "secularization hypothesis" itself has now been largely rejected. Societies have secularized somewhat, but in many parts of the world faith communities are growing. Internationally speaking, faith commitments and communities are alive and well.

Today, many mainstream scholars accept the fact that faith-shaped, well-articulated, winsomely expressed Christian perspectives should be included in disciplinary and cross-disciplinary discourse.

Encouraging Cross-Disciplinary Discourse

Terry Lynn Cornwell

I could not agree more that Christian scholars have a duty to identify truth and faith-based wisdom in tune with Scripture and affirmed by history and empirical investigation. That solid scholarly perspective is ripe for extension into cross-disciplinary discourse.

One relatively new discipline, especially appropriate for examination by Christian scholarship, is the expanding field of animal theology. Examining the work of ethicist and animal theologian Andrew Linzey, for example, allows Christian scholars to initiate cross-disciplinary dialogue between communication studies and animal theology. It also allows them to delve into inter-faith perspectives, which have traditionally been more favorable in their treatment of animals than Christianity. In this context, one communication theory that can be applied to animal rights is Standpoint Theory, which is discussed in relation to my essay on animal theology in Part Two, Chapter 32 (pages 227–230) of this volume.

Certainly, this kind of openness to competing ideas has its downsides as well. I like the characterization that Mark Noll, my very close colleague, has made. He says that except in the hard sciences, it's the intellectual Wild West. If we say the "wrong" thing—potentially offensive to non-Christians—someone might try to "shoot" us down. Culture and politics are very polarizing today. We've always had some of this polarization, but I think that politics has become the religion, even the primary religion, for an awful lot of people on both sides of the political spectrum. Many people, including scholars, have a preset group of loyalties, and they judge everyone according to whose side they think people are on. This makes it difficult to say the "right" things and to communicate well, particularly with people who might be on the other side of the political or culture-war divides. So I think in this intellectual Wild West we Christians need to be friends of law and order, demonstrating the Fruit of the Spirit in how we conduct ourselves.

I like Jonathan Rauch's book, *The Constitution of Knowledge: A Defense of Truth.*[2] He urges us to act with the kinds of checks and balances evident in the U.S. Constitution. Particularly in the age of the Internet and social media, it is easy for us all to pick up false views, spread them, and allow ourselves to become embroiled in the heated rhetoric of the moment. Christian scholars ought to be known as those who really are patient champions of law and order, employing solid evidence, good arguments, and personal integrity—and as those who recognize the same among those with whom we disagree. I have found that when I conduct myself this way, I gain mutual respect from a wide swath of people, except perhaps from those who are vehemently on the oppositive sides of particular issues.

In other words, I think it is important for us to emphasize the integration of Christian scholarship and the Christian virtues. For instance, we should speak the truth in love. And we should treat other scholars as our neighbors, biblically speaking. We should even love our scholarly enemies, to use the biblical language.

One thing that has changed radically since I began as a history professor many years ago is the decreased availability of teaching positions even at major universities. Today, a Christian who wants to enter the Academy and join the project of Christian scholarship faces the potentially disheartening and practical difficulty of finding and keeping a job. Unfortunately, the most difficult disciplines to get jobs in today—such as philosophy, history, and English—are the fields where there has been a renaissance of wonderful Christian scholarship in recent decades.

Then again, when I was a young scholar, even though I had a job teaching at Calvin College, I did not know what the future offered. I had my foot in the Christian academic door, so to speak, and not at a major research university. I worked hard to produce solid scholarship while teaching. I found other, like-minded colleagues to work with and we supported one another.

I also realized early on that I should not be too "Christianly" parochial in my research. I needed to be able to speak to both mainstream scholars and to other Christians from traditions other than my own, conservative, Presbyterian background. At the same time, however, I needed to write about my tradition with a sense of being both appreciative and also fairly critical. I saw this as a way to help myself and other Christians understand where "we" (those in my conservative tradition) came from, what we knew and assumed, and how much of my tradition was shaped by its cultural setting rather than formed by perennial Christian assumptions (root truths—similar to what C. S. Lewis called "mere Christianity").[3] This self-critical work about my own Christian "tribe" turned out to be something that people on the outside were really appreciative of because it wasn't just celebrating or defining my own fundamentalist background, on the one hand, and it wasn't just criticizing and dismissing it, on the other. In a sense, I began doing what all good scholars do—weigh the evidence and make fair judgments that speak the truth in love.

In the end, I think Christian scholarship is a calling. It's risky on many fronts. Yet it can be enormously fun and satisfying—even outrageously so.

Chapter 3

Listening to the Call

NICHOLAS WOLTERSTORFF

[Note: This essay is based on a video interview that Quentin Schultze conducted with Nicholas Wolterstorff for the unconference which Schultze later edited for print.]

Chapter Summary: In this Legacy Scholar chapter, Nicholas Wolterstorff reflects on his journey as a Christian philosopher and scholar. He discusses the evolution of his views on art, particularly in relation to his influential work *Art in Action*, where he emphasized the need to expand the scope of aesthetics beyond high art to include everyday forms of art. Wolterstorff highlights the importance of viewing art as embodied and integrated into daily life. The conversation also touches on the broader trajectory of Christian scholarship, noting the shift from viewing faith as an "add-on" to academic disciplines to understanding it as a perspective through which one engages with various fields and disciplines of study. Wolterstorff reflects on the value of mentoring and offers practical advice for aspiring Christian scholars, emphasizing the importance of passion, skill, and responsiveness to several current and emerging challenges in the Academy.

Quentin Schultze

Hi everybody. I'm Quentin Schultze, retired emeritus professor from Calvin University, and we're shooting this right now here in one of the rooms at Calvin University. With me is a distinguished philosopher, Nicholas Wolterstorff. "Wolterstorff" is hard to spell; look it up. "Nicholas" is easy. But he goes by "Nick." Nick, it's a joy to see you again.

Nicholas Wolterstorff

Thank you, Quin.

Quentin

I arrived at Calvin in 1982, so we overlapped for a few years before you left for Yale in 1989. When I arrived at Calvin in 1982, I had already read some of your books. The particular book I'm going to show here is an old one. It's your 1980 publication, *Art in Action: Toward a Christian Aesthetic*.[1] This book, Nick, had a tremendous influence on how I began to study popular culture and art. Written from a Christian perspective, it gave me an angle on saying that the approach of the Christian to art goes beyond looking at elite or fine art—great as that may be—to looking at art in general.

Nicholas

Right.

Quentin

Art is part of life. So, I want to commend this book to you, our listeners. Then there's another one titled *Works and Worlds of Art*.[2] All of you, especially those in media, should take a look at that one as well. And just before we began this interview you told me about another one on art that has come out very recently.

Nicholas

Yes, it's titled *Art Rethought: the Social Practices of Art*.[3] In that early book, *Art in Action*, I did what you, Quin, report. I argued that we should not just focus on high art: museum paintings, concert hall music, etc. Art is part of life, and we should look at the many ways in which it's involved in life. But I didn't do that in *Art in Action*. I argued that we *should* do that; but I didn't actually do it.

Quentin

Yeah.

Nicholas

Remind me of the publication date of *Art in Action*.

Quentin

It was published in 1987.

Nicholas

It took me almost 40 years to get around to doing, in *Art Rethought*, what I argued in *Art in Action* we should do. For example, in *Art Rethought* I devote a chapter to analyzing how work songs function as an accompaniment to work.

Quentin

Fascinating.

Nicholas

And I devote a chapter to analyzing how the Byzantine icons function, and, more generally, to how liturgical art functions. In a chapter on social protest art, I consider in some detail the powerful work of Käthe Kollwitz, a German graphic artist who worked between the two world wars. So—to repeat—in *Art Rethought* I finally do what 40 years earlier I said we should do. Wow! Forty years.

Quentin

Forty years. I'm glad you stayed with it. Back then, those working in the field of aesthetics concentrated almost entirely on high art. What was it that prodded you, in the 1970s, to argue that the field should be expanded? Why didn't you content yourself with doing what your colleagues in the field were doing? What was the burr under your saddle?

Nicholas

I'm not entirely sure, Quin, but I think the answer is the following. I grew up in a tiny village in southwest Minnesota, Bigelow. My father worked in the local grocery store. In his spare time, he was a craftsman, a woodworker. I can see him yet, lovingly working with wood in the evenings and on weekends. When I became a philosopher and began reading around in aesthetics, over and over I saw the crafts being put down as "mere crafts." There was a pecking order: fine art on top, the crafts below somewhere. I bristled at that. In retrospect, I think what was subconsciously operating in me was that I was convinced that what my father was doing with wood was important. It was not *mere* something. In addition to being a woodworker, my father also did pen and ink drawings. I can see him yet, sitting at the dining room table in the evenings, doing drawings. He never indicated that one of these was superior to the other, that the drawings which hung on the wall were superior to the chairs he made that we sat on. So I think it was being reared in that family.

Quentin

Let me now take things in a somewhat different direction. One of the things that struck me when I became a Christian in my early college days and started reading theology, especially biblical theology, and then later, systematic theology, was the importance for scholarship, regardless of one's field, of the fact that we are creatures: what we're created for, what we can and cannot do by the way we're created, and so forth. Any thoughts on that?

Nicholas

Well, one feature of how we're created is that we're created with bodies. A lot of writing in the field of aesthetics makes it sound as if art is made out of ideas and doesn't involve the body, or matter. So one of the points I was concerned to make in *Art in Action* was that, in creating art, one engages one's body and the material world. It's the experience of painters that their body, in its engagement with the material world, tells them to do something that they had not intellectually anticipated doing. They put down a line, whereupon the line says, "we need another line here." The artist says, "But putting a line there was not part of my plan." The line talks back: "That may be; but we need a companion line here."

Quentin

Again, a change of direction. May I give away your age?

Nicholas

Sure.

Quentin

Okay, I think I've got it right. You're 93.

Nicholas

No, Quin, only 92.

Quentin

Ninety-two. Sorry about that. I don't know what information I was going on, but I was close.

Nicholas

You were close.

Quentin

At any rate, you have been in the business of scholarship as a Christian for a long time. You were into it early on when it was really beginning to take off in different fields: history, sociology, psychology, your own field of philosophy. A lot of people came to you for mentoring; at one point, I did so as well. So what has changed for you, in how you think about Christian scholarship, over the time that you've been involved in it?

Nicholas

Quin, I am deeply grateful to being privileged to have lived through an extraordinary time in the burgeoning of Christian scholarship. In the late 1950s, when I was beginning my career as a professor, I came across a book—I forget its title—that discussed the typical curricula of Christian colleges of the time. Almost invariably what was happening in Christian colleges in the 1930s, the 1940s, and the 1950s was this: the standard subjects were taught pretty much as they were taught everywhere; and then, typically, the college president taught what was called a capstone course. The basic topics in this capstone course were Christian morality, along with arguments for the existence of God, for the reliability of Scripture, and so forth. The basic idea was that Christianity, and religion in general, is an add-on: beliefs about the transcendent are added on to what we all believe about the mundane. You study ordinary sociology, philosophy, etc., and then you add on Christian morality and doctrine. A voluminous and brilliant book on this topic is by the philosopher Charles Taylor, titled *A Secular Age*.[4] In it, Taylor describes in detail this add-on view of religion and then proceeds to powerfully criticize it.

Then what happened in the Christian college movement, in the late 1950s and early 1960s, was the emergence of a movement in which "integration" was the key word, *integration of faith and learning*. The idea spread abroad that Christianity is not just an add-on to standard ways of viewing reality but incorporates a distinct worldview. And the thought was that Christian scholars should integrate the Christian worldview with history, with philosophy, with communications, and so forth. So in the 1960s there were a lot of summer seminars in the Christian colleges devoted to integration. I participated in some of those. But I began to feel uneasy for two reasons. One, Christian worldview. Yes, Christianity speaks to the world and to life in the world, not just to the transcendent; but identifying Christianity with "the Christian worldview" began to feel to me like a prison. For one thing, Christianity is more than a view; it is, if I had to use a single word, an "orientation." And any attempt to formulate a Christian worldview should always be tentative, open to correction by Scripture. Scripture is more fundamental than some worldview that we formulate.

Second, the implicit image is that here is the Christian worldview, and there is philosophy, sociology, communications, or whatever, and the project is now to integrate them, to tie them together somehow. Christian scholarship never felt like that to me. Philosophy never felt like something separate from my Christian conviction which I then had to integrate in some way. I found myself thinking of philosophical issues *as a Christian*. My philosophical self and my Christian self did not come as two separate selves that had to be integrated.

More recently, there has been a third movement—I don't know how widespread it is—epitomized by the titles of some books issued by the Council for Christian Colleges and Universities: *History through the Eyes of Faith, Sociology through the Eyes of Faith*, etc.[5] That seems to me the right metaphor. We don't tie two distinct things together, Christianity with some academic discipline. Rather, the Christian scholar looks through the lens of Christian faith at history, at philosophy, whatever, and describes what they see.

I have lived through these three stages. And somewhere along the line, as the integration view was fading away and the "through the eyes of faith" view was taking its place, what happened was the emergence of societies of Christian scholarship in the various disciplines. Christian historians started a society, Christians in literature did, Christians in visual art— on and on. It was a phenomenal development. In 1978, we Christian philosophers began the Society for Christian Philosophy. The big American Philosophical Society has a sizeable number of affiliated societies. The Society for Christian Philosophy is the largest of these affiliated societies. Several members of the society have been presidents of the APA, Alvin Plantinga and myself among others. It's been a truly remarkable development; I am deeply grateful to have been a participant.

When I entered the field of philosophy, in the late 1950s, I knew of Christians in the field; they were, I would say, guarded. At the time there was a philosophical movement, logical positivism, which argued that religious talk is devoid of sense; it makes no genuine claims. Then, in the late 1950s and early 1960s, positivism collapsed, mainly due to internal difficulties in rigorously and plausibly formulating its basic theses. The floodgates were opened and, as it were, Christians walked through the gates and began to think and write about philosophical issues through the eyes of faith. It was exhilarating.

That was a long speech. Sorry about that.

Quentin

Not at all. That was a great opening for having you address what's going on in scholarship in more recent years with the pluralistic turn, the postmodern turn—whatever you want to call it. I have in mind the movement away from thinking that there is one approach to scholarship and one kind of understanding, whatever field you're in, but multiple approaches. Would you talk about that a bit? It's my impression that a lot of Christian folks are worried about this development.

Nicholas

You're right. A good many philosophers nowadays, maybe most of them, don't think of philosophy as some sort of objective, generically human, enterprise but think of philosophers as approaching the discipline with distinct worldviews: secularists of various sorts with their worldviews, physicalists with theirs, humanists, religious people of various sorts. With our different worldviews we together engage in philosophy, debating the issues, sometimes finding common ground, often agreeing to disagree. That's how most philosophers nowadays think of what goes on in philosophy.

Quentin

And that's been an opening for Christian philosophers?

Nicholas

Definitely.

Quentin

That's certainly also true in my field, the history of rhetoric, which was the earliest manifestation of the academic study of communication. It's wide open, now. Even defining what rhetoric is, proves to be an interesting and controversial issue.

I also want to ask you about the current social context of scholarship: the divisiveness in society, and how that gets reflected in the Academy. A lot of people in the Academy feel unfairly criticized, both by people in the Academy and outside, and they criticize in turn. The present-day Academy does not seem to be, in general, the kind of place where people can engage the differences of perspective very well.

Nicholas

Yeah. There's a lot of talk about political correctness, wokeness, and all of that. I don't doubt that there is a lot of wokeness in present-day universities, more in some than in others. But rather than confining myself to generalities, let me instead talk about the university in which I taught for 15 years, Yale. I taught here at Calvin for 30 years and then taught at Yale for the remainder of my career. My teaching at Yale was not significantly different from my teaching at Calvin. People describe Yale as a secular university; if the occasion is relevant, I correct them and say my experience was that it was, instead, a pluralist university. I was fully honored as who I was; I did not conceal the fact that I was a Christian philosopher.

I was a full professor in Yale's Divinity School, a distinctly Christian divinity school, but also an adjunct professor in its philosophy department and its religious studies department. I taught philosophy at Yale the same way I taught it at Calvin. Robert Adams, an ordained Presbyterian clergyman, was chair of the philosophy department. His wife, Marilyn Adams, an ordained Episcopal priest, taught theology in the divinity school. Bob Adams regularly taught seminars in the nineteenth-century German theologian, Schleiermacher. There was a person in the English department who regularly taught a course in Jewish hermeneutics. There was a course in the law school taught jointly by a theologian from the Divinity School and a law professor. I could go on. Yale, in my experience, was not a secular university but, rather, a genuinely pluralist university. I never felt put down as a Christian scholar.

Quentin

So even at a school which has a phenomenal reputation like Yale and produces so many great PhDs in so many different fields, you felt quite comfortable there, respected.

Nicholas

Yes.

Quentin

So it may be that what we hear about today, and is reported in the *Chronicle of Higher Education*, about all these conflicts, is quite local: certain places, certain personalities.

Nicholas

I don't doubt that it's true at some universities, especially state universities, but let me add a bit to the picture I have drawn.

Quentin

Go ahead.

Nicholas

It's often said that present-day American universities are hostile to the Christian witness. It was my experience, it's much more complicated than that. Every fall, when I was at Yale, I would teach a course in philosophy of religion; typically, about 80 students were enrolled. It was a lecture course, open to everyone.

Quentin

Undergraduate or graduate?

Nicholas

Both. It was basically an undergrad course, but graduate students were welcome to enroll. Yale's departmental boundaries are extraordinarily porous. So there would be law school students in the course, medical school students, and so forth. Almost invariably, about halfway through the semester, a student who had graduated from a Christian college and was now enrolled in the Divinity School would raise his hand—it was always a male— and would say something like, "As Jesus says in John 16 verse 5." As they were speaking, I would look around and see students whispering to their neighbors, putting their face in their hands, saying, I imagined, "Where did this rube come from?" So I would take the student aside after class and say, "You can say approximately what you said, but you can't say it in those words. Remember, this is not a Christian college campfire. This is a Yale University classroom." Typically, the student would reply, "Well, how should I have asked the question?" I replied, "You know, I can't put it into words, but I think if you just listen for a while you'll catch on." Invariably, they did catch on. So it was not hostility to the content of what they said that produced the negative reaction. It was that they had not learned how to speak in a language appropriate to a Yale philosophy classroom.

Quentin

Yes.

Nicholas

They knew how to speak around the campfires of their Christian colleges, but not in this new situation. In my experience, that was usually the source of the hostility.

Quentin

There we go, not understanding the audience. In my field there's a term for this: *code-switching.*

Nicholas

Okay.

Quentin

That's a great example. You have to switch the code. That has also been my experience as a teacher: a different audience requires a different approach, a different code.

Nicholas

The same thing could happen as a teacher, yes.

Code-switching

Elaine V. Fung

Code-switching is when a speaker changes "from one dialect to another," and a dialect is any variant of a language and may include different "pronunciation, vocabulary, and/or grammar."[6] A few examples of English dialects are standard English, British English, and African-American vernacular English.[7] Named by sociolinguists, it was a way to help "understand the phenomena of individuals switching their accents and language to conform or deviate from different social groups or settings."[8]

An example of how code-switching works is in the reality dating television show *Love is Blind*. In this show, contestants got to know each other without seeing but only hearing other contestants. The goal is to make a connection and find a partner. In the first episode of the first season, Lauren, a Black woman, used code-switching when talking with Jon, a White man, when he guessed that she was African-American. Lauren responded, "with a higher pitched, slower, stereotypically White-girl intonation, 'Actually, no, I'm White,'" to which Jon positively reacted back.[9] Rosenboom and Joseph found that while code-switching may help Black women contestants win the game, it is also at their cost of mental and physical health.

When Christian scholars communicate, there should be mindful code-switching depending on the settings and audiences. For instance, Christian scholars addressing a pluralistic audience, as Wolterstorff and Schultze discussed, should package their communication differently than that of a Christian audience.

Two additional readings that are helpful in understanding code-switching are Cadge and Sigalow's "Negotiating Religious Differences: The Strategies of Interfaith Chaplains in Healthcare," and Elkins and Hanke's "Code-Switching to Navigate Social Class in Higher Education and Student Affairs."[10]

Quentin

Let me conclude with this question. You've mentored a tremendous number of people over the years. Especially in philosophy, your influence through mentoring people has been terrific. So if someone just entering graduate school came to you today and said, "Can you give me some advice? I want to be a scholar, and I want to live out my faith as a scholar." What would you say to them?

Nicholas

What would I say to them? Over the years, students would come to me and ask that question, should they go into this, should they go into that. Eventually I learned to put three questions to them.

Quentin

I've heard this before, and it's great. So, listen up, gang.

Nicholas

What do you love? What are you good at? And is it worthwhile?

What do you love? It was my experience over the years with certain students that taught me to ask that question. Every now and then I would have a student, quite often, for some reason, a Korean, who was forced by their parents to go into some well-paying profession, typically law or medicine. But they didn't love it. I had other students who, for example, loved philosophy and wanted to go into it but were not good at it. And then there were those who loved what they were considering going into and were good at it but had never seriously asked themselves whether it was worth doing.

What do you love? Are you good at it? And is it worth doing? You may not be able to find a profession that satisfies all three criteria. But that's what you should look for.

Quentin

And scholarship is one of those things.

Nicholas

Yes. Nowadays I would add a fourth piece of advice: respond to the challenges that fall on your doorstep. Don't have a rigid agenda for your life that you just grind out no matter what. No doubt this reflects an episode in my own career.

In 1976, I was sent by Calvin to a conference in South Africa. There I heard so-called *coloreds* from South Africa issue a pain-laden call for justice. This was in the days when apartheid was still in force. Up to that time I had not thought about justice, not in any sustained way. I had not read about justice, had not written about justice. But listening to these people I had the overwhelming feeling that I could not ignore this cry, that it would be deeply irresponsible for me to do so. I had to put justice on my agenda—as a philosopher, not as an activist, but as a philosopher. Since then, I have thought and written a good deal about justice. Everything I have thought and written about justice is a response to that unexpected call dropping on my doorstep. I have come to think that that is what a Christian should do: listen to the call. Don't just grind out your own agenda.

Quentin

Yeah. I remember one time when I came to you. We sat in the backyard of your house and talked about the field of communication. At a certain point you looked at something I had written and said, "Quin, I don't think you are answering the questions that most people are asking." You probably don't remember that.

Nicholas

Right, I don't remember it.

Quentin

But that's what you said to me. I said, "What do you mean?" And you said, "Well, at any point in time, in any discipline, there are certain questions that people are asking; if you do your work in tune with those questions, people will be inclined to listen."

Nicholas

Yes, that's right.

Quentin

Whereas if you just see yourself as part of the history of the discipline, just connecting to the past and ignoring the current discourse, you'll be ignored by all but a few specialists.

Nicholas

Exactly.

Quentin

People will not be interested in what you are saying, you won't find an audience, and you won't have much of an impact.

Nicholas

On the basis of my thinking and writing about justice, I would now say one more thing to a prospective young scholar. Treat with dignity everyone that you engage. As you will discover, there are a lot of put-downs in the Academy: senior scholars putting down young scholars who they think are threatening or challenging them, and so forth. There's a lot of viciousness. Do not be a part of it. Honor everyone.

Quentin

That may be more significant nowadays than ideological differences.

Nicholas

Yes. It's not just content, but it's also how you conduct yourself, that should bespeak your Christian faith.

Quentin

Thank you, Nick, you're a blessing.

Nicholas

You're welcome.

Chapter 4

Five Root Assumptions for Communication Scholarship

QUENTIN SCHULTZE

*[This chapter is a revised transcript of the author's
unconference video presentation.]*

Chapter Summary: In this Legacy Scholar chapter, Schultze outlines five guiding
faith-inspired assumptions that have shaped his Christian communication scholarship and practice: (1) first, he argues that all communication is action, carrying
moral responsibility toward God, others, and creation; (2) second, he emphasizes
that messaging originates from the heart, acknowledging the emotional depth of
human communication; (3) third, Schultze stresses that the primary goal of communication should be understanding, advocating for listening over speaking to
truly grasp others' perspectives; (4) fourth, he highlights storytelling as the most
powerful form of expression, believing it offers both context and engagement.
Finally, (5) the author concludes by asserting that excellence in scholarship,
teaching, and communication is a Christian calling, urging scholars to serve their
audiences with integrity and skill.

I WOULD LIKE to look at how the Christian faith can inspire, inform, and shape both the
study and practice of human communication. More specifically, I would like to address the
scholarly assumptions (or "root" truths) that can guide us along the way. What might such
fundamental assumptions look like in the field of communication, specifically for Christians who are working either in a mainstream or faith-based university?

I offer five aspects of communication from faith-inspired work that have shaped my
scholarship and teaching at both religious and mainstream universities.

All Speech is Action

First, all human "speech"—all words, texts, movies, podcasts—is action. We communication scholars are in the business of studying what human beings *do*.

This emphasis on communication as action means that we humans inherit responsibility ("respond-ability"). To put it in biblical terms, God creates the world, creates human

31

beings, and puts them *in* the world to take care of it, including to develop it. We humans respond with actions, including communication. And we do it before the face of a living God. We do it according to how and where God calls us. To me, this kind of responsibility is intuitive to all persons regardless of their religious or secular commitments.

If we look at human communication primarily as action, we gain a strong sense of it as an act of responsibility toward others—not just as personal expression. We inherit responsibility toward the Creator, toward others (our "neighbors"), toward ourselves, and toward the "environment" (or "Creation"). As teacher-scholars, we can look at our colleagues and students as our immediate neighbors; they merit careful, ethical consideration in our everyday discourse. Therefore, when I teach or write about human communication, I generally frame it in terms of responsible action—what we *do* and to whom we are *responsible* for doing it. This is why I think we should all consider the importance of Speech Act Theory in formulating our root assumptions about the nature of human communication.

Speech Act Theory

Elaine V. Fung

Speech Act Theory was built upon Ludwig Wittgenstein's ordinary language philosophy, J. L. Austin's foundations, and John Searle's elaboration.[1] Speech Act Theory explains how words not only contain information but also action. There are four types of speech actions: (1) utterance act (speaker's words pronunciation); (2) propositional act (speaker's words about belief); (3) illocutionary act (listener's understanding of the words' intention), and (4) perlocutionary act (listener's behavior change due to the words' effect). Under the illocutionary act, there are five types: assertive, directive, commissive, expressive, and declarative.

Speech Act Theory applies to mediated communication in the sense that the choice of medium for communication is an illocutionary act.[2] Applying and expanding on Quentin Schultze's calling in this chapter, we have the responsibility to serve the audience in our choice or stewardship of specific communication technology or medium. For example, with an online asynchronous course, professors can include videos of themselves as a part of the course so students can have a richer online learning experience.

Two additional readings worth considering on this theory are Sophia Brown and Jonathan Matusitz's "U.S. Church Leaders' Responses to the Charleston Church Shooting: An Examination Based on Speech Act Theory," and Francisco Villarroel Ordenes and colleagues' article "Cutting through Content Clutter: How Speech and Image Acts Drive Consumer Sharing of Social Media Brand Messages."[3]

All Messaging Comes Ultimately from Our Hearts

Second, I assume that all of our "messaging"—our communication, in all media and forms—comes ultimately from our hearts. Jesus Christ offers this rather amazing bit of wisdom (see Matt. 15:17–19). We scholars like to focus on the mind or intellect. But I believe there is a strong affective or emotional dimension to human communication because of our createdness as God's image-bearing creatures. I think that this affectivity separates us, by and large, from the other creatures. We are born to love others, just as God loves us.

In other words, humankind communicates from the heart as well as the mind. We are emotional creatures, often easily hurt as well as encouraged. We worry about what others think about us. Do they like us? Respect us? Love us?

I learned this the hard way as a teaching professor. I had to determine how to engage my heart in my teaching. I realized that as soon as my teaching started gravitating toward the exchange of information, I would lose both the attention and the motivation of my students. I recently wrote an unusual book about my journey toward affective teaching: *Servant Teaching: Practices for Renewing Christian Higher Education*.[4] It is 30 very short chapters, each one explaining by example how I became an affective as well as effective teacher in responsible service to my students. After all, teaching is communication.

Understanding as the Primary Goal of Communication

Third, I believe that the primary thing we should seek in human communication is understanding. Ultimately, communication is shared understanding. This is the humble act of "standing under" God, other people, and even ourselves. We allow ourselves to consider what others are saying. We first listen in order to understand, not to instruct or persuade.

In fact, I believe that listening is the most important human communication skill. Such listening for understanding enables us to know how things really are in the world around and within us. Scripture distinguishes between those who are wise, that is, they understand reality, and those who are foolish. A foolish communicator speaks before listening. They don't know what they're talking about, making a movie about, or texting about. They assume rather than know.

Storytelling as the Most Potent Form of Human Expression

Fourth, I believe that the most potent form of human expression is storytelling—again, in many different media as well as in person. We should be terrific storytellers in how we tell the story of our work, our discipline, our scholarship, and so forth. We are not called merely to transmit information, but to give the field of communication a narrative context.

This is one of the reasons that I generally dislike contemporary textbooks; they don't have a sense of story, and hence they don't have a sense of perspective. Textbooks tend to shovel information, boring the daylights out of students. No student should be bored reading a book about human communication, one of the most interesting, fascinating, and essential parts of our lives.

In all of my teaching and scholarship, I try to contextualize my points by using relevant examples and illustrations in narrative form. Indeed, I see every class meeting with students as part of the story of their lives, my life, and the story of the discipline of communication.

The teachers and scholars who have most influenced me were good storytellers. They used stories to instruct, even to inspire. They engaged students who wanted to go to their classes and to listen to them. Students expected to learn something interesting.

Narrative Paradigm

Elaine V. Fung

Walter Fisher's Narrative Paradigm emphasizes the influence of narratives in helping human beings understand themselves and others.[5] Fisher assumes narration is a part of the very essence of what it means to be human and that storytelling is universal. Narrative *probability* (the coherence of a story) and narrative *fidelity* (the belief of how true a story is) shape the audience's narrative rationality.[6]

Communication scholar Michael Burns explored how stories can help universities recruit prospective students and found that students want to hear stories about students' daily experiences. Explained through the Narrative Paradigm, Burns suggests that "if the stories about normal day-to-day activities have narrative probability and fidelity, students may feel more certain about college and may be able to better visualize themselves at that school."[7] Applied to the theme of Christian scholarship, the narrative paradigm convincingly suggests that sharing stories about the day-to-day activities of a Christian scholar may persuade and encourage other Christian scholars.[8]

Two additional works from communication scholar Quentin Schultze related to Fisher's Narrative Paradigm include *You'll Shoot Your Eye Out!: Life Lessons from the Movie A Christmas Story*, and Chapter 26, "Telling Stories," in *Servant Teaching: Practices for Renewing Christian Higher Education*.[9]

When I wrote a textbook on public speaking from a Christian perspective, I framed all of the major points with stories about former students, friends, and myself—along with a few stories of famous speakers. The subtitle of the book catches this approach: *Serving Your Audience with Faith, Skill, and Virtue*.[10] In effect, the book winsomely introduces even fearful students into a marvelous human gift, namely, serving an audience.

I believe that we humans are made to be storytellers. It is in our bones, so to speak. Scripture comes to us in the form of the story of creation, fall, redemption, and renewal. We frame our own lives in terms within that overarching narrative. We understand ourselves in the light of the narrative that God's faithful servants recorded for us over thousands of years.

My latest book explains how stories function as parables: *You'll Shoot Your Eye Out! Life Lessons from the Movie A Christmas Story*.[11] I got to know the screenwriter, Jean Shepherd, of what might be now the most popular film in America, about young Ralphie's quest for the Red Ryder BB rifle, the Old Man's infatuation with a leg lamp, Flick sticking his tongue to a frozen flagpole, and so many more iconic scenes. Every part of the film works on two levels—as entertainment and as message-rich parable. Shepherd taught me how to think more richly and deeply about storytelling and made me a better teacher and scholar.

Excellence in Scholarship, Teaching, and Overall Communication

Fifth, I believe that we all are called to be excellent in our scholarship, teaching, and overall communication. In fact, I think we are responsible for serving our audiences with excellent listening, expression, and so much more. Those who engage us should be impressed by the quality of our communication, not just by our faith per se. We should be saying to each other, as God is presumably saying to us, "Well done, faithful servants."

There you have them—five root assumptions that have guided me away from anti-intellectualism and toward holistic, faith-shaped teaching and scholarship. I "do" my scholarship under the assumption that it is action, that I have a heartfelt responsibility to serve my audiences, that I must seek shared understanding, and that I must do it all with excellence—often using stories to delight and educate.

Chapter 5

The Christian Mind: Humility
and "World Viewing"

RICHARD J. MOUW

*[This chapter is a revised transcript of the author's
unconference video presentation.]*

Chapter Summary: Legacy Scholar Richard J. Mouw reflects on the intellectual journey within evangelicalism, particularly in light of the seminal works of Mark Noll and George Marsden featured in the CCSN unconference. Mouw shares his personal experiences of navigating anti-intellectualism in his upbringing and the encouragement he received from Christian educator Frank Gaebelein, which affirmed that intellectual engagement could coexist with faithful Christian living. While acknowledging the continued challenges within evangelicalism, Mouw expresses optimism about the flourishing of the evangelical mind, citing examples of influential evangelical thinkers in public discourse. Like other Legacy Scholars, Mouw also underscores the importance of humility in intellectual life, calling for a continuous process described as Christian "world viewing."

GREETINGS TO ALL OF YOU. I'm very pleased to have the opportunity to share with you some important things that are on my mind and, more specifically, to be able to offer my own reflections on two books written by two close friends, Mark Noll and George Marsden—books that have meant a lot to me in my own journey.

When *The Scandal of the Evangelical Mind* came out in the mid-1990s, I read it as I did later with George's book.[1] I read them with great interest, maybe "devoured them" is a more apt description, because they were really speaking to important issues in my own life journey. I deeply understand the scandal of which Mark Noll speaks. I was raised in the evangelical world at a time when the rhetoric of anti-intellectualism ran wild in the sermons that I heard, as well as in evangelistic meetings and at summer Bible conferences. I remember clearly the loud "amens" that came from the congregation when one traveling revival preacher proclaimed that, in contrast to what he had learned in a few seminary courses that he'd taken, "you don't need exegesis, you just need Jesus!" All that the "worldly" intellectuals have to offer, according to another revivalist, is just a bunch of "fool philosophies," and we need not be tempted by any of it. And there was of course much more. Education is good only if you get the victory over it. The only school any Christian needs to attend is the Holy Ghost School of the Bible.

Looking Back: An Intellectual Adventure

Now those were the kind of sentiments I was raised with, but as a sophomore in college, I was actually finding my studies to be exciting. I was feeling like I was on an intellectual adventure, but at the same time I was very much worried not only that I was disappointing my family's hope for me, but also that I was rebelling against the plans that the Lord himself had for my life.

Then one day, a guest speaker came to the Christian college campus where I was studying. His name was Frank Gaebelein, a very familiar name in the old days. Frank was the son of the editor of the Scofield Bible. And Frank himself was a well-known evangelical leader in his own right. He wrote learned articles for Christian magazines and was the headmaster of the Stony Brook School, a prestigious Christian prep school on Long Island. His chapel lecture that day was entitled "The Christian's Intellectual Life," and it gave me a new perspective on the struggles that I had been having. Four decades later I still remember some of the remarks that he made, although I don't have to rely on memory alone since the lecture was later published in a book of Gaebelein essays.[2] "In contrast to the secularist outlook in the academy," he said, Christians must insist that "our intellectual life is infused with faith." But that does not mean that Christian intellectual activity is an easy thing. It's hard work. "We must pay a price," he said, "if we're to use our minds to glorify God, and the price will not come down. . . . It's nothing less," he said, "than the discipline of self-restraint and plain hard work."[3]

Now today that strikes me as a simple and obvious message, but it had a deep impact on me at the time, and I'm grateful that I had the chance to hear his words then. I was at a point in my life when I desperately needed a word of Christian encouragement that I did not have to make a choice between a life devoted to scholarship and a life of obedience to the Lord, that I could be faithful by cultivating a disciplined mind that struggled with deep intellectual challenges, that this intellectual work would equip me to do the required hard work of engaging in the task of Christian scholarship. This task was certainly not made easier by the attitude of unbelievers in the Academy. I ran into some of that during my graduate studies, and so George's insistence on the "outrageous" character of Christian scholarship struck home to me in those times when I did express my evangelical convictions and suffered some measure of outrage from a few people that I studied with.

So as I think about this conference, I'm grateful for this opportunity to look back and see how far we have come since those days. And I agree with just about everything that Mark and George said originally and in their more recent reflections that are now published. What they've said is in fact both wise and insightful. My purpose here is not to disagree with their ideas per se, but rather to express some thoughts of gratitude for how far we have come, and how much of this progress is due in significant part to the two of them and their faithful work.

Looking Forward: A Grateful Critique

Mark, for one, is not that hopeful, not as much as I'd like him to be. He concludes in the preface to the new edition of *The Scandal of the Evangelical Mind*, published in 2022, that the scandal has not yet disappeared. While there are some examples from which he draws some encouragement, he does seem to be almost giving up on the prospect of the evangelical mind. I'm much more hopeful on this score, and I believe that there are important signs that the evangelical mind is flourishing in our own day. Now I think there's a bit of irony in my position, because the belief that the evangelical mind is flourishing is at least somewhat strange in light of the fact that evangelicalism as a whole is not flourishing. Many evangelical intellectuals, in fact, have resigned from the movement. In addition, Mark points out in his 2022 preface that large numbers of White evangelicals are still held captive to conspiratorial nonsense, which reinforces the bad reputation that evangelicalism has in public life for arrogance and simple-mindedness.

In my youth there was indeed a lot of that, though back then it had more of an explicitly biblical cast to it. I remember a revivalist who came to town, and one of his key sermons had this title that he advertised to draw people out: "Are Hitler and Roosevelt Really Dead?" And he argued that both of them were still alive. No one had seen Hitler's body, he alleged, and Roosevelt's coffin was closed when people came to pay their respects. So the argument was that not only were both of these figures still alive, but that they had gotten together and were living together somewhere in South America, jointly plotting a horrible takeover of Western culture and Western life. In my youth a lot of this Hitler-and-Roosevelt-conspiracy-type stuff was actually connected to verses in the Bible. There was a kind of hermeneutic we learned to match current events with biblical names and accounts. So, when the Bible mentions Gomer, it means Germany. When the Bible says Meshach, it means Moscow. And when the Bible mentions the tribes of the north, that was taken as a reference to the global communist conspiracy aiming for world domination. All of this was weird, of course, but at least there was an attempt to be biblical, in its own way. But these days, there's not even an effort to look for biblical support for conspiracies. People get their conspiratorial nonsense, to use Mark's term, simply from social media postings and cable news reports.

Now Mark and George rightly pay attention to the scandals of evangelicalism in public life, and there's certainly a lot to complain about there. But I do see some signs of intellectual progress. Take, for example, what's happened these days at *The New York Times*. Tim Keller, before he died, appeared frequently in the *Times* but asked to comment on important issues of public life, and not just narrow religious concerns. David French is an evangelical who serves as a columnist at the *Times*, assigned to write from a more conservative and more evangelical political perspective on some of the issues of the day. And in fact, there's a whole list, a stable of evangelical commentators whose writings regularly appear in the *Times*. Esau McCauley, who is a Black biblical scholar associated with Wheaton College, writes excellent things in the *Times*. Pete Wehner, who had been a speechwriter for the Bushes, writes really good stuff. Tish Warren, who's a very gifted evangelical Anglican priest, writes in the *Times*. Elisa Wilkinson started as the film reviewer for *Christianity Today*, and after a number of twists and turns she now writes as a film reviewer for the *Times*: an evangelical commenting on the world of film in what's known as our nation's newspaper. Russell Moore of *Christianity Today* regularly appears on "Morning Joe" on *MSNBC*.

I wish that George and Mark paid more attention not only to these noteworthy evangelicals having a significant voice in public and cultural matters, but also to the developments that have been taking place in parachurch ministry. I have often and regularly met with staff members and even board members of organizations like the Council for Christian Colleges and Universities, World Vision, InterVarsity Christian Fellowship, Young Life, the National Association of Evangelicals, and the level of the discussions about important intellectual matters and issues in public life and public faith have been surprisingly rigorous. There are folks in very important and still very successful evangelical organizations who are good friends to the Christian scholarly community, and there is much in their own service that strengthens the evangelical mind.

Now certainly the strengthening of the evangelical mind requires more than intellectual activity. A decade or so ago, the topic of the religious affiliations of U.S. Supreme Court appointments was being discussed in the popular media, and one commentator observed that while evangelicals have a lot to say about matters of legal theory and legal matters pertaining to public life, the nod typically goes to Catholics when it comes to choosing justices who have conservative religious views. On questions of legal theory, the commentator claimed, evangelicals lack intellectual heft. We're not hefty enough. And while I agreed with that assessment at the time, I think that for the most part, evangelical scholars have been increasingly doing their intellectual homework in this area, and I'm impressed with the growing body of literature on legal, social, political, and economic questions by scholars who are intent on making the connections between biblical and theological themes with topics relating to the public square, and doing this in a way that illuminates many important issues of public discipleship. Given these trends, evangelicals may be gaining enough heft to have a fellow evangelical eventually sitting on the bench at the Supreme Court.

Spiritual Formation, Ways of Viewing, and the Christian Mind

But how do we do a better job of bringing the fruits of scholarship of this kind to the front ranks of evangelicalism? An important part of the answer is that more intellectual heft alone is not by itself going to solve the problem. And while we continue to address the important issues of the evangelical mind, we also need to be working on the level of *spiritual formation*—attention to the topic of spirituality for Christian citizenship and Christian intellectual life. Now, Mark and George do acknowledge this. George, for example, commends to Christian scholars the example of Martin Luther King Jr., who he says emphasizes the importance of loving our adversaries and learning from them, which of course requires a strong measure of humility.

Sadly, though, we often come across as arrogant, even in our intellectual lives. This can be seen, for example, in the thinking of nineteenth-century Dutch theologian Abraham Kuyper. Now no one who knows anything about my work will be surprised to hear me say that Kuyper is one of my intellectual heroes from which I have learned so much. However, I wish he hadn't drawn such a hard ontological line between believers and nonbelievers working in the natural sciences. Because he believed that believers and unbelievers face the cosmos from such different points of view, he drew the conclusion that these two categories of people represent fundamentally different kinds of human beings, and that there are therefore two kinds of science: the science practiced by Christians, and then the science practiced by everyone else. Well, I would hate to think that this kind of thinking would influence a graduate of one of our evangelical colleges or universities who is now working on a PhD in microbiology, so that when she's asked by her non-Christian mentor about her career goals, she would respond that she sees herself producing a very different kind of science than the kind evidenced in her mentor's research and teaching. Even worse, imagine her trying to explain that sense of practicing a fundamentally different science than the secular world in a job interview for a position at a secular university. I believe it would be much better for her to talk about what attracted her to microbiology, looking for a way to make a humble reference to her love of created reality and the Creator who made it all.

The Sacred and Secular Divide in Kuyper

Lance Croy

A recent translation of Kuyper's *On Education* may aid in bringing the sacred and secular divide within the sciences closer together. Kuyper said,

> [God] created us as logical beings in order that we should trace his Logos, investigate it, publish it, personally wonder at it, and fill others with wonder. This, too, proclaims the glory of his name. Without scientific research, that treasure remains hidden in the world and does not rise to the surface.[4]

In *The Scandal of the Evangelical Mind*, Mark Noll also cited John Calvin's contributions to warn those in the sciences not to abandon their learning from the Scriptures. Noll described the common grace necessary to help delineate the perplexities regarding the contradictory or confounding results of our studies.[5]

Jesus told the parable of a treasure hidden in a field and a priceless pearl (Matt. 13:44–46). One man stumbled upon the treasure in the field. Meanwhile, the merchant searched for the pearl and found one of great worth. Both sold all they had to acquire it. The former did so with joy. Mouw's perspective on humility recognizes that ardent study does lead to discovery while, at the same time, it can lead to trampling over all sorts of truth. God, in his grace, has interlaced the world with both. Our fields of study should yield an abundance of joy as we proclaim the One who put the treasure there in the first place.

For several decades, I have been teaching about the importance of having a Christian worldview, something that those of us in Kuyperian circles take seriously, as do others these days. More recently, though, I have found myself moving from noun to gerund, speaking now about "world viewing" rather than having a "worldview." I do not think any of us can rightly claim simply to have a biblically based worldview, in the sense of possessing a fully formed vision of the world that provides answers to most, if not all, of our scholarly questions. But we must engage in a "world viewing" process of reflecting on what we encounter as the Word illuminates the new challenges that crop up on our journeys.

I certainly find myself thinking about challenges these days that did not exist when I started my academic career. In this respect, a verse that looms large for me is Psalm 119:105: "Your word is a lamp for my feet and a light on my path." It feels like we're walking a path with many new things suddenly coming into view, and we need help along the way. We turn a corner and suddenly we see something we hadn't thought about, and we have to shine the light of God's Word on that and wrestle with what that light tells us about this new thing that we encounter on our pathway, to make sure that we're viewing things correctly. The writer of Psalm 139 offers strong support for the insistence on being tentative about our own verdicts on things, when he expresses his humble awareness that because God is all-knowing, the contents of God's consciousness, including God's awareness of our own motives and our own cognitive assessments, are open to the correction of God's own scrutiny. Thus we need the persistent posture of saying "search me, O God, search me. See if there be any wicked way in me, O God. Try my thoughts and correct them." The persistent habit of careful self-examination requires a spirit of humility, including in our intellectual lives.

The wonderful French intellectual Simone puts this in a rather bracing way. She points explicitly to the link between intellectual pursuits and spirituality, particularly with respect to humility. She says the virtue of humility "is far more precious treasure than all academic progress."[6] From this point of view, it is perhaps even more useful to contemplate our stupidity than our sin. Consciousness of sin gives us the feeling that we are evil, and a kind of pride sometimes finds a place in that realization. But when we force ourselves to fix the gaze, not only of our eyes but of our souls, upon us, we increasingly realize that we have failed through sheer stupidity, and then a sense of our mediocrity is revealed to us with irresistible evidence. No knowledge is to be more desired than if we can arrive at knowing this truth with all of our souls, and then we shall be established on that right foundation. This sense of humility, I think, is what is so important.

I personally am very grateful for what I have learned from unbelievers. In a very good sermon I heard recently, the pastor asked the congregation to each think of one of the most important spiritual insights into your spiritual life, maybe even the insight that led to your conversion. Who was the person who most influenced you in gaining that insight? Who was the person along the way who inspired you to see things differently in your own life? And yes, that's a very important exercise in which to engage. But I was also very much aware of the fact that there are issues in the intellectual life, and that there are people who have most influenced me in coming to an insight that has been formative in my intellectual development, and that those persons were not Christians, but they did well in helping me to think things through. The writer of Psalm 139, again, offers strong support in his insistence that when he expresses his own humble awareness, that because God is all-knowing, he needs to take a critical look at himself. And very often, it has been unbelievers who have helped me to take a critical glance, maybe even a sustained critical look, at changes that I needed to make in my own thinking.

Conclusion

So I want to say, in conclusion, that yes, there is still some intellectual scandal in evangelicalism. We have a lot of work yet to do, and it's hard work. Gaebelein was right in this. We need to experience the pain of sustained intellectual labor. We can't avoid that, but we can do this work recognizing, as George and Mark rightly do, that spiritual gifts come by the work of the Holy Spirit. For me, this means that we can continue to hope for new manifestations of a revival of mind and heart that I believe has already been happening; in fact, it's been happening with the inspiration that George and Mark have written about in the 1990s and since. So there has been an intellectual revival that has been taking place, and the scandal has somewhat lessened in that process. This is due, in no small part, to the important intellectual contributions of Mark Noll and George Marsden.

Chapter 6

An Outrageous Scandal: Three Rs for the Future of Christian Education

GREG SPENCER

[This chapter is a revised transcript of the author's
unconference video presentation.]

Chapter Summary: In response to Mark Noll and George Marsden's critique of evangelicalism's failure to foster intellectual rigor, Legacy Scholar Greg Spencer proposes three "R's" for reform: (1) *Reframing Evangelicalism*, rethinking or abandoning the term "evangelical," which has become politically charged, and instead focusing on theological depth and intellectual engagement; (2) *Reinforcing the Thinker*, encouraging the development of thinkers who engage deeply with ideas rather than conforming to academic norms; and (3) *Reasserting Wisdom and Character*, integrating moral reflection and community life into education, emphasizing that intellectual growth should be rooted in virtue. Spencer emphasizes that Christian education should cultivate intellectual risk-taking and a holistic, virtue-driven approach to learning.

WE LIVE IN TUMULTUOUS TIMES. That's what we're often told these days. In my lifetime, American power has peaked and is waning, broad-based American evangelicalism has peaked and is waning—and many American Christian colleges are struggling against declining numbers and influence. Among other things, a lack of confidence in truth and traditional morality is changing the media, the church, and the Academy. Anxiety seems to be at an all-time high.[1]

With so many institutions and ideas booming and busting, what is happening to Christian higher education and scholarship? What can be said to inspire the next generation of Christian academics? What prophetic voice needs to be heard? What wisdom is being ignored? In particular, do Mark Noll's *The Scandal of the Evangelical Mind* and George Marsden's *The Outrageous Idea of Christian Scholarship*, powerful messages in their day, point us in some helpful directions?

As I consider these questions—ones posed to all the contributors in this volume—I'm guessing most of us will call readers to continue to correct the scandal Noll highlighted and continue to affirm the outrageousness Marsden argued for. In a lot of ways, I do too, but at times I wonder, am I more a part of the problem or more a part of the solution? Am I too scandalous or am I outrageous enough? Do I have a genuine insight to offer or just a pack of excuses? Am I able to keep coming up with bifurcations like these, or will I run out of them?

We'll see.

How Did We Get Here?

I begin with some recent events, with the overriding question of "how did we get here?"

The 2024 Summer Olympics. My wife and I watched and gloried in remarkable physical achievements, exciting competition, and the camaraderie on the men's and women's gymnastics teams. But other parts were difficult to watch, mainly because of troubling moral assertions. In the opening ceremony, one scene featured two men and a woman flirting brazenly in a library then running down halls and into a room together, obviously about to engage in *ménage à trois*. One man looks to the viewer as he closes the door, as if to say, "uh, uh, uh, you don't get to watch this." Elsewhere in the program, drag queens pranced seductively and a perhaps-unintentional Last Supper parody scene came together. Without sorting out each of these incidents, I simply want to note that most of this content would have been unthinkable not very long ago.

So how did we get here?

Young Christians disillusioned with faith. In our circle, a good number of Christian college alumni, or close friends and relatives, have left the church,[2] or are feeling increasingly discouraged about what they hear from evangelicals in the media. Some say the church seems irrelevant or regressive on sexual issues. Some stopped coming to church during COVID-19 and say they can't get motivated about coming back. Some say they cannot bear Donald Trump being viewed as a political Messiah and spiritual hero. They say, how can a person who appears to be the polar opposite of the qualities in the Beatitudes be endorsed and blessed by the church? They say he's a womanizing, thrice-married, ridiculing narcissist who cozies up to dictators, lies with impunity, and commends the takeover of the Capitol. For the most part, they aren't talking about his political policies. They're talking about his character. When some Trump supporters retort, "Hey, look at the Bible. God blesses and uses bad kings," these friends and alumni say, "Really, *that's* your argument? We should support an immoral leader because God used immoral leaders at times in the past?" The churchgoers against Trump shake their heads and walk away—from church.

So how did we get here?

Troubling assertions espoused by the church. Another recent trend that influences our view of the evangelical mind and the state of Christian academia has to do with the church's susceptibility to illogical and unwise conclusions. Too many Christians gravitate toward fear-based news and conspiracy theories, as if their faith in God makes them less discerning, more open to belief in far-fetched stories. They say that thousands of people in the "deep state" are working behind the scenes to destroy our culture (and these thousands of employees have kept the plot a secret), that Hillary Clinton ran a sex ring from a pizza parlor, that COVID-19 was a government scheme to reduce our population. Or the worst story which, sadly, is one that I know personally, is about a good friend's son who participated in a highly authoritarian church. Eventually, he drifted away from others in that church, and, in some sense, from people altogether, even though he was married and had two children. In his isolation, he started going down internet rabbit trails to QAnon and beyond. Because he ended up believing that aliens had contaminated his own children (and had some kind of psychotic break), he took those children to Mexico and killed them. Obviously, this person had mental illness, and this is an extreme story, but it seems tragically symbolic of the church's abdication of discernment.

So how did we get here?

Many reasons could be offered—but, surely, Mark Noll would say that, in part, one cause is the lack of an evangelical mind: "evangelicals—bereft of self-criticism, intellectual subtlety, or an awareness of complexity—are blown about by every wind of apocalyptic speculation and enslaved to the cruder spirits of populist science."[3] We evangelicals, whom he calls activist, pragmatic, populist, and utilitarian,[4] are too busy crusading in the moment to value the work it takes to process issues as thinkers. And we fail to come at problems as *Christian* thinkers. Marsden argues that though it is permissible, even encouraged, for feminists or Marxists to teach and practice scholarship from their perspectives, "our dominant academic culture trains scholars to keep quiet about their faith as the price of full acceptance in that community,"[5] thus, the *outrageous* idea of actually doing scholarship from a Christian perspective. Among other things, Noll and Marsden say we need forums for deep, rigorous thinking, evangelical places that prize scholarship. They wonder why the Christian college doesn't more often meet this need.

These important concerns aren't new. I'm reminded of Benson Bobricks's terrific book about translations of the Bible into English, *Wide as the Water*. He writes that in the early 1500s when William Tyndale was coming of age, the clergy were an ignorant lot. When the Bishop of Gloucester surveyed 311 deacons, archdeacons, and priests of the Diocese, he discovered that 168 were unable to repeat the Ten Commandments, 31 didn't know where those commandments came from, 40 could not repeat the Lord's Prayer, and 40 couldn't say who the author of that prayer was.[6] In 1709, Jonathan Swift wrote facetiously about a protest movement that wanted to abolish churchgoing. In his satire, Swift says that abolishing the church wouldn't change anything because the church doesn't make a difference in the world anyway, genuine Christianity "having been for some Time wholly laid aside by general Consent, as utterly inconsistent with our present Schemes of Wealth and Power."[7]

One wonders if we have ever achieved this elusive, intellectual Christian community. I've been teaching this material for over 40 years, quoting Harry Blamires's *The Christian Mind*, Os Guinness's *Fit Bodies and Fat Minds*, and Charles Malik's Wheaton commencement address: "evangelicals cannot afford to keep on living on the periphery of responsible intellectual existence."[8] Yet today, the church seems, if anything, worse off intellectually. Are Marsden and Noll and I longing for times that never really existed?[9] And what if it hasn't? Shouldn't we pursue what is the best for the church and for our culture?

And what about counter-evidence to this argument concerning the lack of an evangelical mind? My own personal story doesn't mesh well with the critique. I came to faith as a senior in high school, from outside the church, so I wasn't affected by fundamentalism directly. In college, I gravitated toward InterVarsity Christian Fellowship, which fostered the life of the mind and the integration of faith in all disciplines. I read C. S. Lewis, Francis

Schaeffer, G. K. Chesterton, and many others. I went on to grad school, matriculating as the only Christian in my cohort at the University of Oregon. Then, eventually, I arrived at Westmont College, where I taught for 35 years, and where I found an intellectually vibrant faculty and responsive students. So am I an anomaly? Are these experiences just anecdotes, or have we neglected to tell these kinds of stories?

Another question: is the problem Marsden and Noll outline as much cultural and sociological as it is, as they argue, theological and ecclesiastical? Aren't most large groups of people, regardless of their dogma, beset by anti-intellectualism? Aren't most Americans, as Jim Farrell at St. Olaf College puts it, feeling the social pressure toward "*fun*-damentalism," the norm that "each day should be punctuated by fun"?[10] We just want to have a good time, to veg out, to de-stress, to put our brain in the fridge, to find a way to compensate for and to medicate the anxiety that we feel.

Our editors' prompt for this discussion proposes a positive direction for a response to questions of serious mental engagement and Christian higher education. How can we embrace Kingdom opportunities that our current cultural crises present and offer viable pathways forward? What are some ways through these problems? I am too limited a thinker to attempt to resolve these issues, but I will offer a few discussion points, what I'm calling "three Rs for the future of Christian education."

Reframing Evangelical

First, we need to *reframe "evangelical" or find a new descriptor*. The term evangelical has become so problematic, it may not be able to be revitalized. When I learned the term evangelical as a Christian undergraduate, it stood for a broad swath of groups who held in common a commitment to *sola scriptura* and conversion toward a grace-based faith in Christ's work. During those days I heard Yale historian Timothy Smith make the case that eleven branches of the church belong under the banner Evangelical. I can't remember them all, but they ranged from Mennonite to Pentecostal, from Dutch Calvinist to Black Gospel. It's hard to imagine these groups today rallying around the term evangelical. At least in the public mind, evangelical has been reduced to White populist Republican politics, sometimes tinged with racist attitudes, making it far less of a theological canopy.

As historian Richard Lovelace noted, one secondary element of spiritual renewal across the centuries is a commitment to the community of believers. Before the fundamentalism/liberalism split in the nineteenth century, "qualities which had distinguished the original evangelicals [included] breadth of learning, theological depth, social concern and *striving for ecumenical unity*" [italics mine][11], as well as renewal, nurture, evangelism, and missions.[12] Sadly, as Lovelace notes, the first four qualities tended to be "lost" to the liberal church. We would do well to reanimate the church with a spirit of searching for what we hold in common.

William Blake might inspire us: "I give you the end of a golden string; / Only wind it into a ball, / It will lead you in at Heaven's gate, / Built in Jerusalem's wall."[13] Whatever "evangelical" means, it needs to include searching for that central golden string, concentrating on the intelligent and beautiful love for God seen from Augustine to Teresa to Pascal, from missionaries such as Hudson Taylor to novelists such as Dorothy L. Sayers, from the contemplative life encouraged by Ignatius and Thomas Merton to C. S. Lewis's rousing pub meetings to the enthusiasm of Calvary Chapel, and on and on and on.

Whereas this approach to "evangelical" might provide hope, the current, narrow treatment, for many, leads to despair. As a case in point, there are two or three new churches in Santa Barbara, my hometown, that appeal primarily to ex-evangelicals ("exvangelicals"). I suspect this trend is widespread. Many faculty at Christian colleges are discussing whether to dispense with the word evangelical in defining and public relations documents. But what term would replace it, would describe and provide unity? Traditional? Orthodox? I don't know, but I believe we need to keep searching for the golden string.

Reinforcing the Thinker

My second R is that we need to *reinforce the thinker in the thinker/scholar tension*. Noll begins his book with a substantial citation from Harry Blamires's contrast of the secular and Christian minds, agreeing with Blamires that a Christian mind doesn't exist, and that it hasn't made progress since Blamires's 1963 critique.[14] Though Noll longs for an evangelical "life of the mind," and for greater evangelical forums for scholarship (a research university, a leading scholarly publication, the winning of academic prizes), he does not engage with the preference Blamires has for a certain kind of thinker over a certain kind of scholar. I argue, with Blamires, that the thinker needs more support, more reinforcing. Blamires says it is "a feature of our culture generally, that we are rich in scholars and poor in thinkers."[15] Although the ratio of scholar to thinker varies from age to age, our educational system still tends to repress good, daring, creative thinking. Blamires says public education "is not geared to the production of thinkers. It is geared to their obliteration."[16] That's strong talk. Thinkers are a nuisance. They question foundations, disturb the flow of things.

As Howard Mumford Jones says in his provocatively titled, "The Attractions of Stupidity," most students are like conformist Romans. Only a few are like the Greeks, because the "incessant struggle of the mind to be true to itself, to absorb new truths, to grow, to overcome pressures—these are the painful portion of the independent thinker."[17] Blamires concurs: "The scholar and the thinker are, in some ways, mutually antithetical types. . . . Scholarship cannot endure exaggeration. Thinking cannot thrive without it."[18] He doesn't mean that thinking favors falsehood, but that scholarship is overly cautious, careful not to overstate. Sometimes, when the faculty in our department gathered to compose a few words to praise the winner of our Outstanding Senior, we couldn't find much to say because the student, though proficient in test-taking, had not been distinctive in any other way.

Academic writing, also, can train us toward blandness. Note the importance of the disclaimer. Never put something definitively. Always say "somewhat," "partially," "in a few cases." The value is clear: be careful, measured, don't go out on a limb. As Blamires implies, thinkers poke, cajole, resist typical expectations. He writes, "The scholar evades decisiveness; he hesitates to praise or condemn. He balances conclusion against competing conclusions so as to cancel out conclusiveness."[19]

Although this orientation is not true for all scholars, it is pervasive. I experienced this movement toward circumspection in grad school. Before I switched my emphasis from interpersonal communication to rhetorical theory, my dissertation idea was to study forgiveness in marriage. However, by the time my professors coached me toward operationalizing forgiveness, the term had lost almost every good meaning I thought was associated with it: risk and humility and mystery. Sometimes, at NCA conventions, I wandered from panel to panel in search of someone who would say something seriously challenging, not obscurantist or predictably "party line." Once, when I heard Neil Postman speak on a panel, he seemed dramatically varied from the norm: provocative, prophetic, straight-forward. I still remember the topic: "The De-Meaning of Meaning," pun-intended by him. He was a thinker. And, of course, there were and are many others. But too often in the Academy, intellectual risks are so criticized that all the edges are knocked off, sometimes even for appreciating the good in an idea or in a theory. The norm is to discover what is wrong, to find flaws, to play the doubting game, thus further training us to avoid risk, the risk of criticism.

In addition to promoting good scholarship, we need to cultivate and support substantial, decisive, praising-and-condemning thinkers. Here's a small thing I noticed. In the one-page prompt for the papers that formed the basis for this volume, the word scholar was used four times—and it makes perfect sense given the emphases in Noll's and Marsden's writing. But might this exclusive emphasis on scholarship represent the Academy's understated emphasis on thinking? Some might say we *assume* a commitment to thinking but given the party-line politics of the left and the right, and how driven we are toward the disclaimer, we need to reinforce the thinker more directly. Among other things, let's not merely accept the university's narrow definition of an intellectual life. For example, let's encourage the Christian public intellectual, maybe public intellectuals of all kinds. Wendell Berry, Marilyn Robinson, David Brooks. You have your own list. Let's praise writing that appears in *The Atlantic* and *First Things* and in op-ed pieces in the *Wall Street Journal*, etc. And of course, in promoting the thinker, we should not give license to gross overstatement, nor should we separate thinking and scholarship. Thinkers also study and scholars also think. But in our times, the thinker needs more reinforcement. My mentor at the University of Oregon, a brilliant, wise man, Dominic LaRusso, said that just once, after he gave a speech, he wished someone would come up to him and, instead of saying "good speech," would say "good thinking."

Reasserting the Roles of Wisdom and Character

My third R is that we need to *reassert the roles of wisdom and character in the intellectual enterprise*. Much has been written about this. One example is Jim Taylor's *Learning for Wisdom*.[20] Perhaps I can add to the conversation by weaving together some loose threads. First, the church. One problem is that we tend to articulate faith almost exclusively in two ways: as feelings we have during worship, and as "stepping into the future of some circumstance while trusting God." These are not errors as such, but they often come at the expense of rational reflection and wisdom. We freely say, "I love the awesome worship this morning" or "I'm going to step out in faith" but we tend not to say, "I'm trying to discern what is wise" or "I'm delighted by the brilliant argument that was just presented." The church needs to remember that Jesus's words are as much about wise living as they are about faithful living. We separate them at our peril.

The church also resides in a technological culture with particular challenges. One is the speed of our existence: the ways we hurry through our work, play, and family life. As James Houston says, "If I think faster than I can speak, speak faster than I can act, act more than I have character to assimilate, there is already a basic disjunction within me, which challenges me to live a more integrated, authentic existence."[21] If it is human nature to "outrun" our moral development—and then the pace of our lives leaves our character even more distant from providing a solid foundation for our lives—we should all-the-more seek to integrate wisdom into our curriculum.

Second, in the Academy, we divide faith and wisdom by emphasizing knowledge at the expense of moral practice and community life. We should more closely examine the widely accepted maxim, "learning for learning's sake." The phrase rightly challenges a strictly utilitarian view of education, but it implies that learning is outside the bounds of anything other than itself, including moral evaluation and application. In *The Divine Conspiracy*, as Dallas Willard argues for the reality of moral and spiritual knowledge, he cites a student of Robert Coles's, the Harvard psychologist. The student said, "What's the point of knowing good if you don't keep trying to become a good person?" Willard says the Academy teaches that we can't know the truth of a moral theory or principle: "One can only know about such theories and principles and think about them in more or less clever ways."[22] Learning to be virtuous, to be loving, could consistently inform how we write and teach our subjects. What if a distinguishing feature of Christian colleges was prayerfully applied education?

In grad school, two of my professors offered a seminar on marital communication, during which they asserted that everything they taught in the seminar was "value-free." I asked if I could write my paper on the values they espoused. Though perplexed, they said, "Yes." I did my best to identify their values—and they appreciated the paper. Though professors might not recognize the values they teach, and students might think they are only picking up what is useful for employment, the academic enterprise is not value-free; learning can never be done exclusively for its own sake. We learn and teach according to what we think is wise, and we live in community according to our moral principles, whether we articulate them or not.

In his introduction to Bruce Kimball's insightful book, *Orators and Philosophers*, Joseph Featherstone writes, "The tradition of the philosophers holds that the pursuit of knowledge is the highest good: this is the line from Socrates and Plato . . . to . . . the great research universities of the present. . . . The tradition of the orators, on the other hand, emphasizes the public expression of what is known."[23] The rhetorical tradition (in Cicero and others) argues that the tongue should not be separated from the brain, that the ivory tower, Plato's ivory tower, is too remote. It needs to be an ivory marketplace, an ivory kitchen, and sports field, and film industry. Kimball says that "searching for truth without giving commensurate attention to the importance of public expression inevitably leads the individual to isolation and self-indulgence and the republic to amoralism and chaos."[24] Putting ideas in the public square leads to public scrutiny, which typically leads to thoughtful evaluation about the worth, argument, and moral application of the ideas.

Rhetorical Tradition

Elaine V. Fung

The rhetorical tradition is one of Professor Robert Craig's seven traditions of Communication Theory. Rhetoric started with a focus on speech and persuasion, which has grown into symbolic construction.[25] There are five canons of rhetoric, which include "invention, arrangement, style, delivery, and memory."[26] Rhetoric can be defined in two ways: (1) the art of rhetoric is "the study and practice of effective symbolic expression" and (2) rhetoric as a type of discourse is "goal-oriented discourse that seeks, by means of the resources of symbols, to adapt ideas to an audience."[27]

One scholar found that "Lewis remythologized a hopeless moment to an existence wherein all people were divine and could affect eternity."[28] Perhaps Christian scholars and Christian scholarship can welcome hope amidst hopelessness by encouraging the audience or readers to experience Christian mythos through their research and writing.[29]

Two additional readings that are helpful in this area are Mark A. E. Williams's *Just Words: Lessons of Ancient Education, Classical Rhetoric,* and *Pagan Religion for a Post-Christian World* and Laura Lee Groves and John Hatch's "Prophetic Imagination and Racial Inertia: The Lyrical, Musical, and Visual Rhetoric of 'Is He Worthy?'"[30]

A full-bodied Christian view of learning promotes wisdom, and it promotes thoughtful communication in the community. Our daily rhetoric is the moral test of our thinking and scholarship. In part, this view affirms the classical axiom, *sapientia et eloquentia,* the union of wisdom and eloquence—but as understood under the Lordship of Christ, an ethos-based rhetorical orientation lived out as we love God, and love our neighbors as ourselves—or, we might say, the art of loving appropriately through speech.

On the micro-level, I'm hopeful about the three R's I recommend: reframing evangelicalism, reinforcing thinkers, and reasserting the roles of wisdom and character. Students are remarkably responsive. They want to have their minds awakened, their spirits energized, and their feet mobilized toward faithful, virtuous living. It's our job to help them see their calling as wise and eloquent people before God, as good thinkers in the making.

In light of these recommendations, I return to my original questions. Am I, according to Marsden and Noll, more a part of the problem (resisting a certain kind of commitment to scholarship), or more a part of the solution (seeking to reinvigorate wisdom-based thinking)? Am I too scandalous or not outrageous enough? Do I have a genuine insight or are these ideas just a pack of excuses? Am I able to keep these bifurcations going, or will I run out of them?

For now, I have run out.

Chapter 7

The Humor and Humility
of the Christian Mind

TERRY LINDVALL

*[This chapter is a revised transcript of the author's
unconference video presentation.]*

Chapter Summary: In this Legacy Scholar chapter, Lindvall responds to the challenges presented in Marsden's and Noll's seminal works by articulating four calls that might shape a Christian's scholarly life: (1) *The Call to Action* urges scholars to engage fully their hearts and imaginations alongside intellect and reason; (2) *The Call to the Past* rejects chronological snobbery, urging a return to historical Christian thought, including early church fathers and their teachings; (3) *The Call to Folly* reflects on Noll's critique of evangelical intellectualism, advocating for a scholarly humility that embraces humor and the paradox of Christian identity; and (4) *The Call to Discovery* encourages scholars to engage creatively, using indirect communication methods like parables.

IN 1994 RELIGIOUS HISTORIANS George Marsden and Mark Noll published two books that had a considerable impact on my own mind and at the university at which I worked. In *The Soul of the American University*, Marsden charted and chronicled the decline of Christian faith and thought in the modern Academy.[1] In *The Scandal of the Evangelical Mind*, Noll sent out a clarion call for all of us to think about how to integrate our faith and our particular areas of expertise in the academic work we do.[2] In this short chapter there are four more specific points or "calls" I would like to articulate regarding how to think about the impact of these two scholars: the call to action, the call to the past, the call to folly, and the call to discovery.

The Call to Action

First, there's a clear call to action that flows from these two books. When I and a few of my academic colleagues at Regent University, fellow communication scholars like Michael Graves and Benson Fraser, read these books, we would go out to lunch and would spontaneously argue about how we should respond to these ideas—how we should best do the work that Marsden and Noll were calling us to do. What were we going to do about all of this? How were our lives being changed by these books we're engaging, and how should all this be reflected in what we're thinking and what we're writing?

Graves, for instance, responded to this call by writing extensively about the rhetoric of the Quaker tradition and the archetypal metaphors used.[3] In so doing, he gave all of us a conceptual foundation for what we should be doing. We would look at the Scriptures, and we would talk regularly with one another to try to understand what was important about the task that God had called us to do. So this call worked to bring us out of a mindset we had, or at least I had, in which we would primarily teach out of secular textbooks. We knew in many cases that we were not experts in a certain field, and so we would just follow the textbook, and it was the "easy" way to teach. We came to realize, however, that the approach to education that Marsden and Noll were calling us to involves the heart and the imagination as much as it does reason.

The Call to the Past

And so, from our call to action, we felt that there was a call that was even greater, and that was a call to the past, a call to take history more seriously. C. S. Lewis coined the term "chronological snobbery" to refer to the widespread belief that what is modern or progressive or "new" is inherently better.[4] But of course it isn't. And so, as communication scholars, we felt called to go to the past and try to understand what other people had to say about communication, about rhetoric. That meant not just going back to the ancient Greek and Roman rhetoricians that are regularly taught to undergraduates and graduate students alike, but also to the Hebrew prophets of the Old Testament and the Gospel writers of the New Testament. Amos Wilder did much the same thing in his book on early Christian rhetoric, in which he began to articulate some of the distinctive ways in which Christians communicate—not completely differently, but with a different angle and with a different cluster of reasons and motives.[5]

So we began to explore more fully how other Christians throughout the ages had also communicated their faith. The book of Hebrews tells us that in many ways, many times, and many places, God spoke to us through the prophets and others. And these speeches, these acts of rhetoric, were very different. We could even go to some of the early church fathers. For example, one of my favorites is St. Clement of Alexandria, who is the patron saint of teachers and really old professors. He would argue that we are not to destroy the wisdom of the Babylonians. Rather, we are to find what is good and true everywhere, in the recognition of the fact that, as Augustine would later point out, all truth is God's truth. And in so doing, we find that there is one stream, one stream of living water that takes us to Christ and to God, but there are many rivulets that come in and interact and flow in that same process.

In the third century, St. Alexander used the language of the Gnostics to confront the Gnostics. He used the images that were out there: doves, sailors, ships, anchors. And he used these images to communicate what was essential for what he was doing. Or consider Hildegard of Bingen and the other wild women out there like her, writing dramas that show how the pedagogical is deeply personal. It's not simply rational, but it is something that comes out of our own lives. Likewise, one cannot read Augustine's *Confessions* or *On Christian Doctrine*, or the Apostle Paul's letters, and somehow conclude that they are just speaking to the mind. They are confronting our hearts. They are confronting the way that we, as teachers and scholars, understand what we are about and what we are trying to convey to our students and to one another. So, the call to the past was also a call to become personal as well.

There is an old anecdote about Emerson and Thoreau, who were walking around on the campus of Harvard, and Emerson was boasting about all the branches of learning that were there. There wasn't anything that Harvard was not covering, and these wonderful branches were doing such great work. But Thoreau looked at him, sadly and ruefully shook his head, and replied that perhaps all the branches are there, but none of the roots are. Harvard, Yale, and other storied institutions of higher learning had lost their foundation. They lost their reason to speak clearly and engagingly to what is universally true and what is eternally true. We find, then, that this call to the past can and should awaken in us a call to look differently at the present.

The Call to Folly

After a call to action and a call to the past, there is also a call to folly. The scandal of the evangelical mind is one thing for the Hebrews, but for the Greeks it's a folly. The cross and the resurrection are foolish. Those with a Greek mindset may want to simply be spiritual beings. But for the Christian, the incarnation is very important. The body is a major part of who we are, and so is the folly of our bodies, which is probably God's greatest joke that he has played on us, and one which we much deserve. The folly is to recognize, in humility and in humor, what kind of creatures we are. We are that amazing oxymoron: a spiritual animal. On one side, we're related to everything spiritual and transcendent and eternal and Amish. On the other side, we're related to everything earthly—to weasels, to turkeys, to snakes, and to lawyers. We are these two parts together, spirit and animal. And as we see that we come humbly to what we are teaching and doing.

We find in historical figures like Erasmus, Kierkegaard, and Malcolm Muggeridge this element of humor that we can and should bring to our scholarship, and it makes that scholarship more palatable to others. They can hear us more truly when we speak with a bit of levity. Now, to be comic is not the opposite of being serious. Being comic is the opposite of being tragic or solemn. To be serious is the opposite of being trivial. So one can be trivial and serious at the same time, and one can also be comic and serious. And it is this combination of comedy and seriousness that people like G. K. Chesterton and C. S. Lewis model for us—that ability to speak to ideas in a richer and more compelling way.

The Call to Discovery

But beyond this call to action, this call to the past, and this call to folly, not only to glorify God but also to enjoy him and his world, there's finally a call to discovery. And this call to discovery comes in learning these new ways of teaching and exhibiting our scholarship. My colleague Benson Fraser has written a book recently on parables, on indirect communication,[6] and it is probably one of the most effective ways of communicating our faith to others. Very few people have truly won arguments in public debates. I know that in marriage debate never wins, and that in the classroom it rarely convinces a person. But we can instead make our cases with stories, with parables, and with means by which we can indirectly influence the imaginations and the hearts of our audiences.

Indirect Communication

Elaine V. Fung

Danish theologian, philosopher, and poet Søren Kierkegaard considers indirect communication more effective than direction communication to communicate truth transformatively. As professor of preaching and author Fred B. Craddock explains, Kierkegaard perceived direct communication "as the mode for transferring information" that focuses on the speaker, while indirect communication is "for eliciting capability and action from within the listener," focusing on the listener.[7] As one scholar describes it, indirect communication "conveys truth by way of story, narrative, and symbol"; this is in contrast to direct communication, "which conveys truth by way of logic, reason, and doctrine."[8]

While Kierkegaard uses both indirect and direct communication, his preferred mode is indirect communication in his context of Denmark, where people believed they were Christian because they were either born or lived in Denmark. Kierkegaard found that indirect communication was more effective in sharing the truth as he sought "to awaken his fellow countrymen to the illusion they'd been living and perhaps make them capable of inhabiting a true Christian existence."[9]

Using Kierkegaard's indirect communication can allow faith messages to transform people and communities. In one case, rather than lecturing about self-disclosure, which is a direct approach, a professor used his classroom activity to teach the concept. Students were prompted to ask questions about his life outside the classroom to illustrate the concept of "self-disclosure in relationships."[10] Through the embodied experience and practice of self-disclosure, the professor indirectly communicated to the students about appropriate self-disclosure. This allowed for insights to emerge for students about self-disclosure, which may not be accessible through the professor's direct communication. Additionally, space was created for students to potentially ask questions related to faith and spirituality; thus, the professor's self-disclosure may have indirectly introduced Christianity to the students.

Two additional readings related to indirect communication are Hanisha Besant's article "Captivating the Listener: An Analysis of Audience Responses to

Indirect Communication in a Sermonic Event," and Fraser's book *Hide and Seek: The Sacred Art of Indirect Communication*.[11]

There are folks like Michael Ward, who found this kind of "secret" element even in Lewis's *Chronicles of Narnia*. It's worth recalling that Tolkien hated the *Chronicles of Narnia*. He thought it would ruin Lewis's reputation. He questioned Lewis over what he was doing putting these Norse myths and these Greek myths together in this Swedish sort of snow queen and then Santa Claus, of all people. But Ward discovered that there was method to Lewis's madness, that he was actually using a medieval template of the traits and characters of the different planets in our solar system. And for each Narnian Chronicle, there is a specific planet whose influence consists of bringing forth one feeling, one idea, one total action. So with *The Lion, the Witch, and the Wardrobe*, for instance, we have Jupiter or Jove or the spirit of Christmas, where winter is passing and everything is regal and fun and glorious, and Father Christmas fits into that pattern.[12]

Other scholars and writers of faith have also pursued this call to discovery. Religion scholar Joshua Wright, for instance, has been looking at the idea of comic belief and how those in the church, including Billy Graham and others, used it in the 1950s and 1960s to make the church aware of its own hypocrisy and how it was becoming like Kierkegaardian "Christendom."[13] And so we find that as we read and as we learn, we can find a humorous and indirect way of communicating our faith. In this sense it's valuable to go back and read authors like Dostoevsky and Flannery O'Connor and Pascal. These people awaken us and allow us to discover and see things in new and transformative ways.

Conclusion

I close my reflections in honor of George Marsden and Mark Noll by mentioning two facts about our scholarship that these scholars highlight. One fact is that our scholarship is at the end of time. Remember, Augustine was writing *The City of God* just as the Vandals were coming down and invading Hippo, and indeed they were invading the day he died. Likewise, we write during the end times. We write during a time of the end of Christendom. We write during a time and teach during a time in which disaster is befalling us. But we write and we teach and we stand even as martyrs of the mind to communicate to others our faith.

But we do so in light of the second fact, that our work is and should be seen as work of humility—the kind of humility that comes to us as we take heed of the warnings, from Ecclesiastes and elsewhere, concerning the writing of books. There is no end and the body gets exhausted, but we find a wonderful story of humility coming to us at the end. It's said that Pope Gregory went to heaven, having worked diligently throughout his days on his theory of hierarchies of spiritual powers and principalities, and then promptly found out that he was completely wrong. His reaction? He laughed hilariously. And so, we look at our own humble gift of scholarship that has been inspired by Marsden and Noll and others, and we continue to give it to one another. But we may be wrong, and so we laugh, and we rejoice that God's grace and mercy still cover us.

Chapter 8

A Framework for Biblical Integration in Communication

CALVIN L. TROUP

*[This chapter is a revised transcript of the author's
unconference keynote presentation.]*

Chapter Summary: Christian worldview is a commonplace among Chrisitan educators. But developing a biblical view of life and the world demands intense humility, generosity, and energy for Chrisitan scholars. To acquire agility within the Christian intellectual tradition directly adjacent to the most compelling intellectual work in our respective fields of study means double work—mastering biblical truth at a level that meets or exceeds what our field requires to earn a doctorate. Only such a strong biblical foundation can equip us for professorial service at a level that links disciplinary excellence with wisdom for living. A well-developed biblical foundation makes us deeper, not narrower, and enables us to collaborate and pursue new knowledge as we work with students and colleagues wherever we have been called to serve.

GRADUATE STUDIES can be a blur. But certain moments stick out. One evening a good friend and I were in an Ancient Rhetorical Theory seminar taught by Dr. Gerard A. Hauser, an eminent scholar in the history and theory of rhetoric. Dr. Hauser was trained by Jesuits—his expectations were high, and his pedagogy was demanding, exacting, and deeply formative. My friend Rosa and I were sitting opposite one another at a square seminar table with about ten other doctoral students, some of whom were newbies. We were in a perfect position to keep our eyes on each other and Dr. Hauser at the same time.

Dr. Hauser came in with his books, got out his papers and his notes and, according to his custom, started class by calling on the two people assigned to do that evening's presentations on the readings. The first student was clearly not prepared. Dr. Hauser interrupted the student with a sigh and moved on to the second. Same result. I looked at Rosa in terror. Dr. Hauser looked down and put his books and notes back in his briefcase. He shut the briefcase. He stood up without making eye contact and walked out without saying a word. Rosa and I had to clean up the mess and read the riot act to the newbies.

Mark Noll sent a similar message to us as a classroom of aspiring evangelical minds when he wrote *The Scandal of the Evangelical Mind*. He said: if you believe you belong at the table of scholarship, as a Christian scholar you've got to come prepared. Generously, Noll wrote us this book. He didn't just shut his briefcase and walk away. Christian scholars have been working more diligently at preparation ever since. As Noll deftly pointed out, the evangelical heritage in the wake of the Second Great Awakening, which scholars date as roughly 1790–1840, tended toward anti-intellectualism even as it held fast to biblical orthodoxy.[1] In so doing, he confirmed that a robust commitment to biblical orthodoxy is not anti-intellectual. Recovery of a faithful Christian intellectual tradition based on biblical orthodoxy was his clarion call.[2]

In *The Outrageous Idea of Christian Scholarship*, George Marsden laid the groundwork for how Chrisitan scholars could work faithfully and productively within secularized fields of study. He explained how we could conduct *bona fide* research programs grounded on biblical presuppositions and pursuing pertinent lines of inquiry resonant with the emerging disciplinary knowledge.[3] We might debate how far we've come, but Noll and Marsden charted a course and established conditions on which we could act. Their books demonstrate good scholarship and encourage us to do the same. As a graduate student, I needed people who understood good Christian scholarship and could invite me into that work wholeheartedly.

Today, we depend even more heavily on guides like Noll and Marsden because in the intervening years the secularized academic project has made a decisive anti-intellectual turn. An anti-intellectualism fueled by progressive ideologies has so permeated secularized college and university campuses that the Christian anti-intellectual movement Noll rightly critiqued seems tame by comparison. Conditions that support quality academic scholarship are more tenuous than they were at the turn of the twenty-first century. Reliable guides have become scarce in academia-at-large, making Noll and Marsden's call to establish good patterns and practices more helpful than ever for Christian teachers and scholars.

Faithful Christian Scholarship Means Double Work

Our best work today begins with several old sources that are immediately relevant but may be new to us. But we do so with our eyes fixed on Christ, without nostalgia or sentimentality for the past. We must work in the spirit of Solomon's maxim: Say not, "Why were the former days better than these?" (Ecc. 7:10, English Standard Version). For it is not from wisdom that you ask this. We want to be found faithful in our present moment, tuned to what good Christian scholarship must mean in our own day.

At the most basic level, to turn from the scandal of the evangelical mind and conduct outrageous Christian scholarship demands *double work*. What is "double work?" Double work means developing professional mastery of the Bible while also developing a mastery of the "literature of the Babylonians" (Dan. 1:4, ESV). We need professional mastery of the whole text of the Bible simultaneously with professional mastery as scholars in our respective academic disciplines.

The Literature of the Babylonians

I was initiated into the literature of the Babylonians at Pennsylvania State University in the Department of Speech Communication. At the University of Babylon, Shadrach, Meshach, and Abednego understood their literature ten times better than their Babylonian classmates. The examiners of Daniel & Co. did not inquire about God's Word that they had learned from childhood in Jerusalem. All their work in Babylonian scholarship and service was predicated on the intellectual agility produced through their mastery of biblical truth, understanding, and wisdom (Dan. 2:17–20). They had to do double work.

Even if we don't learn the Babylonian literature ten times better than our colleagues, we must do double work. We must be as strong in our biblical foundations, and in working from those biblical foundations, as we are in the Babylonian literature. As I studied in University Park, Pennsylvania, I quickly realized that I needed to immerse myself in Scripture, more deeply than ever. Biblical truth was absent from the scholarly literature I was reading. The leading schools of thought worked from assumptions that were numb or directly hostile to Christ and His word. If we are going to be wise and courageous enough to be faithful as Daniel was when he advised Nebuchadnezzar and served as a vice-regent over Babylon, we must give ourselves over to the double work that integration of faith and learning demands (Dan. 2:46–49).

Double work is more than shorthand for the common phrase: "integration of faith and learning." The shorthand assumes too much. The "faith" part really means "faith in Christ," not some generic faith associated with a panoply of religions, or a personally defined faith. Faith in Christ might also be termed "The Faith" as received from God through the prophets and apostles, encompassing all the Scriptures of the Old and New Testament. Therefore, we might rightly state the whole as "the integration of biblical faith in Christ and learning."

Coherence and Integration

Some Christian scholars object to the "integration" framework on biblical grounds. We are helped by Nicholas Wolterstorff in remembering that for Christian scholars, all truth, reality, knowledge, and understanding are always already integral. Our starting point is not integration, but the fact of coherence in Christ. And this is eminently true. Biblical faith in Christ begins with Christ as Creator of all things visible and invisible. All things hold together in him. He upholds all things by the word of his power. Therefore, all Christian learning and scholarship begins with the integral coherence of all things.

Shouldn't we simply jettison the "integration" language? Not entirely. Instead of a pre-modern framework that started with an assumption of coherence, modernity came in and said we can study anything as though God doesn't exist, *and in so doing we'll be even more effective in advancing human knowledge.* Accordingly, modernity abandoned coherence. Enlightenment thought resulted in what Francis Schaeffer has called an "upper story" and "lower story" approach to knowledge. In her book *Love Thy Body*, Nancy Pearcey summarizes Schaeffer's point, "In the lower story is empirical science, which is held to be objectively true and testable. This is the realm of public truths—things that everyone is expected to accept, regardless of their private beliefs. The upper story is the realm of morality and theology, which are treated as private, subjective, and relative."[4] The intrinsic coherence in the title *university* has been exchanged for the modern *multi-versity*. We have universities in name only.

In this sense, our need to integrate faith and learning is a response to modernity and its claim that biblical faith in Christ is not a valid starting point for scholarly inquiry. Faith integration language acknowledges the disintegrating shift that continues to dominate at the most advanced levels of higher education today. Nevertheless, the starting point for biblical Christian scholarship is the coherence of all things in Christ—that all the treasures of wisdom and knowledge are hidden in him.

The disjunction between the reality of coherence and the duality of modern thought drives the necessity of double work for Christian scholars. We must understand our academic disciplines on their own terms while we simultaneously develop biblical grounds and maintain biblical fidelity in understanding every academic discipline as contributing within the intrinsic coherence of all things at the deepest (and highest) levels.

Equipping Young Colleagues

When I started as a college president, our provost said to me, "Over the next 10 years, 40% of our faculty are going to be at or beyond retirement age." I responded, "New faculty development in biblical integration will be the most important thing we do for the next ten years. It won't be enrollment, fundraising campaigns, or budget management." Geneva's long tradition of excellence at integrating faith and learning made this work imperative. Since 1968, Geneva's whole core curriculum was tuned to a pedagogy of coherence in Christ, from required Bible and interdisciplinary humanities sequences to communication, composition, and political philosophy courses. We dedicated every department and major course of study to advancing integral work that resonated with the core. Over the years, we have grown to excel at integrating faith and learning in every subject. Here was our dilemma: with our seasoned faculty heading toward retirement, how could we preserve the heritage and strength of the institution in teaching the coherence of all knowledge across the curriculum?

The challenge is simple to explain. Most new Christian professors get terminal degrees from secularized research universities. They have not been professionally equipped for integral Christian scholarship or pedagogy. For example, a new member of our faculty earned a PhD in cancer biology at the University of Michigan. He is a fine teacher but came without training in integrating faith and learning. Most of us come from programs geared to prepare good scholars for posts at prominent research universities. In my case, doctoral advisors discouraged me from involvement in the Religious Communication Association (RCA) because it would hurt my chances to be hired by a major research university. And like an idiot, I didn't go to RCA.

So how could we invite new professors into a school and curriculum that requires double work? To start, we had to find candidates who would understand the work and *want* to participate in a deliberate program of professional development. Then we developed a two-year new faculty development program using a doctoral seminar format. The program prepares faculty to write integral scholarship that might fit in *Christian Scholars Review* or an appropriate journal in their field (often a Christian or religious field-specific journal). We want publication-quality work, not work addressed primarily to an internal, campus audience. New faculty also develop a biblically integral course syllabus for a class they teach regularly, the ultimate end of the whole program. As we worked through these issues with new faculty a framework emerged, a framework that we now refer to as "A Framework for Biblical Integration and Learning."

The framework is founded on biblical literacy. Today, American Christians of every stripe have a very low level of biblical literacy. Thomas Jefferson, who was a deist, was more biblically literate than most believers today. To increase basic biblical literacy is essential for us all. The second level is whole counsel of God, working fluency with the whole Scripture. The third level is understanding of orthodox creeds and confessions of the historic Christian faith. The fourth level is biblical presuppositions—the first principles of all knowledge, understanding, and wisdom from Scripture. These four levels are foundational and essential. Together they constitute the heart of understanding and guide the thoughts of the heart for Christian professors.

Upon the foundational levels stand three working levels. The fifth level is a biblical view of life and the world. The shorthand for this level is "Christian worldview." First, a biblical view of life and the world invites us to examine both the micro level of one person's life and the macro level of the world—from Psalm 139 to Psalm 8. "Christian worldview" is not foundational, but a manifestation of the foundation. Without foundational grounding, ideologues perpetrate great mischief under the banner of "Christian worldview," assuming the authority of Scripture without demonstrating biblical warrant. The sixth level is the Christian intellectual tradition. We need to learn at depth from those upon whose shoulders we stand, particularly in our respective fields. Finally, the seventh level is practical wisdom and subject mastery. The seventh level is the desired end of active engagement with the first six in concert.

The framework works as an Augustinian order, not a formula or method. The levels are organic and permeable; the components co-inform and intersect in practice, reinforcing and advancing one another.

Professorial Biblical Literacy

To begin with, as Christian scholars we need to have been reading through the whole Bible for a long, long time. Reading through the whole Bible is a professional commitment, not a devotional choice. You have to read through the whole Bible regularly. If you're a professional scholar, you can't say to yourself, "I don't know. Read the whole Bible in a year? It's just too much. I think I'll do a three-year plan." Do your work or leave the profession. Treat it like any other professional obligation, whether deadlines on conference papers or publications, book orders, or submitting grades. We need to make expansive Scripture reading a constant practice to gain comprehensive understanding that leads to agility of mind and wholehearted wisdom.

On what grounds? Moses gives such instructions to Hebrew kings in Deuteronomy

17. He says to Israel, you will eventually ask the Lord for a king, and the Lord will give you one. When the king comes to rule over Israel, he should not acquire horses, chariots, wives, and so on. Then Moses says:

> And when he sits on the throne of his kingdom, he shall write for himself in a book a copy of this law, approved by the Levitical priests. And it shall be with him, and he shall read it in all the days of his life, that he may learn to fear the Lord his God by keeping all the words of this law and these statutes, and doing them, that his heart may not be lifted up above his brothers, and that he may not turn aside from the commandment, either to the right hand or to the left, so that he may continue long in his kingdom, he and his children, in Israel. (Deut. 17:18–20, ESV)

God's command was countercultural. Kings did not read and write in this era of history. Scribes and slaves bore the burden of literacy. But Hebrew kings were commanded to read and write so they could become biblical scholars firsthand—to know God's law, His word. They had to write their own copy and read it daily. The consequence would be fulfillment of the first great commandment—hear and do; and the second great commandment—to love their neighbors with all humility.

Christian scholars must read the Bible all the time, so we don't start to think of ourselves as wiser than others. Nothing contradicts the name of Christ more than being wise in our own eyes. The common temptation that threatens to seize us is to think that we're the "smartest one in the room." The practice of reading Scripture—cover to cover, year in and year out, to hear and to do—will produce humility of heart, toward God and toward one another. The path and its consequences are unmistakable.

The Whole Counsel of God

Thorough, active biblical literacy produces mastery of the whole counsel of God. But what makes the whole counsel of God so important for Christian scholars? For every important question in life and in scholarship, we have to go to the whole Scripture. One Bible verse, one passage of Scripture, even one book of the Bible alone will not do. Exegesis of a single verse or passage can be helpful. That's good. But if the goal is to understand something in depth and develop a Christian mind, that's not good enough.

Whole counsel of God understanding means intertextual biblical agility across testaments, times and places, genres, and writers. Not a theologian's construct, the phrase "whole counsel of God" comes directly from the Apostle Paul's final instructions to the Ephesian elders before he departs for Rome (see Acts 20).

Consider the following whole counsel of God case-study. If you wanted to establish a professional consulting partnership in your field, what Bible character would you choose as your partner? You cannot have Jesus. You cannot have the Apostles Peter, John, or Paul. You cannot have Moses. None of the "big names." For example, if you're a communication scholar, you cannot have Aaron either, who God assigned as Moses's mouthpiece. So, who would you choose?

First, you need to know the whole roster of candidates. Who are the best options?

Knowledge of one testament alone will not be sufficient. You will also need to know all the biblical precepts and principles about business and communication. Biblical best practices don't just come in commandment form; many of them come in stories, prophecies, poems, and parables. Many Scriptures apply, but some do not make immediate sense until you put them together with other passages. You have to scour the Scripture, and you need to be able to start in your own mind and heart, just like with all the rest of your best scholarly understanding.

Creeds and Confessions

Creeds and confessions contribute to our knowledge of the whole counsel of God. They teach us that our task is to integrate *the* faith that has been handed down to us from the prophets, apostles, and the Lord Jesus Christ. I am not trying to integrate *my* faith. The Scriptures speak of this faith that we hold together in Jesus Christ. As Augustine notes in the *Confessions*, all truth is a common possession.[5] Only lies are personal property. Therefore, good teaching and scholarship is necessarily communal. Creeds and confessions mark the basic boundaries and the deep content of the faith that we have received and that we profess.

In *Mere Christianity*, C. S. Lewis is talking about *creedal* Christianity. Creedal Christianity is robust and grounded biblically and historically. Lewis talks about it as "The Historic Christian Faith" or H.C.F.[6] Creedal faith insists on major points of orthodoxy—the Incarnation, the Atonement accomplished at the Crucifixion, the Resurrection, the Ascension, the Second Coming, the institution of Christian marriage, of the Lord's Supper, and of Trinitarian baptism. Lewis talks about creedal Christianity as the "great hall." Manifestations of faith in practice—denominational, congregational, personal—are associated with our convictions about *how* to understand these things biblically and faithfully, which Lewis calls the "houses" or "rooms" immediately adjacent to the great hall. It's creedal Christianity that holds us all together.

Aren't confessions a little different? Yes, of course. But like creeds, we do not create our own confessions. Confessions and catechisms summarize basic biblical doctrines *and* instruct us in whole counsel of God grounding from Scripture for basic biblical truths. At Geneva, we rely directly on the *Westminster Standards—the Westminster Confession of Faith, the Larger Catechism, the Shorter Catechism*, and the other Westminster documents—along with the *Testimony of the Reformed Presbyterian Church of North America* as our confessional ground. Other confessional standards include the Lutheran *Augsburg Confession*; the Dutch Reformed *Three Forms of Unity—The Belgic Confession, The Heidelberg Catechism, and The Canons of Dordt*; the Anglican *Thirty-Nine Articles of 1571*; and the *London Baptist Confession of 1789*. All these confessional standards—from the *Westminster Confession of Faith* to the *London Baptist Confession of 1789*—provide confessional ground. Likewise, the Roman Catholic Church has several historical confessions of faith and catechisms.

Christian scholars need a working knowledge of our creeds and agility within our own confessional standards. Confessional ground reinforces the creeds and depends on whole counsel of God approaches to the Scripture. Creeds and confessions instruct us well in how to think as a Christian.

Biblical Presuppositions

Together, biblical literacy, the whole counsel of God, and the creeds and confessions position us to consider biblical presuppositions, which enable us to do Christian scholarship in our respective fields. For example, what basic biblical presuppositions emerge for communication scholars? Word precedes everything. "In the beginning was the Word . . . " is a universal truth, not a religious platitude (John 1:1, ESV). The great truth that word, person, and act are an essential unity in Jesus Christ grounds the whole of human communication; Christ is the image of God, and we are made in the image of God. The spoken word is essential to all human communication. Meanwhile, Psalm 139 teaches that "[the Lord] knows what's on my tongue before I speak it" (Ps. 139:4, ESV). It's his world. It's his word. It's his mouth. Psalm 139 is not just for Christians. It might give you comfort and knowledge as a Christian, but it's true about God for everyone. We have scratched the surface of two basic presuppositions. Christian communication scholars work from a much broader spectrum of biblical presuppositions. The same is true in every subject and discipline.

The foundation of biblical integration—biblical literacy, the whole counsel of God, creeds and confessions, and biblical presuppositions—grounds our teaching and research as Christians. The foundation provides biblical warrants from which we work. When our hearts and minds are tuned to these basics, we can engage at depth in a biblical view of life and the world. When we don't have this foundation, the Christian worldview gets co-opted—ideologically, politically, in all kinds of ways by both the left and the right in American partisan politics.

The biblical foundation also provides intellectual humility and generosity. In Romans 7, the Apostle Paul is asking, "Who am I?" He demonstrates the humility he teaches, confessing that only in the Lord Jesus Christ can he possibly know and live with himself. The humility he practices and calls for invites us to press hard into the Christian intellectual tradition. One example is *Word and Witnesses*, a volume that presents a Christian intellectual history within Communication.[7]

Finally, this biblical framework produces wisdom for living, Christian phronesis, and excellence in scholarship. In *The Outrageous Idea of Christian Scholarship*, Marsden calls us to conduct our work so well that Christian scholarship benefits our non-Christian colleagues, compels them to interact with the ideas, and perhaps even earns their respect.

Conclusion

One day in another Hauser class, Michael Leff, a Jewish rhetorical scholar from Northwestern University at the time, happened to be in town. A friend of Hauser's, Leff came to teach the class and passed out copies of C. S. Lewis's essay, "What do We Make of Jesus Christ?" Leff, as a great rhetorical critic, read through it with us in class, explaining why and how it was good argumentation. I left that class feeling like I had hope, because I realized there are some great scholars in our field who can take Christianity seriously if it is presented to them in a way that makes sense. That's what George Marsden calls each of us to do.

Abiding in a biblical framework constitutes the "double" in double work. What God is preparing you for as a Christian scholar is big, and so it takes double work. Dwelling every day in God's word, meditating on the Scriptures as a regular pattern and practice, is the only way to build a life of teaching and scholarship as a Christian that resides in the world but is not of the world. Only double work in Christ and by his Spirit can produce this fruit; only in double work can we hope that God will confirm the work of our hands.

We are aiming for what Herman Bavinck calls us to in *Christian Worldview*. Bavinck says we need to embed the thought world of Scripture into all our ways of being and thinking and acting.[8] We want to embed the thought world of Scripture, not through some simplistic form of biblical literacy, but by a robust scholarly approach. This scholarly approach comes by reading the Bible in its entirety and getting to know it on our own terms, over and over again.

As we embed the thought world of Scripture into all of our ways of being and thinking and acting, we'll be able, in God's power, to do scholarship that bears good fruit for the people we're working with now and in generations to come. How can we know that a biblical view of the world and life will have such an impact? Because, as Bavinck has reminded us, the biblical view of the world and life fits the world and life.

Chapter 9

Substantive Truth in an Intellectual Pluralism Setting

CLIFFORD G. CHRISTIANS

[This chapter is a revised transcript of the author's unconference video presentation.]

Chapter Summary: Legacy Scholar Clifford G. Christians concurs with George Marsden's critique of secularism in higher education in *The Outrageous Idea of Christian Scholarship* but offers a more nuanced epistemological foundation. He advocates for intellectual pluralism, which goes beyond religious pluralism to argue that different epistemic frameworks—including those rooted in Christian thought—should coexist in academia. The author emphasizes that truth is not merely a cognitive pursuit but a profound, authentic disclosure that challenges the scientific naturalism dominating most scholarship. By reconceptualizing truth as substantive truth, rooted in Christian ontology and theology, Christians offers a counter-Enlightenment perspective that enriches academic inquiry, bridging faith, reason, and creativity in a pluralistic academic environment. His vision aligns with Marsden's call for Christian engagement in academic pluralism but deepens it with an emphasis on faith-informed epistemology.

GEORGE MARSDEN'S *The Outrageous Idea of Christian Scholarship*, which is based on his earlier book, *The Soul of the American University*, accurately documents the radical shift in North American higher education from Protestant establishment to established nonbelief, from education defined by Judeo-Christian values to a secular ethos.[1] In his observation, the hegemony of scientific naturalism places religious studies outside of science and as, therefore, not an academically serious subject. Marsden's notion of rigorous scholarship discourages us from pursuing ill-conceived solutions to this problem. He emphatically opposes a return to a golden age of Christian dominance in higher education, and there is no point to insisting that the charters and constitutions of academic life belong to Christians by birthright.

I mostly worry, as Marsden does, about our responding to the current state of affairs with simplistic fundamentalisms, such as making miniscule claims at the margins that God reigns or resorting to blanket condemnation that the devil is at work in secularism. Given

69

the magnitude of the shift to an ethos of nonbelief in higher education and given our fail-ure historically to demonstrate a credible alternative, the appropriate response is *Christian education*—Christian scholarship developed in colleges and universities in the context of academic pluralism.

A religiously diverse education will be intellectually richer than totalizing nonbelief. As such, Marsden's framework for faith-informed scholarship entails an academic culture of religious pluralism that makes space for Christian perspectives but also for perspectives grounded in Judaism, Islam, Buddhism, Hinduism, and other religious faiths and tradi-tions. This particular academic culture of pluralism should also foster the application of faith-informed perspectives to forms and subjects of scholarship not necessarily seen as traditionally "religious" in concern, for example, African-American studies, feminist stud-ies, and post-structuralism in literature. I share Marsden's broad framework for faith-in-formed scholarship in a pluralistic setting, but while he grounds his ideas in a history of religion and institutions, I arrive at this broad framework by means of epistemology and philosophical ontology, reframing his notion of faith-based pluralism as what I call *intellectual pluralism.*

Let me state the case in cognitive terms for what I mean by intellectual pluralism. All truths, all truth statements, are distinctive in their core beliefs, and biblical truth by defi-nition is consonant with its presuppositions. And in the particular context of the research university, the context in which I work, ideas are ultimately what hold the university to-gether. For the knowledge that we create and teach in our professional life, for our research platform, for our articulation of the rationale of higher education in the world of ideas, truth is the centerpiece. For those of us with a redeemed mind, a biblical understanding of truth as authentic disclosure of inside meaning is a radical alternative to both correspondence and coherence models of truth. It contradicts both deductive rationalism and narrative social construction. It understands correctly that truthfulness is not simply a problem of cognition but is integral to human consciousness and social formation. Truth is the ground of critical thinking in the liberal arts, in contrast with the sort of "objective" and "neutral" truths that characterize laboratory research.

The dominant concept of research, university truth, has been animated by Enlighten-ment reason idealized as scientific naturalism in objectivism, with the aim being true and incontrovertible accounts of a domain separate from human realism. Truth, epistemolog-ically, is conceptualized in terms of representational accuracy, verisimilitude, and natural algorithms. From a biblical frame of reference, on the other hand, is a profoundly mythic character seen in both Hebrew and Greek culture. In this sense, truth is conceptualized as that which is genuinely authentic, open to the inside, expressing and disclosing the heart of the matter. The intellectual tradition of Augustine, John Calvin, and Jonathan Edwards, accordingly, has consistently denied the autonomy and self-sufficiency of human reason. In doing so, these thinkers exhibit the underlying view that scientific truth is not just self-defined, it is not neutral but presuppositional. Mathematical deduction and social sci-entific empiricism are not autonomous abstractions, as conceptualized in Enlightenment thinking; rather, they are interpretations of reality—human and intellectual creations. As hermeneutics in the philosophy of languages made transparent, infinite regression in knowledge, and construction is nihilism. Naturalistic truths cannot escape the classic paradox, that is, one cannot insist on relativism without rising above it, and one cannot rise above it without giving it up.

My concept of substantive truth does not merely critique the fact-value dichotomy of correspondence truth and a relativism-to-nothingness of coherence truth. Substantive truth is an intellectual trajectory that validates faith-informed assumptions and whole-being awareness to replace the North Atlantic "subject-object" dualism that has predominated since John Locke. Substantive truth as academic pluralism is an explicit counter-Enlightenment option. It is empirical without being empiricist. It retheorizes the nature of theory. It enriches our ontology as presuppositional beings rather than more narrow and Cartesian view of human beings as primarily rational beings. It establishes foundations without foundationalism. It exposes the fallacy that reason provides the ultimate truth about reality.

Charles Sanders Peirce established semiotics for the twentieth century. He replaced the dyadic character of the standard theories of meaning with a triadic sign relation. Deduction and induction do not exhaust the field of reason. There needs to be added adduction to account for human creativity—the logic of inquiry that must always accommodate the invention and discovery of ideas and hypotheses—and historicity. My substantive theory of research is abductive for talent. Thomas Kuhn's conception of scientific knowledge is paradigmatic and revolutionary: *abductive* as a complex mixture of innovation, intuition, beliefs, politics, tacit knowledge, and moral discernment. In all this, these different assumptive frameworks for knowledge need to be seen in complementary and dialogic ways: technically justifiable but limiting in their own terms as self-evident, cognitively credible, and each unable to determinatively disprove the others.

Substantive truth engages the university at its most fundamental commitments. Its very reason for being is not merely as an outlier of critique. In the university's world of ideas, when theistic presuppositions come into their own, the underlying idea of the pursuit of truth in the academic world becomes more robust and more edifying. By helping to create and sustain a productive arena for presenting and defending confessional scholarship and in the continuing debates over epistemology, theism will contribute with a prophetic and compelling voice. Creation is not merely raw material but is ordered by the Creator's design. The omniscient and eternal Creator of all things is the source and norm of all truths about everything.

I'm thankful that contending constructively with the idea of cognitive pluralism fits together into the intelligibility of the fullness of what God himself knows reality to be. Substantive truth in a pluralistic setting is my vision for higher education in the days ahead, and it is a vision that I believe deeply reflects what both Noll and Marsden have had to say about distinctively Christian thinking and Christian scholarship.

Chapter 10

A Catholic University: A Religiously Oriented Approach to Teaching and Research

FR. PAUL A. SOUKUP, SJ

*[This chapter is a revised transcript of the author's
unconference video presentation.]*

Chapter Summary: Legacy Scholar Fr. Paul A. Soukup, SJ, reflects on the distinct nature of a Catholic university, particularly through the lens of Jesuit education. He outlines the historical and theological foundations of Catholic higher education, emphasizing the Jesuit commitment to integrating faith with intellectual pursuits. Soukup identifies three main approaches within Catholic universities: (1) adopting a values-based orientation, (2) focusing on purpose-driven education, and (3) ongoing reflection on key principles from the *Ratio Studiorum*. He highlights Jesuit education's emphasis on learning that is rhetorical and active and educates the whole person, fostering community-based learning, and promoting justice rooted in Catholic social teachings.

TO OFFER SOME small contribution to this unconference on Christian education let me stay within the boundaries of what I know—the Roman Catholic educational tradition, and within that, Jesuit education. The Roman tradition differs in some key theological positions from evangelical theology, differences that affect approaches to higher learning. There is, for example, a difference in how these Christian traditions approach the Scriptures and their interpretation. There is also a broader range of acceptance of what fits into the tradition, with less of an opposition between scientific methods and religious understanding. Some of the issues that Professors Marsden and Noll have described do not have the same salience in the Roman Catholic tradition. With the caveat that we begin in different places, here are some reflections on higher education in my own Christian tradition.[1]

The Nature of a Catholic University

I am a member of the Society of Jesus, or the Jesuits. This religious community within the Catholic Church, founded in 1540, has actively educated people across the world since the sixteenth century. At the end of the sixteenth century, a group drafted what they called the

Ratio Studiorum, a guide for schools, a curriculum, and a method of teaching that curriculum. Although these sixteenth-century schools were what we might think of today as combined high schools and junior colleges, the overall educational idea continues to stamp Jesuit schools. It also raises the question about the nature of a Catholic University, since so many of those Jesuit schools have become universities.

In the United States, Jesuit missionaries like those from many other religious communities established schools in the nineteenth century, often to provide education for their co-religionists who had come to the United States, many as uneducated immigrants. The Catholic schools provided basic education and, at the University level, professional qualifications to lift these new immigrants into different roles in society. There was little question about the religious quality or method of the education; everything focused both on religious identity and on cultural placement.

Even after the growth of the schools and the separation of today's high schools from the colleges or universities, the controlling focus of the religious sponsors balanced religious identity and practical learning. Some of the curricula rested on the traditional *Ratio Studiorum* with its emphasis on humanities and education through disputation, but newer subjects embraced the models of scientific education and the cultural ideal of disciplinary education as it grew up in the late nineteenth and early twentieth centuries in German universities and in the United States. Only after the Second World War and an influx of students supported by the GI Bill did many of the Catholic universities professionalize in their approach to teaching and research.

For the Jesuits, the 1960s saw a significant change which involved separating the schools from the religious community. From then on, the universities existed as Catholic universities but sponsored by Boards of Trustees rather than religious communities. That led to further challenges in creating an identity for the schools and for thinking more deeply about what it means to be a Catholic university. In some ways this question is very similar to the question that motivates this unconference: How do we maintain a religious identity in education where the educational system strives for independence from religious dogma or religious influence on teaching and research?

With the Jesuit schools, three approaches emerged. In thinking about this, I will draw on my own knowledge of Jesuit universities and so cannot speak for every Catholic university much less any religiously affiliated university.

Three Approaches to Higher Education

One approach in Catholic universities involves doing what other universities do but with an awareness of one's own values, explicitly taking a *values-based approach*. Catholic theology's reflection on the relationship between God and creation recognizes God's creating act but does not specify how it takes place. Catholic mystics have spoken about "finding God in all things." These values do not make a separation between the goals of science, for example, and God's self-revelation through creation and through the Scriptures. The difference between Catholic universities and many secular universities is that the Catholic university becomes more self-aware of its position vis-a-vis knowledge. Rather than presuming a values-free approach, it acknowledges the values and makes them clear, much as approaches to different kinds of qualitative research encourage us to do.

A second approach resembles what Neil Postman describes in his book, *The End of Education*.[2] He holds that education must have a clear purpose and *values-free education* often lacks that purpose. The clear focus on goals distinguishes the Catholic Jesuit tradition as well as the traditions of many religiously affiliated schools. Postman explains more in his first chapter, which I quote at length:

> To become a different person because of something you have learned—to appropriate an insight, a concept, a vision, so that your world is altered —that is a different matter. For that to happen, you need a reason. . . .
>
> A reason, as I use the word here, is different from a motivation. Within the context of schooling, motivation refers to a temporary psychic event in which curiosity is aroused and attention is focused. I do not mean to disparage it. But it must not be confused with a reason for being in a classroom, for listening to a teacher, for taking an examination, for doing homework, for putting up with school even if you are not motivated.
>
> . . . For school to make sense, the young, their parents, and their teachers must have a god to serve, or, even better, several gods. If they have none, school is pointless. Nietzsche's famous aphorism is relevant here: "He who has a *why* to live can bear with almost any *how*." This applies as much to learning as to living.
>
> To put it simply, there is no surer way to bring an end to schooling than for it to have no end.
>
> By a god to serve, I do not necessarily mean *the* God, who is supposed to have created the world and whose moral injunctions as presented in sacred texts have given countless people a reason for living and, more to the point, a reason for learning. In the Western world, beginning in the thirteenth century and for five hundred years afterward, that God was sufficient justification for the founding of institutions of learning, from grammar schools, where children were taught to read the Bible, to great universities, where men were trained to be ministers of God. Even today, there are some schools in the West, and most in the Islamic world, whose central purpose is to serve and celebrate the glory of God. Wherever this is the case, there is no school problem, and certainly no school crisis. There may be some disputes over what subjects best promote piety, obedience, and faith; there may be students who are skeptical, even teachers who are nonbelievers. But at the core of such schools, there is a transcendent, spiritual idea that gives purpose and clarity to learning. Even the skeptics and nonbelievers know why they are there, what they are supposed to be learning, and why they are resistant to it.[3]

Because the Jesuit tradition emerges within that Western world where "God was sufficient justification for the founding of institutions of learning," the academic parts of Jesuit or Ignatian education flow from a Christian vision of the world in which people love their neighbor, learn to put others' needs before their own, recognize the differences between their motivations, and practice a kind of discernment.

For effective education people need to understand why. For what purpose do we seek education? If the purpose is only economic, one wonders whether this is education at all. To what end do we seek to engage in university education? Why should we pursue research in communication, for example? What do we hope to learn? A religious perspective includes a deeper understanding of how humanity exists in the image and likeness of God. To study, to research, to learn all involves deepening a relationship with God. This end of education distinguishes religious education from what is often the dominant ideology of education in the United States.

As a third approach among the Jesuit colleges and universities in the United States, many have undertaken an ongoing reflection on the key principles elaborated in the *Ratio Studiorum*. Rather than looking at the lists of subjects suggested in that sixteenth-century document, contemporaries have tried to isolate several key principles. Usually they list four things, variously expressed: (1) the mode of education, (2) an approach to the individual, (3) an education rooted in a community environment, and (4) a commitment to justice.

1. *The mode of education.* This was not new to the Jesuits but grounded in the disputations of the late medieval period. This focus on disputation and debate demanded an active education: not rote learning but framing arguments, matching the needs of hearers. This rhetorically based approach should resonate with our communication scholarship. While the world has changed dramatically from the sixteenth century, the idea that teaching should engage students with a purpose remains a solid commitment.

2. *An approach to the individual.* Jesuit schools often refer to "the education of the whole person." Such an educational ideal goes beyond academics. The origins of Jesuit schooling in the sixteenth and seventeenth centuries meant that the students lived at the school, many of them enrolling as young teenagers, and the faculty had charge not only of an academic curriculum but also of the welfare of their students. They saw the students as preparing for life, not necessarily as academics or clerics, but as civic leaders. They taught an education for public life, including its public aspects, exemplified by Jesuit drama and other performance type behavior as was expected in royal courts, courts of justice, and public charities. Beyond that, the schools also had to deal with the social and emotional and religious growth of their young charges. Such comprehensive education meant a preparation for personal and social engagement.

The education of the whole person goes beyond a concern for mental or emotional health. Human beings exist as unities that a disciplinarily focused curriculum often ignores. Every aspect of human identity is inextricably connected to the other parts, and Jesuit schools have over the centuries wrestled with how that education should take place. Students do not separate what university organizational charts do: Student life, athletics, social activities, clubs, politics, activist concerns, and majors and minors happen together. Education of the whole person reflects an understanding of the unity of how people live in the world. To do this well, universities should be small enough for faculty, staff, coaches, and students to know one another and to know what each other does, to model that education of the whole person.

3. *An education rooted in a community environment.* The community forms the environment for education; this frequently appears as "community-based education" but one goes beyond outside activities and internships. To truly work from a Jesuit or Ignatian perspective, the idea of community-based or service learning begins in the education of the whole person. In this sense, the "whole person" must include the community in which that person lives and studies. So education becomes a function of that larger community. Service learning begins as an insertion into the local community, to give both students, faculty, and staff a better sense of the situation of the University (including the religious situation). Rock explains that community-based learning can occur in several ways:

> Bringing community into the classroom manifests typically in one of two ways, with lines between the two often blurred. The first is as place-based learning communities, in which cohorts of students are engaged with local community issues through a series of courses, using the community as laboratory and lens, and developing place attachment in the process. . . . The other is through community-engaged course work in which students work directly with community organizations to identify and develop solutions for those issues.[4]

In addition to this two-fold practice of community-based learning, Jesuit schools have incorporated an awareness of two challenges arising from religious self-understanding: separating community-based learning from simple volunteer work and protecting the local community.

Volunteer work, while valuable in itself, carries the subtle implication that volunteers approach their communities as people who need their help and that they (the students) possess a resource, an expertise, or even a power that local people do not; that the learners provide a service that the communities cannot provide for themselves. To focus on the fact that the students enter the community not to do something for it but to learn from it, Jesuit school programs typically use the "community-based learning" name. Here the emphasis lies on seeing community members as having knowledge, an understanding that community and students help each other, learn from each other. But this raises the second challenge—protecting the community, a need that arises from an understanding of the role of the community. The danger here is that the community, and often the marginalized parts of the community, end up serving the privileged student group. And so, a part of the education of the whole person must involve fostering an understanding of oneself, one's motives, one's prejudices, one's privilege. The model, of course, lies in the Incarnation, in which as St Paul reminds us, the Redeemer emptied himself and took on all of human existence including its suffering; so those who follow the Christian way must also set aside a privilege and temper their pride to understand themselves as called to service.

4. *A commitment to justice.* Current reflection on Jesuit education involves an explicit commitment to justice, which comes directly from Catholic social theology. Taking the lead from encyclicals of John XXIII and Paul VI and the Synods of Bishops in 1971 and 1974, the Jesuit's worldwide policy making 32nd General Congregation's Decree 4 stated, "The mission of the Society of Jesus today is the service of faith, of which the promotion of justice is an absolute requirement. For reconciliation with God demands the reconciliation of people with one another" (#2).[5]

This focus on justice became part of the educational work of the Jesuits, the focus of research, the content of education, and the selection of the student body. Further, the Congregation embraced "a commitment to promote justice and to enter into solidarity with the voiceless and the powerless" (#42).[6] This affects education in two ways. First, the Jesuits decided that "Greater emphasis should be placed on the conscientization according to the Gospel of those who have the power to bring about social change, and a special place given to service of the poor and oppressed."[7]

Second, they chose to

> pursue and intensify the work of formation in every sphere of education, while subjecting it at the same time to continual scrutiny. We must help prepare both young people and adults to live and labor for others and with others to build a more just world. Especially we should help form our Christian students in such a way that animated by a mature faith and personally devoted to Jesus Christ, they can find Him in others and having recognized Him there, they will serve Him in their neighbor (#59).[8]

In this way, the religious commitment leads the entire educational mission and practice.

Conclusion

The Catholic tradition in education aims for a coherent experience for the students, one led by theological and moral commitments. People should feel freedom in the tradition to experiment with new ways to accomplish the goals. And, as Postman urges, everyone should know the purpose, even if they disagree with it.

Chapter 11

Learning, Teaching, and the Christian Mind: A Dialogue

Mark Fackler and Robert S. Fortner

[This chapter is a revised transcript of the author's unconference video presentation.]

Chapter Summary: In this chapter, Mark Fackler and Robert Fortner reflect on their long careers in teaching, highlighting key insights into the relationship between learning, teaching, and the Christian perspective. They discuss how an emphasis on lifelong learning can transform teaching, with both authors advocating for a shift from traditional lecturing to question-based dialogues that foster deeper engagement. The chapter also addresses the challenges of balancing scholarship with teaching, particularly within faith-centered institutions, and the need for faculty to integrate their faith with academic work. Additionally, they emphasize the importance of giving students more autonomy in their learning through project-based assessments, as well as the evolving role of AI in education. Ultimately, the authors encourage educators to seek "gems" in theory, history, and practice, using these discoveries to inspire both personal growth and student development.

Mark Fackler

Hello, everybody. My name is Bob Fortner.

Bob Fortner

No, it's not. Wait a minute.

Mark

Who are you?

Bob

Well, I thought I was Bob Fortner.

Mark

Ah, I guess I'm Mark Fackler.

Bob

Oh, that could be.

Mark

What's funny, though, is that when both of us were teaching together at Calvin College, now Calvin University, we would actually have students confuse the two of us. I had a student approach me in December of one semester, begging me to let him make up the final exam, which he had slept through. And I thought to myself, "Who are you? Do I know you? Has my memory lapsed so much that I could have a student for an entire semester that I don't recognize?" But as it turned out, it wasn't me he was looking for. He was looking for Professor Fortner over here. Once I figured that out, I said, "My friend, you need to go to Bob Fortner, not to me." It's been funny, even at church we've had people confuse us, going up to me or Bob thinking each of us is the other person. But here we are.

Bob

How is that possible, though, since I'm so much better looking?

Mark

Well, there it is, the decision is clear. Anyhow, we're happy to be able to share some of our insights from our long careers in teaching. In fact, Bob is just beginning a new chapter in his teaching career at a local and growing Michigan university. So we may hear something about that, but we're happy to share with you, and we hope that this conference is meaningful to you.

Bob

So, tell us a little bit about your background.

Mark

I went through the process of earning a PhD and beginning my teaching career through the benefits given to me by the Veterans Administration. I was drafted in 1971 and out in 1973, and from there on it was graduate school, and the raising of children, and the beginning of understanding of what was ahead professionally—which started as a one-year gig at a major university in the Midwest and then two faculty positions at Christian colleges, which lasted until my retirement from Calvin 10 years ago. I'm now involved with teaching immigrants and refugees English, in an active program that I'm very happy to be a part of.

Bob

Well, Mark and I both went to the same doctoral program, and both studied under Cliff Christians, although we weren't there at the same time. I left just as Mark was arriving, and for the first decade of my career I served at one public university and also at private, non-Christian universities. Actually, the one I like to bring up is George Washington University, which Chuck Colson, in *Born Again*, cites as among the nation's most intensely secular universities.[1] After this first decade, my career shifted to serving in more faith-inflected and faith-friendly contexts. I taught at Calvin for 20 years, and then left to operate an international research organization called the International Center for Media Studies, which sponsored work primarily in the developing world, working with indigenous Christian denominations (such as the Anglican Church in Uganda) in their operation of hospitals and mass communication outlets. When this organization was forced to close because of economic recession, I went back into teaching, serving at the American University in Bulgaria, then Hope College, and then (finally) Palm Beach Atlantic University. Even after retirement, I'm going back into teaching as an adjunct. So both of us have a variety of experiences teaching at both public and private institutions both Christian and secular. So I think we might have something to say that's useful.

Mark

I'd like to offer a couple of turning points that I experienced in my teaching career, which I think can serve as an incentive to find the "gems" in the theory, history, and practice of communication. The first turning point I'd like to share with you is one that many of you may have experienced already. I thought I was entering a teaching profession, but then I discovered that the profession I had gotten myself into was actually a learning profession. I first started seeing hints of this during my doctoral studies, engaging with thinkers like Paulo Freire. But I began seeing more of this reality at the Pointer Institute of Media Studies, where a wonderful learner—Marty Linsky from the Kennedy School of Government—and I and other faculty were engaged in the task of helping journalists in the 1980s and early 1990s understand their mission more profoundly. Teaching is what I initially thought I had to do. Learning is what I gradually learned I needed to do in order to be an effective teacher. And I found that as I shifted my emphasis from teaching to learning, my teaching got better.

I was more engaged myself in presenting to students things that were becoming important to me as I kept up with the literature. Now, I have to say that this was difficult to do, in large part because the institutions at which I served implicitly saw this learning work as something I needed to do on "my own time," and time was scarce. I recall in those days picking up a book, being so happy to be in it, and then putting it down and not picking it up again for another three weeks, because of the demands of teaching and serving students. Nonetheless, I was able to make this transition, and when I became aware that I was making it, the teaching task became much more delightful. I would encourage each of you to think of yourself as a learner first and then as a teacher who presents your learning as a king of a flowing stream, a spring stream, and then to find the joy of teaching that flows from that stream.

Bob

I basically agree with everything Mark has said. There is always a struggle to balance your own learning with your teaching and, of course, the other demands that your institution will place upon you. We know we are speaking to folks at a variety of institutions, so the things we're bringing up will apply to different people in different ways. But if you are at a Christian-focused institution, the teaching aspect of your work will always be consistently emphasized. All the institutions I know of that have this focus are keenly interested in their faculty members having consistently high-quality interactions with students, and this type of teaching always limits the amount of time you have for thinking, for learning, for imagining how you might approach particular courses differently based on what you have recently learned. None of that is easy, and even though it is necessary for the academic, it isn't something that results in a significant payoff in terms of tenure, promotion, salary increases, and the like. So this work of thinking and learning is done on your own time, and you simply can't rush it. I found that when I was engaged in teaching full-time, I had to basically use my entire summer not to relax, but to spend time on the road, doing research in various parts of the world so that I could learn more and more about the world and bring that into my classroom. And it's exhausting, frankly, never to have had any significant downtime, never to have an extended vacation involving pursuits such as sitting on a beach. I don't know about those things, because we never did them.

Mark

Bob and I had the immense privilege of a common mentor at the Institute of Communications Research at the University of Illinois, Clifford Christians. Hear from him, or perhaps you have already heard from him, because he was surely the most important influence that either of us had in this particular business of understanding our role as learners and teaching from that perspective. Now he won't tell you this, but he slept about three or four hours a night, beginning his own learning curve soon after dinner and on into the morning, getting up early and resuming, and never skipping a beat. This man was an amazing learner, friend, and mentor throughout our doctoral studies. So if there's a lesson in that, find a mentor and learn as much as you can from that person. We co-published with Cliff and basically learned how to do this work by watching and by talking with that amazing scholar, so we're very grateful.

I want to mention briefly my second major "ah ha" moment in my teaching career, and I owe this in large part to Bob. I was into the normal routine of assigning papers, exams, and due dates and prescribing how all of those will be graded. And I said to Bob, "There's got to be a better way, because all of this has just become so routine." He suggested that I try "contract learning." And so I did, and it changed everything I would say to a class. I'd start by telling them that everybody starts at the same level—an F grade—but everybody can get to an A grade. I'll have explaining to do with the dean if I report all As for this class, but you all could make that happen. You just have to show some initiative.

So what I did, instead of offering a standard course of assignments and deadlines, was to offer varieties of pathways to complete the course that students could choose from based on their strengths and interests, all with particular kinds of work and particular deadlines. So I would have 25 different contracts active on any given day in class, and I would urge more. I would tell them, "Let's talk after class, we'll arrange it." I would collect individual assignments as the contract deadlines for them came due. I would grade them, and if they weren't up to speed, I'd offer students a chance to revise and improve their grades. And it worked. I went from papers and finals to projects that individual students agreed to do based on their interests. I told them that this customized work could help them for their future, and it could even result in work product that they could put on their resumes. And I was delighted at their progress, largely because Bob suggested that route as an alternative to the standard curriculum.

Bob

I didn't do exactly the same thing, although I did the contract grading that Mark is talking about earlier in my career. What I did do, particularly toward the end of my career, was give up on the idea that students should be assessed based on regurgitating information that they heard in class or read in the books or did research on themselves. Instead, I assigned them projects. I would say, for instance, in an intercultural communication class, you need to do five projects. There are 12 to 15 of them outlined in the syllabus. You pick the ones that you want to do, and you'll see the requirements for doing each one of them. They all required the students to go off campus, interview people, and come up with an analysis of what they'd heard and talk about the implications of that analysis and, in some cases, apply to a particular theory to that analysis to see how it worked in the real world. Now all of that comes from an understanding, over the courses of a career, that the more interaction you have with students and the more choice you give to students, the more interest they're going to have, and the more or better they're going to do in the end. So, I would say to students that you need to do five projects in order to earn an A, four to earn a B, three to earn a C, and they would get to choose. A student could decide that earning a C is sufficient, so that student would then do three projects. And that was fine, because that was the student's decision. The students will learn just as much, of course, and they're more in charge of their final grade than I am. And I thought, you know, that's a good thing because I don't want to be responsible, really, for evaluating 25 students in a class and trying to come up with the distinction between an A and an A-, or between an A- and a B+. Rather, let the students come to the conclusion of what they want to learn, how much they want to learn, and what they're willing to accept as a grade in this class. And I found this approach to be very useful in all the classes I taught in the latter portion of my career.

Mark

That also prepares students for things like employment interviews or the first year on the job, in which you have to get off your seat and produce and be creative and diligent, as opposed to thinking, "Oh, I'm just sitting here because I need a grade." That's not it. Our effort was to prepare students for the mindset and the incentive that they need to show when they graduate. And we hope that we've accomplished some of that.

The third "ah ha" moment of my teaching career, which perhaps was a result of the first two, was that I went from a lecture presentation to a question presentation. I would try to start each class with questions directed to interests of the day and ultimately to the points I wanted to get across, ultimately to the reading that we had done, ultimately to the theory or history or practice that I was directing the class toward, but questions. And then I realized that there was something to the business of asking questions that could actually help in the era in which we'd been teaching. I think this approach is even more salient in the current political and cultural climate in which we find ourselves—particularly with the intense tribalism and polarization that make genuine dialogue extraordinarily difficult.

Teaching from the standpoint of asking questions, it seems to me, is an important way to create meaningful space in the classroom for precisely this kind of dialogue. I ran across a book written recently by a former congressman, titled *Doesn't Hurt to Ask*; the subtitle,

I believe is *Using the Power of Questions to Communicate, Connect, and Persuade.*[2] I read it, and I thought this would have been a book I would have offered to students to read for credit in almost any class. Learn to ask good questions. Learn to start the conversation by pursuing the interests of the other, and not only in class but also in friendships or mixed circles with different values and perspectives. You might find yourself a lot happier at the end of the day. So in all, I learned well that lecturing ultimately didn't do much for me nor for my students but starting the class with questions certainly did much more. I benefitted from it as well, from my students' feedback and from their reply questions.

Bob

One of the issues I think is important in this unconference that you are attending is one of scholarship. Now I've already said that most Christian institutions do not value scholarship at the same level that they value teaching. But I want to make two points about that. One is that scholarship feeds teaching. If you aren't active as a scholar, what you're probably going to end up doing in the classroom is teaching what you learned as a graduate student while the world moves on, theory moves on, history moves on, ethics moves on. So you can't remain stuck in that historical period of your intellectual development and then expect to have a fulfilling career as an academic who works in the classroom with students. You really need to think of teaching and scholarship as being tied together, with each one feeding the other.

The second thing I would say is to be mindful of the ways in which artificial intelligence (AI) will increasingly affect your work as a faculty member. If nothing else, students are going to be severely tempted to over-rely on it—to have it write their papers or do their research or summarize the readings that you assign them, rather than students doing these things themselves. So I've decided, as I go back into teaching this fall, that the first thing I have to do is to talk to students, on the very first day of class, about why they're there. Because if you're there to learn in an authentic and life-transforming sense, you can't do that by depending on an outside source. There are way too many problems with AI at this point, such that it is most unwise to place uncritical trust in what it produces. I'm going to tell my students that I don't mind if you use AI, but you are ultimately responsible for everything that you submit in this class. So if you depend on AI and it hallucinates, that's your responsibility. And I will catch it, and I will tell you that this sort of thing is not a way that you move ahead as a learner.

All of this isn't to say that AI isn't useful in some ways. I have used it in preparing for classes, and I've found it makes the natural difficulties of preparing for class less onerous. I can say to AI, "Give me a lesson plan about X," and it will create one for me. Then I can look at it and say, "Well, I don't really like that very much," or "I think this is terrific," or "I'm going to use part of this, and not all of it." So it can be a very helpful inventional resource to spur my own ideas and my own thinking about what will happen in my classroom. But in the classroom, you're going to find students who are going to be heavily and unreflectively dependent on AI and who, as a result of that, are not really preparing themselves. Of course, they think they are because they are going to have to use AI in their jobs in the future. And that's true to some degree but using it as a college student to bypass the very thinking process that education is supposed to cultivate in them—that is not going to get them where they think they are going to be. In all this, faculty need to be keenly aware of this issue and be proactive in making the case that depending on their own intellect and their own abilities is far superior to depending on something like AI.

The other thing I want to say about scholarship is that my approach to it has changed over the course of my career. As I said, the first decade of my academic career was outside of a Christian environment. So I wasn't really paying much attention then to the connection between my faith and my scholarship, even though I always saw my work as a scholar as informed by my faith. But as I went back into a Christian environment at Calvin, it became much more significant that I was able to articulate my faith-informed perspective as it applies to scholarship. So between me and Mark, we probably published around 25 books, I would suggest that all of them, in one way or another, were informed by our faith, even if we did not quote John 3:16 or any other Bible verse within the context of the essay or the book or whatever we were writing. It's hard to get away from a worldview once you've adopted it, and you shouldn't be ashamed of that. You should celebrate it and be willing to defend it when you get into a professional meeting or other academic exchange. So if someone asks you why you set up your research questions or your argument in this particular way, you can say that you did so because of how you see the world. That is part of spreading the good news—being willing to articulate your convictions and to be both able and willing to defend them with audiences that are at times unreceptive.

Mark

I'm going to do a 10-second reading that illustrates the last point I'd like to make in this conversation we're having. That point is, find the gems. Find the gems. In theory, history, and practice, focus on the gems as gateways to discovery. I'm going to share from a new book on the First Amendment called *The Indispensable Right*,

> Those who won our independence believed that the final end of the state was to make men free to develop their faculties and that in its government, the deliberative forces should prevail over the arbitrary. They value liberty both as an end and as a means. They believe liberty to be the secret of happiness and courage to be the secret of liberty. They believe that freedom to think as well as you will and to speak as you think are means indispensable to the discovery and spread of truth.[3]

Now, that quote comes from Louis Brandeis in his 1925 U.S. Supreme Court decision in *Whitney v. California*. Brandeis was the first Jewish justice on the Supreme Court, and Anita Whitney was a socialist activist in California who was convicted under criminal syndicalism laws back in the early 1920s. Brandeis's decision in this case had this gem in it, and when I read it, I said, "That's how I would start a class. I would put this quote on display for my class, read it for them, invite them to think about it and/or discuss it together." Find the gems buried away in these obscurities. That's our job. We look for these things, and when we find them, we treasure them, and we share them.

Bob

I'll make one last point as well. I've always thought it was necessary for scholars who have had the good fortune to spend time in doctoral programs, in particular, to take what they've learned and apply it outside the classroom. In so doing, they test theories and methodologies. They learn about other people's lives, and it enlivens them to be able to bring what they've learned in those situations into classrooms and to prove to students that there is value in the history and in the morality and in the theory that they study, because it can be used outside the classroom to assist the world to become a better place. And my career has been full of that, and I'm very grateful for the opportunities I've had to do that sort of thing outside the classroom.

Mark

And my last comment is to take these gems, take these questions, and help students discover the connections to the Gospel; to faith, hope, and love; to your own gratitude for your life of faith and to the challenge that you face as a public intellectual; and to the challenges they will need to face as working professionals in whatever vocational path they follow; do that and you'll end your days satisfied with good work done.

Part II:

Responses to Our Legacy Scholars

Section One:
Foundations and Historical Roots

Chapter 12

What does Alexandria Have to Do with Upland? Classical Theism and the Future of Christian Scholarship

James W. Vining

Response Summary: Noll's *Scandal* points to Christian efforts to establish Christian societies, including education systems, in Plymouth and Geneva as models of faithful Christian intellectual lives. This essay looks instead to the ancient Alexandrian School as a model of faithful Christian scholarship. While initially a persecuted minority community, Christian scholars in ancient Alexandria practiced genuine engagement with pagan scholars in ways that strengthened and expanded their faith and witness, resulting in church growth, intellectual and cultural influence, and theological foundations that continue to shape Christianity today. Contemporary Christian scholars are encouraged to learn from the theological, philosophical, and pedagogical innovations of the ancient Alexandrian School, moving toward scholarly vocations marked by theological confidence, intellectual curiosity, and holistic human formation, and guided by a desire for the redemption of the world.

I GREW UP in the traditions Mark Noll most pointedly critiqued in *The Scandal of the Evangelical Mind*. I was the third-generation member of the Holiness tradition. The charismatic movement influenced the informal network of evangelical teens in my community.

Dispensationalist end-times preachers temporarily captivated me with their claims that the first Gulf War was foretold in biblical prophecy. While I am grateful for the faith of my youth (well, not the end-times preachers), and I think Noll overstated their roles in evangelicalism's anti-intellectualism, I agree with his core critiques of those traditions.

My religious background propelled me to study youth ministry at Taylor University, an evangelical college in Upland, Indiana. Taylor was a model of mainstream evangelical pursuit of Christian scholarship in the 1990s. Christian education professors made me read non-Christian philosophies of education. Bible professors made me study ancient history and contemporary hermeneutics. The bell tower at the center of campus and the tallest structure in Upland had two sides, one representing faith and the other learning, that joined together at the (electronic) bell, an ever-present reminder of the school's task to integrate faith and learning.

Taylor's President Jay Kesler frequently reminded us of that task as he cast a vision for the Christian intellectual life. Decades later, I still discuss his one-liners with my former classmates. Jay, as he insisted we call him, was the first person I remember saying, "All truth is God's truth," challenging my false dichotomy between Christian and secular truth. He regularly reminded us that intellectual pursuits were part of, not a threat to, Christian discipleship, saying in a playful yet passionate voice, "God gave you a brain and wants you to use it." Jay assured us that "When we open a rabbit in a lab at Taylor, it looks the same as it does down the road at Ball State," and encouraged us to be fearless in our research because "nothing is going to crawl out from under a rock and swallow God." However, the most revolutionary Jay Kesler quote for me was, "True Christian scholarship is joyful and courageous." Having spent many formative years motivated by fear of sin and battle with the devil, that simple quote opened me to a perspective on life rooted in a theology of the goodness of God.

Jay Kesler was also the first person I heard mention Mark Noll's *The Scandal of the Evangelical Mind*. His voice shook as he told a chapel full of students and faculty that the book's title grieved him, but he agreed with Noll's evaluation of evangelicalism, and he encouraged us to read the book. That was my introduction to Mark Noll, and speaking more broadly, that was my introduction to the important conversations in this volume.

In this essay, I share thoughts, as someone who spent 15 years as a pastor in evangelical churches and 15 years as a professor in state universities, on a future of Christian scholarship informed by ancient Christian scholarship. First, I briefly reflect on contemporary Christian scholarship, inspired by Marsden and Noll. Next, I look to the ancient Alexandrian School as a model of faithful Christian scholarship in a pluralistic setting. Then, I examine key theological points that were both the outgrowth and the undergirding for Christian scholarship in ancient Alexandria. Finally, I bring recommendations, inspired by the Alexandrian School, for Christian scholars to consider while striving to live their vocation in a pluralistic world faithfully.

Christian Scholarship in the Late Twentieth and Early Twenty-first Century

As evidenced by this current volume, the arguments made by Mark Noll in *The Scandal of the Evangelical Mind* and George Marsden in *The Outrageous Idea of Christian Scholarship* continue to illumine the tensions felt by many Christian scholars in the modern Academy. Tracing the historical roots of evangelical anti-intellectualism, Noll argues that evangelicals had largely abdicated their responsibility to serious intellectual engagement while calling for a renaissance of evangelical thinking. Marsden speaks more specifically about Christian scholars in the Academy, calling for scholarship from a Christian perspective to be considered a legitimate voice among many voices in the modern pluralistic Academy. He advocated for reflective Christian scholarship that would be academically rigorous and explicitly informed by faith commitments.

While there have been changes in both academic culture and prominent Christian thought in America over the past 30 years, the arguments presented by Marsden and Noll in the 1990s continue to generate conversations among Christian scholars. Many Christian scholars, particularly those from evangelical and fundamentalist traditions, feel caught between their religious faith and their vocation as scholars. Religious perspectives can appear at odds with prevailing academic assumptions and have reportedly been a cause for academic silencing. On the other hand, many Christians view academic scholarship with suspicion or indifference, and still others openly claim it is antithetical to Christianity.

Challenges from the Academy

Like Nicholas Wolterstorff in this volume, I cannot think of a time when I was rejected or persecuted for being a Christian in the Academy. This is not to say I have not been rejected, but rather that I do not know that it happened because of my faith in Christ. Most people do not care that I believe the Nicene Creed, if I am doing my job and making good arguments, and I generally find that I am better received at work on the days I manifest the fruit of the Spirit than on the days I grieve the Spirit.

That being said, there are instances when scholars and their scholarship are rejected because of their Christian commitments. Many people reject what they understand to be Christianity, and even in contexts where pluralism, fairness, and rationality are celebrated, some people carry that rejection of Christianity to the intentional rejection of those who identify as Christian. Rejection that is not intentional, religious persecution can occur when people who see the world through different logical frameworks struggle to understand one another, even when discussing the same data or experiences.[1] There are cases where a Christian scholar's intellectually rigorous claims that are filtered through their religious commitments are not recognized as legitimate by non-Christian scholars, not because of an intentional rejection of Christianity, but because they have filtered the same data and experience through different philosophical commitments. While the motivations are vastly different, in both cases, the Christian scholar may reasonably feel that their scholarship was rejected because of their religion.

Challenges from the Church

While Greg Spencer correctly observes in this volume that anti-intellectualism is not exclusively an evangelical problem and that it permeates much of contemporary American culture, he also correctly notes that much of American evangelicalism appears to be worse off intellectually and more prone to wild conspiracy theories now than in the 1990s. Anti-intellectual evangelical voices have amplified despite evangelicals gaining ground in several academic fields. As Noll notes in this volume, evangelicalism at large has not borne the fruit of the labor of evangelical scholars. These scholars face increasing hostility from some anti-intellectual Christians. Some Christians and Christian communities will often reject Christian scholars who study or teach anything not explicitly taught in their (interpretation of the) tradition or Scripture.

Additionally, other Christians view academic work as unimportant or unrelated to God's work in the world. A Christian scholar who feels called by God to shape humans in truth, provide underserved youth skills to prosper in life, or uncover insights into God's world that expand human understanding may be told by fellow Christians they should focus on getting students "saved" because nothing else counts as faithfulness to Christ. Intentional and unintentional rejection from the church can also frustrate and alienate the modern Christian scholar.

The challenges facing Christian scholars, both from the Academy and the church, raise important questions about the compatibility of Christianity and academic rigor. How can Christian scholars maintain theological integrity while engaging productively with diverse intellectual perspectives? What theological resources might enable faithful intellectual work in pluralistic contexts? How can Christian scholars navigate tensions between their religious and academic commitments? These questions invite us to look back in Christian history for models to inform our path forward. While others have looked to Plymouth and Geneva for models, I look to Christian scholars in the diverse intellectual environment of ancient Alexandria.

Christian Scholarship in Ancient Alexandria

Although they lived nearly two thousand years ago, Christian scholars in ancient Alexandria had a context and challenges similar to those of contemporary Christian scholars. Alexandria was a diverse, affluent, and influential intellectual center in the ancient world, and Christianity was one of many philosophical and religious traditions in the city. Christians were looked down upon and frequently persecuted. Under these circumstances, Christian scholars struggled and prospered, generating intellectual work that won over critics, shaped the ancient world, and continues to influence Christians today. Contemporary Christian scholars can look to Christian scholars in ancient Alexandria for guidance on faithful intellectual life in a pluralistic context.

The Alexandrian Context

It is difficult to overstate the significance of Alexandria to the Roman Empire and the ancient Mediterranean world. Founded by Alexander the Great in 331 BCE, the city quickly developed into a diverse, affluent, and influential center for agriculture, trade, military, academics, and culture.[2] As the preeminent center of Hellenistic culture and learning, Alexandria's museums, gardens, zoo, and libraries attracted scholars from throughout the Roman world.[3]

This vibrant port city, second in size only to Rome, hosted a cosmopolitan mixture of Egyptian, Greek, Jewish, Roman, and other cultural influences, creating a unique environment for intellectual exchange.[4] This plurality created what Weinandy and Keating describe as "a cosmopolitan mix of peoples, philosophies, and religions," where different traditions "passionately competed for their rightful place within the polis."[5] Competition between traditions occasionally turned violent, but it also produced fruitful intellectual exchanges.

When Christianity established itself in Alexandria during the first and second centuries

CE, it entered a complex milieu characterized by cultural, ethnic, and economic diversity and robust intellectual exchange among various philosophical and religious traditions.[6] Alexandrian Christians lived, worked, and learned among their non-Christian neighbors. The coexistence was largely peaceful, but violence occasionally erupted between groups, and certain Roman leaders ordered the persecution of Christians.[7]

Christians reflected Alexandria's diversity, reflecting numerous cultural and ethnic backgrounds and socioeconomic positions, including former pagans and affluent and well-educated families.[8] There was also diversity of belief among Christians, including a sharp division between those holding closely to apostolic teachings and the Gnostics, many of whom were deemed apostate.[9]

In this context, a city known for its diversity and intellectual vitality, Alexandrian Christian scholars developed their innovative, rigorous, and theologically rooted approach to education and philosophical exchange. The vibrant intellectual environment, with its diverse traditions in active dialogue about metaphysics, language, and meaning, provided fertile ground for Christian thinkers seeking to understand and articulate their faith in relation to the premier philosophical currents of their time, both as outreach to non-Christian intellectuals and a path for increasing their knowledge of God and God's world.[10]

The Alexandrian School

While many specifics remain the subject of scholarly debate, there is broad agreement that the Alexandrian School was an important site of Christian intellectual activity in which biblical faith and Hellenist philosophy were brought into productive dialogue.[11] From the second to the fifth century, figures such as Pantaenus, Clement, Origen, Athanasius, and Cyril led the Alexandrian School, developing distinctive intellectual practices and theological positions that led to the conversion of pagans and would influence the future of Christianity. Scholars such as Gregory of Nazianzus, Basil of Caesarea, Gregory of Nyssa, Jerome, Ambrose, Augustine, and Aquinas built their theology from the Alexandrian School's intellectual legacy.[12]

Like today's Christian scholars, these ancient Christian intellectuals were regularly challenged and criticized. The Alexandrian School faced opposition on three fronts: non-Christian philosophies and religions that dominated intellectual centers; influential Christian Gnostics promoting deviations from generally accepted Christian traditions; and anti-intellectual Christians who accused the School of forsaking Christianity through engagement with pagan philosophy and education.[13] The Alexandrian School is a model, not for avoiding challenge and criticism, but for faithful Christian scholarship amid those challenges.

The Alexandrian School strove to deepen participants' knowledge of God for union with God. While Alexandrian Christians had clear distinctions between believers and non-believers, they engaged with both groups through what Christians today might consider discipleship, evangelism, and scholarship.[14] The school trained believers, especially new converts, in the life of faith. Learning was integral to their Christian discipleship as Hellenistic education, philosophy, Scripture, and spiritual practices produced knowledge of

God, people, and creation.[15] The school also functioned to explain the faith to non-Christian intellectuals, allowing non-Christians to attend lectures and engage in philosophical debates. The school's use of Hellenistic philosophy in teaching the faith served as an accessible and respectable entry point to Christianity for pagans and Jewish scholars.[16] Finally, in addition to discipleship and evangelism, the school sought deeper understandings of the mysteries of religion, philosophy, and life through study, dialogue, debate, and rhetorical invention.[17]

While many ancient Christians rejected Hellenist philosophy and education as incompatible with Christian revelation, Alexandrian Christians took a different path. They developed an approach that theologian and church historian John McGuckin characterizes as neither "unthinking rejection nor unthinking acceptance" of philosophical traditions.[18] Instead, they engaged deeply with these traditions, maintaining the authority of Scripture and the primacy of Christ while using philosophical concepts and methods to develop and articulate Christian doctrine.[19]

The Alexandrian approach to Christian intellectualism was characterized by detailed and genuine engagement with pagan philosophical traditions.[20] Clement argued that philosophy served as a preparation for the Gospel, suggesting that truth in Greek philosophy came from God and could serve Christian understanding, though finding its fulfillment in Christ.[21] He also said that wisdom was not to be discounted simply because of where it came from.[22] Origen told his students that no field of study was off limits for the Christian because all disciplines pointed toward Divine revelation.[23] The intellectual depth and scope of the Alexandrian School earned the respect of non-Christian scholars and increased knowledge in the Christian community.

In addition to studying and even adopting pagan philosophy and education models, the Alexandrian School engaged scholars and students of other religious and philosophical traditions in intellectual exchange. Non-Christian students could attend at least some classes and lectures in the Alexandrian School.[24] Additionally, Christian scholars in Alexandria collaborated with and even studied under scholars from other traditions.[25] These practices facilitated genuine intellectual exchange and learning between Christians and non-Christians, allowing Christian scholars to share their faith and to have their faith strengthened.[26]

Intellectual exchanges with Jewish, Egyptian, and Hellenist scholars influenced the Christian scholarship in ancient Alexandria. The Alexandria School prioritized the divinity of Jesus and the Scriptures, and they systematically explored the Scriptures in categories and with methods influenced by Hellenistic philosophy and hermeneutics. The biblical stories, poems, and letters were synthesized through and to some extent with Hellenistic intellectual traditions, providing new insights into the truths of Christian faith. These practices laid the groundwork for systematic theology and afforded spiritual and intellectual resources for ongoing engagement with scholars of other philosophical and religious traditions.[27]

Distinctive Theology and Philosophy

The Alexandrian School's distinctive practices were grounded in and helped facilitate distinctive theological commitments. These theological foundations provided rhetorical and philosophical resources for Christian scholars to maintain their faith commitments while genuinely learning from and contributing to broader intellectual conversations.

Classical Theism and Metaphysics

Extensive study of the Scriptures, apostolic teaching, and serious engagement with Hellenistic philosophy and education enabled the Alexandrian School to articulate an understanding of God as not merely the greatest being, but as Being itself—the source and sustainer of all that exists. They taught that nothing has being without God, and no mere being is God. This Classical theistic and metaphysical framework positioned God as deeply present within creation and utterly beyond it.[28] Likewise, for Alexandrian Christians, the material world was not separate from or antithetical to the spiritual world, yet it was only a shadow or faint reflection of the spiritual world.

This theological and metaphysical understanding allowed Alexandrian Christian thinkers to engage diverse philosophical traditions and a full spectrum of disciplines without fearing they were wandering from God's creation. While the Alexandrian School argued against many pagan ideologies, they also recognized those ideologies as incomplete of the fullness of God's revelation about reality rather than some alternative reality. Because they understood God as the source of all being, they could research different traditions and disciplines with what might be called confident curiosity, recognizing that all that is real in the cosmos is ultimately from and points toward God.

Logos Theology

Another significant theological foundation for Alexandrian scholarship was its robust Logos theology. Drawing on the Gospel of John's identification of Christ as the eternal Word (Logos) and philosophical concepts of Logos from Greek thought, Alexandrian thinkers developed a Christology that positioned Christ as the divine reason or logic permeating all creation.[29] As McGuckin explains,

> when Christians confess the Son of God as the eternal Logos of God (the reason, rationale, and wisdom of the deity, which is seeded as the substrate and goal of all created life), they are thereby committed to the fundamental 'faith' that all life is rational, all theology is rational, and therefore in accord with all (true) philosophical or scientific insight.[30]

This position allowed Alexandrian Christians to affirm the value of rational inquiry in all areas of life and from various perspectives while maintaining that Christ, as the divine Logos, was the ultimate source and fulfillment of all truth.[31]

This theological framework had several important implications for intellectual engagement. First, it established that all truth derives from Christ as the Logos. Consequently, truth, including non-Christian philosophical, rhetorical, and educational traditions, could be recognized and valued wherever it appeared. Second, the Logos theology provided a rationale for studying the natural world and engaging with various intellectual disciplines. If Christ as Logos was the rational principle ordering all creation, studying any aspect of creation could reveal something of divine wisdom. Third, this theological framework positioned Christ not merely as one religious truth among many but as the ultimate fulfillment of all humans searching for truth.

Redeeming Creation

Closely related to Classical and Logos theology, the Alexandrian School's theology of creation affirmed the goodness of the material world while maintaining divine transcendence. Unlike many Hellenistic philosophical and pagan religious traditions that viewed matter as inherently evil or meaningless, Alexandrian Christian theology maintained that creation, as the work of God, was fundamentally good and meaningful. They recognized that creation had fallen, lacking the fullness of its intended goodness, but they also believed God was always acting toward union with creation.[32]

This theological commitment had significant implications for intellectual engagement. It affirmed the value of studying the natural world and human culture, since both were understood as created realities bearing divine imprints. It also provided conceptual resources for engaging with philosophical traditions like Platonism without simply adopting dualistic tendencies that devalued material existence. For the Alexandrian theologians, union with God was always the central purpose of creation. God did not reject the flawed creation, but continually engaged creation by calling back to, training, and redeeming it for union with God.[33] This redemptive perspective shaped their understanding of knowledge and motivation for scholarship and intellectual formation.

Knowledge and Knowing

Alexandrian Christian thinkers developed sophisticated epistemological frameworks that recognized multiple ways of knowing while maintaining the primacy of divine revelation. Unlike some Christian and pagan approaches that placed faith against knowledge, Alexandrian theology recognized these as complementary modes of knowledge, distinguishing between different knowledge types without creating stark opposition. The school valued rational inquiry and empirical investigation while acknowledging the limitations of human reason and the need for divine revelation into greater fullness of truth.[34]

This epistemological framework allowed him to engage seriously with pagan philosophical traditions without subordinating Scripture and apostolic tradition. It opened all fields for Christian scholarship and affirmed that everything was created through Logos while accounting for seemingly contradictory insights as different kinds or levels of knowledge. This epistemology was reflected in the Alexandrian School's interpretive approach to Scripture, recognizing multiple levels of meaning—literal, moral, and spiritual. This hermeneutical sophistication enabled productive dialogue with Jewish exegetical traditions and Hellenist philosophy and hermeneutics, while maintaining a distinctively Christian interpretive principle, placing each text in the context of the larger story of God bringing creation back into union with himself.[35]

Intellectual Formation as Christian Formation

Their epistemology that knowledge and faith are complementary coincided with the Alexandrian School's conviction that intellectual formation is vital to Christian formation. The theology that all being and truth are from God led to the belief that, while spiritual union with God ultimately required divine revelation, gaining knowledge of any truth of being was a step toward that union.[36] Influenced by Hellenist education, the Alexandrian School believed that the discipline of gaining knowledge of the lesser truths was preparation for gaining knowledge of greater truths. Hellenistic education also emphasized moral and civic formation, so the school included ethics and practical teachings about life in the church and the polis.[37] The Alexandrian School also taught mystical practices such as prayer and meditation to further a spiritual knowledge of God.[38]

Theological and philosophical positions, including Classical theism, Logos theology, creation theology, and sophisticated epistemology and pedagogy, provided Alexandrian Christians with intellectual resources for engaging diverse traditions without compromising their core commitments. They established what might be called a "confident curiosity" that allowed Christian thinkers to learn from others while maintaining their distinctive theological identity.

Alexandrian School Wisdom for Contemporary Scholars

Having examined both the contemporary challenges facing Christian scholars and the Alexandrian response to similar challenges, we can now consider what contemporary Christian scholars might learn from these ancient predecessors. Below are three Alexandrian insights for navigating today's pluralistic intellectual environments.

Theological Confidence and Intellectual Curiosity

Alexandrian Christian scholars demonstrated that theological confidence and intellectual curiosity can be complementary rather than competing values. This balanced approach stemmed from theological convictions about God, creation, and knowledge that contemporary Christian scholars would do well to recover. Alexandrian theology emphasized divine transcendence and immanence, God as utterly beyond all created beings and intimately present with all creation. This theological framework restrains otherworldly spiritualities and abstractions that ignore the material world and materialist reductions that limit meaning to empirical measurement.

Alexandrian Christian scholars demonstrated intellectual humility and curiosity alongside high Christology and confidence in divine revelation. Their understanding of God as being and truth itself fostered a recognition of the limitations of human knowledge, including their own. As Wolterstorff, Steiner, and Marsden have noted in their contributions to this volume, Christian scholars should recognize that our understanding is always partial and subject to correction. As Mouw and Lindvall have noted in their contributions, this includes a willingness to learn from non-Christians. Our theological claims about God should not be taken as claims about ourselves, our traditions, or even our claims.

The Alexandrian concept of Christ as the Logos provided a theological foundation for integrating diverse fields of knowledge. Rather than working to try to connect faith and learning, this approach saw all knowledge as ultimately connected through its relation to Christ, the Logos, ordering all creation. This theological framework offers a more robust foundation for Christian scholarship and education than many contemporary approaches to faith and learning integration. Rather than treating Christianity as something separate from truth studied in academic disciplines and trying to connect them awkwardly, the Logos-centered approach recognizes the inherent connections that already exist through Christ's relationship to all created reality. Belief in this theology could be similar to what Wolterstorff describes in this volume as looking "through the lens of Christian faith" at one's discipline and describing "what they see."[39] Faith that all creation comes to being through Christ will give us eyes to see and trust that we see the truth.

Redemption Motivation

The Alexandrian understanding that God's essence is love and, therefore, constantly desires union with all creation, provides a powerful motivating framework for scholarship. The act and interpretive framework of intellectual work is God's larger redemptive purpose, not as a rejection of flawed creation but as participation in its ultimate redemption and union with God. Rejecting the Hellenistic idea that the Divine rejects the imperfect and embracing the biblical theme of redemption and God's compassion, Alexandrians saw everything in creation to be studied as potentially redeemable and capable of being transformed toward its divine purpose.

This perspective offers contemporary Christian scholars a compelling theological framework and motivation for their work. Rather than seeing scholarship as a paycheck, a platform, or a culture war weapon, Christians can see their scholarship as understanding and participating in God's redemptive work in the world. This perspective can reveal the cosmic meaning of our work, especially in areas that might seem distant from explicitly religious concerns. It can also release our attitudes from bondage to the cultural outrage of the moment to the outrageous and eternal Divine mercy.

Scholarship as Spiritual Formation

As discussed above, Alexandrian Christian intellectuals viewed knowledge as complementary to, and even an aspect of, faith. This contrasts with the compartmentalization that often characterizes modern academics and religion. Scholarship was understood as part of the larger spiritual journey. Intellectual work was understood not as the entirety but as an essential form of discipleship.

Contemporary Christian scholars should recover this understanding of scholarship as spiritual formation, recognizing that academics is a way to gain knowledge of God and to love God with one's mind. Christian scholars must also lead the way in helping our religious communities recover the discipline of learning truth as an essential part of Christian discipleship. This also means recognizing that learning is never for learning's sake alone but is always embedded in a larger context of moral and spiritual formation. As Spencer argues in this volume, Christian scholarship and education should include wisdom and character formation. Christian scholarship, at its best, aims not merely at acquiring information but also at forming wise and charitable humans who are oriented toward the good of the world and ultimately toward union with God.

Conclusion

Contemporary Christian scholars face challenges that parallel those encountered by their ancient Christian scholars in Alexandria. In both contexts, Christians seek to maintain theological integrity while engaging productively with diverse intellectual traditions in pluralistic environments. I have argued that the Alexandrian School offers valuable insights for navigating these challenges.

The theological framework developed by Alexandrian Christians, with its understanding of God as Being, Christ as Logos, and creation as created and loved by God, as well as its nuanced epistemology and holistic pedagogy, provided intellectual and rhetorical resources for robust scholarly engagement without religious compromise. This approach fostered what I have called a confident curiosity, a stance that allowed Christian thinkers to genuinely learn from diverse traditions with faithfulness to their Christian theological commitments.

Recent discussions of Christian scholarship, from Noll's critique of evangelical anti-intellectualism to Marsden's call for faith-informed perspectives in the Academy, have addressed similar themes from contemporary angles. The challenges they identify within evangelical contexts and in the broader Academy remain relevant for Christian scholars today. The Alexandrian approach addresses these challenges by demonstrating that theological confidence and intellectual curiosity can be complementary rather than competing values. For contemporary Christian scholars navigating pluralistic intellectual environments, this model offers a third way beyond intellectual isolationism and theological accommodation—one that values both theological integrity and intellectual engagement, seeing them not as competing commitments but as complementary dimensions of a faithful Christian mind. Alexandria shows a path to the Christian scholarship Jay Kesler called for, a scholarship that is both "joyful and courageous."

Chapter 13

The Cross-pollination between Athens and Jerusalem

THOMAS J. CARMODY

Response Summary: We must come to see the development of the Christian mind and its expression in our pedagogy as an extension of our faith. Echoing the call of Marsden, we should see our work in the Academy as a calling, an opportunity to model and reflect our faith in all that we do. This is a call to become more than conveyers of information, organizers, writers, speakers and graders to our students and become individuals who reflect the image of Christ whether we are writing a book, teaching a class, grading a paper, or listening to a student's concerns. This is the essence of Christian scholarship according to Noll, whether we serve at a faith-based or pluralistic institution. This essay adapts Archbishop Thomas Cranmer's sixteenth-century prayer for knowing Scripture as a template to hear, read, mark, learn, and inwardly digest our Christian faith and our discipline, so that we can integrate both into a transformative and genuine pedagogy.

As SOMEONE WHO is coming to the end of his active participation in the Academy, I was surprised when I was invited to provide feedback to some of the thoughts and ideas wonderfully articulated at the 2024 Christianity and Communication Studies Network (CCSN) unconference. Yet, my surprise soon changed to gratitude for those people of faith who have gone before me, guided, taught and mentored me in my calling in higher education. So it is with profound gratitude that I offer my small contribution to this essential discussion.

I have spent my career in the academic trenches, primarily teaching undergraduate students how to communicate with clarity, integrity, humility, honesty, and professionalism. And as I was teaching them, they were shaping me, my focus, my attitude, my compassion, my transparency and my faith. We developed a symbiotic relationship. I sought to make them better students, life-time learners, and proficient Christian communicators. They in turn made me a better teacher, researcher, mentor, and minister of the Gospel. Yes, I came into the discipline with academic training, but what I have learned from my students is more than I could have ever fathomed when I accepted the call to serve in the Academy. So it is with this perspective that I humbly offer my thoughts.

In my reflection on how the development and nurturing of the Christian mind pertains to pedagogy, I will begin with Terry Lindvall's accurate portrayal of communication scholars, especially rhetoricians, as those who "call to the past."[1] We often look to the past because in doing so we realize that humanity, at its core, has not changed that much despite our technological advancements. When we read the ancient writers or the Scriptures we can identify with the same types of people: with their emotions, situations, challenges, faults, pride, egos, together with their love, humility, nobleness, self-sacrifice, compassion and faith that we encounter in our courses. We should never assume that those who lived in a different time and culture were somehow less intelligent than those alive today, simply because they did not have all the technological bells and whistles that we take for granted. In the same way, we should not assume that what it takes to be a good teacher or student is somehow different because the modality of the transmission of information has changed. This is especially true for the Christian teacher who views the educational interactions with their students as a calling, a sacred responsibility and true ministry.[2] We may not all wear a collar, but we are all involved in ministry.

It is with this perspective that I look to the past to provide a blueprint for developing and nurturing the Christian mind as it relates to pedagogy. In my view, the formation of the Christian mind and pedagogy must be a natural outgrowth of a genuine Christian faith. This view was also expressed by the Christian writer Madeleine L'Engle, who was asked by a college student and an aspiring Christian fiction writer, who wanted to write Christian fiction, how to accomplish this goal. L'Engle responded to the question this way,

> I told her that if she is truly and deeply a Christian, what she writes is going to be Christian, whether she mentions Jesus or not. And if she is not, in the most profound sense, Christian, then what she writes is not going to be Christian, no matter how many times she invokes the name of the Lord.[3]

I think that this advice gets to the crux of the matter. We must come to see the development of the Christian mind and its expression in our pedagogy as an extension of our genuine Christian faith. What we do in the Academy and in our courses must be an extension of who we are in Christ. Society may encourage us to live a bifurcated existence by advocating that what we believe personally must not infringe on our jobs or professions. But for Christians this is not an option. Our faith should animate our scholarship, perspectives, and teaching. It should transform us from being just conveyers of information, organizers, writers, speakers and graders, to individuals who reflect the image of Christ whether we are writing a book, teaching a class, grading a paper or listening to a student's concerns.

We may shout an "amen" at this suggestion, but how do we do this especially when it seems antithetical to the current culture? I would like to suggest that we can do this by taking as a guide a collect written by Archbishop Thomas Cranmer in the sixteenth century that was most likely influenced by the work of famed Roman educator and rhetorician Marcus Fabius Quintilianus.[4] This collect is usually prayed on the Second Sunday of Advent, what many denominations refer to as "Bible Sunday." Cranmer writes in this prayer:

> Blessed Lord, who caused all Holy Scriptures to be written for our learning; Grant us to hear them, read, mark, learn, and inwardly digest them; that by patience

and comfort of your holy Word we may embrace and even hold fast the blessed hope of everlasting life, which thou has given us in our Savior Jesus Christ; who lives and reigns with you and the Holy Spirit, one God, for ever and ever.[5]

Although Cranmer's prayer is focused on the importance of learning Holy Scripture, it contains elements that every scholar and teacher regardless of discipline, will recognize as essential components of the educational process. Cranmer wrote this collect as a Cambridge-educated Christian academic whose calling led him into the church. However, he never lost his academic perspective, even as he composed the Book of Common Prayer, and it is for this reason that I believe that his prayer provides a template for how the Christian mind can form and transform our pedagogy. Therefore, this essay will follow Cranmer's call to hear, read, mark, learn, and inwardly digest both our Christian faith and our disciplines to integrate both into a transformative and genuine pedagogy, closing the loop between Athens and Jerusalem.

Hear

We must always remember that our students are not a distraction from our scholarship but the reason for it. We should teach, research, and write, always with the focus of reaching our students. This is not just because audience analysis is important as Aristotle taught us, but as Lindvall reminds us, pedagogy is always personal.[6] Our students are our congregation, and we have the privilege to pour into their lives, to teach, mentor and be available to them to discuss our area of study or personal issues they are experiencing in their lives. Let us never forget that many of us are in the Academy because a teacher or teachers came alongside us, as mentors who took the time to do more than convey information. They listened to us, came to know us and inspired us to follow them on our own pathway into the discipline. We stand on the shoulders of those who came before us, and we are blessed to do so.

The same is true of Christianity. We stand on the shoulders of those believers who came before us, for we are participants in the communion of saints. Christianity is not exclusively an individual faith but rather a faith that grows and matures in community, one where we are encouraged to "bear one another's burdens, and so fulfill the law of Christ" (Gal. 6:2, English Standard Version). If we claim to be followers of Jesus, then we must care for the other. This is not an optional add-on to our confession of faith but an essential focus of our maturity as Christians. We were designed for relationship and fellowship, and it is through this process that we are encouraged and strengthened in our faith. So it is not surprising that one of the most important and supporting tools we have is the gift of listening. We listen for inspiration from the Holy Spirit, from the Word, in liturgy, and all these prepare us to be better listeners, more empathic, compassionate and personal. These are the virtues that allow us to graciously interact with the members of our congregation, our students.

Read

Reading is the second element in Cranmer's prayer for learning Holy Scripture, and it is one communication skill that all of us in the Academy needed to master early in our journey. We had to read vast amounts of information to initially learn our area of study, and we continue to do so if we desire to keep abreast of the latest developments. Additionally, we learn early on in our teaching that one of the requirements of our profession is that we must assign and read student papers. I have for most of my career taught the senior thesis course for our department. This requires me to read 45–50-page rhetorical criticism papers. Sometimes this is a blessing, when I realize that a particular student comprehends all I have taught, while at other times it is a cause of extreme frustration and doubt, as I wonder why I even bother with such assignments.

Colleagues ask me if I am a glutton for punishment, subjecting myself to read and grade poor student writing. I remind them that becoming a better writer begins with reading and if I require my students to write papers, they can expect me to read them and respond. I tell the students that I do not have to agree with their conclusions, but I do need to be able to clearly understand what they are arguing. I see this as modeling for my students what I want them to learn and do. As Cranmer's prayer claims, we learn Scripture by reading, and this is the same way we learned our discipline. Reading is a necessary communication skill that we continually use to learn about our area of study, the thought process of our students and most importantly, as a tool to build up our faith.

Mark

I must admit that I mark up things I read, whether it is Scripture, textbooks, journal articles, sermons, student work or anything I want to remember. I did not always engage in this practice because I came from a faith tradition that viewed the Bible as too sacred to be read or comprehended by anyone that was not clergy. So when I came to personal faith during the Jesus Movement, I resisted the urge to write in my Bible, choosing instead to use pieces of paper to indicate important passages I desired to learn.

I kept to this practice until one day, I dropped my Bible, and all my bookmarks scattered on the ground. I was so disappointed when this happened until a friend reminded me that the Bible was a type of workbook that taught us about the God we love and serve. It was still sacred, but I came to realize that it was not designed to remain on a shelf but to be used. To this day, I still mark up my books and I often teach my students how to create their own program for marking up what they read, because it will provide them a way to better learn and remember what they have read. It is a way to personally interact with a text, and with advancements in digital books, students can mark up the texts without defacing the printed word. Students tell me that they learn and remember more from what they read when they mark and actively interact with the text.[7]

Learn

Pedagogy involves more than the regurgitation of memorized information. It requires those in the learning process to be able to demonstrate that they can do something meaningful with what they have received. Theory is good, but education cannot stop there and presume that their audiences are fully educated. In my field, it would be like teaching a basic speech class where the students were taught all the elements of an effective presentation but were never required to present a speech. This situation would lead to deficient learning outcomes and create a faulty pedagogy.

I was told when I began my teaching career that if I truly wanted to learn something I needed to teach it, for teaching is an outgrowth of learning. When I was first offered this observation, I must admit that I had my doubts about its validity, but as I look in the rearview mirror of my career, I have come to recognize the truthfulness of the statement. I think that Cranmer, being trained as an academic, also knew this to be true and therefore he prayed that as Christians, we would come to learn our faith so that we could share it with others. As Christian academics, we study, teach, and engage in scholarship not so that we can become puffed up (1 Cor. 8:1), but so we may communicate the important ideas, concepts, processes, and general information of our discipline to our students. And we do this because we know that those under our tutelage deserve our best efforts. We embrace learning so we can become better teachers and examples of what a Christian academic is and does. In this way our learning, regardless of our discipline, provides us an opportunity to live into our ministry, fulfill our calling and impact the various audiences we are privileged to serve.[8]

Inwardly Digest

When we inwardly digest an idea, concept, perspective, or Scripture, it becomes part of us. This process requires more than simple memorization. Like food when it is digested, it provides us with nutrition, strength, and often pleasure. We must take in food to live and thrive in the same way that Cranmer prays that we make Scripture a part of who we are. We digest it and it provides us with spiritual nutrition. It changes the way we look at others and ourselves. It also changes how we look at what we do, both in our professional and personal lives. By inwardly digesting God's word we will come to define ourselves not solely by our accomplishments but by who we are in Christ.

This is a liberating viewpoint because it frees us to be genuine (not perfect) with our colleagues, students, and all whom we encounter as we move through life. This will not guarantee a trouble-free life, but it will empower us to do what we are called to do, in our teaching and scholarship. If we want to have a fully developed Christian mind, one that will be evidenced in our pedagogy, we must become people who reflect the virtues of Christ in everything we do. It is only when we inwardly digest the Scripture that it becomes a part of us, and it will transform us from the inside out. It will make us better reflections of Christ's love to a world that so desperately needs it. This is the connection between a mature Christian mind and how it is operationalized in our teaching and scholarship.

How Do We Do This?

After we are transformed through digesting God's word, making it a part of who we are not just what we believe, Cranmer claims that we will come to know God better with patience and comfort. As with any long-term relationship, as we come to know God, we will learn to trust him more. We will develop a non-anxious perspective because we will begin to see things from a hopeful and eternal perspective. This is especially needed today when according to the research over 40 million adults in the U.S. have an anxiety disorder.[9]

We are surrounded by anxious colleagues consumed by the "publish or perish" mentality, administrators worried about enrollment and budget issues, students anxious about being able to pay for their tuition, rent, food, whether they will get a job when they graduate or get into the desired graduate program on top of all their interpersonal stressors. And it is into this chaotic whirlwind that we as Christian academics have been called. We can be blown around by all this chaos or we can become a non-anxious presence in the lives of our colleagues, administrators, and students. We can become a safe harbor, a place where they can find a respite from the storms of life at least for a little while, but we can only do this if we are "truly and deeply a Christian."[10] We do not have to be perfect or have all the answers to all of life's questions. But we should be genuine, honest, empathetic, compassionate, knowledgeable about our discipline, engaged in intellectual pursuits, always remembering who we are and representing those we interact with every day. In this way, our pedagogy will become a reflection of our Christian faith and witness.

Chapter 14

Bad Timing: Cultural Redefinitions of "Intellect" at the Beginning of American Evangelicalism

Mark A. E. Williams

Response Summary: The scandalous character of evangelicalism's intellectual thinness is well established in the work of Mark Noll. But the question of how such a scandal came to define evangelicalism is more complex. The failings of the evangelical intellect are rooted, this essay argues, in the historic context which imprinted a set of assumptions upon the movement at its most defining moment. American evangelicalism came into its own in the Second Great Awakening, but that specific historic moment was haunted by a strange redefinition of what it meant to be intellectually mature. The questions of faith had been relegated, by the Enlightenment and Modernist thinkers, to a different domain: individual preference. Because of this, evangelicalism was caught in a scandalous trap—the only way to reason about one's faith was to talk about private experience and personal perspectives. Evangelicalism was, then, incapable of engaging the scientific and material advances of the age without responding to scientific data by assertion. The movement never had a genuine opportunity to develop intellectual depth and was shackled to the corpse of subjective personal experience.

THE CATHOLIC INTELLECTUAL tradition has a fundamentally different history from the Protestant tradition, especially in North America. This distinction inspired very different reactions to both the errors and the accuracies of the Enlightenment and Modernism. Broadly speaking, the intellectual history of Catholicism provided it with methods to reply to Enlightenment and Modern claims that were not available to the evangelical tradition.

Evangelical and Roman Catholic outlooks shared many of the same initial reactions toward Modernism.[1] Both had stringent anti-modern elements and both had camps that attempted to engage Modernism more directly. Despite these similarities, the evangelical's engagement proved more brittle and less sustainable. Fr. Paul A. Soukup's, SJ, superb discussion of Jesuit educational pedagogy hints at some of the reasons for this difference in outcomes, though he focuses on one shared concern between evangelicals and Catholics: how people of faith "maintain a religious identity in education when the educational system strives for independence from . . . religious influence."[2]

In this essay, I wish to contrast Catholic and evangelical tensions within higher education, trying to contextualize the differences between the two in light of their engagements with Modernism. To accomplish this, we must glance briefly at the *premodern* view of the soul in order to understand what Modernism altered, and how that alteration contributed to the now famous scandal of the evangelical mind.

The Premodern Era

The premodern era viewed the human soul as composed of three interactive facets: the intellect, will, and memory.[3] The intellect itself had two separate expressions: what could be known with justified certainty and what could only be embraced with reasonable confidence but not with certainty. The outcome of the intellectual activity that resulted in certainty was called *knowledge*—though *knowing* was an adaptable term, just as it is today. One could know how to ski, or know the population of Albuquerque, or Adam could know Eve. From skill set, to data, to sex, the word *know* has always been versatile. But the Greek and Latin terms have a long history of the more technical definition presented here: *to hold in the intellect, with justified certainty*. The Latin word for such certainty is *scientia* which gives us the word *science*.

Set against this justified certainty was that second expression of intellect: a realm of understanding that could end in reasoned confidence—but not justified certainty. The confidence that was the outcome of this intellectual process was always acquainted with some measure of doubt, always seeking deeper understanding, never a finished project. The word for such conviction in Latin is *fides*, translated as *faith*.[4]

To finish out this premodern picture of the soul in the briefest possible terms, the will was divided into desire and decision; decision was, in the wise, always guided by intellect, that is, by what was known with certainty, and believed with confidence. Desire generally led one astray, unless it was also carefully disciplined and formed (*educare*, in Latin) by knowledge *and* faith. In concert with the intellect and will lay the mystery of memory, in which the powers of the past could assist the intellect in understanding while encouraging the will both to desire well and to choose wisely.

What concerns us most in this moment is the intellect. Prior to the rise of the scientific method, both *knowledge* (in the technical sense) and *faith* were viewed as co-equal aspects of the human intellect. *This must be emphasized.* In the premodern world, faith was an *intellectual* activity; it trained the will and shaped the memory (through Tradition and traditions), but its native land was the soul's intellect. Faith was intellectual because it could give reasons for its conclusions—reasons based in a thoroughly established system of careful reflection, mature emotion, and proven authority.[5]

But the Enlightenment and Modernism rearranged this taxonomy of the human soul. In a nutshell, the movements left *knowledge/certainty* inside the definition of intellectual activity. But *faith/conviction* was relocated to that facet of the soul known as *will*. Increasingly, a person could *believe* whatever they *wanted* to believe. Belief (especially religious belief) became a matter of private preference and individual choice, and in this there was a reflection of broader cultural changes.

The value of an individual *perspective*, trumpeted in the Renaissance arts, slowly morphed in the Enlightenment into the idea of *individual rights*: an emphasis on the limits of the state's power relative to each particular person. In Modernism, this became a kind of *individualism*: an ideology of the autonomous self, choosing its own identity and destiny—especially in the United States, where broad frontiers encouraged an (historically) unusual sense of independent self-reliance.

And with this ludicrously compact narrative of Euro-American developments in one of the most complex transitions in human history, we are ready to explore some of the differences between the Catholic and the evangelical education in the contemporary world.

Differences Between Catholic and Evangelical Education

If we date, as I would, the opening of American evangelicalism to the Cane Ridge camp revival of 1801, then evangelicalism emerged into a culture and at a time when the idea of the intellect had already excluded *faith* from its popular definition.[6] The world in which American evangelicalism was born—or at least came of age—was a world that limited the *intellectual* to the presentation of the scientific, material understanding of natural forces and objects. *Faith*, remember, had already been reclassified as an act of *will*: a desire or a decision made under the authority of a newly minted individualism. Faith was justified by private feeling and personal preference. Evangelicalism, then, began its American pilgrimage with its intellectual hands tied behind its brain. Its arguments for biblical truth, its response to the rising tide of textual criticism (which raised serious questions about the coherence and reliability of the sacred texts), the scope of its possible responses to Darwin's natural selection were all handicapped. There were no intellectual grounds—as evangelicals had inherited the definition of *intellect*—on which to engage these topics as questions of reason *and faith*. The game was rigged: the culture had written *faith* out of the very act of reasoning at the very moment evangelicalism was attempting to begin its journey and give reasons for its faith. And so the response was, too often, a simple, intuitive, enthusiastic assertion of individual will and private preference, backed up by the invocation of *sola scriptura*: the Bible says so (at least to me). Mark Noll's scandal of the evangelical mind was predestined by the very American culture into which evangelicalism was born, historically.

Catholicism, in contrast, began with a more historical understanding of intellect—one that was far broader and more humane, embracing the premodern view of the soul's intellect. Catholicism's educational activities were not, therefore, hog-tied by the culture's current definitions, but contained a vibrant history capable of interrogating (not just reacting to) both Modernism's conclusions and its assumptions. These challenges came from a view of the intellect that was more than capable of going toe-to-toe with Modernism, essentially putting Modernism itself on the defensive: "What scientific evidence can be produced that science is the only intellectual activity?" Beyond this, many of the key players in Modernism's vibrant explorations of nature were Catholic; Catholicism had, for more than 800 years, championed an understanding of nature as one way of intellectually bolstering faith in the Creator of nature.[7] In short, the Catholic educational traditions were already quite comfortable with the idea of exploring nature; these educational traditions were, in fact, on the cutting edge of the emerging sciences and at the same time, they were historically positioned to challenge Modernism's atrophied view of *intellect*. This is not to say the challenges of Modernism were minor issues in the Catholic faith, only that Catholicism's history and assumptions allowed for a more adaptable and deeper response to those challenges.

Noll suggests the evangelical history offers some—but not much—hope, taken from its focus on redemption—a redemption that might reach farther than evangelicals expect.[8] From a Catholic view, Noll's most promising suggestion in that closing chapter is the call to push evangelicals beyond intuitionism, "the rapid move from first impressions to final conclusions."[9] This implies a hopeful beginning in which the justified *enthusiasms* of the evangelical faith might lead not just to proclamations of individual belief, but deep and honest *explication* of their faith. If there is a redemption of the evangelical intellect, it will come not by subverting the mind to personal faith, but by transposing one's personal faith into the broader context of a brutally honest, powerfully humane, carefully systematized intellectual conviction that neither fears nor undermines nor wholly surrenders to scientific knowledge.

It must be noted, in this particular moment, however, that evangelicalism may have already fallen to its own anti-intellectual trajectory. What tomorrow holds is anyone's guess; whether any coherent future evangelical movement can include the past virtues of evangelicalism *and* a rediscovery of the intellect's role in faith is far from certain.

Chapter 15

Lessons from Chautauqua for the Future of Christian Higher Education

JOHN R. TERRILL

Response Summary: The Chautauqua Institution has a rich educational, religious, and cultural history in the United States, dating to 1874. This essay chronicles Chautauqua's meteoric rise, slow decline, and eventual rebirth, with attention directed to lessons it may offer the Academy and church as they seek to recover relevance and public trust. In interaction with Marsden and Noll's seminal thinking on the life of the Christian mind, this review presents Chautauqua as an institutional model for higher education reform and as an exemplar for debunking the compartmentalized, storyless, and ununified academic life. Additionally, Chautauqua serves as a blueprint of intellectual humility, academic neighborliness, and a thick public witness that can penetrate complex and overlapping publics.

"Education, once the peculiar privilege of the few, must in best earthly estate become the valued possession of the many."[1]
— John Heyl Vincent, co-founder, Chautauqua Institution

ONE OF THE MOST influential innovations in Christian higher education dates to the nineteenth century and the founding of Chautauqua. The Chautauqua Institution is unreservedly ecumenical in spirit and believes religion touches all dimensions of life. It revolutionized Christian education, brought literacy and cultural engagement to those not traditionally afforded such opportunities, transformed in-person and distance learning, and established healthy patterns of recreation and leisure to aid intellectual, spiritual, and emotional growth.

During their 2024 unconference, the Christianity and Communication Studies Network explored two landmark books to help chart its future: Mark Noll's *The Scandal of the Evangelical Mind* and George Marsden's *The Outrageous Idea of Christian Scholarship*. Both were published in the mid-1990s, and, for the past 30 years, the perspectives they advanced have influenced Christian higher education and new models of witness and engagement in today's pluralistic university. Marsden has recently identified the Christian study center movement as one of several promising trends. The SL Brown Foundation, for which I serve as Executive Director, maintains membership in the Consortium of Christian Study Centers to which Marsden refers. According to Marsden, Christian study centers "have proven themselves as wonderful communities within the secular Academy where students and faculty can be exposed to the best of Christian thought and sustain high-level inquiry into Christian scholarship and reflections on Christian callings."[2]

Using lessons from the Chautauqua movement over the past 150 years and reflecting on my experiences leading a Christian study center serving the University of Wisconsin–Madison community, this essay explores three ways to strengthen Christian teaching and scholarship in our current academic environment. First, I recount the history of the Chautauqua Institution as a viable model for holistic and scholarly Christian engagement. Second, I present Chautauqua as an institutional model for higher education reform by supporting the organic development of the Christian mind, which can serve as a renaissance for new models of scholarly work and meet the educational aspirations of an increasingly diverse populace. Third, I offer Chautauqua as an exemplar for debunking the compartmentalized academic life. More practically, I offer insights on how academics might reinvigorate Christian scholarship and teaching within the Academy, university-adjacent institutions, and the church more broadly.

More specifically, this essay chronicles Chautauqua's meteoric rise, slow decline, and eventual rebirth, with attention directed to lessons this review may offer the Academy and the church as they seek to recover relevance and public trust. The Chautauqua Institution, its daughter institutions, and the independent and oft-commercialized cross-country Chautauqua circuits embraced fascinating characters from all walks of life. Its dynamic programs featured the talents of artists, musicians, and popular cultural and religious orators of the day. For instance, William Jennings Bryan, Robert La Follette, Jane Addams, and Mark Twain were regulars. Thomas Edison, who married Mina Miller, the daughter of Chautauqua's co-founder, spent regular time on the grounds. Suffragists and women's activists such as Susan B. Anthony, Carrie Chapman Catt, and Eleanor Roosevelt were invited to the platform, as were prominent anti-suffragists. George Gershwin, while visiting, wrote his *Concerto in F*, and Amelia Earhart, upon arrival, landed her plane on the Chautauqua golf course.

In all, nine American presidents have visited. Theodore Roosevelt described Chautauqua as "typically American in that it is typical of America at its best," rephrased by the press as "the most American thing in America." In recent years, Chautauqua has been in the headlines for a more nefarious reason: the location of the brutal stabbing of author Salman Rushdie, who, ironically, was visiting to speak on the United States as a haven for exiled authors and artists.

Historical Background on the Chautauqua Institution

Chautauqua, which celebrated its sesquicentennial in 2024, has four foundational pillars: the arts, education, religion, and recreation. From humble beginnings, the Chautauqua community now includes 750 acres, 1,200 Victorian cottages, condominiums, retail shops, meeting venues, performance halls, and two 18-hole golf courses. Approximately 7,500 individuals reside at Chautauqua on a typical day in season, and over 100,000 visit during its nine-week summer program.

Founded in 1874 on Chautauqua Lake in far southwestern New York, Chautauqua was created to promote religious education and cultural and moral advancement. The Normal Department—to train Sunday School teachers—was its first initiative. As Chautauqua historian and archivist Jon Schmitz observes, the Chautauqua Idea flowed from three historic institutions: the Camp Meeting's regular assembly; the Lyceum's love for lifelong learning; and the Sunday School movement's dedication to Christian education.[3]

Chautauqua was also born with an ecumenical spirit; the early faculties represented most leading denominations. Attendees from many Protestant traditions were "not expected to abandon their church relations."[4] Rather, they were invited "to join in a broad movement for the increase of power in every branch of the Church, and throughout our American society."[5] During the first two-week Chautauqua gathering in August 1874, between ten and fifteen thousand people converged on the site, coming from 25 states and four other countries.

Co-founders John Heyl Vincent and Lewis Miller envisioned education opportunities for Sunday School teachers, uniting liberal arts, pedagogical, and theological training. In the words of Vincent, "The theory of Chautauqua is that life is one, and that religion belongs everywhere . . . Every day should be sacred . . . The cable of divine motive should stretch through seven days, touching with its sanctifying power every hour of every day."[6] In the introduction to Vincent's history of Chautauqua, Miller writes, "Chautauqua was founded for an enlarged recognition of the Word."[7] He continues, "It was the purpose that the scientist and statesman, the artisan and tradesman, should bring their latest and best to this altar of consecration and praise . . . when thus strengthened, return to their respective fields, and there, through the year, weave into the fibre of the homework the newly gathered inspiration and strength."[8]

Those attending the first Chautauqua may have expected a camp meeting featuring preaching, evangelism, and ecstatic communal prayer, which had become popular during the Second Great Awakening in the nineteenth century. What greeted them instead was:

> an enthusiastic company of Sunday School teachers, Bible students, leading educators, a sprinkling of professors of Hebrew, Greek, Latin, and leaders of all religious denominations. Three weeks were given up to study and training in methods of teaching, courses in Bible study, lectures on the models of Palestine park, and the City of Jerusalem, interdenominational conferences, and everything that could make the work of the teacher more intelligent and his sense of responsibility more genuine.[9]

The success of Chautauqua in Western New York gave rise to two other early innovations: independent daughter Chautauqua Assemblies, which totaled nearly 300 by 1904, and Chautauqua Circuits, which, also independent of the mother organization, crisscrossed the country during the summer months as early as 1904.

In its first twelve years of existence (1874–1886), the Chautauqua in New York grew rapidly to a vast network of nearly two dozen projects. The focus was expansive, aimed at professional ministers, missionaries, lay leaders, and general community members of all ages. Among the many initiatives was a School of Theology to train clergy, a Young Folks' Reading Union, a Library School, a School of Physical Education, and the Chautauqua Press.

Chautauqua experienced rapid growth during its first fifty years, but this came at a cost. With a bounty of new buildings and a growing program, Chautauqua was burdened by debt and in 1933, at the height of the Great Depression, entered receivership. Through the help of a benevolent Reorganization Corporation and thousands of donors, including John D. Rockefeller Jr., Chautauqua was saved from dissolution by the end of the 1936 season. However, beginning in the 1950s, the advent of television and internal mismanagement led Chautauqua down another path of decline. With its centennial celebration looming, Chautauqua again pursued needed change, including physical repairs, administrative reform, and new revenue sources from onsite dancing and drinking, activities previously banned since its inception.

The Historical Role of Christian Scholarship in America

Christians in higher education know the institutional challenges colleges and universities face today: weakening demographics; financial and enrollment pressures; affordability; religious and academic freedom; attracting and retaining qualified students, staff, and faculty; political polarization; and governmental disinvestment. A recent bipartisan report on the condition of the United States on 37 different factors is pessimistic across many domains. In terms of diseases and deaths of despair, we rank near the bottom. On political polarization, compared to 92 countries, the U.S. is tied for last for the most polarized. With respect to trust in higher education, out of 28 countries included in the data, the U.S. only outperforms 11% of its competitor nations.[10]

Americans are anxious, depressed, distracted, and distrustful, and our higher education system seems to be contributing to these problems. Marsden opens his book with the attention-grabbing line: "Contemporary university culture is hollow at its core."[11] Historian C. John Sommerville agrees, noting "that the secular university is increasingly marginal to American society," in large part because it is ill-equipped to address religious questions that could, if allowed, be central to the Academy achieving its purposes.[12]

How did we get here? In trying to decipher this geography, Marsden poses the fundamental question, "Why in a culture in which many academics profess to believe in God, do so few reflect on the academic implications of that belief?"[13] He concludes that "our dominant academic culture trains scholars to keep quiet about their faith as the price of full acceptance in that community."[14]

Of course, the record is more complicated, and both Marsden and Noll offer a helpful historical perspective. Higher education in the United States has its roots primarily in the mainline Protestant tradition in the early nineteenth century. While most of these colleges were led at the time by evangelicals, the general outlook was non-sectarian or broadly ecumenical, and in many respects, anti-fundamentalist. To gain legitimacy in a time of significant scientific advancement, these institutions embraced the connection between natural revelation and special revelation. Historian Daniel Williams observes, "The colleges of the antebellum era instilled in students the harmony of empirically based reason, Christian faith, Lockian political thinking, and a common-sense realist form of reasoning."[15] Marsden outlines a similar trajectory; religiously founded nineteenth-century American colleges and universities became "havens for free scientific inquiry," untethered to "appeals to supernaturally based authority."[16] If academic disciplines hoped to advance ideas about Christian humanism and democratic ideals, this posture was essential. As Marsden reasons, "This sharp limit on the bounds of authoritative academic inquiry was not viewed by the university founders as in opposition to Christianity. Rather, they believed that scientific inquiry would advance civilization and hence promote the kingdom of God."[17]

However, as Noll submits, there was a turn in the late nineteenth century. Newer universities embraced a German rather than British model of education—"Not character but research, not the handing on of tradition but the search for intellectual innovation became the watchword."[18] This trend, coupled with a wider incorporation of the Social Gospel, shifted the emphasis from individual conversion to societal renewal, a move broad enough to lure public universities, "which could embrace an ethic of social service without any theological trappings."[19] Thus, as Sommerville suggests in support of Marsden and Noll, "it was largely Protestant liberal academics that brought about the secularization of university education. By relentless opposition to their fundamentalist and Catholic competitors, these Protestants encouraged the *definition* of religion as 'sectarianism.'"[20] These trends, working together, had the paradoxical impact of deterring the development of an explicitly Christian approach to learning and scholarship. In Marsden's view, "Because a broadly Christian outlook could be presumed, not much effort was made to relate Christianity specifically to what was being studied."[21]

Unsurprisingly, in the first half of the twentieth century, "Religion came to be regarded as essentially an extracurricular activity. Mainline Protestants built up ministries on the edges of campus and welcomed Catholics and Jews to do the same."[22] Consequently, the institutional support that might have strengthened the integration of faith, learning, and scholarship waned. The prevailing view was that an explicitly religious mindset was not needed because American values could coexist alongside religious values.[23] As colleges and universities became increasingly diverse, mirroring the larger demographic shifts taking place culturally, "assimilation," "disestablishment," and "nondiscrimination" were foregrounded. Any commitments to sectarianism continued to give way to broader Judeo-Christian or Western ideals. Therefore, according to Marsden, currents flowed in the direction of "standardization and uniformity."[24] Over time, "in place of a Protestant establishment," the American Academy turned into an "establishment of nonbelief," where "the norm for people to be fully accepted in academic culture is to act as though their religious beliefs had nothing to do with education."[25]

Lessons from the Past for the Future

What are we to make of this history in view of our situation today? Drawing on the Chautauqua Idea and the founders who breathed life into it, I will focus on five practical lessons for how scholars in both the Christian and pluralistic Academy might chart a viable path forward for the institutions in which they serve.

Educational Innovation

The Chautauqua Idea spawned innovation within the church, higher education, and the non-profit sector more broadly. Ironically, modernization—the emergence of public schools, libraries, more accessible colleges and universities, movies, radio, and television—contributed to its decline. Today's Academy finds itself at a similar inflection point; of necessity, it must pursue new approaches for long-term viability.

Three notable innovations include the Chautauqua Literary and Scientific Circle (CLSC), the Chautauqua College of Liberal Arts, and the use of recreation, leisure, and the arts to aid one's education. The CLSC, founded in 1878, was referred to by many as the "people's college." The program offered a four-year home reading unit to promote study across multiple disciplines. Not naturally inclined to understatement, Vincent expressed his hope that ten people would register. In the first three days, over 700 enrolled. Ultimately, 8,400 individuals registered for the first class. Four years later, over 1,700 successfully completed the reading course. By the 1920s, 300,000 learners enrolled, and approximately 10,000 circles had been established worldwide.[26] Though only a shadow of itself today, the CLSC has operated uninterrupted since its founding and is often called the first book club.

Five years later, in 1883, the Chautauqua College of Liberal Arts was formed to democratize college education. In Vincent's words, "Here we find provision made for college training of a thorough sort. Students all over the world may turn their homes into dormitories, refectories, and rooms for study, in connection with the great University which has its local habitation at Chautauqua."[27] Unlike the CLSC, the Chautauqua leadership ended this experiment after a decade. Nonetheless, it encouraged the spread of libraries and college extension programs. William Rainey Harper, a young minister and accomplished scholar, who became principal of Chautauqua's College of Liberal Arts in 1886, went on to become the first president of the University of Chicago, where he implemented Chautauqua's model of reading groups into "Great Books" classes and the University's extension learning program.[28]

Lastly, Chautauqua brought innovation to education by intentionally incorporating the arts, nature study, and other recreational activities into its programs, fully aware that individuals change through some combination of head, hands, and heart learning. One early example involves John Heyl Vincent's love of geography. A topographical map of the Holy Lands was built into the Chautauqua grounds as a teaching aid for Bible students, where "children found it a unique playground and raced up and down its miniature hills and fell regularly into the Dead Sea."[29]

Regent College faculty James Houston and Bruce Hindmarsh remind us that "school" derives from the German word, *Schule*, which finds its origins in the Greek word *schole*, which means leisure.[30] "If in Christian higher education we use up all the margins," they write, "we simply fail to allow our faculty, staff, and students to cultivate non-programmatic, non-instrumental ideals, such as those of disinterested scholarship, friendship, and prayer. Like Boaz, we must not glean to the edges of the fields lest we miss the unanticipated grace of a Ruth and Naomi."[31]

Scholars can be tempted to resist innovation, and their ire can be directed at deans and administrators who upset the status quo. Not every idea will work, as proven by Chautauqua, which nearly ran itself into bankruptcy by expanding too quickly; however, some changes will take hold, leading to greater competitiveness and mission accomplishment. No matter our hopes or fears, Christian scholars must learn to work with leaders and trust their motives. Doing so is an important part of Christian witness.

Intellectual Humility

Intellectual humility understands personal and disciplinary knowledge as bounded, and therefore, in need of wisdom and insight from voices in other academic fields. Thus, Christian academics are "set free from the onerous responsibility of being right every time."[32] In this spirit, both Marsden and Noll call for Christian scholarship that generously incorporates integrative and attitudinal commitments. A major step in this direction is demonstrating charity toward those *within* and *outside* our fields, especially across conceptual and departmental barriers. In his afterword, Noll acknowledges the challenges inherent in Christian scholarship. The deep learning required to excel in the modern Academy makes it challenging to find shared language and structures for dialogue across disciplines.[33]

Marsden, reflecting on the life of John Henry Newman, founding rector of the Catholic University of Ireland, mirrors Noll's concerns. "Practitioners of each academic specialty," he writes, "tend to talk only to members of their own discipline or subdiscipline and only in their own specialized language and categories."[34] Agrarian author and philosopher Wendell Berry agrees that specialization has caused the university to grow "not according to any unifying principle, like an expanding universe, but according to the principle of miscellaneous accretion, like a furniture storage business."[35] The problem originates, in Berry's view, when the siloed Academy participants become "makers of *parts* of things."[36] This, inevitably, leads to self-alienation through "the loss of concern for the thing made and . . . the loss of agreement on what the thing is that is being made."[37] In essence, when we lose sight of our academic neighbors, we forget what we are making and how what we are making together contributes to the institution's educational mission.

Valuing the larger educational ecosystem is vital, but so too is embodying the fruit of the Spirit within the ecosystem. Marsden punctuates this point, reminding Christian scholars "that mainstream academic culture and spiritual virtues are often at odds" and there is even a negative correlation between scholarly output and Christian virtue.[38]

Chautauqua avoided academic siloes and for much of its history cultivated Christian devoutness. Vincent captured this idea well: "The college is not a *museum*, —literary, aesthetic, historic, scientific,—but a *gymnasium*, intellectual, moral, personal. Its value is to be determined by the measure of the man who comes out of it, —the measure of his mental, executive, and moral force."[39]

Moreover, Chautauqua is committed to civil discourse and debate and has a long track record of humbly welcoming advocates on opposing sides of an issue. One highly charged example is women's suffrage. Co-founder Lewis Miller was a suffragist, his co-founder John Vincent an anti-suffragist. Chautauqua's two main publications were led by leaders who took different views on the same issue. Theodore Flood, editor of the *Chautauqua Daily*

Assembly Herald, supported women's vote, while Ida Tarbell, journalist, investigative reporter, and editor of the *Chautauquan Magazine*, did not.[40]

In a highly polarized culture, Christian academics have an opportunity to model a more generous dialogue and to carve out a "courageous middle" that refuses to surrender to binary categories. As Shirley Mullen, president emerita of Houghton College, suggests, our failure to accurately interpret and contextualize Scripture "for the new moral and ethical challenges . . . has only made the reductionist approach to biblical authority more costly and painful for the church's credibility over the decades."[41]

A Two-Book Theology

The bifurcated life in academia is undone by a two-book theology—a belief that God is revealed through the books of Scripture and creation. Both Lewis and Vincent "saw religion as belonging to everyday living," where God "was not to be confined between the covers of the Bible."[42]

The Chautauqua movement was born from a deep commitment to Scripture and the centrality of the Bible for instruction in all dimensions of life. Bible study was understood as a gateway for deeper, integrative work involving many academic disciplines and professional fields. Within two years of its founding, in 1876, Chautauqua joined the U.S. Centennial celebrations by extending its season to host a Scientific Congress. In addition to its regular offering of religiously themed lectures, special attention was paid to the relationship between Christianity and science. Lectures such as "Alleged Discrepancies between Science and the Bible" and "The Importance of Science to the Religious Thinker" helped frame the program, as did talks and demonstrations dealing with electricity, light, heat, and astronomy.[43]

In Vincent's telling, "The proper study of the Divine WORD leads to and requires the more careful study of the Divine works."[44] As we engage God's special revelation, we better understand God's natural revelation. When doing so, the secular "loses its hard, metallic ring. It begins, like Aaron's rod, to blossom with spiritual beauty."[45]

Miller and Vincent saw all of life under God's canopy. This remains an important lesson for those who teach, mentor, and lead in the Academy. In Miller's words, we cannot separate the sacred from the secular.

> Away with this dividing-up of things! All things that are legitimate are of God. The human intellect belongs to God, and is to be cultivated for him. And when I see John Wesley, on fire with zeal to save souls, sitting down to write Hebrew grammars, and Greek grammars, and French grammars; when I see John Wesley taking Shakespeare's plays, and so selecting, abridging, and modifying that he could put them into the hands of young people for their culture; when I see what John Wesley did in the promotion of secular culture among his people, that they might be broad as well as intense, —I say again, Away with the heresy that a man is stepping aside from his legitimate work as a Christian minister when he is trying to turn all secular nature into an altar for the glory of God.[46]

A Sacramental Orientation

James Davison Hunter, echoing philosopher Charles Taylor, laments that our buffered and disenchanted world "has left modern and late modern persons without a framework of ultimate and transcendent meaning to order life and to provide a sustaining account of suffering and death."[47] The modern Academy—maybe more than any other institution—lacks a coherent and unifying story. The Chautauqua Idea offers fresh possibilities. In advocating for universal reading and theological reflection, "Chautauqua stretches over the land a magnificent temple, broad as the continent, lofty as the heavens, into which homes, churches, schools, and shops may build themselves as parts of a splendid university in which people of all ages and conditions may be enrolled as students."[48]

According to educator Dennis D. Cali, a sacramental orientation sees the world as "infused with the Divine" and "charged with the supernatural."[49] The Orthodox scholar, Alexander Schmemann, paints a similar picture: "God *blesses* everything He creates . . . He makes all creation the sign and means of His presence and wisdom, love and revelation."[50] A sacralized academic life acknowledges that all dimensions of research, teaching, and serving are touched by transcendent realities. Consequently, the Christian's scholarly vocation rejects the directive Marsden warns against, "that we cannot bridge the gap between empirical truths and wider metaphysical realities."[51]

A goal for academic leaders is to bring a renewed measure of wonder and enchantment to their institutions. To see and experience the world sacramentally is to believe that all people, all professions, all fields of study, all things bear God's image and join in the mutual indwelling of the divine life. As such, one guiding principle for Christian scholars and administrators might be to relate to the Academy as an icon rather than an idol—the university as a gateway to the divine, not the divine itself.

A Thick Public Witness

Finally, Chautauqua is an exemplary example of thick and sustained witness at the seam of complex publics. For over 150 years, Chautauqua has woven threads of faithful presence and action among the church, Academy, government, business, and social sectors—threads that mirror the inter-movement and interrelationships of the Trinity for the *shalom* of God's people.

As missiologist Gregg Okesson reminds us, our "public realms" are highly complex systems shaped by the "interpenetration of many elements."[52] In many church activities, our faith and missiological activities are too thin, never piercing the thick exteriors of the domains they encounter. A thin approach engages the world "one-dimensionally," failing to "enter into and witness to, the interiority of complex, interpenetrating publics."[53] Consequently, Okesson emphasizes the importance of movement, which he likens to weaving or dancing; "Only through the actions of the entire Trinity can salvation be woven into public spaces for the redemption of all things."[54]

Evangelical views of salvation that emphasize personal redemption often fail to consent to God's cosmic restoration project (see Mark 16:15, Acts 3:20–21, Rom. 8:22–23, 2 Cor. 5:17–21; Col. 1:15–20). A first step toward thick witness in a thick public, such as the university, is recognizing that institutional transformation is possible. Doing so requires that we acknowledge that our "publics are not passive" and will respond to "the message being delivered."[55] Institutions are comprised of principalities and powers of both light and darkness. Weaving threads of "faithful presence," as James Davison Hunter describes, leads to "relationships and institutions that are fundamentally covenantal in character, the ends of which are the fostering of meaning, purpose, truth, beauty, belonging, and fairness—not just for Christians but for everyone."[56] Only faithful presence, movement, and weaving a thick public witness over time create the interpenetration necessary to bring lasting renovation.

Conclusion

Commitments to the evangelical mind guided Miller and Vincent in founding Chautauqua. Revolutionary for their time, both men were motivated by a deep commitment to biblical truth, a passion to democratize higher education for the masses, and an ambition to bring the best scholarship and teaching to bear on the life of the church. Theological training in conversation with the sciences, letters, and the arts was considered the most impactful pathway for self-improvement and societal advancement. However, the Gospel's good news for all dimensions of life has been diluted in the Chautauquan context over time, and the "religion pillar" does not bear the weight it did in earlier years.

For those who serve in academic contexts, there is much that counteracts Jesus's message of hope, healing, and transformation. The university prioritizes specialized over communal knowledge, pursues models of scarcity over abundance, affirms the rational over the supernatural, and rewards individual over team accomplishment.

Given what we know to be true about God's redemptive work in the world, I leave you with one final question: Are Noll and Marsden's propositions "scandalous" and "outrageous" enough? The answer is context-specific but deserves our best thought and action throughout our academic careers. The founders of Chautauqua did not play it safe; neither should we. In weaving a thick garment of scholarship, teaching, and service, we are helped by the early Chautauqua Idea, which, "in all its bearings is like a kaleidoscope . . . turned and turned and adjusted to the eye, to see all its beauties."[57]

Chapter 16

Leo Tolstoy's School for Peasant Children

LANCE CROY

Response Summary: The CCSN unconference specifically addressed the scholar-as-teacher, intending to reimagine what it means to teach and publish from a distinctively Christian point of view. During the event, Paul A. Soukup, SJ, presented four key principles based on the Jesuit tradition of Christian higher education: (1) a mode of education, (2) a unique approach to the individual, (3) an education rooted in community, and (4) a commitment to justice. This case study will examine Leo Tolstoy's Yasnaya Polyana School for Peasant Children using that very framework. Interestingly, Tolstoy would critically reflect on the futility of his efforts in running the school. Nevertheless, his insights may offer inspiration for those in the throes of the Academy today.

ONE OF THE TAKEAWAYS from the unconference is the theological and moral commitments required for Christians in higher education. In one of the speeches, Paul A. Soukup, SJ, presented four key principles based on the Jesuit tradition that modern contemporaries use as a framework to visually express these values. They are: (1) a mode of education, (2) a unique approach to the individual, (3) an education rooted in community, and (4) a commitment to justice.[1]

This brief case study will examine Leo Tolstoy's Yasnaya Polyana School for Peasant Children using his "pedagogy-free pedagogy by way of experiment," as he referred to it, and the interesting parallels with these four principles presented by Soukup.[2] The Christianity and Communication Studies Network (CCSN) unconference specifically addressed the scholar-as-teacher, intending to reimagine and reform what it means to teach and publish from a distinctively Christian point of view. Tolstoy offers one such perspective.

Tolstoy, one of the most prolific writers of his time, immersed himself in the administrative tasks of running a school at his estate and committed himself to teaching in the classroom on a day-to-day basis. It is interesting to note that Tolstoy would critically reflect on the futility of his efforts, even sharing many of his regrets and failures.[3] Furthermore, Tolstoy was not trying to provide a "model of what is requisite and necessary for a school, but simply a description of the actual state."[4] Some of Tolstoy's ideas may be radical and impractical today. Nevertheless, it is highly consistent with the evangelical mind of Christian scholars.

A Mode of Education

Tolstoy's school consisted of three classes, 12 subjects, approximately 40 male and female students, and four teachers. Students were not assigned homework or marked tardy, there were no exams, and grades on in-class lessons were used internally by teachers to measure progress. As long as the teacher approved, students could enter any classroom they wanted at any time during the day. They could sit wherever they wanted, usually rearranging the furniture to suit their needs. Tolstoy wrote that some class sessions went several hours longer because students were delighted by the content and demanded more. Other subjects, usually mathematical and grammatical lessons, bored the students and forced the teacher to move on quickly to the next subject. Tolstoy wrote:

> The spirit of the school, for example, is always found in inverse proportion to the compulsion and order required; in inverse proportion to the teacher's interference with the pupil's mode of thought, and in proportion to the number of pupils; in inverse proportion to the duration of lessons, and the like. This school spirit is . . . communicated from one pupil to another . . . expressed in the tones of the voice, in the eyes, in the motions, in the zeal of emulation, it is something perfectly palpable, indispensable, and invaluable, and should, therefore, be the aim of every teacher.[5]

The mode of education was not by rote memorization but by recitation exercises, which took place from five to seven times throughout the day. Students would recite the lesson in their own words, out loud, and all at once. As soon as the clamor became deafening and students shouted over one another, the teacher would call on one student to recite to the whole class. If the student mispronounced something or omitted an important detail, another student would jump in and add their telling of the tale. Interestingly, even the older students who had been at the school longer would occasionally forget names, places, and dates. However, they always recited the events that made the story elements memorable.[6]

Tolstoy once observed a young girl in the commotion narrating the events as if on a stage with grand gestures. As soon as she glanced at Tolstoy, she looked down and began to whisper while everyone else was carrying on around her. It took her two days to build up the courage to speak in front of the class, but when she did, Tolstoy said her remarks were beautiful.[7]

The teachers also kept a diary, which they read to one another, comparing marks and notes about a student's progress. They also passionately disputed and debated with each other and loosely formed the curriculum for the week ahead. Of course, everything could be modified based on the students' needs and demands. The point is that Tolstoy wanted an active education built around communication. He wrote, "Parrot-like repetition of words was not education."[8]

A Unique Approach to the Individual

Tolstoy desired children to read, comprehend what they have read, and develop a love for great literature with an appetite to advance to more challenging works. However, he had to start with books written by and for the people's tastes. The zeal children had for folktales, proverbs, songs, poems, and enigmas would manifest in games and nicknames. The students hungered to have those works read to them again and again. Tolstoy said,

> The teacher's business is merely to propose a choice of all known and unknown methods of possibly helping the pupil in the business of learning. . . . Every pupil represents an individuality with his own needs, to satisfy which freedom of choice is the only possible condition.[9]

Tolstoy allowed each student the choice to employ one or all of the following methods to learn how to read:

1. Students could choose any book and have their teacher read it with them like a child does with their parents. This familial act forges a love for reading together.

2. Students could choose a book and read it by themselves.

3. A child could memorize a book passage and practice it aloud during the recitation sessions, to the delight of both the teacher and the class.

4. Several students could read the same book aloud by taking turns—a practice that was encouraged but not mandatory for the entire school.

5. Finally, students could read to gain comprehension and greater understanding. They relied on their teachers and peers to help clarify and correct any misunderstandings or mispronunciations.

Tolstoy recalled a father telling him that he burned out an entire candle one evening, holding it over his son's book while he read it. Tolstoy, the Jesuits, and Soukup all mentioned that educators should focus on the individual influence of their affective motivations, cognitive faculties, and behavioral interactions, especially with reading and interpreting texts.

An Education Rooted in Community

Tolstoy envisioned a school that benefited the whole community. However, his writings stressed the many failures of that endeavor, which resulted in the school closing and re-opening several times. Tolstoy struggled with whether he should try to educate peasants "out of their sphere" and had to address objections as to why students should be exposed to the arts when they will plow the land for the remainder of their lives.[10]

Art is a powerful medium that gives form to feeling. The artist is bound not only to a time and place but also to available materials. However, the ideas expressed therein can exist in a perceptual space enjoyed time and again by others from various educational, socioeconomic, cultural, and religious backgrounds.[11] For example, movies made in Hollywood can still resonate with audiences overseas. Similarly, movies made in the past can define features of the art form that continue long after the auteur's lifetime. Tolstoy wrote:

> Why is the beauty of the sun, the beauty of a human face, the beauty of the sounds of a popular melody, and the beauty of an act of love and sacrifice accessible to everyone, and why do these things require no preparation? I suppose that the demand for the enjoyment of art and the service of art exists in every human being, to whatever class and environment he may belong, and this demand is legitimate and must be satisfied.[12]

Unfortunately, the existing social structures would prevent the school from breaking out of its place-based model and into the surrounding communities. Many of the social inequities in Tolstoy's time are also true today, leading to Soukup's final point.

A Commitment to Justice

Tolstoy allowed the peasant children to attend his school for free. This outrageous and scandalous experiment occurred because of Tolstoy's moral and religious commitments. Restorative social justice cannot be accomplished alongside cognitive injustice. This means that the Gospel, rightly understood, pushes out my prejudices and presumptions concerning people I am not prone to love. Stated another way, the Gospel gives me a revelatory reason to act lovingly to those I think less about or do not think about at all.

Theologian and author D. A. Carson presented an interesting commentary about educators who forget to serve their surrounding communities. Scholars who live in their heads or are cloistered within the ivory tower without engaging the outside world at a personal, intellectual, and cultural level are "mere quartermasters."[13] The frontlines of evangelism need research publications and scholarly endeavors. Nevertheless, Carson observed that an apologetics professor, for example, becomes a better and more loving teacher by sharing their faith with someone outside the classroom. Carson warned, "Nothing is quite as deceitful as an evangelical scholarly mind that thinks it is especially close to God because of its scholarship rather than because of Jesus."[14]

Despite all the failed experiments at Tolstoy's school for peasant children, one recollection of his is the most relevant to Christians in higher education: the Bible became the foundation for all knowledge-formation, and the students loved reading it. Tolstoy wrote:

> After the Old Testament, I took up the New Testament; they loved learning, and they loved me more and more. . . . In order to open the new world before the pupil, and without knowledge to start him in the love of knowledge, no book is needed but the Bible. I say this even for those who do not view the Bible as a revelation. No, at least I know of no production that unites itself in such a concise poetic form [from] all the sides of human thought as the Bible does.[15]

Therefore, I pray that our pupils and publications are saturated with Scripture. I pray that our failures humble us and help us love Jesus more deeply. May we learn from others, even if their ideas seem radical or impractical. Finally, let us be reminded that there is an art to teaching. Christians in higher education do not merely teach subject matter in a class. Christians in higher education teach subjects (individuals) that matter regardless of their class.

Section Two:
Reimagining the University and
Christian Higher Education

Chapter 17

Reimagining the University: Substantive Truth as the Path to Pluralism

JONATHAN PETTIGREW

Response Summary: Legacy Scholar Clifford G. Christians's vision for the future of higher education is substantive truth within a pluralistic society. The issue facing post-Enlightenment universities, however, is an unwillingness or inability to engage in pluralism. In modern university settings where coalitions of scholars compete for scarce resources and limited decision-making administrative positions, neither coherence-truth nor the correspondence-truth perspectives are well-suited to encourage pluralism. A coherence-truth of narrative constructionism has everything to lose from pluralism because competing narratives might destabilize its power base. Arrogant, naturalistic correspondence-truth similarly does not abide pluralism because it enjoys social privilege. By contrast, the philosophy of Christianity leaves a heritage of free inquiry in pursuit of substantive truth.

"SUBSTANTIVE TRUTH" within the social context of pluralism society is Clifford G. Christians's vision for the future of higher education.[1] His view of truth expertly synthesizes the best of dominant philosophical traditions (like empirical observation) without adopting their fatal intellectual flaws (like relativism or empiricism). He argues, like Marsden, that substantive truth should be a viable option within a pluralistic university setting. While vestiges of pluralism can be found today, for the most part the Academy is not a pluralistic environment—at least not a tolerant one. It is post-Enlightenment, which means that as the Enlightenment project has failed to deliver on the promise of liberating people to live the "good life" outside of dominant power structures, such as those animated by "religion" or "truth."

The key issue we face in post-Enlightenment university culture is an unwillingness or inability to engage in pluralism. Neither coherence-truth nor the correspondence-truth perspectives are well-suited to encourage the pluralism that Marsden and Christians describe. Neither are seedbeds for free, liberal inquiry. Thus, instead of a healthy pluralism that allows proponents of multiple viewpoints to coexist, debate, or marshal evidence for their positions, the philosophical commitments of both postmodern constructivism and modern empiricism are actively opposed to generating a pluralistic environment.

The dominant epistemology of the humanities builds from a coherence-truth of narrative constructionism. This perspective has everything to lose from pluralism because competing narratives with incommensurate truth claims might destabilize the power base of a dominant coalition. Universities are organizations with limited decision-making administrators who direct the university's mission or control the allocation of funds. So faculty in humanities, social sciences, and other colleges who espouse a constructionist viewpoint are interested in "constructing" the Academy in such a way that they can obtain these positions. Manifestations of this hesitance toward pluralism are evident in "cancel culture," which has an insecurity about (at best) or animosity toward (at worst) ideas that run counter to the coherence-truth of narrative constructionism.

The epistemology of the sciences is correspondence to reality, and the dominant form of this perspective in the university is tied to naturalism. This version of correspondence-truth similarly does not abide pluralism because it purports a single, best path that matches its naturalistic presuppositions. Whereas a humble approach to correspondence-truth may allow for pluralism, the arrogance of empiricism narrow-mindedly believes itself to be the only way. The view that all of reality is knowable within closed systems of probabilistic cause and effect allows some room for debate, but it simultaneously safeguards some "truths" like the scientific method. This correspondence view says the "science is settled" and there should be no dissenting views from reasoning persons. It assumes that if everyone could understand the data and its analysis, they would all arrive at the same, correspondence-based conclusion. When people or factions arrive at different conclusions than the "experts," there must be some defect in the person (ad hominem). Like before, this characterization of the correspondence-view also assumes that the university has scarce resources—such as grant dollars—and that only those best qualified to discover truth should be allowed to have them.

By contrast, the presuppositions of Christian epistemology and anthropology (human ontology) ideally encourage pluralism. Christians assume that humans are marked by agency—we have choice, and express it rationally, at times, and often irrationally. Christian ontology places humans as beings who are free. Christianity also assumes, as Cliff Christians points out, that humans are truth-seekers and can be truth-tellers. We may manipulate or lie, but we ultimately desire to know the truth—the authentic heart of a matter. This innate, God-given design bridges correspondence and coherence. A coherent story with no verisimilitude is hollow. Correspondence with no coherence is shallow or disintegrated. When we approach story and fact with the substantive truth lens, our theories can provide deep, integrated insights into reality as a whole.

As the biblical witness puts it, the "truth will set you free" (John 8:32). Christian liberal thought, I argue, is uniquely conducive to pluralism, particularly when compared to modern naturalistic post-positivism and postmodern constructionism. As the heritage of Chrisitan scholarship is lost or forgotten, pluralism becomes less and less tenable as a viable position within the contemporary secular Academy.

Chapter 18

Professor or Poulterer? Cultivating Religious Higher Education in the Postmodern Turn[1]

Craig E. Mattson and Desiree C. Duff

Response Summary: Addressing the emptiness that spurred George Marsden to propose a corrective for the contemporary university and that urged Mark Noll to propose an intensification of evangelical intellection, this essay engages Jean Francois Lyotard's anticipations of professionalized academies. It goes on to search out tendencies toward this postmodern pragmatism in both pietistic and Reformed higher education. The authors offer an alternative to educational utilitarianism with James Carey's notion of ritual communication, which suggests three ways that professors, of both pietistic and puritan leanings, could reorient their pedagogies.

Modern education, C. S. Lewis once insisted, does not teach fledglings to fly; it breeds poultry for public utility.[2] Half a century later, many teacher-scholars soberly agree that the academic aerie has given way to the henhouse. Poet and professor Marion Montgomery characterizes the professionalization of education this way:

> Curricula have been redesigned and marketed in the interest of a product—the most advanced student—in some of the ways we redesign and market new automobiles. Curricula are now sets of tools for adjusting the setting of the intellectual machine so that, when a given raw intellect has gone through the process—has been ground and polished—it may be labeled by its specialty and placed on the open market.[3]

Frank H. T. Rhodes—distinguished geologist, educator, and university leader best known for serving as the ninth president of Cornell University from 1977 to 1995—is less critical of professionalization, but admits nonetheless that the neglect of the humanities has balkanized the "learned professions": "Exhaustively trained, exquisitely skilled, they perform their various functions and exercise their various skills, each constrained and isolated within the enveloping cell of their own professional education."[4]

Those who insist English Catholic, theologian, and philosopher John Henry Newman's culture of the intellect still thrives have to account for the preponderance of professional over liberal arts studies, the prevalence of adult continuing education, and the relatively superior salaries drawn by graduates in information technologies as opposed to their counterparts in the humanities. Observe also the shift from traditional university paradigms to industrial paradigms, the privileging of "money-making" majors, and the marginalization—if not liquidation—of less marketable disciplines. Think of the valorization of the database over the quest for wisdom: the Delphic dictum in the postmodern turn becomes "Access thyself."

Our concern in this essay centers on the state of Christian higher education, so it may seem odd that we turn now to the work of French philosopher Jean-François Lyotard, best known for his work on postmodernism. But we have been impressed with his by now decades-old prophecies about academic henhouses in the era of late capitalism—so impressed that we put his *The Postmodern Condition* in conversation with the history of Christian higher education. What we have come up with is a ludic but hard-to-set-aside analogy between Lyotard's performative professors and pietist and Puritan academicians. Wondering if pietism, Puritanism, and postmodernism had more to do with each other than shared plosives, we have compared our preliminary linkage of the three with our own experience in some five different institutions of Christian higher education. Our hunch has strengthened. Lyotard's prophesies about academic utilitarianism do indeed seem to have found an echo in the widespread pragmatization in the Christian Academy.

Because we have ourselves emerged from a pietistic faith tradition—Independent Fundamental Baptist—we are leery of our own tendency to turn pietism into a whipping boy. ("Evangelical thinkers," remarks James Neuchterlein wryly, "have a remarkable talent for self-criticism.")[5] And despite our own commitment to a reformational worldview in scholarship and pedagogy, we cannot help noting that Lyotard's ideas suggest that the great American Puritan tradition can beat a path to the henhouse door as quickly as the pietist tradition can.[6] In what follows, we first summarize Lyotard's predictions for higher education. Then we suggest some connections between these predictions and religious higher education, first on a pietistic, then on a Puritan model. Finally, we outline three ways that a pedagogy informed by communication historian James Carey's ritual view of communication could help repair the aerie of Christian higher education.

Jean-François Lyotard and Postmodern Poultering

In *The Postmodern Condition*, Jean-François Lyotard predicts that performativity—economic efficiency—will become the chief criterion for education in postmodernity. In his attempt to parse a workable curriculum, he asks the following questions: Who transmits learning? What is transmitted? To whom? Through what medium? In what form? With what effect? To answer Lyotard's questions is to define education, not in terms of the symbolic exchange of meaning, but in terms of bleeps traveling along a wire as a teacher uses signals to influence the student for the betterment of society's performativity. As a result, higher education has to "create the skills that are indispensable to the system."[7] These skills fall into two categories. The first group of skills consists of specialties that contribute to global capitalism, which Lyotard apparently sees as a sort of international barnyard. Students must be trained to become "experts and high and middle management executives in the leading sectors . . . where the action will be;" this "action" pertains to any disciplines associated with technology—what Lyotard calls "telematics."[8] The second group of skills consists of specialties that keep society working—"so many doctors, so many teachers in a given discipline, so many engineers, so many administrators, etc."[9] The problem arises when certain kinds of skills are no longer marketable. Lyotard identifies what he called a "remainder" of young people whom he predicts "for the most part" will be unemployed because they have chosen disciplines in the arts and human sciences.[10]

In addition to training young people to become "capable players" in society, Lyotard predicts that universities will contribute to improving society's performance by assuming a new role—"that of job retraining or continuing education."[11] He predicts that education will not simply be transmitted *en bloc* to young people before they enter the work force but will be "served *a la carte*" to adults who are already working members of society.[12] These adults will return to universities to retool, hoping to improve "their skills and chances of promotion."[13] This conceives of education as the stocking-up of memorable data in neural caches.

The more or less memorable data is the "message" resulting from this "functionalist point of view."[14] This "organized stock of established knowledge,"[15] because of technologies, no longer needs to be transmitted in the traditional lecture, delivered by a professor. If knowledge is that which is translatable into inductive computer language (and indeed, Lyotard suggests that knowledge will exclude anything that is untranslatable into computer language), if there is no need for the abductive, narrative knowledge, then professors can be replaced by computers. The chief end of pedagogy becomes teaching students "how to use the terminals" and how to play what linguists call the game of interrogation—asking the right questions in the right way to get the right results.[16] Lyotard argues that "this partial replacement of teachers by machines" seems unsettling only to people accustomed to metanarratives.[17] If only folks could rid themselves of the bothersome belief in the gradual accrual of wisdom down the millennia—a wisdom somehow embodied in the liberal arts tradition—if only they could muster "incredulity towards metanarratives,"[18] they would have no reason to protest "the knell of the age of the Professor."[19]

In the absence of metanarratives, says Lyotard, institutions will no longer ask "Is it true?" but "What use is it?" This "mercantilization of knowledge," this emphasis on salability and efficiency ensures that the competency that "makes the grade" will be defined by the criteria of performativity (competence in a performance-oriented skill) and transmissiveness (conveying data necessary for that skill).[20] Farewell the verities so long integral to liberal arts education. Even Lyotard, the playful prophet of postmodernism, admits such a farewell may have troubling results. Institutions of higher learning will be called upon "to create skills, and no longer ideals."[21] So far from mentoring future leaders to guide society, the postmodern Academy seeks rather to train future workers to fill "pragmatic posts." Poulterers, in short, have no time for fledglings.

Pietism and Performativity in Christian Higher Education

Linking Lewis's poultry and Jean-François Lyotard's performativity is easier than answering the question, "What hath pietism to do with postmodernism?" Is not Jerusalem closer to

Athens than an earnest, moralistic movement is to a flippant outlook John Fowles once called a "thumbed nose and a salute?" But James Tunstead Burtchaell's *The Dying of the Light* implies a fusion of horizons between the concerns of seventeenth-century religionists (such as Phillip Jacob Spener) and twenty-first century pragmatists (such as Richard Rorty).

Just as postmodernism is most easily defined by the metaphysical rigidity it pragmatically denounces, so pietism is best understood as a practical reaction against what Burtchaell calls a "sclerotic" condition, a rigidified Protestant intellectualism: "The pietist knack is to confront a snarled tangle of custom, construal and protected interests, and to point a prophetic finger at the obscured nucleus of truth within."[22] Pietism's later manifestations in the Awakenings of the eighteenth and nineteenth centuries resulted in the creation of various denominations such as Baptists, Quakers, and Methodists, whose colleges sprang up to educate the children of their parishioners. Such denominations tended to stress "the primacy of spirit over letter, commitment over institution, affect over intellect . . ."[23]—ideas subsequently re-presented in postmodern spirituality, anti-authoritarianism, and sentimentality.

To continue the comparison with postmodernism, pietism maintained these emphases in order to recover performativity. Such emphases, of course, could not help affecting the pedagogical vocabulary: pietists christened some truth sacred and some secular, emphasized ministry instead of vocation, and reduced the liberal arts tradition to what was useful for what came to be called full-time Christian service. This issued forth in a professionalized obedience to the Great Commission in the Gospel of Matthew. As Dallas Willard trenchantly observes, Christian enterprise in recent centuries has shifted its concerns from making disciples—a slow, painstaking engagement—to making quantifiable converts, thus effecting "the Great Omission from the Great Commission."[24]

Although the many pietistic variants held promise for reform in multiple spheres of Christian effort, including higher education, we fear that the pietistic emphasis on performativity has made it vulnerable in the postmodern turn to be transformed into a spiffed-up Spenerism emphasizing marketability, societal efficiency, and technological mastery. As Burtchaell tells the story, the pietists of the past who talked about the point of it all—evangelism—kept the point but forgot the all.[25] We fear that pietists in the postmodern turn may find that when the all goes in Christian higher education, the point is not far behind.[26]

Puritanism and Transmissiveness in Christian Higher Education

Fortunately, the past few decades have seen a resurgent interest in the "all" among American religious higher educators, particularly those of evangelical conviction. Many such scholars have, in good Augustinian fashion, taken up the cause of all truth—not just that part of the truth useful for soul-winning. They have reclaimed Tyndale's dictum that the cobbler is as important as the priest and have pronounced scholarship a valid Christian vocation. The results have been noted even by non-evangelicals. As Richard John Neuhaus has observed in a *First Things* column, "One may reasonably hope that at the end of this new century . . . evangelicals [will have] moved from a still nervous engagement to making substantive contributions that put the whole world in their debt."[27] Alan Wolfe, writing in *The Atlantic Monthly*, has seconded this opinion by proclaiming "The Opening of the Evangelical Mind."[28]

Our own reformational commitments honor scholars such as Nicholas Wolterstorff, Alvin Plantinga, George Marsden, Cal Seerveld, and Clifford G. Christians as contemporary embodiments of that fervent intellectualism that Mark Noll celebrates in Puritan thinker Jonathan Edwards.[29] Indeed, the great reawakening to the American Puritan scholarly heritage that these scholars have helped to affect is a timely one, as J. I. Packer's assessment suggests:

> As Redwoods attract the eye, because they overtop other trees, so the mature holiness and seasoned fortitude of the great Puritans shine before us as a kind of beacon light, overtopping the stature of the majority of Christians in most eras.... [B]ut in Britain and America, the parts of the world that I know best, affluence seems for the past generation to have been making dwarfs and deadheads of us all. In this situation, the teaching and example of the Puritan giants have much to say to us.[30]

So lofty is their pedagogical example that former Wheaton College literary scholar Leland Ryken rightly observes in his book on the Puritans, "Some spokesmen for Christian education today who assume that they stand within the Reformation tradition are in fact outside it."[31]

But what impresses us in Puritan-informed education is not so much the difficulty of achieving as of maintaining a Christ-transforming-culture pedagogy. Indeed, this seems to be a problem in more than one faith tradition, as Burtchaell suggests in his remarks on the children of pietists:

> The authentic pietist speaks to a generation whose life in the church has been hopelessly disordered and makes clean sense of the gospel that is ever ancient, ever new. For them it is a deliverance. But pietists also have a second-generation audience, who now know little or nothing of the tradition. To them, this reformed presentation is wondrously clear, preciously simple, and cogent because so easily comprehended. But they are easily misled.[32]

Similarly, emigrants from pietism like ourselves, who take up the reformational idioms—all truth is God's truth, no square inch Christ does not call "Mine!", etc.—may be tempted by tendencies latent in a newly embraced tradition to take education in a direction out of keeping with the reformational worldview. Such newcomers might, for example, think of education as the transmission of terminology, which brings us back to Lyotard's prophecies.

As noted above, teaching by transmission is precisely what Lyotard anticipated in his series of pedagogical questions listed above. These questions echo the inquiry of the mid-century propaganda scholar Harold Lasswell: "*Who* says *what* in *which channel* to *whom* with *what effects?*"[33] (emphasis mine). Indeed, students of media effects in the Lasswellian tradition will have a difficult time *not* associating the pedagogy Lyotard predicts with the standard media effects models of the past half-century of American communication studies.[34] Still, our linking of Lyotardian transmissiveness with an alleged tendency in the Puritan pedagogical tradition might be a hard sell were it not for the work of communication historian James Carey.

In his work *Communication as Culture*, Carey makes a judicious distinction between two different views of discourse, the first of which he describes as "a transmission view of communication . . . [which] derives from one of the most ancient of human dreams: the desire to increase the speed and effect of messages as they travel in space."[35] He discerns a connection between this Transmission Communication Theory and the reformational tradition in the migration of the Dutch Reformed Church to South Africa and of the Puritans to New England. These Pilgrims saw their voyage in missiological and, therefore, communicative terms. In the New World, they sought not only freedom but also converts. Carey writes, "The vast and, for the first time, democratic migration in space was above all an attempt to trade an old world for a new and represented the profound belief that movement in space could be in itself a redemptive act. It is a belief Americans have never quite escaped."[36] If Carey is right, the reformational tradition's holistic emphases are held in tension with a tendency to see communication as information transport between isolated subjects. A transmissive pedagogy would accordingly entail a sending of data across space—that is, getting what is in the teacher's head into the student's head. Such a model might describe the teacher as a voyager who hopes to make landfall on student shores.

Carey's second view of discourse is called the "ritual view of communication."[37] Students interested in ritual communication attend not so much to the conveyance of data from a speaker to an audience as to the way a speaker and her audience exchange symbols and by doing so, put a world together.[38] Communication breakdown on this model is not a matter of sunken Mayflowers (or torn trans-Atlantic cables) but of fractured worldviews. Because ritual rhetoric is culture-based instead of information-based, ritual theorists will talk about talk quite differently than will their transmissive colleagues. "Instead of using mechanistic terms such as *send* and *decode*," explains communication professor and author Quentin Schultze, "proponents of the cultural approach describe communication with words such as *interpretation, meaning*, and *context*"[39] (emphasis mine). A pedagogy that understands communication culturally rather than transmissively would have more qualities in common with a Eucharist than with a sermon, because the teacher is not so concerned about "the extension of messages in space but . . . [about] the maintenance of society in time."[40] To mesh the Pilgrim imagery with an image of literary theorist Kenneth Burke's, both the student and the teacher are on the same ship on a voyage of discovery.

To think of pedagogy ritually or culturally (we use Carey's two terms inter-changeably, as he does) accords well with the worldview-ish tendencies of the reformational tradition—and, indeed, of any other tradition reluctant to depict the teacher/student relationship in terms of a subject/object dualism. Our point is that a transmissive communication theory, though not essential to, is potential in Puritan responses to pietistic pedagogy. In what follows, we suggest ways that Carey's notion of cultural communication might correct flawed tendencies in both pietist and reformational pedagogies. Not, we hasten to add, that the pedagogical practices Lyotard anticipated in the postmodern turn are devoid of good. The performative tendencies in pietism often speak to students' concerns about getting a job—concerns very much in accord with the longstanding Christian emphasis on vocation.

Furthermore, the transmissiveness more or less latent in reformational thought is particularly effective for communicating terms and propositions systematically. But we think that a ritual pedagogy corrects for viral tendencies in both traditions in three ways.

Implications of Ritual Communication for Pedagogy

First, a ritual pedagogy privileges symbolic exchange over sign usage. Conceiving the classroom as culture rather than as circuitry summons a pedagogy that is, to use Roderick P. Hart's phrase, "addicted to meaning." The "fix" for such a condition is suggested in southern novelist and philosopher Walker Percy's distinction between sign and symbol: in short, a sign points, and a symbol means. A sign, he explains, initiates a succession of time-space events, whereas a symbol performs actions that cannot be described in physicochemical terms—actions such as naming, damning, and affirming.[41] The practicalities of this distinction affect the positioning of teachers and students in the classroom. On the one hand, a pedagogy conceived as the transmission of signs requires a professor to initiate a succession of events in a student's brain, because she and the student stand in opposition to each other as isolated signal receptors.[42] The teacher acts on, instead of with, the student. Pedagogy conceived as symbolic exchange, on the other hand, is cooperative. Instead of standing face-to-face, teacher and student stand shoulder-to-shoulder, looking at the symbolically constructed world they come to share.[43] Whether or not this offers rationale for rearranging classrooms or offices, a professor practicing ritual pedagogy will in any case seek not to transfer her mind into the students' heads, but rather to align her horizon of meaning with theirs.[44]

Secondly, a ritual pedagogy cultivates forgetfulness as well as remembrance. Transmissive pedagogy conceives of lectures in terms of what students should be able to recall. To this end, PowerPoint slides bullet out propositions in mnemonically savvy format. However, such data-mindedness misconstrues memory as a psychological faculty for receiving and containing transmitted signs, which are later to be produced as the answers to fill-in-the-blank questions on the midterm exam.[45] Classroom communication understood culturally, however, allows for the need to reconceive a subject. Gadamer suggests "Only by forgetting does the mind have the possibility of total renewal, the capacity to see everything with fresh eyes, so that what is long familiar fuses with the new into a many leveled unity."[46] What is sought in this fruitful forgetfulness is what twentieth-century scientist and philosopher Michael Polanyi refers to in scientific disciplines as a "breakout" that "bursts the bounds of disciplined thought in an intense if transient moment of heuristic vision. And while it is breaking out, the mind is for the moment directly experiencing its content rather than controlling it by the use of any pre-established modes of interpretation: it is overwhelmed by its own passionate activity."[47] Both the pietist privileging of memorable, useful data and the Puritan love for transmittable, memorable propositions may be reformed by the soul-formative power of a responsibly cultivated forgetfulness.[48]

Thirdly, ritual pedagogy is abductive rather than inductive. Communication scholar Sandra Moriarty's discussion of visual rhetoric works for ritual pedagogy as well: it "may call for a different set of interpretative skills that are more intuitive than conventional, the type of skills used in abductive thinking."[49] But a transmissive, performative pedagogy deploys an inductive method by first laying principular groundwork for grasping a given subject. For example, some professors might feel compelled in their opening lectures to establish a philosophical basis and a clear methodology for the semester ahead. Teachers who think abductively, on the other hand, may displace this linear schedule in order to practice a fore-and-aft movement in their discourse, tacking back and forth between principle and topic, theory and practice, conception and experience.[50] The aim of such a pedagogy, finally, is not syllogistic: the teacher does not seek to make an explicit path from major premises to conclusions. Wide is the gate and broad is the road for transmitting data useful for the job site or the philosophic system, but such explicit inductivity may also create distance between the students and the subject matter.[51] Abductive teaching, on the other hand, enables the learning experience to lose "the character of an observation and . . . become an encounter instead."[52] A semester framed by abductive thinking does not neglect a principular understanding of the subject matter, but rather puts it into conversation with an experiential understanding.

Conclusion

These three depictions of ritual pedagogy hardly exhaust the corrections needed for a performative education that C. S. Lewis predicted half a century ago with his imagery of fledglings and chickens. Nor do these suggestions provide final answers for how to reform a transmissive tendency in higher education that Lyotard anticipated more than two decades ago. But this essay, linking C. S. Lewis and Lyotard in an inadvertently shared prophecy regarding postmodern pedagogy, hopes to open discussion of how James Carey's ritual view of communication might correct some of the corrections already offered for pragmatized religious higher education. Such a view of communication suggests that Christian liberal arts should cultivate meaning through symbolic-exchange, intelligent disremembering, and abductive practice. Our call in this essay to reform the reformers—of both pietist and puritanical traditions—is corroborated by what Montgomery identifies as the vocation of liberal arts higher education: "perfections of intellect."[53] The phrase calls to mind a truth central to all Christian traditions: reform movements are never complete.[54] To cease renovation may well exchange perfections of intellect for increase of poultry.

Chapter 19

Christian Scholarship Thirty Years On

A. Chase Mitchell

Response Summary: This essay revisits George Marsden's vision of "Christian scholarship" amid today's polarized, individualistic, and fractious academic culture. It traces how Marsden's framework, which was suited to the multiculturalism of the latter part of the twentieth century, is not as apt in the present context. The American Academy is now dominated by ideological fragmentation, hyper-partisanship, and misconceptions about Christian scholars' role in secular culture. While praising Christian consortiums like the Christianity and Communication Studies Network (CCSN) for fostering unified witness, the author urges Christian scholars to adapt: to cultivate unity while embracing honest disagreement, tackle contentious issues responsibly, and prioritize Kingdom service over kingdom politics. Christian scholars must resist ideological tribalism and cultivate faithful witness in an age of discord and dissolution—spiritual, political, and cultural.

NEARLY 30 YEARS AGO George Marsden made the case that "Christian scholarship" should be normalized within American academic discourse. He argued that religious views, including Christians', should receive a hearing just as "Marxist, feminist, gay, postmodern, African-American, conservative, or liberal schools of thought."[1] In other words, just because scholars come to their work with particular or even religious moral and metaphysical presuppositions, those presuppositions should not be precluded from driving and even shaping their academic scholarship; provided, of course, that it remains intellectually rigorous and methodologically robust. He makes this claim not (primarily) under the heading of religious liberty, but, rather, because all scholastic enterprise is conducted by human beings. A person, that is, approaches his work with preexisting epistemological assumptions and even moral commitments. Why should one's identity, including their Christian faith, not affect their scholarship?

Jacobsen's Critique of Marsden

In the second edition of *The Outrageous Idea of Christian Scholarship*, which features a new preface and concluding chapter, Marsden reflects on the many changes that have been wrought in American society, culture, and education over the past three decades.[2] While he acknowledges the differences between academic culture then and now, he reaffirms the book's validity: "The essential arguments of this volume remain relevant even in today's somewhat altered context."[3] In a review for the new edition, Rhonda Hustedt Jacobsen gives an interesting perspective on the book's continued relevance. Though she praises Marsden as "a gifted and exceptionally productive historian [who exemplifies] winsomeness, consistently producing work that is empirically sound and generous in spirit,"[4] she also questions the validity of some of his claims in the present context. She writes that "the United States is immersed in a new intellectual milieu in which personal identity has replaced group allegiance as the intellectual standard."[5] She recalls that at the time of the first edition:

> Scholars from different social and intellectual communities of discourse typically saw themselves as representing the perspectives of the groups they identified with, not an individual perspective [. . .] During that time, members of various racial, ethnic, social, and religious groups were prone to reference 'our' truth as it contrasted to the perspectives associated with other communal lenses of interpretation. *But that age of multiculturalism is now past* [italics added].[6]

Marsden's argument, Jacobsen says, was born from a postmodern Western landscape that had already jettisoned capital-T truth and the objective empiricism of the first half of the twentieth century, but still retained a strong social dynamic characterized by group affiliation (whether cultural, political, ideological, or religious). Thus, at the time, his claim that Christians could and should enter the multicultural Academy as one "school of thought," among many, made perfect sense. The idea was that the American university system—which (ostensibly) values fair and free dialogue—would provide the context for rationalistic discourse and debate. Christian scholars, said Marsden, could function as a (relatively) unified voice in the Academy, competing with other groups on equal terms. The problem, Jacobsen points out, is that since then, powerful cultural trends and new technologies have reshaped social dynamics, both within the Academy and in broader culture. In particular, the locus of personal identity has shifted from group affiliation to individual preference/expression. Today, for example, as Jacobsen writes, Americans are more likely to speak about "my truth" or "my faith" than "our truth" or "our faith."

At the cultural level, Westerners have been taught (i.e., catechized) to construct our identity from the ground up. We pick and choose which groups' values (or markers) appeal to us, discard the rest, and integrate the preferred ones into a custom front that suits our tastes. In the Academy, this kind of hyper-personalization is referred to as *intersectionality*. The concept is difficult to define, but it essentially points to a kind of choose-your-own-adventure mode of identity formation. It is the logical conclusion of the postmodern project and is tightly bound up with notions of power, oppression, and victimhood. Although most people have never heard of intersectionality, the "common wisdom" today is that "I decide what my truth is, and that I should tailor life to my own specifications." Social media is inundated by populist adages that are essentially dumbed-down versions of intersectionality wrought in sentimentalized, romanticized, or sexualized terms. *Live your best life, now, boo.*

Just as our secular narratives are becoming more self-referential, so too are our media technologies increasingly self-serving. Social media algorithms provide us with a never-ending stream of curated content that caters to our likes and dislikes; it also gives us a platform to craft and share our ideal self with the world. Streaming media, too—whether video or music—facilitate me-centered experiences. And now, with generative AI, instead of suffering another person in real and sometimes difficult conversation, I can "converse" with ChatGPT, the partner who only speaks when spoken to, knows everything, and only talks about what I am interested in. These technological currents have only intensified cultural fragmentation, including academic discourse and scholarship. As Marsden acknowledges in the concluding chapter of the second edition:

> While sharp ideological conflicts are hardly new to human experience, one of the things that has exacerbated them in recent years has been the digital media. In online exchanges the more extreme views and damning retorts are likely to get the most attention. That invites mutual vilification.[7]

When Marsden forwarded his vision of Christian scholarship in the 1990s, before these trends reached their present intensity, his interlocutors reasonably believed that consortia of Christian scholars would be the most effective means to impress the faith in the academic realm. Indeed, such an approach has borne fruit. To give one example, the Christianity and Communication Studies Network (CCSN)—and this its first unconference—is testament to the fact that Christian scholarship (of the kind Marsden proposed) can make an impact in the Academy. Groups like CCSN are, thankfully, shielded from the worst effects of ideological fragmentation because our members share fundamental beliefs about who Jesus is. Even though cultural changes and political polarization have made it more difficult to articulate a shared Christian vision, such groups remain an indispensable blessing for those of us called to a vocation of Christian scholarship. The fellowship, networking, and publishing opportunities they afford give heft to our collective witness. I am not proposing, then, that we should discard the kind of group-affiliated "mere Christian" scholarship that Marsden proposes and CCSN facilitates. I am suggesting, however, like Jacobsen, that we reconsider the concept of Christian scholarship in this new environment in which we live and work. Indeed, in the new preface of the second edition, Marsden extols us to "think about how the intellectual outlooks of that era [the latter part of the twentieth century] compare with those of [our] own."[8]

Doing Christian Scholarship in the Intellectual "Wild West"

In a talk recorded prior to the unconference, Marsden—discussing his ideas in *Outrageous* and how they have played out over three decades—describes why Christians find it difficult to gain much traction in academic discourse. "Politics," he observes, "has become the primary religion for a lot of people." American Christians, even, adapt their faith according to whichever political ideology they prefer. This observation seems self-evident in today's climate, but what Marsden says immediately after that, I think, belies a deeper issue for scholars. He states, "We need checks and balances, like the Constitution, to temper the intellectual Wild West." Marsden is correct in saying that the Academy has become overly and overtly politicized, and he is right in suggesting that academic discourse needs guard-rails (education, peer review, etc.) to ensure our work maintains intellectual rigor, integrity, and truthfulness. But in comparing academia to an authoritative political text—i.e., the Constitution—he is implicitly claiming that the Academy, like the government, functions to arbitrate and solidify power. It does not. Or rather, it should not.

If Marsden was simply speaking off-the-cuff to combat what he calls the "intellectual Wild West"—that is, if he was using an imprecise analogy to foreground the importance of scholarly rigor—that would be one thing. But his comment echoes what he argues, citing Rausch, in the second edition's concluding chapter:

> In the twenty-first [sic] century, then, we especially need to foster what might be described as constitutional standards for intellectual life that encourage peaceful exchange of differing points of view. [...] the genius [of the U.S. Constitution] is that it tries to prevent one ideological dogmatic faction from taking over the whole government.[9]

In deploying the Constitution metaphor, Marsden belies, I think, a deep-seated con-viction that shapes most American scholars' work. It shows how easy it is for academics—even ones who recognize the pitfalls of politicizing scholarship—to conflate their work with politics. The postmodern paradigm has taken such a firm hold on Western culture that we struggle to disentangle intellectual discourse with partisan agenda. Even Marsden, a Chris-tian scholar aware of the problem, struggles to articulate a vision of Christian scholarship without relying on political analogies. Perhaps that is because, as Jacobsen argues, Mars-den's ideas were formulated at a time when academics participated within a framework of intellectual discourse that was defined by group affiliation: left versus right; Christian versus secular; and so on. Scholars who came of age in that era could identify the fault lines and situate their work according to clearly delineated camps. Now, though, in a world of amor-phous identities and fragmented politics, scholars are often unable to sustain productive discourse, and much less achieve consensus.

How might Christian scholars fare in this new world? Do we have unique resources for reframing and redressing the politicization of the Academy, and thus of Christian schol-arship? What else can we do, in addition to supporting and participating in initiatives like the CCSN, to proclaim Christ in our scholarly vocations? How do we temper the tendency toward disunity in a discordant academic culture? Where do we locate intellectual author-ity, if at all, and what is its relationship to Christian witness? I would like to propose a few brief exhortations that, I hope, help us to begin to address these and related questions.

Christian scholars of various persuasions—including, but not limited to, Catholic, Orthodox, Protestant, evangelical, "conservative," and "progressive"—should continue to strive for unity, even (and especially) in disagreement. We should maintain and cultivate scholarly spaces, like the CCSN, where "mere Christian" scholarship can take root and grow. The recently elected Pope Leo XIV's motto is *In Illo uno unum* (In the one Christ, we are one). Amen. We should strive for common ground and a unified voice as far as possible, and upbuild organizations and initiatives that support it. Christian scholars are called to be salt and light in secular spaces, including academic spaces, that otherwise default to factionalism and divisiveness. We serve as witnesses to God's grace by being charitable to each other in the pursuit of truth.

There is a danger, however, in always downplaying our disagreements. When Christians defer to theological and doctrinal commonality for the sake of unity, there can be a tendency to altogether avoid our real differences—differences that are not just important to believers, but relevant to the broader world. To give one example, many Christians cannot come to consensus on the issue of same-sex marriage. The range of conflicting viewpoints amongst Christians is just about as broad as those proposed in secular societies. Christians have profound and interesting things to say about gender and sexuality, and though we disagree with each other in many cases, by recusing ourselves from that conversation we are depriving the world of our insights and wisdom.

Of course, some would argue that encouraging Christian scholars to tackle contentious issues about which we disagree can harm our public witness. We hesitate to air our dirty laundry for the world. There is truth in that, but I would suggest that such concerns are alleviated insofar as we understand that academic domains are not ecclesial ones. As Christian scholars working in the Academy, we should not imagine ourselves to be agents of doctrinal authority. Rather, we are Christians who think publicly—in explicitly and implicitly theological ways—for the purpose of promulgating rigorous and robust scholarship. As participants in academic discourse, we may articulate how theology informs our respective disciplines and, vice versa, how our disciplines inform theology, but we should not misconstrue our work as theologically authoritative or doctrinally constitutive (unless, of course, our scholarship is sanctioned by Christian institutions, denominations, or traditions).

To put it another way, drawing on the above example: The secular university is a good place for Christian anthropologists, or psychologists, or historians, to bring their expertise to bear on the issue of same-sex marriage, but their primary role as an academic is not to adjudicate, in the authoritative sense, whether same-sex marriage is an orthodox Christian position. Their job, rather—and this is the great strength of the American university system—is to flesh out a particular truth or argument for the sake of understanding, so that others (both within and without the church) can learn from, build on, or refute it in free and open dialogue. This kind of restraint is difficult for many American Christian scholars because, as Marsden pointed out, politics has become "religious" for many people. That is especially true for postmodern secular academics who are eager to live their "faith" by producing partisan scholarship. It is also at least somewhat true for Christian scholars. We see our secular colleagues conflating their scholarship with political activism, and so we are tempted to join the fray by deploying our intellectual resources in a similar manner.

Christian scholars can and should produce scholarship that makes truth claims, but we should guard against a spirit of religious fervor that takes the form of polemical rhetoric, not because our faith should not shape our politics (it should), but because to constitute or exercise authority—whether theological or political—is *not the point* of academic discourse. Can our scholarship be read and referenced by theologians and policymakers? Of course, but the problem is that many academics increasingly see themselves as partisan agents, intellectual warriors whose job it is to set political agendas.

Given the current state of Western culture, then, broadly and within academia—highly politicized and intensely individualistic—Christian scholars would do well to:

- Cultivate unity by maintaining group affiliations (e.g., the CCSN) which presents a winsome witness, from within, to the secular Academy.

- Encourage scholarship about contentious subjects, even theological and political topics, that is both honestly forthright and intentionally ecumenical.

- Reframe scholarship in terms of Kingdom service, rather than kingdom politics. Even though we are citizens of a secular body politic and must abide by the rules of academic discourse in a pluralistic, democratic society, we should not remain content with being one respectable worldview among many. Our vocation is to reveal the true, the good, and the beautiful—in light of Christ Jesus—not to compete for academic prestige, peddle worldly influence, or quietly abide in scholarly ghettos.

Taken together, these scholarly postures can mitigate hyper-partisanship, temper uber-individualism, and foster healthy debate about difficult subjects—both within the church and without. Christian faith is not ultimately heuristic; it cannot be systematized. But these exhortations might help us push back against the prevailing cultural winds of our time.

Chapter 20

A Sacramental View of Communication and Media Studies in the Digital Age

Dennis D. Cali

Response Summary: In this essay, the author reflects on Christian faith in the digital age, focusing on society and academia. He draws insights from the Christianity and Communication Studies Network's inaugural dialogic unconference, especially the ideas of Mark Noll and George Marsden, extending them through a "sacramental view." Cali highlights the challenges Christian academics face amid secularization and postmodernism and proposes the sacramental view as an interpretive lens that recognizes the divine in everyday experiences, reclaims beauty in a commodified culture, and fosters presence with those around us.

THE LEGACY SCHOLARS and participants from the Christianity and Communication Studies Network (CCSN) at their first-ever dialogic unconference inspired deeper thought about the challenges faced by Christian-influenced academics in a rapidly changing world. This essay synthesizes key ideas presented during the event, particularly reflecting on insights from Professors Mark Noll, George Marsden, Quentin Schultze, and Paul Soukup—both the postmodern challenges that they allude to and the hopeful signs that they herald. By extending our understanding of these challenges, I aim to re-cast the contemporary issues in higher education and more broadly in society.

Today's Christian professors confront not merely the singular narrative of the "secularization hypothesis" which Marsden refers to in his chapter but multiple crosscurrents that challenge how we live as Christians and, fundamentally, how we simply live. Viewing these challenges as discourses allows us to imagine our situations as cries emanating from Christ, perhaps in "distressing disguise," a term coined by Mother Teresa of Calcutta to refer to the countenance of Christ she found in "the poorest of the poor" that she served.[1] Beyond this, as Easter people, we are called to reflect as well on how to embody love in our digital age, seeking hopeful signs of Christ's presence among us. Might we view the disturbances in our culture and in the Academy as cries of Jesus Forsaken, and might we view emerging positive developments around us and among us as assurances of Jesus Arisen?

A *sacramental* view offers a perspective by which to engage these important questions. It emphasizes the material world as a means to experience the divine. Everyday elements—nature, rituals, and human relationships—are imbued with spiritual significance. Abraham

Joshua Heschel's line is fitting here: "There is something sacred in every moment."[2] This perspective asserts that the sacred is not separate from the world but intricately woven into it. It invites us to recognize profound connections between the physical and spiritual realms, urging us to look for deeper truths in our common experiences. This view encourages a dual approach: "watch over" and "watch for," recognizing and embracing Jesus's presence in his forsakenness while celebrating his presence in our midst.

In this context, we are reminded that the Academy itself can be a sacred space where learning and faith intersect. The act of teaching, learning, and engaging in dialogue becomes a sacramental practice, allowing us to encounter the divine in our scholarly pursuits. Each interaction with students, colleagues, and community members can be an opportunity to experience Christ's presence, inviting us to reflect on how our academic work contributes to the greater good. Put another way, adopting a sacramental view, we can see the challenges that Noll and Marsden present to us as echoes of the cries of Jesus Forsaken, and we can see the "brighter picture" and "many ways forward," as Noll terms faith-inspired work in the University that he celebrates, as expressions of Jesus in our midst.[3]

Jesus Forsaken in the Device Paradigm

Mark Noll characterizes our current landscape as "treacherous," noting the emphasis students and their parents place on return on investment (ROI). The declining enrollment in humanities disciplines, including the field of communication, exacerbates the challenges faced by those advocating for a more humanistic approach. This is compounded by the ideological biases that have long plagued universities, particularly the secularism that dominates higher education. Noll's insights also echo George Marsden's observation that we live in an "intellectual Wild West," marked by postmodernism's multiplicity of viewpoints.[4]

The challenges we face are not just ideological but also represent modes of consciousness. I propose adopting the terminology of Albert Borgmann or Pope Francis to describe this mentality as the "Device Paradigm" or "Technocratic Paradigm"—a detachment from "the persons, things, and practices that used to engage and grace us in their own right" or "the tendency to see all of reality as a problem awaiting an application of scientific and technological power," respectively—shaping experiences, identities, and interactions.[5] Below, I explore four interconnected sub-themes: (1) identity crises, (2) treacherous environments, (3) perversion of beauty, and (4) disconnection, culminating in the deification of productivity. Each can be viewed as cries from a Forsaken Christ.

Identity Crises

In our digital landscape, many grapple with identity crises rooted in an obsession with authenticity. Social media platforms encourage users to curate idealized versions of themselves, leading to dissonance between real-life identities and online personae. This obsession manifests through body modifications and lifestyle choices aimed at authenticity, yet it often results in a superficial understanding of self. Individuals may feel compelled to perform rather than connect genuinely.

The pressure to maintain an online persona can lead to feelings of inadequacy and isolation when the curated image does not align with reality. The constant comparison to others can exacerbate these feelings, prompting individuals to question their worth and identity. This cycle of performance and validation highlights a broader cultural crisis where authenticity becomes both a performance mask and a commodity rather than a lived experience.

In Christian academic circles, this crisis of identity is particularly poignant. Educators and students alike may feel torn between the pressures of external expectations and the desire to live authentically in their faith. This dissonance can lead to a crisis of purpose, as individuals struggle to reconcile their professional identities with their spiritual beliefs. The challenge lies in fostering environments where individuals feel free to express their authentic selves, grounded in faith, without fear of judgment or rejection.

Treacherous Environments

The digital realm can be treacherous, characterized by echo chambers that reinforce narrow viewpoints and stifle critical discourse. These insular environments create "safe spaces" that protect marginalized voices but can inadvertently suppress intellectual diversity. Furthermore, the pervasive nature of digital media amplifies misinformation, fostering confusion and distrust. The rapid spread of false narratives about viruses and vaccines, climate, election integrity, immigration, historic revisionism, success, progress, and a host of other contemporary discourses cultivates anxiety and isolation, making it increasingly challenging to navigate the complexities of modern discourse.

In these environments, dissenting opinions are often marginalized, leading to a lack of robust debate and critical engagement. The result is a culture that prizes conformity over creativity and innovation. As academics, we must strive to foster spaces where diverse perspectives can coexist, encouraging open dialogue and critical thinking. This is particularly vital in Christian academic settings, where the call to love and serve must include a commitment to truth-seeking and intellectual integrity.

Moreover, the treacherous nature of today's environments extends beyond ideological divides; it also includes the emotional toll of navigating a landscape rife with conflict and division. The challenge for Christian academics is to cultivate environments that promote reconciliation and understanding, drawing on the principles of faith that call us to love our neighbors, even those with whom we disagree.

Perversion of Beauty

In the Device Paradigm, beauty is often distorted and reduced to superficial aesthetics. Platforms like Instagram promote narrow definitions of attractiveness, leading to body dysmorphia and unrealistic expectations. The quest for likes and shares can overshadow the intrinsic value of beauty, commodifying it in ways that erode genuine appreciation for artistic expression.

As art evolves, the emphasis on digital forms can strip away the emotional resonance of traditional media, leaving individuals feeling disconnected from the beauty that once inspired them. This commodification of beauty pressures individuals to conform to curated standards, exacerbating feelings of inadequacy and dissatisfaction. The challenge lies in reclaiming beauty as a profound expression of the divine, encouraging a return to authentic artistic creation that reflects the complexities of human experience.

In the context of Christian academic communities, this perversion of beauty also calls us to reflect on the aesthetics of our educational environments. Are our classrooms and campuses designed to inspire and uplift, or do they reflect the superficial values of a commodified culture? By embracing beauty in our physical spaces and academic endeavors, we can create environments that invite deeper engagement with the divine and foster a sense of reverence among students and faculty alike.

Disconnection

The Device Paradigm fosters profound disconnection between body and soul, leading to disengagement from both the physical world and our embodied experiences. Emotional numbness and superficial engagement replace meaningful interactions and self-discovery. The quest for external validation leaves little room for introspection, resulting in a culture that prioritizes productivity over genuine connection. Many individuals, in seeking connection, find themselves more isolated, as digital communication often lacks depth.

This disconnection can manifest in various ways, from the inability to form deep relationships to a sense of alienation from one's own emotions. The constant barrage of information can make it challenging to pause and reflect, leading to a culture that values speed over depth. As Christian academics, we must advocate for a return to practices that foster connection—whether through shared meals, communal worship, or deep conversations that encourage vulnerability and authenticity.

The challenge here is not just to reconnect with one another but to reconnect with ourselves and our faith. In a world that often pushes us toward distraction and superficiality, we must cultivate spaces for reflection and solitude, where individuals can engage with their inner lives and deepen their relationship with God. This interior journey is essential for fostering authentic community, as it enables individuals to bring their whole selves into their interactions with others.

The culmination of the Device Paradigm is the *deification of productivity*, where individuals are valued primarily for their output. This technocratic mindset prioritizes speed and the ethic of efficiency, often at the expense of well-being.[6] The relentless push for productivity can lead to burnout, as individuals feel compelled to perform constantly. Digital tools, designed to enhance productivity, frequently contribute to stress and urgency, blurring boundaries between work and leisure.

In this context, time becomes a scarce resource, measured in terms of efficiency rather than lived experience. The pressure to be perpetually connected can lead to a loss of personal boundaries, making it difficult to disconnect and recharge. As we navigate this landscape, it is crucial to reassess our relationship with technology, ensuring that it serves as a tool for connection rather than a barrier to genuine engagement.

The deification of productivity also raises important questions about the nature of our academic work. Are we merely cogs in a machine, driven by metrics and outputs, or are we called to be stewards of knowledge and truth? As Christian educators, we must resist the temptation to reduce our work to quantifiable outcomes, instead embracing the transformative potential of education as a means of enriching lives and fostering spiritual growth.

The Device Paradigm, or as Pope Francis termed it, "The Technocratic Paradigm," encapsulates the disconnects in modern life between human activity from ends or purposes shaping perceptions, identities, and interactions. By understanding its implications, we can strive for a balanced relationship with technology that honors our embodied experiences and connections with others. This endeavor helps reclaim our humanity in an increasingly digital world.

The four elements of the Device Paradigm—identity crises, treacherous environments, perversion of beauty, and disconnection—reflect the disfigurement of Christ on the cross. Just as Christ's crucifixion symbolizes forsakenness, these challenges echo a modern-day cry from the cross. Identity crises mirror Christ's disorientation ("Why have you forsaken me?") and struggle for recognition; treacherous environments reflect his "agony in the garden" and ultimate betrayal; the perversion of beauty recalls his disfigurement and contrasts with his grace; and disconnection resonates with the separation, the ex-communication, that he felt in his final moments.

And to complicate things further, in this complex landscape outlined above that permeate our society and manifest in microcosmic but amplified form in college campuses, we encounter all kinds of Christians, each with diverse paradigms and methodologies. While this diversity enriches our community, it also complicates our ability to radiate a Christocentric worldview. Today, we must navigate our expression of faith not only with nonbelievers but also with fellow Christians, running the risks of creating a new Babel among ourselves.

Jesus in Our Midst

The concept of encountering Jesus in our neighbors underscores the essence of community and shared faith. The phrase "where two or more are gathered in his name" (see Matt. 18:20) emphasizes that Christ's presence is alive in our relationships. This theme invites us to see Jesus in each person we meet, enriching our lives and those around us, especially in academic contexts. There are four aspects that are essential to a sacramental view of communication.

To begin, *a sacramental view encourages recognition of the divine in our interactions.* Each encounter—be it with a student, colleague, or community member—becomes an opportunity to experience Christ's presence. Chiara Lubich, founder of the Focolare Movement, termed our neighbor "a sacrament," highlighting the significance of these relationships.[7]

Consider Ana, a dedicated faculty member, and her student Mason, who struggled with academic pressures. During office hours, Ana noticed his distress and chose to listen, creating a safe space for him to share his concerns. This simple act transformed their interaction into a sacred moment, as Ana looked beyond Mason's grades to see his human struggle. By offering empathy and understanding, she embodied Christ's love, fostering a sense of relief and hope.

When we serve our students and colleagues, we participate in a sacred exchange where

Christ is present. Loving our neighbor becomes an encounter with the divine, fostering a community of love and understanding. In vulnerable moments, our neighbors often become the face of Christ, enhancing our spiritual growth and the importance of community.

Second, *recognizing beauty in the world around us* is critical to the sacramental view. Beauty serves as a bridge to the divine, reminding us of God's presence in creation. Whether it is nature, a colleague's kindness, or shared laughter, these moments reflect the sacred.

Jesus often used parables and imagery to convey profound truths. The beauty of creation, in nature and in our own activity, can lead us to a deeper appreciation of God's handiwork. Embracing beauty allows us to become more attuned to the divine in our lives and in our neighbors, inspiring us to create environments where others can experience the sacred. Our field offers unique opportunities to present and to affirm *belles lettres* of ideas beautifully expressed.

Third, the concepts of *present-ness and presence* are essential for understanding our relationship with the Divine. *Dasein*, the uniquely human capacity for uncovering and revealing ourselves and other entities within our surroundings and within a context of relationships, particularly for those who seek to live Jesus's new commandment, emphasizes being fully engaged in the moment.[8] This mindfulness, promised in Jesus's farewell discourse in which he says "Those who have my commandments and keep them are those who love me and will be loved by my Father, and I love them and reveal myself to them" (John 14:21, NRSV, Catholic Edition), enables us to recognize Christ's presence in daily life.

Practicing present-ness—particularly in classrooms or faculty meetings—cultivates awareness that opens our hearts to the sacred. Engaging deeply with those around us, whether asking students what they thought of their presentation or lingering after class with a student or attending a student's performance, fosters authentic presence, where each moment becomes an encounter with Jesus.

Focal practices—i.e., activities that slow us down and help us to connect with ourselves, others, and the world around us—as Borgmann defines them include rituals, preparing a meal from scratch, playing guitar, or shared experiences, for example. Such practices serve as reminders of our faith and connection. We can foster these in our classes, in our discussions, group projects, workshops, and case studies: a Socratic dialogue discussing an ethical dilemma, in group projects in which students form a team to prepare a response to some communication conflict, creative workshop in which students swap drafts of their work critiquing a film and provide each other constructive feedback, or service learning projects in which students partner with a local non-profit and propose a plan for resolving some communication problem. Whether gathering for meals, participating in communal worship, or sharing stories, these focal points remind us of Christ's presence among us.

Finally, *interiority* refers to the inner life of an individual—the thoughts, emotions, and spiritual experiences that shape our worldviews. A sacramental view invites exploration of this inner dimension, recognizing our relationship with God and others as intertwined.

Cultivating our interior life helps us become attuned to the presence of Christ within. This awareness encourages introspection, prayer, and contemplation, allowing us to connect with the divine personally. As we grow spiritually, we see the sacred in our relationships, enhancing our capacity to love and serve. Such pedagogical practices as reflective writing (essays, journal writing), open discussions that invite conversation on personal values and beliefs, incorporation of literature and the arts, exercises that invite reflection on goals and aspirations can help students connect their academic journey to their interior lives

Moreover, interiority encourages confronting biases, fears, and insecurities. Acknowledging these aspects fosters compassion and understanding toward our neighbors. This journey inward deepens our connections, enabling us to recognize Jesus in each person we encounter and Jesus among us.

Conclusion

In closing, the themes of encountering Jesus in our neighbors and recognizing his presence among us are integral to living a sacramental life. By embracing encounter, beauty, present-ness, and interiority, we cultivate a spirituality rooted in community and love. As we gather in his name, we recognize that every interaction—whether with students, colleagues, or fellow members of the CCSN—is an opportunity to experience the Divine, transforming our lives and the lives of those around us.

In this way, the sacramental view enriches our individual spiritual journeys and strengthens community bonds, inviting us to live out Jesus's teachings in our daily lives. Through our encounters, we become vessels of Christ's love, embodying the sacred in a world longing for connection and grace.

Chapter 21

Merging Faith and Intellectual Pursuits in Christ-centered Universities

Donna M. Elkins

Response Summary: Legacy Scholar Richard J. Mouw's work has focused on the intersection of intellectual life and Christian faith. This short essay takes his work a bit further by interrogating the practice of Christian faith in the intellectual communities of Christian institutions of higher education. Using a question and response format, the chapter discusses some of the implications and added expectations for Christians working alongside each other in such a setting. Applying Communication Privacy Management (CPM) Theory is presented as one possible way for Christians to address the tensions of working in a theological, intellectual, and operational environment.

THROUGHOUT HIS WORK Richard Mouw, a professor and former president of Fuller Theological Seminary, has asked the question: What is the role of intellectual life for someone of the Christian faith? Mouw chose to answer the question in his 2014 book, titled *Called to the Life of the Mind*, and makes a clear case that evangelical beliefs and intellectual pursuits are not mutually exclusive. He describes a "meteoric" downpour of fragmented knowledge in our work today and believes that as Christians our hope and humility come from "the ultimate confidence that it all does really hang together" through "the One who is the Truth."[1] We can take heart from the promise that God will eventually lead us in to all knowledge, as we are patient in tolerating the complexities and particularities of what we know in the present.[2]

Based on Mouw's discussion of intellectual life and faith, and his preference for the idea that as Christians we are "world viewing" rather than "having a worldview," the way of interrogating the experience of present-day Christians in the workplace of a faith-based Academy seems best accomplished by asking questions that do not have quick or simple answers. The intellectual life of Christians is often carried out in the classrooms and offices of Christ-centered universities. Three questions are proposed here in relation to the particularities of working in a Christ-centered university where intellectual, professional, and faith lives merge.

Question One: What Makes this Close Combination of Faith and Work in Christ-centered Universities Unique?

The academic workplace, like others, is a site of both challenges and comforts. Those who pursue a position at a Christ-centered institution may not have considered the added pressures in such an environment. Requiring a public integration of faith with daily work can impact relationships between faculty, staff, and students. If you and your supervisor are involved in Bible studies together, how does that change the expectations of the way negative information will be delivered or challenging messages conveyed? What damage is done to people's faith if this communication is not handled in every situation with care? Does it become more or less difficult to correct a person whom you supervise, but with whom you have also prayed and sang during worship in the morning chapel? How do the same general dynamics affect the way you provide feedback or grading to students in your class? Is it possible to maintain "professional" and "faith-based" relationships with individuals without conflicting overlap or intersection?

The secular academic world tends to be skeptical about Christians' ability to separate the intellectual from faith, declaring that Christians struggle to empirically examine their own beliefs. Well-known professor Stanley Fish, though not religious himself, made the case that if one does believe in God, it actually should change everything else and limit the ability to interact with some intellectual ideas.[3] Religious beliefs involve affirmations about reality and values that cannot simply be turned off and on from worship to work.[4] Therefore, engagement with students and ideas in the classroom and colleagues inside the faith-based institution take on a layer of expectation that requires extra navigation.

Question Two: What is the Role of the Christ-centered University?

Though mission statements of faith-based universities may differ, a common essential element is that faith in Christ is part of educating the whole student to spiritual as well as intellectual formation. But what does such a university hold for the faculty and staff members who make it their workplace? Ann Garrido, in her book *Redeeming Administration*, argues that even though those in administrative duties in Christian higher education are motivated primarily to serve others, their work encourages and edifies them in their own spiritual journey as well.[5] Therefore, she presents twelve habits or characteristics that administrators in Christian education environments can develop through challenging encounters and daily activities. One characteristic Garrido addresses is integrity. She asks how one addresses certain personal shortcomings, such as reluctance to work less, meet deadlines, or forgive in a conflict, when expecting the opposite from students or colleagues.[6] Another characteristic Garrido addresses is hope, which she sees exemplified in the role of Christian education administrators, who even in the face of what at times seem insurmountable challenges, maintain hope that they are participating in God's plan. Hope magnifies all of the other Christian habits, Garrido concludes.[7] Is the role of the Christ-centered university therefore to develop values and characteristics in the faculty and staff who work there as much as in the students they mentor?

Question Three: How do Employees at Christ-centered Universities Best Navigate the Challenges of Combining Intellectual Work and Faith with Colleagues and Students?

As described, faculty and staff face unique operational versus theological roles in the Christ-centered university environment. Though there are no easy answers to this question, one communication theory can be of use. In 2002, communication scholar Sandra Petronio published *Boundaries of Privacy: Dialectics of Disclosure*, which included the consolidation of her research about managing privacy. She proposed Communication Privacy Management (CPM) Theory, which features five primary principles related to how individuals regulate disclosing and concealing private information: (1) individuals believe they own their private information and set boundaries around it; (2) individuals therefore believe they have the right to control the flow of their private information to others; (3) individuals develop privacy rules to decide whether to open a privacy boundary and disclose, or rather to keep the boundary closed to conceal; (4) once individuals reveal something private they make others shareholders of the information and presume those others will follow existing privacy rules or openly negotiate to change them; and (5) privacy management issues can become turbulent if there is a disruption or violation of privacy expectations which may result in distrust, anger, suspicion, or uncertainty about relationships.[8]

In the integration of intellectual pursuits, faith, and work, individuals would do well to consider the privacy needs of themselves and others before crossing boundaries and sharing private information widely with fellow Christian students and colleagues. Privacy considerations in this setting mimic those in any professional setting. Therefore, determining boundaries for sharing personal faith and professional operational issues are still needed in the Christ-centered workplace, as is the constant awareness that the methods, tone, and delivery of all communication may face heightened expectations.

Mouw ended his comments during the conference interview with the question: What are we longing for? When thinking about the intersection of intellect, knowledge, business, and faith in the Christ-centered universities of today, that may be the most important question of all.

Chapter 22

Between Technology and Tyranny: Twin Threats for Christian Higher Education

David Dockery

Response Summary: Mark Noll in *The Scandal of the Evangelical Mind* provides a renewed assessment of Christian higher education in this new era. He argues that Christians in higher education continue to face threats from ideologically driven forces and the university's reduction to a mere economic resource. This chapter elaborates on the nature of the threats Noll identifies. It argues that the true purpose of a university is knowledge. The arts and sciences both have their own way of straying from this telos, a danger Christian educators must remain aware of.

IN HIS LEGACY SCHOLAR presentation on the state of the "evangelical mind," Mark Noll notes that while some aspects of the situation have improved, "the landscape remains treacherous."[1] He specifically pinpoints the reduction of the university into a job training center and the growing ideological divide as threats.[2] There is much to say about this topic, but for this brief essay I want to elaborate on the threats Noll identifies. My thesis is that higher education generally, but especially Christian higher education, is endangered by distortions that impose predetermined ends or purposes on the sciences and the humanities. That is, the sciences and the humanities can become directed toward the wrong ends. The sciences, when corrupted, cease to be about discovery and become mere instruments of profit. Conversely, when the humanities become corrupt, they abandon the goal of human cultivation and become over-concerned with power. These two temptations—toward obsession with profit on one hand and obsession with power on the other—constitute twin threats that can destroy the Academy if left unchecked.

Vice and Virtue in Higher Education

As Aristotle taught, virtue is "to act in conformity with right principle,"[3] and this is a good place to start when analyzing the state of higher education. The right principle of higher education is education itself, which is about the pursuit of knowledge for its own sake. For Christian higher education, the pursuit of knowledge is a way of pursuing God, who is the source of all truth. Thus, if a university is virtuous, its main activity should be the search for knowledge.

The university errs when the pursuit of knowledge becomes secondary to something else. "Something else" could be anything—football games, social organizations, politics, or any other activity. It does not matter whether the activity is good or ill; it *becomes* bad when it usurps the university's main mission. A hospital that prioritizes good cafeteria food over healing patients is a bad hospital. In the same way, a university that prioritizes any activity above the pursuit of knowledge is a bad university. It fails to live up to its nature.

Since the subjects of study can be divided into the arts and sciences, higher education is always threatened by vices unique to each. Subjects falling under the genus of "arts" include fields of study such as music, philosophy, literature, and so forth. Also called the humanities or the liberal arts, these disciplines can develop an unhealthy interest in power. The sciences typically include physics, biology, chemistry, engineering—what we now call "STEM" fields. The quintessential STEM vice is the pursuit of technology—the instruments of material domination—over discovery. Of course, there are many other disciplines that straddle both worlds and can therefore suffer from both vices; these include fields such as sociology, communication studies, and psychology.

The Vice of Technology

Within STEM fields, the primary way the pursuit of knowledge can be betrayed is by leveraging it for the pursuit of profit. The sciences are about solving the puzzles of our universe, thereby revealing a greater appreciation for God's work in creation. But some puzzles are more profitable than others, and their profitability can assume oversized importance. Good science should be *objective*, that is, it should be driven by the object of study and not merely the interests of the scientist. However, the potential profitability of a project can threaten the objectivity necessary for a thorough investigation. When the researcher faces pressure to care more about potential technologies and profits from that technology, it compromises the pursuit of scientific knowledge.

Technology represents the instrumentalization of science. It thus abandons scientific study for its own sake. Knowledge ceases to be important just because it is knowledge. The value of knowledge becomes tied to its usefulness. Why should I care about the chemical composition of a rock? What value does that provide to shareholders? Such problems even abound in social sciences. What use is this behavioral theory for selling products? As soon as these questions dominate scientific discourse, science falls into corruption. Its claims to knowledge can no longer be trusted because science has become the mere instrument for achieving the interests of others.

Of course, technology is not intrinsically bad. The problem is the vice of technology, not technology itself. When the goal of a discipline is the discovery of technology, such as in certain engineering disciplines, it makes perfect sense. In other, non-technology focused sciences, technological discovery is fine *so long as it is not the main point*. It should be a byproduct of genuine discovery.

For the Christian, the vice of technology is a spiritual danger as well. To see a truth of nature is to recognize the hand of the Creator. By abandoning objectivity, the scientist loses the ability to appreciate God's world and reduces his work to raw material. Furthermore, abandoning the spirit of objectivity often coincides with pride. Objectivity requires emptying the self to fill it with knowledge of the object of study. Reducing science to a mere instrument, however, puts the self at the center of investigation. The question is no longer "What has God made?" but "What's in it for me?" Thus, technological vice is a spiritual danger scientists and Christian universities should avoid.

The Vice of Tyranny

If the vice of the sciences is instrumentalization, the vice of the humanities is an unhealthy pursuit of power. This may, at first glance, sound ridiculous. It is hardly as if academic rhetoricians and philosophers hold significant political power. Yet in an indirect sense, they do. Scholars of the liberal arts craft the social theories that permeate public discourse and shape the public mind. These become the basis of political action. What lawyer or politician achieves their aims without some understanding of human nature, without the ability to bend the public will? Diligently pursued, the humanities can lead to great power—sometimes at the expense of their *telos*.

Traditionally, the humanities have been about human cultivation. Hans-Georg Gadamer is representative of this view when he describes the humanistic pursuit as "rising to the universal."[4] More colloquially, one might call it being "well-rounded." Humans have latent abilities that need to be exercised to achieve their full potential. Appreciating music, understanding literature, engaging in philosophical debate, and reading history are activities that elevate the human out of living a mere animalistic existence. Engaging in them is not merely an exercise in power. The true student of the humanities pursues them simply to become better at being human.

Christians should especially care about the humanities because the call of God is to become truly human. Humans were made in God's image, yet we have rejected that image through sin. The humanities are one way of reclaiming our original purpose: To glorify God by reflecting him in all we do. God has imbued in each human soul a tiny sliver of his divine majesty: the ability to create, the power of language, the sensitivity to beauty, and the wisdom to see beyond the surface of matters to the truth. Every Christian should care about engaging the abilities God has given them, to become an encompassing thinker who integrates all of life into the divine image.

Yet scholars of the humanities lately have zeroed in on one specific part of humanity: power. Look at the syllabi of the average graduate course in rhetoric, particularly at elite universities. Comb through leading journals in disciplines such as literature and philosophy. Check what books are coming out of the prominent university presses. Does power not feature prominently in most, if not all?

There is a place for studies of power, especially in disciplines like rhetoric. However, it increasingly creeps into every aspect of academic inquiry. For instance, it is highly unlikely that one will publish a paper of rhetorical criticism that focuses on whether a speech was beautiful or truthful. Reviewers are more interested in analyses of power relations. Asking

"Is the speech beautiful?" is likely to be considered less interesting than "Who does the concept of beauty marginalize?" There is a place for such questions, but not at the expense of other interesting questions.

Purposefully or inadvertently, many humanities scholars have replaced human cultivation with the love of power—in other words, tyranny. For in David Roochnik's reading of Plato, the love of power *is* the definition of a tyrant.[5] Certainly, not all scholars of the humanities who study power are tyrants. It is possible to know power without loving it. But the general tenor of disciplines like literature, art, and communication suggests that a good many have slipped into an unhealthy love of power. When every discussion is about who should have power and who should not, when every theory is a lens for finding subtle power relations in literature, when humanities scholars routinely dream of changing (or destroying) the System, when these theories go unquestioned because they have been rendered unquestionable—one knows the love of power has taken root.

This love of power is directly contrary to the goal of the humanities. Part of being an encompassing thinker is learning to master the inner tyrant. The humanist transcends the self by learning to take a broad perspective, to see the world from many angles, and to contemplate higher truths. Tyrants can see it from only one: Who has power and who does not. Consequently, there can only be one question: How do we change this situation? The very question presupposes that scholars have the authority to answer it. This narrowing of one's vision represents a surrender to the inner tyrant and a failure of humanistic education.

In the spirit of charity, one must acknowledge that these discussions of power are often framed within the context of justice. But justice, much like truth and beauty, have been flattened in many of these conversations. One is told that justice is a matter of power, much like how claims to truth disguise power. Genuine discussions of justice are important—important enough to recognize the inherent nuances of the concept. The theories driving scholarly discourse seem uninterested in them.

The vice of the humanities, then, is the vice of tyranny. It is abandoning the quest to grow into the image of God and replacing it with the quest for human power. The study of power is important, but when it is not tempered with developing other aspects of the human being, it narrows one's vision. Insofar as humanistic education is about becoming a well-rounded person, it is directly contrary to it.

Finding the Virtuous Middle

Even within the context of Christian higher education, it is all too easy to fall into these vices. There is constant pressure to raise enrollment and promise "good" jobs for graduates. Administrators and scholars should not be blamed for struggling with the complicated academic environment of our world. Finding a middle way through the vices can be difficult.

Despite these challenges, it is crucial to remain true to higher education's calling. Giving in may provide short-term benefits, but it will result in long-term destruction. Nothing can save an institution that has abandoned its reason for being. Once people realize that there is nothing Christian about this Christian university anymore, it will become just another secular college competing with much larger and stronger secular colleges. Even if it succeeds, it will be a hollow victory. For in the words of Jesus, "What good is it for someone to gain the whole world, yet forfeit their soul?" (Mark 8:36). That is the danger: Losing the university's soul.

Fortunately, it is also true that "God did not send his Son into the world to condemn the world, but to save the world through him" (John 3:17). No Christian university that remains true to its calling will finally be condemned. It may lose the prestige of this world, it may suffer at the hands of those who have succumbed to these vices, it may even have to close its doors. But it will not lose its soul. Nothing can take that away except itself.

The commendation of our Master is greater than any prize this world can give. It should therefore be pursued with the utmost vigor, at the expense of everything else. The unique way a Christian university can pursue this is by creating a community of scholars who diligently and effectively labor to equip and empower students to earn an authentically Christian education.

Such an education pursues knowledge itself, and in doing so, encounters the author of all knowledge. It cultivates the character of students so they can experience the full range of humanity God has bestowed on each one of them. When these pillars stand, everything else can find its true purpose. Such a university has no cause for shame.

Noll was right: The landscape of higher education is treacherous. That treachery, I contend, comes from both the arts and the sciences. Both have their own way of betraying what it means to be a Christian university. Yet when pursued correctly, Christian universities still have tremendous potential to illuminate the universe and cultivate the image of God present in all. It is for Christian higher education to pursue that calling.

Chapter 23

Communication Challenges for Christian Higher Education

REID VANCE

Response Summary: This essay extends Marsden's reflection in this volume on the unique role Christian higher education might play in restoring biblical truth in the Academy. The author suggests that Christian faculty and administrators must first answer three essential questions regarding their institutions: (1) Who are we, and who are we not? (2) What makes us distinct? and (3) how can this be our moment? Additionally, faculty and administrators must answer questions about the distinctions between their universities and other Christian colleges in areas such as student life, commitment to service, faith and learning integration, and vocational preparation. In so doing, challenges await regarding institutional identity, cultural representation, and value creation. Christian institutions that can meet each challenge will be those that emerge from a time of uncertainty as healthy institutions.

ALTHOUGH GEORGE MARSDEN, in *The Outrageous Idea of Christian Scholarship*, focused on the possibilities for faithful teaching and research by Christian scholars at any college or university, he highlighted the unique role of Christian higher education.[1] While he has since noted that some of his detractors have called his ideas "loony," his thinking about faith and scholarship has endured and remains relevant to Christian professionals in the academic and administrative ranks at any institution.

Christian higher education indeed remains in a unique position to build on Marsden's invitation to offer an educational experience characterized by both academic excellence and theological fidelity. As a professor of communication in Christian higher education who aspires to think and act and write and produce work in a way that is faithful to biblical truth, promotes the common good, and sets a good example for my students and colleagues, Marsden's words are both hopeful and challenging to me. They should also be hopeful and challenging to everyone in Christian higher education who has the task of communication in their job description—that is, *everyone* in Christian higher education.

Specifically, I and my fellow Christian college communicators must stand ready to provide answers to three essential questions that demand reflection, discussion, and action. First, who are we, and who are we not? Second, what makes us distinct? Third, and finally, how can this be our moment? As an important part of addressing these questions, we must also be prepared to address the three challenges of identity, culture, and value.

Who are We, and Who are We Not?

In his 2024 remarks to the Christianity and Communication Studies Network (CCSN), Marsden identified the defining characteristic of Christian scholarship: the role of personal faith in the life of the scholar. Marsden identified a Christian scholar as one whose faith largely shapes their scholarly agenda.[2] What makes a particular exercise in scholarship Christian is less about its content (to appropriate an overused term in contemporary media) and more about the faith commitment of the individual scholar. The scholar's commitment is to the discovery and interpretation of truth that is brought forth by and presented in a way consistent with Christian belief and behavior.

The parallels associated with this categorization are true for persons in any number of communication-related fields. For example, a Christian journalist would likely claim his commitment to uncovering and reporting facts is guided by a work ethic that aligns with values such as the Golden Rule. A Christian public relations practitioner would likely perform her duties in such a way to meet the highest professional standards without resorting to actions that might distort facts, manipulate people, or violate Christian ethical standards.

So, too, Christian scholars should be dedicated to the highest ideals of the scholarly vocation, employ best practices available to all scholars while avoiding methods and habits that might violate biblical standards or bring disrepute to the Christian community. But at a deeper level, it is not enough for Christian scholars to allow their faith commitments to serve as hedges against the worst in professional practice. The faith commitment of a Christian scholar should serve as a motivation for doing the best work possible in ways that honor God and enhance the reputation of the Christian community.

What is true for individual scholars is true, too, for Christian colleges and universities as institutions. Like their secular counterparts, Christian colleges and universities should be devoted to the highest ideals of scholarship. No matter how individual institutions choose to express their faith commitments as institutions, those commitments should, in fact, *be* expressed. If they are not, what truly sets Christian colleges and universities apart from public or other institutions of higher learning?

Therefore, it is how a Christian college expresses its faith commitments, and how those commitments are communicated to various audiences, that sets it apart from public and other private colleges and distinguishes it among its peers. The defining question for Christian higher education leaders and communicators—"Who are we, and who are we not?"—is central to its institutional identity.

Christian higher education is more diverse in its identity formation and approach to scholarship than might be realized. On one end of the faith and learning spectrum are fundamentalist-oriented Bible schools or undergraduate schools operated by evangelical seminaries. Christian scholars at these institutions may or may not be compelled to abide by interpretations of Scripture that, while promoting doctrinal purity with the institution's particular theological tradition, may, in some ways and to varying degrees of effectiveness, limit what can and cannot be taught. As a result, such institutions are often misperceived by many outside their tribe (and especially by scholars in secular higher education) as being unserious about scholarship.

On the other end of this faith and learning spectrum are Christian institutions that have loosened if not entirely shed their church or denominational affiliations and abandoned their fidelity to and promotion of explicitly Christian beliefs and practices. Though founded by Christian churches and denominations, they've made intentional decisions to no longer be known by their Christian heritage. Scholars at these universities that remain Christian (often literally) in name only are free to pursue truth wherever the discovery process leads, but Christian beliefs have no bearing on their teaching or research. In fact, outright hostility to orthodox Christian faith can increasingly be found among scholars at these institutions.

Most Christian colleges and universities, however, are situated in a vast middle religious ground of the faith and learning spectrum. Most of the universities in this middle space of Christian higher education have retained an emphasis on the authority of the Bible, how the Bible speaks to the values that should guide intellectual inquiry, and an appreciation of church history that continues to guide community formation and cultural engagement. In practice, they reject the extremes of the spectrum. In scholarly engagement, admissions practices, and cultural engagement, they focus on how biblical truth should inform both scholarly pursuits and student development.

Marsden suggests that this middle ground offers the wisest path forward for Christian colleges and universities in their quest to be taken seriously as places of scholarly inquiry. "Liberal arts colleges with strong religious identities and some openness to the larger academic community" he writes, "are in the best position to encourage serious Christian academic discourse."[3]

What does this mean for the Christian college communicator? If "Who are we, and who are we not?" is the defining question of Christian higher education, the most important task of professional and scholarly communicators at Christian institutions is to provide clear and honest answers to that question. No matter where an institution is on the spectrum, Christian college and university communicators must be proactive, confident, truthful tellers of their institution's story.

For better or worse, Americans' perceptions of Christian higher education are shaped by mass and social media. Christian higher education professionals have the responsibility to make the best possible use of media strategies and channels at their disposal to tell their stories in ways most journalists cannot or will not do. The story of Christian higher education will be told with or without the people who know and value its contributions to scholarship and cultural engagement. It is in the interest of each Christian college or university to be intentional about shaping that narrative.

What Makes Us Distinct?

"Even when schools retain a substantial church affiliation," Marsden notes, "most of what is taught in their classrooms, except for Bible and theology courses, is indistinguishable from what is taught in state universities."[4] I have never personally engaged the author on this point, but I doubt that Marsden meant this observation as a compliment to Christian colleges and universities. The second key question for faculty and other leaders in Christian higher education, therefore, is "What makes us distinct?" And again, it falls to the communication professionals at Christian institutions to provide a clear and compelling answer to the question.

Marsden alluded to the appropriate answer and focus in his remarks to the CCSN audience, claiming that "[w]e seek to identify root truth, faith-based wisdom, *in tune with Scripture* but also proven by history and empirical investigation"[5] The idea of being "in tune with" the teaching of the Bible is something that secular higher education simply cannot do.

Yet even among Christian institutions, there is room for variety in response. "Different Christian theological and biblical traditions," in Marsden's view, "often bring their own strengths to the general goal of Christian scholarship."[6] In essence, not all Christian colleges and universities need to be the same. This is good news! Such conformity is both impractical and unhealthy for the body of Christ.

Think of the Baskin-Robbins ice cream experience. The famous Baskin-Robbins shops offer a broad variety of ice cream and other frozen treats. Indeed, the company made its name by deviating from the once standard and limited options of vanilla, chocolate, or strawberry. For Burt Baskin and Irv Robbins, no fewer than 31 flavors were enough! Today, the company boasts over 1,400 creative options for their customers.[7] Yet every flavor is of the same, time-tested, inherently desirable product that never disappoints on a warm summer day: cold, delicious, flavorful, hand-scooped ice cream.

There's room for many flavors of Christian higher education, too: Reformed, Pentecostal, Baptist, Wesleyan, fundamentalist (and perhaps even Catholic if the definition is stretched beyond Protestantism). Distinctions abound among each flavor of Christian college. Yet, generally speaking, enough commonality exists among Christian institutions that most are willing, through voluntary associations, to self-identify with other colleges and universities that take similar approaches to faith and learning.

One prominent example is the Council for Christian College and Universities (CCCU), a nearly 50-year-old organization of more than 170 schools worldwide whose mission is "to advance the cause of Christ-centered higher education and to help our institutions transform lives by faithfully relating scholarship and service to biblical truth."[8] CCCU members see themselves as different from secular colleges and universities, and their tent is big enough to include a diverse number of colleges and universities who fully integrate biblical truth into the college experience, seek to advance the spiritual and moral formation of their students, and produce graduates who do good in the world.[9] The continued relevance of Christian higher education depends on administrative and faculty communicators at these institutions who can contrast the mission and work of their colleges and universities with that of their secular counterparts.

Yet even within the larger-than-perceived tent of Christian higher education, distinctives thankfully persist. The result is both friendly cooperation on important scholarship and other initiatives and healthy, engaging competition among Christian colleges. Especially as it relates to enrollment strategies, the work of professional communicators within Christian higher education often reflects the reality of such competition.

Communication professionals must therefore prepare key university faculty and administrators to answer questions about the distinctions between their universities and other Christian colleges in areas such as student life, commitment to service, faith and learning integration, and vocational preparation. They must develop strategies and employ tactics to gain the attention of a pool of prospective undergraduate students often focused as much on student life as academic reputation. (Indeed, Christian higher education communicators have, in the past, often focused primarily on aspects of student life to differentiate themselves from the competition, especially to parents increasingly unsold of the value of college in general and wary of what much of public and non-sectarian private higher education has to offer.) And they must also help graduate school enrollment personnel tell the institution's story to audiences of non-traditional college ages and seasons of life who are increasingly focused on value and convenience.

In fact, the answer to the question "What makes us distinct?" becomes essential when prospective students and their families begin to compare the cost of a Christian higher education with one from a public higher education. Communication professionals may exercise little control over such a decisive factor. But they should advocate for having their voices heard in their institution's fiscal planning. For families who are looking for every edge in affordability, a commitment to Christian scholarship and the values and practices that accompany such a commitment may make a wary parent more likely to trust a son and daughter with a Christian college rather than with a state or other private university. It is no stretch to believe that the answer to the question, "Why should students choose a smaller, usually more expensive Christian college over a larger, often more affordable state university?" may represent the greatest challenge for Christian higher education communicators today.

If only for the sake of institutional survival, therefore, families of all religious backgrounds, or none at all, must be given compelling reasons to choose Christian higher education. Faculty and administrators at Christian colleges and universities must know what makes their institutions distinct, and they must articulate those distinctions in such a way that prospective students from all faith backgrounds or none at all see the value in what their peculiar brand of higher education has to offer.

How Can This Be Our Moment?

Research suggests that students of all religious backgrounds—and those having no religious background at all—expect their college experience to be one that engages them with matters of life purpose and meaning, and they expect college faculty and administrators to help them find it.[10] This finding is good news for Christian higher education! As Marsden noted, "Church-related liberal arts colleges are finding that, having preserved some of their traditional ways, they are now offering more of what people are looking for in higher education and hence are ahead of the game."[11]

As much of American higher education has become commodified and homogenized, and as many campuses are only now emerging from years of social, political, and cultural controversies, the opening exists for Christian colleges and universities to truly stand out among the increasing number of educational opportunities that include, among other options, in-person courses, online instruction, and self-paced learning. In fact, Christian higher education would be wise to continue the development of each of these delivery systems in developing new and culturally engaging scholars.

It follows that if the product—a degree, an experience, a micro-credential, or something else—is no longer packaged as one-size-fits-all, Christian college communicators need to be ready to employ a variety of tactics to reach their institutions' goals regarding enrolling, retaining, and graduating their students. Specifically, three challenges await faculty and administrators whose job it is, on any number of levels, to get the word out about what Christian higher education and their particular institutions have to offer.

The Identity Challenge

This challenge relates to the question of "Who are we, and who are we not?" More precisely, it is about what kind of an institution each Christian college or university wants to be in the public eye. For some universities, being a *Christian* college may be enough of a separator. For example, a smaller university in a largely secular region of the U.S. will likely stand out among other post-secondary options. For universities that remain only loosely tied to mainline Protestant denominations and to those colleges that remain tightly bound to their Christian roots, the identity challenges may center around how their institution is different from private higher education at large.

But for most Christian universities, the identity challenge involves to what degree they are willing to embrace the idea of being *evangelical*. Unfortunately, the term evangelical in the public imagination is increasingly associated with something other than a faith commitment or a set of religious principles. Instead, it is taken on political and ideological meanings, much to the dismay of many Bible-believing, evangelism-focused Christians and their institutions who now struggle with determining how much the label evangelical is worth fighting for.

For those evangelical colleges and universities that remain committed to the label, their identity challenge will be to provide clarity on what exactly they mean by their use of the descriptor. As Marsden noted in his comments to the CCSN, "Politics has become the religion, even the primary religion, for an awful lot of people on both sides of the political spectrum."[12] Christian colleges and universities that choose to identify with any one political ideology or movement may find their reach limited to members of that tribe.

Some institutions will no doubt follow the pattern of local churches which create statements based on, and often using the exact words of, Scripture itself. Functionally, this method is not difficult. Thousands of dollars and hours have spent by local churches in creating mission statements that the typical faithful Bible reader could create with a simple Mad Lib's-style exercise. Other institutions may choose to use comparative terminology to set themselves apart not from public and non-sectarian private colleges but from other Christian institutions. Denominational affiliation may continue to play a key role in these college's identification effort.

In any case, clear and concise communication of a Christian college or university's identity will be a growing challenge in the future. The words that Christian college communicators use to define their institutions, and how they communicate who they are to any number of publics, may matter now more than ever.

The Cultural Challenge

Closely associated with the identity challenge is a cultural challenge facing Christian college communicators. Christian colleges and universities have always shaped culture to a lesser degree. At the very least, Christian colleges have shaped a particular sub-culture, members of which have spent a great deal of time responding to or (often poorly) imitating culture at large. This trend is especially evident in the arts where Christians tend to be consistently a few years behind the culture in producing mostly imitative work.

More often, however, Christian colleges and universities have occupied a defensive position regarding culture. We have been known by what we are against, what we do not allow our students to do, and what we do not tolerate on our campuses. These postures, though they may be appropriate given an institution's histories and faith commitments, may be perceived as problematic if not discriminatory by large segments of the public.

How should Christian communicators in the faculty and administrative positions respond? Marsden, in his comments to CCSN, gives us a helpful framework: "Christian scholars ought to be known as those who really are patient champions of law and order, employing solid evidence, good arguments, and personal integrity, and as those who recognize the same among those with who we disagree."[13]

One could make an argument that Christian higher education has the opportunity to shape a new counterculture, one that could match the influence of mid-twentieth century radicalism but without the violence. "It is important," Marsden declared, "for us to emphasize the integration of Christian scholarship and the Christian virtues. . . . We should speak the truth in love."[14] Such an approach clashes with contemporary societal discourse which promotes the notion that political and cultural opponents are best eradicated. The triumphalism of extremes may be socially ascendant, but humility, service, and respect remain fundamental virtues for both the Christian and the Christian higher education communicator.

The Value Challenge

Finally, every faculty member and administrator at a Christian college or university must understand that Christian higher education will never cost less than it does today. You do not need to be an economist to realize that, on average, the costs of goods and services never go down. I say this with great respect for my fellow Christian college professionals: If we are waiting for our institutions to become less expensive to attract the students we want, we are ignorant, delusional, or both.

And like every other industry, Christian higher education has exercised in recent years three options: cut expenses, increase revenues, or a combination of both. Many Christian colleges have already cut expenses. Academic programs have been shuttered. Faculty have been laid off, regardless of tenure. Administrative staff have been let go.

Athletics programs have disappeared overnight. Buildings have been closed. Online in-struction has been embraced as a possible cost-savings move or as an institutional savior (though in reality, it is neither).

Still other Christian university leaders have looked for new revenue streams. They have diversified their institutional portfolios. They have begun to recruit more non-tra-ditional demographics. They are dabbling in real estate development. They are partnering with secondary education. They've renewed church and denominational affiliations long strained by the independent trustee movement of the late twentieth century. Such efforts may indeed be worthwhile and can provide valuable financial lifelines.

But most Christian colleges and universities will continue to both cut expenses and work to increase revenue. Most institutions are likely to explore any combination of the options noted above. Like other businesses, the fiscally fittest will survive while others likely will not. And like other businesses, those Christian colleges and universities that can offer the best overall value in a college education will find students and their families willing to pay.

Therefore, all Christian colleges and universities, along with their faculty and admin-istrators, must be good marketers and public relations practitioners. They can no longer assume that people know of their existence much less naturally want what they have to offer. And they can no longer assume that prospective students and their families will instinc-tively value what they have to offer more highly than that of the competition simply because of their institution's claim to a Christian commitment.

Based on media portrayals of varying degrees of accuracy, potential students and their parents are right to question the current value and values of American higher education. In a world where "Is college worth it?" is now a legitimate question, Christian colleges that can't convince prospective students and parents that the educational opportunities they provide will produce real value will not survive—and deservedly so. But those Christian institutions that can demonstrate real value to students, offer clear and compelling answers to questions of institutional identity, and provide a campus climate in which students can become shapers of culture have a moment ready to be seized.

Chapter 24

The Catholic University: Preserving the Mission Amidst Contemporary Pressures

Kathleen M. Edelmayer

Response Summary: Higher education in the United States faces financial, ideological, and functional challenges and pressures from society and from within the Academy. Additionally, debate continues regarding the intersections of faith and reason in higher education within public and private institutions. Previous research by Mark Noll and George Marsden examined the role of Christian scholarship in higher education. This essay reflects on those works as well as their recent essays and Fr. Paul A. Soukup's essay on Catholic education. It examines current pressures on higher education, the impact on Catholic universities, and offers strategies Catholic institutions might enact to uphold their unique identity and mission while addressing financial pressures, a more diverse student body, and social and political challenges.

OVER THE YEARS, much has been written about the role of the Catholic university. In the U.S., major documents range from the *Land O'Lakes Statement* (1967) to *The Application of Ex Corde Ecclesiae for the United States* (1999).[1] Contemporary papal documents include *Fides et Ratio* (1998) and *Ex Corde Ecclesiae* (1990).[2] While there is debate and competing interpretations of documents, through all, one concept is consistent: faith and reason are intertwined and fundamental to Catholic education.

According to the Association of Catholic Colleges and Universities, there are approximately 230 Catholic colleges and universities in the United States, not including seminaries. Most of the institutions identify with a specific religious order, tradition, or diocese.[3] While there is no single framework for Catholic universities, there are several beliefs they hold in common. Paul A. Soukup, SJ, provides an extensive description of the nature of Catholic higher education, with an emphasis on the Jesuit tradition.[4] The parallels between the Jesuit tradition and the Felician Franciscan tradition, of which imbues Madonna University, are extensive.

In this essay, I will discuss current pressures on higher education and offer strategies Catholic institutions might enact to uphold their unique identity and mission while addressing financial pressures, a more diverse student body, and social and political challenges. This reflection will engage with Paul A. Soukup, SJ's and Mark Noll's unconference essays as well as Mark Noll's and George Marsden's works from the 1990s. I will begin, however, with a brief description of my personal experiences as it influences this writing and then address many of the strengths in Catholic higher education today.

As a Catholic, my faith influences both my personal and professional life. I attended Catholic schools from fifth through 12th grade. However, my undergraduate and graduate experiences were at large-scale public universities studying economics and communication. My teaching experiences have been at public universities, a Lutheran college, a college in the "Methodist tradition," and, for the past 26 years, Catholic institutions. Throughout this time, even in state universities, I have not experienced religious hostility or unacceptance. In fact, my experience was the opposite; religion was not a topic to be shunned but instead proactively discussed, and I was able to follow my research interests in political and religious communication. Though, clearly, this is not the experience for many.

Strengths of Catholic Higher Education in the United States

Throughout the unconference essays, there is broad agreement that there is indeed much to celebrate in regard to Christian scholarship. This is the case in the Catholic context as well. Drawing on Soukup's framework, I argue many of the strengths of Catholic higher education parallel the four key principles of Jesuit education: "(1) the mode of education, (2) an approach to the individual, (3) an education rooted in a community environment, and (4) a commitment to justice."[5] That is, learning should be engaging and purposeful to match the needs of the students. Education should address the "whole person" including their spiritual and social formation to recognize and honor the unity of all people of the world. And with that unity in mind, students should engage the local community through service and develop a life-long commitment to "build a more just world."

My institution, Madonna University, is a Felician Franciscan university rooted in the beliefs of St. Francis of Assisi. The Association of Franciscan Colleges and Universities describes the three characteristics of the Franciscan Tradition as sacramental, relational, and grounded in Gospel values.[6] It is sacramental as "all creation is in the Incarnate Word;" all creation reflects God's goodness and beauty and, therefore, diversity is to be celebrated, and all creation must be respected.[7] The Franciscan Tradition focuses on relationships among all people, promotes peacemaking, gives voice to all, and promotes justice. The tradition is grounded in the Gospels through both belief and action. Based on these characteristics, a Franciscan education should recognize education as a gift to be developed and shared; service to others is essential, and one should engage ethically to serve the larger community. Madonna University applies the Franciscan Tradition through the Felician values of respect for the dignity of each person, peace and justice, reverence for creation, and education for truth and service. These values are foundational to all aspects of our university. Similar values are reflected at Catholic institutions throughout the country.

Service is one value that is prevalent at many Catholic colleges and universities. The Association of Franciscan Colleges and Universities supports its 22 member institutions through its mission of "providing exceptional education, fostering compassion, and instilling a sense of service."[8] Service connects the institutions with the community. Service may be through academic service-learning opportunities, clinicals, advocacy for community groups, offering support services to K–12 communities, and extensive academic programs for "service" professions as health care, social work, education, and criminal justice.

A second value evident in many Catholic institutions is the work with various cultures and religions. At our institution, we have worked with the Felician Sisters of North America to develop a bachelor's degree in business for students in Haiti. While their program is fully online, many can travel to campus to participate in commencement celebrations. We also have degree completion programs with a university in Dubai. On our own campus, we have ethnic, religious, racial, and international diversity in our student body. Many Catholic colleges and universities have developed interfaith dialogue departments or programs. Select examples include Madonna University, Catholic University, Benedictine University, Xavier University, St. Francis College, and the College of St. Benedict's/St. John's in Minnesota. Such interfaith programs are rooted in the ecumenical framework of Vatican II.

Finally, academic excellence is a value of all Catholic institutions. One example of such excellence is The University of Notre Dame's Department of Theology which was ranked best theology, divinity, and religious studies department in the world by QS World Rankings, the fourth such honor since 2020.[9] Boston College and KU Leuven were the two other Catholic institutions in the top 10.[10]

The "Treacherous Landscape" Applied

Although progress continues, there are still many struggles. In his unconference document, Mark Noll notes that "the landscape is treacherous."[11] Many of the concerns he identifies are relevant to public and private higher education, including the "economic self-interest . . . to find their first money-producing job" and political partisanship and identity politics.[12] In this section, I will address how these challenges are reflected in Catholic higher education today.

Social and Political Environment Challenges

The first challenge is the financial pressures on the American system of higher education as a whole. In large part because of these pressures, institutions are making major cuts to personnel and academic programs. In addition, students and parents are understandably concerned about employment opportunities, future salaries, and large student debt, and colleges have responded in part by emphasizing the sciences and professional and pre-professional majors at the expense of other areas. In Catholic institutions, unfortunately, the largest cuts are often in the humanities and specifically in theology and religious studies programs. Recently we have seen the elimination of theology and religious studies at Marymount University in Virginia and St. Mary's University of Minnesota in 2003 and St. Norbert College in Wisconsin in 2025,[13] to name a few. These developments are particularly disturbing since theology and religious studies are one of the major foundations of a Catholic university.

Since the start of 2025, there have been unsettling developments related to government policies concerning higher education, specifically with respect to identity politics.

The February "Dear Colleagues" letter from the United States Department of Education calls for, among other things, institutions to abandon DEI initiatives under the guise of "discrimination."[14] In April, the U.S. Supreme Court heard the Oklahoma case addressing whether public funds could support a Catholic charter school (*Oklahoma Statewide Charter School Board v. Drummond*).[15] Many Catholic institutions would argue that diversity, equity, inclusion, and belonging are inherent in the Gospel message and integral to Catholic education. While the debates over vouchers and prayer in public schools are not new, the blurring of lines between church and state can create new challenges to the free exercise of religious faith. How these debates continue to play out may threaten the Catholic identity of academic institutions. Unlike the 1800s and 1900s, lay leadership in religious institutions also opens the universities to more direct attacks from government. Massimo Faggioli, professor of theology and religious studies at Villanova University notes that "Priestly ordination or membership in a religious order gave university presidents a kind of protection from government interference or threats; lay presidents don't have quite the same immunity."[16]

Internal Catholic Challenges

The landscape is treacherous not only from the outside, but also from within the Catholic community itself. I will address two of the internal challenges pressing against the essential mission of Catholic educational institutions: (1) the elimination of theology and religious studies programs, and (2) the spectrum of conservative Catholics including "evangelical" and "rad trad" (short for radical traditionalist) who reject many Vatican II documents, their implications, or both.

While a result of the financial challenges addressed above, the elimination of theology and religious studies programs cuts into the core of the identity and mission of a Catholic university. Massimo Faggioli of Villanova University has written extensively about the damage these cuts will have on the quality of a Catholic education.[17] He notes, "Despite all the DEI (diversity, equity, and inclusion) initiatives, the disappearance of theology will make our Catholic campuses less diverse and inclusive. It will also make them less Catholic and less well rounded."[18]

The second major challenge within the Catholic community is the tensions between those who have fundamental differences in interpretations of Vatican II. In his 2022 text, Noll identifies specific problems of "fundamentalism" as "anti-intellectualism," "hardening conservative evangelical commitments," and "having a chilling effect on the exercise of Christian thinking around the world."[19] These concerns are particularly visible in the Catholic landscape in the United States today. Often called "evangelical Catholics" and "rad trad Catholics," they long for a return to "authentic" Catholicism as they define it. Faggioli describes this perspective as an "anti-*aggiornamento* Catholicism" and a "wave of theological traditionalism," a "quest for continuity to the exclusion of the dynamic character of the tradition" and "not just 'trad' ideas coming from a few marginal intellectuals. Catholic anti-liberalism is part of a broader phenomenon, a new quest for Catholic identity that takes various expressions—liturgical, doctrinal, political, and educational."[20]

While not a new phenomenon, the pressure from the evangelical Catholics has certainly grown in recent years with modern media, including electronic and social media.

They are suspicious of the Catholic theology from the past 60 years, including the wonderful, complex work conducted by modern Scripture scholars. Rather than expanding outreach, the goal is often just proselytizing and converting, not openness and acceptance. One way this is exemplified by their identification of a "Catholic" college or university. Although there are more than 200 institutions of Catholic higher education in the United States as noted above, the Cardinal Newman Society identifies only 17 that are "model institutions that refuse to compromise their Catholic mission" and three which are marked as receiving "provisional recognition."[21] Another way these beliefs are shown is their labeling of Pope Francis. Many, including scholars and priests, rejected Pope Francis and described him as heretical and a threat to the true church.[22] Conversations continue today as the church waits for the start of the papal conclave; many are advocating for a "traditional" pope who will return the church to its true path. Those who have a nuanced understanding of Vatican II are often undercut by those accusing them of being heretical.

Preserving the Mission

Institutions of Catholic higher education should take the lead by embracing roots and by maintaining an unapologetic stance regarding the centrality of the mission, the integration of faith and reason, and the need to engage with and support others.

First, Catholic institutions of higher education must integrate their espoused missions throughout the institution. Each institution's mission is unique, rooted in its culture, heritage, and founder. And, for institutions affiliated with a religious order, the mission is also tied to the order's charism, the distinct character and spirit of the religious community. The mission must be embodied through its academic and social policies and programs. Institutions cannot back down from their mission. Rather, institutions must embrace its centrality as the dean of Georgetown University's Law School did when the U.S. Department of Justice demanded the deletion of "diversity" programs. Dean Trainor replied to the government in his most articulate letter:

> As a Catholic and Jesuit institution, Georgetown University was founded on the principle that serious and sustained discourse among people of different faiths, cultures, and beliefs promotes intellectual, ethical, and spiritual understanding. For us at Georgetown, this principle is a moral and educational imperative. It is a principle that defines our mission as a Catholic and Jesuit institution. Georgetown University also prohibits discrimination and harassment in its programs and activities and takes seriously its obligations to comply with all federal and local laws.[23]

Second, Catholic higher education must continue to integrate faith and reason. This union assists as well in addressing essential questions about the nature of the world, what it means to be human, the reason for existence, and creating a just society. Faggioli notes,

> The need for theology hasn't changed. . . . But, if anything, it is more important than ever. One of the ways to reposition it in a less marginal role, especially in Catholic higher education, is to claim a commitment to theology as faith working

with reason in an incarnational-sacramental imagination—a new phase in the *aggiornamento* of Vatican II, with an ethos that continues to be critical but dares to be unapologetically ecclesial.[24]

The humanities, theology, and religious studies remain in core curriculums. They are not only valuable in their own right, but are also critical components in the STEM, criminal justice, and health care programs in that they provide a framework for ethical, moral, and just decisions. The University of San Diego has established the Humanities Center to emphasize these inherent connections. Noell Norton, the dean of the College of Arts and Sciences explains, "We want to make sure that the intersection of the human to science, technology, the social behavioral sciences and the arts is really clear."[25]

Finally, Catholic institutions of higher education must build bridges, engage with the world, and promote fundamental values such as proclaiming the dignity of the human person, embracing all peoples, and living the Gospel message. Interfaith dialogue must continue, and it must be spurred by academic institutions. We must continue to open the doors to those who have not had post-secondary educational opportunities. We must continually work for justice, grounded in the Gospels and Catholic Tradition. And we must build commonalities in the spirit of the late Pope Francis.

We are not alone. Organizations such as the Association of Catholic Colleges and Universities exist to support the institutions. The ACCU's mission is clear: "To stand firmly at the intersection of higher education, the Catholic Church, and contemporary society in order to listen to, anticipate, and respond to the realities of Catholic higher education."[26]

It is critical to support Christian scholarship in all its forms, both within the Academy and through engagement with the community. Faggioli articulates the significance, "The fate of Catholic theology in the Western world is inseparable from the fate of academic theology, which in turn depends not only on universities, but also on wider spheres of publishers, academic journals, magazines, grade schools, and seminaries."[27] We must actively work to preserve the mission of Catholic higher education, especially during such turbulent times.

Chapter 25

Christians' Progress Through the Academy:
The Need to Journey Together

ELAINE V. FUNG AND BRANDON KNIGHT

Response Summary: In light of Marsden's and Noll's call for scholarly and supportive communities for people of faith, this contribution explores how the gathering of Christian scholars might help re-imagine and reform higher education. The solution to the challenge of loneliness, isolation, and individualism that higher education is actively facing is community. An academic faith community like Kristos Logos Paideia helps cultivate faithful and hope-filled emerging Christian scholars, who may become future teachers, researchers, administrators, and beyond.

JOHN BUNYAN'S CLASSIC *A Pilgrim's Progress* underscores the importance of *community* regarding the narrow path leading to the celestial city.[1] Christian, the seemingly solo protagonist of the story, demonstrates how there truly is no way in which a believer can complete the journey without others aiding him along the way. Consider the role of Evangelist, who holds him accountable, or Goodwill, who gives advice and encourages Christian to keep going. We need other Christians to continue the straight and narrow path of the Christian life.

The same lesson of *community*, applied specifically to academic life and vocation, is addressed in George Marsden's *The Outrageous Idea of Christian Scholarship*. In this classic work, he discusses the peculiar situation of Christians within the Academy. When noting potential paths forward for Christian scholarship, he posits that much of the future hinges on academic *community building*. For instance, he states: "Contemporary Christian scholarship will not receive its potential unless it can establish a strong institutional base. . . . Scholars, like everyone else, depend on communities."[2] Therefore, the essential nature of Christian community remains an important truth that must be taken to heart. Nevertheless, as Marsden illustrates throughout the history of the Academy in America, Christians are tempted and willing to carry the burden of individualism and, therefore, often partake a lonesome and dangerous journey of scholarship wrought with hazards that can potentially wreck one's faith.

That State of Community and Belonging

Sadly, people—both Christian and not—are isolated and longing for community. According to the Pew Research Center's January 2025 study, "about one-in-six Americans (16%) say they feel lonely or isolated from those around them all or most of the time—including roughly equal shares of men and women. About four-in-ten adults (38%) say they sometimes feel lonely."[3] The U.S. Surgeon General Vivek Murthy declared loneliness a national epidemic, making loneliness a nationwide issue as well as a higher education issue.[4] Specifically, higher education faces the challenge of loneliness, as "adults younger than 50 are much more likely than those ages 50 and older to say they often feel lonely (22% vs. 9%)" and "adults with some college or less education, those with lower incomes and those who are not married are among the most likely to say they feel lonely all or most of the time."[5]

College students who moved away from home for the first time in college are faced with increased daily stress, loneliness, and depression, while daily happiness decreases.[6] Even more, Rutland Gillison laments the built-in individualist structure of academia. This includes undergraduate education having an individualist structure, which parallels how academics often do their work individually, subjecting undergraduate students to an isolated and individualistic academic culture. The problem, as she sees it, is that such a structure is unrealistic and does not prepare students for their future vocations which will inevitably be part of a community. She states, "Modern occidental mainstream society has historically enshrined the ideal of the autonomous individual."[7] Students completing degrees at Christian universities are not, therefore, immune to this problem.

Gallup found in 2024 that 20% of US adults felt loneliness "a lot of the day yesterday."[8] Daily loneliness is connected to wellbeing, for example, "those experiencing daily loneliness are nearly five times as likely as those who do not report daily loneliness to rate their current life poorly (14% to 3%)."[9] Not only does loneliness have ramifications for the present but also the future as "lonely adults are 23% less likely to be optimistic about their future lives than are their not-lonely counterparts (64% compared with 83%)."[10] The issue of loneliness highlights the human need for relationships. As Galioto et al. highlight, there is a "primal need of humans to connect with others" as seen with Maslow's hierarchy of needs.[11] This aligns with Genesis 2:18, as before the fall, there existed relationships: "The LORD God said, 'It is not good for the man to be alone. I will make a helper suitable for him'" (Gen. 2:18).

While there is an issue of loneliness, there are also several solutions to reduce loneliness. Community and a sense of belonging are important for students not only as a way to reduce loneliness, but also as they hold other positive academic results, such as "levels of academic engagement, motivation, and persistence."[12] Mary Ann Covey, former director of counseling and psychological services at Texas A & M University, observed that there was a growing interest in creating student organizations that help build and cultivate student connections.[13] These connections could be a start to building community and a sense of belonging among students. Additionally, the process of creating a student organization allows students to come, communicate, and create together. As Schultze describes, "as we communicate, we form relationships that become our communities."[14] There are three aspects of well-being to reduce experiencing loneliness: career wellbeing ("liking what you do each day"), physical wellbeing (being "active and productive every day"), and social wellbeing (an "ability to see friends, family, and coworkers in person").[15] Additionally, Galioto et al. propose that "both online and offline connections" need to be cultivated "to promote general wellbeing."[16] Another recommendation is hope, as it brings out resilience.[17] Therefore, a community that cultivates hope and wellbeing directly addresses the issue of loneliness.

The community in general has multiple benefits addressing the issue of loneliness, but there are some distinctions for a Christian community. Schultze explains that "the words 'communication' and 'community' stem from the same Latin root, *communicatio*, which literally means 'to make common.' Historically, the term was even used to refer to 'possession of a common faith.'"[18] Bonhoeffer views the Christian community as "a gift of grace, a gift of the Kingdom of God."[19] Bonhoeffer states that "our community with one another consists solely in what Christ has done to both of us."[20] Unity in and through Christ aligns with Scripture, as seen in the body in Christ. Both 1 Corinthians 12:12–27 and Psalm 133:1 state "How good and pleasant it is when God's people live together in unity!" Christ is the focus and reason for gathering in the Christian community as Bonhoeffer suggests that Christians can "have access to one another, joy in one another, and fellowship with one another."[21] One of the unique aspects of a Christian community is that it "remains for all the future and to all eternity."[22]

Just this year the Barna Group recently found that "66 percent of all U.S. adults say they have made a personal commitment to Jesus that is still important in their life today."[23] This is a 12% increase from 2021, when commitment to Jesus was the lowest across three decades of tracking. Specifically, Gen Z (born between 1997 and 2012) and Millennials (born between 1981 and 1996) have a significant increase compared to Boomers (born between 1946 and 1964) and Gen X (born between 1965 and 1980), who have remained flat. Barna Group recommends that ministry leaders celebrate and steward as "People are open—perhaps as much as any time in recent memory—to Jesus. Churches that can meet people in this openness—with authenticity, humility and a focus on discipleship—may find fresh opportunities to minister."[24] At the same time, there is the challenge of people who are spiritually open and are not affiliating or attending churches. CEO of Barna, David Kinnaman, suggests that this is an opportunity for "cultivating deep-rooted discipleship."[25] A question arises from this research as to what role a Christian undergraduate honor society can play in meeting this essential, albeit overlooked, need?

Kristos Logos Paideia: Establishing an Academic Faith Community

In his 2024 Christianity and Communication Studies Network (CCSN) unconference Legacy Scholar presentation, Greg Spencer highlights how Noll and Marsden have made similar critiques about evangelicals' lack of intellectual and relational depth. Whereas Noll sets sights on the lack of long-term orientation among evangelicals, Marsden critiques the failures of Christian institutions who have over time failed to produce thoughtful students with a vision and depth for future cultural impact. Spencer specifically underscores the historic theme of shallowness regarding the Christian Academy: "Among other things, Noll and Marsden say we need forums for deep, rigorous thinking, evangelical places that prize scholarship. They wonder why the Christian college doesn't more often meet this need."[26]

Similarly, over 20 years ago, Marsden articulated solutions to the historic problems facing Christian scholarship in the Academy. Of those noted, he contends that Christian scholarship in the Academy must rely on "sub-communities" within various disciplines; otherwise, they will be fully reliant on the structures that already exist. He even shares a few academic societies, like the Society for Christian Philosophers, which "has been remarkably successful in reestablishing Christian perspectives in that field as acceptable, if not always welcome."[27] This is where the recent formulation of honor societies like Kristos Logos Paideia (KLP) can cultivate students committed to integrating the Christian faith with communication.

Kristos Logos Paideia launched in January 2024 by the CCSN. It is the first of its kind, namely a Christian-based undergraduate communication society whose purpose is to inculcate a Christian vision of the discipline to change the trajectory of the future. KLP's mission statement reads: "We are dedicated to recognizing and celebrating excellence in communication scholarship while fostering an environment where students can explore the integration of their Christian faith with the academic study of communication."[28] Although an academic honor society in the discipline is not necessarily what Marsden and Noll had in mind as both critiques and praise were offered regarding evangelism in academia, it is plausible that such a community can meet an essential need. The honor society already within its first year and a half boasts 20 students from major Christian institutions of higher learning throughout the country: Biola University, Palm Beach Atlantic University, East Texas Baptist University, and William Carey University.

With community building in mind, KLP is set to be a quite useful node of networking within the Academy unobtainable in previous years. For instance, all members of the honor society have free admission to the CCSN unconferences. Last year, four undergraduates attended, served, and networked with Christian scholars in the discipline. Additionally, all members are given free admission to the CCSN Summer workshops which serves both in networking and academic training, but just as important, such experiences allow undergraduates to listen and speak with some of the greatest thinkers in the discipline. We will continue to community-build, per Marsden's challenge, by adding other academic layers to encourage students to consider graduate school because, after all, "undergraduate teaching is the heart of higher education."[29]

KLP's sponsoring organization, the CCSN, was founded in 2014 and has, in many ways, paved the way for such an undergraduate honor society to be created from scholarly networking, collaboration, and publications. Following the lead of Marsden in particular, KLP seeks to enact measures that will both help counter secular pressures in the Academy as well as encourage and inculcate the Christian faith in the discipline of communication and rhetorical studies. The hope of KLP and CCSN's investment into undergraduate scholarship is a hope for the future and a potential solution both for the lack of community and the secularization of the field.

Communication scholar Ronald Arnett posits that such needed spaces in academia can best be labelled an "academic home." By this concept, Arnett means "a meaning structure that embraces a feeling of having a place from which to stand and contribute to education on a campus."[30] The key to building this "academic home," he contends, is through a dialogic orientation which requires community, dialogue, and authenticity. KLP's mission statement demonstrates a desire to carve out a unique space for Christian communication scholars wherein the discipline can be explored through a faith-based lens. This invitation to Christian belonging is not offered in several academic institutions or societies. But, even more, the organization is committed to building future opportunities for students to connect, dialogue, and, hopefully, add to the discipline even at this early stage in their academic careers.

As learned from Christian in *The Pilgrim's Progress*, community is the sustenance that aids the believer on his road to the celestial city. This truth is even more significant for Christians in academia where loneliness abounds, and community is not deemed a virtue.[31] The creation of Kristos Logos Paideia is a humble yet bold attempt to build community and encourage faith integrative scholarship in only one of the many fields of study God has gifted us with through his creation.

Section Three:
Communication, Pedagogy, and
Intellectual Formation

Chapter 26

The Unlikely Intellectual:
How Reuben "Uncle Bud" Robinson's
Rhetorical Invention Challenges Noll's *Scandal*

ABRAM J. BOOK

Response Summary: At first glance, the great Holiness evangelist Reuben "Uncle Bud" Robinson personifies the type of shallow theology and intellectual suspicion that Noll argues has traditionally doomed evangelicalism. Robinson was an uneducated, backcountry preacher who is credibly said to have won more than 100,000 conversions through his use of rural metaphor and simple folksy imagery. However, a closer look at Robinson's rhetoric indicates an underlying depth of thought that forged incredible bonds between Uncle Bud and his audiences. This essay makes three major points: (1) the importance of rhetorical devices in preaching and discourse, (2) grit and ethos as ideals of intellectual communication, and (3) the importance of counterpublics in persuasive message appeal.

IN HIS LANDMARK WORK *The Scandal of the Evangelical Mind*, Mark Noll suggests that American evangelicalism and anti-intellectualism are virtually synonymous. Within his overall critique of what he refers to as the intellectual disaster of fundamentalism, Noll reserves particularly scathing criticism for Pentecostals and Holiness advocates, arguing that in their pursuit of the practical presence of God as the primary spiritual goal, they doubled down on dispensationalism and spurned the life of the mind.[1] The problem, Noll, explains, was not that Holiness adherents pursued closeness to God as a spiritual goal, but that the movement assumed that one must reject the world's knowledge to be effectively spiritual.[2] Noll writes: "The movements that seemed to do such damage to evangelical thought—Holiness, Pentecostalism, Dispensationalism—hid the most important thing behind a veil of secondary concerns."[3]

Reuben "Uncle Bud" Robinson, an early twentieth-century Holiness evangelist, offers a surprising counter-narrative to Mark Noll's critique of evangelical anti-intellectualism in *Scandal*. Robinson was an uneducated, backcountry preacher born into the depths of poverty at the dawn of the Civil War in the Appalachian hills of East Tennessee. As a young man he relocated with his mother and siblings to Texas, where he worked as a ranch hand before being converted under the preaching of a Methodist circuit rider. "Uncle Bud," as he came to be called, received an exhorter's license from the Methodist Episcopal Church South in 1880, despite having no formal education, being only semi-literate, and suffering from a stammer and recurring epileptic seizures. Methodist historian Steven Cooley writes: "Robinson came to the holiness movement from an iteration of that poor plain-folk culture of the South memorialized in Steinbeck's *The Grapes of Wrath*."[4]

On the surface, "Uncle Bud" seems to personify exactly the kind of cheap populism, shallow theology, and suspicion of intellect that Noll argues has traditionally marred evangelicalism. "The fundamentalist movement reinforced the dogmatic power of populist teachers," Noll writes, and "with the universities and their formal learning suspect, the spokesperson who could step forth confidently on the basis of the Scriptures was welcomed as a convincing authority."[5] The truth, however, is more complicated and interesting. While Robinson's folksy preaching style and lack of formal education might initially align with Noll's thesis, his rhetorical strategies reveal a sophisticated engagement with theological ideas that fostered unity and spiritual depth. In this essay I argue that Robinson's use of rhetorical devices, personal ethos rooted in grit, and creation of counterpublic communities provided an antidote to the intellectual shallowness Noll excoriates.

After a brief stint as a Methodist circuit rider himself, Robinson instead decided to engage in itinerant evangelism, becoming known early in his preaching career as "The Cowboy Evangelist." Upon his death in 1942 at the age of 82, Robinson had traveled more than two million miles in itinerant evangelism, preaching more than 33,000 times to adherents of more than 70 denominations. He is credibly said to have won more than 100,000 conversions through his use of rural metaphor and simple folksy imagery. Robinson was also instrumental in the formation of the Church of the Nazarene in Texas in the earliest years of the twentieth century and became a central figure, personally and rhetorically, of early twentieth-century Holiness revivalism. Cooley writes: "While other holiness revivalists acquiesced to the modern pressures of reality, Bud Robinson took license from the humorist's wink to cut the language free of reality for the playful imaginative exploration of its felt symbols . . . and stretched the Methodist vernacular out beyond even its own expansive limits."[6] Noted Holiness author and historian Darius Salter even goes so far as to refer to Robinson as the Holiness movement's Will Rogers.[7]

It is worth noting first that Robinson personally financed the college education of more than 30 young ministers over nearly two decades. He and his wife, Sally, often boarded students in their Peniel, Texas, home while the students attended Texas Holiness University. Moreover, Bud himself wrote that had life afforded him a realistic opportunity to do so, he would have taken four or five years to get a good education and that doing so would have made him an even better preacher and evangelist.[8] Robinson's case at least anecdotally suggests that rather than rejecting worldly knowledge out of suspicion or piety, some Holiness preachers of the early twentieth century simply did not have access to educational opportunities and had to teach themselves how to preach and make theological interpretations. Furthermore, the evidence strongly suggests Robinson recognized that furthering education and cultivating the life of the mind were worthwhile and necessary pursuits despite his own lack of formal learning.

The presence of several highly educated figures within the ranks of the Holiness movement somewhat ameliorates Noll's scandal on its own and challenges stubborn stereotypes of Holiness folk as unlearned fanatics. Robinson was sanctified under the preaching of the Asbury-trained William Baxter Godbey and became close friends with many seminary-educated evangelists, among them John Lakin Brasher, A. M. Hills, and Henry Clay Morrison.[9] Brasher, a Methodist Episcopal Evangelist who served as president of two different Holiness colleges, conducted many a revival meeting alongside Bud. Despite the chasm between Brasher's considerable education and Robinson's lack thereof, Brasher later wrote glowingly of Robinson and his preaching: "Instead of being a hindrance, his slight lisp and hesitation of speech made what he said more interesting and people did not want to miss a word. His quaint, hillbilly pronunciation caused what he said to stick and be remembered. A college education would have been the ruin of him."[10]

A Different Kind of Intellectual

Noll writes that for Holiness adherents of the nineteenth and early twentieth centuries, simple biblical truth was key: "Where learned elites were proposing pragmatic, democratic, and social-scientific solutions to the gravest modern problems, Holiness advocates offered the Holy Spirit."[11] Robinson and his contemporaries used terms such as "the higher life," "victorious living," "a deeper walk of grace," and "entire sanctification," when preaching and teaching, suggesting to hearers that living a sinless life on earth was possible and that the Holy Spirit could be tangibly experienced in that day and hour.[12] This "let go and let God," mentality, Noll further argues, led to a retreat from evangelical intellectual engagement and to a broader suspicion of the Academy brought on in no small part by populist and revivalist preachers. Salter expresses similar sentiments but aims his broadside directly at Robinson and his peers, suggesting they oversimplified complex theological truths and advocated outlandish interpretations of Scripture in their preaching: "The witticisms, eccentricities, and antics of William Godbey, Uncle Bud Robinson, Beverly Carradine, and John T. Hatfield were expected and enjoyed by their admirers but served to alienate the movement from the evangelical mainstream," Salter writes, "Holiness celebrities were not held accountable for outlandish biblical interpretations and prophecies."[13]

I submit that the truth surrounding the intellectual indictment of the Holiness movement is more nuanced than Noll or Salter might admit. In fact, Robinson's preaching and writing synthesized simplicity and depth, using rhetorical practices to bridge divides and model an alternative evangelical intellectualism. His use of rural metaphors related to farming and frontier life helped make theologically abstract doctrines like entire sanctification relatable to what were largely "plain folk" audiences similar to those of his upbringing.[14] One anecdote Bud told went as follows: "One of the most beautiful things about our Nazarene boys up and down the land is that they are so busy following the Lamb, that they have no time to ride the goat. While they are not lodge fighters, thank the Lord, they are not goat riders!"[15] In this way, he explained the life of Holiness as being primarily about "following the Lamb" (Christ) while avoiding messy worldly distractions and temptations (riding the goat), perhaps loosely echoing metaphorical language from Jesus's own teaching on "the sheep and the goats" (Matt. 25:31–46, New American Standard Bible).

This and similar metaphors Bud used deeply connected with small town and rural audiences of the early twentieth century. Robinson's grandson, William Welch Jr., who served as his driver in the final years of Robinson's itinerant ministry, wrote of his grandfather in an unpublished family memoir: "While his Tennessee mountain speech was a curiosity, what he said, substantive or playful, overflowed with affection for his hearers and was mixed with laughter and tears. Somehow, the space between speaker and hearer disappeared."[16] His storytelling went beyond the use of metaphor to mirror inductive methods, allowing listeners to "discover" truths alongside him rather than being lectured about them.

Multiple scholars who have examined the early twentieth century Holiness movement have concluded that Holiness folk seemed to speak a language only they understood. The preaching style of Robinson and his colleagues, Brasher writes, "flowered in the distinctive constituency of Holiness camp meetings and the emphases of holiness theology."[17] Cooley writes that as a young man he received a copy of Robinson's autobiography, *Sunshine and Smiles*, from his grandmother, and that Robinson's use of language was so curious and unique that Cooley could not understand it despite his extensive training and reading in the early Methodist tradition. "[I]f Methodist/holiness people talked to one another in this way," he notes, "then the language must have had rules of usage and meanings to these users, an understanding of which would have implications for our own fuller and wider understandings of this specific religious culture and perhaps for the faith itself."[18] The development of this level of synthesis of thought and mind and highly coordinated management of meaning that both Cooley and Brasher detail, regardless of the specific words or niche linguistic conventions used, can only be described as deeply intellectual.

Thus, Robinson's uncanny ability to connect with his audience through simple but strategic rhetoric cannot be dismissed as theological ignorance. What Bud and his Holiness contemporaries lacked in formal education, they made up for through a relatable use of language and a keen spiritual and practical awareness of rhetorical situation. Robinson's preaching synthesized simplicity and depth, using rhetorical practices to bridge divides and model an alternative evangelical intellectualism. Furthermore, his simplicity was strategic, not anti-intellectual. After all, theological purism and doctrinal fidelity mean nothing if the hearer cannot understand the words. Robinson alluded to this when he wrote of a time he sat under the preaching of a highly educated pastor in a large church:

> I sat in a $500,000 church and listened to a preacher take the most of his time explaining what a great German scientist had discovered in a single grain of sand. The crowd went to sleep and left him to discourse on the sand. The poor people did not get anything worth their time. They were going to church where their hungry hearts were not fed, and where they did not get once encouragement to help them in the battles of life.[19]

This is not at all to say that highly educated pastors cannot achieve the kind of coordinated management of meaning that Robinson did with his Holiness audiences. It also does not imply that self-taught preachers are in any way better at doing so, though they may feel the need to work harder at doing so to supplement their lack of education. The late pastor, author, and Emory University professor Fred Craddock, who shared notable biographical similarities to Robinson's, found ways to connect with his audiences through story, narrative, and collective experience much like Robinson did.[20] What Robinson's case demonstrates is that intellect extends far beyond book learning to include the learned (and perhaps sometimes inherited) ability of indirect communication.

Grit as Intellect

Noll's critique of the Holiness movement and its concomitant dispensationalism almost completely fail to account for intellect acquired and fostered through lived experience. Grit and resilience, properly regarded as components of Aristotle's concept of ethos, are created through personal narratives, and they create empathy and strengthen persuasive appeals. Bud Robinson is emblematic of the hardships and poverty many frontier Holiness preachers endured during the late nineteenth and early twentieth centuries. Illiteracy until age 20, epilepsy, an unusual condition in which his shoulders became randomly dislocated from their sockets, and a stammer he eventually overcame without any treatment or therapy: all of these positioned Robinson as a "wounded healer," embodying a perseverance and grit that authenticated his message.

Psychologist Angela Duckworth defines grit as the combination of passion and perseverance directed at long-term goals.[21] Duckworth further explains that grit is not simply talent or luck, how intensely someone may want something in the moment, or even about one's level of educational preparation. Instead, grit is about maintaining a steadfast commitment to a goal you care deeply about, and persisting with effort and interest over years, even in the face of setbacks, slow progress, or failure. Professor Joe Gorman similarly suggests resilience as the operative word: "No matter how fierce the pain or deep the humiliation, resilient ones get back up one more time than they fall down. . . . Resilient people weather adversity. . . . Resilience is a journey."[22] In Robinson's case, the cause he cared deeply about was preaching the Word of God and he exhibited unabated resilience in doing so despite unimaginable setbacks throughout his life.

The pivotal point in Robinson's life and ministry and that which most embodied his ethos of resilience occurred in San Francisco in June of 1919, an incident Robinson referred to simply as "my smash-up." Later, he published it in book form as *My Hospital Experience*, and the story became a hallmark of his preaching during the second half of Robinson's itinerant ministry. As he crossed a street on the way back to his hotel room from an evening revival service, Robinson was hit by a car and severely injured. His description of his injuries is not only explicit but typical of the grotesque prose that defined the rhetoric of Southern writers like William Faulkner and Flannery O'Connor.[23] In *My Hospital Experience*, Robinson wrote:

> My left arm was pulled bottom-upwards, and the bone broken about an inch and a half below the joints and the bone running down to the elbow was split. My right arm was broken . . . so badly slivered that a number of pieces of the bone went out into the muscle, and the long end of the bone was driven right through the muscle and through the undershirt sleeve and top shirt sleeve and coat sleeve, and the end of the bone came on over and struck through my coat into my chest, and when I reached the Emergency there were two inches of

the arm bone sticking out through the flesh and my clothes. My left knee was smashed and my left leg was broken, and my left ankle was pulled apart and the foot turned around in the joint.[24]

Resilience and grit are oft-neglected aspects of ethos, but they are central to the development of the rhetor's character and credibility. As persuasive proofs are concerned, logos is probably more often associated with intellect than ethos, but it is through the resilience and grit that make up ethos that Robinson's flaws, failures, and hardships became tools for spiritual and rhetorical authority. Audiences are far more likely to identify with a rhetor's words when they understand the extent to which the speaker has weathered similar adversity. That is, Bud Robinson's audiences listened and responded to what he said not because he said it eloquently but because they understood it as an embodiment of their own spiritual, physical, and psychological struggles. In those ways, grit functions as a type of indirect communication. Robinson's rhetorical grit ultimately demonstrates that evangelicalism's "mind" need not reside in academia but can thrive through persuasive, experiential communication.

Holiness as Unifying Discourse

Noll's critique of the Holiness movement hiding the most important things under the veil of secondary concerns is well-placed. For decades in the American Holiness movement, legalistic theological viewpoints and practices, such as biblical literalism and not wearing jewelry, dominated the way of Holiness and distracted from matters of true spiritual importance. However, when Holiness adherents willingly discard practical and theological legalism, the way of holiness itself emerges as a unifying discourse that can bring together discordant messages. Once again, Bud Robinson's example is an instructive one. Robinson would likely have described himself as somewhat legalistic in personal practice but during his five decades as an evangelist, he worked alongside more than 70 denominations—an indication that his Holiness message effectively spanned theological divides and that his particular brand and language of Holiness contained within it not only significant intellectual vein but an inherent rhetorical accessibility.

Interestingly, Noll admits that learned intellectualism undergirded by theism and Christian norms has been abandoned by values-neutral approaches to truth and with liberation from dogma as a primary motive.

> The issue specifically is whether there is any good reason, apart from an active deity, to take for granted the regularity, communicability, universality, durability, and repeatability that are so basic for so many intellectual endeavors. But even that significant contextual assertion has been advanced only rarely by Christian thinkers in the modern marketplace of ideas. The much more obvious reality is that scientists, philosophers, historians, and critics have long been acting as if general theistic considerations, much less explicitly Christian concerns, were irrelevant.[25]

That passage strongly suggests that while Noll extolls the virtues of intellectualism and intellectuals on one hand, he seems to recognize intellectualism's slide toward secular progressivism and its abandonment of or at least unwillingness to embrace theistic foundations on the other. I would argue this is the primary reason for evangelicalism's suspicion, if not outright rejection, of intellectualism. Evangelicals and perhaps especially Holiness adherents have picked up on what they justifiably perceive to be the increasingly secular nature of intellectualism and higher education and want little to do with it. That is perhaps a microcosm of the disdain educated elites have long held toward the working class—the kind of "plain folk" to whom Robinson and his contemporaries preached and from whose ranks many of them emerged. Again, Robinson's approach to rhetoric can be helpful in bridging this ever-widening gap. His sermons attracted urban and rural, educated and uneducated audiences alike, creating a space where holiness transcended social divides.

While Noll's criticism of the evangelical abandonment of the life of the mind has merit, adherents of intellectualism and higher education have almost completely abandoned theistic and Christian considerations in research, scholarship, and rhetoric. The scandal of the evangelical mind is not a one-way scandal. The scandal of intellectualism, in fact, is that it has largely failed to embrace theism or any notion of absolute truth. Evangelicals cannot wholly mitigate the scandal of the evangelical mind until secular and theistic intellectuals commit to mitigating the scandal of the intellectual spirit. This requires evangelicalism and secular intellectualism embracing each other as cooperative rhetorical publics where practical, even if they may differ on philosophical or theological specifics. Though one could point to many examples, one way in which Robinson did so is worthy of special consideration.

Robinson supported the ministry of the famous African-American intellectual Booker T. Washington, even though he may not have necessarily agreed with all of Washington's political, racial, or social views. After attending a speech Washington delivered at Vanderbilt University in 1907, Robinson encountered Washington on a train after the event and the two held an extended conversation. Robinson wrote of Washington's Vanderbilt Speech in the *Pentecostal Herald*, a periodical widely read within Holiness circles at the time, "Nobody can listen to Booker T. Washington and go away unconcerned. He will make any man think that sets and listens to him."[26] Washington said that the Vanderbilt speech was one of the few opportunities he ever had to speak to Southern White men at a college.[27]

Robinson then proceeded to summarize Washington's speech in his own words and expressed his support for Washington's efforts to educate his fellow African Americans. Of the train conversation, Robinson wrote: "He told me that he had about fifteen hundred students in his school. I was pleased to know he is doing a great work amongst his people. He deserves the prayers and support of all the United States. Every church in the land ought to help Booker T. Washington with these boys and girls."[28] Washington's speech and subsequent conversation with Robinson is instructive in evangelicalism's attempts to address anti-intellectualism by bridging social divides.

This episode is significant because Robinson often preached to Southern Whites in the segregated South and wrote a weekly column for the *Herald of Holiness* (and regularly for other Holiness publications prior to it) for at least 30 years of his itinerant ministry. His words thus reached hundreds of thousands of people beyond just those to whom he preached. Noll criticized evangelicals and particularly the Holiness movement for being culturally disengaged and more focused on dispensationalism and what might be considered legalistic aspects of theology than in cultural contemplation or engagement. Thus, it is important that Robinson used his column and considerable platform in the *Pentecostal Herald* to put forward his favorable impression of Booker T. Washington and to urge Holiness adherents to support Washington's work. In this way, Robinson's language focused on communal transformation over doctrinal nitpicking. By embracing and promoting Washington's social efforts, Robinson used rhetoric to attempt to forge a shared identity in Christ amongst those traveling the way of holiness and likely even some who were not. This stands in stark contrast to the fragmented picture of evangelicalism and the Holiness movement and the anti-intellectual attitudes that Noll and Salter argue resulted from that fragmentation.

Conclusion

Finally, if evangelicalism is to reclaim its intellectual vitality, then its representatives must use all of the tools at their disposal to do so. While university learning is one of the most powerful such tools, the recovery efforts should not be limited to knowledge and information passed down through the halls of colleges and universities. Intellectualism, for its part, must be willing to embrace theistic means of understanding the world. Knowledge gained through higher education can be severely limited if presented entirely or largely from a standpoint of secularism or rejection of absolute truth. Rather, evangelical intellectualism should be reevaluated to include the role of indirect communication, rhetoric, grit, and resilience in bridging theology and practice. Robinson's considerable success at evangelism and soul winning challenges Noll's notion that intellectual depth requires academic rigor. Instead, his model suggests that evangelical vitality can be found in rhetorical engagement—connecting the truth to lived experience. It also suggests that evangelicals be willing to put aside the social and political differences they may have with certain social causes and work with such publics to accomplish Kingdom goals. To be most effective, today's evangelical preachers, teachers, and writers must take their cue from Robinson and learn to balance doctrinal fidelity with accessible communication.

Chapter 27

Jest the Facts

LANCE CROY

Response Summary: Søren Kierkegaard mastered the art of indirect communication through the use of parables. He authored rich imagery that sets the scene on the dramatic stage of life. All good parables are characterized by aesthetic balance and brevity, metaphorical and trenchant imagery, limited character development, plot twists or reversals, and easy memorability. This short essay will paraphrase a few of Kierkegaard's parables, displaying the drama necessary to be silly about some sobering truths.

THE COMEDIC IRONY necessary to discuss truth through parables, stories, supposition, and poetic language requires wisdom and witticism. Christians teaching in higher education and producing scholarly publications should consider persuading their audiences through Søren Kierkegaard's method of indirect communication. According to Christopher Ben Simpson:

> Kierkegaard's method of indirect communication has to do with communicating to one in the midst of an illusion. . . . Paradoxically, this loving and "Christian" manner of communicating truth entails a certain deception—for to address one in the midst of illusion [one] begins by taking the other's delusion at face value . . . by stepping into a life-view as a lived actuality. . . . The goal of the communication intended in Kierkegaard's work is to help the reader change their viewpoint, their life-view, and so the way they live.[1]

According to Thomas C. Oden, all good parables are characterized by their aesthetic balance and brevity, metaphorical and potent imagery, limited character development, plot twists or reversals, and easy memorability.[2] Fitting this characterization, many of Kirkegaard's parables have been retold or passed down throughout history. Therefore, the following short essay will paraphrase a few of Kierkegaard's parables, displaying the irony necessary to be silly about some profound and sobering truths.

Seeking God First

Ludwig is a seeker. He wants to seek God first. However, he must be educated first. Then he must pass his exams. Now, he is off to seminary. Eight years later, he is ready to seek God. But he now needs a job. He fills out his resume and submits dozens of applications. He finally finds a congregation. He must work his way up the hierarchy. He is tired and wants to be nursed by his future wife, but he has to be engaged before that. Many years pass. Finally, Sunday arrives, and Ludwig steps into the pulpit to preach. Strangely, the Scripture reading for that day is, "But seek first the kingdom of God" (Matt. 6:33, English Standard Version). After all that time, Kierkegaard writes,

> The clergy's whole profession (not to mention the rest of us good Christians) is a constant practice of this: first the earthly and then the kingdom of God, first regard for what the fear of man bids or forbids and then the kingdom of God, first a living and then a funeral.[3]

Loving Others

Suppose there are two painters. One says, I have traveled the world and still cannot find my muse or even a man worth painting. In every face I have studied, I can see one little fault. The other painter says, I am not well-traveled and have only stayed in my small circle of friends, but in every imperfection I have noticed, I can show them something beautiful. Kierkegaard states that love requires that we are "able to find some lovableness in all of us, consequently loving enough to be able to love all of us."[4]

Soul-body

Let's compare a house to what it means to be human. Suppose this house contains a cellar, ground floor, and premier *ètage* (first floor) delineated by rank. Kierkegaard writes,

> The soulish-body synthesis in every man is planned to be spirit . . . but the man prefers to live in the cellar. . . . And not only does he prefer to dwell in the cellar . . . he becomes furious if anyone would propose to him to occupy the *bel ètage* which stands empty . . . for in fact, he is dwelling in his own house.[5]

The Word of God

Think of a man who has received a letter from his lady love. Suppose the letter was written in a language the man did not understand. Suppose the letter also contained a desire that the lady wanted her beloved to satisfy. Suppose that when the two lovers finally reunited, she asked him if he accomplished it. Now, the man could only confess that he had spent most of his time reading dictionaries to translate the letter and get the wording right. Thus, there is a distinction between reading and reading. Kirkegaard warns:

Let us not dismiss this picture too soon. . . . If there is a desire, a commandment, an order then (remember the lover!), then be off at once to do accordingly. "But" you perhaps would say, "there are so many obscure passages in the Holy Scriptures, whole books which are almost riddles." To this, I would reply: I see no need to consider this objection unless it comes from one whose life expresses the fact that he has punctually complied with all the passages that are easy to understand. Is this the case with you?[6]

The End of The World

Finally, Kierkegaard's most famous parable is worth quoting directly:

> It happened that a fire broke out backstage in a theater. The clown came out to inform the public. They thought it was just a jest and applauded. He repeated his warning, they shouted even louder. So I think the world will come to an end amid general applause from all the wits, who believe that it is a joke.[7]

When I read these and other parables of Kierkegaard to the class, I often ask them to respond with a word picture that speaks indirectly or in a roundabout way. I am always amazed at how difficult it is for them. The students default to statements with an explanation devoid of any story elements. Lindvall referenced Benson Fraser's book, which provided this important observation, "Just presenting 'the facts' or articulating an argument, no matter how true, oversimplifies the process of communication and totally dismisses the variety of ways by which Scripture itself imparts truth."[8]

Kierkegaard mastered the art of indirect communication by using parables. He authored rich imagery that sets the scene on the dramatic stage of life. The comedic irony, as Kierkegaard would note, is that when the curtain falls, the one who played the Beggar and the one who played the King are one and the same.[9] Kirkegaard describes the actualized life as an actor who realizes God not only authored the play but also sits in the balcony seeking an honest portrayal. Even if an actor forgets a line and must be prompted, the audience applauds the actor, not the stagehand who delivered the cue.[10] Therefore, the humble learn to live truthfully, serving the scene and ensemble. Their soul and body are imbued with the Word of God as they seek first their first love and then love their neighbor as themselves before the grand finale. May we be content to play for an audience of One.

Chapter 28

Dorothy Sayers: The Gospel and
The Power of Indirect Communication

Kim Okesson

Response Summary: Christian scholars are challenged by Mark Noll and George Marsden to develop robust frameworks for thought and scholarship, not allowing space for society or the Academy to assert scholarship by Christians is of lesser value or rigor. An important strategy for credibility for the Christian scholar is consistently communicating ideas in the public sphere with excellence and relevance. This essay provides a brief overview of the life and writings of Dorothy Sayers as an exemplar scholar who utilized her academic understanding of language to impact varied sectors of society as a scholar, a writer, and a public speaker. The excellence she brought to her work amplified her ideas throughout British society. She used her profound communication skills to influence British society both inside and outside the church, through her effective communication of the Gospel to a nation which largely misunderstood what it means to be Christian.

DOROTHY SAYERS (1893–1957), a prolific author, theologian, and playwright, moved in the same intellectual circles as C. S. Lewis and J. R. R. Tolkien. She was not one of the original "Inklings," but she was already a successful author by the time she engaged in philosophical discussions and debates with that influential group and enjoyed their friendship.[1] She was a gifted communicator and knew the power of narrative to teach spiritual truth.

Sayers was known for her ability to wordsmith.[2] Gospel themes are evident throughout all of her writings.[3] She made important contributions to the church and society through her writing, yet few, according to Laura Simmons, have explored it in depth.[4] Simmons, a professor at George Fox University at the time of writing her book about Sayers's theology, attributes this to the huge volume of her writing and the massive variety in her writing.[5] Her published work includes poems, short stories, plays for radio and the stage, children's books, novels, letters, literary reviews, essays (including theological, political, creative commentary) and translations (most notable her translation of Dante).[6] Her impact as a female scholar during her lifetime, as a peer of male scholars still viewed as giants today, is significant. She not only had a place at the table, but she led the way for many women, years after her death, who would pursue meaningful academic careers.

In addition to her other writing gifts, Sayers was masterful at indirect communication. As she sought to display the Gospel in her writings, she wrote almost as much fiction as she did non-fiction. Similar to G. K. Chesterton, she wrote mysteries. In all this, she contributed to both our understanding of theology and communication.

Biographical Background

Sayers was an only child, born in Oxford in 1893. Her father, Henry Sayers, was a chaplain and her mother, Helen Mary Sayers was the headmaster at Christ Church Choir School.[7] Dorothy was taught at home; her lessons were alternately taught by governesses, her father and her mother.[8] Her father taught her Latin and started her lessons when she was only six. Her parents were known for their love of theater and took her to London annually to see productions. She also was encouraged to play-act and regularly identified herself with her favorite characters in books.[9] As she grew, she also produced plays, made costumes, props, and programs as well as authored long narrative poems which she illustrated herself.[10] An artist of her caliber, from a young age, naturally turned her everyday life experiences into art.

Before she became a teenager, her parents anticipated her attendance at university and chose Oxford as the best university for her.[11] They planned her high school years accordingly, choosing an elite boarding school for her preparation. She enrolled at Oxford, even though at the time Oxford only admitted female students but did not confer degrees on them. In 1920, when Dorothy Sayers was 27, Oxford University changed their policies on conferring degrees and began recognizing women as graduates.[12] Dorothy Sayers was one of the first female graduates of Oxford University: she was awarded with bachelor's and master's degrees in modern languages.

After her graduation, Dorothy Sayers went on to a lifetime of writing. Although her writings included both fiction and nonfiction there was nothing frivolous about her personality or her publications. Simmons describes her as both a participant and an observer in society, which afforded her a unique perspective.[13] Sayers was a very intentional author; she sought to communicate foundational truths about God and humanity in all of her works.

Despite the quantity and quality of her work, she has been pointedly understudied and rarely regarded as a theologian.[14] Few have examined her important contribution to the church in this regard.[15] "Her vocation as a writer was a vital part of what equipped her to be an especially effective lay theologian."[16] Her skills in communication were a gift to the church and she sought to use them to bring the church into right relationship with the God it claimed to worship.

Lay Theologian

Dorothy Sayers was not an ordained member of the clergy but was considered an intellectual member of the laity in the church. She was regularly invited to write letters and plays to help explain Christianity and make it accessible to the common person. James Beitler, Director of the Wade Center at Wheaton College, praises Sayers for her ability to illustrate and teach hard truths realistically through drama, which had a profound impact on the church.[17] In 1940, Sayers had taken the clergy of England to task over their lack of ability and motivation to teach the creeds in a way that people understood them to be relevant to their everyday lives. According to Sayers, the clergy failed to view Christianity rhetorically and by doing so, made no effort to communicate to the audience in a way the audience could understand.[18] Her exasperation was expressed in her statement, "They've got the most terrific story in the world and they don't tell it."[19] James Beitler brilliantly states that "the stage was at one and the same time Sayers's workplace and her pulpit."[20] Sayers stewarded her gifts and talents to use art to communicate spiritual truth.

Sayers's goal for her audience was transportation, in other words, a complete immersion in the experience of the narrative. According to Beitler, her work showcases Quintilian's concept of *energeia*.[21] Energeia is the realistic depiction of an event, done with such excellence, persuasion, and emotion, the event seems real to the audience.[22] Sayers was an author and playwright who gave much time and attention to the poetics of space. For example, in her greatest mystery novel, *The Nine Tailors*, she hired an architect to draw the parish church, so she could realistically set scenes in the space through her writing. Through her dramatic works Sayers sought to connect with her audience in ways the traditional teaching in the church could not.

A central question that theologian Fred Craddock pointedly asked was how does one person communicate the Christian faith to another?[23] This question was one that Dorothy Sayers asked as well, as she saw the church in England not communicating the Gospel nor the doctrines of the church effectively. She spent much of her career writing and speaking toward that end. Craddock stated that many an author and rhetor has had to face the hard reality that although truth is available to all, it does not mean it is understood nor is it enacted.[24] As Craddock remarked, "there is no lack of information in a Christian land; something else is lacking, and this is a something which the one man cannot directly communicate to the other."[25] Even though Sayers wrote broadly and across numerous genres, she was singularly focused and committed to honoring people and the message by seeking understandable avenues of communication.

Dorothy Sayers knew her stories were theological, even though she did not attend a seminary or have an official position in the Church of England. This idea is supported by C. S. Song in his book on "Story" theology.[26] All people, all over the world, from all of time were and are storytellers. Song states,

> A story worthy of its name grips you in the depths of your heart and mind, forces you to look deeply into yourself and into human nature, and compels you to examine relations between you and other human beings, between human beings and the world, nature and creation, and relations between human beings and God. If this is what story does, it is profoundly theological.[27]

Sayers believed that creative work was of the highest order; since all of humanity bears the image of God, then all creating is in the image of the divine act of creating.[28] The doctrine of the Trinity, the three in one, represented for her the creative process as a three-fold work.[29] This three-fold work of human creation includes idea, power, and energy.[30] Idea, power, and energy are all part of the same creative conceptualization process; they are one, like the Father, Son, and Holy Spirit.[31] "Idea," analogous to the Father, is the creative concept that starts in the mind of the artist.[32] "Energy," analogous to the Son, is the process of making the conceptual material.[33] "Power," analogous to the Spirit, is the effect this materialized concept has on the audience.[34]

Sayers's work was all the more valuable to the church in England as she understood the myths, concerns, and questions of the society around her. She knew British culture, which means that she knew well the myths present in British society. Song speaks to the importance of theology being the matrix in a story, thus myths give the rhetor insight into what a community believes about the big issues of life: birth, death, creation, good, evil, right and wrong.[35] Through understanding the myths in a culture, the rhetor or author can craft stories with the same concerns or values, which then also communicate ultimate truth.

Writing Genres and Theology

Advertising, detective fiction, translation, and playwriting are the genres through which Sayers's theological voice was heard the strongest. Each of these four genres had a particular characteristic or set of characteristics which illustrated her gift for speaking theologically through text.

Advertising

Sayers's early career was in advertising. A successful advertiser must know and understand the culture she is selling to and must also have a writing ability which is succinct, yet meaningful. Sayers was notable for her economy of words.[36] There were three ways her experience in advertising helped her write theologically. First, Dorothy Sayers was trained to identify unclear writing.[37] If an advertisement in the newspaper left the public wondering what it meant, the advertisement was useless. Similarly, clergy who spoke and wrote using lofty theological sentiment or antiquated language left the public wondering what it all meant, rendering the message useless. Sayers could not tolerate this kind of ambiguous and ineffective communication. Second, advertisers were attentive to the details of the ordinariness of life, how people thought, and what was tolerable. Sayers wrote *Creed or Chaos* to address the very common misunderstandings people in England had about Christianity. The traditional teachings of the church were a challenge for the average person to understand, thus she put the teachings and the misunderstandings in dialogue with each other, to create clarity.[38] Finally, her experience in advertising improved her own clarity of writing and the impact of her religious works.[39]

Detective Fiction

Detective fiction was a common genre in the early twentieth century. Interestingly, the skill Sayers developed in writing detective stories aided her in communicating the Gospel. In a detective story, the author must map out a story with enough logical sequence so the plot is believable for the reader.

Authors of detective fiction also craft arguments. The clues along the way must lead to a logical conclusion. This is evident in her essay "Creed or Chaos?" Here, "she anticipated the responses of the uninstructed person to the various doctrinal assertions of the Christian faith."[40] Crafting this type of argument or plot requires research on the part of the author to create realistic settings both architecturally and geographically, lifelike relationships between characters, historical accuracy, and attention to detail of language and dialect. Sayers studied campanology, the art of bellringing, for two years before she wrote her novel, *Nine Tailors*. The story of *Nine Tailors* opens with a nine-hour pealing of the bells. Additionally in the plot, a lost and then discovered document, which must be decoded for the mystery to be solved, required the main character to have knowledge of bell ringing and bell towers.

Finally, good detective fiction allows the author to present the same story or the same situation from the perspective of many different people. This grants the author the opportunity to gift the story both a richness and a depth.[41] Sayers was concerned with what was being proclaimed from the pulpit in the church as well as what the person in the pew heard. This dual perspective allowed her the unique position of "explaining theology from the inside out."[42] This is evident in her novel, *The Documents in the Case*, in which the case is told from multiple perspectives. Lastly, her creativity and artistic ability in writing detective fiction employed her imagination. She created people and places, conversations and concerns, destiny and dynasties, all from within her own mind. She lived in this creative space and had no tolerance for people and institutions of influence who had a platform for proclamation yet were utterly lacking in imaginative ability to communicate with their audience.[43]

Translations and Plays

Similarly, Sayers's work in translation helped her to hone her skills which were useful for communicating theologically. Translation work from antiquated language to modern language assists the public to hear a timeless message in a new light. The Church of England still used the King James Version, which although it had beautiful Shakespearean English, was largely unrelatable to the average person in the twentieth century. When she translated the Gospels to write *The Man Born to be King*, she used modern language, which succeeded in shocking and impressing her audiences.[44] As traditional language had lost its meaning, her goal was to have people hear doctrine and theological truths for the first time in a way they could understand and as relevant to their lives.[45] Writing this play was an incredible artistic labor as she translated it from the original Greek and created her own synthesis of the four Gospels. She then wrote the play in such a way as to make the story coherent.[46] This play showcased her writing capacity and ability. She wrote one coherent story, to be performed as twelve radio segments with each segment capable of standing on its own, in and of itself. C. S. Lewis testified Sayers's play moved him so deeply that he re-read it every Holy Week.[47]

As a playwright, Dorothy Sayers brought history and theology to life. She was convinced that a play would have more impact on society than volumes of theological texts.[48] Sayers was persuaded that the majority of the people in the church "are exceedingly surprised to discover that the creeds contain any statements that bear a practical and comprehensible meaning."[49] She believed the incarnation was the most wondrous part of Christianity, yet tragically the incarnation was also one of the least understood doctrines in England. Determined to address this, Sayers allowed the dogma to "speak for itself" by putting it on stage with passion.[50] She read the story of Jesus's life through the lens of great drama and it thrilled her soul.[51]

In *The Dogma is the Drama*, she chastised the church for making Scripture boring despite their best intentions to teach it well. She noted this was a particular tragedy as they had bored people ". . . in the name of the One who assuredly never bored a soul in those thirty-three years during which he passed through the world like a flame."[52] In response to hearing one of her plays on the BBC, one listener stated, "We quickly felt the wild, unruly, unfriendly atmosphere of the inn and as the play progressed and as we followed each sidelight on the environment of the little family the whole scene became amazingly vivid. . . . None of us realized before how much we had just accepted the story without properly visualizing it."[53] Audience members who attended her play, *The Man Born to be King*, responded to it with statements that included: "enthralling," "deeply moving," "made it come alive," "better than dry as dust sermons," "real humanity," "the scene and people came alive," "it took me back through all the ages to the cave at Bethlehem."[54]

Women and Feminism

Dorothy Sayers was a strong and outspoken advocate for women. She had lively debates with C. S. Lewis about the ordination of women in the Church of England, after he initiated a dialogue with her about her thoughts on the issue in 1948.[55] Through her life, she modeled the impact a woman could have by stewarding her gifts with excellence for the building up of society and the church.

In *Are Women Human?* Sayers rebuked the common rhetoric of human rights and human issues consistently attributed to men, while women's rights were another category altogether. At this point in history, men's choices defined human choices.[56] Women were still denied opportunity to vote and were denied access to certain careers. Although Sayers had earned her degree from Oxford and had the distinction of being one of the very first to be granted her degree, she had to wait 10 years after completing her coursework before Oxford determined it was acceptable to confer degrees on women.[57] Tischler writes, "her graduation was an unforgettable, life-changing moment for all that it symbolized, both for her [personal] intellectual achievement" and also for what it demonstrated about the recognition of women as scholars.[58] For 40 years prior to Sayers enrolling at Oxford, women had been fighting for equality in opportunity education, degrees, and professional life.[59] Women were prohibited from many professions and marriage was considered the highest goal for all women. To Sayers, this was a profound waste of human potential and resources.[60]

Sayers used her fiction writing to illuminate the tragedy of the wasted lives of women. In *Unnatural Death*, she illustrated a healthy perspective of women as her characters were strong women, devoted to their faith, capable in their work and fulfilled.[61] Sayers insisted that work was given to humanity by their Creator, not just to men, or just to women.

Conversely, God gave each person gifts and abilities; those gifted for the work, should do that particular work. Gender, according to Sayers, was not a qualification for work, for "[t]he purpose of work must be found in the value of its product, which must be of the quality that it glorifies God. As creators, people must make themselves subservient to the work for which they are best suited, in order to bring into being that which they were created to create."[62] In her perspective, humans are made to work, and work is not something one must do to live, but rather what one lives to do.[63] Work is God-given and is not discriminatory based on gender.[64]

Sayers did not see a distinction between men and women for work or any other aspect of life. In *Are Women Human?* she had a forceful response to the "imbeciles" who asked her to speak about the topic of detective fiction "from a woman's perspective": "Go away and don't be silly. You might as well ask what is the female angle on an equilateral triangle."[65] Her goal for all women was for them to think of themselves as human, equal, not inferior or superior, to all other humans.[66] *Gaudy Nights*, one of her detective novels, also illustrates this belief. In this novel, Sayers placed the main character, a woman, in a university as a leader and an intellectual, who used her intellectual skills to solve the crime.[67] This was the first novel, in the genre of detective fiction, to highlight a woman.[68]

Most of the authors who have written on Sayers mention the lack of scholarship surrounding her life and work. In fact, Simmons's 2005 book, *Creed without Chaos*, is one of the first to present research on Sayers as a theologian, and this is despite the fact that her writings effuse theology. Her life was theologically informed, as was her thinking and writing. She may have been overlooked because she was a female scholar, or it may be that Simmons was correct in attributing it to the vast variety and volume of her work. There seems to be enough theological material in her fiction work alone, however, that a lifetime of study could be done to reach the depths of her theological themes and instruction.

Sayers, according to Simmons, "had a unique combination of talents: a keen theological sense coupled with tremendous writing skill and a concern for how ordinary people understood Christianity" —talents, Simmons posited, which are vital and relevant for today.[69] Although Dorothy Sayers wrote in the twentieth century, tempting one to discount her work as irrelevant for a modern audience, her mastery of transportation in teaching Christian doctrine is as important today as when she originally wrote. Her passion for the reality of the *imago dei* and the life-altering ramifications of this reality for all of humanity, is a relevant example of God's perspective and intentions for humanity, even in the twenty-first century. Christian communication scholars can learn a tremendous amount from the example of her life and writings. Her commitment to excellence, her love of doctrine, her incredible attention to detail, her expansive knowledge of her culture and society, her insatiable appetite for learning, and her humility in continually working to become a better writer, and therefore a more effective communicator, are all characteristics which made her an effective and influential communicator and are qualities worth emulating for any communication scholar.

Chapter 29

All Truth is Still God's Truth: Christian Scholars Modeling Reality

NICK PERTLER

Response Summary: This response explores a transformationalist approach to culture, which holds that Christianity should actively engage and reshape secular culture. Pertler begins by discussing this historical perspective and its influence on Christian thought as embodied by Augustine. Augustine's embrace of classical learning for Christian purposes, namely rhetoric, illustrates the enduring significance of the idea that "all truth is God's truth." He then explores how this principle should inform contemporary Christian scholarship. By considering the concerns raised by Mark Noll regarding evangelical anti-intellectualism and the neglect of the life of the mind and George Marsden concerning the exclusion of Christian viewpoints and their potential to enrich the university, he argues that when Christian scholars model the implications of the reality that all truth is God's truth, they contribute meaningfully to broad academic discourse.

IN THE LAST DECADE of the twentieth century, two foundational texts with serious implications for Christian scholars were published. The first, Mark Noll's *The Scandal of the Evangelical Mind*, claims that evangelical Christianity has neglected the life of the mind and has become significantly anti-intellectual, which hinders the faith's overall credibility when it comes to engaging with the secular Academy.[1] Noll's work was followed by George Marsden's *The Outrageous Idea of Christian Scholarship*, which advances the claim that the inclusion of more Christian viewpoints would enrich the university and should be more welcome as they are largely excluded at present.[2] Marsden's argument seems to follow naturally from Noll's: if there is really no such thing as good Christian scholarship to a substantial degree, then perhaps it is no wonder that we do not have more of these voices represented in the secular Academy.

In the recent years since, updated editions of Noll and Marsden's books have been published, both noting slight optimism that in some ways things are improving. An underlying presupposition that Noll and Marsden both share is that Christian scholarship matters for society at large and not just for the church alone. Christian scholars operating in obedience to the Scriptures are called to "do all to the glory of God" (1 Cor. 10:31, English Standard Version). As a result, Christian scholars should be known as those who strive to do good work. Further, all Christian scholars walking faithfully with their Lord are directed to live and conduct their work in a way that exemplifies humility, honesty, and love. These characteristics, when put into practice, also benefit the secular Academy and, as such, Christians can provide a model of scholarship that is credible and useful for all. However, whether this benefit is apparent to non-Christian scholars is an open question. Christian scholarship *should* matter to the secular Academy because Christians sincerely and authentically engaged in the enterprise of scholarship are operating in good faith that all truth is God's truth, and as such, they have the potential to provide genuine and unique insight for everyone.

This essay proceeds as follows. First, I explore the historical approach that believes Christianity should transform secular culture. Next, I take a closer look at a figure who embodies this approach, Augustine, and explore the philosophical importance of the concept all truth is God's truth. Finally, I argue that the concerns of Noll and Marsden can begin to be addressed when Christian scholars model implications of the reality that all truth is God's truth, which is beneficial for the whole Academy—Christian and non-Christian alike.

Christianity and Culture

Believers in Jesus Christ are called to be in the world but not of the world (John 17:14–18). This means that Christians are to engage with culture in some capacity, but not to the extent that they lose sight of their heavenly priorities. The way this has looked across time and space has been by no means uniform. For some have served God and those of the world by physically disengaging, while others have engaged with culture critically and redemptively.

In a classic treatment of the subject, Richard Niebuhr's *Christ and Culture* identifies some of the various approaches the church has followed over the generations when it comes to the issue, broadly speaking, of how to relate to culture: (1) Christ is against culture, (2) Christ is of culture, (3) Christ is above culture, (4) there is a paradox of Christ with culture, and (5) Christ is the transformer of culture.[3] Each of these positions are worth examining and have similarities and overlap in places; for the purposes of this essay, though, I will be focusing on the last one.

Before looking at this particular framework for cultural engagement in more detail, it will be helpful to establish a basic working definition of culture. Niebuhr describes culture as human activity as distinct from the natural world. Culture is not only social but also human achievement, "the work of men's minds and hands,"[4] that must constantly be developed and maintained. This necessity to preserve culture is important when seen against the backdrop of the value judgments it implies. The culture we create displays certain purposes we have in mind for humanity, so too the culture that we preserve. Taking the institution of learning as an example, Niebuhr warns, "Let education and training lapse for one generation, and the whole grand structure of past achievements falls into ruin."[5] Keeping these factors in mind is helpful for Christians as they recognize the pluralistic tendencies of the cultures within which they find themselves, particularly in the context of the life of the mind and what is taught in their educational institutions.

Fundamental to the framework of Christ as transformer of culture are the beliefs that "culture is under God's sovereign rule, and that the Christian must carry on cultural work in obedience to the Lord."[6] Niebuhr characterizes this framework as more hopeful than some of the others, and he proceeds to list some of the theological convictions underpinning such a conversionist approach. The first is a profound acknowledgment of Christ's sovereign creative activity in the present moment, ordering the affairs of society according to his purposes, with or without a degree of cognizant participation on the behalf of humanity.

Second, these conversionists tend to emphasize a view of the world in general and humanity in particular as created good but now living under the corruption of sin because of the Fall. Niebuhr describes this corruption as inordinate or a type of misdirection for humanity:

> He loves with the love that is given him in his creation, but loves beings wrongly, in the wrong order; he desires good with the desire given him by his Maker, but aims at goods that are not good for him and misses his true good.[7]

Thus, culture needs to be transformed to achieve rightful order.

The third and final distinctive theological conviction for conversionists has to do with a view of history that focuses on the eternal present. In other words, this approach tends to draw attention to God's capacity and willingness to work in the present moment of history with a responding humanity, as opposed to emphasizing the past or future works in time. Here we have "[t]he divine possibility of a present renewal,"[8] to which Christ's transformation of culture is part. As identified by Niebuhr, one of the key representatives of this perspective is Augustine. As Niebuhr puts it,

> The Roman rhetorician becomes a Christian preacher, who not only puts into the service of Christ the training in language and literature given him by his society, but, by virtue of the freedom and illumination received from the gospel, uses that language with a new brilliance and brings a new liberty into that literary tradition.[9]

When placed in the context of how he makes continued use of his educational training in rhetoric, both in his thought and lived experience, Augustine embodies the Christian cultural transformation approach.

All Truth is God's Truth

As the dominance of the Western Roman Empire drew to a close, the fifth century AD was a time of great social reform. Augustine (AD 354–430) preserved the premodern rhetorical tradition amidst great turmoil and, ultimately, appropriated classical rhetorical theory toward Christian ends—a move that remained intact throughout the early Middle Ages. Augustine defends the role of rhetoric in Christian learning because he recognizes that "every good and true Christian should understand that wherever he may find truth, it is his Lord's."[10] Augustine retrieves the best of pagan learning, including rhetoric, to bring it into God's service. Augustine believes in the necessity of rhetorical education for Christian use because through rhetoric one learns how to express one's thoughts adequately.[11]

Through Augustine's work in *On Christian Doctrine*, the premodern rhetorical tradition receives validation and simultaneously becomes modified for Christian ends. In *On Christian Doctrine*, Augustine's educational perspective follows from the idea that learning should be attentive to moral and intellectual formation, which, for the most part, harmonizes with classical culture. Augustine clears the way for Christians to make use of the liberal arts curriculum. Augustine keeps the unity of eloquence and wisdom intact and helps the intellectuals of his age to see the benefits of pagan learning in the attainment of truth and virtue when filtered through Scripture.[12]

As a classically trained orator, Augustine brings rhetoric under the Christian umbrella because he understands its value. Augustine understands the value of rhetoric for persuading his followers to act upon the beliefs they already hold. Augustine's rhetoric and philosophy of education, or what James Murphy calls his metarhetoric, centers on the idea that,

> each man is an individual learner, placed in the universe by a God who has given him, as an individual, the means by which he may learn about the universe, therefore about God, and therefore about the role in the universe which God intends him to play.[13]

Augustine exhibits a rhetorical mindset that he obtains through classical learning, learning that he finds necessary for proper interpretation of difficult Scriptures. Augustine rejects certain aspects of the pagan arts but praises the process of learning as a cultural ideal—an ideal that finds fulfillment when united with Christian objectives. Gerald Press shows the foundational part *On Christian Doctrine* plays in bringing the premodern rhetorical tradition into Christian education. Press identifies that the doctrine in Augustine's Christian educational commitments makes up for certain things he finds lacking in classical learning.[14] In particular, the unity of Christian doctrine provides an intelligible view of the world, whereas much of pagan learning has contradictory tendencies. Augustine also sees a more complete morality and pathway to happiness through the Christian doctrine that preaches salvation, redemption, and forgiveness—ideas that are foreign to pagan ears. Most importantly, Augustine makes learning a form of piety.[15]

Augustine understands the importance of learning how to speak truth well, because it makes it more accessible to diverse audiences. Augustine not only authorizes the adoption of pagan learning when used in ways that do not contradict Christian teaching, but he also sees its relative benefit for advancing Christian doctrine. The principle that permits Augustine to adopt pagan learning alongside Christianity, that all truth is God's truth, discloses itself as typically rhetorical. Thus, Augustine defends elements of human custom while simultaneously appropriating it to the needs of his historical moment.

Several decades ago, Arthur Holmes wrote a book titled, *All Truth is God's Truth*.[16] In examining the concept expressed in the title, Holmes emphasizes the point that this does not mean that all truth whatsoever is to be found in Scripture. Scripture does claim that the Bible contains all truth needed for living a godly life (2 Pet. 1:3), but not everything possible for living a productive life on earth. There are many areas of truth and knowledge that can be learned apart from the Bible. Additionally, the concept that all truth is God's truth does not imply that human beings are necessarily able to grasp all truth, but it does suggest an intelligibility to the world based upon rational, non-contradictory principles. Arguably the most important thing about the idea we are examining is that

> the truth about Christ is the focal center to which all other truth about everything in creation is ultimately connected. Whatever we understand about nature is ultimately about his creative wisdom and power; whatever we do in human art and science ultimately comes from the creative and rational potential that God invested in men by making us in his own image.[17]

For those Christian academics who live by faith in this reality, it should impact not only scholarship but also broader cultural engagement.

Modeling Reality

Augustine's thought, all truth is God's truth, is not only a helpful reminder of the need for Christians to engage with secular scholarship, but also, perhaps just as important, that there are implications for such an approach in terms of how modeling this reality might influence non-Christian scholars. Modeling is a form of indirect influence. Since all truth is God's truth, Christian scholars have reason to be confident and, as such, they should demonstrate the behaviors and values that result from this conviction, with the hope of creating a contagious atmosphere that unbelieving scholars will implement and benefit from. In this final section of the essay, I will discuss the significance for the secular Academy when Christian scholars model implications of the reality that all truth is God's truth.

But before getting to these main implications, I digress for a moment to examine George Marsden's helpful distinction of Christian versus non-Christian scholarship. Marsden reminds us that when we are dealing with "facts" in scholarship, there should be nothing to distinguish that content when relayed from a Christian scholar or a non-Christian scholar. Mathematical equations have the same answer regardless of worldview. The differences may start to appear when we are discussing interpretation of facts, and perhaps even more so when the scholarship lead to questions of moral action. As Marsden explains, "at one level such differences might look like mere partisanship, at a deeper level they have to do with large-scale beliefs about what the world is, or should be, like."[18] An additional general difference could be the research questions being pursued. Christian scholars will likely have research priorities influenced by their faith, which shapes their scholarly agendas.

Marsden lists some ways in which the Christian faith ought to impact one's scholarship, which is not to imply that these are unique and do not apply to non-Christian scholars, but they should be considered foundational for Christian scholars. First, the motivation to do the work well can be greatly influenced by one's faith commitment. Second, just like many nonreligious scholars who approach their work with altruistic motives, even more so should Christian scholars be asking how their work is making a tangible difference in people's lives, especially since Scripture commands such a posture. Third, this type of posture could lead to the direct opening of specific faith-based research avenues or communities that would otherwise not exist. Fourth, the tendency of Christian scholars should be to look at their work as contributing to larger questions of meaning and purpose that would otherwise not arise apart from a prior faith commitment.

Marsden also draws attention to a potential pitfall of Christian scholarship when approached in the wrong way. Robert Wuthnow's review of Mark Noll's *The Scandal of the Evangelical Mind* provides an entry point. He states that

> good Christian scholarship may be virtually indistinguishable from scholarship done by anyone else. In my own discipline of sociology, for instance, studies of impoverished families, community service, personal morality, health reform, sexuality, and values have flourished in recent years—much of it compatible with a Christian worldview, and yet little of it flaunts that perspective.[19]

Marsden picks up on Wuthnow's use of the word "flaunts" in his evaluation of Noll's thesis. One thing all Christian scholars should be wary of is giving the unintentional perception that because one's work is presented as explicitly conducted under the framework of a Christian worldview, that therefore one's conclusions are automatically superior to others or even worse, "as claiming divine sanction for one's point of view."[20] This does not mean that all viewpoints are equally valid or that the Christian scholar should not challenge other points of view; rather, Christians practicing the virtues of charity and humility should engage in what Marsden calls "fair-mindedness." Attempting to truly understand a topic from multiple viewpoints and not using one's Christian faith commitment as a short cut for hard work, will lead to greater engagement with non-Christian scholars.

We are now able to see how the concerns of Noll and Marsden can begin to be addressed when Christian scholars model implications of the reality that all truth is God's truth. First, by remembering and acting upon the belief that all truth is God's truth, Christian scholars have the basis to exemplify courage while engaging with the scholarship of the secular Academy. Just as Augustine took a courageous position to engage with the best of secular learning for God's purposes, which was by no means a uniform opinion within the church of his day, so too Christians today can and should be characterized by those who support the marketplace of ideas. Christians will not only continue to benefit from the genuine insights of the secular Academy but also put themselves into a more credible position when seen as academics who are not afraid to engage with provocative ideas and can instead model the type of respect they hope to receive even if they cannot ultimately agree.

Next, Christian scholars who take seriously the idea that all truth is God's truth must understand how important it is to have their voices included in the Academy because they are people deliberately pursuing ideas through the framework of a Christian worldview. As such, they believe they are potentially contributing life-giving content into a scholarly conversation that could otherwise be, from their view, misdirected. This is not the false mindset mentioned earlier of assuming that their scholarship is divinely sanctioned; rather, it is a type of God-honoring humility in that sincere Christians and scholars are owning their predisposition while operating under strong conviction to do honest work so that they may help others (Eph. 4:28). Doing honest work includes doing hard work and doing it well. These first two points fall under Marsden's discussion of faithful presence in academia, which can be achieved "simply by carrying out high-quality work and attending respectfully to the work done by others."[21]

Finally, in this postmodern age whereby the dominant viewpoints of the Academy have grown less homogeneous, the Christian perspective is theoretically well-positioned. Of course, to be credible and relevant Christian scholars must continue to enter in through the preestablished gates initiated by non-Christian thinkers who are hallowed in the modern university, for as Noll reminds us, "they have set the agenda for what goes on throughout the Academy."[22] While perhaps the Christian perspective remains a minority in the Academy, in the context of the United States, Christian scholars must remain advocates of free speech while recognizing that this potentially protects speech of other minority groups whose views they challenge. But by modeling the courage of Augustine, they can strive to find the useful and helpful out of that which is misguided.

Conclusion

Ultimately, the work and lives of Christian scholars present the opportunity to be witnesses of their faith in the secular Academy. For C. S. Lewis, "culture is a storehouse of the best (sub-Christian) values,"[23] which means it contains relative goods that should be identified as precursors to something better. For example, Lewis thinks Christians should celebrate the value of honor in European literature and recognize it as a potential foretaste of courage, "the ideal of knighthood may prove a schoolmaster to the ideal of martyrdom."[24] In the same way, Christian scholars who engage with the best ideas of the secular Academy can find the ways in which these ideas connect to the larger framework of unified knowledge. By modeling an approach where they are finding the good in the secular Academy, they can affirm sub-Christian ideas while witnessing to the reality that all truth is God's truth.

Chapter 30

Christianity and Communication:
Faith-inflected Scholarly and Pedagogical Praxis

JANIE MARIE HARDEN FRITZ

Response Summary: Christian intellectual traditions find common ground in a moment that challenges assumptions about the real, the right, and the good. Christian scholars are called to embrace excellence of disciplinary practice while remaining faithful to a Christian worldview. We enact a dual commitment to academic excellence and a vocational call, the latter of which provides a "why" for the "how" of our scholarly endeavors, just as our students need a "why" for the "how" of their educational pursuits. Although Christian mission-based educational institutions and secular institutions offer different contexts for the work of Christian scholars, both can be engaged faithfully. This reflection on the contributions of Fr. Paul A. Soukup, SJ, George Marsden, Mark Noll, and Calvin Troup to the Christianity and Communication Studies Network's 2024 unconference recognizes the need for venues like this one for support and encouragement of Christian academics.

THIS UNCONFERENCE, the first offered by the Christianity and Communication Studies Network (CCSN), is exactly the gathering I had longed for and hoped for as a PhD student. Questions about the intersection of faith and intellectual life, how a Christian worldview might speak to issues in the Academy, how persons of faith might offer a robust account of how assumptions and presuppositions of Christianity could be directed to intellectual issues of the day and could be reasonable and even compelling—these issues absorbed me even more than my studies in communication; they pointed toward a foundationally meaningful project. As I came to learn over the course of the years, persons of faith have been engaged in this project for a very long time. Indeed, as I began to discover the contours of faith-engaged reason, or reason-engaged faith, I gained hope and encouragement in my intellectual life and my understanding of what it means to be a person of faith seeking to understand human communication as a defining feature of human being and existence. I kept pursuing this question, and when I arrived at Duquesne University, the question continued to compel my research and teaching. I learned more about Christian tradition and encountered multiple voices from past and present offering coordinates for this very important quest.

Called to Faith and Reason

Just before leaving Madison, Wisconsin, where I completed my PhD in communication arts, I had begun to subscribe to *First Things*, a remarkable interdisciplinary publication that invites public intellectuals from Jewish and Christian tradition to reflect on what Richard John Neuhaus had called the "naked public square"—the eclipse of faith perspectives or religious tradition(s) as legitimate contributors to public discourse—and related issues of faith and culture. What role has religion to play in public life? This question is not far from Tertullian's question, which has continued to reverberate over the course of centuries: What has Athens to do with Jerusalem? Quite a bit, we have discovered through figures such as Augustine and St. Thomas Aquinas, the Reformed tradition, and many others down through the ages who hail from Catholic, Protestant, and Orthodox perspectives and who have sought to show forth the image of God in their intellectual work.

I remember, in my early days at Duquesne, reading Mark Noll's *The Scandal of the Evangelical Mind* and George Marsden's *The Outrageous Idea of Christian Scholarship*. How good it was to see them as required reading for the first CCSN unconference and to hear again the voices of these towering intellects! I can imagine no better theme for a conference in which we met to engage questions specific to the field of communication, media, and rhetoric as they speak to larger questions of faith and the Academy. What we have learned from this conference will help us reflect on the contours of education from a faith-informed perspective—a Christian perspective, broadly conceived. The Catholic intellectual tradition, the Reformed intellectual tradition, the evangelical intellectual tradition—outrageous and scandalous as they may be, each with various strands and approaches to scholarship and learning taking place in multiple institutional environments—have insights to offer each other for a deeper and more textured understanding of the life of the faith-informed mind in the Academy. As we live out our callings, as Fr. Paul A. Soukup, SJ, notes, we will be equipped to serve our surrounding communities as we seek to form whole persons through education as we remain faithful to our academic calling, our good work in the world, our labor worthy of being done.

Certainly. the institutional location where we live out our vocation will shape the extent to which we will work explicitly or implicitly toward that formation, as will the larger environment, as Soukup goes on to observe. Looking at the United States as a cultural context, we see evangelical and Catholic scholars wrestling with what it means to work as an academic and a person of faith. In their videos for the unconference, we hear Marsden and Noll offering their perspectives on decades of development of what it means to work within two communities: the academic community and the community of faithful Christian practice. We understand that these communities have, in some cases, been happily joined, as Soukup notes. This integration has typically found a home in religiously grounded educational enterprises, but it has also found pockets of welcome in secular institutions as teachers and scholars of faith have inflected their studies with assumptions and presuppositions of faith, inflections that have gained some degree of welcome in a world of multiplicity and difference, as Noll suggests.

Common Ground and New Opportunities

To trace the history of secularization and of faith-grounded considerations of investigation, learning, and knowledge is beyond the scope of the conference and of this reflection, but what I see emerging is a new partnership across strands of historic Christianity that share in common what C. S. Lewis calls "mere Christianity," also addressed by Marsden in his presentation. The hegemony of empiricist and materialist understandings of the world is no longer in play as it once was; even philosophy has opened possibilities for understanding questions of human life and being that press beyond purely secular approaches, harkening back to a pre-modern worldview that acknowledged a Creator and human accountability to something—or Someone—beyond our control. As Marsden notes, today's historical moment sees an expansion of possibilities, with legitimacy offered to diverse points of view. Science, with its assumed ontology and epistemology, which relegated religious thinking to the background, is no longer the architectonic framework for engagement. Modernity has given way to postmodernity and its welcome of difference. In this sense, we see Lyotard's notion of petite narratives emerging as an opportunity for Christian perspectives to take their place in the public square and in the Academy, as our speakers have noted.

Marsden articulates a key presupposition of a Christian worldview: We live in a created universe in which there is a right and wrong; we inhabit a moral order that is not constructed or arbitrary. Although we do not understand this world perfectly, being limited in our understanding and recognizing our identity as existentially flawed creatures, we are feeling our way along as best we can and with accountability for what we do know. Soukup notes that the assumptions underlying the Catholic intellectual tradition and the Jesuit approach to education share some commonalities with evangelical approaches, but because of the history of a Catholic understanding of the relationship between faith and reason, or Scripture and science, particular issues will not be of as much concern to Catholic tradition, which works from a different hermeneutic starting point. Nevertheless, both perspectives have excellent representatives who have worked to bring a Christian perspective to various academic disciplines over the decades—indeed, over the centuries.

The questions scholars bring to their disciplines and fields are driven by their assumptions and perspectives. There is no neutral ground, so making assumptions clear is important. Noll notes the need for Christian analysis of the surrounding culture. In this sense, we are called, as Soukup suggests, to community engagement that is actually cultural engagement—in this case, the community is the larger society, including the mediascape, the institutional environment, and all elements of our social world. But as Noll also suggests, we see challenges to research that appears to question current cultural assumptions based in values centering on human choice and inclination—political polarization has left no one unscathed. Assumptions about human persons, the human body, and the relationship of human beings to institutions drive almost everything we research and publish. It is difficult to find an objective or neutral perspective that would judge between competing claims, particularly when there is disagreement about foundational issues and starting points—the rules guiding play, so to speak. We do well to provide clear ground and starting points for the work we do, as so many scholars connected with this unconference have done.

One must choose elements of reality to focus on and issues to think about out of the many, many options available; those choices are guided by assumptions and by the goods we protect and promote. As Christians who follow a scholarly vocation seek to be faithful to their calling, they must, as Calvin L. Troup notes in his reflection, do double duty: learn the wisdom of the Babylonians and remain deeply steeped in a faith tradition. The CCSN has provided a welcome place to publish unapologetically Christian work in the field of communication, filling a great need on the part of faith-based educational and scholarly enterprises.

In 2017, I gave a talk that became an essay published in the *Journal of Communication and Religion* that traced understandings and elements of (the) Catholic intellectual tradition(s), noting how this tradition of scholarly practice responded to various historical moments, eventually focusing on the United States as a context for consideration of questions Catholic intellectuals and academics were asking. Historical, cultural, and intellectual developments shaped the institutional development of Catholic universities, as we note in Soukup's discussion of Jesuit education, a tradition with a storied history. As I look back, I am struck by what used to appear as parallel paths of evangelical and Catholic thinkers and scholars gradually converging, or at least intersecting in fruitful ways.

As secularization and cultural changes continued, as noted by James Davison Hunter in his now-classic *Culture Wars*, strands of religious traditions that once considered themselves enemies cast new eyes on each other, finding common ground on minimalist understandings of historic Christian tradition while maintaining important doctrinal distinctions on key issues.[1] *Evangelicals and Catholics Together*, a volume edited by Charles Colson and Richard John Neuhaus 30 years ago, provided evidence of what would have been thought impossible in the early years of the twentieth century and certainly prior to that time.[2] The fault lines shifted, and a "why" for the "how" of finding common ground emerged.

A "Why" for the "How" of Excellent Practice: Living the Christian Academic Vocation

A "why" for the "how" is needed more than ever today in multiple contexts, and a central one propelling this unconference is education. Soukup cites Nietzsche through the reflection of Neil Postman on the importance of a "why" for education beyond temporary motivation, a "why" that keeps students engaged even when they do not feel like it. This "why" propels the will to keep going. This "why" for education is also relevant for those of us who teach and do research in the Academy where we will teach those students who need a "why" for the "how" of pressing on when they'd rather be elsewhere.

For academics, Noll notes, that "why" can become localized to the desire to impress one's peers. To some extent, that "why" has a place if it is directed not toward acclaim for its own sake, but toward excellence defined by goods internal to a given set of practices. A broader "why" that is related, but not identical, to the desire to impress one's peers is the desire to do one's best at an enterprise, to incorporate, as far as they do not transgress the grounds of faith from which we work, the practices of the field in which we find our vocations. Sometimes we may redefine those standards of excellence, but only once we have become experts, true craftsmen in that practice, perhaps even standard bearers of excellence in that practice. That is exactly what many Christian scholars have done, in fact, with the outrageous idea of Christian scholarship.

Alasdair MacIntyre, in his classic treatment of the state of philosophy, specifically regarding moral philosophy and questions of the good, in *After Virtue* (now in its third edition), speaks of traditions, of communities of practice marked by characteristic virtues.[3] Quentin Schultze raises this point in his conversation with George Marsden—that there is a way of approaching the task of intellectual activity that is marked by a set of virtues. Sloppy scholarship and ill-informed teaching are problematic for everyone and do no credit to those engaged in them or to the communities they represent. Even perspectives one does not agree with—for instance, approaches or methodologies that emerge as hegemonic for some time—may be acknowledged, even as one's own direction moves differently. The task becomes making one's presuppositions clear and accounting for the scholarly moves one makes, demonstrating how one is following a scholarly tradition of practice even as one walks on different presuppositional ground. When presuppositions suggest different approaches, offering a "why" for that "how," just as qualitative and interpretive scholars offered a rationale for different ways of knowing based on different ontological presuppositions for phenomena, Christian scholars can provide the "why" for the "how" of their approaches, even if others may challenge those approaches.

Marsden's "why" points to a conviction that one's work matters, and that one's calling to do scholarship that brings glory to God can be that "why." His work reflecting on and considering his own faith tradition with both critique and acclaim is a helpful example. When Christians take on the vocation of academic pursuits, they form a new community of practice, one that has to do the double duty, as Troup points out, of engaging two sets of expectations and bringing them together, remaining faithful to each. It is hard work!

Soukup's discussion of Jesuit education shows a focus on a particular tradition of practice that has engaged education and scholarship in response to various historical moments, developing distinctiveness in specifically articulated ways that can serve as a guide. His reflection runs parallel to that of Troup, who articulates a position from a Reformed perspective. Different approaches to Scripture and interpretation and to the life of faith yield different understandings of what it means to integrate faith and reason, Christianity and education. One is more implicit and the other more explicit in approach. Both have solid, tested ground and practices, but the emphasis is different in each case, which also reflects commitments to an individually centered compared to a community-centered understanding of the meaning of the church. Both traditions certainly have concerns for the person and the community, but different theological understandings move these traditions in different ways. The differences are valuable, however, and combine to offer a welcoming place for taking on the scholarly and educational task at hand. I am grateful to Robert H. Woods Jr. and the CCSN for such a place and look forward to the next gathering!

Chapter 31

Reimagining Evangelical Communication: John Wesley's Three Rules as an Antidote to Mark Noll's *Scandal of the Evangelical Mind*

ABRAM J. BOOK

Response Summary: Mark Noll's now classic book *The Scandal of the Evangelical Mind* indicts evangelicalism's intellectual poverty, but his analysis largely overlooks a critical dimension: how communication practices shape—and sabotage—evangelical engagement with ideas. By applying John Wesley's three rules ("do no harm," "do all the good you can," and "attend to the ordinances of God"), this essay argues that redeeming the evangelical mind requires reforming not only what evangelicals think but how they communicate. Wesley's framework, rooted in grace-oriented dialogue and communal discernment, offers a path to heal the fractures Noll identifies.

JOHN WESLEY, ACCORDING TO observed professor and theologian Vinson Synan, was not only "the indomitable founder of Methodism," but was also "the spiritual and intellectual father of the modern holiness and Pentecostal movements, which arose from Methodism in the last [nineteenth] century."[1] Wesley, an English clergyman, theologian, and evangelist, was educated at Oxford University. While there, he and his brother Charles, in association with George Whitefield, formed the "Holy Club," a group dedicated to spiritual discipline and social outreach.[2] In 1738, he experienced a profound spiritual awakening, describing his heart as "strangely warmed" during a Moravian meeting. This event catalyzed his evangelistic career and theological convictions. Wesley's emphasis on personal holiness, social reform, and the doctrine of Christian perfection distinguished his movement, leading him to preach open-air sermons across Britain and establish a network of Methodist societies.[3] Furthermore, Wesley's prolific writing, organizational skills, and tireless itinerant ministry left an indelible mark on Protestant Christianity, influencing religious revival, social reform, and the abolitionist movement in both Britain and America.

Mark Noll rightly recognizes Wesley and several of his contemporaries as believing that diligent, rigorous mental activity was an important way to glorify God. At the same time, he places much of the blame for what he refers to as "the scandal of the evangelical mind" at the feet of Wesley's Holiness descendants. "None of them," he declares, "believed that intellectual activity was the only way to glorify God, or even the highest way, but they all believed in the life of the mind, and they believed in it *because* they were evangelical Christians."[4] In contrast, he argues that modern evangelicals "have not pursued comprehensive thinking under God or sought a mind shaped to its furthest reaches by Christian perspectives."[5] Anti-intellectualism is not just a lack of thinking, however; it is a failure to communicate thoughtfully, exacerbating harm to the church's witness. Noll's "scandal" persists, not merely because of the overall lack of evangelical scholarship nor evangelicalism's long retreat from academia, but also because evangelicals lack grace-filled communication structures.

Wesley's "three rules" offer a tangible framework for cultivating that kind of communication, as well as an antidote to the lack of intellectual rigor or curiosity that Noll argues has permeated American evangelicalism for decades. The rules are "do no harm," "do all the good you can," and "attend to the ordinances of God." The General Rules of the Methodist Church, as published in the *United Methodist Church Book of Discipline 2016* state that doing no harm means "avoiding evil of every kind, especially that which is generally practiced."[6] Doing all the good one can means "doing good of every possible sort, and, as far as possible, to all men."[7] Finally, attending to the ordinances of God (sometimes referred to as "means of grace") can be defined as maintaining faithfulness and consistency in all public and individual acts of glory to God.[8] Ordinances of God can include but are not limited to the reading of Scripture, study, meditation, fasting, and prayer. When studiously and consistently applied to everyday conduct and discourse, Wesley's three rules offer a way for evangelicals to approach and frame public conversation and discourse in ways that both honor God and stimulate the mind.

"Do No Harm": Communication as Invitational Dialogue

Noll correctly critiques evangelicalism's intellectual superficiality but pays little attention to how communication styles affect the scandal. One example of this can be observed when evangelicals engage in combative rhetoric aimed at strongly supporting specific, perhaps dogmatic, positions while actively attempting to undermine opposing views. Sermons or media that preach only to the already convinced, confirm preexisting biases and actively avoid engagement with dissenting views also perpetuate the crisis. Finally, dismissive rhetoric on the part of evangelicals, such as labeling academic inquiry "worldly" to avoid engaging in uncomfortable debates or dialogue, also worsens the intellectual scandal.

Under Wesley's rules, and particularly the "do no harm" rule, communication should be understood as an ethical obligation. Wesley's rule to "do no harm" specifically condemns speech that divides or degrades. His *Advice to the People Called Methodists* (1746) urged followers to avoid "controversial preaching" that might inflame hatred.[9] Wesley's insistence on "peaceable" and "gentle" speech (Jas. 3:17), for example, should challenge today's evangelicals to stop weaponizing dehumanizing terms like "libs" or "snowflakes." Second, Wesley's journals regularly show him listening humbly and engaging atheists and Anglicans alike and sometimes at the same time—a model for answering critics without compromising conviction. Furthermore, "doing no harm" means redefining what is considered "biblical" communication. Scripture includes nuanced genres such as lament, parable, and poetry, and thus reducing public discourse to mere slogans, as evangelicals have seemed inclined to do, harms the Christian witness and the evangelical obligation to communicate biblically.

In fact, Wesley's *Earnest Appeal to Men of Reason and Religion* (1743), invites dialogue with skeptics.[10] This stands in stark contrast to some rhetoric of modern-day evangelical leaders, many of whom dismiss professors and elite universities as socially and theologically irredeemable. The evangelical mind will never grow or expand if such dismissive rhetoric is allowed to remain the norm regarding institutions of higher education. Doing no harm and treating communication with the ethical care it deserves in part means being willing to dialogue even with challenging ideas and perspectives. Wesley's second rule builds upon the first by moving the evangelical mind from engaging in open dialogue and avoiding destructive rhetoric to using communication as a tool for civic bridge-building.

"Do All the Good You Can": Communication as Civic Bridge-building

Noll effectively chronicles evangelicalism's retreat from academia but neglects how poor communication alienates broader society. In essence, one of Noll's blind spots in his critique of the evangelical mind is the civic cost of poor dialogue. Polarized rhetoric (e.g., framing climate science as "anti-God" or immigration reform as "racist") undermines evangelical credibility on issues like environmental stewardship. Wesley's admonition to "do all the good you can" means actively confronting those civic costs by using speech as a redemptive force for the common good.

Furthermore, Wesley's second rule demands communication that helps society to flourish. For example, Wesley humanized the poor through stories in his journals, rather than treating "the least of these" simply as statistics or data. Thus, modern evangelicals should prioritize telling the stories of marginalized people over data-based lobbying as a way of using communication as a vehicle for public good. Finally, Wesley offers an example of what could be considered digital discipleship when he harnessed print media in the form of pamphlets and journals to spread ideas.[11] One way Wesley's example might apply in contemporary evangelical contexts is through doing good by using social media to amplify nuance rather than outrage. The Methodist practice of "conferencing"—communal discernment—could reshape online discourse. Imagine evangelical leaders hosting Twitter spaces not to lecture but to listen to LGBTQ+ Christians or scientists.

Noll is correct to be concerned about the evangelical mind and the broader evangelical retreat from all things academic. However, Wesley's second rule demonstrates that an effective evangelical mind is not just well-read but also skilled in communication that builds bridges instead of bunkers. Wesley's third rule expands again upon his second, suggesting redemptive speech can be activated as a spiritual discipline or communal means of grace for intellectual hospitality.

"Attend to the Ordinances of God": Communal Practices for Intellectual Hospitality

Noll prioritizes rehabilitating individual evangelical thinkers but underestimates how communal practices shape intellectual culture. In this way, Noll's prescription is somewhat incomplete. Wesley's third rule appeals to communal aspects of spiritual growth tied to structured practices ("ordinances"). In short, Wesley's perspective could be interpreted to suggest that he viewed communication as a spiritual discipline and his own communication serves as evidence of that. Wesley, for example, calmly debated detractors who openly threatened him or questioned his theology often choosing to preach in open air environments such as fields, marketplaces and in front of walls—a stark contrast to the one-way, authoritarian pulpits common today. Though it was seen as indecent and ungentlemanly in Wesley's time, field preaching allowed his words to reach people who probably would otherwise have never set foot in a church building.[12]

Just as Wesley saw holy communion as a means of grace by which believers receive Jesus's presence, listening to "the least of these" (Matt. 25:40) could become a spiritual discipline.[13] If evangelicals are to alleviate Noll's scandal, they must devote themselves to true listening and re-cultivate communal habits of understanding rooted in loving God and neighbor first. The famed therapist M. Scott Peck wrote: "Since true listening involves a setting aside of the self, it also temporarily involves a total acceptance of the others. Sensing this acceptance, the speaker will feel less and less vulnerable, and more and more inclined to open up the inner recesses of his or her mind to the listener."[14]

While this should not be taken to mean that evangelicals cannot harbor or express theological opinions (quite the contrary), evangelicals must become better at recognizing when to attend to the means of grace. This means setting aside dogmatic feelings in favor of love, understanding, and productive dialogue. As Richard Foster points out, God richly and profoundly guides individuals, but "he also guides groups of people and can instruct the individual through the group experience. . . . The superintending Spirit would utilize the checks and balances of different believers to ensure that when their hearts were in unity they were in rhythm with the heartbeat of the Father."[15]

Second, the communal nature of early Methodist class meetings required collective confessing of "uncharitable words,"[16] a practice that might serve to temper online vitriol today. The decline of Sunday School, a Wesleyan innovation for lay education, mirrors evangelicalism's retreat from structured dialogue. Reimagining small groups as spaces for intellectual exploration (for example, discussing race and theology) could revive that tradition. The "ordinances of God" include practices that train believers to think and communicate collectively, resisting the individualism that fuels anti-intellectualism. While Noll's call to rehabilitate individual evangelical thinkers is a good one, it must be accompanied by a call to rehabilitate communal structures that allow for collective spiritual formation within the evangelical tradition more broadly if the scandal is to be fully remedied.

Conclusion: Toward a Communicative Ethos of Grace

Noll's "scandal" persists not merely because evangelicals lack scholars but because they lack grace-filled communication structures. By framing communication as both moral duty and spiritual discipline, evangelicals can develop a communicative ethos of grace, thereby addressing Noll's scandal at its roots. Elizabeth McLaughlin makes a similar argument related to Wesley's example of communication: "In a context where religion seems damaging to the public good, Wesley's notion of gift, choice, and action can offer an alternative witness, as embodied faith can speak louder than words."[17] Wesley's "do no harm" triad offers an even more specific corrective: First, by doing no harm, evangelicals can reject speech and communicative acts that dehumanize. Second, by "doing all possible good," evangelicals can not only avoid dehumanizing rhetoric but harness the power of dialogue for Kingdom benefit. Third, by attending to the ordinances of God, evangelicals can cultivate vital communal habits of humble listening and collective guidance.

Chapter 32

Communication Standpoint Theory and Animal Theology: Applying George Marsden and Quentin Schultze

Terri Lynn Cornwell

Response Summary: Communication scholars George Marsden and Quentin Schultze provide a theoretical foundation for application of a specific theory of communication—Standpoint Theory—to a relatively new discipline: Animal Theology. This case study begins with Marsden's four ways religious faith can interact with scholarship and applies Schultze's root assumptions for communication scholarship. With Marsden's and Schultze's work as fundamental, Standpoint Theory is then applied to Animal Theology. Standpoint Theory emphasizes the importance of the perspective of marginalized groups—in this case animals—in creating a more just society. Applying communication theory to Animal Theology also provides a valuable avenue for inter-faith dialogue, especially enlightening for Christians since faiths other than Christianity are often more compassionate to animals.

In his classic text *The Outrageous Idea of Christian Scholarship*, George Marsden outlines four ways religious faith can have an important bearing on scholarship. In addition to motivating the scholar, determining applications for research, and shaping sub-fields about one's work, faith can have an important bearing on how the scholar sees her field and how it fits into a larger framework of meaning, especially when one is dealing with "interpretations about humans and their relationships to the world and to others."[1] Examining human relationships to others, including all creatures created by God, can provide greater depth to our understanding of the fundamental tenets of communication (God/human, human/human, and human/animal).

In giving examples of how Christian theology might be integrated with other scholarship, Marsden first discusses the doctrine of creation. After questioning the weaknesses of methodological atheism, which rejects the doctrine of creation and posits that moral standards evolved as survival mechanisms and to serve cultural interests, Marsden suggests that Christians should embrace in their scholarship the doctrine of creation, which includes God-created laws. For example, "the principle of altruism—that the weak should be cared for by the strong—is not just a cultural norm but a norm given by God to all of humanity."[2] Inserting the doctrine of creation into a researcher's scholarship substantially changes how she thinks about human rights and moral principles—and, one would suggest, how that researcher thinks about animal rights and moral principles involving non-human creatures.

Building on Marsden's tenet of faith-based wisdom for Christian scholarship, while wholeheartedly embracing Christian theism (and the doctrine of creation, in particular) as the foundation for their research, communication scholars can then apply the root assumptions for communication scholarship proposed by Quentin Schultze. Schultze's first two assumptions set the stage for a discussion of Standpoint Theory in the realm of human/animal communication.[3] The first is "All Speech Is Action," suggesting that the language used in animal/human communication indicates an inherit responsibility toward all living things regardless of their standpoint; and the second is "All Messaging Comes Ultimately from Our Hearts," suggesting that the powerful (humans) should consider the standpoint of the powerless (animals).

Introduction to Animal Theology

Ancient Hebrew practices involving animals included animal sacrifice, which paralleled the predominant interpretation of Scripture, particularly from the Book of Genesis, which suggested humans were given "dominion" over the animals. While early Christianity abandoned animal sacrifice, the concept of human's power over animals continued as the predominate interpretation of Scripture. After the Scientific Revolution and Enlightenment, this interpretation was strengthened as Christianity "severed ties with the rest of nature, seeing humanity at the top of the hierarchy," and animals merely as "objects purely for utilitarian use."[4] Since the Enlightenment, "animals have been, for the most part, left off the pages in Judaism, Christianity, and Islam," but non-human creatures have been more prominent in Hinduism and Buddhism, as well as other Eastern religions, which have been more compassionate in their treatment of animals.[5]

Christian voices asking theological questions about animals, however quiet, have been a small part of spiritual deliberations over the centuries. Augustine and Aquinas excluded animals from considerations of justice,[6] but John Calvin emphasized that laws against maltreatment of animals in Deuteronomy indicated that God would condemn such cruelty against animals.[7] In the eighteenth century, John Wesley also spoke against animal cruelty, and in the nineteenth century Christians campaigned against animal cruelty and vivisection.

Voices emphasizing compassion for animals became more vigorous in the twentieth century, following the lead of the fledgling animal rights movement, and scriptural interpretations highlighting compassionate care for animals became more prominent. The story of Noah, which includes animals as partners with humans in God's covenant promise mentions "every living creature" six times in God's announcement of the covenant.[8] The poetry of Job contained in God's response shows God's concern for the wellbeing of animals (Job 12:10 and 38:39–41), and Psalms 104 and 145 outline God's compassion for all creatures (Ps. 104:10–15; 27–28 and Ps. 145:9).[9]

As the twenty-first century has progressed, more Christians have been concerned with the suffering of animals both from natural disease and human-inflicted pain like certain practices of factory farming. As author and professor of theology John Schneider observes: "How could such horrific suffering exist within the good creation of the omnipotent, omniscient, and morally perfect Christian God?"[10] Additional concern by Christians in the growing movement of Creation Care ministries indicates more interest in compassion for animals as part of God's creation. Furthermore, the relatively new profession of Animal Chaplain has brought compassionate care surrounding animals and their human companions to the forefront.

Animal theologian Andrew Linzey (b. 1952), an Anglican priest, faculty member of the Faculty of Theology at the University of Oxford, founder and director of the Oxford Centre for Animal Ethics, is a leading voice in Christian compassion for animals. Linzey's major theological principles include recognizing a reverence for life, the responsibility not to inflict pain, and the rights of animals as sentient beings. These tenets, clearly part of the Christian faith regarding human beings, are extended by Linzey to animals. In other words, reverence, responsibility, and rights are provided to the weak (animals) as a moral priority with humans as the servant species. Here the connection to communication Standpoint Theory becomes clear.

Bridge to Communication Standpoint Theory

Standpoint Theory has its roots in feminist ideology, which seeks to highlight women's voices, long silenced over millennia. In recent decades, the theory has been applied to other low power groups, most notably indigenous peoples.[11]

Standpoint Theory begins with the premise that people whose standpoint includes power and privilege generally want to maintain the status quo with little consideration of those who live from a disadvantaged standpoint. Furthermore, proponents of the theory state that to create a more just society, the perspectives of all should be considered—especially those who are powerless. This theoretical perspective accordingly emphasizes that "[t]hose with power define what is true and good,"[12] but people at the margins have a unique standpoint because they have nothing to lose and therefore can be more honest about reality. Thus, the marginalized are exactly the group who should be heard first.

Given the principles of Standpoint Theory, communication scholars, including those working from within a Christian perspective, can logically place animals in a marginalized group with each animal species having a unique standpoint. Carefully observing the standpoint of animals would enhance human/nonhuman animal relationships. For example, a growing number of scientists are studying emotions expressed by animals and how they are communicated to humans.[13] In addition, other researchers are looking at ways animals seem to exhibit compassion.[14]

Another way to employ Standpoint Theory would be to examine the critical need for certain dog breeds to have work to do (e.g., border collies, military dogs, service dogs). The standpoint of animals is also helpful when examining the animal industrial complex, as noted in the work of Temple Grandin, an autistic person who has used her autism to bring more humane practices to factory farming.[15]

Combining Linzey's Animal Theology with Standpoint Theory provides a path to increasing compassion for animals in Christianity and, if grounded in Marsden's and Schultze's tenets of Christian scholarship, would serve to advance the dual disciplines bringing a fresh voice to both.

In conclusion, Marsden's work laying out a foundation for Christian scholarship is especially appropriate when considering the intersection of Communication Studies and Animal Theology. This unique scholarship fits into the larger framework of meaning that Marsden emphasizes. For example, the Christian tenet of caring for the weak by the strong gains an additional layer of meaning when applied to animals. Furthermore, Schultze's assumption regarding the relationship of speech to action provides a way to examine how humans relate to all living creatures by studying their language about animals. Finally, Schultze instructs that all messaging comes from the human heart, thus suggesting that powerful humans should understand the standpoint of powerless animals and extend to them heartfelt compassion.

Chapter 33

Rethinking the Role of Dialogue in Persuasive Risk Communication: Introducing Normatively Responsible Instructional Advocacy

Timothy L. Sellnow and Deanna D. Sellnow

Response Summary: This essay introduces Normatively Responsible Instructional Advocacy (NRIA) as an innovative approach to risk communication steeped in the principles of Christian scholarship introduced by George Marsden in his book, *The Outrageous Idea of Christian Scholarship*. Traditional approaches to advocacy are typically situated in an atmosphere of winning and losing. Thus, these approaches tend to "absolutize one dimension of human experience and to subordinate all else to it."[1] Conversely, NRIA invites the co-creation of solutions together with audiences in the spirit of a "unifying experience" in the love of God.[2] The authors describe the process of NRIA as focused on achieving a balance among cognitive, affective, and behavioral learning via agile co-creation that honors the normative needs and expectations of diverse audiences.

ADVOCACY IS AN AMBIVALENT PHENOMENON. On one hand, advocacy is understood as persuasive communication in which one policy or approach prevails over competing proposals.[3] In this sense, advocacy ultimately produces winners and losers, which can also promote perceptions of arrogance on the part of the *winners* and resentment on the part of the *losers*. We instead propose conceiving of advocacy as speaking on behalf of—or better still, in concert with—risk bearers to co-create solutions to social problems at both the individual and community levels.[4] This form of advocacy cannot reach its potential unless it is inspired by compassion and love.

In this essay, we propose Normatively Responsible Instructional Advocacy (NRIA) as it eschews manipulation intended to "absolutize one dimension of human experience and to subordinate all else to it."[5] In contrast, we argue that NRIA is built on a foundation of compassion and loving God as a "unifying experience."[6] This unifying love for God and all of God's creatures opens the way for agile collaboration and the co-creation of solutions that honor the norms and expectations of diverse people and groups. The following paragraphs describe the nature of NRIA and clarify its potential for addressing George Marsden's call to Christian scholarship.[7]

NRIA as Dialogue

Initially, we situate NRIA in dialogue. Dialogue has long been a central feature in risk communication and is increasingly emphasized as a best practice for crisis communication.[8] The hope is that, through dialogue, solutions to the threat of risks and the immediate danger of crises can be co-created through shared dialogue among government agencies, organizations, and risk-bearers.[9] Four criteria must be met for NRIA to thrive:

1. NRIA message content must strive to achieve a balance among cognitive, affective, and behavioral learning outcomes.

2. Rhetorically sensitive improvisation must be an integral factor when co-constructing NRIA message content.

3. Agility is essential when distributing NRIA message content to diverse audiences.

4. NRIA message content must honor the norms and expectations of diverse audiences.

NRIA and Christian Scholarship

We believe this conceptualization of normatively responsible instructional advocacy fits particularly well with Marsden's call for Christian scholarship in two ways. First, we agree with his critique of pragmatism. Our approach to NRIA embraces some of the pragmatic functions (e.g., tolerance, openness, dialogue, civil discourse) that John Dewey and others secularized as a "common faith."[10] From a risk communication perspective, however, pragmatism all too easily presents these virtues as functions that can be practiced void of compassion and love. An example is the frequency with which comments such as "our hearts go out to the victims" have moved from virtuous sincerity to strategic obligation by crisis response spokespersons.

Second, to answer Marsden's call, we take solace in his theological context of the human condition. To achieve normatively responsible instructional advocacy, practitioners must speak from a place of compassion born in selflessness. Outside a theological perspective, such criteria for success may appear weak or naive. Conversely, we agree with Marsden that "loving God is a unifying experience."[11] We contend that NRIA draws its credibility, reason, and influence from this unity.

NRIA and Risk Communication

On a broad level, NRIA conceptualizes risk communication through the lens of learning. For instance, those at risk learn from subject matter experts who simultaneously learn about the nature of the audiences they serve. The balance of affective, cognitive, and behavioral learning ensures that all engage in the complete cycle of learning.[12] Affectively, the emotional toll of a risk must be recognized and treated with compassion. Cognitively, the risk must be understood on a practical level by those at risk, while subject matter experts simultaneously respond compassionately and sincerely to the personal needs and fears of their audience, providing a unifying message of love. Behavioral learning involves the ultimate co-creation of protective actions that are meaningful to and achievable by those at risk.

Commitments to both improvisation in creating messages and agility in delivering them is essential to meet the criteria of NRIA. Improvisation reflects an ongoing willingness by all participants in the communicative exchange to adapt their message content based on what they learn, as well as on the vacillating needs expressed by their audiences. Agility in message distribution entails a recognition that access to technology varies among audiences and that in-person communication is often the richest and most trusted form of interaction.[13]

Finally, a willingness to listen and learn from others, including those who are unlike us and potentially even classified as enemies, can and must occur through the unifying expression of love. Any communicative strategy perceived as manipulatively strategic is not normatively responsible. In this case, normative responsibility is indicative of the unifying love Marsden describes.[14] Thus, NRIA cannot be achieved without a willingness to offer grace in the communicative exchange.

Conclusion

In summary, we believe normatively responsible instructional advocacy is an apt alternative to traditional conceptualizations of risk communication as persuasion. NRIA is distinct from existing studies that seek to determine how and why various target populations are best persuaded or manipulated. Whereas a strategic approach is sender-focused and based on an assumption that experts know best, NRIA is instead grounded in co-creation as a "normatively desirable argumentative practice."[15] NRIA assumes that what people impacted by risk have to say is important.[16] It also invites those engulfed in high-risk situations to co-create meaning, strategies, and policies for managing risk and promoting safety through dialogue.[17]

Most importantly, NRIA resists any temptation to manipulate the actions of others through strategy. Instead, normatively responsible advocacy reflects the "outrageous idea" that pillars of Christian faith such as honesty, compassion, and empathy can and should be central features of risk communication.[18] We steadfastly maintain that NRIA is a realistic, pragmatic, and altruistic alternative to callous technique. Despite its promise, NRIA has received limited consideration in risk communication contexts. As Daniel O'Keefe explains, no generally accepted framework exists for normatively good—and as we extend, faith-based—argumentation.[19] Hence, this essay takes a step toward refining the form and function of NRIA as an alternative to sender-focused, winner and loser outcome-driven persuasion in risk contexts.

Chapter 34

Art in Action: The Metaphor and the Image on the Move in Evangelistic Thought and Practice

GILLETTE ELVGREN

Response Summary: Nicholas Wolterstorff's seminal book on aesthetics *Art in Action* provides a foundational look at a more progressive and ubiquitous need for and use of art creation both in secular and faith-based environments. This essay sources Wolterstorff's coverage of this Creative Mandate, primarily in providing an overview on the importance of metaphor and image creation in terms of their application to soteriological expressiveness. Using primarily examples of art in action from the theatrical genre, scriptural references, and dominant art and religious personalities, art as an active force in the church, university, and marketplace environments is examined. The essay concludes with an overview of the correlation of evangelism and artistic expressiveness as compatible entities.

NICHOLAS WOLTERSTORFF in his Legacy Scholar unconference presentation (Chapter 3 of this book) states:

> Well, one feature of how we're created is that we're created with bodies. A lot of writing in the field of aesthetics makes it sound as if art is made out of ideas and doesn't involve the body, or matter. So one of the points I was concerned to make in *Art in Action* was that, in creating art, one engages one's body and the material world. It's the experience of painters that their body, in its engagement with the material world, tells them to do something that they had not intellectually anticipated doing. They put down a line, whereupon the line says, "we need another line here." The artist says, "But putting a line there was not part of my plan." The line talks back: "That may be, but we need a companion line here."[1]

The above is the essence of Wolterstorff's contribution that so excited me in his seminal work, *Art in Action*, in which he concludes that art is more than just an idea or a theme, rather, it is the primary vehicle for feeling and physical integration with one's emotional and immediate environment.[2] Art then has a meaning that is more than cognitive, but which touches on the essence of creation in terms of our experiential lives in the workplace as well as being a mystery with its sources in metaphoric unfolding. Thus, it can be suggested that art is perhaps as important a vehicle in terms of soteriological thought and expression as are more academic or theological contributions.

My career has primarily been composed of telling stories in space, which is probably an appropriate definition for all art itself. Art is a created or made unity expressed in terms of movement, sound, rhythm, color, words, but also created within consciously created frameworks such as, stage space, frames, canvas, time limitations, applied non-realistic transitions, a plethora of styles and, of course, meaning. All of these are the elements of art in action which serve as the investigative aesthetic of Wolterstorff's book by that title. His contribution in this interview has ignited areas of interest in terms of my work in the arts as well, especially in an expanded concept of the word "action" and in the live performance venues. Thus, the following remains at the forefront for creative investigations in determining how art can serve as a more active creative element in evangelistic thought and practice. This essay will look at the concept of art in action in its as yet unrealized ability to serve as a vehicle for soteriological expression within an ongoing metaphoric creative tapestry.

The Metaphor and Image as Action

Going back to the source of things: in Genesis 1:27 God tells us that we are made in his image, which implies that we should become image makers ourselves as well. Thus, one of the primary *actions* of our very being is to fulfill this imitative process entitled the Creation Mandate. Our ability to communicate verbally and to write comes from this endowed gift. Through these mechanisms we can imagine and articulate, to a degree, the mysteries that surround us, including the reality of God himself. Metaphors describe actions and objects in ways that are not literally true but can help elucidate an idea, say like conversion, through experiential analogies. In a sense, it is another way, which can use beauty and other associative indicators, into encouraging and establishing the need for action. Through embracing the "other worldliness" and of playing a part in terms of soteriological expressiveness, the metaphor can become an essential descriptive vehicle. Conversion implies new relationships through spiritual interaction and an entire new set of action words that metaphorically describe this process such as "born again," "journey to enlightenment," "spiritual awakening," and "as a caterpillar becomes a butterfly," and so forth.

Christ refers to a Kingdom of God metaphorically being like this landowner or that lost coin. He grounds the ineffable in identifiable imagery that quickens and challenges our imaginations as he reconstructs what "the kingdom of God" is like. And in doing so, he embraces worlds of analogical thought and expression. His parables reflect the actions of those immediately existing in his environment, working and planting fields, growing vineyards, traveling dangerous roads, buying and selling, and the like. He transforms material reality through symbolic actions, healing blindness with mud in the eyes, embracing a dove as an image of the power of the Holy Spirit, and describing himself as the bread of life. The physical world becomes the plaything of the multi-dimensional nature of existence as he transports boats through time and space, transforms water into wine, dialogues with iconic Old Testament figures on the Mount of Transfiguration, and somehow through his blood sacrifice takes upon himself the sins of the world.

So how can metaphor making be looked upon as an action in itself? First, by creating a mental image the "action" is to encourage a new or alternative way in which reality can be perceived, appreciated, or understood—which was a major aspect of Christ's mission here on earth. The metaphor maker is invigorating another's imagination through the artful construction of images. It is a tool for investigating another way of understanding and influencing behavior through evocative imagery. It is truth telling using a creative context, rather than as information or syllogistic logic, because it is often endowed with an emotional context and purpose. It is essentially associative and requires active engagement hopefully resulting in self-discovery. And metaphor making shares consciousness as art, of ones identifying the images used as a common phenomenon. It expands our shared humanity and ultimately encourages a search in a greater aesthetic universe of the very questions of worldview: where did we come from, why are we here, and where are we going? But it does this not in terms of scientific language, in terms of academic sureties, but in terms of the demands for unity and meaning in all areas of our cultural awareness and activity.

An overview of a few of the approaches to the idea of art as action that have been elucidated through history and reflect on and contribute to Wolterstorff's thesis are provided below beginning with Aristotle. Though not connected with the evangelistic impulse, his contribution in terms of the liveliness and impact of art on an audience starts the dramatic aesthetic ball rolling. Students today regularly study his *Poetics* in terms of dramatic structure, characterization, and intent.[3]

Aristotle notes that tragedy is an imitation of an action. But it is not just any action: it is an action that is pivotal, life changing, challenging, and loaded with potential meaning. And it all points toward "catharsis" which is the process of art identification that causes a sympathetic change in the viewer. Wolterstorff would agree with Aristotle that the experience of art should not be one of mere contemplation, which separates art from the so-called masses of society, but truly engage the observer phenomenon in the process of actual change/catharsis or at least in increased self-perception.

When we think of the role of art in evangelization, we should not just think of so-called sacred art. It is more inclusive than that, or so notes St. John Paul II, in his letter to artists:

> Even beyond its typically religious expressions, true art has a close affinity with the world of faith, so that, even in situations where culture and the Church are far apart, art remains a kind of bridge to religious experience. In so far as it seeks the beautiful . . . art is by its nature a kind of appeal to the mystery. Even when they explore the darkest depths of the soul or the most unsettling aspects of evil, artists give voice in a way to the universal desire for redemption. . . . Evangelization is really nothing other than helping people see what it is they're really longing for. And what we're all really longing for is to participate fully in everlasting Beauty.[4]

C. S. Lewis points us in this direction when he contends that the "very essence of our life as conscious beings, all day and every day, consists of something which cannot be communicated except by hints, similes, metaphors, and the use of those emotions . . . which are pointers to it."[5] He further adds: "We do not want merely to see beauty. . . . We want something else which can hardly be put into words—to be united with the beauty we see, to pass into it, to receive it into ourselves, to bathe in it, to become part of it."[6]

Here Lewis literally describes the appreciation of beauty in terms of mystery and action, nothing passive about it. We receive it into ourselves in a process reminiscent of the indwelling of the Spirit itself. We want to be filled with the beauty moment like we want to be filled with the Spriit. It speaks of an encounter, of change, of a mystery. It speaks to the empty vacuum in those whose salvation needs are calling out to be filled.

In her search for effective action through art American essayist and novelist Flannery O'Connor notes:

> I have often asked myself what makes a story work, and what makes it hold up as a story, and I have decided that it is probably some action, some gesture of a character that is unlike any other in the story, one which indicates where the real heart of the story lies. This would have to be an action or a gesture which was both totally right and totally unexpected; it would have to be one that is both in character and beyond character; it would have to suggest both the world and eternity. The action or gesture I'm talking about would have to be on the anagogical level, that is, the level which has to do with the Divine life and our participation in it. It would be a gesture that transcended any neat allegory that might have been intended or any pat moral categories a reader could make. It would be a gesture which somehow contacts mystery.[7]

The key word here is "mystery," for as O'Connor would suggest, art is meant to engage us at personal, physical, and metaphysical levels that are not immediately cognitive, but which are still a meaningful aspect of our existence in this God-charged universe.

Jonathan Edwards (1703–1758) believed that God's beauty, as expressed in creation and art, was a powerful tool for evangelism. As one gives himself to moral and expressive beauty, people's lives could be changed as they were drawn to God through art.[8]

When noted literary critic, philosopher and communication theorist Kenneth Burke writes the following he joins the Wolterstorff's art in action ensemble:

> To consider language as a means of information and knowledge is to consider it epistemologically, "semantically" in terms of science. To consider it as a mode of "action" is to consider it in terms of poetry. For a poem is an act, the symbolic act of a poet who made it—an act of such a nature that, in surviving as a structure or object, it enables us as readers to re-enact it.[9]

Here Kenneth Burke acknowledges that depicting language primarily as a means of touting information is akin to a materialistic viewpoint. Burke is proposing that language is an "act" or "action" exemplified by poetry. The poet is creating a symbolic action which puts forth metaphoric language that projects meaning within its creation and that challenges the reader to interpretate and identify with the truth expressed through symbolic poetic art. So language for Burke becomes more than meaning and structure—it is an active contributor to the way we see things and motivates how we participate in the world. His insights into the action description of language are also easily transferred to the other art expressions of language in theatre, film, and musicals.

Shakespearean language with its extended metaphors and poetry often encapsulates and defines the scene, and the action intent, the beauty of language as persuasion and description. As he says in *Hamlet* when the players are addressed: "Suit the word to the action and the action to the word."[10]

In the fall of 1966 members of the Moscow Art Theatre, the most proximate inheritors and practitioners of Stanislavski's acting theories, visited Tulane University where I was pursuing a master's degree in Theatre. They were asked if they could identify or perhaps distill the most important aspect of acting that Stanislavski came up with and their response was "physical action." To sum up, this implies that the actor, while onstage, is continually pursuing a physical action in relation to his objectives or wants. "I want to touch, to dominate, to get out of here, to seduce, to get her to do what I say . . ." But what if the script doesn't have you touching that other character? You still want to, and badly. The physical action still exists, even though it might not be realized, the result being a palpable tension created by the actor in terms of *wanting* to realize the motivational complex which are realizing the character's immediate desires and needs. All words become actions on the stage. And they are supported by the gestural life of the characters in a symphony of breaths, motions, rhythmic changes, and reactions. The phrase "acting is reacting" is familiar to every student of the art.

Gesture is an additive to this action complex that needs to be studied and realized as an important communication vehicle for supporting evangelical rhetoric as something more than theological postulating. Gestures represent action as image—not always realistic, but almost always creating an understanding between those sharing the expressive moment. Gestures lend themselves to helping define and communicate metaphoric or more abstract concepts. They originate as physical acts or actions that provide context in terms of understanding what is not present. And they provide an added visual expressiveness as well as emphasis to the images being actualized. They function as the natural expressive tool to all language and therefore is it out of the realm of possibility that a "gestural language" could be imagined even in approaching evangelical opportunities? Expressive dance would seem to fit into these gestural prerogatives.

Imagery itself could be considered an aggregate of metaphoric language creation. Paul Pastor, in his article "Treasures of Darkness," comments on the persuasiveness of imagery in terms of how it works and why we need it.

It is easier to describe the effects of *image* than to define it. The effects are of a kind of haunting—"pictures" that bleed from a story, painting, film, poem, etc., back into one's life. The mind returns to a complex image or set of images; finds itself wanting or needing to be inside them, to touch and interact with them. These images are multifaceted, magnetic, inherently interesting, and capable of sustaining long attention, continuing to reveal gifts for a very long time. Dream-stuff. Icon-stuff.

Image and intuition, the "gut" element of creativity, seem to have become spiritual and artistic treasures that Christian writers today cannot (or do not) intentionally or skillfully access. And yet, they are among our heritage, both as humans and as Christians. Both seem foreign to us. They are ours by birthright, but we have lost them.[11]

If as Wolterstorff and others suggest that art is action, and if it is the immediate result and fruit of our creative mandate, then utilizing its innate power focused on conversion awareness would seem to make sense. In addition, because all of this speaks to us emotionally as well as intentionally and is an essential part of our oneness with the Creator, would not it seem that the literary, poetic, gestural, and dialogic rhetoric of our active language could find more footholds in its usage through the arts to assist in bringing people to a personal knowledge of the Lord?

In looking at the communication through the arts in terms of evangelistic verbal and gestural expression, certain areas of contemporary practice need to be accounted for if there is going to be a working and meaningful transformation of the use of the arts in soteriological thought and practice. Where does it fall short, or manifest a culpability in ways that can be addressed with the idea of promoting a more ubiquitous acknowledgment of the power of artistic persuasion and expressiveness as a meaningful evangelical tool?

A brief overlook at art in the church, the universities, and in the marketplace will emphasize some areas for further consideration.

The Church

The church needs to become more aware of the use of the potential power of using art and to challenge certain negative opinions that have been perpetrated over the ages. Antipathy to the dramatic arts goes all the way back to Plato's *Republic* in its condemnation of the performing arts, casting "image making" as a sin and the actor as an essential liar. The early church continued and built on this antipathy toward the performing arts in its response to Roman secular productions, considered to be antithetical to Christian ethical standards in the way that communion, baptism and the crucifixion were satirized. The church therefore forbade actors to be baptized unless they swore off any involvement in thespian pagan practices.

Seminary students need to be educated as to how the arts can function in approaching the seeker as to holistic needs, i.e., emotional and aesthetic life which can be readily expressed and also understood through affective artistic expression. How might the spiritual and artistic landscape of this nation be transformed if churches would consider the artist in residence with the same consistency that they might promote seminary students?

The Faith-based University

The university needs to re-prioritize its commitment to arts programming, which is usually among the first to be downgraded when finances become tight. The recent COVID-19 onslaught witnessed a plethora of schools turning drama and film majors into minors and cancelling programs altogether. Somehow the legitimacy of arts instruction and performance is not regarded academically as significant as the sciences, psychology or history, though the sheer depth of student experience with cell phone use and TV cultural consciousness far outweighs experience with what is considered to be the more academically respected venues. At the University of Pittsburgh, we put together drama teams of actors to meet with and create drama vignettes that spoke directly to the area of scholarship that requested them. Drama students interacted with law, medicine, psychology, English classes and dialogued afterward concerning the content presented with students in class. How could faith-based universities benefit from having drama-oriented teams interfacing with their academic offerings? The purpose would be to more effectively integrate the art form with the discipline to focus on art as a necessity rather than an imposed curiosity.

Revivals at many faith campuses are vociferously prayed for, but what does a renewed and regenerative positioning of art within the faith spectrum actually look like? Where are the examples we can refer to? Some programs offer playwriting classes, but few regularly support new work productions. Politically or theologically conservative faith-based universities are known to forbid dance representations, which includes musicals, and a shutdown of anything physically expressive. The metaphor and the image become suspect because they do not represent action in immediate cognitive language terms but are expressed through movement. A Florida college staged a drama that had a scene at a school dance in it. The dance was consequently staged but could only be seen when a door opened to show moving figures in the background. The administration ultimately pulled the show from its scheduled run entirely. A Christian artist created a series of sculptures representing scenes from Revelation and displayed them in my church's foyer. They were ultimately removed because people said they did not understand them.

In the Marketplace

When Gerald Manley Hopkins writes that "the world is charged with the grandeur of God," he is expressing the fullness of the vision that not only nature has brought to our expressive appreciation, but to being a statement of our calling, to 'charge' our total environment with works that identify and glorify the presence of God in our lives.[12] Faith expression is not just found in a Sunday morning worship service, but has to enter into our daily vocational work and all that it entails. And it cannot do this by just sitting in museums to be contemplated. Art is not just fine art but is engaged in just about every aspect of our lives. This is a constant theme emphasized by Wolterstorff: "And then, once you've seen that, that art is just embedded deeply in human action, once you've seen that, then it seems to me that you and I as thinkers about art, instead of focusing on just one action, that of aesthetic contemplation, we should take note of the absolutely unbelievable variety of ways in which works of art enter into our lives."[13]

Pete Hammond, InterVarsity's former director of Marketplace Ministry pushes this concept of the dangers of the immobilization of the Sunday-Monday morning gap further: "This immobilization of 99% of God's people is both unbiblical and discriminating, while making our task of world evangelization impossible."[14]

My wife and I have traveled to Chester and York England to view their reenactments of the Medieval Mystery Plays that originated in their towns during the fourteenth through the sixteenth centuries. These dramas depict the epic biblical story beginning with creation and ending with the second coming and final judgement and represent the actualization and idealization of the idea of Marketplace evangelization. Originally, they were approved by the church and anonymously written and performed by the local trade guilds, being performed on decorated wagons that were pulled through the town by horses during Corpus Christi celebrations. For example, the Shipwrights performed the Building of the Ark, while the Butchers played the Death of Christ or Crucifixion. The Bakers, of course, would dramatize the Last Supper, while delighting audiences with loaves of bread thrown from their wagon. The entire population of the town and surrounding areas would come out to celebrate the holiday as up to 48 different wagons depicted 48 different scenes from Scripture, in a panorama that could last for up to 20 hours as each wagon stopped at several locations repeating their dramas.

The local folk often were ignorant of the written word, and these Mystery Play presentations were at the time the most effective communicative device of spreading the Gospel stories to their essentially illiterate audiences. It was also a celebration and brought together all classes of citizens sitting on the ground or on benches or pews moved out of doors. I recall a particularly festive moment in Chester where the "Bakers" guild had put together several long tables, with loaves of bread, but enough room to dance on, which they did as they enacted the last supper while drinking pints of Ol' Peculiar Ale. The contemporary audience was treated to an old and classic biblical narrative, enacted by their own market amateurs in the local bakery business.

Another instant where the crossover of the dramatic arts into the marketplace took place was in Pittsburgh, when a company that I founded, Saltworks Theatre Company, received a grant to present short sketches in the lobby of Alcoa Aluminum Headquarters at lunchtime. Saltworks is administered and staffed by Christians, and though the topics presented weren't always directly confessional, the subjects dramatized dealt with issues such as gossip, eternity or wanting to live forever, the meaning of life, the question of God's existence, and the vacuity that needs filling in our lives. Lively reactions were encouraged after each presentation and dialogue with the audience ensued and bore fruit.

Other examples that could encourage the use of dramatic arts in the marketplace took place in Pittsburgh. Teams of actors were put together to bring paintings to life in museum environs; in presenting musicals and improvised parable sketches in malls that gather crowds and encourage audience participation in training faith-based artists how to integrate their work and faith practices in the marketplace. A performance barge was used to tour the Ohio River and enact the historical and musical narrative of the steel industry along with stories and myths of Pittsburgh and environs in front of steel town riverbanks.

I was invited to attend a pensioner's picnic for a steel company's retired workers, so I brought along a bevy of Pitt grad students with tape recorders to record their stories. Out of this came a rather epic production of a musical theatrical documentary entitled *Steel/City*, in which the third act was a staging of the picnic complete with kielbasa cooking onstage. I had been given a semester off from the university to research, write and then direct this show and we filled the balcony with retired workers and their wives, most of whom were from eastern Europe and had never seen a live production. As the action of the picnic commenced the actors told the stories that the workers had related word-for-word at the picnic and the balcony exploded as the retired workers actually stood up and shouted things like "Hey Sam, you hear that, that's my story," and in turn the entire audience clapped and cheered. Faith stories were shared. These men's lives as steel workers were being presented in an artistic context that made what they had lived through, their life, work and faith struggles, better understood and appreciated by the entire city.

I return to Wolterstorff to sum up his take on the "marketplace" view of things. Christians should engage in the arts as attendees to the human action which surrounds them in their daily pursuits. His goal is to urge his fellow Christians to engage in the arts, not from the standpoint of the contemporary Western way of thinking about the arts, but rather through a more Christian framework of the arts as servants to human action, for "the purposes of art are the purposes of life."[15]

A mobilization of marketplace Christians is essential if the Sunday-Monday gap and the goal of world mission is to be accomplished. Wolterstorff continues: "And then, once you've seen that, that art is just embedded deeply in human action, once you've seen that, then it seems to me that you and I as thinkers about art, instead of focusing on just one action, that of aesthetic contemplation, we should take note of the absolutely unbelievable variety of ways in which works of art enter into our lives."[16]

These comments represent only three areas of focus; however, many others could be subsumed within the subject of evangelism itself, which will be the primary area covered in the concluding thoughts of this essay.

Art, by its very nature of presenting a veil of paint, musical notes, dance steps, and imitation of thought, word, and actions in describing emotion and meaning as they interpret reality, is often viewed as suspect in terms of being a vehicle for evangelistic encounters. This has resulted in a kind of literalism of artistic expressiveness, for the more abstract the process of representation becomes, the more hesitant is the conservative evangelical to apply it to their favored and supposedly safer modes of expression. Art is appreciated at several aesthetic and cognitive levels, often meaning different things to different people, the result being a threat to what are the inviolable truths in Scripture. After all, feelings, which are the proper stuff of art, are elusive, subjective, and not immediately identifiable as a means of interpreting the truths of Scripture. This might imply that when our traditional interpretation of temporal reality as sequential and tied to a predictable unfolding of calendar events, and space as defined by where we are now, as something knowable and safe, is transformed within the expressive creation of an art gesture, that it becomes therefore suspect and even potentially dangerous. What happens to mystery in this mindset? Can we only know and experience the truth as an explicit and knowable event?

Mystery by itself is a condition of our visitation to this universe and we should celebrate its gift to us by our Creator. It can be and usually is a thing of beauty by itself, unknowable, but sustaining, elusive but comforting in revealing that we are part of something far larger than we can imagine and as an aspect of God's character and grandeur. It is the basis for the promises that he has revealed to us in terms of the relativity of time and space, and how and what we, in our Christ imaging, will share with him throughout eternity. I get excited at some of the mechanics of the new physics that are being revealed. Are these dimensional clues that provide insight into the mysteries of the universe also revealing of the mysteries of God himself? Is the fact that an electron can be in two different places at the same time reflective of the realities that we, as spirit filled creations of God, are blessed in being in his Kingdom at the same time as we occupy this material landscape? How can our art better express this phenomenon linguistically and visually? And could not this revelation through our art offer the same drawing power toward salvation as evangelistic rhetoric?

Christ presents this challenge as he meets Nicodemus at night to answer questions dealing with who Jesus is and what does he represent. When he says, "I tell you the truth, no one can see the kingdom of God unless he is born again," he is presenting one of these mysteries using the metaphor of birth as the analogical reference (John 3:3). It is knowable, however, in the heart to a degree as our Lord meant it to be. But Nicodemus's response as a student of Scripture, a leader in his assembly, an obedient follower of the Law, is totally literal: "How can a man be born when he is old?" Nicodemus asks "Surely he cannot enter a second time into his mother's womb to be born!" (John 3:4).

Jesus presents a mystery through metaphoric descriptiveness because the subject matter is beyond the knowable logic of space-time reality. He has used an artistic metaphoric device to tell the truth as well as suggest a new and transforming direction for Nicodemus. Could not we also in this contemporary evangelistic journey of describing the salvation process to the seeker use the words and actions and images through art expressiveness which could more effectively draw the seeker into the world of awe and marvel and wonder and mystery that makes life itself so delightfully unpredictable and compelling?

If art is action, then should we not wield it as a tool and as an appeal to the lost side of anyone that longs for something more in this mundane world than is presently being encountered? If, in our abstractions, we are only a step away from cognitive understanding, let us celebrate that it is only a step, and that what the seeker will take away will continue to challenge, motivate, and change his ongoing state of being. We do not need to articulate Jesus as all that we know him to be and include every aspect of his saving presence in every artwork that we create. This can often result in a feeling of being subjected to spiritual propaganda. We do not need to attempt to solve the mystery of every spiritual reality that we are confronted with. But at the same time, we need to find a new, fertile, captivating, unique and omni-presently human and feeling expressiveness.

Perhaps we have to rethink the use of the "Four Spiritual Laws" as a primary tool of presentation in the salvation moment? I am not denigrating the use of or results of these "laws" as effective evangelical tools, but just the reference to the idea of "laws" somehow restricts the resultant freedom and wonder that is encased in the salvation moment. Why not refer to the mystery of the Holy Spirit as an ineffable gift that results from the confession of sin and of an enlivened spirit? Why not mention that now you will be introduced to multiple worlds of spiritual dimensions, and that a destiny and purpose to one's life will become a driving force? You will now be inculcated into a life of action, of becoming a child of the Lord. Your entire reference to the major issues of life and of the small willful choices of a moment will become God oriented and hopefully God ordained.

The following questions need to be addressed and discussed by artists and Christian communication scholars regarding questions dealing with persuasion in the arts in terms of an active evangelistic focus:

- Can evangelism actually be a purpose of art?

- What are the contradictions between proselytization and art production?

- How does art as action differ from the immediate intent of evangelization?

- Is the demand for clarity in terms of faith in art production by reference reflect a demeaning of the arts' ability to communicate through indirection, subtext, and metaphorical representation?

- Do the sought-after tenants of evangelization by themselves run counter to the artistic sense of action in terms of context and meaning?

- How can imagery speak louder than words in terms of evangelistic intent?

Art is not about religion. It is active and more about relationship. It is an expressive language that accompanies this new relationship and should provide a new way into experiencing the unique birth that is promised us as we discover the length and depth of God's ongoing revelation in our lives.

Chapter 35

Spiritual Growth in a Digital Age

Kim Okesson

Response Summary: The author echoes Noll's concern regarding the church's intellectual and spiritual formation, now challenged by digital saturation. Drawing on insights from Sherry Turkle and others, Okesson explores how technology reshapes attention, memory, and relational depth—undermining practices essential to spiritual maturity. Her call to "a long obedience in the same direction" resonates with George Marsden's vision of cultivating Christian virtue within modern cultural frameworks. This brief reflection urges communication scholars to model countercultural habits that foster enduring spiritual growth in a distracted age.

IN MARK NOLL'S BOOK, *The Scandal of the Evangelical Mind*, he reminds the church of the importance of intentional formation and transformation of one's intellect. This was true in the cultural and societal context of 1995, when his book was first published. Although the cultural context of the twenty-first century has shifted dramatically due to communication technology, his exhortation to the church is as relevant as ever. As societal and technological realities battle against the right formation of intellect and the use of our minds, it also fiercely challenges our capacity to do the hard work of persevering in spiritual growth. Living in an instant society, saturated with easily accessible information, tempts us all to seek instant spiritual growth, understanding, and wisdom.

The evidence of the many faceted ways communication technology has contributed to a rapid decline in communication skill, increases in mental health illnesses, as well as altered brain function and shortened attention span, is legion. The works of Sherry Turkle, Quentin Schultze, Larry Rosen, Jonathan Haidt, among others provide a wealth of data, insight, and instruction about the effects on individuals, families, and communities.[1] An area that is overlooked, however, is how these thinking, relational, and societal changes impact spiritual growth.

Spiritual growth has been famously described by Eugene Peterson as "a long obedience in the same direction."[2] He wrote a book with the same title more than forty years ago, yet the message still resonates today. Deep faith, spiritual insight, and wisdom are not accomplished instantly. Similar to the shaping of a person's character, the honing of spiritual faculties and sensibilities takes time, experience, reading, learning, relating, and growing.

Technology that shortens attention spans and changes the way our brains store long-term information pose serious challenges to some of the most basic and critical Christian practices. For example, of crucial importance in the life of a Christian is the discipline of reading the Bible and memorizing Scripture passages. Sadly, reading has largely been replaced with skimming or scrolling. Memorization has been shortchanged as information is stored and retrieved digitally.

In light of the stark contrast between how spiritual growth occurs and the effect communication technology has on us, what are some key practical commitments we can make to ensure our own spiritual growth? How can we model countercultural thought and behavior for our students? As communication scholars, let us commit to doing some of the very things the authors listed above exhort us to do. Together, let us expect more from each other and less from technology. Let us strive for and lead others toward virtue in a digital age. Let us create a climate conducive to conversation, that pushes back on environments harming mental health and encourage one another in the long obedience in the same direction.

Chapter 36

Counter-cultural Christians in a World of High-speed Communication

KEVIN SCHUT

Response Summary: George Marsden suggests that Christian scholars should move beyond an a-religious, secular practice of scholarship. In the author's media studies practice, that means mapping the contours of our media environment to identify some of the pitfalls of our contemporary culture to identify lived practices that would enable Christians to have a Christ-centered revolutionary perspective in our culture. In this short essay, Schut discusses the problems of a media environment that is highly transactional, algorithmically individualized, insanely fast, and cacophonous. He suggests, in line with other Christian critics, that learning to slow down and invest in physical space is an act of Christian counterculture.

FOR MANY PEOPLE, the term "video games" conjure images of high-speed action, bullet sprays, explosions and body counts. And not without reason: the militaristic *Call of Duty* franchise and crime simulator *Grand Theft Auto* series are fast-paced and violent, and they also dominate headlines due to their financial success. The top tier of game seller Steam's list of highest grossing games of 2024, for instance, is only populated by action and combat games—not all of them are bloody, gory messes, but they all involve fighting.[1] Nevertheless, people who really know gaming can find oases of calm in the midst of frenetic shooters.

Townscaper and *Tiny Glade* are inviting simulators with peaceful soundtracks that give players the opportunity to build quaint towns or medieval castles and manors.[2] *Dorfromantik* does the same with tiles that make a pretty countryside.[3] For those who are more puzzle-minded, the mysterious *Blue Prince* has a player build and rebuild an entire house with floorplans; there's no rush and certainly no mayhem.[4]

These slow, gentle games provide a kind of counterculture to the dominant culture of all-the-time motion: they suggest that video games can be something more than what we typically assume, that they can emphasize thought over constant movement, that they can feature building instead of destruction. Not everyone needs to play such games, but their very existence suggests there is more to this medium. In this sense, I think they are a good model for Christians trying to be faithful in an increasingly fast-paced world.

In *The Outrageous Idea of Christian Scholarship*, George Marsden argues against the notion that academics leave their faith commitments out of their research. Scholarship in North America has become predominantly secular in character, but Marsden argues this is neither necessary nor desirable. After tackling common arguments against a more explicit role for religious faith in the Academy, he argues Christian beliefs, ideas, narratives, and traditions bring a variety of benefits. Christian scholars bring a strong moral framework to their work and counter problematic tendencies of contemporary scholarship like naturalistic reductionism. His call for Christian scholars is to engage their faith in a way that shapes their research, writing, and teaching. So how can scholars who study media and culture apply these insights?

Jacques Ellul argues that "the situation of the Christian in the world is a revolutionary situation."[5] He doesn't mean this in the ordinary political sense; rather, he believes that society and culture of the world operate according to a soul-crushing logic, and that Christians must provide an alternative. Building this counterculture starts with awareness and knowledge, but cannot stop there: "Christians ought to try to create a style of life which does not differentiate them from others, but yet permits them to escape from the stifling pressure of our present form of civilization."[6] As James K. A. Smith explains, our lives are liturgical—our everyday practices constitute embodied ideas.[7] Meals and shopping and forms of entertainment and more all demonstrate and give form to what we really believe.

Proper Christian communication scholarship, then, should guide us to healthy, counter-cultural communication practices that embody a different way of living and being. This will not mean just one thing. Some scholars focus on interpersonal communication, like Bill Strom's research on covenantal relationships.[8] Quentin Schultze's *Habits of the High Tech Heart*, as another example, focuses more on the cultural impact of our digital media environment and the necessity of Christian virtue in these spaces.[9]

My own work (similarly to Schultze) draws on Media Ecology Theory and its emphasis on the impact of our media environment on our culture and cognition. The work of theorists like Marshall McLuhan, Elisabeth Eisenstein, Walter Ong, Neil Postman, and others points out that our tools of communication directly impact what and how we can meaningfully interact. For example, Ong argues that the creation of writing tends to lead to a decreasing capacity for memorization;[10] Postman argues that television encourages a culture to turn all public discourse into a form of entertainment.[11]

Today's digital media environment has many other features worth mapping and considering as Christians to determine how we might best be the revolutionary presence Ellul envisions. I would identify a number of culturally impactful and prominent key features of much of today's media: our digital communication is often highly transactional, it is algorithmically individualized, it is insanely fast, and it is cacophonous.

Just like many video games, much of our media today keeps track of our score. Our TikTok videos rack up view counts, our posts on Instagram generate likes. Our communication is not about building relationships so much as earning relational points. If we play the game well, we ascend to the godlike S-tier of major social influencers, who continually hawk products in order to pay the bills. The message: we become valuable not for who we are, but by performing the right way—and the right way is one that generates de-humanized numbers and encourages shallow consumerism.

In addition, much of our material is highly tailored to individualized tastes, following the logic of often-complicated algorithms. TikTok has reached the apex of today's media landscape by catering to users' tastes in a never-ending stream of bite-size chunks of video. Many fans feel like the service knows exactly what they want. Even legacy media like print and television, now that they have been digitized, are much more precisely targeted than they were in the late twentieth-century era of broadcast media. The implicit idea here? We deserve exactly what we want, when we want it, and we should not have to deal with other people's perspectives, ideas, values, and humanness. Our curated content is just so much perfectly tailored (as opposed to mass produced) junk food to enjoy and dispose of.

The media environment we live in is also overwhelmingly fast—and this is not just limited to the action video games already discussed. Action and reaction happen as quickly as fingers can type or reactions can be filmed, unlike the days when mass media required extensive organizational support, complete with gatekeepers and necessary delays. In 1990, only the live TV networks could instantaneously deliver information and opinions to the masses and did so at tremendous expense largely due to the complexity of that undertaking. Today, *everyone* can do the exact same thing for any and every purpose at a very low cost. We get impatient waiting a few minutes for an email or text message or a social media direct message, let alone several days or (the horror!) a week or two. Speed can be exhilarating but also gives us no time for thoughts or emotions to bake or settle or mature.

All these features and several others lead to a media environment that is incredibly cacophonous. The medieval market fair was full of loud merchants and town criers and bards, but it was limited to a few thousand people, and at the end of the day everyone went home to a small, quiet community. Today's culture enables everyone with a phone to speak and speak and speak. And while every wannabe influencer knows it is hard to gain an audience, the fact is that the most obscure YouTube post can blow up overnight and reach many millions or even hundreds of millions of people. And since we are all incentivized to get contacts and fans, and since we've been trained to think that our tastes and opinions are exceptionally important for no other reason than the fact that we have them, and since there really is not much of a filter on posting often and rapidly, we are encouraged to speak a lot. Many of us indeed do so, nearly constantly, on every imaginable topic. And when content producers "flood the zone" with so much stuff that we become disoriented and have a hard time making sense of anything, we descend into the meaningless noise implied by the term "cacophony."

So what is a Christian scholar of communication to call for here? What is a meaningful revolutionary counterculture? I do not think there is just one right path here. But just as slow games show us that video games do not all have to be *Call of Duty*, healthy Christian ways of living can show our culture that not everything has to be a chase for points, or highly individualized, or fast paced, or overwhelming.

In this volume, for instance, Quentin Schultze calls us to develop the practice and skill of *listening*—something that demonstrates an interest in the value of others, implies a kind of humility that is a clear alternative to lionized consumer individual, and reduces the volume of the constant stream of chattering voices. Robert H. Woods Jr. and Paul D. Patton call for *Everyday Sabbath*—a conscious, careful set of practices aimed at entering into God's peace and rest.[12] Christians need to model the value of quietness, both physical and mental, the ability to put away our devices, close our email client, turn off the apps, and ground ourselves in the physical world and in face-to-face relationship building. Real Christian community that is careful, loving, joyful in non-digital interaction (and digital relationships too!) provides tangible liturgies that are counter-cultural and give space for God to enter into our day-to-day actions.

I do not think every Christian can or should take a complete digital off ramp. Not everything about the constantly blinking lights of our phones is inherently wrong (I am a scholar who studies the video games he loves to play—I am not going to tell you they are all bad!). And in any case, the church needs people fluent in the culture of the digital world: we need podcasters and influencers and comedians and singers and dancers and recipe makers spreading salt and light at light speed on social media apps. But we should be clear that this *way* of communication is not significantly counter-cultural. Some people in the church at least should be modeling a way of living significantly different from our always-on electronic world. And all of us should be sometimes practicing it.

Marsden's insights still hold today: a Christian scholarly take on our media landscape should not attempt a kind of detached neutrality. The goal should be to analyze our tools of communication in order to identify its strengths and weaknesses so that we can help Christians imagine a way to be truly countercultural. Faced with an often dehumanized, self-centered, rapid, and overwhelming communication environment, Christian scholars would be missing their revolutionary calling if they did not help reveal the pitfalls of our contemporary culture and suggest some different ways of living. Sometimes, it means putting away our phone and taking a walk in the woods. In many cases, it may be a conscious limiting, quieting, and centering of our social media use. And sometimes, it may be as simple as putting down our virtual blaster, and instead building some quiet, quaint pastel villages.

Section Four:
Personal and Vocational Reflections

Chapter 37

The Christian Professor in the Twenty-first Century

GERALDINE E. FORSBERG

Response Summary: In *Scandal*, Noll laments the lack of Christian thought applied to all areas of life. Meanwhile, Marsden, in *Outrageous* discusses how Christian ideas are often ignored or marginalized within the university. In this essay, written more than nearly 30 years later, the author argues that Christian educators in the twenty-first century must reject propaganda, embrace intellectual discipleship, and demonstrate Christlike integrity in every part of academic life. By cultivating wisdom based on Scripture and embodying truth in love, professors can give a faithful witness in classrooms and institutions—offering students not just knowledge but the transformative hope found only in Jesus Christ. In today's Academy, marked by fragmentation, relativism, and moral drifting, Christian professors are called to develop a Christ-centered mindset, courageously stand for truth, and bring the living presence of Jesus Christ into the core of the university.

IN THE SOUL *of the American University: From Protestant Establishment to Established Non-belief,* George Marsden explored the twentieth-century movement of American universities away from their Christian foundations to a state of nonbelief, even total rejection of any truths associated with the eternal God, the Bible, and prayer.[1] He followed up with his book, *The Outrageous Idea of Christian Scholarship,* in which he discussed the Christian neglect of scholarship and the need to bring Christian scholarship back into the university.[2]

In his 1994 book, *The Scandal of the Evangelical Mind,* Mark Noll analyzed the anti-intellectualism movements in the nineteenth and twentieth centuries that fostered Christian skepticism of academic pursuits.[3] The church at large emphasized personal conversion instead of intellectual understanding.

We are now deep into the twenty-first century, and life in academia has changed. At the November 2024 conference titled "Re-imagining Christian Thinking and Scholarship in an Age of Tribalism and Ideological Resentment," sponsored by the Christianity and Communication Studies Network (CCSN) and held at the New Orleans Baptist Theological Seminary, Marsden, Noll, and many other Christian scholars and authors addressed the current state of the university. Readings were assigned before the conference, and the authors' video presentations were viewed in advance. Then, discussions took place on contemporary changes in the university and the implications for Christian scholars.

I led a discussion session on the role of the Christian professor in the twenty-first century. The following thoughts represent ideas based on the readings, presentations, and discussions. The question we posed was: What is the role of the Christian scholar and professor in the twenty-first century, and how do our responsibilities differ from previous eras? It was concluded that more today than ever, as professors, we need to develop a Christ-focused mind, take a stand for truth, and bring Jesus Christ to our students and universities.

Develop a Christ-focused Mind

Billy Graham, the great evangelist of the twentieth century, affirmed the need for Christian professors to consider the state of our universities, young people, and colleagues. He wrote,

> Therefore, if evangelization is the most important task, the task that comes immediately after it—not in the tenth place, nor even the third place, but in the second place—is not politics, nor economics, nor the quest of comfort and security and ease, but to find out exactly what is happening to the mind and the spirit in the schools and universities. And once a Christian discovers that there is a total divorce between mind and spirit in the schools and universities, between the perfection of thought and the perfection of soul and character, between intellectual sophistication and the spiritual worth of the individual human person, between reason and faith, between the pride of knowledge and the contrition of heart consequent upon being a mere creature, and once he realizes that Jesus Christ will find Himself less at home on the campuses of the great universities, in Europe and America, than almost anywhere else, he will be profoundly disturbed, and he will inquire what can be done to recapture the great universities for Jesus Christ, the universities which would not have come into being in the first place without Him.[4]

The great challenge and task of the Christian professor in the twenty-first century is to develop a burden for the university and to acknowledge that there is no real hope for the university and society apart from Jesus Christ. The Christian professor must understand the importance and the significance of developing a Christ-focused mind. The Christian intellectual's first responsibility is to foster a mind transformed by Jesus Christ. Calvin L. Troup, the president of Geneva College, emphasized this in his concluding keynote message. He noted how he is responsible for hiring professors, and he wants to employ excellent Christian professors. However, these professors must not only be outstanding in their disciplines, but they must also be grounded in biblical thought. Most new PhDs are coming out of secular universities where a biblical foundation is not part of their education. Therefore, Troup has created a two-year biblical education program for the professors at his college, emphasizing biblical literacy, the counsel of God, the creeds and confessions, and a biblical worldview.[5]

Troup wants his faculty to be outstanding in their academic disciplines and faith, and he notes how this requires "double work" on the part of the Christian professor; he wants his professors to develop the mind of Christ.[6] Many biblical references focus on the importance of the mind. We read David's instruction to his son Solomon from the Old Testament Scripture. He said, "And you, my son Solomon, acknowledge the God of your father, and serve him with wholehearted devotion and with a willing *mind*, for the Lord searches every heart and understands every desire and every thought" (1 Chr. 28:9). From the New Testament, we are told to think with the mind of Christ. For example, the Apostle Paul said, "Let this mind be in you which was also in Christ Jesus, who, being in the form of God, did not consider it robbery to be equal with God, but made Himself of no reputation, taking the form of a bondservant, and coming in the likeness of man" (Phil. 2:5–7, New King James Version). As believers, we have the mind of Christ (1 Cor. 2:16), which can be developed and nourished. The Apostle Paul emphasized the development of the Christian mind when he reminded us to "not be conformed to this world, but be transformed by the renewing of your mind, so that you may prove what the will of God is, that which is good and acceptable and perfect" (Rom. 12:2, New American Standard Bible).

When we have the mind of Christ, we seek to serve rather than be served; we love our students and colleagues. We have a mind that does not condemn but brings hope and help. We have a mind filled with humility rather than pride. We have a mind filled with gratitude and praise for our heavenly Father—a mind filled with mercy, compassion, and kindness. We have a mind that meets others where they are. We can only have the mind of Christ when we allow him, in the power of the Holy Spirit, to flow through us. We can have the mind of Christ as we let his Spirit work in us, drawing us to himself, filling us with his perspective, and enlightening our minds and thoughts. We cannot think and believe Christianly without Jesus Christ living through us. The mind of Christ is evident when we live in faith and obedience to him.

Therefore, the Christian mind is a mind filled with the Holy Spirit. I am afraid that, at times, we intellectualize the discourse on faith so much that we lose the object of our faith and the object of the Christian mind—Jesus Christ. As intellectuals, we must constantly affirm that knowledge *about* God differs from a relationship *with* God. As the Bible says, even the demons know of and believe in God (Jas. 2:19). The "Christian mind" is not based on biblical knowledge alone (although biblical knowledge is essential), nor is it based on belief alone (even some of Jesus's disciples believed but left him); rather, it is based on a miraculous trust in Christ and an acceptance of Christ into our lives, to give us his mind, his way of thinking, his perspective on life. The Christ-controlled mind is a mind that deals not only with abstract knowledge but also with concrete, obedient action.

One characteristic of a Christ-controlled mind is that it is filled with God's word. Jesus either quotes or refers to Genesis, Exodus, Leviticus, Numbers, Deuteronomy, 1 Samuel, 1 and 2 Kings, 2 Chronicles, Daniel, Psalms, Isaiah, Hosea, Jonah, and Malachi. In Matthew, Mark, and Luke, the temptation of Jesus is recorded, along with his response. When Jesus was tempted to satisfy his hunger by turning stones into bread, Jesus responded by quoting Deuteronomy 8:3: "Man shall not live on bread alone, but on every word that comes from the mouth of God." When Satan tempted Jesus to test God by throwing himself off the highest point of the temple, Jesus responded by quoting Deuteronomy 6:16: "Do not put the Lord your God to the test." When Satan tempted Jesus to bow down and worship him, Jesus quoted Deuteronomy 6:13: "Worship the Lord your God and serve him only." Jesus's mind was filled with Scripture. If we are to have the mind of Christ, we must fill our minds with Scripture.

As a child, I was blessed to have a grandmother who enrolled me in the Bible Memory Association (BMA). Throughout the early years of my life, I would memorize Scripture and then go to someone who would listen to me quote the word. At the end of the year, I attended a camp where theologians came and provided expository teaching on the Scripture I had memorized. This has helped me keep God's word in my mind and thoughts. We must meditate daily on God's word and let it guide us in approaching our disciplines from Christ's perspective. As a Christian professor, knowing God's word and hiding it in our hearts is essential for Christian witness.

Charles Malik, the philosopher and former President of the United Nations General Assembly, put it well when he said, "The greatest revolution ever was Jesus Christ himself; not his ideas, not his teachings, not his moral principles, but he himself; for nothing is greater, more revolutionary and more unbelievable than the Gospel of the Crucified, Resurrected and Glorified God who is to come again to judge the living and the dead."[7] Malik references Blaise Pascal, who said:

> Not only do we only know God through Jesus Christ, but we only know ourselves through Jesus Christ; we only know life and death through Jesus Christ. Apart from Jesus Christ, we cannot know the meaning of our life or our death, of God or of ourselves. . . . Thus, without Scripture, whose only object is Christ, we know nothing, and can see nothing but obscurity and confusion in the nature of God and in nature itself.[8]

As Christian professors, intellectuals, and students interested in academic pursuits, we need to reaffirm the importance, significance, and efficacy of Christ's mind being lived through us. Christ's mind and life were supportive of both the heart and the intellect. He not only cared about our physical needs, as shown by his healing of the blind, the crippled, and the deaf, but he engaged the intellect of those he encountered by constantly giving evidence that they could not refute, causing them to question their own thinking. For example, when the crowd wanted to stone the woman caught in adultery, Jesus said, "Let any one of you who is without sin be the first to throw a stone at her" (John 8:7). Jesus challenged the religious leaders to examine their own lives and their thinking.

To bring the mind of Christ back into the university, we must get to know the mind of Christ. What was important to him? How did he respond to people and situations? What were his values? How did he view the world? How did he view our role in the world? When we develop biblical literacy, it is not for knowledge's sake. Having Christ's mind is to come to know the One who created us and formed us while we were still in our mother's womb. It is to come to know the One who designed us individually for a specific God-ordained purpose. It is to go to Scripture to develop an intimate relationship with the God who created us to have a personal, loving relationship with him. Then, our role as Christian professors in the twenty-first century is to bring Jesus Christ back to the university: to our students, our scholarship, and our colleagues. We can do this by practicing the habits of Christ's mind—humility, truth, love, compassion, empathy, kindness, mercy, wisdom, and peace. Christ was filled with the Holy Spirit. He was conceived by the Spirit, identified by the Spirit at his baptism, and led by the Spirit all throughout his life. To bring Christ back into the university we, too, must be filled with the Holy Spirit and led by him.

Reaffirm Truth

A second task of the Christian professor in the twenty-first century is to reaffirm the pursuit of truth. We know that early universities in Europe, Africa, Asia, and America were founded to seek truth. The University of Oxford proclaimed "*Veritas liberabit vos*" (i.e., the truth will set you free). Harvard stood for "*Veritas*" (i.e., Truth). Yale University had as its motto "*Lux et Veritas*" (i.e., Light and Truth). And yet today, truth is often scorned or dismissed with hostility in public universities. Relativism continues to dominate the message in the classroom. Students are told there is no absolute truth, only various opinions. Today's universities have favored pragmatism, commercialism, ideology, and technology rather than philosophical, historical, and theological inquiry. Even science has been seized by political and biased bureaucratic systems.

Amid the university's deemphasis of truth, Christian professors must take a revolutionary stand for truth—and they are. In our discussions, Mark Noll explained that Christian professors now more boldly communicate truth than when he wrote *The Scandal of the Evangelical Mind*. Christian professors are taking a stand for truth in universities worldwide through efforts such as The Society of Christian Philosophers, Veritas Forum, CCSN, InterVarsity, Global Scholars, the Global Faculty Initiative, Faculty Forum, Christian Studies Centers, Academic Connections, and many discipline-specific Christian societies. Books like *Professing Christ: Christian Tradition and Faith-Learning Integration in Public Universities*,[9] *A Grander Story: An Invitation to Christian Professors*,[10] and *Finding God at Harvard: The Spiritual Journeys of Thinking Christians*,[11] are just a few books that explain how Christian professors are bringing their faith to bare in their scholarship and with their students.

In upholding truth as a fundamental aim of the university, Christian professors must, with all humility, guard against adopting the political and ideological propaganda so prevalent in contemporary culture. I like the way George Marsden expressed this. He referred to Jonathan Rauch's book *The Constitution of Knowledge: A Defense of Truth*. Marsden states,

> He urges us to act with the kinds of checks and balances evident in the U.S. Constitution. Particularly in the internet and social media age, it is easy for us all to pick up false views, spread them, and allow ourselves to become embroiled in the heated rhetoric of the moment. Christian scholars ought to be known as those who really are patient champions of law and order, employing solid evidence, good arguments, and personal integrity—and as those who recognize the same among those with whom we disagree. . . . In other words, I think it is important for us to emphasize the integration of Christian scholarship and Christian virtues. For instance, we should speak the truth in love. And we should

treat other scholars as our neighbors, biblically speaking. We should even love our scholarly enemies to use the biblical language.[12]

I am reminded of *The Treason of the Intellectuals* written in 1927 by Julien Benda, the French philosopher, novelist, and cultural critic.[13] Although, to my knowledge, Benda was not a believer, he thought that it was essential that scholars, professors, intellectuals, and what he refers to as scribes maintain their passion for the spiritual and not be consumed by the temporal and political world. Benda writes, "The modern scribe's function is to pursue eternal matters, yet he believes he will become greater by concerning himself with public affairs."[14] Benda's writings are as relevant today as they were in the early part of the twentieth century. The "intellectual elite" have often adopted the political and ideological values of the media, and they are most vulnerable to propaganda.

Jacques Ellul, the French professor of law, sociology, history of institutions, and lay theologian, addressed the same issue in his book *Propaganda: The Formation of Men's Attitudes*.[15] He believed that intellectuals were the most susceptible to propaganda. According to Ellul and summarized by Konrad Kellen there are three reasons this is so:

(1) they absorb the largest amount of secondhand, unverifiable information; (2) they feel a compelling need to have an opinion on every important question of our time, and thus easily succumb to opinions offered to them by propaganda on all such indigestible pieces of information; (3) they consider themselves capable of "judging for themselves." They literally need propaganda.[16]

Christian professors must prioritize truth in our thinking and scholarship. We must be careful not to buy into the propaganda of the Left or of the Right. This is a challenge we need to address in our highly propagandistic media world.

In his book *Christ and the Media*, Malcolm Muggeridge noted the importance of keeping Jesus Christ as the focus of our attention. He said, "I am more convinced than of anything else that I have ever thought, or considered, or believed, that the only antidote to the media's world of fantasy is the reality of Christ's Kingdom proclaimed in the New Testament."[17] As professors in the university, we need to develop an awareness and discerning attitude toward the media and its effects on us and the world around us. As my late professor, friend, and media critic Neil Postman so aptly wrote, we live in a culture where we amuse ourselves to death.[18] As Christian professors, we must immerse ourselves in the eternal Kingdom through the power of the Holy Spirit and allow Christ to live his life through us.

Another warning Ellul gave to Christian professors, intellectuals, and church leaders was to avoid mixing theology with ideology, particularly Marxist thought. In his book, *Jesus and Marx: From Gospel to Ideology*, Ellul elaborates on this issue, explaining that virtually all European intellectuals have adopted Marxist thinking.[19] Ellul himself moved away from the Marxist paradigm. In our current universities, the Marxist theory of wealthy oppressors versus poor oppressed individuals, along with the patriarchal Western civilization versus marginalized women and minorities, significantly influences much of academic discourse. This has contributed to the polarization we observe in our universities and society. At the conference, George Marsden addressed the political and polarizing challenges faced by

Christian scholars in our contemporary society. He states, "We've always had some of this polarization, but I think that politics has become the religion, even the primary religion, for an awful lot of people on both sides of the political spectrum."[20] As Christian scholars, we need to examine our foundational presuppositions. Are our foundational presuppositions biblical or ideological? What theoretical frameworks have we embraced in our scholarship, and are those frameworks ideological or biblical?

Jesus Christ declared that he is the truth. He stated, "I am the way and the truth, and the life" (John 14:6). As followers of Christ, we must reaffirm our love for truth and the significance of truth-seeking within the university. In his conference presentation, Terry Lindvall reminded us of Augustine's words, "All truth is God's truth."[21] The university's core mission should focus on the pursuit of knowledge and truth, requiring commitment to learning that goes beyond ideology and pragmatism. As Christian professors, we must uphold the higher purpose of scholarship. George Marsden also reminded us, "We should speak the truth in love."[22] We should introduce truth to the university with love, respect, and humility.

Make Jesus Christ Known in the University

A third task of the Christian professor in the twenty-first century is to intentionally make Jesus Christ known in the university. Jesus Christ and his word can transform the individual, the university, and society. As Christ-followers, we must more fully understand how God's Word changed all Western civilizations, and we need to impart that knowledge to our students. Vishal Mangalwadi's *The Book that Made Your World: How the Bible Created the Soul of Western Civilization*,[23] and *This Book Changed Everything: The Bible's Amazing Impact on Our World*,[24] are must-reads to build confidence in the transformative impact of God's Word in our world. Mangalwadi clearly explains the power of God's Word in shaping the foundations of the entire university, our laws, our hospitals, and science. Our students need to understand this truth. A student told me recently that in her class, a professor told the students that there is no such thing as truth, that Christianity is evil, that Jesus, as a man, is largely to blame for our patriarchal society, and that anyone who believes in him is contributing to an evil society. Christian professors need to help set the record straight. We must confidently bring the truth to our students and colleagues. We can do this both in the classroom and in our writing.

Christian professors can also restore the significance of objective reality at the university. The university has embraced the philosophy that there is no objective reality, only multiple realities. However, the truth is that an objective reality exists. If a plane crashes, there is the reality of the passengers' deaths. If a married couple divorces, there is the reality of a divided home. If a student does not achieve passing grades, he may lose his place in the university. If an infant is aborted, there is the reality of a child's death. There is an objective reality. Once rooted in objective reality, science has now been compromised by political interests. Journalism was once founded on objective reporting; now, it is influenced by ideological activists. Objectivity needs to be reinstated at the university. The Christian professor can uphold rationality, logic, and objectivity as standards.

At our unconference, Calvin L. Troup spoke on the importance of professors embracing the Bible as a foundation for scholarship. The Bible gives us a historical grounding for our place in history. The Bible provides us with an understanding of who we are as human beings created in the image of God. We are given life by the Holy Spirit, who breathed life into us. We are not merely material beings. The Bible explains our purpose for life—to know God and to have a relationship with him. The twenty-first century student is searching for purpose, meaning, and significance; when they cannot find it, they suffer from loneliness, depression, and mental illness. The Christian professor can bring a solid foundation of truth back to the university. We can do this in our classrooms and our scholarship. This past year, Western Washington University had two students on our campus who committed suicide. I told my students that I would be remiss if I did not tell them that there is a God who knows them, hears them, and has a wonderful plan for their lives. Their lives have meaning and significance. I let the students know that if they were ever depressed or overwhelmed with life, they could share with me, and I would gladly pray for them. Some students came to me with appreciation. There was also a student who gave me a negative review on a course evaluation as a result. This is what we face when we share Christ in the university. The Christian professor must have courage, as we have been told we will face persecution for taking a stand for Christ.

As Christian professors, we can explain to our students the importance of growing and developing as well-rounded individuals. I asked my students last quarter if their professors had discussed their character development. They all said no. So this quarter, I explained to my students that I am an Ellul scholar, a Postman scholar, a McLuhan scholar, and a Jesus scholar. I noted that Jesus provided a model for human development and learning. The Book of Luke states that Jesus grew in wisdom (intellectually), stature (physically), and in favor with God (spiritually), and favor with man (socially).[25] I explain to my students that as they navigate the university, it is essential for them to develop as whole individuals intellectually, physically, spiritually, and socially. Jesus developed as a whole person and was interested in our development as whole people. He spent significant time teaching, healing, building relationships, and demonstrating how we should live. Our students need to understand the relevance of Jesus Christ in our lives today. It is also essential for our universities to emphasize character development. Christian professors in the twenty-first century can reintroduce this as a vital dimension of education.

There is no doubt that universities today are struggling. They have lost their original mission and calling as they have shifted toward a market mentality. Students have followed suit, often entering college without a purpose other than obtaining a degree, graduating, and earning money. The Bible states, "Without a vision, the people perish" (Prov. 29:18). Without vision, the university is in decline. Paul A. Soukup, SJ, in his conference presentation, "A Catholic University: A Religiously Oriented Approach to Teaching and Research," referred to Neil Postman's book, *The End of Education*.[26] In that book, Postman writes that students need a "why" for their education. Soukup writes, "For effective education, people need to understand why. For what purpose do we seek education? If the purpose is only economic, one wonders whether this is education at all. . . . A religious perspective includes a deeper understanding of how humanity exists in the image and likeness of God. To study, to research, to learn all involves deepening a relationship with God."[27] Even in a pluralistic educational system, the Christian professor can bring back the need for a transcendent purpose or end for education. At this time in history, the educational system and universities need a clear vision of what education is really about. The Christian professor can help restore vision for their students and the university. The Christian professor is uniquely positioned to provide a vision that fosters an emphasis on God's creativity, beauty, humor, humility, and love. The Christian professor in the twenty-first century can help elevate humanity toward a more civil, kind, respectful, and compassionate society—a much-needed society in the twenty-first century.

Christian faculty can also help restore a world vision in our universities. Professors and students worldwide are coming to know Jesus Christ. In North America, Western and Eastern Europe, Asia, India, South America, and Africa, professors and students are turning to Christ as our only hope. In a ministry I serve with, Faculty Commons, professors travel from U.S. campuses to other nations to speak on university campuses. In the process, the U.S. professors gain a vision for the world, and often, the students and professors they meet come into a relationship with the Lord. It will be wonderful when more Christian professors from other nations come to North America to be witnesses in our universities. We need their voices to be heard. Christian professors living out faith in the twenty-first century need to take a role in bringing global awareness and the transcendent to our campuses. Our God is a God of the universe. And the university is a global institution in need of him.

In *The Two Tasks*, Charles Malik asks a probing question for believers. He asks, " . . . If Christians do not care for the intellectual health of their own children and for the fate of their own civilization, a health and a fate so inextricably bound up with the state of the mind and spirit in the universities, who is going to care?"[28] I believe that in the twenty-first century, more and more Christians are aware of the university's power to influence our society for good or ill. Christian parents know the power of professors and the university to shape and influence their children. Christians do care, but often they do not know what to do about it. It is up to the Christian professor to more intentionally bring Christ into the university. Christian professors in the twenty-first century have this as our unique role and calling. We must give ourselves to it completely with heart, mind, and soul. We must genuinely love our students and colleagues as we do ourselves.[29]

Chapter 38

Reflections on Christ-centered, Holy Spirit-inspired Learning in an Age of Propaganda and Polarization

William J. Brown

Response Summary: This essay is inspired by Marsden's advocacy for twenty-first century Christian scholarship characterized more as winsome rather than outrageous. In an age of propaganda and polarization, Marsden points to a great need for Christian scholars to provide new vision for Christian higher education nourished by the bonds of Christ-like humility and unity of the spirit. First, the author argues for the necessity of judging ourselves and our own susceptibility to be manipulated by fear and false information from both governments and media sources anchored in divisiveness. Second, drawing on a recent book on Christian higher education, the author argues for consideration of a balanced approach to learning that equally values cognitive learning centered in the mind, spiritual formation centered in the heart, and practical service brought about through the work of our hands.

Fifty years ago during my freshman year as a young engineering student at Purdue University, one of the most respected Bible teachers among my Christian mentors, Bob Mumford, who continues to sustain a vibrant ministry today, spoke a simple yet profound message that created an anchor for my life.[1] Based on I Corinthians 11:31, Bob taught that there are two ways to walk with the Lord: the easy way, which is to judge ourselves, or the hard way, which is to be judged. I especially like the Amplified Bible translation: "But if we evaluated and judged ourselves honestly [recognizing our shortcomings and correcting our behavior], we would not be judged." Considering how we might make our future scholarly contributions as Christian scholars more relevant and useful to both the believer and unbeliever, we could benefit greatly by acting on the Apostle Paul's admonition as an academic community of Christians committed to loving God and our neighbor as Christ commands.

The purpose of this short essay is to raise provoking questions that might lead us to deeper self-reflection about our current influence on American society and Christian higher education. This essay is inspired by the invaluable contributions of two of the leading evangelical scholars of the past 50 years: George Marsden, Emeritus Professor of History at the University of Notre Dame, and Mark Noll, Research Professor of History at Regent College and former Francis A. McAnaney Professor of History at the University of Notre Dame. I also was stirred by Joel Carpenter's recent essay, "Reawakening Evangelical Intellectual Life: A Christian Scholar's Review,"[2] and intrigued by Amos Young and Dale Coulter's recent book, *The Holy Spirit and Higher Education: Renewing the Christian University*.[3] My musings here are informed through the lens of media research, as opposed to theological or philosophical scholarship.

I begin with this question for reflection: How might we more prudently judge ourselves as Christians and scholars who love God and one another and who seek knowledge and wisdom in our divisive and deceitful culture? We should reflect deeply on what it means to love God as we listen, learn, teach, and share what we believe to be truthful within our Christian communities and to those who have not yet surrendered their lives to Christ. During the past 75 years, we have witnessed an intensified assault on the idea that it is still possible to ascertain and teach truth, or wisdom, a closely related terminal value that Milton Rokeach, former Professor of Communication and Psychology at the University of Southern California and one of my most cherished professors, described as an "end-state of existence" that guides the development of a mature life.[4]

Communication about truth and wisdom within our Christian scholarly community ought to contrast from the world's deliberations about such things. If not, we are failing to offer the "distinct perspectives" that George Marsden indicates "ought to change the contextual framework for thinking about just about everything" and should guide our scholarship and educational endeavors.[5] Yet, if we as Christian scholars sound like the world when we discuss our differences, how will the world discern our distinct perspective? Our trumpets of truth and wisdom will be lost in the cacophony of the many voices of error and foolishness.

In Joel Carpenter's fine essay on reawakening evangelical intellectual life, which merits contemplative reading, he challenges evangelical scholars to "bless others with wholesome, creative, and constructive thinking and living rather than continuing to try to impose our will on others" and to seek our "own integrity and renewal in the faith and do not focus on judging others."[6] Scripture obviously has much to say about truth and falsehood and about judging others. We need remind ourselves that to abandon our commitment to live by truth is to live by lies, as Alexander Solzhenitsyn warned in his famous essay, "Live Not by Lies."[7]

In her experience of teaching theological truth to Christians raised in Communism, Esther Ng finds it challenging to educate and empower Christians to embrace truth and reject the lies perpetrated by the government, society, and the corrupt systems of this world controlled by powers of darkness. She states:

> We live in a time when it is often difficult to distinguish between truth and falsehood, or between right and wrong. Thus we encounter imitation merchandise and counterfeit money; lies and half-truths spoken by politicians and journalists; hoaxes and emails, text messages, and social media; distortions in historical accounts, in reports of scientific research, and even in presentations of religious convictions. Under such circumstances, how should Christians live?[8]

Scripture states that God hates lying and bearing false witness and detests those who create and disseminate lies to mislead and oppress others. Christian scholars should agree that a genuine commitment to Christ implies an uncompromising commitment to truth. Yes, you may reply, but which truth when everyone claims they know the truth? Perhaps this is where we turn to scholarship to help distinguish between truth and falsehood.

We have many contemporary examples where scholarship is needed to sift through the falsehoods, propaganda, and disinformation that have created divisive opposing narratives that have trapped Christian scholars into destructive conflicts. Consider, for example, the following opposing narratives: (1) the January 6 capital protests versus the capital insurrection, (2) the unquestionable legitimacy of the 2020 presidential election voting practices versus the consequential documented election fraud, (3) the U.S. Government's COVID-19 campaign to protect the public from the pandemic versus the U.S. Government's coercive and unscientific mandates and social media censorship, and (4) the scientific arguments for declaring man's production of CO_2 emissions as the cause of harmful climate change versus the scientific arguments supporting the claim that man's contribution to climate change through CO_2 emissions is negligible. Many of us hold divergent beliefs about these events and policies.

Although pursuing the truth about such matters is important, we may find ourselves entangled in unproductive caustic debates that play into Satan's well-known strategy to divide and conquer Christians and to make them impotent as peacemakers and agents of reconciliation in a fractured culture. In addition to these volatile issues, there is the divisive nature of differing political judgments among Christian scholars and educators regarding our last two U.S. presidents across the political spectrum. Communication about these differences often have not been conducted in a way that protects the unity of the church and advances the Gospel. The social media posts of Christian scholars often do not embody the Christlike love, patience, and forgiveness that God commands us to practice. I am challenged by George Marsden's call for Christian scholarship in the twenty-first century to be characterized as "more winsome than outrageous."[9] This leads to my second question for reflection: How might we as Christian scholars communicate about social and political differences with a quickness to listen and a slowness to speak and a commitment to share what we believe to be truth with humility and in love?

Age of Propaganda and Polarization

As persuasion scholars Anthony Pratkanis and Elliot Aronson declared in their 1992 book, *Age of Propaganda*, we now live in a mediated society filled with disinformation, factoids, misleading narratives, and manipulated messages that violate the norms of truth-telling and the free exchange of information.[10] If we ignore this reality, we do so at our own peril. Let me provide a potent example in a subfield of communication study of my expertise. One of my areas of specialty is health communication. I have published numerous health communication studies and have served as a blind reviewer for many decades for two of the leading health communication journals. When the COVID-19 pandemic descended upon us, I immediately went to the health communication literature to learn what we knew and what we did not know about COVID-19 and how best to protect ourselves.

As a media scholar, I recognized the nature of the U.S. Government's $1.5 billion dollar propaganda campaign to convince Americans to take one of the three experimental COVID-19 vaccines as one of the largest in history.[11] The U.S. Government has a rich tradition of creating propaganda campaigns, defined as organized communication systems that apply the "techniques of mass persuasion" to influence large populations "through the manipulation of symbols" that "play on our prejudices and emotions."[12]

The U.S. Government's COVID-19 campaign successfully used high fear appeal messages to both persuade and coerce Americans to follow their mandates of wearing masks, social distancing, not interacting with other people in small group or large group settings, and getting COVID-19 vaccines.[13] That strategy completely opposed the basic health principle that *the more society can function normally during a pandemic—the better the people will manage and survive*[14] (emphasis mine). Not long into the pandemic, it became clear that U.S. and world health agencies, including the NIH, NIAID, the FDA, the CDC, and WHO, along with news media organizations, medical establishments, universities, tech companies, and social media companies "were suppressing and continue to suppress the early and very effective treatments for COVID-19" that were successfully being used by doctors throughout the world.[15]

High fear appeal messages are very effective in gaining compliance and were used extensively during the COVID-19 pandemic to persuade people to take COVID-19 vaccines.[16] Despite the claims made by the U.S. Government and much of the U.S. news media, the scientific data indicate the lowest COVID-19 death rates occurred in countries, states, and regions of the world that used therapeutic drugs like Ivermectin, Hydroxychloroquine, and others; while some of the highest death rates occurred in the most vaccinated nations of the world like the United States.[17]

There are many prominent writers of various political perspectives that document the COVID-19 propaganda campaign and the inefficacy of the COVID-19 vaccines and mandates to stop the pandemic, including Peter R. Breggin and Ginger Ross Breggin's *COVID-19 and the Global Predators*,[18] Sharyl Attkisson's *Follow the Science*,[19] Naomi Wolf's *Facing the Beast: Courage, Faith, and Resistance in a New Dark Age*,[20] and Robert F. Kennedy Jr.'s *A Letter to Liberals: Censorship and COVID: An Attack on Science and American Ideals*.[21] One of the most troubling facts of the COVID-19 years was the systematic censorship of Americans, including scientists and medical doctors, who challenged the scientific validity of the U.S. Government's COVID-19 mandates.[22] Even more disturbing was that many Christian families, friends, and churches allowed the COVID-19 pandemic and government mandates to create conflicts, harm relationships, and create divisions. I wonder how well as a community of Christian scholars we might have helped to mitigate these divisions instead of contributing to the divisiveness.

Our academic community of Christian scholars loses credibility when we make hasty judgments of the spiritual condition and heart motives of our social, cultural, and political leaders and their supporters based on media portrayals rather than first-hand information based on interpersonal interactions. More than 60 years of media scholarship provides us with important research findings that we ought to consider. First, as noted earlier, we live in an "age of propaganda."[23] Pratkanis and Aronson's late twentieth-century declaration is still valid today, as AI is enhancing the creation of propaganda.[24] Second, there is a clear relationship between what information sources we drink from and what we believe to be true.[25] John Demuyakor notes that "the powerful elites in the society who control media find it easy to automatically influence ideological developments that are either allowed or outlawed from being broadcasted."[26] The role of spiritual forces at work in propaganda cannot be ignored, as the Apostle Paul reminds us that we are not to be ignorant of the schemes of the devil and must stand against them (2 Cor. 2:11, Eph. 6:11). Third, we also live in an age of polarization as manifested in our highly polarized social and cultural environment that pits a loosely organized pool of urban minorities and wealthy intellectual and progressive elites against a loosely organized pool of conservative professional and working-class populists. Samuel Perry states that despite the centrality of religion in American society, "America's divides has largely shifted toward partisan identity, political ideology, race, and class interests" and that "religion remains powerfully implicated in all dimensions of American polarization."[27] This leads to my third question for reflection: Given the challenges of propaganda and polarization, how might we as Christian scholars not allow differing social and political perspectives to impede our efforts to maintain the unity of the spirit in the bond of peace that we have as Christians (Eph. 4:3)?

The Holy Spirit and Higher Education

I now turn to the question of how the community of Christian scholars might forge a way through the political divisiveness of our propaganda-filled mediated society to create vibrant institutions of higher learning that protect free speech and yet debate ideas and differing perspectives in mutual respect, kindness, and civility that is a contrast to the vitriolic and harmful speech that daily spews out through all forms of media. If we adhered to the Apostle James's (Jas. 1:26) command to control our speech, the unwise and often embarrassing pronouncements that Christians post on social media or disseminate through other mediating communication channels would cease. There are many good reasons why King David refused to curse King Saul, reflected in the personal prayer that he recorded in Psalm 19:14.

In their recent book, *The Holy Spirit and Higher Education: Renewing the Christian University*, Amos Yong and Dale Coulter describe their vision for a Spirit-infused institution of higher education.[28] Despite some of the shortcomings of their work as noted in Timothy Larsen's excellent critique, their ideas and vision are worthy of reflection by Christian scholars.[29] Yong and Coulter envision a Holy Spirit-infused university or college as a place of learning whose purpose is "to inculcate a habitus in students in which moral formation, encounters with transcendence, and investment in mission now orient them."[30]

They insinuate that in *The Scandal of the Evangelical Mind*,[31] Mark Noll incorrectly positioned Pentecostalism as anti-intellectual, observing that new religious movements often attract social and intellectual elites. Noll's critique of Pentecostalism and higher learning was much more nuanced, as Noll does not argue that the leading of the Holy Spirit in the intellectual life of the believer leads to anti-intellectualism. Noll is clearly aware that since God is the source of infinite knowledge and wisdom, not man, then man must look to the guidance of the Holy Spirit, who leads us into all truth in each of our intellectual endeavors (John 16:13).

What Yong and Coulter might have accurately observed is that Noll privileges the cognitive processes of learning over two other equally important processes that occur through the heart or spiritual center of a person and through the hands which embody acts of service. This tripartite understanding of higher learning, expressed as a "head-heart-hands" model, is what I would like to consider in my final reflections.

We now live in an age of artificial intelligence, an age with implications that will far exceed the age of propaganda and age of polarization. AI makes much of what we do in higher education increasingly irrelevant, since knowledge is at everyone's fingertips and is no longer a scarce commodity. This leads to my fourth question for reflection: Since scarceness leads to value, how do we as Christian scholars create value for our degree programs when students no longer need our knowledge?

I offer a couple of recommendations. First, we need to shift the higher learning model espoused by Yong and Coulter to the issues of the heart, that is, spiritual formation, and to teaching skills to those whom God has called to work with their hands. When we look back on our most profound and transformational experiences attending a college, university, or formal educational program, few of us would state it was the knowledge we gained that was most important. Rather, was it not the people we were with, the friends we made, the spiritual leaders who mentored us, and the experiences we had outside of the formal learning environment that were most transformative? These are the intangibles that are not likely described in our marketing materials for prospective students or featured on our college and university websites. How can we make the heart formation of the believer a priority in all of our educational programs?

Second, we need to consider what educational programs we can provide that facilitate teaching students the various vocations and professions in which they work with their hands. In 1 Thessalonians 4:11, the Apostle Paul encourages Christians to lead a quiet life and to work with their hands. The need for vocational and professional degree programs in the United States is increasing, especially in light of the federal government's efforts to increase manufacturing throughout the United States. If our first reaction to a skill-based curriculum is that we are not in the trade school business, we may be overlooking what God has called us to do. Jesus could have chosen any profession; he could have been a scholar, but he chose to work with his hands as a carpenter. The best practices of apprenticeship programs blend a focus on character formation with a focus on skill development.[32] Vocational educational and training programs lead to innovation and growth.[33]

Developing vocational degree programs that blend spiritual formation and mentoring with vocational skill development and training should have a place in the Holy Spirit-inspired universities of the future. This leads to our last question for reflection: What might we do as Christian scholars to facilitate the development of new vocational and professional degree programs in the colleges and universities where God has placed us?

In conclusion, my purpose here has been to inspire reflection on first, how we might judge ourselves as we make corrections that enable us to be salt and light in our heavily propagandized and polarized society; and second, to consider how God might use us to advance our efforts as a community of Christian scholars to advance balanced "heads-hearts-hands" learning programs that serve the church more effectively and advance God's kingdom and purposes in the organizations in which he has placed us. I hope your reflections might be fruitful.

Chapter 39

Long Walks of Teaching and Faith

Douglas Kelley

Response Summary: The author uses the image of walking on the road to Emmaus as a metaphor for developing the "Christian" mind in pedagogy. Leaning into the unconference theme of faith integration in the public sphere (particularly as developed by Legacy Scholars Noll, Marsden, and Spencer), he emphasizes dialogue as human encounter and creating space where good things can happen through a process of letting go of ego and development of academic humility. Learning spaces then become co-creations between teacher and student as Christian faculty learn to embody their own faith in the classroom.

I HAVE LONG LOVED Robert Zund's painting, *The Road to Emmaus*—the pastoral scene, the travelers in rapt conversation. Along with the characters in Luke 24, I am drawn to the discovery of new truths and experiencing the fire within as I walk with Jesus and other companions seeking to experience truth. My life has been a long walk with Christ, listening to parables, aphorisms, and proverbs as we have traversed varied terrains together.

My teaching spaces have been designed as long walks as well. I have had no desire to write trade books and hit the circuit as a popular speaker. Rather, my place is in the classroom, in which students and I walk with one another as we form long-term mutual-learning relationships, with our mutual travel characterized by trust, connection, disruption, insight, and transformation.

I see my writing as creating similar transformative spaces. This has been problematic for me as a social scientist, in which the orientation is biased toward "significant" findings and answers. Of course, I have provided these elements when needed, but more so I have invited my readers to join me on long written walks to explore various subject matters. In this sense, my writing and research are heuristic. Each individual effort is a part of a longer journey, not an end point. Together, they weave a tapestry of ideas that bring reader and author closer to their shared humanity and hopefully to the One who is our Ultimate Creator.

These long walks of learning have not differed much across context, contrary to the overly binary distinctions suggested by some. With some regularity, certain Christian individuals, upon finding out that I was teaching at Arizona State University, would give me a knowing look and ask, "How's that going?" This experience parallels Mark Noll's description in his essay for this volume: "I feel that in my academic life, I can't tell people that

I'm a serious church member. I feel at church that I can't tell people I'm committed to the academic life."[1] I have felt the same, but gratefully, as I tried to distance myself from being considered a "Christian scholar," a non-Christian colleague encouraged me to keep bringing my faith perspective into my work. He saw both church and university as places where moral questions could still be considered. Some may question that basic assumption, but it was in that spirit that my teaching at Seattle Pacific University (Christian) and Arizona State University (public) differed little from one another—genuinely engaging students in both places as we courageously encountered course content.

Where is the "Christian" in all of this? I would argue that this is the wrong question. For me, it is impossible to separate faith from the rest of my life—both personal and academic. My teaching at SPU and ASU sprung forth from what I call my genuine teaching self or what Parker Palmer terms, the undivided self.[2] My faith heightens my awareness to certain ideas, perspectives, themes, happenings. My awareness and interest piques as students and I explore ideas of love, justice, intimacy, and forgiveness. Mark Noll states, "It is not 'the evangelical mind,' 'Christian thinking,' or such categories that are important. It is rather the specific task needing research, the nagging problem requiring further thought, and the current field to which one has been called."[3]

As a communication scholar I am prone to learning and understanding through dialogue. Specifically, I have been drawn to Buber's notion of *genuine dialogue*: "Whether spoken or silent . . . where each of the participants really has in mind the other or others in their present and particular being and turns to them with the intention of establishing a living mutual relation between himself and them."[4] When my students or readers and I can approximate genuine dialogue, learning and knowing emerge.

As an undergraduate religious studies major at Arizona State, I was fortunate enough to take courses with Del Brown, a Christian professor who introduced me to liberation and existential theologies. Much more liberal than I was, Del was bright, articulate, and had a beautiful mind for the faith. I have fond memories of walking together after classes chewing over course concepts, while at the same time talking openly about his concern for his own son's faith.

This approach to nurturing the mind was formative for me. In later years I would connect it to Paul's injunction to have the mind of Christ: "who . . . did not count equality with God a thing to be grasped, but emptied himself, by taking the form of a servant" (Phil. 2:7, English Standard Version). I have truncated Paul's statement to highlight two aspects that have characterized my hope when writing and teaching. The first aspect is self-emptying—to let go of ego in the service of others. Closely related is the aspect of academic humility—to cease grasping after being a "god," but rather to become human to my students and readers.

As we release ego and embrace humility, we *create spaces in which if good things can happen, they will*. I first proposed this idea in *Just Relationships* as a means of interpersonal advocacy.[5] As advocates we create space, invite others into that space and, if they come, then begin to co-create space where good things can happen. This process recognizes our own agency, but it also emphasizes our lack of control of other individuals. As teachers, we are advocates for our students. As such, we create safe spaces for learners to risk disruption and consequentially to experience the opening of their minds to new ideas and new actions.

This kind of genuine teaching is a humbling process, void of ego, in that it recognizes that we do not control the outcome. Once students are willing to enter into this rather sacred space, we join together in a long walk of mutual learning and potential transformation. For me, some of today's public scholar talk is filled with too much certainty. As Christian scholars, we can find ourselves in this same position: too confident in what we think we know. And, as Greg Spencer argues in his contribution to this volume, we are in danger of avoiding the practice of good thinking that is willing to endure risk.

Examples of safe spaces for co-learning occurred frequently in my forgiveness course. In the third week of the semester, I would host a panel including a Christian pastor, a rabbi, the head of the local Muslim congregation, and a Buddhist priest (and, no, they do not all walk into a bar). Each panelist would provide an overview of their religion's understanding of forgiveness. Then the class session would be opened for questions. In the spirit of full disclosure, during the class period before the panel I would share my own faith background related to forgiveness.

The point of these forgiveness panels was not to offer information as much as it was to create a space where good things could happen. Talking to a Buddhist priest is different than reading about Buddhism. A tone was being set for the rest of the semester—we could safely broach a wide variety of religious perspectives together as part of our class discussions and assignments.

The panel also provided the opportunity for students to watch me learn and be challenged. Like it or not, I became an imperfect embodiment of the Christian faith for many students. I say this not to exaggerate or place undue pressure on our roles as professors. However, my *how* became an important contribution to *what* the students were learning. As Marsden comments in his contribution to this volume, "This self-critical work about my own Christian 'tribe' turned out to be something that people on the outside were really appreciative of because it wasn't just celebrating or defining my own fundamentalist background, on the one hand, and it wasn't just criticizing and dismissing it, on the other. In a sense, *I began doing what all good scholars do—weigh the evidence and make fair judgments that speak the truth in love* [italics mine]."[6]

Release of ego and embrace of humility opens space for the embodiment of faith in our classrooms and writing. It is part of the long walk that cultivates the mind of Christ in us all. It creates space where good thinking and learning and discovery and transformation can, and do, happen. As Parker Palmer reminds us: "Good teaching comes from the identity and integrity of the teacher."[7] For me this has meant bringing my genuine teaching self to my students and writing as honestly as possible—long walks together in hope of hearing the Shepherd's voice along the way.

Chapter 40

Christian Pedagogy:
Formation vs. Indoctrination

Rick Olsen and Julie Morgan

Response Summary: This essay explores three themes that run through insights by Marsden, Lindvall, Noll, and Spencer in their Legacy Scholar presentations. The authors call on faculty to teach Christian things, integrate a Christian point of view when teaching non-Christian things, and to be humble and humorous as an expression of "salt and light" (Matt. 5:13–16) in the Academy. Each of these distinctives should be carried out within a larger attitude of formation rather than indoctrination. This posture of ongoing formation should be modeled by the faculty member as well. These imperatives must also be carried out in ways that demonstrate excellence in both pedagogy and curriculum design.

I (RICK) NEEDED TO facilitate a hard conversation with two students who were claiming they had been emotionally and mentally harmed by the other. My colleague, David, also attended the meeting. I wanted to say, "you are both being petty, say 'I'm sorry' and let's get back to the point of college!" What took place instead was a circuitous dialogue that eventually resulted in disclosures by both students about diagnosed depressions, childhood trauma, and other issues that informed their interaction patterns. One student eventually said, "You are not in this alone." It took patience to find the moment of transformation.

David and I made room for this meeting because we had a mutual hope that we could get to a place of mutual positive regard. It was exhausting. I felt a bit like the biblical figure Jonah who desired the quick wrath of God only to realize he was called to love others into a right relationship with God. A heart *for* God is easy, having the heart *of* God for others is hard.

So it is with teaching. Many of us would prefer a quick, direct, methodical approach to subject mastery. But students are more than just students, and teachers are more than just teachers. We meet as communities of learners and journey together for a while. To what end? We argue that a faculty member of faith should ask "What actions or responses by me will most likely foster formation in my students?"

The contributions in this volume speak to the importance of Christian thinking and faith-informed scholarship. We are often told that research informs teaching. But that is not automatic, and neither is faith-informed teaching. In this essay, we briefly contrast teaching and scholarship, identify some common ground, and connect insights from several of the Legacy Scholar contributions in this volume to the ground-level challenges of the college classroom. We call on faculty to teach Christian things, integrate a Christian point of view when teaching non-Christian things, and to be humble and humorous as an expression of "salt and light" (Matt. 5:13–16) in the Academy.

Differences and Commonalities in Pedagogy and Scholarship

Much of scholarship involves the joys and challenges of writing to fellow experts. It is ideally somewhat linear and cumulative. Scholarship builds on itself, and the literature review reveals our new starting line. We make transparent use of endorsed methods to arrive at our best current thinking about a problem of interest.

Teaching is a bit more cyclical. We are brain farmers with a new crop each semester. The students and the popular culture that informs their worldviews changes rapidly; spiritual orientations, biblical and cultural literacy are always in flux. Our role as instructors becomes one of adapting to the conditions in the field each season and embracing the pattern of the seasons. There are shared characteristics. In both scholarship and teaching, we are engaged in sensemaking and formation. We lead our students through a process of discovery—even if the discovery that is new to them is known to us. There is still a hope that they have grown through navigating the challenges of our curriculum and now, they too, have new starting lines for their thinking and doing.

There are numerous perspectives on how to think like a Christian. What might it mean to teach like a Christian? We can adapt George Marsden's agenda: "Why do I teach, who am I trying to serve? What good am I trying to bring about?"[1] Our faith, peppered by Lindvall's call for humility and humor, can foster unique classroom cultures and interaction choices that help us "teach better" than others, but that is not guaranteed. One of us teaches at a large public institution (Rick) while the other teaches at a small, private religiously affiliated institution (Julie).

Over the past 30 years, we wrestled with these questions as we constructed our syllabi, managed our classrooms, and engaged with our students (in addition to how we approach our research and service). These questions guided our conversations with the student who "forgot" that there was a final exam, the student who confessed they had not been sober in any of our classes, or the student who could not seem to stay awake in our morning class because they also worked from 10:00 pm to 6:00 am. We responded thoughtfully, not because we wanted to be good teachers (which was true), but because we wanted to figure out how our faith can make a tangible difference in these moments. What does God call us to do to foster the student's ongoing formation? And, as it turned out, processing these questions helped us to refine our thinking and our faith. We are in an ongoing formation journey as well.

The sentiment for a Christian distinctive is not sufficient. There is also a need to do great teaching by the standards of the Academy, using the basic concepts, principles, and tools of the trade to foster excellent curriculum design and pedagogy.

As we reviewed the Legacy Scholar essays by Noll, Lindvall, Marsden, and Spencer, and considered our own experience as educators, we identified three teaching opportunities or perhaps mandates. Each is complicated by the growing lack of biblical literacy and more broadly, the diverse worldviews of students, parents, cultural Christians including Christian nationalists, the broad array of cultural influencers and other factors such as delayed maturation due to COVID-19 and other factors beyond our control. We must address such complications with curiosity and compassion, not judgement or frustration.

Teach Christian Things

Our first admonition is for Christian academics to teach Christian things. That is, to integrate explicitly Christian concepts when they are relevant to the outcomes of the course or the informal teachable moment. This might mean very broad concepts such as love and sacrifice or more specific concepts such as the symbolism of communion. Faculty of faith should seek out opportunities to integrate faith as a normal variable and topic of discussion and critique. In Rick's research methods class, he has quotations from Proverbs in his syllabus that directly deal with the learning outcomes of the course and during an early lecture. He reminds his students of faith that "we are called to think on whatever is true, noble, right, pure, lovely (Phil. 4:8–9). But let us emphasize that the first descriptor is that it must be true! And that is why research, critical thinking, wisdom, and discernment are so important."[2]

In his Legacy Scholar presentation, Mark Noll recounts how many scholars of faith find it difficult to integrate both identities (scholar and Christian) with their peers in each community. The classroom is a strange blend of neither and both of those spaces. It is a learning community in which we have a unique place of leadership and influence. But it is important to remember that it is not just the secular culture that has made it difficult to bring Christianity into the classroom. The Legacy Scholars in this edited volume wrestle with the fundamental truths of the faith. American Christianity is full of dysfunction and excess: Christian nationalism, the prosperity gospel and the hate-filled rhetoric of some faith communities often make headlines and go viral. Noll's challenge of integrating both identities is complicated by the challenges of responding to faulty orthopraxis as well as faithfully conforming to orthodoxy. As teachers, we find the challenge is less around correcting the beliefs or practices of our students and colleagues and more around navigating the negative perceptions from others, if and when we explicitly identify as "Christian." In the classroom, Rick will usually say "I'm a member of a faith community" or other labels that seem more invitational and carry less semantic baggage than "Christian."[3]

The work of bringing faith into the classroom should generally be aligned with the learning goals of the course and demonstrate the integration of critical thinking and faith. Such integration is likely more effective if we can do so with humor, humility, and, in Legacy Scholar Terry Lindvall's words, "a bit of levity."[4]

Teach Non-Christian Things from a Christian Point of View

Our second admonition for Christian academics is to teach non-Christian things from a Christian point of view or at least integrate a distinctly Christian perspective with the various perspectives to be covered. I (Rick) will note in my research methods class that "even if we are looking at issues of faith such as 'Does prayer lead to faster healing?' we need to focus on measurable material evidence and good research practices." And then I move on. As Marsden notes: "We Christians use the same types of reason, evidence, and questioning that other scholars might employ—although our underlying assumptions and questions might be different and our conclusions different because of our own, faith-shaped examination of the issues and disagreements addressed."[5]

I (Julie) teach at a private, faith-based university. I can round out secular theories of interpersonal communication by raising the idea of interpersonal communication within the context of a Judeo-Christian assumption of a fallen and broken world. For example, I use the lens of faith to examine the popular communication theory called Coordinated Management of Meaning (CMM).[6] This broad theory centers on the idea that each person has a truth or a story of lived experiences that inform interaction patterns with themselves and others. And, listening to each other's truth with respect and curiosity opens the door for true dialogue. Julie extends this theory into the possibilities for co-created spiritual experiences. In the semester after George Floyd was murdered, a White male student shared that he wanted to be a police officer while one of her Black male students shared how his dad had been stopped many times by the police without clear cause. In the practice of CMM, they were able to lean into a taboo topic and listen to one another. Students were changed by the experience and modeling of what it looked like to truly listen and lean into difficult conversations. It was evidence of spiritual formation and love for one another that integrated CMM and Ephesians 6:12 that speaks to broken systems and powers all around us.

Teachers as Salt and Light

Our third admonition for Christian academics is to be well known as teachers who are "salt and light" (Matt. 5:13–16) in the lives of our students. This means we strive to teach with joy and be as interruptible as Jesus was with children and others that were culturally invisible or unimportant. This approach calls for discernment. When will it foster formation to extend grace? When will it foster formation to express a hard truth in love and emphasize accountability?

Both of us fondly remember Dr. Ray Penn, a Christian professor who met with a Christian student who had over-extended themselves and did not finish an independent study research project. This student was notoriously hard on themselves. Ray said "I'm going to give you an A that you do not deserve, so that you better understand grace and can extend it to yourself and others. Remember this." There were tears and hugs and this former student went on to become a professor. This story also reminds us that we should not assume that the Christian students will naturally be better students. They are on their formation journeys, too.

Conclusion

This essay has explored several through lines in the essays by George Marsden, Mark Noll, Terry Lindvall, and Greg Spencer. We urge faculty to embrace humor and humility and approach their role as guiding students (and themselves) through the ongoing challenge of formation. These efforts would ideally show up by teaching Christian things as normal and natural, offering relevant Christian perspectives on non-Christian content, and being "salt and light" (Matt. 5:13–16) in our daily conduct and interactions.

Legacy Scholar Greg Spencer concludes his call with the "need to reassert the roles of wisdom and character in the intellectual enterprise."[7] He further notes that a "full-bodied Christian view of learning promotes wisdom, and it promotes thoughtful communication in the community."[8] We agree. Wisdom is the synthesis of critical thinking and humility. We submit to the larger mystery even as we discern what to do next. A key barrier to sharing faith in the classroom is the arrogance of certainty. Humility, including intellectual humility, is exhibiting salt and light to our students. Showing them that a central goal of the educational enterprise is about empowering them to navigate ambiguity for the rest of their lives leaves much room for God and faith to be part of the conversation and their journey of formation.

Chapter 41

A Scandal of Evangelical Pedagogy:
An Outrageous Idea of Christian Teaching

Adam Sonstroem

Response Summary: This anecdotal reflection and teaching analysis is based on my personal experience in Dr. Noll's class and how his teaching emphasized building the mind and character through relationships. Dr. Noll was not just a scholar *par excellence* but a man who humbly lived out his call to teach and train young scholars. What made Dr. Noll's teaching truly outstanding and counter-cultural was that he embodied the role of the servant scholar whose faith and humility shaped his interactions with students. His humble, faith-full approach to scholarship and teaching deeply transformed my own teaching.

THE SCANDAL of the Evangelical Mind and The Outrageous Idea of Christian Scholarship were released in the mid-1990s, a few years before I entered Wheaton College in the fall of 1998.[1] During my undergraduate studies, I had the privilege of reading both of these works and taking a church history class with Dr. Noll. Up until that point, I had not necessarily considered a calling to the life of the mind, let alone what a life of the mind looked like for a Christian. I had always been taught to do my best academically and honor God with my whole self (including my mind), but that was essentially where my consideration ended. To do anything other than honor God with my mind seemed like a foreign concept to me. What I was not sure about, though, is what honoring God with my mind actually meant, beyond just doing my best in school.

What Marsden and Noll presented in their works that was equally outrageous and scandalous was an approach for Christians in the Academy that called for intellectual, scholarly excellence in their respective fields rooted in relationship building and moral character development. Christians were not called simply to think deeply to flaunt their God-given intelligence or elevate their own intellectual status, but instead to use that knowledge to cultivate relationships to grow the kingdom of God. They argued that scholars should integrate their faith (including biblical and theological knowledge) into scholarship and ask questions that challenge core beliefs for the purpose of building a stronger faith. In addition, this academic rigor and excellence needed to be paired with a focus on godly character and covenantal relationships. While a thorough analysis of the two works is beyond the scope of this pedagogical reflection, my purpose here is to recount a story about Dr. Noll that truly reflected his approach to academic rigor rooted in relationships. Instead of merely critiquing and lamenting the lack of intellectual rigor in the Christian Academy from a lofty tower, Noll actively sought to develop the mind and character of his students by investing intellectually and relationally in us, so that we in turn, could invest in others. These uncommon and Christlike pedagogical practices influenced my own approach to teaching.

In the fall of 2001, with the world reeling from the events of 9/11, I finally had the privilege and honor to take a church history class with Dr. Noll during my senior year. While my previous experiences with professors in the Wheaton history department were exceptional and shaped my approach to the content I would teach in American and European history classes, I was excited for the opportunity to study under Dr. Noll—an opportunity that had previously eluded me. Little did I realize in those first days of class that I would undergo a transformative experience that profoundly shaped not only my scholarship but also my future teaching career as well.

Let me begin this story by saying, in an academic world dominated by publishing credentials, rank, and tenure, Dr. Noll was at or near the top of any list of accomplished professors and scholars. His published works alone spoke for themselves (and they honestly did speak for themselves because he never once made mention to his accolades, accomplishments, or intellect inside or outside of class). Instead of a professor who was compelled to show the class how smart he was, I encountered one of the most humble and gracious men I have ever met in the academic world. He was (and is) an accomplished and respected scholar in his field, but he treated the class like colleagues in learning instead of academic inferiors to be merely tolerated. After knowing him only a few weeks, he offered to write letters of recommendation for me if and when I applied to graduate school (I wish I could say I took him up on his offer). He was humble and unassuming, truly embodying the concept of servant scholar.

As I learned from him over the course of the semester, his depth of understanding, mastery of course materials and academic rigor were clearly conveyed every class session. We began each class reflecting on a particular hymn and walking through the time periods and themes associated with our textbook (which Dr. Noll had written). From content delivery to theological analysis and discussion, we discussed Christology and creeds, monasticism, crusades, and schisms, hitting in depth theological insight along with historical turning points. During lecture and discussion, I clearly remember Dr. Noll's patience, humility, and unassuming demeanor.

When it came time for the final paper, I selected a topic and buried myself in books and research during the latter half of the semester to ensure I delivered a work worthy of the class and the professor. When I received the paper back, I was devastated. The entire first page was bleeding from red pen marks and suggestions for edits and revision. I could have easily put up yellow crime scene tape and walked away from the paper and waited for the police to arrive to declare my academic prospects and future as an educator dead on arrival.

Let me step back for a minute and explain. My approach to writing had always been to spit out as much information on paper as needed in as few words as possible. Some might call my style concise, while others might conclude I did not have a lot to say or needed to do more research. To explain ideas or to develop a thesis statement was very difficult. I did not like to write nor was I particularly good at it, but I did work hard at writing during high school and in my early undergraduate studies to improve. My primary motive for improvement, though, was to please my teachers. I wanted to demonstrate how hard I worked and to hear that they were proud of me for the papers I submitted. If a teacher suggested revisions or tore a paper apart, I often saw it as a personal slight, an insult to my character, or a reflection on how I fell short as a person and not just as a student. I did not want it to appear that I had slacked in my work or had overlooked simple and correctable mistakes.

Jumping back into the flashing police lights and yellow crime scene tape that was once my beloved church history paper and the death of my aspiring teaching career, I learned my most valuable pedagogical and life lesson that day from Dr. Noll. With his academic credentials and extensive list of publications, this man did not need to give me, a nobody undergraduate, the time of day or engage in any way with my paper to help improve my writing. He could have easily skimmed it and at the end written, "This is terrible!" He could have moved on without a second glance. Instead, he elevated me, that same nobody undergraduate, who was desperately trying to produce a worthwhile paper, and saw fit to encourage my writing. He took the time to explain why certain words or phrases worked better than others. He explained to me ways to improve my writing. Instead of assuming I could never be academically on his level and treating me like an intellectual peon, he spoke into my writing and helped me improve the paper.

This lesson stuck with me on two fronts. First, if Dr. Noll, an extremely well accomplished and respected scholar, could take the time to comment and invest in me as a scholar, how much more could I, even without his academic credentials and respect, invest in the lives of my students and their writing? Second, his approach completely shifted my perspective on feedback. While I cannot say that I have joyfully welcomed critique on every paper I have written since then, his constructive criticism of my work has led me to believe that my teachers through the rest of my academic studies did not have it out for me or saw me as less of a person if I did not produce a perfect paper on the first (or second or, let's be honest, third) draft. Instead, they were also continuing to invest in me as a person and a scholar.

What *The Scandal of the Evangelical Mind* and *The Outrageous Idea of Christian Scholarship* taught me was that academic rigor came in challenging ideas and critiquing writing but, more fundamentally, that it was embodied in relational, godly character that was humble with a servant's heart. It was tough love that made me a better teacher, scholar, and person—not for the purpose of ultimately flashing my credentials and academic accomplishments—but to pass on that knowledge. Demonstrating Christ's love for my students was to invest in their academic future, to hold them accountable and expect excellence (seasoned with grace). Academic rigor was not to puff myself up or to think more highly of myself based on academic accomplishments. Instead, I could serve students and encourage them to realize a life of the mind was an essential part of loving Jesus and that academic rigor was not somehow contrary to a life of faith. Like Christ himself, this approach of integrating faith and learning with relationships is often seen as countercultural or even contradictory in the Academy. Dr. Noll demonstrated to me how important it was to flip the proverbial cultural script, being excellent in things of the mind but combining it with godly, authentic relationships and humility.

I will be forever indebted to Dr. Noll for what he taught me about church history in the fall of 2001 (I even taught my first church history course 23 years later) but I am even more indebted to him for how he invested in me as a person and a scholar, and that true scholarship, the true scandal, in my mind, was that an academic life was not a call to hold yourself higher than everyone else as a philosopher king. Rather it is a call to model Jesus by serving others with our lives and our minds. True Christian scholarship and excellence must be accompanied by relationships and godly character. This is the legacy that Dr. Noll left with me.

Chapter 42

The Call to Folly: Creating a Breakthrough in Teaching and Learning

DAVID ENNS

Response Summary: This short reflection explores how a blast of comedic "folly," in the spirit of Lindvall, can succeed where pragmatic solutions fall flat. The author recounts a youth camp performance where his horn act replaced a divisive rock-versus-hip-hop concert format. The result was a startling breakthrough: a fractured audience unified in a single wave of laughter. The piece argues that this event is a vibrant case study for Lindvall's theology of humor, where embracing the absurd disarms hostility and teaches humility. While event planners sought a logical fix, it was an outrageous, faith-led act of unorthodoxy that honked a clear path to community, proving that God often uses the most unsuspecting tools to accomplish his beautiful work.

ONE SCORCHING SUMMER in the Ozarks, I arrived at a church's high school camp to perform in the slot that had annually been their Friday night concert. They had only recently broken the tradition of hiring a band to bring in a comedy variety act such as mine. The event coordinator explained their rationale: they used to book alternating rock and hip-hop bands, hoping to satisfy every musical taste, but recently found that more of their students light up and get involved with comedy. As George Marsden puts it, some faith-led callings are "enormously fun and satisfying—even outrageously so"—and in this case, what began as a programming shift turned out to be a faith-shaped act of unity that reached across student divisions in ways music had not been able to.[1]

What followed affirmed the unexpected strength of that shift. Before incorporating comedy into the lineup, the participation breakdown of the camp had been reasonably consistent each year. However, the demographics of each group shifted depending on the type of music being performed. Typically, about 10% of the audience was fully engaged—dancing, cheering, and visibly excited—while another 45% appeared to enjoy the show passively. The remaining students often meandered around the edges or remained disengaged, suggesting that the music was not connecting across the board. However, the dynamic shifted dramatically when the event organizers switched to hosting a comedy night. Participation surged to over 90% across the crowd. Intrigued by those numbers, I caught myself mentally mapping audience engagement in real-time as muscle memory carried me through the show that night. Through musical gags, spontaneous crowd interaction, and a rhythm-driven comedic style, my antics created a shared experience that cut across personal preferences. Students weren't just watching; they were laughing, clapping along, volunteering, and actively engaging with the show's energy.

Recalling Terry Lindvall's emphasis on humor as a path to disarm hostility, I marvel at how comedic folly overcomes stylistic boundaries.[2] Instead of splitting students into tribes—hip-hop fans here, rock loyalists there—a comedy act invited them into a moment of shared joy. That moment is a practical example of Marsden's encouragement to let Christian convictions shape cultural practices in surprising ways—not by drawing lines but by entering shared spaces with humility and a faith-driven sense of purpose.[3] Rather than mimicking mainstream concert culture, the camp's pivot to comedy reflected a faith-shaped undertaking that might have appeared odd by cultural standards yet served as a bridge across differences, grounded in faith.

For years, event leaders in the Ozarks had scrambled for pragmatic solutions to unify the crowd. Their well-intentioned efforts often reinforced stylistic divisions rather than dissolving them. While Mark Noll emphasizes the importance of intellectual rigor, he also affirms that many effective paths forward emerge when faith convictions are creatively expressed in public spaces.[4] The shift to comedy was not just strategic—it was spiritual. The event team had been praying for ways to foster a faith-filled atmosphere that transcended musical tastes. They hoped to gather students around a deeper purpose rather than letting genre preferences overshadow spiritual growth.

Watching skeptical high schoolers from opposite musical worlds converge around a comedy act reminded me that bridging divides is not always about logic or persuasion. Playful humor often accomplishes what rational explanations cannot. Lindvall sees humor as a teacher of humility that helps us stop taking ourselves so seriously and opens our eyes to the unexpected ways God can unify us.[5] In this case, comedic folly eclipsed years of programming frustration in a powerfully connective night. That, in a nutshell, is how a seemingly outrageous, faith-shaped comedic act facilitated genuine togetherness beyond any standard formula. After all, as the Apostle Paul reminds us, "For we live by faith, not by sight" (2 Cor. 5:7).

And so, the call to folly became a breakthrough, proving that joyful, faith-shaped risk can open space for unity, growth, and unexpected grace. What began as an unconventional booking became a sacred moment that affirmed how faith, when expressed creatively, can draw even the most skeptical hearts toward something deeper.

Chapter 43

Remember Who You Are: Confession, Memory, and the Formation of Ethos

ANNALEE R. WARD

Response Summary: This essay explores how the rhetorical canon of memory, when re-envisioned through Augustine's theology, can restore character (ethos) to the center of public speaking. Building on George Marsden's call for faith-informed scholarship and James K. A. Smith's insights on formative practices, it argues that memory—understood as a confessional act before God—shapes speaker identity and moral integrity. In contrast to the prevailing focus on performance and technique, this approach prioritizes virtue, humility, and spiritual reflection. Integrating memory as a practice of confession in pedagogy forms speakers who embody credibility through character, renewing public discourse with ethical and faithful communication.

GEORGE MARSDEN CHALLENGES Christian scholars to let their beliefs about God shape academic inquiry.[1] This call is particularly urgent in the field of rhetoric, where the role of character—central to both classical rhetoric and Christian virtue—has been increasingly sidelined. While Marsden emphasizes faith's intellectual implications, I build on his vision with James K. A. Smith's reminder that our practices shape us.[2] I argue that the rhetorical canon of memory re-envisioned as a practice understood through Augustine's theology is vital for cultivating speaker ethos and restoring a character-centered approach to public discourse.

The Crisis of Character in Public Speaking

The erosion of character in public communication is evident not only in secular politics but also within Christian circles. Scandals involving religious leaders—ranging from financial misconduct to moral failures—reveal a troubling disconnect between message and messenger. This widespread character deficiency in speakers is not just an ethical concern; it is a formative issue. Generally, public speaking as currently taught emphasizes performance and effectiveness over moral formation. In doing so, it neglects the foundational rhetorical principle that *ethos*—a speaker's credibility—is deeply rooted in character. Textbooks may nod to ethos alongside logos and pathos, but they generally prioritize research, logic, audience analysis, style, and delivery over the speaker's character. Ethos is often framed in terms of reputation and ethical citation of sources but rarely extends to personal virtue.

In public speaking education, this means more than adding a Bible verse to a syllabus. It requires a reorientation of pedagogy to prioritize virtue over technique, faithfulness over expediency. If our academic work is to reflect our faith, we must reintegrate the moral and spiritual dimensions of communication.

Historically, rhetoric has recognized the inseparability of moral character and persuasive power. Quintilian famously defined the ideal orator as "a good man speaking well,"[3] and Seneca asserted, "as a man speaks, so is he."[4] Most importantly, Jesus's teaching affirms this principle: "What comes out of the mouth proceeds from the heart," and "by your words you will be justified, and by your words you will be condemned" (Matt. 12:33–37, English Standard Version). Together, these voices affirm that persuasive speech is inseparable from moral integrity.

Despite these enduring insights, the reduction of ethos to surface-level credibility or reputation continues. Ethical considerations, when included, often focus narrowly on issues like plagiarism rather than the speaker's integrity. This reductionist view is a problem that Christian educators must address.

Memory as a Formative Practice

Memory—an often-overlooked rhetorical canon—may be key to recovering authentic speaker ethos. Over the years scholars have contributed insight into character formation. For example, Aristotle encouraged the application of practical wisdom (*phronesis*).[5] Scottish-American philosopher Alasdair MacIntyre emphasized the power of practice in virtue formation.[6] American journalist and non-fiction author Charles Duhigg clarified how habits are formed.[7] Yet little attention has been given to memory as a confessional practice—remembering who we are before God—as a means of shaping moral integrity.

When taught in public speaking, memory focuses on recalling the speech in the moment. Linking memory to self-reflection makes it a tool of character formation. In Augustine's *Confessions*, we encounter a redeemed use of memory that provides a corrective to today's light version of speaker ethos.[8] He provides a theological framework for understanding memory as more than recall; it is a spiritual practice that shapes identity and cultivates virtue.

In his *Confessions*, Augustine devotes an entire book to the topic of memory, describing it as vast, complex, and fundamental to identity. For Augustine, memory is the gateway to self-knowledge, confession, and ultimately, communion with God. He portrays memory as the repository of experiences and knowledge but also as the means by which one encounters God. This view of memory is not just introspective; it is transformative. Augustine scholar Gary Wills summarizes his work on memory: Augustine saw memory as "dynamic, constructive, predictive, constitutive of identity, the meeting place with other humans, and the pathway to God."[9] Through memory, we reflect on our lives, acknowledge our failings, and orient ourselves toward divine grace. In the context of public speaking, this reflective process can anchor a speaker's ethos in humility and authenticity.

Augustine expounded on the Jewish and Christian Scriptures, which place a significant emphasis on remembering, both individually and communally. In Scripture, God repeatedly calls people to remember, turn from their sinful ways, and live their lives with God at the center. Central to the call to remember is God's call to repent and obey. In Christian churches today, this call manifests in Catholic and Reformed liturgies, in particular, as the service of penitence or service of confession. Confession requires the discipline of memory in looking back at our failings as individuals, as a church community, and as a society. Engaging our memories in self-examination forces us to face our moral failures, mistakes, and misdeeds. We recognize our lack of virtue and character because we see it in the light of God's call to perfection in Christ. For as Richard Mouw asserts, "the persistent habit of careful self-examination . . . requires a spirit of humility."[10] And humility goes a long way to temper a speaker's ego.

Yet memory, in Augustine's framework, does not trap us in guilt. It is also the means by which we praise God and remember his mercy. Similarly, within Christian liturgy, the practice of confession is followed by an assurance of God's forgiveness. This dual function—confession and praise—enables memory to shape us positively, even when our recollections are incomplete or flawed, notes Augustine. Even misremembering, if done in the context of glorifying God, can positively shape our moral formation. When memory is oriented toward God's glory, it becomes a tool for moral and spiritual formation.

A Vision for Christian Scholarship in Rhetoric

Marsden envisions an approach to scholarship that is not only intellectually rigorous but also spiritually grounded. He argues that American higher education should be more open to discussions about how faith intersects with learning. A Christian approach to scholarship decenters the self in order to better love God and neighbor. In the discipline of rhetoric, this means recovering the moral dimension of communication and embedding it within our pedagogical practices. Engaging the memory in the practice of individual and communal confession has the power to temper speaker illusions, self-justifications, and ego manipulations.

Speakers may achieve persuasion, but without a moral compass, they risk manipulation and self-deception. If, however, educators prioritize character through the lens of memory and confession, they can help students become not only better speakers but also more virtuous people.

By reminding students to regularly examine their lives in the presence of God, we engage a pedagogy that reflects God's Kingdom. As students inhabit a practice of confession, both communally in a faith community and individually, they are more likely to develop the humility and integrity essential for ethical communication. This is where Marsden's call becomes urgent: Christian educators must engage their disciplines in ways that reflect the holistic implications of belief in God.

This reimagined approach to public speaking centers character at its core. Thus, memory becomes central at the start of speech preparation—not merely a tool for delivery. It calls for these practices:

1. Self-Reflection: Encouraging students to engage in regular self-examination in light of Scripture and theological truths.

2. Confessional Memory: Integrating practices of remembering and confessing as part of speech preparation.

These practices align with Marsden's vision of Christian scholarship as deeply connected to the human condition and responsive to God's call. They also echo Augustine's understanding of memory as a tool for spiritual growth and identity formation.

Conclusion: Memory, Character, and Faithful Communication

Marsden's call for Christian scholarship urges us to take seriously the integration of faith into our academic disciplines. In public speaking, this means reclaiming the formative power of memory as a means of cultivating character. Scriptural teachings, as illustrated in Augustine's *Confessions*, offer a theological model for how memory can shape ethos, moving speakers toward confession, humility, and grace.

Our concern for character, virtue, and ethics in communication—particularly in religious discourse—reflects a desire to improve the world, build trust, and inhabit truth. Without deliberate self-examination in the light of divine accountability, communicators risk falling into rationalization and self-deception. A utilitarian approach to ethics suffices only for expediency; a more profound commitment to character formation requires memory as a practice of confession and renewal. In doing so, we honor the rhetorical tradition that values ethos and reinvigorate public speaking with a moral and spiritual foundation that strengthens both the individual speaker and the broader public discourse.

If we want to produce communicators who speak truth with integrity, we must go beyond technique and strategy. We must form students who remember who they are before the face of God. In doing so, we will not only honor Marsden's vision but also contribute to the restoration of public discourse through the formation of virtuous speakers who embody the Gospel in word and deed.

Chapter 44

A Ticket to the Big Game: How Lesslie Newbigin, Michael Polanyi, and George Marsden Gave Me Plausibility during Perilous Doctoral Research and Post-pandemic Teaching

MICHAEL A. LONGINOW

Response Summary: In their seminal works, Noll and Marsden raise questions in the late twentieth century about the failure of evangelical Christian colleges and universities to distinguish themselves as centers of intellectual rigor. Noll claims secular universities, with a fervor for research and cutting-edge thought, have long outpaced the work of Christian scholars in the creation of critically important knowledge. Marsden traces evangelical scholars' lack of fervor through a history that involves an inevitable slide out of Christian mission into secularity and obscurity within American higher education. This essay challenges Noll and Marsden on several key assumptions and conclusions by drawing on personal experience and the plausibility structures of Lesslie Newbigin and Michael Polanyi, among others, to bridge rigorous Christian and secular thought.

To be a faculty member in a Christian liberal arts college or university in the early decades of the twenty-first century entails paradoxes that would delight G. K. Chesterton.[1] It is a blending of identities. It requires teaching with a grasp of (even if in disagreement with) what Mark Noll suggests has been a long-brewing anti-intellectualism within evangelical culture.[2] At the same time, it requires shrewd faith integration into one's discipline, along with skill at crafting intellectual inquiry capable of publishable, peer-reviewed research.

George Marsden's inquiry into the soul of the American university speaks to this mix. He contends that the history of meaning in American universities, Christian or otherwise, lies not in the quest for new knowledge. Our attention need not be diverted by the replacement of theology as "queen of the sciences" with science as a faith system devoid of any awareness of God.[3] What matters instead is a tracing of academics' pursuit of what to do with that nagging sense of the numinous underlying all thoughtful inquiry, or that something from which morality springs, that something which is beyond reason and experience.[4] Historians of American higher education differ in their engagement with this contention, but they generally agree with Marsden's claims.[5]

Marsden's point, along with Noll's, bears heavily on the future of the Academy, and academics, in colleges and universities that claim a Christian mission. Most of these schools are particularly tuition dependent.[6] Stability in enrollment drives the viability of academic programs, curricula, even institutions' very existence. The paradox is that for a school to be measurably Christian, it must defend its biblical mission; yet to pursue viability can require compromises of institutional conscience aimed at increasing or preserving enrollment.[7]

A driving factor in this equation is students. They are a paradox as well. University leaders are eyeing their concerns.[8] Students believe in God, but they do not; many bring questions about whether biblical principles can align with, let alone be woven into, the fabric of their academic discipline, or their daily lives.[9] Students' peripheral vision is on business or ministry start-ups, social media influencers and entrepreneurs.[10]

My Plausibility, the Life of the Mind, and Christian Liberal Arts Education

This essay will use the theory of plausibility structures as a tool to question and refute Mark Noll's claim, in *The Scandal of the Evangelical Mind*, that teaching-focused Christian liberal arts colleges and universities lack the capacity to form the kinds of wide-ranging knowledge that have value when juxtaposed with the scholarly output of land-grant and private research universities. It will also use plausibility structures as handholds to underscore the claim made by Arthur Holmes that the very act of integrated teaching, that is, a systematic blending of biblical truth with a given academic discipline, is, itself, an act of scholarly work.[11] Noll's definition of scandal, I will suggest, is far too sweeping a term. Noll's denigrating of scholarship and intellectual pursuits among evangelicals could itself be called scandal. My aim in this chapter will be to support the complicated, often misunderstood quest of making the synthesis of career-focused pedagogy within a liberal arts education meaningful to students in the twenty-first century. My argument will focus on the work of Christian academics, but it has implications for those with evangelical beliefs outside academia.[12]

I am uniquely equipped to confront these paradoxes as an academic because I entered the Academy without what Lesslie Newbgin (and Peter Berger) would call a necessary plausibility structure for scholarly success.[13] Having been raised in Chicago, having completed a Master of Science in news journalism at the University of Illinois, my move from the newsroom to the classroom was driven not merely by Midwestern pragmatism, but by a sense of calling, one I considered biblical, to uncover hidden truth and bring societal remedies for injustice. My career journey after graduate school, which was in part a response to a deep reading of *All the President's Men*, entailed two years of city news reporting near Chicago.[14] Then I moved to Georgia where I encountered geographic marginalization (Northern-born reporter seeking answers in the Deep South), which led me to get training in document-driven investigation. That new skill helped me examine unethical bank lending practices, systemic racism in business, and local government corruption through political cronyism. The year before signing my first faculty contract to teach English and journalism, I took my press pass into a convention complex in Atlanta, interviewing and photographing presidential candidates at the Democratic National Convention. Before that, I met and interviewed Mujahadeen fighters in a Georgia hospital recovering from battle wounds in Afghanistan; and I studied the protest strategies of ACT UP, an activist LGBTQ+ movement that helped to shake the national discourse on gender.[15]

But I found that my commitment to investigation leading to change through journalism had no clear equivalent in Christian undergraduate academia. My very choice to enter this world was challenged by a hiring committee at Asbury University that questioned the legitimacy of a media professional's contributions in a liberal arts setting. They doubted the value of my skills-driven Master of Science degree and whether it gave me the scholarly tools necessary to enhance the life of the mind they believed true academia required. Despite some committee misgivings, I was hired on tenure track and given seven years to complete a doctorate. Few guided my steps into those doctoral studies. What could a news reporter possibly bring to the intellectual table?

Finding the Handholds:
Newbigin, Polanyi, and The Sympathizers

The answer lay waiting in archived documents in scholarly libraries. Much in the way I had approached public records in my investigative journalism, I looked deeply into these documents, i.e., collected papers, correspondence, publications, and found a mostly-ignored thread of Christian faith commitment and revivalist spirituality that, by means of media voices, linked aspirations of the earliest colonial colleges and universities with the development of modernist and postmodernist thought in twentieth-century universities. Marshall McLuhan's contention that the medium—in this case higher education—was the message became my vehicle forward.[16]

A parallel help were the plausibility structures embraced by Lesslie Newbigin. A sympathetic scholar at Asbury Theological Seminary introduced me to Newbigin's work; that writing, in turn, introduced me to the thinking of Michael Polanyi and Peter Berger.[17] I had read a bit of Berger, specifically his *Sacred Canopy* in college but it had little resonance for me in the sheltered Christian liberal arts setting where I was rarely challenged in my theories of knowledge.[18] I hit those challenges in my doctoral coursework. Faculty there embraced and invited me into the thinking of Michel Foucault, Richard Rorty, Friederich Nietzsche, Paulo Freire, and Kenneth Bruffee, among many others.[19]

It was Newbigin's (and Berger's) theories of plausibility that gave me a kind of deflective shield against postmodern critics: religious beliefs, I found, are maintained by social networks and rituals whose value is undeniable in existential ways.

Plausibility structures, as described by Newbigin, are concepts borrowed from Polanyi, whose sense of personal knowledge pushes back against the systematic skepticism inherent in pluralistic thinking. That pushback is grounded in an awareness of God's place in the universe and the sense that truth is out there to be found.[20] I needed this reassurance, for in my doctoral studies I navigated an intellectual world where scholars viewed history and truth as fungible, subject to the intimations of Reader-response Theory and socially constructed meaning.

Another help came from Roman Catholic scholar Walter Ong's seminal research in orality and literacy, which gave me a theoretical handhold on the very meaning of oral cultures inherent in reporting practices of journalism for print, broadcast and digital news in Western cultures.[21]

Berger was a sociologist, but his work had implications for communication within religion (I could situate journalism within these) as systems informed by God's design in human encounter.[22] From Martin Buber's 1937 classic *I and Thou*, I found ways to situate even as mundane a journalistic procedure as the news interview in significant theory of discursive meaning. Buber, bringing his Jewish cultural thought to my work, helped me explain how the pursuit and conducting of journalistic interviews could exhibit biblical wisdom, empathy and compassion.[23]

Newbigin, the Scandal, and my Doubt of the Doubters

To find a plausibility in my stance as a Christian researcher amid doubting faculty in my doctoral classes was a relief at many levels. Doubting my doubters there built a kind of intellectual muscle that gave me confidence. From Newbigin I learned that postmodern assertions about the incapacity of religious faith to survive under intellectual scrutiny were a kind of dogma, a faith perspective;[24] my dissertation chair and committee accepted my scholarly propositions better when I was able to converse with their assertions about truth. Fearlessness in the face of their questions and criticisms brought respect for the intellectual moment. My doctoral committee announced my dissertation approval with what felt like a grudging respect.

Back on my own campus, I confronted doubters of another kind. I was able to bring a plausibility to my stance of practical journalist, with one foot firmly in the camp of experiential news-industry preparation for students, and scholar of media history and communication, with the other foot also firmly in the camp of theorists probing the meaning of orality, literacy, and media identities in a digitizing world. Within weeks of my dissertation defense, I was called before the same faculty review committee that, with misgivings, had hired me, and this time for tenure review. I was granted tenure; the committee chair wrote that my portfolio was overwhelming in its defense of criteria.

Through all these experiences, I brought plausibility to the notion that Noll and Marsden had each, in their own way, erred in their criticisms of, and generalizations about Christian higher education. As I had done earlier with Newbigin's guidance, I doubted their doubts. Noll was wrong in his doubts about Holiness scholars. True, there was in my experience some angst, discussion, and frustration about the role of research and intellectual inquiry among Holiness scholars.[25] I find in both Noll and Marsden evidence of a hubris of Calvinist thought that disdains any scholarly approach other than theirs. Having lived and researched alongside many of Holiness scholars, I found enormous intellectual strength in their inquiry. Yes, they held the power of the Holy Spirit in high regard, but this did not make them a people prone to "letting go and letting God," as Noll put it. Marsden was accurate in tracing the slow erosion of biblical mission in many Christian colleges and universities in the United States over time. He does have some suggestions for better scholarship by Christians in the twenty-first century.[26] But he glosses over those whose convictions for biblical integration stood firm.

Where Noll claimed that no significant research was emerging from the relatively tiny Christian colleges and universities across the U.S., I consistently found significant new inquiry getting published by my colleagues at Asbury and at other smaller schools in the Council for Christian Colleges and Universities. Yes, their research got attention at evangelical scholars' gatherings, journals, and books, which was necessary and significant dialogue, but it was also published in notable university presses in the United States and in Europe. And it emerged as part of significant intellectual conversations with scholars who, even if not part of a Christian community (they were often Jewish, Muslim, Hindu), respected their questions and suggestions about morality, ethics, and the ways humans should live beside each other.

Where Marsden claimed that secular, pluralistic trends bring an inevitable destruction of biblical mission in serious higher education, his tracking of this concept was limited to the thinking and policymaking of leaders in offices and board rooms of administration buildings. What he missed was the very potent undercurrents of the extra-curriculum within all higher education. Social historian Helen Horowitz and others note that there are worlds that students create within any college or university that have lasting impact on their minds and lives. In some respects, this is more significant for careers and human development than university policies or students' majors, and which can even shape policy and curriculum at these schools over time. This trend is no less true at Christian liberal arts colleges and universities; the internationally acclaimed "outpouring" at Asbury University in 2023 is one recent manifestation of this.[27]

What neither Noll nor Marsden take into account is the significant, very intellectual work of Holy Spirit-led integration of biblical principles into innovative pedagogy and curriculum. Such integration is hard work; not all faculty invest in it, but many scholars do.[28] It is a commitment many faculty pursue across the hundreds of Christian colleges and universities nationally. Having served on search committees for new faculty, and having been part of new faculty orientation workshops, I have been consistently impressed with the newly minted PhDs and even faculty from research universities who come to evangelical Christian universities excited about weaving biblical insight into the humanities, business, the arts, or sciences. Faculty from Biola's Rosemead School of Psychology produce nationally recognized research on such topics as anxiety, attachment theory, suffering, discrimination, and cultural humility. The Crowell School of Business at Biola in the last two years, has built a center for biblical understanding and practices of artificial intelligence, a crucial topic for all in higher education. Biola's School of Fine Arts and Communication has launched a Winsome Conviction Project aimed at the study and practice of biblically grounded civil discourse in our divided nation. At Wheaton College, where Noll taught for many years, psychologist Mark Yarhouse, formerly at Regent University, has taken leadership of the Sexual and Gender Identity Institute, fielding research that is cutting-edge for not just Christian educators but any college or university seeking to understand student thinking and formation in understanding of the self.[29]

Scholars such as Noll and Marsden who dissect and speak critically of American higher education, and Christians within it, will be with us for the foreseeable future. Yet the calling and work of biblical integration into undergraduate education remains. I have chosen it. And I have found that parents of students in evangelical homes (and in homes with little to no faith commitment) remain fascinated by, even hungry for such integration, and they will pay for it. And as I suit up to join the faculty of my university for commencement ceremonies each spring, I am reminded again that I am not alone.

Chapter 45

Not That Kind of Horn Guy:
An Auto-ethnographic Reflection on Faith
Leading the Way and Intellect Bringing the Assist

DAVID ENNS

Response Summary: This case study tunes the scholarly debates of Marsden and Noll to the peculiar key of a musical comedian. Specifically, it engages Marsden's call for faith to serve as the animating force in a vocation and Noll's lament over the evangelical neglect of the mind. Drawing on his auto-ethnographic experiences as "Dave the Horn Guy," the author examines how to orchestrate a faith-led calling in the public square. When confronted with a cacophony of risqué humor, he argues that faith must take the lead, with intellect providing the nimble assist. Through anecdotes from baseball stadiums and international television, the piece demonstrates how to puncture innuendo with a well-timed comedic riff, offering a unique model of cultural engagement that is both joyful and theologically grounded, proving that a Christ-oriented witness can be profoundly serious and seriously fun.

CHRISTIAN SCHOLARS George Marsden and Mark Noll challenge believers to resist compartmentalizing faith and intellect.[1] Marsden emphasizes that faith should serve as the animating force behind one's professional or scholarly calling, while Noll laments the evangelical neglect of the mind and calls for a more robust intellectual witness. In response to their work, this reflection explores how their debate plays out within the unconventional realm of my musical comedy act as Dave the Horn Guy.[2] Specifically, I have repeatedly encountered risqué humor in my performances—moments where I have found that faith must take the lead, with intellect providing the assist.

"Shame on you!" came the indignant cry from the phone operator, who glanced at my email address mid-conversation. My domain—davethehornguy.com—had clearly sparked a misunderstanding, and I instantly realized she had assumed something salacious.[3] After an awkward pause, I clarified, "No, no—I'm not that kind of horn guy. I literally have 25 horns strapped across my body for a music variety comedy act." To clarify: two octaves of hand-squeezed horns—rubber bulbs, brass bells, each with its own pitch. She sputtered apologies, but her reaction was unforgettable. It was the first of many times people would misconstrue my comedic horn persona. Moments like these taught me that a faith-led calling, especially one so unconventional, requires the ability to shift between modes—a practice Nicholas Wolterstorff describes as code-switching, initially explored in sociolinguistics by John Gumperz.[4] This approach helps navigate routine misunderstandings, engage with scandalous heckling, and, most importantly, articulate an intellectually grounded response that honors the deeper motivations within such an outrageous vocation.

Imagine a person (me) in a vivid orange jumpsuit—something straight out of a mechanic's garage or a prison yard—adorned with 25 chromatically tuned bulb horns. All strapped to armpits, legpits, neckpit, elbowpits, chest, thighs, everywhere. Depending on what I flex or bend, I get different melodies and chords. I will crank out three- or four-part harmonies of Super Mario Brothers, patriotic medleys, radio hits, college fight songs, and the like. From U.S. arenas to overseas TV gigs, this eclectic horn act shoots out confetti, mixes through a loop station, pulls up volunteers, parachutes horns over the audience, and creates big smiles wherever I can honk.

Despite pouring my energy into crafting these blasts of joy, I cannot avoid the barrage of sexual humor that people commonly assert upon my act. On a larger scale, sexual sins and scandals have repeatedly eroded trust in churches and Christian leaders, making even playful innuendos feel fraught with more profound potential consequences. Given that, I have come to see each performance not just as entertainment but as a chance to carry a faithful, evangelical witness into whatever venue I am in. It is for these reasons that it became critical how I would prepare for each gig, a career inevitably loaded with unsolicited sexual joking.

An Outrageous Calling

The impetus for my unusual act was not based on a business plan, but a sense of faith-led conviction akin to what Marsden refers to as the outrageous idea of openly Christian scholarship. In a recent conference hosted by the Christianity and Communication Studies Network (CCSN), Marsden stated that faith commitments could and should fuel our creative, academic, or vocational endeavors.[5] Although his claim focuses primarily on academic settings, I see a direct parallel in the entertainment world that education prepares performers for. While my comedic performance might understandably look unconventional, it originated in a deep sense that God gave me this peculiar idea as an opportunity to brighten people's lives and kindle hope for faith-centered conversations.

Even as Noll challenged evangelicals to cultivate greater intellectual depth, my journey highlights the need to integrate faith and intellect rather than treat them as competing commitments.[6] In my case of dealing with inappropriate heckling, faith propels me onto the stage while intellect refines my technique, shaping verbal comebacks. After all, 1 Peter calls us to "always be prepared to give an answer . . . " (3:15) implying a readiness rooted in spiritual conviction and thoughtful articulation. Whether I am hooking up 25 horns to my bright orange jumpsuit, brainstorming comedic dialogues, interviews, or Gospel messages, I see how faith leads while the mind strengthens and sharpens.

Puncturing Innuendos in Baseball and Beyond

Early on, my faith–intellect balance was tested at baseball stadiums. Between innings, I would energize crowds with peppy horn tunes and then mingle with fans. Often near the beer tent, the conversation would turn from curious to risqué—someone would grin and ask, "You must be pretty horny!" and then they would follow it up with talk about squeezin' bulbs or blowin' horns in sexual contexts. At first, I would just half-laugh or shrug, unwittingly encouraging off-color banter. Over time, I developed a more deliberate response. I might blast an interruptive honk with my horns or tease, "That's between me and my wife, buddy!" Such responses are fun enough not to kill the vibe but still draw a moral boundary. In keeping with serious-minded reflection, I started mentally rehearsing these comebacks, ensuring I neither compromised my convictions nor came across like a holier-than-thou police officer, slapping troublemakers with spiritual misdemeanors.[7]

Those comedic boundaries faced another challenge when I landed on a British television show. Mid-interview, the host lobbed pun after pun about "finding my horn," "replacing my horn," and "losing my horn," casually slipping sexual undertones into every verb. Unfamiliar with UK slang, I initially hesitated but soon realized he was steering the dialogue in a lurid direction—and proud of himself for doing so. My human nature told me to grin and roll with it, but my faith-led conscience objected. If I played along, I would validate an innuendo-laden humor that clashed with my values. In a pinch, I improvised a comedic pivot: "Not that kind of horn guy (honk honk)—mind if I rock out a horn-o-gram for your show? (honk honk honk . . .)" At first, he continued, but I kept censoring out his more explicit lines with brassy riffs and readied comebacks, redirecting the spotlight toward quality fun rather than crude implications. This careful shifting of language and tone preserves my integrity while remaining accessible and lighthearted.[8]

Faith and Wonder as Catalysts

In my experience, faith has this unseen, powerful capacity, like spiritual adrenaline, that thrusts us into settings we might never choose rationally. Marsden explained how faith-based commitments can be a wellspring of motivation. Similarly, I often stand behind stage curtains—dressed in this outlandish jumpsuit, horns clicking against one another—realizing how improbable a horn guy can make a living. In many ways, I see it as stepping out in the same spirit that calls biblical figures to do unusual, seemingly irrational things in obedience. Hebrews 11 is full of such examples. The intangible wonder of faith is also akin to a creative spark: fans who approach me afterward are not simply curious about technique; they express awe at the mystery of it all. "How'd you ever dream this up?" or "What made you think of such a crazy but joyful act?" they ask. As unique as it is, God gave me a straightforward story to tell because its roots are in the church.

That opens a natural path to share how I consider it a calling, my attempt to bring positivity and reflection into everyday life. The intellect then supports this faith impetus: I discuss my hours of rehearsal, the design of new prop prototypes, or the business model that allows me to keep traveling. Faith-led creativity still demands thorough, methodical planning—whether for comedic engineering or bridging conversations. And, of course, there is the biblical reminder that we must have answers ready "with gentleness and respect" (1 Pet. 3:15).

Synthesizing Faith and Intellect

Though I lean heavily on faith-led impetus, mirroring Marsden's encouragement to let Christian assumptions shape the entire enterprise, I realize that pure zeal without method can lead to comedic flops.[9] Trust me, the blooper reel is long—but I will spare you for the sake of the argument. Much as Marsden reasons that a Christian scholar ought to be thinking about how their faith shapes their scholarly agenda, I, too, must keep faith at the forefront. But I do not dismiss the mind. Instead, I recall Noll's admonition that evangelicals sometimes lack scholarly discipline. Here, comedic discipline involves carefully orchestrating routines, analyzing crowd dynamics, and formulating reasoned responses for off-colored encounters.

In his Legacy Scholar chapter, Wolterstorff emphasizes that Christian conviction must emerge from within, shaping character before expression.[10] In light of that, I have seen my comedic identity as something cultivated from spiritual integrity, not layered on as a moral performance. Whether blocking off vulgar innuendo with a quick horn blast or referencing Scripture subtly in backstage show planning, the comedic approach and the faithful orientation intertwine seamlessly. The greatest commandment emphasizes the importance of engaging our reasoning and understanding as part of our devotion and love of God (see Matt. 22:37).

Conclusion

From baseball games to international television, my verbal navigation aligns with Marsden's vision that Christian faith should not retreat from the academic or public square but instead inform and animate the full range of cultural engagement—even in places as unexpected as deflecting suggestive humor. At the same time, it responds to Noll's charge that evangelicals must reclaim the life of the mind; while not every moment lands perfectly, I strive to shape my comedic cues and crafted responses through careful planning, ethical reflection, and theological awareness. Faith compels me to stand on improbable stages, trusting God in a surprising vocation. The intellect emerges in the structured comedic routines and the deliberate rhetorical strategies that handle crowd reactions. I eventually developed a talk that played on the horn guy versus porn guy antics—pairing research on addiction and a faith-led call to purity as a proactive measure to help people shed harmful habits.

Ultimately, this experience might seem unconventional, but I have witnessed how a faith-led comedic approach with robust intellectualism can unify diverse groups, disarm risqué humor, spark curiosity, and encourage people to decide to follow Jesus Christ. The horns are only an entrée—my real aim is to let faith and wonder lead the way, with the mind providing the scaffolding that enables me to honk out a Christ-oriented witness that is as joyful as it is grounded.

Chapter 46

Producing "Procedural Rationality"

Robert Stephen Reid

Response Summary: In this response to the reflective assessment of Noll and Marsden—30 years after they first placed the challenge before Protestant Christian leaders and educators to advance the intellectual and theological work of Christian scholarship—the author turns to a challenge Marsden originally made and reaffirmed in his unconference Legacy Scholar presentation. Marsden maintained that Christian scholars must produce scholarship that relies on the "procedural rationality" of the Academy but also rely on their own faith convictions "to animate" their scholarly effort. Reid reflects on key moments in the development of his scholarly project as a vocational participation in this calling and points forward to how this vocation must continue to be met by the next generation of Christian scholars.

THERE ARE ENOUGH QUESTIONS posed by the Legacy Scholars of this dialogic unconference on Christian scholarship to fill several volumes. I was particularly intrigued to hear what Mark Noll and George Marsden would share almost a third of a century after their two books spoke to a generation of scholars, like me. I benefitted hearing from the variety of contributors, but it was their reflections that both brought me to the "Where are we now?" question. It also led to my own vocational reflection on the part I played in this calling.

Noll's *The Scandal of the Evangelical Mind* was an important word to hear in the 1990s. I received my MDiv degree from Fuller Theological Seminary in 1979. I served as an ordained pastor for a decade before pursuing a second MA degree and a PhD in Communication. I received the latter degree in the summer of 1994, the year *Scandal* was published. I was well aware of the anti-intellectual, provincial hermeneutic of biblical interpretation Noll documents as still pervading too much evangelical thought. It was one of the reasons I pursued further educational preparation. I wanted to be able to practice a more inclusive hermeneutic of intellectual engagement while advancing the interests of Christian scholarship in a chosen field of disciplinary inquiry.

George Marsden's scope was wider in his 1997 work, *The Outrageous Idea of Christian Scholarship*. He was responding to secular critiques of Christian scholarship, critiques reflective of a mindset that too often resisted hiring faculty who acknowledged their faith or who saw faith as a constitutive aspect of their scholarly identity. He challenged Christian scholars to engage the cultural and intellectual questions of their disciplines with a "faith-informed" perspective, not the least because, the institutional culture of most academic universities is "hollow at the core."[1] In their effort to pursue the liberal agenda of a pluralistic society, he believed that academia had illiberally rejected the legitimacy of faith-informed reasoning in playing a part in contributing to advancing disciplinary knowledge.[2] As a result religious thought grounded in faith traditions, thought that forms the original basis of all modern value systems, was often no longer welcome to have a seat at the table of academic inquiry. Marsden called for Christian scholars to adopt the "procedural rationality" of the Academy without leaving their faith-informed perspective at the gates of those educational institutions.[3] Marsden's reflection, in particular, led to my own personal review of my disciplinary journey into this calling to contribute to the *Outrageous Idea*. What follows is my scholarly story of participation in Marsden's vocational challenge.

My "Procedural Rationality" Faith Journey

I served as a pastor for the decade after receiving my MDiv degree from Fuller Theological Seminary in 1979. In 1988 I took up graduate work in the University of Washington's Department of Communication, receiving an MA degree in 1990 and a PhD degree in 1994. While pursuing graduate education at UW, my religious belief was not an issue. My PhD dissertation committee was comprised of an Episcopalian, a Lutheran, a Catholic and a Presbyterian—all of whom held leadership roles in their congregations. A sign of this academic openness in matters of religion came with encouragement to write my MA thesis as a reader-response, rhetorical analysis of the Gospel of Mark. While in the PhD program I submitted an essay for publication that extracted a revealing insight from my thesis work. The article was accepted and published in *Quarterly Journal of Speech*.[4] With its publication the career path of my scholarship was set. I had become a rhetorician whose focus would be consideration of the rhetoric of religious discourse whether ancient or modern.

I held several senior lecturer positions (including a year at the University of Washington itself) before accepting a faculty appointment to the Communication Department at the University of Dubuque in Iowa. As a private Presbyterian university UD welcomed my scholarly interest in religious rhetoric. The year before accepting this appointment I had already published the rhetorical commentary on the Gospel of Mark derived from my MA thesis and had co-authored a homiletics book on the rhetoric of American preaching. I published several essays in the area of classical rhetoric and religious rhetoric in those first years. However, the next opportunity to step up to the actual *outrageous* call came at the invitation of Martin Medhurst, editor of the journal *Rhetoric & Public Affairs*. He chose to dedicate a special edition of that journal to invited essays from rhetorical scholars representing as many different religious and theological traditions as he could imagine. His question to each of us was how our own faith tradition served as a source of rhetorical invention in our lives and our scholarship.[5] My contribution, an essay entitled "Being Baptist," was divided by four headers: a personal social history of my "Becoming Baptist" in my late teens, what "Being Baptist" entails, identification of distinctive tropes that serve as "Baptist Sources of Invention," and finally what "Thinking like a Baptist" might look like in print. I ended the essay, after noting that denominations all too often represent historical "frozen controversies" that can constrain as readily as they serve the faith identity of a scholar:

> In all of this I have come to believe that a denomination's constitutive rhetoric can function as a core capability for argument invention. But core capabilities invariably become core rigidities if they become insular, overconfident, and dogmatic. If Baptist thought remains irrevocably fixed in a bygone era's strategies of persuasive invention, it is inevitable that pathos will be increased to supply the seeming deficit of a failed logos—the homiletic equivalent of the sermon manuscript with the scrawled marginal note "Weak point; pound pulpit."[6]

I confess that I had Mark Noll's *Scandal* book in mind as I wrote those words.

In December of 2005 I received another email request from Medhurst. It was sent to various authors of the books and essays he planned to use in a fall 2006 graduate rhetorical criticism seminar at Baylor University. He asked each of us to respond to the questions: (1) "Is there such a thing as a Christian approach to criticism?" and (2) "How does your own Christian commitment affect the way you think about and do criticism?" He had just raised the same question in his 2004 essay "Religion and Scholarship: A Pluralistic Conversation."[7] His contention was that that a distinctive Christian approach to criticism needed to be articulated for the twenty-first century. His own proposal was that, in offering critique of civic discourse shaped by Christian belief, a critic would need to be able to relate conclusions drawn from insight from biblical revelation, from church history, and from the teaching authority of the church.[8] He believed that critique that makes present the underlying religious ethos communicated in expressions of public discourse helps explain the appeal of religious candidates by "a people, a demos, hungry for spiritual values and willing to support those who articulate with clarity and passion the specifically moral, ethical, and spiritual dimensions of their public policy choices."[9]

The same year Medhurst published a demonstration essay using this critical approach to analyze the significance that the faith convictions expressed by both candidates Bush and Gore during the 2000 presidential campaign had on the final outcome of the election. He analyzed how both candidates drew upon their own religious faith in making appeals to the American public in their 1999 presidential campaigns. Medhurst finds that American acceptance of the Supreme Court's final resolution of the contested vote to be remarkable. He proposes that the moral and religious rhetoric of that contest, in which both men spoke to a hunger for spiritual values in the American populace, held the middle-left-and-right mass of the electorate together. The uncontested acceptance of the religious faith commitment of both candidates became the glue of a "democratic ethos" that held the nation together through that resolution.[10]

Having offered his theory and critical practice of it in print, he challenged other Christian critics to make a similar bid to identify what should count as a specifically Christian theory of rhetorical inquiry for the twenty-first century.[11] His email was, in effect, asking others of us to step up. I devised my answer to his question and sent it in brief form as an email response several days later. Full publication of that briefly sketched proposal came in

2008 with my "A Rhetoric of Contemporary Christian Discourse" published in *The Journal of Communication and Religion*.[12] I began by considering the stumbling block of a prior effort to determine whether there is such a thing as a stance of Christian criticism. That question had been debated in a 1986 conference on Christianity and Literature, where they pondered "What's a critic to do?" But the conference participants could not agree which doctrine(s) and whose versions of those doctrines would matter in critical assessment. I located my own theory in the narrative turn made by North American theology in the 1980s that made Christian identity a matter of narrative rather than doctrinal knowing.[13] Stated succinctly, my abstract proposed,

> [A] rhetoric of Christian discourse that provides for the possibility of a set of critical moves by which the coherence of public expressions of a Christian ethos that "dwells rhetorically" in discourse (Hyde 2004) can be assessed. Three domains of identity are explored as a narrative rather than doctrinal conception of Christian identity configured in oral and written discourse: a tradition-based reasoning, a narratively shaped worldview, and a hope engendered identity and ethic of responsibility.[14]

I argued that a Christian critic should be able to examine the intersection between the cultural consciousness presuppositions and faith consciousness presuppositions a faith communicator is negotiating, how that negotiation gets expressed in talk or print as a narrative identity, as well as the degree to which the moral vision of hope expressed is characteristic of a Christian ethos and an essential Christian *mythos*—and all of this revealed in the communicator's discourse *whether or not the argument of the work considered is purposefully religious*.[15] I concluded this proposal by indicating my understanding that in proposing this theory of a Christian rhetorical criticism, I was participating in Marsden's *Outrageous Idea* challenge. I wrote,

> Of necessity [this] proposal offers a broad statement in order to avoid reifying a particular, univocal conception of Christian belief as the actual faith practice of all Christians—or worse, reifying the assumption that such a rhetoric need not be identified because everyone knows (remembers) what it is when they see it.[16]

The following year, I provided a demonstration essay that used these three "critical moves" to analyze the Christian coherence of the narrative identity revealed in Aleksandr Solzhenitsyn's 1978 Harvard Commencement Address, "A World Split Apart."[17] His "A World Split Apart" speech clearly stands with Churchill's 1946 Westminster College "Sinews of Peace" speech as one of the most significant commencement addresses of the twentieth century. Yet even 30 years after the speech was presented in Harvard Yard, as news coverage reported his death in the United States, this one speech more than all his written work was invariably mentioned. So many who heard the literary giant speak that day came away believing that he was deeply insensitive, even ungrateful, to the country that had been hosting his exile from the Soviet Union. They had no 'ears to hear' a Christian prophet's indictment of America as equally complicit in its version of materialistic obsession as the Soviet Union was to their version of it. Ronald Berman's published volume *Solzhenitsyn at*

Harvard offers the official English translation of the speech followed by twelve news stories of reaction and six more thoughtful academic responses.[18] The reaction was mixed at best. America was not ready to hear that Solzhenitsyn used the address to name America's many failures to live into its original Christian civilization vision as equally tragic to that of the Soviet Union's failure to live into the Eastern Orthodox church's vision of it in Russia. *New York Times* columnist James Reston quipped that "for all its brilliant passages, it sounded like the wanderings of a mind split apart."[19]

Was the speech incoherent? I set as my essay purpose to examine the narratively constructed ethos of Solzhenitsyn's Christian civilization with a view toward identifying what Michael Hyde calls "the ethos of an identity that dwells rhetorically" in a speech.[20] To do this I employed the resources of the theory of contemporary Christian discourse I had articulated as a means to consider the coherence of a Christian speaker's narrative identity, his moral vision, and his voice as a cultural consciousness negotiating what counts as truth in light of his faith consciousness. The essay reveals a great irony that the coherence of the speech's faith consciousness was grounded in a genre born in Harvard's own origins—the American Jeremiad. A sermon form designed to list the many reasons that demonstrate a need for people to repent was lost on a now secular audience content with its material gains. Lutheran historian Martin Marty, then editor of *Christian Century* magazine wrote that he came away from the speech reaffirmed in his belief that Solzhenitsyn was "one of the great moral prophets of our time."[21]

Conclusion

Marsden began the *Outrageous Idea* book by asking, "Why are there in mainstream academia almost no identifiable Christian schools of thought to compare with various Marxist, feminist, gay, post-modern, African-American, conservative, or liberal schools of thought?"[22] His assessment three decades later, in the dialogic unconference is that this pluralism itself eventually created a situation where no one school of thought dominates. It increasingly makes room for people of faith, whether Christian or theists committed to other traditions of faith, to be able to join the table. The criterion, however, is that they must be willing to adopt the "procedural rationality" of the Academy in the conduct of their scholarly inquiry. I would add, however, that the question of whether their voice will be heard in disciplinary inquiry still rests on whether they have developed a mode of inquiry that is *critically* shaped by their faith. The latter was inherent in Medhurst's two email questions: (1) "Is there such a thing as a Christian approach to criticism?" and (2) "How does your own Christian commitment affect the way you think about and do criticism?" These were "school of thought" questions as Marsden had phrased the quest.

The volume *Professing Christ: Christian Tradition and Faith-Learning in Public Universities* was an initial effort to address a dimension of the second question. In that volume's Foreword, Mark Noll provides an image grid that synthesizes ways individual essayists envisioned their institutional identities in their engagement with students and in their departments within the institution.[23] But the question of critical engagement—how does one's faith influence critical engagement of the subject of one's discipline requires that we ask how our faith affects the way in which we seek to advance disciplinary inquiry.[24] Marxists, feminists, womanists, deconstructionists, and post-colonialist scholars traditionally approach their disciplinary work with a clear sense of how these ideological perspectives directly shape their disciplinary inquiry in the critical questions they ask. What does that look like in Christian inquiry?

Catholic scholars have been asking this disciplinary inquiry question for some time. David Tracy's *Plurality and Ambiguity: Hermeneutics, Religion, Hope* was a profound engagement of it posed in print in 1987.[25] I find Stephen Webb, a Catholic who ruminates about how Protestant thought might illuminate the canvas of this question, offering a provocative consideration of the rhetoric or Protestant scholarly inquiry in "Reviving the Rhetorical Heritage of Protestant Theology."[26] At present I look to Catholic philosopher Charles Taylor who would locate whatever form this critical practice would take as necessarily an issue of an ethic of faith consciousness rather than a set of theological commitments.[27] But, like Medhurst, I believe there is work yet to do. We need to identify what would constitute a specifically Christian approach to critical inquiry. Medhurst put his oars in this water as I have done. The invitation to continue the work is no longer *outrageous*. But it is still necessary if Christian thought is to be received as consequential in disciplinary inquiry.

Chapter 47

Horns and Holy Nudges:
A Faith-led Journey Beyond the Classroom

David Enns

Response Summary: This short think piece charts a faith-led journey that began not with a bang, but with a holy nudge—a quiet prompting that led to a life in a jumpsuit full of horns. The author chronicles a cross-country move that defied logic but followed faith, connecting this experience to Mouw's conviction that intellectual seriousness must be integrated with spiritual formation. The piece argues that while faith may compose an improbable melody, intellect and Mouw-inspired "uncommon decency" are crucial for navigating the dissonant notes of skepticism and doubt. It is a story of how an outrageous vocation requires a finely tuned spiritual posture, proving that sometimes God's call asks us to trust his plan and, eventually, learn to play the horns.

As GEORGE MARSDEN CONTENDS, integrating Christian conviction into public and professional life is not only possible—it is essential for cultivating vocations that reflect the fullness of faith.[1] Similarly, Mark Noll's challenge to evangelicals to engage more deeply with the life of the mind pushed me to think critically and intentionally about how to embody theological seriousness—even in a calling so unconventional it involved relocating our family from California to Colorado and strapping horns to my body.[2]

I was happily settled as a church music pastor in Sacramento when I felt compelled to pursue a bizarre yet fascinating idea: attaching bike horns to my body to play *Jingle Bells* at our church's Christmas show. To make it work, I tuned the reeds inside standard rubber bulb horns to specific musical pitches and attached them to various joints, pits, and other points on my body. To my surprise, the quirky experiment became a full-time act.

People might assume the success of this venture virally sprang from sheer luck, but it was propelled by a faith-led whisper so unusual that I needed every ounce of intellect to validate each new step. In *The Outrageous Idea of Christian Scholarship*, Marsden argues that Christian vocation should be shaped by theological commitments rather than conventional success metrics—a truth I came to understand firsthand through a cross-country move and a jumpsuit full of tuned horns.[3] In the following years, my journey exploded into a life far beyond standard career formulas—one that intellect alone could never have orchestrated.

My faith-led whisper did not start with honking horns, but when my wife and I responded to the Holy Spirit prompting us to move to Colorado Springs. At that time, we had three young children, not exactly the ideal season for a major relocation without a clear job lined up. Whimsy had no place in our decision; we were far from seeking a reckless adventure.

Richard Mouw's Legacy Scholar presentation emphasizes how intellectual seriousness and spiritual formation need not be separated.[4] He reflects on his conception of the evangelical mind as a heart posture encouraging believers to work diligently and practice spiritual humility. Such was the case in our move. We prayed and worked hard to discern God's voice through a unique season. Time would reveal that the horn act would find surprising traction.

Looking back, if we had approached this transition in life by logic or intellect alone, we would not have concluded that it made sense. As Noll emphasizes in *The Scandal of the Evangelical Mind*, the neglect of serious intellectual engagement has weakened the church's witness; in our case, resisting that trend meant allowing reason to serve faith, not override it.[5] While faith and intellect worked together to set us on the road to Colorado, the next question became: how would we navigate those roads, literal and metaphorical, with grace? Would we travel humbly and patiently or succumb to spiritual road rage toward those who doubted or misunderstood our journey?

This process required more than surface-level patience—it demanded the kind of uncommon decency and spiritual humility that Mouw calls essential to the Christian intellectual life.[6] Amid the uncertainty, we sought to stay open to God's leading with the posture of Psalm 139:23: "Search me, God, and know my heart; test me and know my anxious thoughts." Not everyone saw our move or this new career as worthy; some dismissed it as a novelty, while others questioned its theological grounding. Mouw's reflections affirm the kind of response we hoped to embody—one that listens with humility, engages with conviction, and welcomes critique without defensiveness.[7] When faced with skepticism, I began to see each conversation not as a threat to my calling but as an opportunity for faithful dialogue—grounded in joy yet willing to be sharpened by critique.

The same principles apply in our research or writing: study as though it depends on you, pray as though it depends on God. Sometimes, we realize that an outrageous calling is precisely where faith can soar—supported by minds ready to explain, strategize, and celebrate all our creative Lord sets before us. But this journey also requires gracious perseverance, the ability to remain calm, steadfast, and kind when faced with challenges, doubts, or criticism. This faithful endurance reflects Christ's character, showing that the academic roads we trailblaze can be navigated with conviction and compassion.

Chapter 48

The Rabbit Room: An Outrageous Perspective of Christian Communication

Kate Mead

Response Summary: This short case study provides a reflection on the author's dissertation research in light of George Marsden's *The Outrageous Idea of Christian Scholarship*. Referencing her dissertation that studied the online communication present within an artistic community called The Rabbit Room, it considers the author's Christian faith in three ways: (1) how it influenced her research direction and analysis; (2) how it encouraged her to consider existing critiques on existing assumptions on the nature of communication and community; and (3) how it encouraged her to note both the spiritual and the physical in the research analysis. This case study concludes that the Christian faith is a valuable interpretive lens within academic communication research.

IN THE OUTRAGEOUS *Idea of Christian Scholarship*, religious historian George Marsden considers a range of arguments for bold synthesis of faith and the Academy.[1] He articulates four significant influences that faith may have on academic scholarship, two of which this short essay aims to discuss. First, faith may direct researchers to certain applications of their research and, second, faith may enable researchers to see a field through a different viewpoint or "larger framework of meaning."[2] Marsden further claims that Christian influence "involves a characteristic set of questions and larger perspectives which . . . permeate inquiry in many subtle ways."[3] Noting the benefits of addressing subjects from a number of perspectives, Marsden references historian Harry Stout as he claims that Christian scholarship can also aid in critiquing existing assumptions.[4] In these respects, studies on communication done from a Christian perspective may present findings and/or interpretations that may contradict or complement other academic findings, thus adding value through Christian research.

My own experiences as a graduate student affirm Marsden's assertions. My doctoral dissertation was developed partially because my own graduate studies had opened my eyes to the intersection of communication and religion. While working on my MA degree, I developed an interest in both historical and contemporary instances of communication within religious contexts. Strongly encouraged and supported by faculty members at a large public university, my interest grew as those faculty expressed their fascination with what

Christian communicators chose as their message content. This academic support proved a foundation for my eventual doctoral studies that would begin years later, when my attention turned away from traditional religious communication done by church leaders in church contexts to a less-studied group: Christian nonprofit organizations.[5]

The Rabbit Room

Influenced significantly by my Christian faith, my attention turned to nonprofits because they specialize in particular religious activities but remain generalized in the Christian audiences they target. Therefore, I anticipated that studying them would provide insight into Christian culture as well as group communication patterns and tactics. My doctoral research focused on one organization as a case study: the Rabbit Room. The Rabbit Room is a nonprofit organization based near Nashville, Tennessee and developed as an online community that encourages Christian musicians, writers, and artists through community and artistic support. The Rabbit Room's mission is summarized as the cultivation and curation of "story, music, and art to nourish Christ-centered communities for the life of the world."[6]

Operating under the assumption that communication is a building block for creating and maintaining social reality, the study was designed to analyze how one organization utilized communication to create culture.[7] The study uncovered several communicative themes that contributed to the organization's culture, themes that were significantly spiritual in nature. Perhaps most interestingly, though, was the culture that was observed within the Rabbit Room, a culture that encouraged participation by both artists and non-artists alike. Since the Rabbit Room is an artistic organization, it was unexpected to discover that a segment of its intended audience was non-artists.

Like the analogy in Marsden's work, this view of the Rabbit Room's *cockpit* requires interpretation. What should be made of an organization that seeks to provide community and resources to artists but does so by reaching out (at least in part) to non-artists? What is there to be discovered in an organization that, rather than minutely segmenting to reach its audience, widens its scope to others?

Much of the logic behind the Rabbit Room's general approach is found in the organization's communicated themes. Two themes of note are (1) the distinction between "good" art and "bad" art, and (2) the idea that art nourishes community and community nourishes art.

These themes give insight into the organization's view of community—one that reflects biblical principles but also supports additional communication research that focuses on the bridging of differences rather than mere unification in similarities. Communication professor Eric W. Rothenbuhler contends that community (mediated or otherwise) does not always imply cohesion.[8] Rather, community is often used as a tool for the working out of differences, because members who join together are not identical and may not even be inherently alike. Communicative efforts seek agreeing audiences, and if those audiences do not yet agree, communicators seek to achieve agreement. Within the Rabbit Room, and particularly within its communicative focus of addressing both artists and non-artists, communication was found to be unifying in nature through an examination of the organization's two communicated themes.

To begin, a central communicated theme of the Rabbit Room is the differentiation between good art and bad art. In this theme, artists are called to work hard to improve their artistic skills. They are called to take their creative work seriously, learning from others and refining their trade so that the things they present to their audience increasingly speak of beauty and truth in the service of God. Art that does not do this—does not reflect beauty and truth or does not endeavor to do it well—is considered bad art. This then offers direction for both artists and non-artists. Non-artists are called to become more thoughtful consumers of art, immersing themselves in good art and further learning of the ways that art can speak beauty and truth into the world. This theme fosters both creators and consumers of good art, which sets itself apart through its reach toward what is good and true. This theme aimed to consider existing definitions of art and to unite its audience in its understanding of good art.

Another theme reflects the claim that art is not meant to exist in isolation, because art is further prompted and refined through the contribution of others. Artists generally voice consistent feelings of isolation, and the Rabbit Room's communication encourages consistent community, aiming to build consensus and community where they previously did not exist. In effective community, the artist labors in her art to present it to an audience. This is the role of the non-artist. This audience, then, responds by offering knowledgeable support to that artist. This unifies the artists and non-artist as they work together to provide an atmosphere where artistry is of benefit to all. In addition, because the Rabbit Room expands the definition of art to include things that are outside the bounds of traditional art (things like home décor or gardening), the organization implies a call to all humans to both create good art and help others to create it. This is an inclusive call, one that reaches to a wide rather than segmented audience. This theme, again, seems to aim for unification despite differences.

In both of these themes, consumers of art are enriched because of the art that exists in their lives. Without art, lessons may remain unlearned, and truth may remain undiscovered. Through connection with the artist and his work, a reader, listener, observer, or viewer can enter into an artistic space that emphasizes aspects of reality that are often unseen or lost in daily life—even if they are not artists. These two sides of the artistic relationship are interdependent: the artist needs support, and the audience needs the art. It is assumed that the artistic community becomes better at creation and using art to find truth and beauty when they do so together as they refine each other and teach each other, fostering greater unification.

It is likely this cockpit of artistic culture found in the Rabbit Room would have been interpreted differently by an individual unfamiliar with the language or knowledge of Christian faith. Themes revolving around art and redemption hold deeper spiritual meanings for Christians. They may be taught to view themselves as artistic because God himself is artistic, noting that they are created in the image of God. They may also see themselves as called to redeem the world through art, by using it to bring light to the darkness of the world—light imparted to them by Christ.

Ultimately, what I found while doing my expressly Christian research was twofold. First, I discovered that research topics informed by the Christian faith can be of use to others within the Christian faith. My doctoral work was one area where Christian research could prove to be of benefit to Christian community, online or otherwise. As Christians, we will be better informed if Christians are willing to study through an expressly Christian lens. Second, I realized that communication assumptions widely accepted by the academic world should be challenged. As Rothenbuhler noted, unchecked assumptions can limit interpretation of studies and may imply that differences are inherent threats to community, despite researched evidence to the contrary.[9]

In studying communication through a Christian lens, truths found in Scripture find a home even in a largely secularized Academy. In this Rabbit Room case study, we find affirmations of the beauty of a diverse body of Christ, which alludes to the requirement in 1 Corinthians 12 that all parts accept each other and work together in purpose. We also find the building of community rather than an assumption that it already exists, which alludes to the exhortation in Philippians 2 not to give in to the divisive nature of selfishness or vanity but to be unified in love, spirit, and mind. This is an active undertaking that assumes difference but prompts individuals to actively unify—a perspective that echoes Rothenbuhler as he warns of the danger of blindly accepting that community can only be studied where it already exists.[10]

One value of Christian research, as Marsden claims, is that it encourages the consideration of the spiritual in addition to the physical. It is essential to consider, whether in religious or secular contexts, how "we may see God working in the ordinary, if only we have the eyes to see."[11] The value of Christian scholarship becomes harder and harder to deny when it is done more and more. Only then might we Christians help the world notice its absence.[12]

Chapter 49

I Have a Vision

JOHN R. PECK

I HAVE A VISION . . .

Of a church whose worship seeks out all the resources of its members and utilizes all their skills. Where the hymns are sung with zest, perception, and expression, and accompanied by every instrument anyone can play, including hands, and feet and smiles. And where the unfamiliar music of another generation is learned until it is loved.

A church with liturgies that are never mechanical, and spontaneity that is never trivial.

Where the least of its meetings are conducted like royal appointments, and its greatest days are marked with solemn hilarity.

Where organizational efficiency is always at the service of caring love.

Where even poor efforts are done with painstaking diligence and commended with tolerant hope.

Where brilliance of mind or skill only serves to light up Jesus Christ and his Gospel; where no one can hog the limelight, no one gets too much attention, and no one gets left out.

Of a church where outsiders get as much welcome as old friends; where no one stands alone unless they need to; where the awkward ones are accepted, and the pleasant ones are disturbed by hard realities.

Where the first to hear a complaint is the offender, and the last to air it is the sufferer.

Where peoples' interests are worldwide, without being worldly, and personal without being petty.

I have a vision of a church which shares an invincible passion for learning and giving, whose life is energized by a glad acceptance of the Cross as a way of life.

Whose self-critical humor puts people at ease, and whose self-denials disturb and brace them.

Whose sympathies are so warm and imaginative that no one has the nerve to indulge in self-pity; and whose ideals are so high that slightly soiled notions are shamed into silence.

Whose convictions are firm without being rigid; whose tolerance extends even to the intolerant; whose life is an admonition, whose love learns even from its opponents, and whose faith is infectious.

I have a vision of a church that is like that because from time to time it hears its Redeemer's voice speak with such authority that nothing will do but obedience, nothing matters but God's love, and others coming in can only wonder, and wish, and ask.[1]

Section Five:
The Church, Public Witness,
and Evangelical Identity

Chapter 50

The Rise of Managerialism in the Evangelical Mind: A Historical, Theological, and Organizational Analysis

R. Tyler Spradley

Response Summary: This essay explores the rise of managerialism in evangelical churches, a paradigm prioritizing efficiency, consumerism, and organizational strategy, which has eclipsed the theological and intellectual heritage of evangelicalism. Noll and Marsden's seminal accounts of the historical decline of the evangelical mind provide insight into rise of evangelical anti-intellectualism, which is argued to enable and exasperate entertainment, market-driven cultural shifts in worship practices and church polity. Calling for a renewed mind in church growth processes, this essay critiques evangelical churches that adopt corporate models and proposes five mindful counterstrategies—theological education, communal worship, critical technology use, humble leadership, and discipleship focus.

"But we have the mind of Christ" (1 Cor. 2:16b, English Standard Version). Where is the mind of Christ in the evangelical movement and its churches? Addressing this question means taking note of the rise of a corporate, managerial approach to church affairs. A corporate, managerial approach emphasizes efficiency, consumerism, and organizational strategy and has extended its tentacles into evangelical churches. Organizational decisions and strategies eclipse evangelicalism's theological and intellectual heritage. Simply, the infiltration of managerialism into ecclesiology contributes to the erosion of the evangelical mind. As a result, evangelicals should counter the mindless embrace of show business and crowds by balancing intellectual rigor and doctrinal purpose. Ultimately, churches must heed the call to return to a holistic Christian mind.

Mark Noll and George Marsden document intellectual decline in evangelicalism. In *The Scandal of the Evangelical Mind*, Noll traces evangelicalism's prioritization of revivalism and pragmatism over rigorous scholarship beginning in the nineteenth century.[1] He contends that evangelicalism forsook intellectual engagement in favor of emotional experience, resulting in anti-intellectualism within the movement. Similarly, Marsden notes how the fundamentalist-modernist controversy of the early twentieth century further entrenched anti-intellectual views.[2] The outcome of this controversy was a broader withdrawal of evangelicals from cultural and academic domains. While well supported, are Noll and Marsden's contentions sufficient explanations for the decline of the evangelical mind and the rise of anti-intellectualism? Arguably, there is another contributing factor to document—the ascension of managerialism.

Larger cultural shifts, particularly in the areas of entertainment and media, erode critical thinking in society and its institutions, including evangelical churches. In *Amusing Ourselves to Death*, cultural and media critic Neil Postman asserts that the shift from a print-based to a visual, entertainment-driven culture prioritizes spectacle over substance.[3] Could this be true for evangelicalism? Yes, it could and is. The logic that has prevailed is that spectacle produces larger numbers—the metric of success in both business and evangelicalism. In her book *Reaching Out Without Dumbing Down*, Marva Dawn critiques the evangelical tendency to oversimplify theology.[4] Fueling oversimplification, evangelicals seek to appeal to consumerist audiences rather than disciple congregants. Dawn contends that oversimplification of theology undermines the depth of Christian thought. Furthermore, David F. Wells explains in *No Place for Truth* how evangelicals have succumbed to cultural pressures to adopt therapeutic and market-driven approaches to church and neglect theological rigor, resulting in larger but less intellectual congregations.[5] Likewise, Carl R. Trueman, in *Reformed or Deformed*, describes how the prioritization of cultural relevance over doctrine has given rise to a "mindless" pragmatism mirroring secular managerialism.[6] Collectively, Postman, Dawn, Wells, and Trueman illustrate an evangelical trajectory toward managerial and consumerist, entertainment-driven perspectives that are reshaping its ecclesiology.

The Christian Mind

The Christian mind transcends mere intellectualism but does not preclude it. This section focuses on what mind is and should be within evangelicalism before examining how managerialism has undermined it. Mind is a disposition holistically oriented toward God. In the Old Testament, the Hebrew term *leb* (heart/mind) implies this holistic disposition. In the Shema expressed in Deuteronomy 6:5, loving God should include the heart, soul, and might, thus employing all faculties in the experience and expression of godly devotion. In the New Testament, the Greek term *nous* (mind) harkens back to Deuteronomy 6:5 as Luke writes, "You shall love the Lord your God with all your heart and with all your soul and with all your strength and with all your mind" (Luke 10:27, ESV). Notably, Luke adds a reference to mind, but in both passages, a comprehensive devotion to God integrates intellectual, emotional, and physical faculties. Complementing this holistic devotion, Paul writes in Romans 12:2 that the renewing of the mind enables the Christian to resist secular conformity and discern the will of God. Therefore, the Christian mind is wholly devoted relationship with God and discernment of God's purposes.

If a Christian mind is to be wholly devoted and discern God's will, then a Christian mind should pursue intellectual excellence as a virtue. Two biblical examples emerge. First, King Solomon is rewarded for asking God for a discerning mind in 1 Kings 3, and second, the Apostle Paul is rewarded with a preaching opportunity because he reasons with Jews in the synagogue and Epicurean and Stoic philosophers in the marketplace in Acts 17:16–34. Once more, the book of Proverbs advises mindful Christians to get wisdom and insight (4:7) and get understanding rather than riches (16:16). Pursuing intellectual excellence is a virtue, but without the Christian mind, pursuing intellectual excellence for its own sake is folly (1 Cor. 1) and vanity (Eccl. 1:12–2:26).

Additionally, the pursuit of intellectual excellence benefited Christendom historically. Augustine of Hippo, Thomas Aquinas, and C. S. Lewis advanced apologetics. Augustine's *City of God* and *The Confessions*, read for centuries, advances a philosophical defense of the Christian faith. Aquinas's *Summa Theologica* influences apologetics and rhetoric by systematically engaging in intellectual debate to support Christianity. C. S. Lewis's apologetics demonstrates intellectual rigor without devolving into Gnostic heresy, which elevates knowledge over faith.[7] Other example figures emerge in the Protestant Reformation such as John Calvin, who emphasized the study of Scripture for Christians to renew their minds, discern God's will, and resist the corrupting power of sin over the mind.[8] Another example from the Great Awakening, Jonathan Edwards saw the mind and religious affections as intertwined producing intellectual understanding and heartfelt devotion.[9]

With a wealth of theological resources, it is difficult to imagine evangelicalism abandoning the Christian mind and the virtue of intellectual excellence. Yet the infiltration of managerialism into evangelical ecclesiology demonstrates a trade-off. Whereas the heritage of evangelicalism embraced the disposition of holistic devotion, including intellectual excellence, at present evangelicalism embraces managerialism.

Organizational Drift

The Industrial Revolution's principles of efficiency, measurable outcomes, and organizational growth permeate evangelical churches. While these principles initially guided industrial production and migrated into business models like Total Quality Management (TQM), the Industrial Revolution's long-term significance is far-reaching.[10] Originally, the managerialist paradigm functionally shaped industrial production and business, but it permeates ecclesial structures, often under the pretext of advancing evangelistic goals. Citing the Great Commission to make disciples in Matthew 28:16–20 and Acts 1:8, evangelical goals focus on numbers—numbers of attendees, numbers on member rosters, numbers of confessions of faith, numbers of web clicks, numbers of sermon downloads, and numbers of baptisms. This section further illuminates the effects of managerialism on evangelicalism.

The Managerial Turn

The managerial turn in evangelical ecclesiology demonstrates how managerialism has co-opted the religious structures of churches. Organizational communication scholar Stanley Deetz critiques the "corporate colonization" of organizations that displaces organizational purpose for economic growth.[11] By internalizing market logics into church practices, managerialism colonizes the church and reduces human interactions to transactional exchanges. The seeker-sensitive church is a prime example of corporate colonization. Emphasizing measurable outcomes for organizational growth, the seeker-sensitive model uses marketing strategies to attract unchurched community members and increase congregation size. The seeker-sensitive model demonstrates many of the challenges to the evangelical mind regarding corporate growth and compromised purpose. To illustrate, megachurches like Willow Creek Community Church adopt TQM and marketing strategies to attract the unchurched.[12] By doing so, Willow Creek Community treats churchgoers as consumers. In turn, they use market data to appeal to consumer preferences that attract and retain them. Similarly, Saddleback Church, under the leadership of Rick Warren at the time, leveraged data-driven outreach and purpose-driven branding, derived from Warren's widely popular *The Purpose Driven Life* and *The Purpose Driven Church*.[13] Saddleback Church achieved megachurch status with a celebrity pastor and international reach with their brand.[14] Esteeming consumer preferences, applying metrics, elevating pastors to celebrity status, building multimillion-dollar facilities, integrating secular amusements (e.g. coffee shops, bookstore), and generating entertainment-driven services transforms evangelical churches and their services to mirror corporate enterprises and product launches.

Adopting Corporate Identity

Adopting managerialist practices corrodes the identity of evangelical churches. In the managerial turn, the evangelical identity morphs into a corporate identity. Author Mary Jo Hatch argues that adopting consumer models causes organizations to lose their distinctiveness as they prioritize market demands over purpose.[15] Thus, evangelical churches become indistinct from their secular counterparts. In evangelical churches, this shift in priorities manifests as a shift from biblical ecclesiology to business metrics, where success is measured by budgets, attendance, engagement, buildings, and media presence.[16] Author Mara Einstein explains this identity shift as the sacred becoming secularized.[17] The pursuit of scale and spectacle in this identity shift crystallizes in the example of Lakewood Church in Houston, Texas. With a $95 million annual budget and a 16,800-seat facility, Lakewood Church's identity appears more corporate than evangelical.[18] As author David Wells points out, scale and spectacle mask a quest for human-centered rather than God-centered glory.[19] The effect of this identity shift prioritizes external perceptions over substantive practices.[20] Organizational scholar Mats Alvesson warns that "empty signifiers" detach an organizational identity from its foundational values.

Yielding to Technology

With the advent of the Industrial Revolution, Taylorism and scientific management introduced efficiencies and technologies that transformed workplaces, and as evangelical churches have been colonized by managerialism, churches have likewise been transformed by these efficiencies and technologies.[21] Scholars have long warned of the totalizing effect of technology on culture. In *Technopoly*, Neil Postman claims that technology reshapes society, its institutions, and individuals.[22] MIT professor Wanda Orlikowski's concept of "sociomateriality" and University of Montreal professor François Cooren's concept of "ventriloquism," provide a elucidate how technological determinism is co-opted by evangelical churches in the managerial turn.[23]

First, Orlikowski provides a framework for understanding the relationship of technology, people, and organizations. "Sociomateriality" integrates the social (e.g., people, practices, culture) and the material (e.g., technology, objects) into one term to communicate how the social and material are entangled and mutually constitute one another.[24] In relationship to the managerial turn in evangelical churches, sociomateriality is observable in the ways multimedia worship systems, streaming platforms, and data-driven outreach and decision making shape how ministry and worship services are enacted. In *Brands of Faith*, Mara Einstein explains how technologies are integrated into church branding and marketing.[25] For example, North Point Community Church uses light, sound, and video production design to create immersive and globally streamed worship services. Orlikowski's notion of sociomateriality illuminates how technology and experience are interwoven to mutually constitute the worship service; nevertheless, technologies are not neutral tools. The light, sound, and video production design shapes how North Point Community Church organizes and enacts its worship service and how attendees—in person and online—experience it. Technology, in this case, privileges spectacle over substance.

Second, Cooren explains how non-human actors such as technologies and metrics powerfully shape organizational practices. Cooren goes as far as to assert that non-human actors speak. How is this possible? Cooren proposes the process of "ventriloquism."[26] Through communication, non-human actors are made to speak or are animated.[27] Consider how a report generated by ACS Technologies or Ministry Platform software on church metrics is animated by references to that report in a church leadership meeting. A pastor may say something like, "The report justifies increased visual demonstrations in sermons because of engagement metrics." The verbal references to that report affects decisions made in the meeting. It is important to be mindful of the persuasive, but limited, nature of technologies and the reports they generate. Such metrics are designed with specific intent, which demonstrates non-human agency in the construction and use of results. Evangelicals must be mindful of how human and non-human puppeteers do not always shape strategy using sound doctrine.

Technological determinism, sociomateriality, and ventriloquism attest to the ways evangelicalism has uncritically yielded to technology. Those witnessing its effects note the negative impact on diminished communal worship and the growth of individualized, entertainment-driven worship, the relationship of technology to faith branding, and the overreliance on data analytics and metrics to evaluate church effectiveness.[28] When faced with the avalanche of technology use, questions arise as to what extent evangelical churches are critically engaging with technologies, questioning whose purposes these technologies serve, or considering the managerialist paradigms underlying the technology adoption.

The Impact of the Managerial Turn

Managerialism has profoundly impacted Western Christianity and evangelicalism. According to sociologist James Davison Hunter, evangelicals have been in a spiritual literacy decline since the 1960s.[29] Supporting this decline, Barna Group found that only 17% of practicing Christians in the United States regularly read Scripture outside of church services.[30] Concerns emerge as to the depth of belief and devotion if so few self-proclaiming

Christians are reading their Bibles. Moreover, Scott Thumma and Dave Travis, authors of *Beyond the Megachurch Myths*, demonstrate how spiritual literacy declines correlate with the rise of corporate models of church like megachurches.[31] Furthermore, managerialism displaces the church's purpose, prioritizing numerical growth and other measurable outcomes over discipleship. Arguably, evangelicals have lost their Christian minds trading the faithful fulfillment of the Great Commission for organizational expansion. The managerial turn in evangelicalism results in evangelical mindlessness.

Evangelical Mindlessness

Evangelical mindlessness is, in part, a product of the managerial turn. Defined as a departure from a biblically grounded, heedful disposition toward God, evangelical mindlessness is a stark contrast to the Hebrew and Greek words *leb* and *nous*. Drawing on organizational scholars Karl Weick and Karleen Roberts's seminal work on collective mind, there is a dramatic contrast between heedless and heedful as well as mindless and mindful.[32] Heedless and mindless action results from habitual behaviors. Such behaviors are performed thoughtlessly without considering context, responsiveness, adaptivity, or outcome. Conversely, heedful and mindful action results from a set of behaviors that account for context, learn from failures and near misses, avoid oversimplifications, match complexity with complexity, adapt accordingly, and defer to those with the most expertise. While Weick and Roberts focused their attention on high-risk organizational contexts, the general phenomenon of heedful mindfulness versus heedless mindlessness crosses organizational types, including evangelical churches. The aim of collective mind is to both explain and control organizational action leading to performance reliability. In the context of evangelical churches, performance reliability may be reconceptualized as enacting the Christian mind. Considering the managerial turn in evangelicalism, questions emerge as to how mindlessness has decayed reliable performances. The remainder of this section attends to the ways evangelicalism has mindlessly valued pragmatism over principle, consumerist worship over communal worship, technology over skepticism, celebrity leadership over humble leadership, and profit over discipleship.

1. Pragmatism

Evangelical mindlessness prioritizes pragmatic outcomes, such as quantifiable metrics for attendance, engagement, and financial growth, over principle. While much easier to measure, quantifiable metrics eschew assessment of congregants' holistic devotion to God, discernment of God's will, biblical literacy, and pursuit of Christian intellectual excellence. Weick and Roberts describe how mindless action interrupts collective purpose and values, whereas mindful action aligns behaviors with the collective principles.[33] Integrating metrics to judge organizational performance, churches fail to reflect on their theological implications or fit.[34] Even Willow Creek Community Church, which fully adopted the seeker-sensitive consumerist model of ecclesiology, revealed that their model failed to foster Christian mindfulness. A 2007 internal study by Willow Creek Community Church concluded that their pragmatic, seeker-sensitive model successfully contributed to increased attendance but neglected spiritual growth among church members.[35] Willow Creek Community Church's preoccupation with numeric success blinded them to failures to fulfill biblical purpose. Harkening back to Weick and Roberts's research on *collective mind*, pragmatism fractures alignment between churches' organizational structures and practices. Moreover, pragmatism may subvert who they are—their very identities. Rather than evoking Weick's concept of *sensemaking* to collectively critique pragmatism's effect on evangelicalism, evangelical pragmatism has bypassed sensemaking.[36] In doing so, evangelicalism has not discerned how business models fit with or fragment biblical ecclesiology.

2. Consumerist Worship

Consumerist worship services use market research and entertainment media to tailor to individual preferences rather than prompt communal, biblically modeled worship services. Consumerism does not reflect collective mindfulness, nor does it foster collective identity and purpose. Organizational scholars Mats Alvesson and Hugh Willmott critique consumerist organizational cultures. They argue that these cultures sabotage collective identity by prioritizing market-driven preferences over a shared sense of identity and values.[37] Driven by consumerist models of concert-like worship services, evangelical churches sell "worship experiences." Such experiences are widely available in-person and online at churches like Hillsong, Bethel, Elevation, North Point Community, or Gateway. With mood lighting and pop-style music, services cater to cultural tastes. Church members become audiences as high-production value hides low theological fidelity. Dawn explains that sacred worship spaces have been corrupted and transformed into entertainment venues.[38] The effect of this corruption and transformation is a highly attractive and marketable emotional experience at the expense of theological substance.[39]

3. Technological Acquiescence

Churches employ digital platforms, electronic giving, streamed services, multimedia services, social media engagement, and multimedia marketing. Acquiescing to technology, churches have not critically assessed how these digital tools align with their purpose and identity. Many in evangelicalism may not realize that their churches are technopolies. Mindless adoption of technology permeates ecclesiology. Without mindful skepticism of technology's reach and effect, churches are evolving into virtual products. Author John Sanders describes an example of technological acquiescence at Life.Church. The church's internal social media software is endowed with an algorithm to track member engagement and giving patterns, and, in turn, Life.Church uses data for organizational expansion.[40] This is a picture of technological determinism, but it is not a picture of mindful technology use. Instead, technology further entrenches business models into churches. Additionally, churches are moving more of their services, events, and interactions online to virtual communities. The effect is not necessarily greater performance reliability. In a 2020 Pew Research study investigating virtual church experiences during the COVID-19 pandemic, findings demonstrated that 79% of U.S. Christians attending virtual services felt less connected to their churches.[41] Thus, quantifiable clicks and views may not be the best metrics for communal engagement. Overall, technology as a tool has merit in evangelicalism, but a dose of skepticism is needed for mindful technology use.

4. Celebrity Leadership

Evangelicalism's embrace of the celebrity pastor promotes a human-centered glory, a heedless departure from Christ-centered humility. Mindful leadership, according to Weick and Roberts, is accountable to the collective.[42] Furthermore, the individual leader's effectiveness is determined by the collective pursuit of the organization's purpose. In contrast to mindful leadership, the celebrity pastor prioritizes personal image over the collective identity and purpose of the church.[43] The church's emphasis on the celebrity pastor overshadows the priesthood of believers (see 1 Pet 2:9) and consolidates authority in the influential status of the celebrity. Stewart Clegg offers a general critique of celebrity leadership. Clegg warns that celebrity leadership generates a power imbalance, tipping the scales toward the leader's individual agenda over collective goals.[44] Marti and Ganiel, in their book *The Deconstructed Church*, describe celebrity pastors as religious entrepreneurs adopting trends in business, entertainment media, and politics.[45] Celebrity pastors like Elevation Church's Steven Furtick use social media to brand and self-promote, often under the auspices of extending their ministry's reach.[46] However, celebrity leadership undermines the evangelical church as the church becomes dependent on the charismatic figure rather than on the communal identity in Christ.

5. Profit Pursuits

Evangelical churches are not corporate enterprises. Yet the prioritization of financial growth and multimillion-dollar budgets over spiritual formation mindlessly redefines the church. While churches must attend to ethical, responsible financial practices, churches are tempted to think bigger is better. Chasing profit, churches reflect the heedless focus on short-term, material gain over long-term reliability.[47] Matthew 28's Great Commission (vv. 19–20) is not a call to numbers, per se, but a call to make disciples. Discipleship is undercut when churches invest the bulk of their time and energy into financial growth.[48] Furthermore, church budgets and buildings are powerful non-human actors, influencing organizational decision-making.[49] If a church's budget and buildings reflect a corporate model, then the organization becomes subservient to the needs of generating the revenue to fund the budget and buildings. The problematic nature of budget and building authority is clear when a celebrity pastor falls from grace, subsequently impacting the church's attendance and giving. Mars Hill multisite megachurch in Seattle, Washington, and Gateway multisite megachurch in Southlake, Texas, know all too well how a celebrity pastor's publicly grievous sin disrupts the corporate model of churches. For reliable performance, profit-driven decision-making must give way to discipleship-driven decision-making.

Mindful Practices for Evangelical Institutions

Evangelical mindlessness is marked by a lack of heedful interrelating and uncritical corporate colonization of churches.[50] This section focuses on the biblical mandate to counter mindlessness and realize mindfulness. To begin, Romans 12:1–2 illustrates God's means of mindful practice, "be transformed by the renewal of your mind, that by testing you may discern what is the will of God, what is good and acceptable and perfect" (ESV). Countering evangelical mindlessness must include resistance to worldly market logics that do not comport with Scripture. In 2 Timothy, Paul admonishes Timothy and the church universal to reject unsound teaching and doctrine. Paul writes, "but having itching ears they will accumulate for themselves teachers to suit their own passions, and will turn away from listening to the truth and wander off into myths. As for you, always be sober-minded, endure suffering, do the work of an evangelist, fulfill your ministry" (4:1–5, ESV). If evangelicals are to recognize unsound teaching and doctrine to be wholly devoted to God, discern the will of God, and pursue Christian intellectual excellence, which is Christian mindfulness, then evangelicals must resist the mindless effects of the managerial turn. The following five recommendations address the five aforementioned mindless threats to evangelicals.

1. Theological Education

To counter profit-driven mindlessness, theological education equips Christians to renew their minds and discern God's will amidst cultural pressures. If "rightly handling the word of truth," evangelicals could resist corporate colonization and its pragmatic metrics for decision-making. Mindful organizations use sensemaking to resiliently respond to pressures threatening collective purpose.[51] Deetz argues that communicative practices should be rooted in shared meaning to resist market logics.[52] With that in mind, mindfulness in the evangelical context converges on the teaching of sound doctrine. There are a series of mindless effects to be corrected through theological education. Noll suggests that anti-intellectualism begets theological weakness, which begets poor witness.[53] Prioritizing theological education prioritizes the shared evangelical purpose to witness. The integrity and soundness of witness is dependent on the witnesses' theological fidelity, not on profit-driven market logics.

2. Communal Worship

To counter consumerist worship, communal worship equips Christians to overcome worldly preferences. Communal worship emphasizes participatory and God-centered adoration, which is in opposition to the consumerist spectacle dominating evangelical services. This shift in worship services is a call to resist the cultural tug to commodify worship.[54] Alvesson advises organizations to align practices with identity and purpose to withstand market logics.[55] Are there churches that emulate resistance to consumerist culture? How can churches align practice with identity and purpose? Consider Redeemer Presbyterian Church in New York City. As a smaller congregation, church services feature participatory liturgy, Scripture reading, exegetical preaching, prayer, and traditional hymns.[56] Unplugging the mood-lighting effects and focusing on substance, evangelical churches may experience increased collective spiritual engagement. In a 2019 Barna Group study, 68% of Christians attending liturgy-focused churches reported deeper spiritual engagement compared to their counterparts in megachurch churches.[57] Communal worship services are plausible answers to heedful, unifying worship experiences.

3. Limited Technology Dependence

Technology should be used as a tool in service of evangelical identity and purpose and not function as its master. Limited technology use heeds Paul's words to the Corinthian church, "All things are lawful, but not all things are helpful" (1 Cor. 10:23, ESV). Heedful organizations use tools to ensure alignment with their identities and purposes.[58] Therefore, churches should pause before jumping on the digital bandwagon and consider the need and consequences of technology adoption. For example, All Souls Church in London uses technology selectively. They offer online sermon streaming but prioritize small, in-person groups to maintain relational bonds.[59] Like-minded churches seeking evangelical mindfulness should treat technology as a tool to foster biblical community.

4. Humble Leadership

Instead of promoting celebrity culture, evangelicals should promote humble leadership. The self-serving image of the celebrity pastor contrasts with Scripture. Philippians 2:3–4 exhorts: "Do nothing from selfish ambition or conceit, but in humility count others more significant than yourselves" (ESV). Distributed and servant leadership reverberate with humility. Organizational scholar Barbara Czarniawska maintains that organizations with distributed leadership are more resilient because their processes and outcomes are not overly dependent on an individual.[60] Comparably, the Leadership Network concluded that servant leadership resulted in higher congregational trust and longevity.[61] Humble leadership cultivates the evangelical mind because it is aligned with Christlikeness and the collective interests.

5. Discipleship Focus

Profit-driven metrics should be sidelined in favor of spiritual-growth metrics. Discipleship aligns with the call of the Great Commission in Matthew 28:19–20 to: "Go therefore and make disciples of all nations, baptizing them in the name of the Father and of the Son and of the Holy Spirit, teaching them to observe all that I have commanded you" (ESV). To this end, Richard Osmer encourages churches to use formative practices such as mentoring to engender spiritual maturity.[62] Organizational scholarship comports with the focus on formative practices over profit. Alvesson and Willmott found that emphasizing intrinsic organizational goals over extrinsic measures helped organizations to thrive.[63] A discipleship focus at Navigators ministry is realized through one-on-one discipleship using mentoring models and biblical curriculum. In a 2018 study, Navigators found that 82% of mentees increased in their biblical literacy through their discipleship model.[64] If churches want to track metrics to assess their success, a discipleship focus rather than a profit focus will prompt greater organizational reliability.

Conclusion

The rise of the managerial turn in evangelicalism reflects a failure to enact Christian mindfulness and pursue intellectual excellence. As Noll and Marsden critique the anti-intellectualism stemming from revivalism, pragmatism, and fundamentalism, this essay focuses on managerialism.[65] Consumerist ecclesiology ushered in following the Industrial Revolution threatens the evangelical mind. Threats manifest as pragmatism, consumerist worship, technological acquiescence, celebrity leadership, and profit. Such threats may guise themselves in the intellectual garb of management and business research, models, and practices, but the managerial turn has not yielded greater depth of the evangelical mind nor Christian intellectual excellence. Yet evangelical churches can reassert their identities and counter mindlessness in the wake of the managerial turn. Through theological education, communal worship, critical technology use, humble leadership, and a discipleship focus, evangelical churches are poised to renew their minds in the spirit of Romans 12:2.

Chapter 51

The Christian Mind to Serve the Church: Thinking Pastorally about the Contemporary Value of Noll and Marsden

Mark Allan Steiner

Response Summary: This chapter revisits the enduring relevance of Mark Noll's *The Scandal of the Evangelical Mind* and George Marsden's *The Outrageous Idea of Christian Scholarship*, arguing that both works remain vital for confronting two persistent challenges within American evangelicalism: cultural co-optation and a diminished intellectual engagement with Scripture and the natural world. Steiner warns that U.S. evangelicals often reflect secular values—individualism, consumerism, and moral blind spots—more than biblical distinctiveness, echoing Noll's critique of anti-intellectualism. Drawing from Marsden, he calls for a more integrated Christian scholarship rooted in epistemological humility. Ultimately, Steiner contends that a robust evangelical mind is not merely academic, but essential for the church's faithful discipleship, cultural discernment, and theological maturity.

THERE'S A LOT OF SENTIMENTAL VALUE for me to have been a part of this gathering of scholars and thinkers because I discovered both books during my time in graduate school. I was honestly struggling then to figure out how to relate together two things I was passionately wanting to do. I wanted to learn the field, to teach rhetoric and communication well, and to do quality scholarship that genuinely served the field. At the same time, I wanted to bring my faith in Christ to bear on all this so that my teaching and scholarship would also accomplish meaningful Kingdom work. I am greatly indebted to both Noll and Marsden for helping me to cultivate a vision to excel in both of these vocational missions and to see both of them in an integrated way.

My purpose in this brief chapter is to stress why these two books are still relevant, and why they are still important for the church, particularly the evangelical church in America. I will admit upfront that my comments here are more pastoral than they are academic, reflecting my heart as someone who wants my intellectual work primarily to serve the church, to help the church to be more faithful in its important work on earth. Accordingly, I am focusing my remarks here on two major issues that we as U.S. evangelical Christians face that Noll and Marsden really help us to engage in our own day.

Cultural Co-optation

The first major issue is the reality that cultural co-optation is a fundamental problem for the U.S. evangelical church. In his letter to the Romans, the Apostle Paul admonished them not to be "conformed to the pattern of this world" (12:2). The sad reality, unfortunately, is that the U.S. evangelical church has been far more conformed to the pattern of this world than we realize or would like to admit. To be sure, we have some practices that make us at least slightly different than people outside the church. We tend to go away to a building on Sunday mornings more than other people do. We tend to abstain—or think we abstain—from certain things in ways that most people outside the church do not. Even so, there are important ways in which we really do live out or are in danger of living out the values of our culture and bearing witness to our culture, much more so than bearing witness to the God that is revealed in the Bible.

How do we do this? First, I think we tend to emphasize the sins of people who are not like us and turn a blind eye to those sins in which we indulge. In doing this, we turn away from the biblical witness to humanity, which makes clear that even for *believers*—i.e., those who have been saved from the penalty of our sin, who have the Holy Spirit living inside of us, and who have the ability to resist sin and not be imprisoned by it anymore—there is still a sin nature that we struggle with, and we still have hearts that are deceitful and corrupted by the stain of our sinful nature. Instead of maintaining a sober self-awareness of this biblical reality, we embrace the cultural idea that we are basically okay, we are basically above-board, and we are wholesomely authentic in our identities. We embrace the deep-seated belief that if we engage in certain formulaic practices, then we are the good guys, and, of course, people who are not like us are the bad guys.

Noted evangelical author Jerry Bridges's book *Respectable Sins* spotlights this exact problem.[1] It is a candid and forceful inventory of those pervasive sins regularly committed and indulged by U.S. evangelical Christians—sins such as discontentment, unthankfulness, pride, selfishness, lack of self-control, anger, and judgmentalism. He shows that we, as a religious subculture, have become quite adept at tolerating, minimizing, or ignoring these sins. And if it is true that we take our cues about ourselves and our own moral standing from our culture and not from the Bible, then this approach to our own sin makes perfect sense.

How else do we show our conformity to the pattern of U.S. culture? A second way is in how we have internalized and practiced the contemporary cultural values of individualism and consumerism and even infused them with a spiritual justification. We all too easily think of ourselves as consumers as we relate to God. We all too easily think that we have a right to a pleasant, comfortable life, and that (like a good customer service provider) God owes this kind of life to us.

What are the results of this mentality? The George Barna Research Group has done substantial sociological research over the years on the practical beliefs and behaviors of U.S. evangelical Christians, and this research has been cited in several books, including Ron Sider's *The Scandal of the Evangelical Conscience*.[2] One aspect of this research emphasizes how the behaviors of evangelical Christians compare with the general population on certain matters. What are the divorce rates like? What are the domestic abuse rates like? What is the extent to which we engage in pornography? What are the levels of giving, i.e., how generous are we and how cheap are we? On these types of questions, this research has strongly suggested that the people inside the church are not significantly different from those outside the church. We inside the church may say or even earnestly believe that we follow biblical values and directives, but on a day-to-day level we think and live pretty much like the rest of the world does. I think a major contributor to this problem is the reality that, as Noll has said, there is simply not much of an evangelical mind, which is largely as true in 2024 as it was in 1994.[3]

When we do not practice a responsible intellectual existence in the church, we are far more vulnerable to exactly these types of cultural conformity and co-optation. It takes a serious life of the mind, which involves both a carefully trained mind and a carefully trained heart, to be able to see these cultural and ideological forces that are profoundly difficult to see. And if we cannot see these forces, we are not going to be able to make sense of them from a biblical perspective. And we certainly will not be able to resist them in any meaningful way.

What the church needs to do is similar to what William Deresiewicz, in his book *Excellent Sheep*, says college students in general need to do. He suggests that they need to strive for and earn an authentic education that enables them to recognize these cultural influences.[4] Deresiewicz uses the Platonic term *doxa*, roughly translated as "opinion," as a contrast to "knowledge," to describe these cultural influences that are all around us. These forces subtly, gradually, and powerfully squeeze us into particular ways of thinking, seeing ourselves, and valuing certain things over others. Deresiewicz claims that it takes serious education to recognize *doxa*, to see it, to see around it, to see past it, and to resist it.

I believe that this is also exactly what people in the church need to do. A responsible intellectual existence and a vibrant evangelical mind are critical to help the church offer a collectively authentic and countercultural witness. We simply cannot do that if we are conformed to the pattern of this world and do not even realize it and thereby offer a witness to what our culture is like instead of offering a witness to what our God is like. So the problem of cultural co-optation is an important reason why we need to take the life of the mind much more seriously, and why we need to be very intentional in cultivating a more intellectual and theological culture in the church.

The Bible and the Natural World

We should do all of this in response to a second major issue as well: the real natures of the Bible and of the natural world, which both come from God and reflect what God is like. The Bible and the natural world are not uniformly simple, and they are not uniformly plain. Rather, they are wonderfully complex and mysterious, which means that it takes a disciplined heart and a disciplined mind to properly engage them, to see their majesty, and ultimately to glorify God for them.

I think the call for more of an evangelical mind flows naturally from a high view of Scripture: that it is divinely inspired, that it is fully authoritative on all matters of faith and life, and that it really is truth in the fullest sense of the word. Part of the unseemly witness of the U.S. evangelical church is that we have implicitly turned away from this high view of Scripture by "shoehorning" it into a narrow epistemological mold, essentially reducing it to a massive series of acontextual and propositional claims of fact. Both Noll and Marsden have written extensively about this epistemological shoehorning, and an important practical consequence of this is that it all too easily leads us to misread and even abuse the Scriptures. For example, I can think of how U.S. evangelicals have used verses like Jeremiah 29:11, Philippians 4:13, and 2 Chronicles 7:14. Typically, verses like these are stripped from their cultural, rhetorical, and literary contexts and made to say something completely different from their original meaning. They are read instead as promoting ideas like "God is my co-pilot," or "God will empower and bless whatever I want to do," or "God will give me political victory if I just follow the right formula." Misuses of the Bible like this not only make it say things it was never intended to say, but also more fundamentally cheapen our understanding of what truth is and what the Bible is.

To reclaim a high view of Scripture, then, we need to embrace the reality that it has a mysterious and complex character that reflects the God whose Word it is. That means, in part, that there are many important places in which the Bible speaks with clarity. In other words, the most important basic truths necessary to know God and live in right relationship with him are broadly accessible. One need not be a scholar to engage and be transformed by the truths of God's special revelation—to grapple with, understand, and respond to the Gospel message and embrace Jesus Christ as Savior and Lord.

But at the same time, the Bible is like an onion. As we dig deeper, we find that there are layers of it that are more complex, requiring the kind of reading and interpretive skills that any serious literary artifact would require. Then there are layers that require formal theological and language training to engage well. And then there are layers that are so mysterious and frustrating that even professional theologians struggle mightily and are forced to reckon with their own limitations as the finite and fallen creatures that all human beings are. What this all means, then, is that to fully engage with and follow the voice of God in Scripture, we need modesty. We need to place ourselves into the grand narrative of the Bible. And we need to bring to these tasks serious and earnest intellectual and theological effort. A vibrant evangelical mind, then, is indispensable to reading the Bible well and living the Bible well.[5]

Since the natural world, like the Bible, was created by God, it should not be a surprise that the natural world has the same onion-like character that the Bible has. There are definitely numerous aspects of the natural world that are clear, accessible, and easy to grasp. Pretty much everyone can understand that gravity is a thing, right? And yet, if we think more deeply about what gravity is and how it works in the way that physicists have explored it for most of the past 100 years, we quickly realize that there is actually very little that is simple about gravity. Think about it: the idea that space bends, the idea that time bends—who would have thought of this? This is exactly the kind of thing that no one would just commonsensically come to, right?

So, the natural world, like the Bible, has a profoundly counterintuitive character, having many features that we would not naturally come up with on our own. It is wildly complex. It is mysterious. And if you want further proof of just how utterly grand and incomprehensible God's creation is, just think about astronomy and the good work that astronomers have done, particularly in the last several decades.

To properly approach and glorify God with how we approach the Bible and how we approach the natural world, then, we need the heart attitude of modesty, but we also need serious intellectual and theological effort as well. Again, this is because the Bible and the natural world have that divine spark in them, and so they have a complex, mysterious, and counterintuitive character that God also has. If we are to fully glorify God, then, we simply must have more of an evangelical mind. So in all the ways I have discussed in this short chapter, I think we see the practical witness of Noll's and Marsden's work for the church. It really is not just about being better scholars, as important as that is. More fundamentally, it is about how we can better disciple the church to grow in sanctification and in faithful witness. To me, that is ultimately what makes their work particularly valuable for our own day and age.

Chapter 52

How Scholars Can Serve the Church

BRIAN D. MATTSON

Response Summary: The author reflects on the growing disconnect many Christian scholars experience between the culture of the Academy and that of the local church. While an academic's professional life is shaped by the pursuit of excellence and inquiry, the church often values immediate relevance, pragmatism, and narrowly defined spiritual contributions. This mismatch can leave Christian scholars feeling spiritually homeless and vocationally disoriented. As Mark Noll lamented, the scandal lies not merely in the lack of intellectual seriousness among evangelicals, but in the church's failure to recognize the life of the mind as integral to faithful Christian witness. The author suggests that scholars can serve and partner with the church in service of the church's mission not by abandoning academic identity but by embodying three vital habits: curiosity, collegiality, and concentration. These practices can help bridge the gap between scholarship and discipleship, helping the church reclaim a more holistic vision of vocation and learning.

AS ACADEMICS, we are marked by a persistent, even relentless, orientation toward excellence and advancement. Our scholarly pursuits are animated by a commitment to producing high-quality research, and our institutions consistently demand excellence in both teaching and service. This drive for achievement is not incidental—it is deeply embedded in our formation, cultivated from the earliest stages of education and intensifying throughout our academic trajectories. From primary education through graduate school, the momentum of advancement has shaped our habits and aspirations. The pursuit does not conclude with the conferral of a terminal degree; rather, it accelerates as we publish articles, contribute to edited volumes, submit book proposals, and pursue tenure and promotion. Institutional incentives such as rank, tenure, and professional recognition reinforce this striving, often consuming much of our energy and imagination.

Yet, this deeply ingrained academic drive often clashes with the culture of the local church, which may not share the same priorities regarding individual achievement or scholarly excellence. Whether the church ought to value such pursuits is a broader question beyond the scope of this essay. However, for Christian scholars, especially those within evangelical traditions, the contrast can be disorienting. The intrinsic motivation for intellectual and professional advancement may be neither expected nor encouraged in congregational life. As a result, evangelical scholars may experience a sense of displacement within their own faith communities. Their training, insights, and abilities are frequently underutilized or even overlooked by church leadership. Despite having much to contribute to the theological, educational, and strategic life of the church, many scholars struggle to find meaningful opportunities to serve.

This raises a pressing question: What is the role of the scholar in the church? How might academics faithfully and fruitfully offer their gifts in communities that may not immediately recognize their value?

The Current Situation

This disconnect between the Academy and the church is particularly acute for scholars whose fields lie outside of biblical studies or theology. While pastors and church leaders may recognize the relevance of theological expertise for preaching, teaching, or doctrinal formation, they often struggle to see the value of disciplines such as philosophy, history, the natural sciences, literature, psychology, or the arts.[1] The intellectual contributions of these fields are frequently marginalized within evangelical ecclesial contexts, in which theological authority tends to dominate conversations about truth, ethics, and spiritual formation. As a result, scholars working in non-theological disciplines often find themselves without a clear ecclesial role or vocational outlet for their academic gifts.

This marginalization can stem from a variety of factors. First, there exists within segments of evangelicalism a functional anti-intellectualism—an enduring suspicion of the Academy, particularly when it comes to secular institutions or disciplines perceived as morally or ideologically ambiguous.[2] Fields that raise critical questions about power, gender, race, history, or epistemology may be viewed as politically charged or even spiritually dangerous. Second, many evangelical churches operate within a highly pragmatic orientation toward ministry. Church programming is often assessed based on perceived immediate relevance or measurable outcomes—metrics that tend to favor activities like evangelism, worship production, or small group growth.

Scholarly engagement, by contrast, operates at a slower pace, is more nuanced, and rarely yields quick, quantifiable results. Third, churches may lack a theological vision that affirms the intrinsic value of all forms of knowledge as part of God's good creation. Without robust doctrines of creation, vocations, or the intellect, churches inadvertently communicate that only certain kinds of knowledge—namely, explicitly biblical, theological, or pastoral—are spiritually significant.[3] Fourth, many individuals in the church receive more discipleship from the news media than they do from the church. The news media serve as a powerful source of information that not only shapes peoples' political but also their spiritual ideologies.

For scholars in disciplines within the sciences, humanities, or social sciences, these dynamics can be alienating. Their research, teaching, and professional commitments may be met with indifference, misunderstanding, or even suspicion. Over time, this alienation can foster deep vocational tension: the scholar may feel spiritually homeless, deeply committed to the church as a community of faith, yet at the same time intellectually disconnected from its rhythms and discourse. This dissonance is not merely a personal struggle; it reflects broader ecclesial deficiencies in how evangelical churches understand vocation, knowledge, and the role of the laity.

Consequently, many scholars find themselves asking: Is there space in the church for the contemplative and critical habits cultivated specifically in the Academy? How might a biologist or political theorist or poet offer their expertise in a way that strengthens the life of the church, rather than remaining on its periphery? These questions deserve serious theological reflection and ecclesial attention. They also invite scholars to consider how they might translate their intellectual gifts into forms that are intelligible, accessible, and fruitful for the church community—without compromising academic integrity or diminishing the depth of their discipline.

How Can Christian Scholars Help the Church?

Christian scholars do not have to hold leadership positions within the church to have a lasting influence within their local church contexts. As faithful members of evangelical churches, scholars can model the very habits that made them scholars in the first place. Many scholarly habits could be mentioned, but three are particularly important within the current cultural milieu: curiosity, collegiality, and concentration.

Curiosity: A Vital Virtue for the Academy and the Church

In an era marked by technological saturation and the acceleration of artificial intelligence, the practice of curiosity is at risk of diminishing. As Barbara Blodgett argues, curiosity appears to be waning in contemporary life, particularly in educational settings where students increasingly depend on digital search tools rather than cultivating the intellectual discipline required to formulate meaningful questions and patiently pursue answers.[4] This reliance on instant information, while efficient, may undermine the deeper processes of inquiry, reflection, and learning that form the bedrock of personal and spiritual growth.

The implications of this decline in curiosity are not limited to the classroom—they reverberate profoundly in the context of Christian life and discipleship. The very heart of Christian practice involves an earnest seeking after truth, meaning, and communion with God. Jesus's exhortation in the Sermon on the Mount encapsulates this spirit: "Ask, and it will be given to you; seek, and you will find; knock, and it will be opened to you" (Matt. 7:7–8, English Standard Version). The imperative to seek reflects an epistemological and spiritual posture of curiosity, a readiness to explore the mysteries of faith and the kingdom of God.

Blodgett defines curiosity as "asking the right sorts of questions at the right time with the right purpose in mind while creating the right context for the conversation."[5] However, historical perspectives complicate this view. Augustine of Hippo, for instance, offered a critique of *curiositas*—a disordered desire for knowledge disconnected from its proper end. In his *Confessions*, Augustine expresses concern over the pursuit of knowledge for its own sake, or worse, for the sake of self-aggrandizement. James K. A. Smith summarizes

Augustine's position as a warning against curiosity that is motivated by pride or a desire to be seen as wise.[6] The real issue, Augustine contends, is not knowledge itself but the *telos* of learning—the kind of love that fuels it.[7]

Despite Augustine's critique, a redeemed vision of curiosity remains essential, particularly within scholarly and ecclesial contexts. Many academics begin their journey not out of a desire for prestige or power, but from a sincere love for discovery. The joy of posing a thoughtful question, designing a method of inquiry, and pursuing new understanding is a deeply human experience. While such endeavors might bring external rewards, they are often undertaken for the intrinsic delight of learning. This posture of wonder and attentiveness challenges the utilitarian tendencies of modern knowledge consumption and presents a compelling alternative.

For scholars who also serve in congregational settings, curiosity becomes a powerful bridge between the Academy and the church. The intellectual habits cultivated through research—attentiveness, humility, rigorous inquiry—can be translated into pastoral attentiveness. Curious scholars are not merely interested in abstract ideas but also in the lived experiences of the people around them. They can create spaces where questions are not only permitted but cherished—spaces in which individuals are encouraged to express doubt, seek wisdom, and encounter truth without fear of judgment.

Moreover, by modeling curiosity in our approach to Scripture and theology, scholars can inspire a similar posture in others. When we engage the biblical text with seriousness, ask difficult questions, and respond with awe rather than anxiety, we nurture a spirit of exploration in our communities. This practice fosters a mature faith—one that is not threatened by complexity but energized by it.

The evangelical church is particularly in urgent need of this revitalized curiosity. In a cultural landscape marked by rapid change and profound confusion, rehearsed answers and rigid formulas often fall flat. Curiosity enables the church to rediscover timeless truths and communicate them in ways that resonate afresh. It empowers believers to engage culture with wisdom, courage, and creativity—not as mere defenders of tradition, but as seekers of truth grounded in love.

Curiosity is not a luxury or an academic indulgence; it is a spiritual discipline and a moral imperative. It invites us into deeper communion with God, richer understanding of others, and more faithful engagement with the world. In a time when "answers" are easy, but wisdom is rare, curiosity beckons us to slow down, ask better questions, and trust that seeking, in its truest form, will lead us to the One who is the source of all knowledge and the fulfillment of all longing. Let the church, and those who serve within it, become a people who cultivate, embody, and celebrate holy curiosity.

Collegiality: A Model for Unity in the Church

Scholars acquire the habit of collegiality through years of rigorous academic training. Many recall their experiences with group projects both enriching and frustrating. These mixed perceptions remain consistent across generations of students. As an educator, I frequently underscore to my students the essential nature of collaborative work. It is imperative they recognize and appreciate the diverse talents each member brings to a group endeavor. Learning to identify individual strengths and strategically apply them toward shared objectives is vital for success.

Moreover, I remind students that they often do not get to choose their teammates. This reality mirrors many life situations: one may choose a spouse, but not the spouse's family; one may choose an employer, but not one's coworkers. The ability to work effectively with unfamiliar individuals, embracing their differing perspectives and experiences, lies at the heart of collegiality. When this practice is embraced, teams not only function—they thrive.

What might it look like for this habit of collegiality to take root in the church? Theologian Norma Cook Everist explores this very notion. She writes, "To be collegial is to have eyes wide open to the gifts of all, knowing that we are part of the priesthood of all believers."[8] For Christian scholars, this perspective resonates deeply. Faith in Jesus Christ re-creates humanity through the power of the Holy Spirit. The church thus becomes a community of Spirit-transformed individuals, called to live and labor together "as partners in ministries of reconciliation in a hurting and hurtful world."[9]

The New Testament consistently calls believers to such practices. In 1 Corinthians 12–14, the Apostle Paul challenges the Corinthian church to embrace unity amidst diversity—a theological expression of collegiality. In 12:4–11 (ESV), Paul articulates the foundational principle of spiritual giftedness:

> Now there are varieties of gifts, but the same Spirit; and there are varieties of service, but the same Lord; and there are varieties of activities, but it is the same God who empowers them all in everyone. To each is given the manifestation of the Spirit for the common good. For to one is given through the Spirit the utterance of wisdom, and to another the utterance of knowledge according to the same Spirit, to another faith by the same Spirit, to another gifts of healing by the one Spirit, to another the working of miracles, to another prophecy, to another the ability to distinguish between spirits, to another various kinds of tongues, to another the interpretation of tongues. All these are empowered by one and the same Spirit, who apportions to each one individually as he wills.

Within the church exists a diverse array of people, endowed with varying gifts and callings. Yet this diversity is not chaotic—it is unified by the common origin of these gifts: the Spirit of God. Paul insists that these gifts are to be exercised not competitively, but collaboratively, toward the mission of the church.

Paul's rhetorical illustration in 1 Corinthians 12:14–26 exposes the absurdity of disunity within the church. Using the metaphor of the human body, he shows that just as a body cannot function if its parts reject one another, the church likewise ceases to thrive when its members fail to recognize their interdependence. Each part—no matter how small or seemingly insignificant—has a unique and essential role. No part can dismiss another as unnecessary without damaging the whole. God has intentionally arranged this diversity so that all members share in one another's suffering and joy, cultivating mutual care and honor. Any assertion of "I have no need of you" within the body of Christ signals a breakdown of communal integrity and a rejection of the very design God has given for the church to flourish in unity amid diversity.

This vision resonates deeply with the academic habit of collegiality. In scholarly life, we learn to collaborate across differences, recognizing the varied strengths of our colleagues and working toward shared intellectual goals. Translating that posture into the life of the church means embracing a culture where every gift is valued—not only pastoral or theological, but also academic, artistic, scientific, and more. Collegiality calls us to practice humility, to listen well, and to labor together as partners in ministry. When scholars embody this virtue in the church, they help cultivate a Spirit-shaped community that reflects the diversity, interdependence, and mutual respect envisioned by Paul—a church where no one says, "I have no need of you."

The Apostle Paul concludes the chapter by affirming God's purposeful distribution of roles and gifts:

> Now you are the body of Christ and individually members of it. And God has appointed in the church first apostles, second prophets, third teachers, then miracles, then gifts of healing, helping, administrating, and various kinds of tongues. Are all apostles? Are all prophets? Are all teachers? Do all work miracles? Do all possess gifts of healing? Do all speak with tongues? Do all interpret? But earnestly desire the higher gifts. (1 Cor. 12:27–30, ESV)

Diversity within the church is not accidental; it is divinely orchestrated, reflecting the manifold wisdom of God and the varied gifts of the Spirit. For Christian scholars—individuals deeply formed in the disciplines of collaborative inquiry and respectful intellectual exchange—this diversity is not a problem to be managed but a gift to be stewarded. Trained in the art of collegiality through years of academic formation, scholars are uniquely positioned to model and nurture this essential virtue in the life of the local church.

But how does collegiality take root and mature within the ecclesial community? Paul's answer, as found in the oft-quoted but rarely fully appreciated "love chapter" of 1 Corinthians 13, is strikingly clear. Written to a fragmented and competitive church, Paul's words are not abstract ideals but practical imperatives for relational life: "Love is patient and kind; love does not envy or boast; it is not arrogant or rude. . . . It bears all things, believes all things, hopes all things, endures all things. Love never ends" (1 Cor. 13:4–8a, ESV). These virtues—patience, kindness, humility, endurance—are not merely personal dispositions but the moral infrastructure of true collegiality. In both Academy and church, collegiality requires the humility to listen deeply, the discipline to collaborate generously, and the courage to honor others' gifts without defensiveness or rivalry.

In practice, scholars can embody this in concrete ways within their congregations. A historian might partner with a pastor to develop a church education series on Christian responses to social change, bringing both academic insight and pastoral sensitivity to the conversation. A scientist might join a missions committee to help evaluate international partnerships through lenses of sustainability and ethics, modeling the respectful, interdisciplinary discernment they practice professionally. A literature professor might facilitate a book group that invites theological reflection through narrative, showing how reading together can become a deeply communal act of discipleship.

Beyond formal roles, scholars can practice collegiality by intentionally affirming the gifts of others in the congregation—administrators, artists, stay-at-home parents, trades-people—recognizing that every member brings vital wisdom to the body. In leadership meetings, they can help cultivate a culture of mutual respect and thoughtful dialogue, re-sisting the temptation to dominate discussions with expertise and instead asking better questions, promoting clarity, and encouraging shared ownership.

Collegiality, when rooted in *agape* love, becomes more than a social skill; it is a theo-logical act. It mirrors the unity-in-diversity of the Triune God and offers the church a com-pelling witness to the reconciling power of the Gospel. In an age of fragmentation, scholars who practice collegiality faithfully help the church recover its vocation as a body—many members, one Spirit, and a shared call to love.

Collegiality in the church is not merely a social strategy; it is a theological imperative grounded in the Gospel of Jesus Christ. As members of one body, we are called to engage in shared ministry, mutual support, and spiritual growth. This collective effort requires more than cooperation—it demands a posture of love, humility, and deep respect for the Holy Spirit's work in each individual. Collegiality, then, is both the method and the goal of Christian community: a means by which the church becomes a visible sign of God's reconcilia-tory work in the world. When practiced with intentionality and faith, collegiality reflects the very nature of the Triune God—diverse in personhood yet unified in purpose—and becomes a witness to the transformative power of Christ among his people.

Concentration: A Scholarly Virtue for a Distracted Church

A vital but often overlooked scholarly habit that holds profound significance for both the Academy and the church is concentration. In a world awash with digital me-dia, relentless multitasking, and constant notifications, the ability to focus has become increasingly rare and precious. These cultural patterns of distraction not only affect indi-viduals during worship services, sermons, and personal spiritual disciplines, but they also infiltrate the institutional life of the church itself. As congregations attempt to navigate an entertainment-driven, fast-paced culture, traditional rhythms of worship and formation are frequently dismissed as tedious or irrelevant. Consequently, churches often feel com-pelled to adopt gimmicks or reinvent their identity in pursuit of engagement, potentially diluting their core mission and exhausting their members with overly busy calendars and diffuse priorities.

Within this context, the academic life offers a powerful counterexample. The prac-tice of concentration is the lifeblood of scholarly vocation. Every semester, educators make strategic decisions about what content to prioritize, how to structure learning, and which topics must be deferred. Scholars are trained to hold fast to the larger mission of education despite political, social, or economic disruptions. As Amos Yong reminds us, we pursue learning not merely as an intellectual exercise but as a vocation shaped by beauty, truth, and virtue—even amidst the instability of our time.[10]

Scholars can model this same discipline of concentration within the church. Our expe-riences sitting through—and delivering—countless lectures, both engaging and otherwise, have taught us the value of attentiveness. If we expect students to offer their presence and attention, then we, too, must embody that same posture during worship. Attentive body language, mindful listening, and deep engagement with Scripture and liturgy can serve as quiet yet powerful testimonies to the importance of presence in a distracted age. In treating church services with the same seriousness we expect in the classroom, we dignify both the speaker and the gathered body.

Beyond modeling personal concentration, scholars can also contribute to the structural clarity of the church's mission. We are uniquely positioned to ask clarifying questions about vision, strategy, and execution. What is the church truly called to do? How do its current programs align with its theological commitments? Is there coherence between the stated mission and the actual calendar? All too often, churches embrace a breadth of programming that leaves leaders burned out and congregants fatigued. The oft-quoted maxim that "20% of the people do 80% of the work" is symptomatic of deeper issues: unexamined assumptions about effectiveness, unchecked activity, and a failure to prioritize.

In contrast, the academic mindset understands the necessity of limitation. No professor can cover the entirety of a discipline in one semester; therefore, we choose wisely, teach deeply, and trust the process of formation over time. The church can benefit from this wisdom. Scholars can help local congregations streamline their activities, pruning excess in order to concentrate on practices that truly form disciples and embody the church's mission. This is not about doing less for the sake of convenience, but instead about doing less for the sake of doing what matters most.

In an age of fragmentation, the church needs more than clever strategies or novel programming—it needs a renewed capacity for holy concentration. Scholars, with their cultivated habits of focused study and disciplined inquiry, are uniquely equipped to help the church recover this virtue. By embodying attentiveness in worship, asking hard questions about mission, and resisting the allure of endless activity, we can help the church resist cultural currents of distraction and rediscover the depth and beauty of its calling.

Concentration is not merely a mental discipline; it is a spiritual posture. It calls us to be fully present to God, to one another, and to the tasks entrusted to us. In modeling this posture, scholars can become agents of renewal—quietly yet persistently guiding the church toward a deeper, more purposeful, and more faithful witness in the world. Let us then offer the gift of our focused presence, believing that in doing so, we help others see more clearly the One who calls us to a life of worship, wisdom, and love.

Conclusion

Ultimately, bridging the gap between the Academy and the church will require mutual humility and imagination. Church leaders must broaden their vision of Christian vocation to affirm the intellectual life as a legitimate and vital expression of faithfulness. At the same time, scholars must be willing to serve with patience and discernment, finding ways to embody curiosity, collegiality, and concentration in the shared life of the church. In doing so, they may help reawaken in the church a more expansive theology of learning—one that honors not only those who preach and teach theology, but also those who labor in the diverse fields of human knowledge, bearing witness to the breadth of God's truth in the world.

Chapter 53

Exposi-story Preaching

JOHN R. KATSION

Response Summary: This essay takes Mark Noll's charge for evangelicals to develop a deep reading of Scripture by encouraging preachers to preserve biblical narratives in their original story form rather than reducing them to traditional three-point sermons, using a method called exposi-story preaching. This author demonstrates the primacy of stories in Scripture, Jesus's extensive use of narrative teaching, and how humans are neurologically hardwired for stories rather than abstract propositions. The proposed exposi-story methodology combines expository verse-by-verse analysis with narrative's inherent power through thorough contextual research, identifying the story's main point(s), crafting vivid details, and making applications naturally within the story's flow rather than forcing artificial divisions. This approach trusts the Holy Spirit and narrative's power to transform listeners' hearts, ultimately encouraging preachers to simply tell the story.

I WANT TO ENCOURAGE practitioners of the art of preaching to think about using a method I like to call "exposi-story" preaching or, to put it more simply, just *tell the story*. So often in preaching, pastors and teachers take a beautiful story found in Scripture and then turn it into a three-point speech with an introduction and a conclusion. But it was written as a story, and when we make that conversion, we destroy the power of the story. Instead of keeping it as a story, we squeeze it into what we are used to: a speech with main points a congregation or an audience can remember.

Mark Noll, writing in *The Scandal of the Evangelical Mind*, observed, "Finally, if evangelicals are ever to cultivate the mind, habits of intuitionism—the rapid movement from first impressions to final conclusions—must be changed."[1] He goes on to encourage a deep reading of Scripture, stating that

> [t]o realize that the Bible is narrow ('these are written that you may believe that Jesus is the Christ') is to make it deep—like a well dug down and down until it refreshes all those who draw from it for every task of life. To pursue the Bible, as it reveals God-in-human-flesh, is to find not just Christ but the world that Christ created, the humanity that he joined, and the beauty that he embodied in himself.

To move from a broad to a deep reading of the Bible might be a hard thing, but picking up the book was even harder.[2]

I believe exposi-story preaching, by insisting on engaging with the narrative form found in Scripture, pushes back against the oversimplification and reductionism Noll laments while allowing for a more thorough contextualization and examination of the Word. I hope this method encourages speakers and preachers to resist the temptation of intuitionism and not reduce the beauty and complexity of a biblical story down to a three-point "how-to" sermon.

I believe that what we need to do instead is tell the story as written in Scripture because it was written in that form. It will have a power and way of connecting with an audience that will be missed if we take it from its story form and put it into the form of a Western-style three-point speech. This method I have called exposi-story preaching. I believe this delivery method remains true to the particular passage laid out in Scripture, while preserving the power of the original form.

This essay will lay the preliminary groundwork for the exposi-story method. To do that, I will first examine the primacy of the narrative form in the Bible; then, I will ask the question: Why? Why would the God of the universe use narrative as his primary means of communication? In answering that question, I will demonstrate that one of the powers of narrative is that it is made for the way God created our brains to think and process information. And if that is true, why do we turn these stories into expositional speeches? It destroys the very power that God intended for that story. This essay ends by providing a brief overview of the exposi-story method.

The Primacy of Story in the Bible

Professor of Systematic Theology Jo Ann Davidson, in writing about the use of narrative in Scripture, writes: "Biblical narrative is not an inconsequential part of Scripture. Indeed, it is a major literary form."[3] The Bible Project, a leading producer of educational videos about Scripture, states that narrative makes up a whopping 43% of the Bible.[4]

As another evidence of the primacy of story, look no further than Jesus. He, the master teacher, used stories extensively in his teaching ministry. One form his use of story took was his use of parables, which the Gospel of Mark points out Jesus never taught without (see Mark 4:34). Now, his use of parables was often used as a form of judgment, obscuring the Gospel's message to those who would not listen. However, parables simultaneously revealed the Gospel's truth in compelling and fruitful ways for those with spiritual eyes and ears to hear it (see Matt. 13:10–13). Matthew Henry, a Presbyterian theologian, and pastor said this about Jesus's use of parables: "he preached by parables, because thereby the things of God were made plainer and easier to them who were willingly ignorant; and thus the Gospel would be a *savour of life* to some, and *of death* to others."[5]

Whether for judgment or enlightenment, parables allowed Jesus to use the power of the story to change listeners' lives. During his earthly ministry he spoke between 35 and 40 parables, depending upon definition.[6] These stories involved plot twists, compelling characters, images, and situations listeners could relate to—all aspects of great storytelling. Jesus used the power of story and was considered a great teacher who taught in compelling ways and with authority. So if nearly half of the Bible is in narrative form and Jesus himself taught with story, why did God choose to work this way to convey spiritual truth? The answer is that the God who created us knows that humans are built for stories.

Modern neurological research is beginning to reveal that the human brain is hardwired to be particularly receptive to narrative forms of communication. They have found that sensory, motor, and emotional regions light up in brain scans when people listen to a story, showing that when a person hears a story, they react as if they are experiencing those events for the first time.[7] The brain engages in neuro-coupling when listening to a story, which means that the brains of the storyteller and listener are synchronized. Hasson et.al. explain neuro-coupling this way "the neural processes in one brain are coupled to the neural processes in another brain via the transmission of a signal through the environment."[8] As the speaker tells their story the regions that are lighting up in their brain begin to light up in the audiences' brains leading to brain synchronization or neuro-coupling. Matt Johnson, writing in *Psychology Today*, states it simply: "When you're the speaker, your goal is to replicate the same pattern of brain activity that you have in your head inside the head of your conversational partner."[9] This neuro-coupling leads to an enhanced understanding from the audience.[10]

Studies of the brain have also revealed that stories help us in pattern recognition and memory, which means we remember a story far better than just cold, hard facts.[11] Finally, brain researchers have found that stories trigger a chemical called oxytocin, which leads to feelings of empathy and fosters a bond between the speaker and the listener. Neuroscience confirms that the human brain is not just receptive to stories but is fundamentally organized to process, remember, and share information in narrative form. This hardwiring explains why stories are powerful for communication, learning, empathy, and social cohesion.[12]

The reality that humans are bent on a good story is supported not only by neuroscience, but also by intellectual developments in the subjects of argumentation and reason. In developing the narrative paradigm, Walter Fisher renamed humanity *homo narrans*, declaring that "[t]he idea of human beings as storytellers indicates the generic form of all symbolic composition . . . symbols are created and communicated ultimately as stories meant to give order to human experience."[13] He argues that we make decisions based on whether the story someone has told us holds up to scrutiny rather than for just rational reasons. We decide if the story has good reasons by applying the tests of narrative probability and narrative fidelity. I believe God chose the narrative form because he knew that is what moves us, and to persuade us of his truth, he needed to tell good stories. So if it is true that humanity is physically and socially constructed to be persuaded and moved by stories, why would we want to change that form when wrestling with the stories of the Bible? What I want to offer next is a method of delivery for narrative passages in the Bible that preserves the author's original intent while keeping the form the story inhabits. I call this method exposi-story preaching.

Expository preaching is a tried-and-true method of preaching that is defined as the "communication of a biblical concept derived from and transmitted through a historical-grammatical and literary study of a passage in its context, which the Holy Spirit first applies to the personality and experience of the preacher then through him to hearers."[14]

Expository preaching begins with a passage. It develops a proposition based on that text. Next the preacher then shows how the ideas in the text help support the proposition, or the "big idea" that they are wanting to convey to their congregants.[15] It takes as its starting point a specific text, which is part of a larger expositional project. The goal of the preacher may be to preach through a particular book in the Bible verse by verse, or to just deal with one passage but still go through it verse by verse. What the preacher of narrative needs to do is to keep the concept of expositional preaching while maintaining the storytelling form. So how does one do it? This is where I want the speaker to think of exposi-story delivery.

First, the preacher begins with the story. It is good to remember that a story contains the following: exposition, rising action, climax, falling action, and resolution. To tell a great story, it should involve all five elements, and when interpreting the passage, you need to see all five elements in it.

Once the passage is chosen, the preacher needs to study the theological meaning of the story but will also need to research the passages' historical and cultural contexts to bring life and color to the story. I like to think of filling in all the facts that are there but are not explicitly stated. For instance, I am interested in the length or look of the objects the characters are using. I am very interested in distances and time: how far is this town from where the character came from, what elevations they covered, and so on. I am interested in any cultural customs that would be important to remember, such as eating times, relations between men and women, fathers and children, the type of money they used, to name but a few. I want to build up the historical and cultural context of this story.

Once I do that, I try to establish the main point of this story: Why is this story here at this place in the larger story of the book or the even larger story of the Bible? Finding out the story's main point helps me see the flow of the story or any minor applications that might be occurring on the way to the big idea of the passage. If one main point does not come out, though, I do not worry, as maybe there is not a main point I need to make. Maybe the point of the story is for multiple points to come out, and those need to be addressed instead. Remember, we are trying not to force the story into some Western notion of propositional speaking. However, since a lot of narrative in the Bible is written to make a point, sometimes a single point can be found, but be open to there not being one and having multiple applications. All in all, the reason for the story needs to be fully in mind, whether there is one or multiple.

Once I have done this preliminary research, I begin to envision in my mind the world this story lives in. In many ways, I start to create a movie of this story in my mind. I then write that movie down as a story, using word choices that help the audience imagine the world that the story is creating. I use the details I fleshed out from the context to build the world the story inhabits.

Like any great movie, I start with a hook: What would hook the audience into watching this movie or listening to my story? Maybe I begin with a scary scene near the end of the story or in the middle of the story. After describing the scene, I ask the audience how they got here, who this person is, and why they are in this predicament. Following this, I go back and begin at the beginning of the story. That is one hook I often use. Many Bible stories are compelling enough and have their own natural hook; either way, I need to think of a way to get my audience involved and grab their attention.

Once I grab the audience's attention, I then tell the story. I try to apply good methods of storytelling, one of which is detail: the more detailed your description of the scene, the characters, and the events, the better the story. Seasoned writer and storyteller September Fawkes's advice to writers is just as applicable to preachers when telling a story: "Appealing to the senses and attention to detail is what will ground your reader and bring your story to life. Details often make it so that your reader experiences your story, instead of just reading about it."[16] Another thing I do is reference the text while telling the story. I will cite a specific verse that helps to point out the details of the story as found in Scripture. It also adds to the expositional nature of my storytelling and the fact that I am not making this story up out of thin air. As a storyteller, I am constrained by the text's boundaries. I will let my imagination soar, but only as far as the text of Scripture allows.

I type this story out, and I write like I am speaking. After writing out the story as it unfolds like a movie in my brain, I go back and look for moments of application. Are there moments in this story that lend themselves to congregational application? Are those applications in the text, or am I forcing those applications into the text? A good example is from the story of the prophet Elijah found in 1 Kings. In chapter 19 verses 1–9, we meet Elijah running out of fear from Jezebel and her threat to kill him. He is scared and disappointed in God and Israel and finds himself in the middle of the desert of Horeb. Here, God asks him to rest under a broom tree. He does and falls asleep. He then wakes up, and an angel is there and asks him to eat some food, and drink some water, and then go back to sleep, for he has a long journey ahead of him. Elijah then wakes up and begins a 40-day trek to the mountain of God. At this moment in the story, it feels natural to apply ideas about rest and how your body needs a break, and if you do not get enough rest, you will fall into depression, just as Elijah did here. That seems to fit the story, and I have heard two sermons with that application at that moment in the story. But my question is this: is that application intended by the original writer of the story? Did the writer tell the story in this way so that, at that point, the original readers would make the connection that God expects us to get enough rest to not fall into depression and discouragement as Elijah did?

I do not think the writer meant for that application, and in my opinion, at that point, you are forcing the story to say something it was never intended to say. But when a natural part of the story, these applications can be very powerful moments in the sermon. So how should the preacher apply this moment in the story? Should they apply it all and just keep on telling the story? Those questions are out of the scope of this essay, and ultimately, that is up to the speaker and the Holy Spirit to decide. I also want to clarify that I do not wait until the end of the story to make those applications, I make them in the moment as the story unfolds. But there are times I have preached sermons where I have not applied any part of the story at the moment, rather leaving it to the Holy Spirit and the story to do its work. It is a hard thing to do as someone brought up on Western notions of speech construction, but I want to do more of it. I believe if I trusted God, the Holy Spirit, and the power of narrative, I would do it more.

This leads me to the biggest point I would like to get across with the exposi-story method, and that point is this: *try just telling the story*. The expositional sermon, proclaiming the Word of God verse by verse through a book is the foundation upon which good preaching rests. I am asking you not to abandon that approach but instead to change the form you fit that approach into. If it is a story, keep that form. Try not to turn the story into three main points with a poem in the conclusion. Instead, try telling the story. God wrote many of his truths in story form; let the story God wrote do its work. Tell the story.

At the end of one of my exposi-story sermons one Sunday, an elementary-aged girl walked up to me with her mom and dad in tow and said, "Thank you for making the Bible interesting and in a way I can understand." And that is something that I think is sad. God wrote a lot of Scripture in such a way that all ages can understand, but we often mess it up. This is a telling fact: I never have to explain to kids what I am doing when I preach to them through story; in contrast, I always must explain in advance to my adult audiences what I am doing; otherwise, they think I am talking down to them. But I keep thinking: if a story is good enough for God, it should be good enough for us. And what happened to us adults that we cannot enjoy a good story anymore? I believe it is still there; we just need to start recovering the art of storytelling in our preaching.

And remember that there is a grand story that God is telling in the Bible, and we are part of it. It starts in Genesis and ends in Revelation. It is a wonderful story full of many ups and downs, setbacks and successes, culminating in the greatest act of mercy accomplished by Jesus on the cross. It is a story that starts with a fall but ends in redemption. It is a story begun by one man bringing sin into the world and ends with one man dying on the cross but rising triumphantly from the grave and who one day will return as King of Kings and Lord of Lords. We are part of that story that one day will end, but with Jesus, we then begin a new story, or as C. S. Lewis so eloquently put it in *The Last Battle*: "All their life in this world and all their adventures in Narnia had only been the cover and the title page: now at last they were beginning Chapter One of the Great Story which no one on earth has read: which goes on forever: in which every chapter is better than the one before."[17]

Chapter 54

The Role of Christian Magazines in Christian Scholarship

KEN WATERS

Response Summary: Building on the foundational analyses of Mark Noll and George Marsden regarding the challenges and marginalization of evangelical scholarship, this essay advocates for expanding the reach of Christian academic work beyond traditional outlets. Waters echoes Noll's call to engage the broader public square and addresses the persistent lack of recognition for Christian scholarship within churches and society. He proposes that evangelical magazines—such as *The Christian Post*, *Christianity Today*, *Sojourners*, and *World*—serve as vital platforms for disseminating research and fostering dialogue. By leveraging these publications, scholars can influence opinion leaders, enrich congregational understanding, and contribute to the ongoing narrative of faith's interaction with culture and politics. Waters concludes that Christian magazines not only propagate ideas but also provide valuable primary sources for scholarly research and historical analysis.

I RECENTLY HAD two reactions to Mark Noll's analysis of evangelical scholarship decades after he and George Marsden's groundbreaking books. The first centers on the need for us to widen the lens of our scholarship and address areas where faith and the public square interact. Of the lack of recognition for our scholarship, Noll told the 2024 Christianity and Communication Studies Network (CCSN) unconference that:

> Such a lack of attention indicates the need for those interested in Christian learning and committed to the life of the mind as believers to consider the broader landscape in which ideas, arguments, and meaningful discussions occur. The churches have not been welcoming places for that kind of wider dissemination.[1]

In other words, let's find ways to engage more people with our research and analysis results. It is still an unfortunate fact that many church-goers are not receptive to the life of the mind we represent, even after some 30-plus years of our excellent research and publishing of books and academic articles.

So how do we reach evangelicals with what we feel are research observations and analyses that can enrich their lives, their churches, and our culture, politics, and society? We need to find more avenues for disseminating our scholarship than just in our classrooms or through an occasional journal article or scholarly book read by a handful of like-minded scholars. Noll challenges us with this statement:

> However, good quality work will not have the kind of impact it could have if no attention is paid to the means of propagation, publicity, and presentation of solid work worldwide. Although there are some healthy signs, Christian academics and scholars have been slow to realize how important it is to think about communicating in the broader realm.[2]

Reaching Beyond the Gates of Academia

I want to suggest a partial answer to this dilemma and suggest that evangelical scholars consider this source of wider publicity as a source of information and observation that can enrich our studies. Regarding the first suggestion, Greg Spencer provides a partial answer in his presentation to the unconference when he notes that Christians should contribute to and promote the works of public intellectuals whose influence extends beyond academia and the church. He lauds thinkers such as Wendell Berry and David Brooks, among others, for their work published in *The Atlantic*, *First Things*, and *The Wall Street Journal*. Here, he says, are potential landing sites for well-argued and occasionally outrageous thinking by Christians engaging with our culture's big ideas (and the influential decision-makers).

As a way of extending Spencer's suggestion, I recommend we include evangelical magazines in this mix of outlets for reasoned, accessible commentary on current events as seen from a Christian worldview. This recommendation is based on my recent research on the content found in four evangelical news and commentary publications.[3] The four I studied—*The Christian Post*, *Christianity Today*, *Sojourners*, and *World*—aim to educate and encourage opinion leaders within the evangelical movement. Millions of online page views are recorded monthly for just these four publications. Millions more readers engage with other publications for Protestant and Catholic believers. Within the pages and pixels of these publications, one can find top-notch thinking where the Christian worldview is fused with insight into the events of the day, week, month, or year.[4]

Other publications providing insight into conservative Christian thinking include The Gospel Coalition's website, whose audience is primarily Reformed believers. Religion News Service functions similarly to the Associated Press by providing news articles on a subscription basis to various publications. *First Things*, founded by public theologian Richard Neuhaus in 1989, is an Institute for Religion and Public Life imprint. *Charisma* is read mainly by charismatic evangelicals. *Relevant* started as a publication meeting the needs of younger Christians. *Christian Century* caters to a more progressive wing of Protestantism, much as *Sojourners* centers its focus on evangelicals concerned with peace, justice, and an end to oppression worldwide. So far, I have mentioned publications targeted mainly toward White Christians, although *Christianity Today* increasingly features articles of interest to people of color written by people of color and faithfully describes itself as impacting Christian communities of color.

Communication scholar Quentin Schultze argues that Christian media—magazines, radio talk shows, podcasts, and the like have fostered a rhetoric of communication and discernment for believers. "In the United States," he writes, "the religious press has been one of the most important vehicles for bringing people of faith into a shared public space to converse about the broader society."[5] As these media extended their influence, they also extended a conversation about topics of concern across time and space, ethnicity, theology, doctrine, and social class. "Tribal journals extend the specialized conversations across geographic space, organize collective sentiment, focus the discussion, and somewhat centralize the ways that the participants imagine their faith in the world," he adds.[6] Sometimes the information comes from writers or editors assuming a prophetic role, providing "an ongoing critique of the life of the church and the wider society."[7]

Evangelical Christian newspapers and magazines predate the American Republic. The earliest publications printed news about the homeland (England) gathered from arriving ship crews. They also reprinted sermons by well-known evangelists residing in the Colonies or visiting from Great Britain. In the early days of the Republic, until the present, evangelical publications have also shared news of advocacy campaigns attempting to support special causes. Publications against slavery and alcohol consumption, and promoting worldwide missions, women's rights, and the eradication of poverty and slavery, appealed to Christian readers. "Abolitionism was a religious movement, emerging from the ferment of evangelical Protestantism," claims historian Richard Hofstadter.[8] "The profusion of anti-slavery and abolitionist books, newspapers, pamphlets, reports, printed speeches and other publications which appeared in those three decades were an essential feature of this evangelical movement," he adds.[9]

Today, a handful of evangelical publications, like those I studied, can move the needle on public discussion, interjecting a credible biblical perspective. One need only consider the public reaction, not to mention that of President Donald Trump, when Mark Galli, then editor of *Christianity Today*, used biblical values and Scripture to encourage the U.S. Senate to convict the president of "high crimes and misdemeanors" during Trump's first impeachment in 2019.[10] *Sojourners* and its leadership, specifically Adam Taylor and Jim Wallis, also called for Trump's impeachment. Trump certainly raised the public profile of *CT* when he took to Twitter to call the publication a "far left magazine" and declared that "[n]o President has done more for the evangelical community, and it's not even close."[11]

Calling for the removal of Trump, which contradicts the generally accepted viewpoint of his popularity among the faithful, may not be the encouragement some scholars need to consider submitting an opinion article to one of these or other Christian magazines. But it does illustrate that opinion articles published in the evangelical press are not all apologies for the Religious Right. Academic pollsters synthesizing the results of their studies are among those contributors who are often published in Christian magazines. So, too, are Christian philosophers and ethicists. Perhaps the easiest way to increase the number of discussions based on our scholarly discoveries is to submit our analyses and conclusions from our research and academic efforts to these publications.

The pastors and lay leaders who subscribe to evangelical publications are important in disseminating the practical applications of Christian scholarship to their congregations. We know from the Two-step and the Multi-step Flow Theories of Communication that opinion leaders, such as pastors, can play an essential role in passing on what they have learned to others. Suppose pastors possess the knowledge and nuanced analyses found in Christian publications. In that case, they may feel more emboldened to help their congregations understand how the Bible interacts with the issues of the public square in our divided society. In doing so, pastors may ensure that our outrageous scholarship, if more of it finds its way into these publications, becomes knowledge Christians need to grow in their relationship to God and for their leavening influence on society. A straightforward suggestion is that those who create Christian scholarship subscribe to a few evangelical publications and gift those subscriptions to their pastors.

Magazines' Contribution to Scholarship

One final observation from the remarks of Noll and Spencer is that evangelical publications represent a fertile source for research and discovery. The holy grail of historical and rhetorical research is to find and analyze primary sources such as diaries and letters. Evangelical magazines may also provide essential and valuable resources for our studies. Yes, these publications are curated, and editors and publishers may influence the presentation of the facts and observations they contain. But it is important to note that the publications often present credible, fact-based information and analysis. Their editorial leadership possesses a minimum of a bachelor's degree in the liberal arts or business. Usually, their top staff hold a theology degree. That alone does not guarantee the trustworthiness of their observations or the opinions they express, of course, but should put their content on an even playing field with that contained in the nation's other public information sources. Additionally, the perspectives and concerns of millions of conservative Christians are not presented by prominent national news outlets. When they are presented, the narrative is often skewed by bias or inadequate understanding of the deeply nuanced Christian worldview.

Today, the best publications for rhetoricians and historians to study for accurate and fair news from a Christian perspective are independent of a denominational or advocacy agency ownership. It certainly is true that every news and opinion site—mainstream and religious—is subject to censorship or meddling by its owners, as we have seen in recent incidents involving the *Los Angeles Times* and *The Washington Post*. However, Christian media owned and operated by an independent board of directors is slightly likelier to publish, free from potential meddling by an individual owner or an activist board member with a strong ideological bent. For the most part, even though Christian publications approach their news and opinion essays from a Christian worldview, they still insist that their writers hew to established journalistic values of accuracy, fairness, and openness to potential dialogue with those who disagree with their fact-finding or viewpoints.

Scholars may also find surprises in their reading and research into the content of Christian publications. For instance, from 2015 to 2025, a period dominated by Donald Trump's influence, the publications provided nuanced and sometimes contradictory narratives to our generally accepted beliefs, cultivated by mainstream news articles that treat evangelicals as a mass movement fully supportive of President Trump and his policies. That is not always the case. Indeed, the pushback against some of these political moves is infused with biblical reasons why Christians should oppose them.

Additionally, these publications provide information of importance to the church when mainstream publications do not. *Christianity Today* generally avoided "investigative" news stories involving other Christian ministries.[12] But in 2020, it published a series of articles exposing the sexual misdeeds of the late evangelist Ravi Zacharias.[13] The magazine's editors explained: "*Christianity Today* doesn't undertake the long and expensive work of investigating accusations to create a list of notorious sinners. Our aim is correction, not just of the leaders we're reporting on, but of all of us."[14] A few years later, the magazine turned its lens on itself, admitting that over 12 years, it allowed a pattern of sexual harassment by two men: its just-retired editor, Mark Galli, and former advertising director Olatokunbo Olawoye.[15] *Christianity Today* published the full text of an external investigation commissioned by its Board of Directors, along with an explanation and apology from the company president.[16]

Until 2021, *World* called its editorial philosophy "biblical journalism." Coined by its long-time editor, Marvin Olasky, biblical journalism teaches writers to report news events through a lens of what the Bible says about human existence. His justification for this approach is that all news media reflect the bias of their writers, editors, and publishers. Olasky encouraged his writers to recognize their bias as Christians and to present the information, quotes, and other facts with accuracy and integrity, but to do so through the lens of a Christian worldview. "[This] reporting is designed to show readers the salient facts in Bible-based contextualization and allow them to agree or disagree with the conclusions reached," he said.[17] In his ground-breaking analysis of Christian journalism, he claimed that "[a] solidly Christian news publication should not be balanced. Its goal should be provocative and evocative, colorful and gripping, Bible-based news analysis."[18] Under Olasky, journalistic practices and values-informed news stories reported from the scene on many interesting issues. One distinctive of such an approach is that it "provides necessary insight for believers in a culture that has taken pluralism to new heights and has often pushed what's been called traditional Christian values into minority status."[19]

Conclusion

Together, evangelical publications also give scholars insight into the rhetorical devices of a given era and what the late Phillip Graham, then owner of *The Washington Post*, called the first draft of history.[20] Scholars of the interaction of faith, politics, and culture should consult Christian magazines and online sites with the same zeal they pursue diaries, oral interviews, and personal correspondence of people they study.

As Noll notes, Christian scholarship is no longer an inherently scandalous idea. However, challenges remain if we are to widen the scope of our studies and, in particular, address areas where the public square interacts with our Christian faith. As Noll further notes, one of these challenges is disseminating the results of our study to believers. Even if churches and pastors seem hesitant or hostile to the notion that we should discuss current events, faith, the veracity of scientific observation, and critical thinking, Christian scholars need to ensure their discoveries and observations find acceptance from more evangelicals. I have suggested that Christian scholars take some time (even if it is not rewarded in the tenure and promotion process) to share the results of their study by writing articles for the Christian press. Additionally, with caution and discernment, we can share with pastors and church leaders the growth in the faithful that results from embracing the idea that Christian scholarship improves the lives of the faithful. Finally, when appropriate, consider consulting these Christian publications as a critical and valuable source of the first draft of history.

Chapter 55

Techne and Testimony: The Mandate for Christian Scholars in a Digital Age

Franklin Nii Amankwah Yartey

Response Summary: The author proposes practical ways for Christian scholars to engage in conversations shaping academic and civil discourse beyond the confines of the Academy. Drawing on St. Paul's Epistle to the Ephesians (4:7–13) describing the purpose and mission of teachers, the author argues that Christian scholars should actively use current social technologies to fulfill their calling. We must use the grace apportioned to us by Christ to "equip his people for works of service, so that . . . " (Eph. 4:12) we can fulfill the will of God and thus "become mature, attaining to the whole measure of the fullness of Christ" (Eph. 4:13). Building on Mark Noll's emphasis on the importance of "communicating in the broader realm," the author conceptualizes these social technologies as tools (*techne*) that align with God's plan for humanity.

IN HIS ADDRESS to the 2024 dialogic unconference held by the Christianity and Communication Studies Network (CCSN), prominent American historian Mark Noll acknowledges that Christian scholars do not dominate the academic and public sphere. However, there is now a large body of scholarship by individuals and groups identifying themselves as Christian scholars who strongly believe that their intentional thinking, creation, and shaping of pedagogy and research is a calling from God.[1] Noll adds that never in our nation's history have we seen what is happening now with Christian pedagogy and scholarship. It is now more critical than ever for Christian scholars and experts to affirm the importance of disseminating their work to a broader public by putting this into practice. In this short essay, I theorize and propose practical ways for Christian teachers and scholars to engage in the conversations that are shaping academic and civil discourse beyond the confines of the Academy. Specifically, I invite and encourage them to utilize social media platforms to share their ideas and engage with the broader public.

In his legacy lecture at the unconference, Noll states:

> It has taken me quite a while to realize that the American context constrains what academics can accomplish among academics, but even more in the world at large. There may be good quality thinking in the churches and by Christians in

the Academy. However, that good quality work will not have the kind of impact it could have if there is not also attention to the means of propagation, the means of publicity, the means of presentation of solid work in the world. Although there are some healthy signs, it seems to me that Christian academics, along with scholars in general, have been slow to realize how important it is to think about communicating in the broader realm.[2]

Social media is one channel through which to disseminate work to the public. Building on Noll's emphasis on the importance of "communicating in the broader realm," I conceptualize these social technologies as tools (*techne*) that must align with God's plan for humanity—serving as an Ark to advance his purposes rather than a Tower of Babel fostering self-serving division. Christian academics must explore where to disseminate or discuss their work to benefit society. As Noll asserts that "the American context constrains what [Christian] academics can accomplish," I want to expand this notion of the American context to include social media platforms because these are the platforms where most debates and conversations occur; for one's ideas to reach a larger number of people, it may be helpful to engage on these platforms. For their ideas to resonate beyond the Academy, platforms like X (formerly Twitter), TikTok, Facebook, Instagram, Snapchat, and Pinterest, among others, could be utilized. Many will argue that social media platforms such as TikTok or Instagram may not be the appropriate channels to disseminate Christian academic work because some platforms are associated with uncivil interactions. However, we live in an age where we are constantly sharing information "to a generation attuned to listening [and watching] rather than reading."[3]

The Challenges of Speaking in Social Media Spaces

It is not uncommon to believe that it is not simple to add one's voice to online conversations in the age of *The Death of Expertise*.[4] A belief we see sweeping social media platforms and online forums suggests that experts are not needed and that "almost any challenge, from running a lab to running a country, is relatively easy, and that almost anyone can do it if they watch enough YouTube videos."[5] Varying levels of hostility are shown toward experts, be they academics, politicians, or people who have been trained and possess specialized knowledge. According to Tom Nichols, author of *The Death of Expertise*, there is hostility toward established knowledge, and some believe that every opinion and subject is as good as any other.[6] Is this part of what Mark Noll means by *American context constraints*? These are some issues that academics face while engaging on these platforms. The abundance and almost limitless supply of good and bad information on the internet allows citizens to "mimic intellectual accomplishment by indulging in an illusion of expertise."[7]

As Christian academics, we must not be discouraged by these obstacles of social engagement; instead, we must focus on the mandate given to us by God. We do not encounter many stories of technology in the Bible, but we should not forget that in Genesis, God created the heavens and earth and deemed everything good. The matter that God created was taken by us (humans), and we, in turn, created many things, including technology. Though I do not consider technology as neutral as the Greek Orthodox do, I do agree it has the potential to be used as an instrument for good or evil. In Genesis, God instructed Noah to build an ark (technology) used as God instructed to save humankind.[8] Contrasting that technology with the Tower of Babel, in Genesis 11:4–5, the people decided to build a tower and they said to themselves, "Come, let us build ourselves a city, with a tower that reaches to the heavens, so that we may make a name for ourselves; otherwise we will be scattered over the face of the whole earth." God was not pleased with this technology, creating confusion among the people, which permanently halted their project. Since then, humans have created millions of tools, including social media platforms, used for good and evil. Though the church may not be an innovator of new technologies (from the era of the Gutenberg press to our digital revolution), it has always used these technologies to share the Gospel (for example, thousands of churches have a social media presence). Christian academics should therefore consider taking inspiration from this history and the opportunities presented to us by social media.

The Opportunities and Obligations to Speak in Social Media Spaces

It is critical for Christian academics to lead by example in disseminating and discussing their work through these social media platforms. I am not asking scholars to sign up for every social media platform but to consider picking one or two and establishing an online presence, creating a space where ideas can be shared in non-complex forms, and employing the techniques of storytelling to engage potential audiences.[9] Drawing on St. Paul's Epistle to the Ephesians (4:7–13) describing the purpose and mission of teachers, Christian scholars should actively use current social technologies to fulfill their calling. We must use the grace apportioned to us by Christ to "equip his people for works of service" (Eph. 4:12) so that we can fulfill the will of God and thus "become mature, attaining to the whole measure of the fullness of Christ" (Eph. 4:13). As Christian academics we have to start somewhere, and I invite you to discern which social media platform or public engagement forum best aligns with your temperament, vocation, and audience that will facilitate the sharing of your ideas.

The suggestion to sign up for a social media platform may be daunting for some, and social media is not for everybody; some choose to stay offline, and I respect that. However, for those of us who are a little adventurous, we are presented with an opportunity to build a community online and create a presence in the digital public square. While not all callings require social media engagement, Christian scholars, when appropriate, should consider employing current social technologies as part of their calling. Some examples of Christian scholars meaningfully engaged in online conversations include:

- Dr. Esau McCaulley, a contributing opinion writer for *The New York Times*, author, and associate professor of New Testament and public theology at Wheaton College.[10]

- The Reverend Tish Harrison Warren, a writer and an Anglican priest, former contributor to *The New York Times*.[11]

- Dr. Gavin Ortlund, a pastor, author, speaker, and apologist for the Christian faith.[12]

- Father Justin Sinaites, a Greek Orthodox monk and St. Catherine's Monastery librarian at Mount Sinai in Egypt. He has been digitizing a vast collection of ancient manuscripts and books to make them more accessible to academics.[13]

- Father Maximos Constas, a writer of numerous scholarly articles including "Attentiveness and Digital Culture."[14]

Across four social media platforms (X, Facebook, YouTube, and Instagram), author, professor, and public theologian Dr. Esau McCaulley has over 241,000 followers/subscribers. Some of them engage with him on various subjects based on the clips he shares from his podcast, which are not limited to conversations about culture, theology, history, politics, and the church.[15] He also amplifies the ideas of other scholars by sharing links to books by other Christian scholars, allowing his audience to engage with them. A medium like X that enables users to share short snippets of text and embedded video allows for various degrees of interactivity, allowing audiences to have a direct conversation with the authors.

Similarly, Anglican priest and author Tish Harrison Warren also has over 56,000 followers across three social media platforms (X, Facebook, and Instagram), where she has adapted to these digital mediums by having direct interactions with her followers and the public at large. Like Esau McCaulley, she shares excerpts from her writings and publications with a broader audience, engaging in public digital conversations.

Pastor, author, speaker, and apologist for the Christian faith, Dr. Gavin Ortlund, has over 177,000 followers/subscribers across four digital platforms (X, Facebook, Instagram, and YouTube). On YouTube, he creates content to help strengthen the church and engage culture.[16] Father Justin Sinaites has a public blog where he shares iconic images and snippets of information with the public, in addition to playing a leading role in digitizing manuscripts.[17] The Very Rev. Fr. Maximos Constas also runs a YouTube channel with over 179,000 subscribers where information is shared to further the mission of Orthodox Christianity.[18]

Given the limitations of some digital platforms, the Christian scholars discussed above have adapted to various mediums by tailoring their messages to resonate with their audiences, using accessible language, and creating both short video clips and long-form videos on platforms like YouTube and X to connect with them. They offer diverse perspectives on cultural issues and debates through a spiritual lens. True, theological depth is often lost when interacting on platforms like X, due to the restrictions on the number of words one can type at a time and the brevity of these digital mediums. Beyond these formal limitations, most people use social media to consume short pieces of information, and one runs the risk of non-engagement with audiences or followers if the information shared is too lengthy and does not resonate with a particular digital culture, such as X or Instagram. However, by utilizing these digital platforms, Christian scholars have a greater degree of editorial freedom, thereby bypassing traditional gatekeepers. Furthermore, having a digital presence is not all rosy, as some of these scholars have also experienced unwarranted criticism. For example,

Esau McCaulley shared a post promoting a yet-to-be-released book. Though an audience member had not read the book, that person decided to leave a negative comment for Esau McCaulley.[19] Tish Harrison Warren's X post on refugees also received quite a number of discouraging comments.[20] It is essential to note that by signing up to engage on these digital platforms, we relinquish some degree of privacy and open ourselves to potential negativity as well. But we must not forget that we also make ourselves accessible to those who will not have the opportunity to interact with us offline. Thus, we connect with a broader audience and open ourselves to learning from others.

Despite the drawbacks of these platforms, these Christian scholars appear to be thriving on social media; they continue to gain new followers and subscribers, and they also receive positive feedback from their audiences. For example, one of Gavin Ortlund's followers, Bruce Clark, writes:

> Dr. Ortlund, I am a recent "follower" having discovered your video dialog with Dr. Cooper over baptismal regeneration. I am a minister of the Gospel, Southern Baptist, and have been in dialog with a couple of friends who have recently left the Baptist tradition and become Lutherans. After spending quite a bit of time in dialog with them, I came across your video and larger body of work. Your position on baptism is nearly identical to my own. I will be reviewing more of your work and I appreciate your graciousness in dialog on these issues. Thank you for your service![21]

The comment above illustrates that Dr. Ortlund is providing value to his followers and is successful in connecting with his audiences. These Christian scholars (Dr. Esau McCaulley, Tish Harrison Warren, Father Justin Sinaites, Dr. Gavin Ortlund, and Rev. Fr. Maximos Constas) have created online communities where they not only practice digital theology and share faith-based information but also extend their pastoral care within these digital platforms. These scholars among many not identified in this piece, demonstrate that Christian academics can thrive in online digital spaces despite the uncivil language and behavior that pervades them. Their engagements online invite us to consider how we can also meaningfully contribute to the various digital conversations. We must use the grace given to us by Christ to share the message of God through our inventions (scholarship and intellectual ideas). In so doing, we must also strive to think, critique, write, and engage in conversations not just from a Christian framework as Noll proposes but also be willing to do this from other frameworks.[22]

In Acts 17:16–34, we read of Paul engaging the philosophers at the Areopagus in Athens. Paul's conversation with the philosophers is an illustrative example, and Christian academics should also consider engaging with mainstream scholars, publications, and media conversations. There is a need for them to establish themselves as rigorous thinkers and credible scholars. As I have indicated in the previous paragraph, several scholars are doing this, which is inspiring. As the philosopher, diplomat, and politician Charles Malik said, there is "infinite value of spending years of leisure in conversing with the greatest minds and souls of the past and thereby ripening and sharpening and enlarging [. . .] powers of thinking."[23] We must be willing to step out of our epistemic bubbles to engage with others not of our faith without judgment.[24] By engaging other viewpoints, we invite others to do the same, so let us step into these digital spaces, not for our egos but for the glory of the One who called us to think, teach, and serve.

Chapter 56

Reflections on Pragmatics and Excellent Communication

ISAIAH LIN

Response Summary: In their respective ways, Wolterstorff's and Schultze's contributions in this collection call us to appreciate what is beyond mere words. The former case involves the occasional necessity of code-switching. The latter case involves the importance of Speech Act Theory. Part of the wisdom on offer in both cases is the insight that excellent communication goes beyond mere semantics. Drawing on H. P. Grice's work on conversational implicature, the author reflects on Schultze's recommendation to reframe "evangelical." The simple overarching point is that the mature Christian must master contextualization. Excellent communication turns on it.

IN OUR PRESENT MOMENT, the Christian call to excellence in communication feels weightier than ever. More and more it seems to hang on how well we are able to communicate. Failure to communicate well will stunt both our relationships as well as our witness. I am encouraged to see thoughtful Christians continuing to give the nature of communication scholarly attention.

In their own ways, Nicholas Wolterstorff's "Listening to the Call" and Quentin Schultze's "Five Root Assumptions for Communication Scholarship" both gesture at what is beyond the mere semantic contents of the words we use.[1] In the former case, we see the occasional necessity of *code-switching*—a kind of audience-based contextualization for a given message. In the latter case, we see the insights of Speech Act Theory, which is in part a recognition that communication is, at its heart, something we *do*. The phenomena here are distinct and so are the respective points that Wolterstorff and Schultze are making, but there is a shared wisdom on offer in both cases.

Shared Wisdom on Excellent Communication

Wolterstorff recalls a commonplace sort of occurrence in his courses at Yale, one in which a divinity student, having graduated from a Christian college, failed to appreciate the context of the Yale University classroom. This failure inevitably led to a negative reaction from the other students. By Wolterstorff's lights, this failure was the result of the student's having not yet learned how to speak in a language appropriate for the Yale philosophy classroom. "You can say approximately what you said, but you can't say it in those words," had been Wolterstorff's admonition to the student.[2] It was not a failure in content, but mode. The lesson is intuitive. Different social contexts require adherence to different linguistic norms. The excellent communicator understands these differences and masters how to negotiate them. Her success as a communicator depends on it.

Analogously, Schultze brings Speech Act Theory to bear on our assumptions regarding the nature of human communication. Once the Christian sees that speech is something we *do*, we immediately recognize a host of natural implications, most notably about responsibility—toward the Creator, creation, others, and ourselves. Importantly, we therein see that speech, like any other action, is a way to express our fundamental purpose: to love God and to love others. Any action which fails in this regard is an unmitigated failure. So the excellent communicator loves by way of his speech. Indeed his success as a communicator depends on it.

I think we can now see in plain view that the above two insights give us a third. Even if communication is largely about accurately transmitting information, and a purely semantic account can be given for its success, it does not follow that communicating well is a purely semantic phenomenon. Wolterstorff appreciates this in referencing the role of social context. Schultze appreciates this in referencing the moral ends of our speech acts. Both recognize that excellent communication—the kind we are to strive for—goes beyond mere semantics or locution. The Christian call to excellence here makes demands not just on the content of our speech, but the mode of presentation—and not just on what we say, but the end for which we say it.

Pragmatics and Excellent Communication

As we take seriously what true communicative success includes, I think we will find that H. P. Grice's work on implicature is illuminating.[3] Grice famously offers a theory which explains and predicts conversational implicatures, acts of meaning one thing while saying another. One reason his work is helpful here is that it explains how pragmatics help to determine what speakers communicate in speech. A core insight in the theory is that communication is collaborative. Speakers and listeners cooperate to achieve effective communication. Grice's observation is that communication often depends not on what is literally said, but on what is meant in context. I think this expands the shared wisdom from above. One substantive implication of this is that if we are blind to certain conversational features, such as what our audience antecedently believes or present social goings-on, we can accidentally communicate something we do not intend. So the excellent communicator must not only master the mode of presentation and speak for the right ultimate ends but must also have a keen awareness of her conversational context and milieu.

I think we can bring all of this to bear on one of Greg Spencer's concerns in "An Outrageous Scandal." Spencer notes that the term "evangelical" is now so saturated with problematic sociopolitical baggage that Christians face the question of whether or not to dispense with it altogether. It seems to me the Gricean insight reveals how deep the problem might be. When a term like "evangelical" evokes a host of unintended implications, reframing may not be a live solution, especially if what that amounts to is simply intending something else as we use the term. The speaker must reckon with what the hearer hears, which for better or worse is largely shaped by the sociopolitical world outside of our churches. And if a word has become so contextually laden with negative associations that it no longer functions effectively—or worse, functions counterproductively—maybe what we ought to do is not to fight for its semantic purity but find language that better achieves our ultimate ends. I personally do not know whether we have arrived at that point or not. Either way, I say the master communicator appropriately thinks beyond his own intentions to the way his speech lands on his audience.

Conclusion

So what are we to do? If my analysis is more or less accurate, the problem is largely pragmatic, rather than semantic. Ultimately, the problem lies primarily in what "evangelical" signals in various contexts, which we would be wise to consider. Further specification of what we mean when we use the term runs the risk of missing the problem altogether. It stands to reason then that a viable solution will also be largely pragmatic, rather than semantic.

I think we have made some philosophical progress here, but I do not have a sophisticated, pragmatic solution to offer. I do not have an unsophisticated one either. I hope those much smarter than me continue to discuss these things. In the meantime, while we prayerfully seek such a solution, whether we use the word "evangelical" or not, I will remind us that our fundamental burden is the same—to be faithful and to love. Perhaps the most fitting way to end this reflection is simply to reiterate the practical, Christian wisdom that Wolterstorff, Schultze, and Spencer themselves give us. Treat all interlocutors with dignity. Honor everyone. Responsibly serve your audiences. Seek shared understanding. Reassert the roles of wisdom and character. And do it all with excellence.

Chapter 57

Cross-fertilizing the Evangelical Mind in the Current Media Age

Joshua D. Hill

Response Summary: Hill examines Noll's insight that a healthy evangelical mind requires cross-fertilization between different groups, especially between evangelical academics and non-academics. This cross-fertilization has become more difficult, Hill claims both because choosing the right medium has become difficult and because the culture has shifted toward an oral-aural mindset, creating both communication and identification problems. By profession, academics preserve a literacy mindset, but lay, or non-academic, evangelicals operate more in an oral-aural mindset. Hill argues for "crucicentric" approaches (i.e., focused on the death of Christ on the cross and his resurrection) to these problems, recommending that academics draw on examples from evangelical missions and initiate more in-person conferences and gatherings that intentionally bring evangelical academics and non-academics together.

ONE KEY INSIGHT Mark Noll gives in his original *Scandal of the Evangelical Mind* and updates in this volume is that evangelicals need intellectual cross-fertilization to maintain a healthy mind. In his 1994 book, Noll explains that separating Christian colleges, evangelical seminaries, and secular universities provided "religious security" but lost the "ideal of Christian intellectual life in which theologians, biblical scholars, and scholars from other disciplines work in constant connection . . . promoting first-order reflection about the whole world under the lordship of the one true God."[1] We need interaction between these different evangelical spheres to love God with our shared evangelical mind.[2]

In his Legacy Scholar presentation, Noll sees the "most serious problem as the disconnect between the academic world and the churches," and he notes the modern reality that the intellectual life of the church is affected inordinately by social media, whose "masters . . . tend to be partisan, populist, conspiracy mongers for whom . . . disinterested scholarship is a dirty word."[3] Noll focused on intellectual cross-fertilization between spheres in academia in 1994, but now he sees the "most serious problem" as the interaction between evangelical academic and lay spheres, impaired by social media. Noll says,

[T]he churches mostly exist in a world where attitudes, outlooks, impressions, presuppositions, are dominated by what comes through social media and popular communications. It has taken me quite a while to realize that the American context constrains what academics can accomplish among academics, but even more in the world at large.[4]

Noll recommends that evangelical academics invest in communicating with pastors and lay evangelicals, crossing media and social boundaries to model the incisive questioning, adherence to evidence, caution in conclusions, humility in the face of contradiction, generosity of scholarly listening, and other aspects of the academic ethos that Noll portrays as essential to the evangelical mind.

I agree with Noll that the evangelical mind needs this cross-fertilization of intellectual perspectives across evangelical spheres. But current underlying factors make such communication across spheres more difficult: currently valued media distort complex issues, lay evangelical culture is harder to reach because of its shift toward orality, and this culture change makes disagreement dangerous and difficult to navigate. For each of these three complications informed by a Media Ecology framework,[5] I suggest "crucicentric" approaches that emphasize the medium over merely the message—incarnation and death to self over mere exposition. As Christ and his disciples communicated by modeling a "way of life," so also can evangelical scholars follow that same pattern in their cross-fertilizing communication.[6] Finally, I suggest academics do so using evangelical missions as a model and cross-group in-person conferences as a strategic tool from evangelical tradition.

The Media is the Mess in this Messy Age

Recognizing the impact of media forms, Noll says, "good quality work [of evangelical scholarship] will not have the kind of impact it could have if there is not also attention to the means of propagation, the means of publicity, the means of presentation of solid work in the world."[7] He mentions television as one of those "means,"[8] gesturing to the evangelical pattern of jumping to use each medium without also studying its impacts, from print to radio to the web to social media.[9] With Noll, we should ask which media are most apt to promote the life of the evangelical mind; that is, what medium or media of communication guide and support the habits of thought, habits of communication, and habits of socialization that create and maintain the kind of intellectual engagement Noll hopes for? Are we hoping for a renaissance of the printed, written medium (exemplified by this volume)? What about the democratized medium of short videos on YouTube, Vimeo, or even TikTok? Will those support the evangelical mind? Or perhaps the long-form podcast is the happy intersection between the discursive style of evangelical scholars and the new oral-aural habits of the population. And what about the medium of in-person face-to-face communication. Where does that fit in?

I argue that we should avail ourselves of the already-existing scholarship in Media Ecology before throwing energy into our Christian academic TikTok accounts aimed at local churches. Many Media Ecology scholars are implicitly or explicitly Christian in their analyses of media (e.g., Marshall McLuhan, Neil Postman, Walter Ong, Fr. Paul A. Soukup,

SJ), and some are within the evangelical pale (e.g., Jacques Ellul), but their consensus that *the medium changes the game* cannot be ignored.

A full exposition of how different media change the game in communication is beyond the scope of this essay but consider this brief example. The habit of reading a physical book builds the capacity for attention, provides the time for memory processing, and relaxes the human physiologically. Reading the same book online shortens the attention span, changes the eye behavior on the page itself, reduces comprehension, and keeps the nervous system in a state of high arousal.[10] Reading physical books supports logical processing and creative thought—the elements of what we normally consider "the life of the mind"—more than reading online.

Can a free or reduced-cost evangelical ebook disseminating key scholarly insights about recent linguistic and archaeological contexts for interpreting biblical texts, for example, make academic scholarship more accessible to a broad audience—sent, say, to a massive email list of pastors? Certainly. But that accessibility must be weighed against the impact of the medium itself: how the medium "leans" away from critical thought, how emails with free resources are "disposable," and how poorly the free ebook competes for attention with a six-minute YouTube video giving a simplified version of that information in a visual-aural way.

Paying "attention to the means of propagation," then, means that evangelical academics need to learn the tradeoffs inherent in different media forms. Pastors have recently been confronted *en masse* with the complexity of this issue in the wake of the COVID-19 epidemic, as many were forced to experiment with digital remote church services but now find themselves having to negotiate a balance between the returned face-to-face crowd and their "digital crowds."[11] It is clear that the media mix affects the identity and community of those churches, and such media, similarly, affect the interaction between Academy and church.

The measuring stick of evangelical populism has long been the "effectiveness" of the medium, though what "effective" has meant is questionable.[12] Number of decision cards sent in? Number of people attending the service? Number of downloads, or likes? Worse yet, the amount of money taken in?

I suggest a cruciform baseline medium and measuring stick for evangelical academics: the medium of in-person communication and the criterion of relational depth built through long-term engagement rather than broad, shallow, and quantitative popularity. Jesus, also seeking to share knowledge, spent time with people in an internship mentor role over years, even when they clearly were not paying attention to the lecture and failed in the lab portion. As repeated often in John 17, he saw his work as "these men." How might evangelical academics invest in in-person relationships with people in their church community—say, 12 people in their social circles of Christian lay people, explaining how Christianity intersects with the pursuit of truth in the scholar's field? How might evangelical institutions of higher learning shift their tenure criteria so that alongside the criteria of publications and formal service, they also ask Dawson Trotman's favorite question, "Where are the [people] you are discipling" in the community?[13]

This is cruciform because choosing commitment to relationships is hard, much harder than (though no more laborious than) maintaining an active academic portfolio online and posting academic messages on the relevant social media. Focusing one's impact on a small set of clearly flawed, flighty human beings through the friction of face-to-face communication also feels like a shakier foundation for a legacy than the frictionless ideal of publications and videos that garner likes and theoretically touch every corner of the earth but require nothing.

Echoes of the Oral-Aural Mind

Media and culture have a reciprocal relationship. Above, I suggested that Christian academics choose the medium that best promotes thinking and relationships, but the other side of that problem is that fewer lay evangelicals may have "ears to hear" what academics say because of the cultural shift toward orality.

I make this observation through Walter Ong's paradigm of the "literate mind" and the "oral-aural mind."[14] According to Ong, the type of medium used habitually to communicate not only affects the message but also changes the kind of thinking that is normative in the person and group inundated with that kind of medium. The kind of thinking academic scholars aim for prizes objectivity, acknowledges multiple interpretations, separates interpretation from facts/data, and welcomes reasonable correction. These are all characteristics of mind made possible and undergirded by print culture. Cultures without print (primary oral cultures) or cultures where the impact of print is on the wane (our current culture) operate according to different normative pathways. Those oral-aural cultures aim to reinforce group solidarity, to sort or reframe facts/data to favor one's position, to find and exploit weaknesses in one's opponent, and to signal the virtues and identity markers of one's group, often in memorable and clearly recognizable shared language.[15]

The literate mind seeks to build an edifice of truth while continuously remodeling whole wings of the castle and critiquing its own builders and materials, while the oral-aural mind inhabits one of the received castles quickly and arms itself to defend those walls to the death. I am painting both sides with a broad brush, obscuring the complexities of their differences and the ways in which they overlap. However, readers can relate if they have spent time with non-academics discussing conclusions as "tentative" or exploring the possible interpretations of a set of data. Often, the first question that makes its way past the general puzzlement of our oral-aural conversation partner is "but whose *side* are you on?"

Those familiar with Media Ecology might find this explanation unneeded and lacking nuance, but my point is that we have to navigate this gap in mindsets when trying to cross-fertilize lay evangelical communities with academic ones. Even when evangelical academics do shoulder the burden of communicating to pastors and laypeople, choosing a medium that promotes careful attention and thought, the audience might not have ears to hear because of the sea change in mass culture away from the literate mind.

Are we academics doomed to speak only among ourselves in a form of language that may as well be Latin, as has happened in Western culture before?[16] No, we are not doomed, but we must be more cunning (see 2 Cor. 12:16). One solution is unlikely: delete all new media forms and double down on education in deep literacy. Realistically, we can hope to inculcate deep literacy in only the few students we entice into the reading and thinking habits of higher education.

The other solution is the one Jesus modeled by the sacrifice of his incarnation. The incarnation was the most radical, most humbling, act of translation imaginable. The communication problem Jesus faced was more dire even than ours. How did Jesus address that communication gap? Through in-person modeling ("if you have seen me, you have seen the Father"), in-person application ("But that you may know [this principle]," he demonstrated it), multiplication of those models by open-ended opportunities ("You give them something to eat"), and the verbal combination of oral-aural teaching modes with challenges to application ("Blessed are those who hear the word of God and keep it") (see John 14:9; Matt. 9:4–6; Mark 6:37; Luke 11:28, New King James Version).

Because the gap between literacy cultures is so much wider now, evangelical academics must translate concepts and written words into embodied communication, leaving the safe space of academic publications and calling evangelical laypeople out of the "safety" of cyberspace to struggle together with communication in a shared social world.

Taking Up the Cross in a Tribal Culture

Our historical moment demonstrates not only the *difficulties* but also the *dangers* implicit in a cultural shift to an oral-aural mind. Ong says that the literate mind is "irenic"—peaceful in that it tends to *explore* more than *defend* its positions—while the oral-aural mind is "agonistic"—aggressively attacking other positions or defending its own.[17] Our culture seems to be moving toward the latter, toward identity groups, tribes, that are focused on attack and defense rather than exploration.[18] Emotionally, this defensiveness manifests as fear and anxiety. Cognitively, this defensiveness manifests as avoiding direct engagement with the "enemy," refusing to listen and dialogue.[19] Asking people to reconsider their evidence or explore multiple interpretations may be received as an attack on their very being.

When we teach in a multi-perspectival manner or dialogue from a neutral vantage point, our actions may be perceived by oral-aural evangelicals as a cover-up for a manipulative agenda, an attempt to corrupt and "un-man" the youth, or evidence that we are eggheads caught in a sucker's game. While, as Noll says, the quality of evangelical scholarship has gone up, the distrust of the ethos of scholarship among lay evangelicals has skyrocketed.[20] Communicating to lay audiences has always had its difficulties—relying on popular writers to simplify and amplify academic arguments—but the level of challenge has increased. If evangelical academics are not presenting their work in a stark enough framework to agonistically "own" the libs, the atheists, or some other group, they may find themselves outside the camp, disowned as insufficiently loyal to the evangelical tribe.

Jesus again provides us with a model for how to maintain a strong distinction between two kingdoms while also resisting the call to swear loyalty to tribal camps locked in agonistic combat. His irenic mode of engagement can provide a model for us in our communication conundrum.

Jesus taught in a culture in which Jews who cooperated with the "big government" of Rome were marked as the worst of traitors ("tax collectors"), in which interaction with Samaritans was avoided, in which one's doctrinal, educational, socioeconomic, or actual tribe could serve as unreflective criteria for including or excluding conversation partners:

Pharisee, Sadducee, unlettered poor, Zionist, or someone, say, from the Nazareth ghetto. Jesus not only refused to be identified strictly with any of these groups, but he also spotlighted the artificiality and unhelpfulness of many of these tribal markers by the way he taught. He told parables about good Samaritans, and he talked to bad Samaritans. He called tax collectors to his side, healed the Romans and gentiles he was *not* called to minister to, publicly excoriated the hypocrisy of the most respected scholars, and dialogued earnestly and freely with people in any of these groups who came with open ears. And, for his pains in refusing to take a side in the political chessboard of his culture, he was crucified.

If all truth is God's truth and our calling as academics is to find, test, and disseminate the truths of our field, we can legitimately follow Jesus's model to engage in truth-telling and truth-seeking across social boundaries without fear. Could we then follow Christ typologically to some form of crucifixion, such as being "canceled" online? Yes, but as Christians, not just academics, we know that "to live is Christ and to die is gain" (Phil. 1:21, NKJV). Many of us have long prepared our hearts to suffer for Christ under "Pilate," the secular academic hegemony, but the shift away from a literacy mindset among lay evangelicals means we should be prepared for the cross from that direction as well.

Crucifixion in secular academia might mean being rejected from journals because we own the confessional warrants undergirding our research. But among evangelicals, the cross could mean being called into the dean's office of our confessional college or university and being warned to stick to certain political narratives in our field lest the school's donors be offended. Taking up the cross does not mean belligerence or acting as a Romantic martyr but instead refusing persistently any "spirit of fear" in favor of doing academic work in "a spirit of power, of love, and of a sound mind" (2 Tim. 1:7, NKJV).

Cross-fertilization: Future Directions

Let me summarize and then deliver on the final part of my thesis. Noll "realize[d] that the American context constrains what academics can accomplish among academics, but even more in the world at large," and he exhorts evangelical academics to bridge the gap with pastors and other evangelical people in the churches, while also noting how the online world has widened that gap.[21]

I have said Amen to Noll while also developing three Media Ecology challenges to Noll's exhortation. First, academics should choose media forms that will strengthen, not weaken, the evangelical mind. Second, evangelical academics should communicate strategically to bridge the gap between their "literate mind" and the "oral-aural mind" of the evangelical layperson. Third, academics should communicate *courageously* because the agonism of the oral-aural culture can be dangerous, bypassing rationality entirely in a defensive-tribal reaction to perceived danger. I have argued that, as *evangelical* academics, we are called to apply the "cruciform" part of Bebbington's definition to our communication across groups, especially in an age when "cross-fertilization" of ideas is itself felt as a threatening move to many in our target audience.

But how should evangelical academics communicate as a "way of life," not just as words through lectures (or podcasts, webinars, books, articles, blogs, YouTube vlogs, graphic novels, or raps)? I suggest that we draw on two communication strategies from the historical tradition of evangelicalism—cross-institution coalitions/conferences and in-person communication based on cross-cultural missionary work—to bridge the gap developed in my three themes above. These two approaches to communication resist the tendency to oversimplification, hard tribalism, and defensiveness.

Medium of Public Evangelical Academic Conferences

Evangelicalism is a coalitional movement that has historically tied different Christian groups together through interpersonal networking, shared mission-focused publications, and shared evangelical activity. Mark Noll, David Bebbington, and George Rawlyk note in their transnational study of evangelical history that "[f]rom the days of Whitefield, Wesley, and Edwards [on,] the interconnections among British, American, and Canadian evangelicals, as also their brothers and sisters in many other areas of the world, have been foundational to evangelicalism," and that "[i]nnovative networks of communication have sustained the transnational character of evangelicalism and given it much of its distinctive shape."[22] George Marsden suggests that evangelicals maintain unity as an "organic movement" based in "common traditions and experiences" and, more narrowly, an explicit "transdenominational community with complicated infrastructures of institutions and persons who identify with 'evangelicalism.'"[23]

Much of this transnational cross-fertilization between different evangelical churches, parachurch organizations, and missions happened in print culture, but it also depended heavily on in-person interactions at conferences and in shared evangelical outreaches. Of many examples, Edith L. Blumhofer's portrayal of the early Pentecostal movement is instructive. She notes that "[b]oth women and men apparently had the resources to travel widely and frequently to conferences and camp meetings."[24] In the movement overall, having "a single charismatic leader . . . mattered less than their presence, and having the same people on every conference roster helped unify disparate groups."[25] Those of us who have moved in circles affected by Billy Graham crusades know, too, how very different churches and groups strengthened their evangelical identity through shared in-person action across the city.

As Noll notes, evangelical academics have begun reaching out to lay communities through in-person events such as the Veritas Forum and Christian Study Centers, but I suggest that such venues be pursued further to increase the interaction of scholarly and lay evangelicals.[26] Dialogue among a diverse range of scholars and non-scholars stimulates the thinking of each individual mind at the conference and creates a ripple effect as participants go back to their home spheres. Can people get some of the same information through internet browsing? Yes, but internet engagement does not lead consistently to networks of relationships, further dialogue in written academic mediums, or charitable explorations of participants' different interpretations. We should move online interaction to in-person contexts to keep it real, memorable, and incarnationally communal.

One intriguing possibility of using electronic media to initiate and organize in-person conferences is reported on by Molly Worthen, who profiles "The Liturgists" podcast, whose listeners have started moving from listening individually to "find[ing] one another" and "conven[ing] events where fans eat, drink, and worship together."[27] One of the podcast hosts, Mike McHargue, explains that listeners cannot be left to listen to information alone: "[w]e have to draw them into some kind of communal practice."[28]

In contrast to the ease of a quick podcast or YouTube video, attending in-person conferences costs time, attention, and money, a cost we feel even when conferences are a normal part of our profession. Taking the further step of organizing such conferences, inviting lay evangelicals, and ensuring that the presenters are communicating incarnationally with the lay community would be quite the cross indeed.[29] But the conference medium has evangelical precedent and Media Ecology theory to recommend it.

The Cross-cultural Missions Paradigm

Missions is the core activity built into evangelicalism that continually cross-fertilizes it, revitalizing its strength through diversity and countering the movement toward insular tribalism.[30] Most missions crosses some cultural barrier and engages in some level of cultural dialogue—listening and translating between "other" cultural groups. Christ's mission is the overarching model; intercultural missions provides a diverse array of cultural challenges and possible solutions, providing a paradigm for evangelical academics in their listening, considering, valuing, and speaking—not least because the literacy of academic culture and the orality of lay evangelical culture create a communication gap similar to that between missionaries and their target peoples, who are often oral-aural.

In communicating to lay evangelicals like missionaries, scholars should consider the scholarly diction barrier, the research tradition barrier, and the statistics barrier, among others. As evangelical scholars, examining missions also helps us examine ourselves ethnographically. We are often no less insular, no less prejudiced in favor of our own disciplines' warrants, methods, and language.

Many of my own evangelical prejudices have been exposed by my readings in missions, specifically by on-the-ground stories that challenged my assumptions. Growing up with a typically zealous evangelical devotion to the faithful translation of the Bible, I was challenged, for example, by the translation choices for the Motilone people: Bruce Olsen felt he had to switch wording from the "house built on a rock" to the "house built in the sand" in Jesus's parable because that switch communicated the truth best to the Motilone, whose best houses are built in sand.[31] Another example: I was formed by a modern evangelical devotion to rational, linear exposition, so I was challenged by Honduras church-planter George Patterson's own confession of shame. He had been observing a church plant in a network he was responsible for, and he was mentally critiquing the church leaders, who had not explained the communion elements they were serving, but when Patterson looked up, he saw all the people eating the bread and weeping. The native leaders gave very little rational explanation of the ritual, but all the people experienced Christ. Patterson, and I, realized there was more to the communion service than a full and proper exposition of the symbolism.[32] This thoroughly Christian revelation broadened my perspective and gave me my own evangelical framework for understanding and evaluating what I later read in philosophical hermeneutics. These examples and more shaped my attitude and strategies for communicating my own research to evangelicals with more oral-aural mindsets.

We need to learn to listen. Non-academics in our culture need to be approached with language they can receive. At the ground level, this means that we need to learn to tell better stories, narratives faithful to our research but also accessible and interesting to our non-academic brethren. Narratives do not have to be simple; even traditional narratives in tribal cultures were polyvalent, inviting the listeners to think through the possibilities and engage in interpretation.[33] But stepping out of our disciplines' language conventions is difficult. Finding narratives and accessible language to communicate to a lay audience is labor-intensive and frustrating. Writing and speaking to our own academic culture is difficult enough. Who would want to put themselves through the trials of translating their work for people with a mindset so foreign to our own?

This is where the example of Christ pertains as the original missionary, the one with the biggest cultural gap to bridge. He could only indirectly and in bits and pieces communicate "heavenly things," and when he used stories and metaphors from people's lives like gardens and fish and leaven, they often still did not understand. He was frustrated, too. "How is it that you do not understand?" he asked (Mark 8:21, NKJV). But he continued, in the flesh, to teach in words, demonstrate in deeds, and maintain a personal relationship with as many as would stay and listen to him.

Conclusion

I have tried to lay out some Media Ecology coordinates of the communication problem involved in cross-fertilizing academic and lay evangelical spheres. Oral-aural culture is more cued to agonistic rhetoric than irenic exposition, more interested in choosing sides than probing nuances of the truth, and trained by a steady diet of "interruption technologies" to seek strategic knowledge in ever-shorter and more extreme expressions.[34] To meet our lay brethren where they are, we need to engage with them personally and in-person, on the model of missions, instead of broadcasting words into this mission field from afar. Further, pursuing the in-person venues of evangelical mixed-group conferences is one way we might attempt such dialogue. Coming alongside Noll, this is how I suggest we pursue cross-fertilization and demonstrate the character of Jesus in our scholarly calling.

Chapter 58

Toward a Rhetorical Evangelical Mind

Ben Voth

Response Summary: In his Legacy Scholar presentation at the unconference, respected religious historian Mark Noll argues there are problems in the ongoing emergence of Christian academic thought in the twenty-first century, specifically suggesting that "evangelicals" expressed undue skepticism of COVID-19 protocols. This essay argues that skepticism and the larger intellectual process of debate and refutation play an essential role in the ongoing reality of the Christian mind. Jesus's adaptation of the Shema compels us to love God with our mind, and Christian praxis as seen in authoritative biblical texts indicates reasoning and argument play a necessary role in mental discipleship. This essay reconsiders Noll's warnings about "evangelical" skepticism about COVID-19 protocols to better assure the path of abundant life Jesus assured his discipleship will bring about even in the twenty-first century.

THE SCANDAL AND OUTRAGEOUSNESS of evangelical intellectual life remain salient in 2025 as when first expounded by Mark Noll and George Marsden in the 1990s.[1] Noll provides an update in a new preface and afterword.[2] Despite optimistic notes about its possible progression, the rhetorical situation for the Christian mind in academia is more conflicted than ever. As proposed by the Christianity and Communication Studies Network (CCSN) unconference, conflict is driven by an increasing sense of tribalism wherein political intensity acts to divide individuals from faith as a test toward ideological fidelity before those two things are allowed to coexist in peace. Despite the looming shadows of American partisanship, a consideration of the status of the evangelical mind is possible. More specifically, is a Christian academic mind possible? Beginning with the central figure of Christianity—Jesus—the answer is inevitably "yes." The prominent reasons are twofold: Jesus is a teacher, and he acts and instructs upon the emergence of our mind.

In the aftermath of Jesus's resurrection, a woman is offered as having the first insight to this pivotal reality. She says "Rabboni," which means "teacher" (see John 20:16). For Mary, Jesus was intrinsically a teacher. This identification with the role of teacher informs Christianity of the importance education has within discipleship. Secondly, Jesus comments directly upon the mind in his adaptation of the Shema. Deuteronomy 6:4–9, states: "Hear, O Israel: The Lord our God, the Lord is one. Love the Lord your God with all your heart and with all your soul and with all your strength." The original and intellectual exercise offered in the Torah stresses a central personal discipline of loving God with all our heart, soul, and strength. Jesus adapts this greatest commandment to include his emergent Kingdom of the mind: "Love the Lord your God with all your heart and with all your soul and with all your mind" (Matt. 22:37). Jesus's addition of mind is transformative to global politics because human communities were previously organized around notions of dominion or physical power.[3] This explanation given to "an expert in the Law" provides a political hinge upon which a sophisticated version of politics ruled by reason rather than force. The Deuteronomy rendering of the Shema emphasizes physical strength. This is consistent with William Barret's analysis of the Hebraic man.[4] Barrett posits a development in human thinking between the Hebraic and Greek view. A key part of the emergent Greek view is the prominence of the mind over the body. Jesus's adaptation of Jewish thinking with an emphasis to love God with our mind, creates an impetus toward the continual renewal of the mind. The Academy is a central human repository for the cultivation of the human mind and so as Christian academics, our leadership on this renewal is paramount.

Critical Theory is among the most important transformative epistemologies shaking academic disciplines. The root of Critical Theory is lodged in the twentieth-century endeavors of the Frankfurt School. Among the important participants from the standpoint of communication study is Jürgen Habermas. Despite his intensive secular and socialistic convictions, Habermas makes this pivotal assessment of Christianity's position in the advent of the twenty-first century and the wide array of global challenges facing academia's growing concern with social justice:

> Christianity has functioned for the normative self-understanding of modernity as more than a mere precursor or a catalyst. Egalitarian universalism, from which sprang the ideas of freedom and social solidarity, of an autonomous conduct of life and emancipation, of the individual morality of conscience, human rights, and democracy, is the direct heir to the Judaic ethic of justice and the Christian ethic of love. This legacy, substantially unchanged, has been the object of continual critical appropriation and reinterpretation. To this day, there is no alternative to it. . . . Everything else is just idle postmodern talk.[5]

These published words from a leader of the Frankfurt School could hardly be worded more decisively in favor of Christianity's intellectual headship. Many of our most important contemporary academic values of the twenty-first century are rooted in the critical tradition of Christianity. Jesus's kingdom of the mind reigns supreme in the judgment of Frankfurt scholar Jürgen Habermas. His 1976 work, *Communication and the Evolution of Society*, posits societies advance best when affinities for communication competence abide. Habermas is one of the most quoted experts in the realm of communication, and his theoretical insights about the necessity of the public sphere ground important parts of the communication discipline. Habermas concludes "there is no alternative to [Christianity]," demolishing pretense of epistemological pluralism, and he further deigns supposed alternatives to be "idle postmodern talk."[6] Given such profound reluctant testimony for the supremacy of Christianity, we can consider how Christian academics themselves take hold of their own reconsiderations in this realm. Some secular and Christian academics dispute Habermas's claim.[7] In interviews Habermas has been asked about the quotation and does not say it was a misquote.[8] Habermas's contention that almost every aspect of Critical Theory judgment is derived from Judeo-Christian thinking is consistent with Jesus's own epistemological ownership in the Gospel of John 10:1–18.

At the heart of this reconsideration is the argument of "anti-intellectualism." Perhaps derived from the absurd renderings of the *Scopes Monkey Trial* featuring Clarence Darrow and William Jennings Bryan, a reductionist story found in the film *Inherit the Wind*, imagines how fundamentalists rebuked the science of evolution. From this Hollywood heuristic of 1960, Christianity must exit gracefully from the learned halls dominated by good science.[9] The charge that evangelical Christianity is anti-intellectual has not abated in the twenty-first century. In his own 2022 attack, Noll accuses Christians of taking an anti-intellectual view of the COVID-19 pandemic with their poor cooperation with COVID-19 protocols. It is a difficult allegation to confront because of an enduring Judeo-Christian insight about knowledge is poorly understood even among Christian academics.

The Knowledge Problem

In many respects, Christianity is intrinsically anti-intellectual.[10] From the problematic centering of the "tree of knowledge" in the opening of Genesis to the central dialectic of Jesus in verbal combat with teachers in the Gospels, the human acquisition of knowledge is biblically recognized as fraught with peril. Our pursuit of knowledge as an intellectual can easily put us on a prideful path that endangers not only us but our surrounding community. Grappling with this overriding problem cannot be comforting for Christians entering the Academy and seeking knowledge.

One of the more annoying allegations emerging from the strawman evolution debate concerns the Genesis story—itself ripe with misunderstanding. In the strawman portrayal, the only argument Bryan and his intellectual heirs are making is about the age of the earth. The arguments between Darrow and Bryan were more substantial. At the center of the creation story stands "the tree of knowledge." As early as Chapter 2, Genesis explains: "In the middle of the garden were the tree of life and the tree of the knowledge of good and evil" (v. 9). Further in the narrative, God commands that "you must not eat from the *tree of the knowledge of good and evil,* for when you eat from it you will certainly die" (v. 17, emphasis added). The tree of knowledge contains fruit the humans can pluck for themselves. Struggles over "literalism" miss the larger theological point. Knowledge that we take for ourselves independent of God is the inception of our downfall. The common truism "knowledge is power," is suited to the warning found in Genesis 2. Knowledge acquisition is intrinsic to being human—we are curious. However, pursuit of knowledge can yield deadly results when sought apart from the presence of God. The Genesis account is a responsibility test about whether humans can walk with God or must rebel and seek their own knowledge. The dangers of knowledge are apparent in the framework of humanity offered in the outset of the Bible.

The problem of anti-intellectualism is bound up in Jesus's conduct as well. Most of

Jesus's conflicts focus upon debates with scholars and knowledge experts. The adaptation of the Shema was consequent to many "tests" administered by fellow teachers eager to "catch" Jesus in rhetorical missteps. The problem revealed in Jesus's stories and dialogues is the teachers had acquired knowledge/power in a manner that served their selfish interests rather than people's needs. No one is criticized more severely than the intellectual leaders of Jesus's era. Among the mildest summaries of the dialectic is the conclusion of the Gospel of Matthew (23:26–28). The summary in John is more antagonistic and goes to the heart of the knowledge/power problem that haunts humanity to this day. Jesus compares the pharisees to thieves, robbers and killers. Jesus's rhetorical sophistication provides a repudiation of his rival teachers as "thieves coming to kill and destroy" (see John 10:7–10). The point is amplified by the killing of Jesus required because of what the teachers profess to "know" about Jesus.

Today, Christian academics need to consider what a full emulation of Jesus entails. It entails more than being a supporter of good deeds. Christian discipleship expects knowledge mastery can inherently check the bad human motives in knowledge acquisition that are deadly in consequence. This is arguably a pivotal theological error surrounding one of the most treasured evangelical verses found in the profound Pauline prose of Romans 6: "But thanks be to God that, though you used to be slaves to sin, you have come to obey from your heart the pattern of teaching that has now claimed your allegiance" (v. 17). Paul concludes in a crescendo: "For the wages of sin is death, but the gift of God is eternal life in Christ Jesus our Lord" (v. 23). Much like the error of the fruit of the knowledge tree imputing a genetic sin to humanity, contemporary Christian life imagines Paul to say, the *cost* of sin is death, when he, in fact, says the *wages* of sin is death. This implies a political economy of sin. The legalistic framework—of which Paul was once a powerful part—was a teaching/knowledge system that was deadly. The new knowledge framework frees the mind from this deadly aspiration.

Noll's skepticism and concern about the Christian mind is motivated by his observations about "evangelical" responses to COVID-19. Other strong Christian thinkers have observed Noll's disposition on this question. In an essay analyzing the COVID-19 crisis, Mark Denison explains that "Noll . . . exposes the deep antipathy to intellectual excellence that exists among many Christians. The more we have faith, the less we will have doubts and the less we will need to understand our faith—or so we think."[11] Denison agrees with the allegation made by Noll that Christians display an antipathy toward intellectuals regarding COVID-19, writing that "[i]n the preface, he [Noll] describes the tension this caused him as a scholar and a committed Reformed Christian. 'The thought has occurred to me regularly, that, at least in the United States, it is simply impossible to be, with integrity, both evangelical and intellectual.'"[12]

The idea that someone cannot be an evangelical and an intellectual is a serious ethical charge made by Noll. It is an allegation that deserves scrutiny—especially among Christian academics who might continue to think of themselves as "evangelicals." The question is clear even in the promotion of the new edition—*Booklist* is offered as an endorsement of Noll's view, "[t]hat anti-intellectualism is not inherent in evangelicalism Noll demonstrates by presenting evangelical intellectual history, primarily in the U.S., . . . Noll well exemplifies what he prays evangelicals generally will learn to value again: thinking like a Christian."[13]

This promotional quotation printed with the 2022 book suggests evangelicals have stopped thinking like a Christian. Understanding Noll's charge regarding "evangelicalism" and intellectual life does not require a resort to rhetorical lenses of "partisanship." The Bible provides a warning that knowledge acquisition will bring with it a risk of rebellion to God. That is our political citizenship ultimately—obedience to God. Members of the American left and right objected to the draconian aspects of COVID-19 stricture. A centerpiece of Noll's argument involves Francis Collins. Collins, as the head of NIH, is undoubtedly an important embodiment of Christian excellence within science. Noll makes this strong criticism of "evangelicals" in the 2022 preface:

> The recent pandemic well illustrates this conflicted relationship. Francis Collins, director of the National Institutes of Health, has explained how C. S. Lewis's *Mere Christianity* turned his life around. . . . Many evangelicals, however, have turned aside from such research-supported voices to heed advice from figures who have mastered social media, but nothing else.[14]

The skepticism criticized by Noll is well-grounded and arguably the *veritas liberabit vos* Jesus sought in the eighth chapter of John. Noll's skepticism regarding evangelicals and COVID-19 are observed in his preface:

> These evangelicals have been least likely to seek vaccination against the coronavirus, least likely to believe that evolutionary science actually describes the development of species, and least likely to believe that the planet is really warming up because of human activity. White evangelicals are also most likely to repudiate the conclusion of impartial observers and claim that the 2020 presidential election was "stolen." They are most likely to regard their political opponents as hell-bent on destroying America. They are least likely to think that racial discrimination continues as a systemic American problem. And in response to a question that is usually formulated poorly, they are most likely to believe that Scripture should be interpreted "literally." In each of these spheres, White evangelicals appear as the group most easily captive to conspiratorial nonsense, in greatest panic about their political opponents, or as most aggressively anti-intellectual.[15]

Much of Noll's sense of proper COVID-19 protocols is rooted in a respect for the leadership of Francis Collins during the pandemic. Collins's advice on COVID-19 was not fully transparent. In June of 2021, Collins told a publication the COVID-19 virus likely developed from natural origins:

> Far and away, the most likely origin is a natural zoonotic pathway from bats to some unidentified intermediate host to humans . . . the possibility that such a naturally evolved virus might have also been under study at the Wuhan Institute of Virology and reached residents of Wuhan—and ultimately the rest of the world—as the result of a lab accident has never been adequately excluded.[16]

In hindsight, almost no convincing evidence has emerged to deny the virus originated in the Wuhan lab. There is no practical evidence that the virus had a natural origin.

Anthony Fauci played an important role in discrediting efforts to clarify the virus's lab origins.[17] That origin is important because the American scientific community played a role in rationalizing gain of function research at the lab, in conditions that would likely not be approved in the U.S. Noll and Collins remain adamant social restrictions such as masking were obviously effective in the COVID-19 era. Scientific journals blocked valid research experiments showing masks increase the intake of CO2, which can lead to health hazards.[18] In 2025 many empirical claims regarding masks and other restrictions on life have proven to be true. The hindsight of three years after Noll's critique of "evangelicals" suggests skepticism about protocols was warranted and the quest to squelch dissent was not. There is credible scientific evidence that does not reduce the risk of disease transmission.[19]

Damage was done to individuals who were fired from their jobs for refusing to take the COVID-19 vaccine. Under oath and testimony, lead scientist Dr. Anthony Fauci acknowledged the six-foot rule imposed upon American society had no basis of medical prevention in scientific literature.[20] A better Christian epistemic ought to embrace skepticism of the certitude of pharisaic leaders interpreting the law to their own selfish ends. Jesus's teaching aims squarely in this case at the radically closed society and anti-Christian governance of the Chinese Communist party. The millions of deaths resulting from the COVID-19 pandemic remain one of the most important atrocities of the current era. Multiple international intelligence agencies confirm the virus originated in the military research lab at Wuhan. Chinese government officials strong-armed their propaganda about the virus not being airborne from the outset of infections. The Communist government banned domestic travel while allowing international travel in 2019 and 2020. All of this points to malicious military-based misconduct with catastrophic consequences experts warned about regarding gain of function research for decades. China faces no serious penalties for this deadly result killing more than 7 million people worldwide. The government of China falsely brags 83,000 people in China died from the virus hiding more than a million deaths.[21] Focusing blame on evangelicals deflects from the worthy blame the government of China should face regarding COVID-19.

The Alternative: Empiricism and Beloved Community

Jesus associated with lepers and unclean individuals who under therapeutic designs of national law were banned from social contacts. Jesus's breaches of protocol with lepers and women with issues of blood point to a deliberate skepticism cultivated by his teaching method (see Matt. 8:1–3, Luke 17:11–19, Mark 1:40–45, Luke 8:43–48). Jesus appears to directly engage the false therapies of the Pharisees. Jesus saw in the therapeutic approach of Jewish law offered by local authorities an overbroad interpretation and a practical threat to individuals living in the authority of these intellectual leaders. The global public needed more freedom of information, not less, in the recent pandemic. Collins himself lamented the openness of American society and appealed for more draconian power.[22] American Christian preacher Howard Beecher observed: "Free speech is to a great people what winds are to oceans in malarial regions, which waft away the elements of disease and bring new elements of health; and where free speech is stopped, miasma is bred, and death comes fast."[23] The ideal Christian view is not anti-science. Jesus's rhetorical divorce of disease from sin, created a free-minded world where alternative causes to illness could be discerned. In fact, Jesus defended an intellectual standard of empiricism. Regarding his own teaching and the testing everyone must do, he urged that "we judge things by their fruit" (Matt. 7:20). The point here is not to reciprocate the failed rhetorical paradigm and make political demons out of Fauci and Collins. It is important to remain faithful to the critical hermeneutic embodied by the master teacher of Jesus. Science can become scientism that resembles a cultural tower of Babel rather than the reciprocal clarity of Pentecost.

Noted science historian Thomas Kuhn describes the rhetorical work of science. He provides insight about how "revolutions" take place and a problem in science that we likely witnessed in the events of the pandemic:

> Yet that element of arbitrariness is present, and it too has an important effect on scientific development . . . the activity in which most scientists inevitably spend almost all their time, is predicated on the assumption that the scientific community knows what the world is like. Much of the success of the enterprise derives from the community's willingness to defend that assumption, if necessary at considerable cost. Normal science, for example, often suppresses fundamental novelties because they are necessarily subversive of its basic commitments. Nevertheless, so long as those commitments retain an element of the arbitrary, the very nature of normal research ensures that novelty shall not be suppressed for very long.[24]

The stifling of viewpoints regarding COVID-19 regimen are apparent in the many lawsuits now being won by individuals denied employment for failing to adhere to demands of COVID-19 regimen.[25] An essential ingredient of science is that its conclusions must be falsifiable.[26] Most science is normal science and has a rhetorical tendency to suppress novelties delaying the inevitable revolution in science.[27] It is important to understand Christianity played an arguably inescapable role in innovation when Jesus challenged his disciples and the larger intellectual culture about why a certain man was blind.

We may fear there is no practical alternative to the criticisms made by Noll. The American Civil Rights Movement of 1942–1967 was predicated upon a praxis of Christianity called "beloved community." Martin Luther King Jr., James Farmer Jr., and John Lewis often spoke of this paradigm. The group did embrace other theological perspectives; all participants were practitioners of "loving your neighbor as yourself" and believed "beloved community" could rectify the problem of segregation.[28] The primary mode of change was deliberative conversations with engaged leaders who through thoughtful conversation came to change their minds about segregation. The effort was bipartisan. James Farmer Jr. ran for Congress in New York as a Republican and worked in the Nixon and Lyndon B. Johnson White Houses. Farmer believed Black people should not be exclusively voting for one party over the other. The empirical success of Beloved Community remains credible in the twenty-first century for a means of how the evangelical mind can work toward the good.

Because Christianity maintains the radically open and idealistic mind, it will tend to come under withering rhetorical attacks from the conventions of present culture.[29] The risk-taking innovation required is more easily ventured in a world where the impossible is possible. That is the work of faith as small as a "mustard seed." The fact Christians disagree with "normal science," is not a point of discredit.[30] It is an important part of "setting us free" in a truth process not bound by predatory authorities that seek punishment for thoughts outside their defined box.[31] The mysterious embodiment of a truth system where the law is not abolished but grace supersedes the dehumanizing intimidation common to an over-zealous interpretation of the laws is the key to success. Jesus taught and lived that paradigm that anchors the proper Christian mind of the twenty-first century.

The idea Christianity might be anti-intellectual should not surprise us. It certainly did not surprise the intellectuals and academics rooted in the academic institutions of Jerusalem of the first century. Precisely as foreshadowed in the serpent's discussion with Eve about having knowledge without God (Gen. 3). Jesus's confrontation at the temple in Jerusalem at the nation's academic pinnacle was a predictable narrative consequence to a story peppered with accusations and defiance as Jesus answered questions from academics across the nation. Jesus observed that the teachers corrupted the knowledge of God into a deadly weapon utilized against the people of God. Our ongoing intellectual abilities to misinterpret God and leave him entirely out of our academic equations is perfectly consistent with the rhetorical arc of the Bible.

As Orwell observed, the price of telling the truth in times of mass deception can easily be the loss of human life. The Communist Party of China excels at mass deception and intimidation and consequently executes thousands of people every year—exponentially more than any other government in the world.[32] Easter centers the resurrection like an intellectual diamond amidst the absurdity of global *Gleischaltung*.[33] The Christian belief in the resurrection is the truth that sets us free because it can by faith place our mind beyond the reach of fear induced by deadly genocidaires who kill the innocent in public as a rhetorical means of gaining the consent of masses. Death is not the last word in political argument. It can be an idealistic beginning. The public killing of the innocent has always been among humanity's worst features. The resurrection of Jesus is offered as an important and necessary alternative to that shrewdly crafted world.

Conclusion

The evangelical mind is inherently "scandalous" and problematic because as an emulation of Jesus—the master teacher—it is a challenge to present orders. The status quo is an entrenchment of knowledge traditions. Understanding and acting upon various academic disciplines and better understanding the limitations of the known world, requires inherent faithful Christian believers meant to bring change to the world as presently ordered. Jesus is disruptive. The Gospels make clear, and Jesus assures his followers a struggle will ensue in the choice to be a disciple. As iron sharpens iron, Christian academics can challenge one another in pursuit of the truth that sets us free.

Mark Noll's seminal work on Christian academics—*Scandal of the Evangelical Mind*—remains important and foundational. The 2022 version with a new preface and afterword provides an important measure of where this important collective mind might be. Noll's comments in 2022 are more pessimistic. There is good evidence Noll misjudged the status of the evangelical mind. There are two primary reasons for this regarding the central arguments Noll makes: (1) Jesus was opposed to the excessive health protocols imposed by intellectual leaders of the day, and (2) there is a growing body of evidence such as Fauci's admission the six-foot rule had no scientific basis—that many of the COVID-19 strictures were overzealous. This essay establishes an alternative to the current paradigm by suggesting an emphasis on deliberation comparable to "beloved community" of the American Civil Rights era. There is a credible alternative to believing the evangelical mind has dangerously lost its way. The alternative embraces debate, deliberative modes of communication, and a profound realization of Jesus's affiliation with those marginalized by intellectualized systems has a proven track record of improving the human condition.

Chapter 59

The Scandal of *The Evangelical Imagination*

Abram J. Book

Response Summary: Karen Swallow Prior argues primarily that the way evangelicals have chosen to frame their faith and represent it in words has repeatedly resulted in ineffective witness and negative press and that a reframing and re-imagining of collective evangelical vocabulary is needed. In his Legacy Scholar presentation, Mark Noll provided an endorsement for Prior's book, referring to it as, " . . . an indictment . . . but an indictment with hope because of evangelical engagement with the gospel."[1] This review focuses on how Prior's book specifically extends Noll's ideas, as articulated in *The Scandal of the Evangelical Mind*, and what Prior's conclusions mean for the future of communication scholarship within evangelicalism, in particular.

MARK NOLL WRITES in his 1994 legacy work, *The Scandal of the Evangelical Mind*, that the scandal has "at least three dimensions—cultural, institutional, and theological."[2] Generally, Noll argues that evangelicalism is plagued by anti-intellectualism, which is problematic for both practical and historical reasons. Specifically, Noll places blame for what he identifies as evangelical anti-intellectualism at the feet of cultural forces such as populism and pragmatism, as well as theological forces like revivalism, fundamentalism, and the Holiness movement.

In her recent book, *The Evangelical Imagination: How Stories, Images and Metaphors Created a Culture in Crisis*, Karen Swallow Prior, a scholar of Victorian literature, suggests that the problem plaguing American evangelicalism does not merely concern the absence of the evangelical mind, as Noll argues in *Scandal*, but extends to the more fundamental failure of the evangelical imagination.[3] While Noll critiques the anti-intellectualism within evangelicalism, focusing his attention on the lack of significant evangelical contributions to arts and sciences, Prior examines the evangelical social imaginary, analyzing stories, images, and metaphors that have molded evangelical culture. As language, the ether of all metaphor and story is a primary tool of the intellectual mind, Prior's book offers a useful perspective to communication scholars, particularly those working within the humanities.

To that end, Prior closely examines 10 categories that have shaped the evangelical imagination: awakening, conversion, testimony, improvement, sentimentality, materiality, domesticity, empire, reformation, and rapture. Noll addresses some of these issues in passing, but he is writing primarily from the perspective of twentieth-century evangelicalism and its historical roots. Furthermore, Noll focuses on intellectual trends and their impact on evangelicals' engagement with politics and science. Prior extends that critique, exploring the development of evangelical imagination over the past three centuries while considering literature, art, and popular culture to unpack evangelical concepts and practices.

Very early in her book, Prior offers a metaphor to help the reader understand her thesis:

> If evangelicalism is a house, then . . . unexamined assumptions are its floor joists, wall studs, beams, and rafters—holding everything together but unseen, covered over by tile, paint, paper and ceilings. What we don't see, we don't think about. Until something goes wrong and needs replacement. Or restoration. Or reform.[4]

This is an ironic way to open the book considering a major component of Prior's thesis is that underlying assumptions and metaphors have continually shaped evangelical culture, often for the worse, yet it is a particularly fitting metaphor to describe the theological blinders so common to evangelicalism.

Another such metaphor is domesticity, a concept Prior suggests is rooted in the Victorian era. She explains that domesticity has led to the idolatry of the physical home, to the inherent felt need to protect one's personal property and to consumerism taking on the form of religious practice. Prior argues that much of what evangelicals assume is biblical regarding domesticity is actually a product of Victorian-era norms. Prior writes, "Just as the home at times came to replace the altar, so too the family (or at least the father) could become confused with God."[5]

Stylistically, Noll's *Scandal* takes a more academic and critical tone consistent with its thesis, while Prior writes in a more engaging and accessible style. On the surface, that might indicate Prior is guilty of exactly what Noll argues—essentially, the dumbing down of language and theological specificity to make the tenets of evangelicalism easier for the layperson to grasp. However, the ability to make abstract, complicated ideas accessible to audiences without robbing the ideas of their power, meaning, or impact is the essence of intellectual communication. Prior's thesis indicates that she likely agrees with Noll regarding what he identifies as the three major causes of the scandal, yet her analysis is almost entirely cultural in tone and substance. Prior focuses on reforming the evangelical imagination through a better understanding of its cultural foundations, while Noll emphasizes the need for greater intellectual engagement and rigor within the evangelical community. These approaches are not adversarial nearly as much as they are complementary.

Both authors agree that there are significant issues within evangelicalism that need to be addressed and there are similarities in their arguments, to be sure. Prior and Noll share a common goal of fostering a more thoughtful, biblically grounded, and culturally engaged evangelicalism while approaching their respective critiques from different angles. Prior's critiques zero in upon areas where evangelical culture has diverged from Scripture, urging a reformation of the imagination. She does not offer a concrete definition of imagination but instead suggests that "imagination" does not fit neatly into boxes. Imagination, Prior explains, is a mediating power that bridges the objective and subjective aspects of the human experience and that is essential to cultural meaning-making.[6] Prior calls upon evangelicals to "immerse ourselves more deeply in the stories, images, and words that reflect what is good, true, and beautiful: yes, Scripture, but also the human applications of Scripture that express the fulness of its teaching."[7] While one could argue that imagination and its products are natural derivatives of the mind, intellectual discourse and creative imagination often diverge in priority and consequence, which places Prior's recent *Imagination* as a necessary extension of Noll's earlier *Scandal*.

Prior's chapter on conversion, for example, offers some of her most pointed critiques. While Noll briefly mentions the conversionist history of evangelicalism in *Scandal*, Prior expands upon Noll's idea of conversionism when she writes that the Great Commission exhorts Christians to "go and make disciples," not to "go and win converts." Furthermore, while conversion is important, Prior argues that evangelical literature and practices have consistently overemphasized the drama of the conversion experience at the expense of other equally consequential aspects of the Christian life. As evidence, Prior offers Ebenezer Scrooge's sensational moral and spiritual metamorphosis in Dickens's classic *A Christmas Carol*.[8] While she does not discount the importance of the conversion experience to Christianity, Prior also does not mince words when she criticizes the shortcomings of conversion narratives: "It is nearly impossible within evangelicalism to separate the importance of conversion itself from the importance of telling the story of it."[9] Prior, in turn, suggests that such emphasis on dramatic conversion stories has become problematic for the evangelical imagination in the sense that the most spectacular testimonies are typically the most celebrated—overshadowing less colorful but equally valid experiences. Additionally, the focus on quick and dramatic conversion experiences has fostered an attitude of instant gratification when it comes to the Great Commission and, as Prior argues, this cocktail of factors has created an over-reliance upon conversion testimonies as uncritically accepted sources of religious authority.[10]

In *Jesus Christ and the Life of the Mind*, Noll writes:

> If evangelicals are to make a genuinely Christian contribution to intellectual life, they must ground faith in the great traditions of classical Christian theology, for these are the traditions that reveal the heights and depths of Jesus Christ. Intellectually, there is no other way . . . He is, among his many other titles, the Christ of the Academic Road.[11]

Though she would likely agree in principle with Noll's argument regarding classical Christian theology, Prior responds to Noll's metaphor with one of her own, contending that Jesus is not simply a road *to* something, rather he *is* the road.[12] For Christian communication scholars, this means not only that human communication is one of God's gifts to humanity to be used for his glory, but also that Jesus Christ is the very essence of human communication.

Chapter 60

We Should Talk: G. K. Chesterton and Lesslie Newbigin Respond to George Marsden and Mark Noll

Michael A. Longinow

Response Summary: Mark Noll and George Marsden have made sweeping claims about the slow and steady slide among Christian evangelical colleges and universities from biblical foundations into a kind of surrender to secular approaches to higher education and a dispensing of spiritual formation in favor of humanist approaches. This chapter puts Noll and Marsden in an imagined conference session with G. K. Chesterton and his insights into the life of the mind and soul that inspired C. S. Lewis and Lesslie Newbigin. Lewis's and Newbigin's unpacking of plausibility structures offers Christians confidence that a life of faith is not only possible in intellectual contexts, but preferable.

Picture a ballroom in a conference hotel. You are attending a plenary session. Up front on a stage are two tables with a podium, and four tabletop microphones. Big screens on either side of the stage will give visibility for those in the back. And it is a big room. At one table are Mark Noll and George Marsden. It feels like the Twilight Zone, but at the other table are G. K. Chesterton and Lesslie Newbigin. This panel will be unpacking whether, as the first quarter of the twenty-first century unfolds, the evangelical mind is still scandalous, and in what condition we find the soul of the American university—evangelical Christian universities, included.

The panel topic is aimed at academics, specifically, faculty at Christian colleges and universities. The room is filling up because of the intense scrutiny Christian faculty are facing from many angles. Their viability as a profession is in question.[1]

Most in the room teach at colleges and universities that are tuition driven. Numbers of incoming students, post-pandemic, have been dropping at their schools. And part of the reason is that increasing numbers of Americans simply do not believe in the assumptions of previous generations that a four-year undergraduate degree is either necessary or worth the significant investment. Research into that trend includes Christian families.[2]

All on this panel have some insights into this crucial moment in American history. Each has thoughts for academics at explicitly Christian colleges and universities not only about their role in wider American culture, but about pressures some feel in an era of postmodern cancel culture.[3] Will the panelists agree? Can they? This essay will suggest that after the dust settles from some robust debate, they do. My arguments will be divided into segments based on the panel speakers: Noll will lead off, followed by Marsden. Chesterton will then contribute, followed by Newbigin.

Noll and The Ongoing Scandal

Noll opens the panel by telling the gathered academics that *The Scandal of the Evangelical Mind* was not written directly to address laments with faculty culture or Christian academia; but he points out that he still believes there are lapses in the scholarly elements of undergraduate liberal arts programs in schools of the sort in membership of the Christian College Coalition and the Council for Christian Colleges and Universities. In the first edition of his book, he had given a shout-out to a few schools (Calvin, Messiah, Redeemer, Samford, Steubenville, Wheaton) which he said had "made some progress in the postwar years at promoting scholarship alongside the more general goals of broad learning and basic Christian orientation."[4] Faculty from some of those schools are in the room.

Noll points out his sense, from the book, that the Christian liberal arts university in the late twentieth century was, for the most part, a collection of teaching institutions that contributed little to generating new knowledge beyond the repetitive discussions of doctrine, philosophy, and cultural change.[5]

One critic of Noll's 2022 re-publication of *The Scandal*, now seated in the front row, had said in *The Christian Scholar's Review* that Noll's original laments had not changed much even two decades later.[6] He limits himself to a muted "that's right!" but wants to interrupt Noll to say that "If anything, they've become more pointed." Noll did admit in the new edition of *The Scandal* that the very term "evangelical" had become so spongy as to be useless as an identifier.[7]

Noll repeats to the room what he had said in a column in *First Things* that he was "largely unrepentant" about his book's claims. But he admitted in that column that based on some reader feedback, he would allow today that the problem is not just with Christians, but with "intellectual weakness" in American culture writ large—difficulties of an "advertisement-driven, image-pre-occupied, television-saturated, frenetically hustling consumer society."[8]

With a glance around the ballroom, Noll reinforces his claim that Christian liberal arts colleges and universities have had an "appalling thinness" in their approach to intellectual encounter with culture and ideas, and a preference for quick, trendy answers to societal issues, particularly as these responses bring in new students or donations to their school's ongoing funding base.[9] But he gives a nod to a particular audience member, Nathan Tilley, whose unpublished research cast doubt on "whether intellectual life is a viable Christian vocation," and "whether Christian thinking necessarily involves explicit or distinctive Christian content."[10] Noll also gives a smile to attendee David Bundy, whose critique of *The Scandal* noted the ways that Noll had glossed over scholarly contributions of Holiness, Pentecostal, and Dispensationalist thinkers and the robust colleges, universities, and seminaries in their traditions going back centuries.[11]

Marsden and the Soul of American Universities

None of this is new, says Marsden, picking up the discussion. He notes that Carl F. H. Henry had some pointed words for evangelicals in the 1940s about their lack of critical thinking and practical faith. Henry did not call it a scandal but suggested that evangelicals had reason to search their consciences.[12] Marsden catches the eye of Richard Mouw, sitting up front; he had endorsed Henry's thoughts, having been at Fuller Seminary when Henry was one of the founding faculty.[13]

What you are a part of, Marsden reminds the room, is a game—a game within an experiment. To be a member of the Academy in the United States has always had rules, some written, many unwritten.[14] And the ability of Christian faculty to win at that game has gotten more complicated in recent decades.

American higher education from its earliest years was an attempt to recapture the ethos that was the European medieval university, that elite network of cultures which, by the time Harvard opened its doors, had begun fading as the sole source of spiritual and intellectual meaning in western societies.[15]

What we now call Ivy League schools began with the purpose of training clergy and did so by developing mind and character through a grounding in theology. Theology, in fact, was called the queen of the sciences. It is no more, particularly in the best-funded research universities.[16]

In the earliest North American colleges and universities, faculty and administrators were mostly clergy. They were often the best-educated in a community and their commitment was to guiding students in the life of the mind while cultivating their souls.[17]

Higher education in the pre-colonial United States was guided by a widely accepted subculture of Protestant Christian faith, a subculture that extended into the mid- to late twentieth century.[18] But as the twenty-first century has begun, "You might have noticed a diminishing of that subculture," Marsden says without smiling. Frank McVey, a former president of the University of Kentucky wrote that there is a spirit in every college and university.[19] But that spirit has for decades shifted away from one of spiritual formation to one focused on a new faith and a belief in the mind alone, and human will as preeminent in societal progress.[20]

Tenure is not the guarantee it once was of acceptance into favor in universities of any description. But it remains a kind of coin of the realm.[21] And to earn it in most disciplines requires getting one's research published in peer-reviewed journals or getting a peer-reviewed research papers accepted at prestigious conferences.

Yet Christian academics in the twenty-first century—if they dare pitch research to the peer-reviewed journals and conferences controlled by postmodernist scholars—have cause to fear rejection. In many academic disciplines, there is a kind of inverse proportion between one's commitment to biblical topics (or even to fixed meaning in texts, truth to be found rather than created) and one's being heard, published, or publicly respected among some scholars in the arts, sciences, humanities, or social sciences.[22]

G. K. Chesterton

Chesterton, when it is his turn to speak, needs a nudge. He has been gazing at some action out in the hallway. Has he been listening? Of course. He tosses a wadded-up sheet of hotel note paper at the front row. "We need more imagination in here," he says with a chortle. "We've been so fixated on the life of the mind that we're going to make each other a bit crazy. Imagination does not breed insanity, you know. What does breed insanity is reason." He gives a wink at Noll and sighs. "Ah, the scandals. How we love them and loathe them. And how much more interesting they make our lives." Chesterton tells Noll that his fixation on the evangelical mind is a puzzlement. To Chesterton, the mind in pursuit of Christ is one with a sweeping breadth that covers evangelicals, Catholics, Orthodox, that is, anyone who trusts Christ for salvation.[23]

But he tells the room that Noll's contention that Christian thinkers lack pugnacity is quite on point. The truths of Christ are not merely adequate for discourse in intellectual circles; they are the superior direction, the very truths for which many skeptics secretly long. And the more the skeptics and doubters come at us, Chesterton says, the more doubtful we should become of their doubts. It was doubts, in a sense, that brought him to Christ.[24]

Chesterton tells the room that he shares a sense he has gathered from Noll and Marsden that Christian scholars need to get up, give an answer, fight back with the best scholarly tools. Unless you bring it up, you lose an opportunity to add to what James Carey, seated in the third row, calls the ongoing conversation of communication.[25] Jesus calls us to go into all the world and make disciples; all the world includes the classrooms, laboratories, and studios of American colleges and universities. But how do we go? "Not by retreat," he says.

Evangelicals have shifted to the back foot: they are retreating, turning toward each other when they should be advancing, reaching into new spheres, Chesterton says. And evangelical scholars' recessive stance suggests they do not really grasp the truth of God's sovereignty over the natural realm, over the academic enterprise.

Postmodern higher education, the Academy in the twenty-first century is not evil, not an enemy, he tells the room, with a glance at Marsden. If there is pain involved in the new struggles that Christian faculty have, C. S. Lewis would say, perhaps it is God's megaphone getting their attention.[26] Lewis was a reader of Chesterton, and he has just taken a seat in the back.[27]

The thinking of postmodern academics, and perhaps even some doubting evangelicals is not bad, says Chesterton. "In some ways," he adds with a grin, "it is far too good," noting a line from his book *Orthodoxy*. "It is full of wild and wasted virtues."[28]

Chesterton pauses, then confronts Noll's claim that the scandal of the evangelical mind was evangelicals' lack of presence in the intellectual marketplace of ideas. Yet they had been there all along, he says. Noll had admitted that a key means of the advance of Christian culture and thought through the centuries had been media. He saw most of it as lacking both intellect and influence.[29]

"Define influence and intellect," Chesterton says to Noll. He recounts his story, from his book *Orthodoxy*, of a man in a boat who believes he has found an uncharted land, claiming it for England. He believed he had left the past and found the future, a new place. The paradox was that his bold venture to what he thought was a distant place was, in reality, a return home.

The last line in Noll's *The Scandal of the Evangelical Mind* is telling. He says pursuit of the mind is the pursuit of God. And anti-intellectualism among evangelicals is, in part, a myopia bred of over-emphasis on doing rather than thinking.[30] But Niebuhr would differ with Noll on this: belief necessitates action as much or more than words, he claims.[31] Niebuhr is seated on a back row.

Plato would tell Noll that an intellectual mind is not merely a function of schools; it is a thing created by community, or people to people. Dewey would pick up this notion by saying that community, in turn, emerges through a robust press and people who follow it.[32] Historian Nathan Hatch, among others, has argued that media narratives were integral to the growth and spread of evangelicalism in the United States.[33] Hatch, seated near the front, smiles at Chesterton's point. His sense is that the life of the evangelical mind, over time, spread by word of mouth and shared publications, not merely in scholarly settings. Hatch called the early American republic a collection of mostly common people whose collective commitment to know God, and learn about God, was profoundly committed to "the vernacular in word, print and song."[34] Revivals, or awakenings of faith, were more than emotional reactions to God in the history of American evangelicalism. They were also a turning to a life of the mind in pursuit of God in his Scriptures and writings about it.[35]

Lesslie Newbigin

Newbigin, as attention turns to him, smiles at the crowd and the other panelists. The last on any panel suffers from the largesse of those listed first, he says. He has a little time left to make his points. But he begins by telling the audience to consider the space in which they are sitting. Some are close to the stage, some far away. Where each chose to sit determined their perspective on the action, and part of the scandal that Noll speaks of stems from this truth. Reinhold Niebuhr argued that positional stance is, itself, a means of understanding the world. Where one chooses to see things, and those with whom one sees them, is an interpretive community.[36]

Too many evangelicals, he says, whether in the Academy or not, have stepped back from a crucial dialogue. To limit one's intellectual encounters only to those with the same theological vocabulary is a mistake. The skepticism of naturalists and postmodernists is every bit a faith perspective as is a Christian's conviction that God is real and alive in their lives and in history.[37] When a naturalist or postmodernist is willing to admit this reality, Christian intellectuals can come alongside this unbelieving neighbor and say, "stand with me and see if you don't see the same pattern I do."[38]

Perhaps there does remain a scandal among evangelical thinkers, Newbigin says; the question of whether the soul of the American university can be revived is still salient. But our task in the twenty-first century is not what to think about it—it is who we are thinking with. The focus must be on strategic encounter. Scholars who claim Christ as Lord must find ways of asking research-based questions that explore the wonders of God's order in any academic discipline. And the nomenclature, the very rhetorical stance of such questions must consider who will read or do peer review on the research. The Apostle Paul's example at the Areopagas is instructive: he knew the poetry of his hearers, as well as the faith systems they either held or understood. And it framed his presentation of Christ (see Acts 17:22–31).

The dogmas that skeptics of Christian thinking hold are dogmas so pervasive that they appear invisible to the skeptics. They are a set of beliefs that cannot be easily changed, Newbigin says. It does no good to attack these dogmas, or those who hold them. A combative stance only alienates.[39]

With that, the moderator points to his watch and apologetically closes the session, inviting anyone with more questions to come forward. The aisles immediately fill as scholars approach.

Chapter 61

Developing the Ethos to be Outrageous and Scandalous: Preparing for the Inspiration to Change the World

STEPHEN D. PERRY

Response Summary: How do Christian scholars effectively provide outrageous ideas that will be considered and debated by other scholars? This essay argues that scholars must build a track record and develop the credibility to say things outside of the mainstream, get them published, and have them considered. The ensuing ethos becomes one of the mechanisms that can convince others to pay attention to outrageous ideas. Christian scholars should show that they can speak to communication issues in ways that advance knowledge both in secular as well as in specialized faith spaces. Making research progress on secular fronts is not a waste of time for the Christian scholar. It, in fact, may well be necessary both from the perspective of advancing human flourishing and to set the stage for how faith integrates with those ideas. The author demonstrates the advantage of developing ethos by relating the trajectory of his own experience as a scholar in the Academy.

I ATTENDED A CHRISTIAN COLLEGE and studied mass communication. We had a Christian music radio station on campus and were sharing the Gospel though the words of songwriters and artists who recorded Contemporary Christian Music (CCM). We wrestled with how to behave as a Christian in the profession of media, asking questions about whether we could take jobs at secular radio stations that played music filled with lyrics of lust or greed, sung by musicians who were often in the news for drug use and sexual deviance.

It was only in my philosophy and theology classes that were part of the general education core, however, that we really dug into deep faith questions. At least one professor, whom I still disagree with in nearly every one of his posts on Facebook, seemed to be a true thinker. And, no, Facebook is not a venue where I find it worth engaging him with my disagreements.

Unfortunately, my Christian college education introduced me to this scholar who was at times outrageous as a thinker but did not prepare me to truly engage in Christian thinking. In fact, I do not think most of my professors were more than practitioners who liked to teach. They were fine men and women, and I thought I was getting a good education. But the truth is, if they had been the scandalous, outrageous thinkers that behaved like Jesus, they would not have had a job at my institution for very long.

Jesus was outrageous and scandalous. It was outrageous to tell people that the meek will inherit the earth or that they are blessed when they are persecuted because of righteousness. It is outrageous to believe that we should rejoice when people insult us and persecute us and falsely, say all kinds of evil against us because of Jesus. Should we get upset and defend ourselves? Oh, but if we are to become academic prophets who challenge the power structures in our field and the status quo of scholarly orthodoxy in communication, we will be like the prophets that Jesus talked about who were persecuted in the same ways and yet continued to prophesy (see Matt. 5:5–12).

And what if we must absorb ridicule, anger, a lost job, and other hardships? Jesus was outrageous about that, too. If someone sues you and takes your shirt, give him your coat as well? If they force you to go one mile, go two miles (Matt. 5:40–41). Never mind that when his time came to challenge the top brass, he did not ride in on a horse to "show them," but chose a donkey to enter humbly (Matt. 21:5–8). When someone was needed to help with the washing, he bent down and washed dirty feet, all the while knowing that all things were "under his power" (John 13:3–5).

Perhaps after we examine Jesus we think, "Well let's just head recklessly down the path of being outrageous." Maybe you've seen those panels at academic communication conferences, in which scholars present their research on body piercings in strange places or on the rhetoric of breasts or on the sh**ification of Twitter.[1] There have even been reports of conference presentations done in the nude. Those are outrageous and scandalous as well. Maybe a Christian communicator should be equally outrageous in some other direction. I am not sure what that would look like—but while you think that over, let me stop you there.

There needs to be much preparation before you engage the outrageous as a Christian scholar. Just think of the times Jesus kept his outrageous actions and teaching a secret for a time. The leper was not to tell anyone (Matt. 8:4). The disciples were not to tell anyone he was the Messiah (Matt. 16:20). The transfiguration scene witnessed by Peter, James, and John was to be kept a secret until Jesus was raised from the dead (Matt. 17:9; Mark 9:9). Healings were sometimes to be kept secret (Mark 7:36; Luke 8:56). Buy why? In Jesus's case it may have been because it would have brought trouble on him from the authorities too quickly for the timeline to the planned crucifixion. But also, the outrageous sometimes needs to be supported by ethos, and ethos comes with time. Let's talk about that next.

Earning the Right to be Outrageous

New PhDs often make breakthroughs. But there are very few who do that in a notable way. For some, it is the good fortune of mixing past experiences with new communication knowledge. For others, perhaps it is their personal brilliance and the support of a reputable faculty who help push forward the new breakthrough. While those things happen, for most of us, we need to build credibility in the field for several years to gain a reputation that allows us to challenge entrenched beliefs. If you are that new scholar, it might take discernment to know within which of those camps you are, but most fall into the latter camp.

Well-trained Christian scholars will have some insights that allow them to combine Christian experience and theological knowledge with theories in the field of communication. But those insights are not automatic, and if they are not handled well, they may struggle to gain support from those who have believed competing views for years. So are outrageous ideas to be tossed out into the academic mainstream frequently and furiously, or should they be handled more internally, within a supporting group of Christian scholars, as the ideas are refined and honed into something that can compete well in the field?

Earlier I pointed out where Jesus told people to keep certain acts or knowledge secret for a time. He knew there was wisdom in waiting. However, he did not perform all of his miracles or teach in private. He declared the outrageous ideas in the "Sermon on the Mount" in front of a large crowd. Herein is the tension as we try to be the outrageous Christian thinkers that Spenser and Marsden encourage, while still being "shrewd as serpents and innocent as doves" (Matt. 10:16, Christian Standard Bible).[2]

The tension comes as scholars avoid faith topics to earn a position on an esteemed university's faculty or to earn tenure. That may be humanly wise or shrewd. But the conflict comes when the faculty member goes down a path of research that makes it hard to integrate faith-themed ideas post tenure. It is like hiding your faith from your neighbors for six years and then suddenly trying to witness to them.

And what can scholars teach in the classroom? If their ideas have not been published and vetted through peer review, or at least editor review in a reputable outlet, can they teach it to students without difficulty from administration? Even after publication, teaching the content may raise complaints. So how should Christian scholars make their impact?

I am not advocating for a single "right" way in this essay, but I am working toward giving you permission to earn your place in the field before trying to be outrageous. That does not mean I encourage hiding your faith. All scholars, even non-Christian and atheistic ones, ought to know what the faith variable does as part of our communication experience. But there are questions related to faith that you should be brave enough to address and then there are things that would be considered outrageous to a person who has no Christian understanding. Those latter items may need to wait until you have the ethos to propose them.

In my early career I published research on Christian music (CCM) radio formatted stations with my accomplished thesis advisor.[3] I authored work on the meanings of the music of a CCM recording artist to his fans.[4] And I even published research on religious broadcasting in Australia, comparing the government policies there to those in the U.S. and looking at the resulting religious media landscape.[5] But I also published secularly on the Freedom of Information Act, on the influence of humorous advertisements and comedy programming, and on exemplar theory and the spiral of silence before being considered for tenure. Was I wasting my time working on secular ideas?

If academia is of any value to the world, we should understand our secular work as part of helping human flourishing. It helps us prepare students to excel at their communication craft as it works its way into textbooks and lectures. We do not know how our research will be used, ultimately, so if our research goals are in the service of our neighbor whom we are to love, even researching secular topics can be regarded as work in God's service. But while we do that, we also build a reputation for doing solid research.

Now, fast forward to my years as a senior professor. I had edited a top 10% journal in the field successfully. I was asked to serve as the chair of the research committee of the Broadcast Education Association. I had co-authored a theory textbook. So in about 2015 when God clearly said, "I want you to write a conference paper on peace journalism," a subject I had thought about from a Christian integration perspective but had never written about, I had both the ethos and the call to begin being outrageous and even scandalous.

Becoming Outrageous and Scandalous

I had been introduced to peace journalism as an editor, when I accepted an article for publication in *Mass Communication and Society* written by Lee and Maslog.[6] It turned out to be one of my favorite articles that we published during my editorship. But I had a problem with it. Some of the assumptions of peace journalism were at odds with what Christian theology teaches about human nature and our propensity to do evil. Most of the scholarship at that time examined direct violence, the kind that is easily seen as bullets and bombs fill the pages and packages in the news. Scholars assumed that if we could just have journalists write in such a way that we would de-escalate violence, people would stop killing each other. It assumed people would be reasonable and look for paths to peace if the media did not provoke confrontation.

The theory discussed cultural and systemic violence as well, but little of the research investigated those kinds without still prioritizing direct violence. There was little mention of how to handle leaders in the mold of a Pol Pot or a Mussolini or a Hitler. The subtle undertone was that it would be better to allow leaders to subject a certain people group to low wages, poor living conditions, and few rights than to have actual fighting to save them. Is that right from a Christian perspective? Initially I simply pushed back and pointed out how the vulnerable, sick, and poor were the ones dying under sanctions that were meant to pressure governments prior to war. In fact, claims were that more people died from sanctions prior to the Iraq War than the number who died from direct violence during the war. I argued that ethically, we must consider the faces of both those who die during war and those who die from the sanctions and other evils of rulers whose actions have precipitated the perceived need for war in the first place.[7] Quoting from an episode of *Madam Secretary*, I noted that "War is always wrong . . . always! But some things are wronger."[8]

That article began a line of research for me on peace journalism. Much of it was mainstream, simply measuring various aspects of how the media dealt with conflict. I taught graduate seminars on the topic, directed dissertations, co-authored with students, and my students even edited and authored books on peace journalism after their graduation. Then I was given the opportunity to author an article in *Journal of Broadcasting and Electronic Media* on the state of Peace Journalism as an area of research. Benefitted by the ethos of years of publishing scholarly research, I crafted an essay based in the literature of peace journalism but cross-examined it with a theory from philosophy of Christian realism. I talked about Luther and Calvin and Augustine's philosophy about just war and raised questions about how journalists should evaluate conflict situations using a framework to assess which side demonstrated true motivations to help people.[9]

I received strong support from two reviewers of the article and strong opposition from a third. But ultimately, I was able to persuade the editor that the specific objections of the third reviewer ran counter to the desires of the first two (objections that seemed clearly motivated against Christian integration), and the article was accepted. The ethos of years in the Academy, I believe, were important to that acceptance. And out of that article, two of my students recently published their own follow-up study in *Journalism and Mass Communication Quarterly* using the moniker "just peace" journalism—extoling equitable peace that is lasting rather than a false peace that allows injustices to simmer.[10] It is the concept of *shalom*.

It is outrageous and scandalous to many in Christianity as well as to peace studies and peace journalism advocates that the integration of Just War Theory with Peace Journalism leaves open the possibility of necessary war. Just War Theory pulls heavily from Scripture and Christian forefathers to make its case, but the claims are not universally accepted. Pacifist groups like the Anabaptists would certainly think differently, as do many academics who claim that violence simply begets violence.[11] So to many, this work is scandalous. The outrageous idea of this Christian scholarship is that it should provide for robust debate both from a secular and from a Christian perspective. Yet, I am convinced that if we are to love our neighbor, we must think like Dietrich Boenhoffer, who believed that to watch the genocide of the Jews and do nothing was more evil than to try to kill Adolf Hitler.

I have a few years left to engage that idea and introduce new faith inspired integrations, both through my students and through my writing and speaking. Most recently, I was inspired to introduce a new paradigm of what news should be. In my recent talk to the Christianity and Communication Studies Network (CCSN), I emphasized the need to move from a "fourth estate" mindset to a "jubilee" mindset.[12] Perhaps that should be thought of as a "human flourishing" mindset in the long run, but my first writing was a book chapter on how to embrace jubilee principles rather than being tribal.[13] I continue to advance that work.

That effort, like my peace journalism research, was Holy Spirit inspired. God spoke to me as I read the book of Leviticus. He planted an outrageous idea in the mind of someone who has just enough ethos and enough protection at my Christian university employer to attempt this outrageous idea. To those who have conflated politics and Christianity, this may also be scandalous in the church. But if God blesses, it will help solve a dilemma in journalism that secular ideas have not yet found a solution to.

In conclusion, I encourage you to listen to the voice and timing of God. Put the other projects on the shelf if necessary to take up what he tells you to research. Be hesitant to make the outrageous your goal until he calls. Until then, be faithful with research that loves your neighbor and loves your God but always be looking and listening for how the Holy Spirit may inspire new outrageous ideas.

Chapter 62

Theorizing the Supernatural: Exploring Spiritual Interaction through Social Science

Jonathan Pettigrew

Response Summary: What makes the study of human communication distinctly Christian? This case study considers how a social scientist might approach theory development from observations about human experience recorded in Scripture. The Bible repeatedly illustrates that human beings interface with demonic and angelic spirits, not to mention with God himself. A researcher might design a study to pursue questions like: When does the unseen spiritual realm show up within the perceptible? How does exorcism work? The case suggests studies that would put questions into limited, but testable models to explore supernatural communication.

CHRISTIAN ACADEMICS, researchers, and students have an opportunity to derive theory from Scripture and then go about refining the theoretical links and boundary conditions for which the theory holds. Because the Bible and Christian theology teach that reality includes both natural and supernatural aspects, we can theorize from this ontological position. Participating in this type of theory development would begin to elucidate communication between the spiritual and natural parts of reality and contribute toward a more holistic communication theory that does not simply ignore the supernatural but seeks to expose and understand it. For example, we might generate hypotheses about prayer as a conversation with the Divine or attempt to derive principles for managing conflict in organizations. These would subsequently be translated into testable, theoretical models of human communication.

Here is an example of how this might look in practice. Scripture illustrates that humans interface with demonic and angelic spirits, not to mention with God himself. Throughout the Bible, angels interact with humans. In the Christmas story, for example, Gabriel announces the birth of Christ to Mary (Luke 1) and in a dream, Joseph is warned by an angel to avoid the jealousy of Harod and move to Egypt (Matt. 2:13–15). It was not just the key players in the story that met the angelic, either. Angels visit unnamed shepherds pulling a graveyard shift (Luke 2:8–18). Demons also speak to Jesus and his disciples. Remember these statements? "My name is Legion" (Mark 5:9); "Jesus I know, and Paul I know about, but who are you?" (Acts 19:15). The Gospels also record times when Jesus and his disciples speak to demonic beings. During his 40-day temptation, Jesus speaks directly to Satan (Matt. 4:4, 7, 10) and Christ and his disciples speak to unclean spirits.

So a Christian approaching the study of human communication might ask: How do people communicate with God and spirits? When does the unseen spiritual realm show up in perceptible ways? How do people obtain authority over supernatural beings? These questions would need to be put into a limited, but testable model.

Take the idea of exorcism and communicating with evil spirits, for example. One approach is to identify variables, define them, and then develop some propositions that put these into relationship.[1] These could take the form x causes y, for p population under z conditions. We might observe in the Gospel accounts that commanding/rebuking demons causes distress (sometimes violent physical convulsions) and then dramatic relief. Further, the pattern seems to depend on a close association with Jesus. Luke 10 shares about 70 who went out, amazed that demons were subject to their authority. But another story in Acts 19 shares about the seven sons of Sceva who were beaten and stripped and sent running from the man possessed by demons. The Gospels also include an account where Jesus's disciples cannot exorcise a demon (Matt. 17:14–21). Given this pattern in Scripture, we might then theorize that when people closely associated with Jesus rebuke/command demonic spirits, subjects who are chronically oppressed by demonic spirits will experience distress (perhaps even physical convulsions) followed by a dramatic relief.

Moving to the level of study design, an experiment could be ethically questionable. We cannot randomly assign people to a demon-oppressed condition and others to a control condition. It also might be difficult to recruit a sample of demon-oppressed people. So naturalistic observation would be a more practical approach. We might travel with a team who perform exorcisms and take field notes or locate Christian ministries who perform spiritual deliverance, such as Francis MacNutt.[2] We might interview pastors of various Christian denominations and inquire about their experiences with the demonic. These observations would provide a lens through which to test the theoretical proposition that x causes y for p population under z conditions. We also might collect narratives from those who claim to have experienced spiritual deliverance. Such a project could utilize a narrative analysis to discover the commonalities among a corpus of stories and discern patterns of experiences.

This example seeks to illustrate that Christian thinkers and social scientists could derive theory from Scripture and perform sets of studies, using various methods, to expand, refine, discard, or modify those theories. By theorizing the unseen, spiritual realm, scholars provide a pathway for subsequent study, debate, and engagement. Theory is how data are translated into meaningful ideas and a way to illuminate aspects of reality that are otherwise ignored. Thus, developing social scientific theory is a significant and opportune task for Christian academics.

Chapter 63

Book Review of *Beyond Equality: Women Leaders in Higher Education*

Elizabeth B. Jones

Response Summary: During the author's time at the CCSN unconference, her discussion with colleagues focused on how to traverse disagreements and build trust and respect among Christian scholars. Gender roles surfaced as one such potential difference among Christians that might play a role in navigating disagreements and fostering trust. In *Women Leaders*, author Savanah Landerholm posits that gender equality is a needed prerequisite for cultivating women leaders but is in and of itself inadequate to surmount the unique structural, cultural, and nurture challenges that women face when summiting the academic ladder. Although the text is not written from an explicitly faith-informed viewpoint, Landerholm identifies these challenges, presents archetypical ways women have navigated them, and offers thoughts on cultivating responsive agency for women leaders.

In BEYOND EQUALITY: *Women Leaders in Higher Education*, Savanah N. Landerholm celebrates that women today have more access to workplace opportunity than ever before.[1] Women have entered the workforce en masse and earn more undergraduate and graduate degrees than men. Why, then, with this pipeline of qualified candidates, do women still comprise a tiny proportion of senior leadership in higher education? Landerholm posits that gender equality, understood as parity of "status, rights, and opportunities" is a needed prerequisite for cultivating women leaders but is in and of itself inadequate to surmount the unique challenges women face when summiting the academic ladder.[2] She acknowledges the complexity of changing gender roles in society and notes that her research findings may at times also apply to minorities or working parents more generally. However, she maintains that biological characteristics (such as pregnancy, childbirth, lactation) and traditional conceptions of gender (such as man as leader and provider, woman as follower and nurturer) continue to permeate women's workplace experiences. She notes that although women have experienced dramatic improvements in workplace discrimination over the past century, "the problem still exists; it is yesterday's news *and* today's news but hopefully not tomorrow's news."[3] And indeed, the book's central thrust is how women leaders in higher education navigate tricky terrain, make severely constrained choices, and exercise a significant degree of agency in their professions despite the odds stacked against them.

The book's five chapters contextualize and elucidate the varied career trajectories embodied by the senior-level leaders in higher education Landerholm interviewed to inform the text. Chapter 1 provides a succinct and helpful introduction to the framework that informs her investigation. She first notes that many of the obstacles to leadership faced by women in academia are rooted in beliefs that have been operative for much of human history. As Landerholm notes:

> Women are considered less powerful—less strength, less endurance, less force. Women are considered less qualified—less educated, less knowledgeable, less experienced. Women are considered less capable—less dominating, less aggressive, less decisive. Though these are *just* stereotypes, the message is crystal clear that women are less than men.[4]

Landerholm then contends that it is challenging for women to attain senior leadership positions because these gender stereotypes infiltrate multiple layers of higher education; namely, "*structure* (policies and procedures), *culture* (internal and external pressures), and *nurture* (models and mentors)."[5] She notes that although women benefit from legal protections that often preclude overt gender discrimination, structural barriers remain at least subtly operative. Glass ceilings prevent ascending leadership ladders, sticky floors anchor women in low-prestige positions, and maternal walls dictate if and how women will work once they are mothers. Cultural strictures involve shared values and beliefs and encompass concepts like expectations for working mothers to perform tirelessly and proficiently across the spheres of home and work, which Landerholm identifies as two "greedy institutions" that demand total commitment.[6] Women also benefit from career-focused nurture that manifests through modeling, mentorship, and support; however, it can be challenging for women to develop these kinds of leadership development networks. Higher education leaders' careers exist at the nexus of structure, culture, and nurture.

Although each woman called to lead responds creatively to the opportunities and constraints of her context, Landerholm asserts that three archetypes emerge for women leaders in higher education: "passers," "pushers," and "peacekeepers." Chapters 2, 3, and 4, respectively, elucidate these archetypes. Landerholm's assertions are drawn from her personal interviews with 41 women senior-level administrators including deans, provosts, vice-presidents, and presidents from a diverse range of institutions. Those leaders identified as passers ascended to leadership positions by positioning themselves as "one of the guys" and downplaying their perceived difference or femininity. They tended to be goal-oriented, assertive, and career-focused. Many chose to overcome structural and cultural barriers to leadership by sequencing their family life and careers; namely, by waiting until their children were older to go "all in" on their demanding career trajectory. Pushers were passionate about furthering gender equality within their institutions and serving as a catalyst for change. Many identified as feminists. Landerholm characterized pushers as principle-oriented, aggressive, and women-focused. They desired to model work-life balance through positive deviance; for example, by bringing their children to work events. Peacekeepers, in contrast, tended to work within existing systems. As Landerholm noted, "Others describe them as sweet, kind, dedicated, loyal, deserving of leadership. They earned their way to a position of leading."[7] Peacekeepers were described as relationally oriented, empathetic, and family-focused. Women situated in this archetype tended to experience the most self-doubt in their leadership abilities when compared to the other archetypes, a phenomenon often labeled as *imposter syndrome*. Landerholm challenges this label by noting it places the onus on women to stop doubting their own qualifications and abilities, rather than acknowledging the pervasive gender stereotypes that promulgated such beliefs in the first place.

Chapter 5 concludes by providing an ethics of responsive agency intended to move women leaders in higher education beyond equality. Landerholm notes, "Responsive agency, an embodied theological response to gender oppression, offers a way forward for women looking to advance in the workplace and to move beyond equality."[8] Responsiveness involves awareness of the strands of structure, culture, and nurture that inform workplace experiences, and an understanding of persons' relationship with these forces. Agency, then, builds on this awareness to acknowledge women's ability to act meaningfully in their situation. Landerholm asserts that "women must be agents for their own liberation" who seek to free all others as well.[9] The flux of higher education today is presented as an opportunity for women to move beyond equality and to create structures, cultures, and nurturing relationships that make profoundly difficult and constraining choices between work and family less common.

This slim volume possesses overarching strengths that make it well-suited to several audiences. The book is brief and accessible, while still offering robust academic support for its claims. Thus, anyone involved in administration or faculty development could glean insights helpful in cultivating women leaders in their own institutions. The book would be an edifying balm for many women in any phase of the academic journey, though perhaps particularly suited to early-career scholars. As noted in the text, Landerholm's interest in this research topic surfaced from her affinity for leadership and having a baby while in graduate school. Many of the author's observations resonate with my experiences as a working mother of four who has navigated her academic career to date while pregnant or parenting young children. As Landerholm notes, "Children are not the problem; children are indeed gifts from God, the author and creator of the universe."[10] And yet, many working mothers can identify viscerally with Landerholm's simultaneous contention that, due to societal and organizational pressures, "[a] woman must be more even when her tank is empty."[11]

Although *Beyond Equality: Women Leaders in Higher Education* is not written from an explicitly faith-informed viewpoint, this work is valuable reading for Christ-following communication scholars. This book emerged as a title worthy of review based on my unconference experience. We learned from renowned Legacy Scholars prior to the unconference who thoughtfully extended the themes of Noll's and Marsden's texts to consider Christian teaching and scholarship today. I was challenged and inspired by each presenter and observed—with curiosity rather than evaluation—an absence of female voices. During the conference my discussion table focused on traversing disagreements and building trust and respect among Christian scholars. One of our discussion prompts was: how can we navigate profound differences and work together in meaningful ways that maintain healthy relationships? Gender roles surfaced for me as but one such difference. Landerholm acknowledges that religion has been used as tool of oppression against women.[12] It is imperative to note these abuses of power and to work against them. It is also important to acknowledge that varying traditions within Christianity hold different perspectives on the roles of women and that these beliefs may tangibly influence women's leadership experiences. As a Christian female scholar who teaches at a faith-based institution rooted in gender egalitarianism, my own experiences and convictions inform my perspective. Neither I nor my tablemates left our discussion with glib platitudes on navigating profound differences among believing scholars. However, like Knoll, Marsden, and our Legacy Scholars, I remain hopeful. *Beyond Equality* reminds us that people's embodied, lived realities matter. Communication can be life-giving, and we can partner together to create flourishing *shalom* communities for all within our institutions.

Despite the book's considerable strengths, I found myself at times wishing for additional nuance and information given the complexity of these gender-related topics. Detailed discussions of the study's methods and findings, as well as further discussion of the theological concepts briefly alluded to within the book would strengthen the manuscript. In addition, although I appreciate the agency and creativity afforded to individual women leaders in the book's final chapter, there is some inconsistency in the attribution of responsibility to context versus the individual. Many of the most interesting points in the study are found in the end notes, and after reading these, I often wished for even more of the author's astute insight. The lack of nuance at points is not a fatal flaw of the manuscript but rather reflects the inevitable tradeoffs between complexity and accessibility Landerholm navigates. In sum, this book is not written from a Christian or communication perspective, but it nonetheless offers helpful insight for those of us who wish to promote flourishing within our institutions. May we remember: "There is neither Jew nor Gentile, neither slave nor free, nor is there male and female, for you are all one in Christ Jesus" (Gal. 3:28).

Afterword

Communicating Scholars

Kenneth R. Chase

Response Summary: This volume provides occasion for gratitude and lament, appreciating the contributions of Mark Noll and George Marsden to Christian intellectual inquiry yet sharing the disappointment that growth in Christian scholarship has not seen a commensurate growth of Christian intellectual influence in church and society. Given this disappointment, Christian communication scholars have distinctive opportunities for inquiry. The author highlights how Noll, Marsden, and others within this volume conceive of these opportunities. Then, building upon these, he offers two additional directions for Christian communication inquiry: (1) reflecting upon the formation of a Christian mind, and (2) conceptualizing communication not merely as a means but as integral to the practices of Christian faithfulness.

Gratitude

THIS COLLECTION reminds us of the awe-inspiring and joyful truth that Christians ought to love God with their minds. Those of us called to be Christian scholars have particular occasion to give thanks for the profound and godly influence of Mark Noll and George Marsden, whose modeling of love in word and deed have shaped not only our personal lives (I, for one, have been blessed with the indelible imprint of Noll's scholarship), but extends to scholars and academic disciplines across the Academy, including the discipline of communication represented by the existence of the Christianity and Communication Studies Network (CCSN) and this volume.

Our gratitude, though, is accompanied with deep concern. As Noll and Marsden note, both in this volume and in the new editions of their now-classic books, the admirable growth in Christian scholarship since the original publication of *Scandal* and *Outrageous* three decades ago is paralleled by what appears to be a dismissal of the Christian mind by millions of self-identified evangelicals. For many of our Christian brothers and sisters in the U.S., the "scandal of the evangelical mind" is the fact of its existence, not its absence. The haunting truth is that many evangelicals, particularly White evangelicals, believe that Christians entering higher education are risking their faith through the seductions of a "woke" liberalism that elevates critical reasoning, multi-culturalism, and social justice above the truth of God's Word.[1] In a recent *Christian Scholar's Review* forum devoted to Marsden's updated edition of *Outrageous*, Marsden states this bluntly: "we have not been successful in reaching most of our most natural constituencies, which would be evangelical churches and communities."[2]

Of course, a lot of Christian scholarship points directly to the very causes of this evangelical suspicion toward the Christian mind. Not the least of these, of course, is Noll's own analysis in *Scandal*. For several authors in this edited volume, bridging the gap between church and Academy is a pressing challenge for the Christian mind. Noll is explicit: "For the life of the mind, I would identify the most serious problem as the disconnect between the academic world and the churches."[3] This is a particularly salient problem for those of us whose scholarship is in the communication discipline. After all, we ought to be the scholars supposedly knowledgeable about the dynamics of connecting and disconnecting. Therefore, what do we offer as Christian communication scholars to advance Christian scholarship in our churches?

This communication challenge is not limited to believers in the pews. Noll also identifies the pressing need of developing alternative delivery systems for Christian scholarship, combatting the mediated populism dominating both church and culture and exploring, in contrast, "the means of propagation, the means of publicity, [and] the means of presentation" through which our scholarship can have its rightful impact.[4] As Noll sees it, therefore, Christian communication scholarship focuses on how Christian intellectual reflection is brought to bear on church and society.

Marsden, too, recognizes the ongoing need for the influence of Christian scholars, particularly in the Academy. As he notes in this volume and explains in more detail in the newly added content for the 2024 edition of *Outrageous*, highly politicized approaches to academic disciplines and deeply held objections to Christian moral commitments provide new forms of resistance to distinctively Christian scholarship.[5] How, then, do Christian scholars move forward in such a climate? This edited volume provides numerous answers, particularly for communication scholars. After briefly summarizing a few of these answers, I suggest two additional directions for communication scholars: first, reflecting on what it means to develop a Christian mind, and second, conceptualizing communication as an ends, not merely as a means, of Christian practice.

Moving Forward

Where do Christian communication scholars go from here? Marsden's answer in this volume is similar to his answer 30 years ago. Although he is not as explicit as Noll in naming this as a challenge for communication scholars, it is every bit as much a communication-focused answer. Christians ought to operate as pluralists in the Academy, Marsden says, modeling the sorts of citizenship conducive to intellectual inquiry and the respect for diverse views. Or, to put it another way, Marsden urges the Christian scholar also to be a certain kind of communicator. As he states in the 2024 edition of *Outrageous*, "Christians should strive to preserve rules of civil discourse that protect the expression of diverse views. And rather than being always ready to fight, they should be always willing to listen, to give opposing viewpoints a fair hearing, and to value careful argument over facile rhetoric."[6] Indeed, this master historian also would be a delightful guest lecturer in any Communication 101 course: be civil, listen rather than fight, provide opportunity for opposing viewpoints, and use argument rather than "facile rhetoric."

We find these sorts of recommendations scattered throughout this collection, giving depth and color to Marsden's summary. The values guiding Marsden's pluralism could be right at home, I suspect, with the value-laden commitments of Jesuit education, as Fr. Paul A. Soukup, SJ, documents. Quentin Schultze provides his own list overlapping Marsden's, with the added benefit of providing strategic insight into message effectiveness. Greg Spencer's commitment to wisdom and character could be an eloquent gloss on the entire list, reminding us that Marsden's pluralist behaviors are rooted in character formation. Any institution operating according to Clifford G. Christians's epistemology of intellectual pluralism would benefit from the collegial ethic Marsden recommends. And Nicholas Wolterstorff's story about his student's impertinent quotation of a Bible verse concludes with the wise, pluralist advice of how the student could improve class participation: "You know, I can't put it into words, but I think if you just listen for a while you'll catch on."[7]

Both Noll and Marsden, therefore, provide Christian communication scholars with some initial directions and purpose. Communication equips and enables believers and nonbelievers to enter into the life of the mind. This is a matter of expanding influence, of having our communication scholarship advance Christian intellectual inquiry. If we take the Christian mind to be marked by a careful consideration of Scripture and the world (to do "double work," in Troup's felicitous phrasing), then communication scholarship must take seriously the very challenge to scholarship within the Academy. In his pointed observations on the church's co-optation by secular values, Mark Allan Steiner states the path forward this way: "we need to be very intentional in cultivating a more intellectual and theological culture in the church."[8] Perhaps Richard Mouw's question is the key to this entire volume: "how do we do a better job of bringing the fruits of scholarship of this kind to the front ranks of evangelicalism?"[9]

Thus, either explicitly or implicitly, this volume places communication at the front and center in the challenges facing Christian scholarship. So what ought we think of this prospect for communication scholarship? The invitation of this volume is to press forward and not merely celebrate gains or to ponder resistances. By pulling through some of the threads of the Legacy Scholar essays in this volume, I provide two additional recommendations.

1. Reconsider the Christian Mind

This collection assumes we ought to have a Christian mind, which is called forth in the command to love God and practiced through scholarship witnessing to the beauty and glory of his creation. For the advance of Christian communication scholarship, though, this assumption ought to be reflectively examined. I do not mean that Christians ought not use their minds (!), but that what we mean by "mind" ought not be "mindlessly" accepted.

In his 2022 Preface to *Scandal*, Noll characterizes the Christian mind as a "creative, outward-looking, self-confident, and open-minded intellectual life" marked by humility, self-criticism, and eagerness for God's truth.[10] For Christian academics, this is an encouraging and straightforward list of traits. Although we could press into each of these, seeking nuance of definition and variance of application, the list is suitable for opening the conversation about a Christian mind and its relative presence or absence in church, Academy, and society. My recommendation, though, works a different angle. I propose we critically reflect on the animating ideal of the Christian intellectual underlying this list, that we consider further the subjectivity often presumed within our deeply imagined vision of how to live, teach, and study in ways that characterize us as having Christian minds.

I raise this issue because it is all too easy to presume, within the way we imagine the life of the mind, the very sort of subjectivity challenged from all quarters and through multiple diverse orientations within the Academy. Within the communication discipline, and particularly within rhetorical studies, a phrase such as "Christian mind" already presumes too much about human subjectivity to be accepted uncritically as the cornerstone of Christian intellectual inquiry. The historical accounting of today's Christian mind, as we find in Noll and Marsden, may too easily be located within the contours of a modern subjectivity formed, as a Foucauldian would say, through structures of power/knowledge. Today's rhetoricians would see an appeal to this "mind"—and the particular selection of traits associated with it—as weighted ideologically and inseparable from troublesome modern intellectual ideals.[11]

Thus, from this disciplinary perspective, what counts as appropriate operations for the Christian mind, even how we operationalize loving God with one's mind, is an advocated and ideologically inflected position rather than a starting point. Even those other terms used in this volume to ground the work of Christian intellectuals would be viewed suspiciously, such as "academic excellence," "scholarship," and "pluralism." Rhetorical scholars might identify these starting points as ideographs, terms through which the ideologies of modern subjectivity and the modern Academy are condensed and made rhetorically effective by combining and associating them with selected Scriptures about love, faithfulness, witness, and character. Or, to rely on another rhetorical perspective, we could identify this collection of admirable traits motivating the Christian intellectual as "god-terms," or "ultimate terms," of the Christian scholar's calling.[12]

Although we may question the secular intent to dissolve all we cherish into the historical constructions of power and the machinations of rhetorical appeal, we also ought to take heed of Terry Lindvall's charge to approach our tasks with a comic humility befitting our human frailty and see where such challenges might take us.[13] At the least, a disciplinary critique of subjectivity challenges us not to beg the question of what we take to be the Christian mind. Indeed, this question of intellectual subjectivity is not merely a passing fancy of the secular intelligentsia. Willie Jennings, former dean of the Yale University Divinity School, has given much thought to the ways Christian scholars imagine the ideal of intellectual formation. In his influential book, *The Christian Imagination*, Jennings places contemporary Christian thought and practice into the historical context of colonialism. In a more recent book focused directly on the intellectual formation of Christians within divinity schools (and also within many other Christian educational institutions, he surmises), Jennings reflects on the impacts and alternatives to the colonial legacies. The received ideal of a highly educated Christian mind, Jennings claims, is imagined as a "white self-sufficient man, his self-sufficiency defined by possession, control, and mastery."[14] By "white" here he is not specifying "people of European descent" (although those of us who are White males of European descent are likely carriers of this imagined construct) but a "way of being in the world and seeing the world" structured according to the homogenization of affect and cognition.[15]

Jennings's historical and structural analysis requires much more comment, of course. For my purposes here, though, we can treat his lament about a commonly imagined ideal of a Christian mind as provoking ongoing Christian intellectual inquiry. He does so not only through critique but by exploring an alternative. Rather than imagining the Christian mind as organized around the pursuit of knowledge, Jennings returns to the biblical picture of a people yearning for deep and profound relationship with God and with one another. The formation of a Christian intellectual, then, begins not with the "commodities of learning" but with the ideal of "belonging"; it begins by imagining "the deepest sense of God-drenched life attuned to life together, not with people in general but with the people that comprise the place of one's concrete living and the places (the landscapes, the animals, and the built environments) that constitute the actual conditions of one's life."[16] Sharpening the contrast, Jennings speaks of this alternative in the context of teachers and students: "We too often still imagine our students as guests in a world that we host, rather than as the host of a world we have entered as guests."[17] Jennings's emphasis on belonging is not dismissive of a teacher's knowledge. Rather, he locates knowledge within the priority of relationally oriented learning: "learning not only our students' abilities and interests, but the worlds—social, cultural, geographic—out of which they come."[18] To teach in this way would require, for many of us, that we examine and alter the tacit assumptions shaping what it is to be an educated person, what it is to have a Christian mind. Our calling is not to grasp knowledge and then lead others into aligning their minds and bodies with that knowledge. It is a calling rather to cultivate our intellectual inquiries by joining with others in yearning for, and giving presence to, the intimacy of shared lives through the hope of Christ's redemption.

How this works out in practice within the Academy will vary by persons and situations, of course. For now, though, we may begin by simply shifting a metaphor of the Christian-academy relationship. Taking Jennings's perspective, we would be less inclined than Marsden to affirm Noll's reference to today's Academy as an intellectual "Wild West."[19] This phrase is rhetorically troublesome, metaphorically placing the Christian mind as a centered and authoritative vantage point by which peoples and lands are surveyed and tamed; we (and I certainly am implicated in this rhetorical construction) gather knowledge, evaluate alternatives, and strategize our settlements. The alternative image, then, is of guests and hosts; we approach the Academy as guests, attentive to and appreciative of the diverse persons (faculty, staff, administrators, students) who are our hosts.

Although Jennings offers his alternative imagining of Christian intellectual formation for those within higher education, we also could imagine this as the relationship of Christian intellectuals within a local church or even within secular communities. How might we, as Christian scholars, prioritize belongingness as we live with church congregants, community neighbors, and fellow citizens? Christian communication scholars, in particular, ought to be wary of imaging our scholarship as forging or translating communication knowledge in order to conform churches into our preferred understandings of culture, politics, and worship. Rather, our first task, as those gifted and trained into loving God with our minds, is to shift our imagined ideal of communication scholarship from *transferring knowledge* to *belonging with*. We find guidance for this shift sprinkled throughout this volume, such as Spencer's emphasis on "good thinking" that opens, explores, and risks;[20] Lindvall's illustrations of relationally shaped action and discovery;[21] Wolterstorff's encouragement to live with gratitude and passion within academic communities;[22] Mouw's preference for "world viewing" rather than the formation of "worldviews";[23] Fackler and Fortner's conversation about teaching as learning;[24] and Soukup's account of education "rooted in a community environment."[25]

Reimagining the Christian mind as constructed within and through a pursuit of localized and intimate belongingness will have notable impact on the way we conceive and study communication. As an impetus for one of these ways, I offer my second recommendation.

2. Consider Communication as Ends (Not Merely Means)

In his contribution to this volume, Quentin Schultze begins his list of "root truths" by affirming "all speech is action."[26] This is crucial, especially if we situate this truth within a reconstructed sense of Christian mind as formed from, within, and toward the end of Christ-centered intimacy and belonging. Conceiving communicative activity as first and foremost action, then, shifts our focus away from communication primarily as a means, or a tool, and, instead, toward communication as inseparable from the end, as the active and faithful practice of God's reconciling and redemptive work through all creation. Christian communication is the very practice of living faith.

The challenge of placing communication as the ends and not merely a means within Christian practice is familiar to several of this volume's contributors through the prodigious and influential work of Jacques Ellul.[27] Throughout the latter half of the twentieth century, Ellul warned us that means-dominated thinking, which he calls "technique," had become the primary way of thinking and acting in the Western world. He was particularly concerned that Christians were no different than nonbelievers in this regard, increasingly allowing questions of know-how to substitute for questions of purpose, of letting means-based thinking overwhelm reflective and prayerful considerations of the ends. The result, Ellul claimed, is the loss of human freedom: Christians cease to live reflectively about their purpose and actions and, instead, act according to reflexes shaped by the dominance of technique. Having become slaves to technical mastery—of guiding life and thought according to what is practical, successful, and efficient—Christians are conformed according to a practice of rationality that strips away their authentic witness of God's revolutionary redemption.[28]

In the decades since Ellul's death in 1994, we have not seen much in evangelical churches that would alter Ellul's concerns. To the contrary, the typical Christian approach to communication aligns more often than not with the priority of technique. A lack of Christian commitment to intellectual inquiry in church, Academy, and society—as noted throughout this edited volume—illustrates Ellul's diagnosis. For many Christians, the goals or ends of Christian existence have been collapsed into the means of doing Christianity such that Christians seek what every other social collective seeks, to have our beliefs and values respected and empowered, to gain advantage within the marketplace of products, ideas, and politics, to grow our membership, and to calculate how we might maximize desired outcomes through the efficient use of our resources. Communication media within the evangelical subculture, such as print publications, radio, Bible conferences, YouTube, social media, and church growth programs, prioritize communication technique as both the means of disseminating Christian teaching and as the means by which one grows the church, builds Christian citizens, and strategizes spiritual maturity.

Of course, many believers would be quick to claim these communication techniques are not used mindlessly but are, contrary to Ellul's claim, focused on achieving ultimate kingdom goods, such as saving sinners or shaping culture. The problem with such a response, though, is twofold. First, the "end" is conceived as that which is achieved through communicative means. Thus, the value criterion of means-based thinking—namely, that our actions are assessed in terms of success in meeting specified outcomes—becomes the value criterion of Christian practice. Second, the theological-biblical identification of the kingdom end(s) most likely has been hermeneutically sifted (and proof-texted) to justify the technique. So for example, Christians seeking cultural acceptance of biblical morality may link that acceptance with the desirability of bringing more people to Christ. Yet, the scriptural or theological basis for a causal connection between public acceptance and an increase in conversions is itself mired in technical thinking, partly dependent on the heritage of revival techniques (as Noll documents in *Scandal*) but also on the techniques of public opinion formation and culture-making, which became ubiquitous in the work of twentieth-century sociologists and social psychologists and continue to shape the study of Christian influence today. In other words, the dominance of technique in the life of believers, and in the study of Christian communication, is pervasive.

The alternative course of thought and action for the Christian, says Ellul, is to subordinate technique to the inaugurated presence of God's kingdom. "In God's action," Ellul writes, "the means never appear except as the realized presence of the end."[29] The Christian's communication, therefore, is not primarily a technique useful for something other than communication, as if it is a step ladder allowing self and others to reach kingdom goods. Rather, communication is elemental within the presencing of the Kingdom's promise for self and others. We do not communicate to achieve or accomplish a goal separable from that communication; we communicate as the influential presencing of God's Kingdom.

Placing the instrument of communication within the ends of kingdom practice also puts the very idea of communication into question. When communication both reflects and constitutes the very presencing of redemption, then we no longer presuppose communication as a fixed entity, as if it is a process existing independently of God and his suasory movement in the creating, sustaining, and redeeming of all creation. Thus, to enter into the study of communication is to enter into sustained reflection on the richness and the mystery of God's influence in the world. Practically, this foregrounds the need for wisdom within the Christian mind, a practice encouraged throughout this volume, particularly by Mouw and Spencer. Dependent on the wisdom from above, Christians make daily practical communicative judgments reflecting, and performing, the Kingdom (see James 3:13–18).

Studying communication, therefore, pushes the Christian communication scholar in the direction of lived communicative wisdom rather than settled technique.

Imagining Communication

Christian communication scholars are great at asking the "how" questions, often at the expense of reflecting upon the "why" questions. I have seen the drive toward technique in my own work, seeking mastery in the know-how of communicating faith in church and society. We also can see it in this volume. As I noted above, one of the primary purposes of this edited volume is to advance Christian scholarship—and Christian communication scholarship in particular—into the church, the Academy, and society. If by this we mean that Christian communication scholarship facilitates the *transfer* of knowledge to church and world, or identifies more or less desirable ways to *convey* Christian values and commitments to the Academy, or specifies ways of *propagating* thoughtful Christian knowledge, then communication becomes a tool in the scholar's toolbox. And if this is all we do, then we will have reduced Schultze's first "root truth"—that communication is action—to a truism of the technological age rather than as an incitement to explore what it is to live as the very presence of God's people.

There is more to Christian communication scholarship than building quality toolboxes. Toolboxes remain useful, of course. But we ought to carefully interrogate our imagined ideals of Christian intellectual work so that communicative tools are subordinate within the communicative character of God's Kingdom ends. Thus, communication is not merely applied by Christian minds, nor merely operationalized by Christian minds, nor merely used to influence Christian minds. Communication is all of these, of course, but first and foremost it is integral to the very contours of that mind, of the mind in action as yearning for, living into, and constituted by the movement of Christ's redemption to call a people into intimacy with God and each other.

Regardless of how we proceed—of which ideals, techniques, or ends shape our work—the path forward for Christian communication scholarship is blessed with an abundance of resources. Among the most helpful are the contributions of Mark Noll and George Marsden. Joined by the many other scholars and colleagues in this collection, we all can relish a supportive and faithful community of learners pushing us to the love of God and others with ever greater insight into the practices and divine glories of our communicative existence.

Notes

A Liturgy for the Knowledge Seekers
Donna M. Elkins

[1] Richard J. Mouw, *Called to a Life of the Mind: Some Advice for Evangelical Scholars* (Grand Rapids, MI: Wm. B. Eerdman, 2014), 33, 47.

[2] Todd C. Ream, Jerry Pattengale, and Christopher J. Devers, eds., *Habits of Hope: Educational Practices for a Weary World* (Downers Grove, IL: InterVarsity Press, 2024), 36.

Foreword
J. Matthew Melton

[1] Mark A. Noll, *The Scandal of the Evangelical Mind*, 1st ed. (1994) and 2nd ed. (2022) (Grand Rapids, MI: Wm. B. Eerdmans).

[2] John A. Stormer, *None Dare Call It Treason* (Florissant, MO: Liberty Bell Press, 1964).

[3] Martin Buber, *Between Man and Man*, trans. Ronald Gregor Smith (London: Kegan Paul, 1947), 184.

[4] George M. Marsden, *The Outrageous Idea of Christian Scholarship*, original ed. (1997) and updated ed. (2024) (New York: Oxford University Press).

[5] Mortimer J. Adler, "The Great Conversation Revisited," in *The Great Conversation: A People's Guide to Great Books of the Western World*, 2nd ed. (Chicago: Encyclopædia Britannica, Inc., 1990), 28.

[6] Alasdair MacIntyre, *After Virtue* (Notre Dame, IN: University of Notre Dame Press, 1981), 263.

[7] J. Matthew Melton, "The Medium is the Master, Barbarians of the New Dark Ages" (chapel presentation, Lee University, Cleveland, TN, September 7, 2006).

[8] G. K Chesterton, *Orthodoxy* (San Francisco: Ignatius Press, 1995).

[9] MacIntyre, *After Virtue*, 263.

Introduction
Robert H. Woods Jr. and Mark Allan Steiner

[1] See http://website.archivenatcom.org/about-nca/what-nca.

[2] Harry R. Lewis, *Excellence Without a Soul: How a Great University Forgot Education* (New York: PublicAffairs, 2006), xiv–305; and John M. Ellis, *The Breakdown of Higher Education: How It Happened, the Damage It Does, and What Can Be Done* (New York: Encounter Books, 2020).

[3] Mark A. Noll, *The Scandal of the Evangelical Mind*, 1st ed. (Grand Rapids, MI: Wm. B. Eerdmans, 1994) and 2nd ed. (Grand Rapids, MI: Wm. B. Eerdmans, 2022); George M. Marsden, *The Outrageous Idea of Christian Scholarship*, original ed. (New York: Oxford University Press, 1997) and updated ed. (New York: Oxford University Press, 2024).

[4] C. S. Lewis, *Surprised by Joy: The Shape of My Early Life* (New York: Harcourt, Brace and World, 1955), 254.

PART ONE: LEGACY SCHOLAR PRESENTATIONS

Chapter 1
The Scandal of the Evangelical Mind: Then and Now
Mark A. Noll

[1] Jonathan Pettigrew and Robert H. Woods Jr., eds., *Professing Christ: Christian Tradition and Faith-learning Integration in Public Universities* (Pasco, WA: Integratio Press, 2022).

[2] Mark A. Noll, *The Scandal of the Evangelical Mind* (Grand Rapids, MI: Wm. B. Eerdmans, 1994).

[3] Paul Miller, *The Religion of American Greatness: What Is Wrong with Christian Nationalism?* (Downers Grove, IL: IVP Academic, 2024).

[4] Edward J. Carnell, *Television: Servant or Master?* (Grand Rapids, MI: Wm. B. Eerdmans, 1950).

Chapter 2
Mere Christian Scholarship
George Marsden

[1] George M. Marsden, *The Outrageous Idea of Christian Scholarship* (New York: Oxford University Press, 1997).

[2] Jonathan Rauch, *The Constitution of Knowledge: A Defense of Truth* (Washington, D.C.: Brookings Institution Press, 2021).

[3] C. S. Lewis, *Mere Christianity* (London: William Collins, 2012).

Chapter 3
Listening to the Call
Nicholas Wolterstorff

[1] Nicholas Wolterstorff, *Art in Action: Toward a Christian Aesthetic* (Grand Rapids, MI: Wm. B. Eerdmans, 1987).

[2] Nicholas Wolterstorff, *Works and World of Art* (Oxford, England: Oxford University Press, 1980).

[3] Nicholas Wolterstorff, *Art Rethought: The Social Practices of Art* (Oxford, England: Oxford University Press, 2015).

[4] Charles Taylor, *A Secular Age* (Cambridge, MA: Harvard University Press, reprint edition, 2018).

[5] Ronald A. Wells, *History through the Eyes of Faith* (San Francisco: HarperOne, 1989); David A. Fraser and Tony Campolo, *Sociology through the Eyes of Faith* (San Francisco: HarperOne, 1992).

[6] Clella Iles Jaffe, *Public Speaking*, 7th ed. (Boston: Wadsworth, 2013), 199.

[7] Jaffe, *Public Speaking*, 199; Helen Rosenboom and Ralina L. Joseph, "'What Makes You Think I'm African American?': Identity Performance, Code-switching and the Strong Black Woman on *Love Is Blind*," *Critical Studies in Media Communication* 41, no. 3 (2024): 276–281.

[8] Rosenboom and Joseph, "'What Makes You Think I'm African American?'" 279.

[9] Rosenboom and Joseph, "'What Makes You Think I'm African American?'" 277.

[10] Wendy Cadge, and Emily Sigalow, "Negotiating Religious Differences: The Strategies of Interfaith Chaplains in Healthcare," *Journal for the Scientific Study of Religion* 52, no. 1 (2013): 146–158; Becki Elkins and Eran Hanke, "Code-Switching to Navigate Social Class in Higher Education and Student Affairs," *New Directions for Student Services*, no. 162 (2018): 35–47.

Chapter 4
Five Root Assumptions for Communication Scholarship
Quentin Schultze

[1] Stephen W. Littlejohn, Karen A. Foss, and John G. Oetzel, *Theories of Human Communication*, 12th ed. (Long Grove, IL: Waveland Press, 2021).

[2] Thomas W. Simpson, "Telepresence and Trust: A Speech-Act Theory of Mediated Communication," *Philosophy & Technology* 30, no. 4 (September 2017): 443–59.

[3] Sophia Brown and Jonathan Matusitz, "U.S. Church Leaders' Responses to the Charleston Church Shooting: An Examination Based on Speech Act Theory," *Journal of Media and Religion* 18, no. 1 (2019): 27–37; Francisco Villarroel Ordenes, Dhruv Grewal, Stephan Ludwig, Ko De Ruyter, Dominik Mahr, and Martin Wetzels, "Cutting through Content Clutter: How Speech and Image Acts Drive Consumer Sharing of Social Media Brand Messages," *Journal of Consumer Research* 45, no. 5 (2019): 988–1012.

[4] Quentin Schultze, *Servant Teaching: Practices for Renewing Christian Higher Education* (Grand Rapids, MI: Edenridge Press, 2022).

[5] Walter R. Fisher, *Human Communication as Narration Toward a Philosophy of Reason, Value, and Action* [Reprint] (Columbia, SC: University of South Carolina Press, 2021).

[6] Stephen W. Littlejohn, Karen A. Foss, and John G. Oetzel, *Theories of Human Communication*, 12th ed. (Long Grove, IL: Waveland Press, 2021).

[7] Michael E. Burns, "Recruiting Prospective Students with Stories: How Personal Stories Influence the Process of Choosing a University," *Communication Quarterly* 63, no. 1 (January–March 2015): 114.

[8] Burns, "Recruiting Prospective Students," 99–118.

[9] Quentin Schultze, *You'll Shoot Your Eye Out! Life Lessons from the Movie A Christmas Story* (Grand Rapids, MI: Edenridge, 2024); Quentin Schultze, *Servant Teaching: Practices for Renewing Christian Higher Education* (Grand Rapids, MI: Edenridge, 2022).

[10] Quentin Schultze, *An Essential Guide to Public Speaking: Serving Your Audience with Faith, Skill, and Virtue*, 2nd ed. (Grand Rapids, MI: Baker, 2020).

[11] Schultze, *You'll Shoot Your Eye Out!*

Chapter 5
The Christian Mind: Humility and "World Viewing"
Richard J. Mouw

[1] Mark A. Noll, *The Scandal of the Evangelical Mind* (Grand Rapids, MI: Wm. B. Eerdmans, 1994); George M. Marsden, *The Outrageous Idea of Christian Scholarship* (New York: Oxford University Press, 1997).

[2] Frank Gaebelein, *The Christian, the Arts, and Truth: Regaining the Vision of Greatness*, ed. D. Bruce Lockerbie (Portland, OR: Multnomah Press, 1985).

[3] Frank E. Gaebelein, "The Christian's Intellectual Life," in *The Christian, the Arts, and Truth: Regaining the Vision of Greatness*, ed. D. Bruce Lockerbie (Portland, OR: Multnomah Press, 1985), 154–155.

[4] Abraham Kuyper, *On Education*, ed. Wendy Naylor (Bellingham, WA: Lexham Press, 2019), 156.

[5] Noll, *Scandal*.

[6] Simone Weil, *Waiting for God*, trans. Emma Craufurd (New York: Harper & Row, 1951), 105.

Chapter 6
An Outrageous Scandal: Three Rs for the Future of Christian Education
Greg Spencer

[1] See Jonathan Haidt, *The Anxious Generation: How the Great Rewiring of Childhood is Causing an Epidemic of Mental Illness* (New York: Penguin, 2024).

[2] See https://www.pewresearch.org/religion/2019/10/17/in-u-s-decline-of-christianity-continues-at-rapid-pace/. "More than eight-in-ten members of the Silent Generation (those born between 1928 and 1945) describe themselves as Christians (84%), as do three-quarters of Baby Boomers (76%). In stark contrast, only half of Millennials (49%) describe themselves as Christians; four-in-ten are religious 'nones,' and one-in-ten Millennials identify with non-Christian faiths."

[3] Mark A. Noll, *The Scandal of the Evangelical Mind* (Grand Rapids, MI: Wm. B. Eerdmans, 1994), 14. See also Richard Mouw, *Called to the Life of the Mind: Some Advice for Evangelical Scholars* (Grand Rapids, MI: Wm. B. Eerdmans, 2014); Douglas V. Henry and Bob R. Agee, eds., *Faithful Learning and the Christian Scholarly Vocation* (Grand Rapids, MI: Wm. B. Eerdmans, 2003).

[4] Noll, *Scandal*, 12.

[5] George Marsden, *The Outrageous Idea of Christian Scholarship* (New York: Oxford University Press, 1997), 7.

[6] Benson Bobrick, *Wide as the Waters: The Story of the English Bible and the Revolution It Inspired* (New York: Penguin Books, 2001), 90.

[7] Jonathan Swift, "An Argument to Prove That the Abolishing of Christianity in England May, as Things Now Stand, Be Attended with Some Inconveniences, and Perhaps Not Produce Those Many Good Effects Proposed Thereby," in *The Prose Works of Jonathan Swift*, ed. Herbert Davis (Oxford, England: Basil Blackwell, 1966), 28.

[8] Charles Malik, "The Two Tasks," *Christianity Today*, November 7, 1980, 40.

[9] See George Steiner, *In Bluebeard's Castle: Some Notes Towards the Redefinition of Culture* (New Haven: Yale University Press, 1971), "Most history seems to carry on its back vestiges of paradise. . . . Behind today's posture of doubt and self-castigation stands the presence, so pervasive as to pass largely unexamined, of a particular past, of a specific 'golden time,'" 4.

[10] James Farrell, "Cultural Disobedience," Chapel Talk at St. Olaf College, September 24, 2003.

[11] Richard Lovelace, *The Dynamics of Spiritual Life* (Downers Grove, IL: InterVarsity Press, 1979), 321.

[12] Lovelace, *The Dynamics of Spiritual Life*, 315.

[13] William Blake, *The Complete Poetry and Prose of William Blake*, ed. David V. Erdman (New York: Anchor Books, 1988), 231.

[14] Noll, *Scandal*, 5.

[15] Harry Blamires, *The Christian Mind: How Should a Christian Think?* (Ann Arbor, MI: Servant Books, 1963), 50.

[16] Blamires, *The Christian Mind*, 52.

[17] Howard Mumford Jones, "The Attractions of Stupidity," in *Introduction to College Life: A Book of Readings*, eds. Norman T. Bell, Richard W. Burkhart, and Victor B. Lawhead (Boston: Houghton Mifflin, 1962), 44.

[18] Blamires, *The Christian Mind*, 52.

[19] Blamires, *The Christian Mind*, 51.

[20] Jim Taylor, *Learning for Wisdom: Christian Education and the Good Life* (Abilene, TX: Abilene Christian University Press, 2017). Taylor understands education in terms of learning for wisdom about truth, goodness, and beauty. See also Darin H. Davis, ed., *Educating for Wisdom in the 21st Century* (South Bend, IN: St. Augustine's Press, 2019). This volume of essays includes "Slow Wisdom as a Sub-Version of Reality" by Walter Bruggemann, in which he helpfully contrasts the "fast" triad of control (might, wealth, and wisdom) and the "slow" wisdom of fidelity (steadfast love, justice, and righteousness). Both are indispensable.

[21] James Houston, *I Believe in the Creator* (Grand Rapids, MI: Wm. B. Eerdmans, 1980), 27.

[22] Dallas Willard, *The Divine Conspiracy: Rediscovering our Hidden Life in God* (San Francisco: HarperOne, 1997), 5.

[23] Joseph L. Featherstone, "Foreword," in *Orators and Philosophers: A History of the Idea of Liberal Education*, by Bruce A. Kimball (New York: Columbia University Teachers College Press, 1986), ix–x.

[24] Bruce A. Kimball, *Orators and Philosophers: A History of the Idea of Liberal Education* (New York: Columbia University Teachers College Press, 1986), 238.

[25] Stephen W. Littlejohn, Karen A. Foss, and John G. Oetzel, *Theories of Human Communication*, 12th ed. (Long Grove, IL: Waveland Press, Inc., 2021).

[26] Littlejohn, Foss, and Oetzel, *Theories of Human Communication*, 37.

[27] James A. Herrick, *The History and Theory of Rhetoric: An Introduction*, 5th ed. (New York: Routledge, 2016), 24.

[28] G. Brandon Knight, "Myth Maker, Myth Maker, Make Me a Myth: C. S. Lewis, Mythopoiesis, and the Rhetoric of Glory," *Journal of Communication and Religion* 42, no. 1 (2019): 83–98.

[29] Knight, "Myth Maker," 96.

[30] Mark A. E. Williams, *Just Words: Lessons of Ancient Education, Classical Rhetoric, and Pagan Religion for a Post-Christian World* (Pasco, WA: Integratio Press, 2024); Laura L. Groves and John B. Hatch, "Prophetic Imagination and Racial Inertia: The Lyrical, Musical, and Visual Rhetoric of 'Is He Worthy?'" *Journal of Communication and Religion* 43, no. 1 (2020): 5–25.

Chapter 7
The Humor and Humility of the Christian Mind
Terry Lindvall

[1] George M. Marsden, *The Soul of the American University: From Protestant Establishment to Established Nonbelief* (New York: Oxford University Press, 1994).

[2] Mark A. Noll, *The Scandal of the Evangelical Mind*, 1st ed. (1994) and 2nd ed. (2022) (Grand Rapids, MI: Wm. B. Eerdmans).

[3] See, for instance, Michael P. Graves, *Preaching the Inward Light: Early Quaker Rhetoric* (Waco, TX: Baylor University Press, 2009).

[4] C. S. Lewis, *Surprised by Joy: The Shape of My Early Life* (New York: Harcourt, Brace and World, 1955), 254.

[5] Amos N. Wilder, *Early Christian Rhetoric: The Language of the Gospel* (Cambridge, MA: Harvard University Press, 1971).

[6] Benson P. Fraser, *Hide and Seek: The Sacred Art of Indirect Communication* (Eugene, OR: Cascade, 2020).

[7] Fred B. Craddock, *Overhearing the Gospel*, Rev. and Exp. (St. Louis, MO: Chalice Press, 2002), 4.

[8] Fraser, *Hide and Seek*, 2.

[9] Fraser, *Hide and Seek*, 21.

[10] Joseph Sowers, "Pay Attention and You'll Overhear Me: Søren Kierkegaard's Theory of Indirect Communication," *Journal of Communication and Religion* 44, no. 3 (Autumn 2021): 110.

[11] Hanisha Besant, "Captivating the Listener: An Analysis of Audience Responses to Indirect Communication in a Sermonic Event," *Artifact Analysis* 1, no. 4 (Fall 2022): 38–59; Fraser, *Hide and Seek*.

[12] Michael Ward, *Planet Narnia: The Seven Heavens in the Imagination of C. S. Lewis* (Oxford, England: Oxford University Press, 2010).

[13] Joshua Wright, *Comic Belief: Religious Irreverence and Irreverent Religion in Cold War America* (PhD diss., Harvard University, 2022).

Chapter 8
A Framework for Biblical Integration in Communication
Calvin L. Troup

[1] Joseph Conforti, "The Invention of the Great Awakening, 1795–1842," *Early American Literature* 26, no. 2 (1991): 99–118; Mary Cayton, "The Expanding World of Jacob Norton: Reading, Revivalism, and the Construction of a 'Second Great Awakening' in New England, 1787–1804," *Journal of the Early Republic* 26 (May 2006): 221–248; Richard Rogers, "The Urban Threshold and the Second Great Awakening: Revivalism in New York State, 1825–1835," *Journal for the Scientific Study of Religion* 49, no. 4 (December 2010): 694–709.

[2] Mark A. Noll, *The Scandal of the Evangelical Mind*, 1st ed. (1994) and 2nd ed. (2022) (Grand Rapids, MI: Wm. B. Eerdmans).

[3] George M. Marsden, *The Outrageous Idea of Christian Scholarship*, original ed. (1997) and updated ed. (2024) (New York: Oxford University Press).

[4] Nancy Pearcey, *Love Thy Body* (Grand Rapids, MI: Baker Books, 2018), 12–14.

[5] Saint Augustine, *The Confessions of Saint Augustine*, trans. John Ryan (New York: Image Books, 2014), XII. xxxiv, 34.

[6] C. S. Lewis, *Mere Christianity* (London, England: William Collins, 2012).

[7] Robert H. Woods Jr. and Naaman K. Wood, eds., *Words and Witnesses: Communication Studies in Christian Thought* (Nashville, TN: B&H Academic, 2020).

[8] Herman Bavinck, *Christian Worldview*, eds. and trans. Cory Brock, James Eglinton and N. Gray Sutanto (Wheaton, IL: Crossway, 2019).

Chapter 9
Substantive Truth in an Intellectual Pluralism Setting
Clifford G. Christians

[1] George M. Marsden, *The Outrageous Idea of Christian Scholarship*, original ed. (1997) and updated ed. (2024) (New York: Oxford University Press); George M. Marsden, *The Soul of the American University: From Protestant Establishment to Established Nonbelief* (New York: Oxford University Press, 1996).

Chapter 10
A Catholic University: A Religiously Oriented
Approach to Teaching and Research
Fr. Paul A. Soukup, SJ

[1] In this I draw on an essay I published in 2023 in volume 7 of Explore, the journal of Santa Clara University's Center for Ignatian Education. See Paul A. Soukup, "The Jesuit Educational Tradition: A Personal View," *Explore* 7 (2023): 4–11.

[2] Neil Postman, *The End of Education: Redefining the Value of School* (New York: Vintage Books, 1995).

[3] Postman, *The End of Education*, 8–9.

[4] Amy E. Rock, "Bringing Geography to the Community: Community-based Learning and the Geography Classroom," *GeoJournal* 87, Suppl. 2 (2022): S236–S237.

[5] "Thirty-second General Congregation of the Society of Jesus," *Decree 4: Service of Faith and the Promotion of Justice* (Rome: Institute of Jesuit Sources, 1975), April 6, 2023, https://www.scu.edu/ic/programs/ignatian-worldview/stories/decree-4-gc-32-service-of-faith-and-the-promotion-of-justice.html

[6] "Thirty-second General Congregation."

[7] "Thirty-second General Congregation."

[8] "Thirty-second General Congregation."

Chapter 11
Learning, Teaching, and the Christian Mind: A Dialogue
Mark Fackler and *Robert S. Fortner*

[1] Charles W. Colson, *Born Again* (Grand Rapids, MI: Chosen Books, 2008).

[2] Trey Gowdy, *Doesn't Hurt to Ask: Using the Power of Questions to Communicate, Connect, and Persuade* (New York: Forum Books, 2020).

[3] Jonathan Turley, *The Indispensable Right: Free Speech in an Age of Rage* (New York: Simon and Schuster, 2024), 10.

PART TWO: RESPONSES TO OUR LEGACY SCHOLARS
Section One: Foundations and Historical Roots

Chapter 12
What does Alexandria Have to Do with Upland?
Classical Theism and the Future of Christian Scholarship
James W. Vining

[1] I also believe there is hope for shared understanding! See Kenneth Burke, "Terministic Screens," in *The Philosophy of Literary Form: Studies in Symbolic Action*, 3rd ed. (Berkeley: University of California Press, 1973), 44–62.

[2] Kurt Anderson, *Clement of Alexandria for Beginners: Bridging Classical Philosophy and Early Christianity* (Kindle Books, 2024); Thomas G. Weinandy and Daniel A. Keating, *Athanasius and His Legacy: Trinitarian-Incarnational Soteriology and Its Reception* (Fortress Press, 2017).

[3] David Bentley Hart, *Atheist Delusions: The Christian Revolution and Its Fashionable Enemies* (New Haven, CT: Yale University Press, 2009); Arthur F. Holmes, *Building the Christian Academy* (Grand Rapids, MI; Wm. B. Eerdmans, 2001).

[4] Henry Chadwick and J. E. L. Oulton, Alexandrian Christianity (Philadelphia, PA: Westminster Press, 1977); David Robertson, *Word and Meaning in Ancient Alexandria: Theories of Language from Philo to Plotinus* (Aldershot, England; Burlington, VT: Ashgate, 2008); R. S. Soloviev, "Philo and Numenius in the Neoplatonist-Christian Struggle for True Philosophy in the Third Century," *Litera*, 2023, https://aurora-journals.com/library_read_article.php?id=40567, paras. 1 and 2.

[5] Weinandy and Keating, *Athanasius and His Legacy*, 2.

[6] George Hinge and Jens A. Krasilnikoff, eds., *Alexandria: A Cultural and Religious Melting Pot* (Aarhus: Aarhus University Press, 2009); Holmes, *Building the Christian Academy*.

[7] AnneMarie Luijendijk, "Did Early Christians Keep Their Identity Secret? Neighbors and Strangers in Dionysius of Alexandria, Presbyter Leon, and Flax Merchant Leonides of Oxyrhynchus," in *Religious Identifications in Late Antique Papyri* (Abingdon and New York: Routledge, 2023); Christopher Haas, *Alexandria in Late Antiquity: Topography and Social Conflict* (Baltimore, MD: Johns Hopkins University Press, 1996); Hart, *Atheist Delusions*.

[8] Luijendijk, "Did Early Christians Keep Their Identity Secret?"

[9] Birger A. Pearson, "Christians and Jews in First-Century Alexandria," *The Harvard Theological Review* 79, no. 1/3 (January–July 1986): 206–216.

[10] Holmes, *Building the Christian Academy; Kevin McGinnis, Scripturalizing Educational Elitism: Social Formation, Mythmaking, and Symbolic Labor in Origen* (Claremont, CA: Claremont Press, 2018).

[11] Annewies van den Hoek, "The 'Catechetical' School of Early Christian Alexandria and Its Philonic Heritage," *The Harvard Theological Review* 90, no. 1 (January 1997): 59–87.

[12] Anderson, *Clement of Alexandria for Beginners*; Ronald E. Heine, *Origen: An Introduction to His Life and Thought* (Eugene, OR: Cascade Books, 2019); Joseph McLelland, *God the Anonymous: A Study in Alexandrian Philosophical Theology* (Philadelphia Patristics Foundation, 1976); Philip Schaff, *The Complete Works of the Church Fathers* (Kindle Books, 2016); Hans Urs von Balthasar, *Origen: Spirit and Fire: A Thematic Anthology of His Writings* (Washington, D.C.: The Catholic University of America Press, 2001).

[13] Chadwick and Oulton, *Alexandrian Christianity*; Mark Edwards, "Clement of Alexandria and His Doctrine of the Logos," *Vigiliae Christianae* 54, no. 2 (2000): 159–177; Pearson, "Christians and Jews in First-Century Alexandria;" Ilaria L. E. Ramelli, "'Ethos' and 'Logos': A Second-Century Debate Between 'Pagan' and Christian Philosophers," *Vigiliae Christianae* 69, no. 2 (2015): 123–156; Samuel Rubenson, "From School to Patriarchate: Aspects on the Christianisation of Alexandria," in *Alexandria: A Cultural and Religious Melting Pot* (Aarhus: Aarhus University Press, 2009), 150–159.

[14] Anderson, *Clement of Alexandria for Beginners*; Rubenson, "From School to Patriarchate."

[15] Winrich Lohr, "Christianity as Philosophy: Problems and Perspectives of an Ancient Intellectual Project," *Vigiliae Christianae* 64, no. 2 (2010): 160–188.

[16] McGinnis, *Scripturalizing Educational Elitism*; Ilaria L. E. Ramelli, "Origen, Patristic Philosophy, and Christian Platonism Re-Thinking the Christianisation of Hellenism," *Vigiliae Christianae* 63, no. 3 (2009): 217–263.

[17] Anderson, *Clement of Alexandria for Beginners*.

[18] John Anthony McGuckin, *The Eastern Orthodox Church: A New History* (New Haven, CT: Yale University Press, 2020), 297.

[19] McLelland, *God the Anonymous*.

[20] Hart, *Atheist Delusions*; Holmes, *Building the Christian Academy*; Schaff, *Complete Works of the Church Fathers*.

[21] Clement of Alexandria, "Exhortation to the Heathen," in *The Writings of Clement of Alexandria*, Vol. 1 (Edinburgh: T. & T. Clark, 1867); Ramelli, "'Ethos' and 'Logos.'"

[22] Clement of Alexandria, "Stromata: Book 1," in *The Writings of Clement of Alexandria*, Vol. 1. (Edinburgh: T. & T. Clark, 1867).

[23] Hart, *Atheist Delusions*; John Anthony McGuckin, *Origen of Alexandria: Master Theologian of the Early Church* (Lanham, MD: Lexington Books, 2022).

[24] Rubenson, "From School to Patriarchate."

[25] Hart, *Atheist Delusions*; Holmes, *Building the Christian Academy*; Soloviev, "Philo and Numenius."

[26] Anderson, Clement of *Alexandria for Beginners*.

[27] Anderson, Clement of *Alexandria for Beginners*; McGinnis, *Scripturalizing Educational Elitism*; McLelland, *God the Anonymous*; Ramelli, "Origen, Patristic Philosophy, and Christian Platonism."

[28] Clement, "Exhortation to the Heathen;" Clement, "Stromata;" Origen, "On First Principles."

[29] Edwards, "Clement of Alexandria and His Doctrine of the Logos;" Ramelli, "'Ethos' and 'Logos.'"

[30] McGuckin, *Origen of Alexandria*, 34.

[31] Holmes, *Building the Christian Academy*.

[32] McGuckin, *Origen of Alexandria*.

[33] McGuckin, *Origen of Alexandria*; Clement, "Stromata."

[34] Anderson, *Clement of Alexandria for Beginners*; Schaff, *Complete Works of the Church Fathers*.

[35] Henri de Lubac, *History and Spirit: The Understanding of Scripture According to Origen* (Ignatius Press, 2007).

[36] Anderson, *Clement of Alexandria for Beginners*.

[37] Holmes, *Building the Christian Academy*; Lohr, "Christianity as Philosophy."

[38] van den Hoek, "The 'Catechetical' School."

[39] Nicholas Wolterstorff, "Listening to the Call," in *From the Outrageous to the Scandalous: Re-imagining Christian Thinking and Scholarship in an Age of Tribalism and Ideological Resentment*, eds. Robert H. Woods Jr. and Mark Allan Steiner (Integratio Press, 2025), 23.

Chapter 13
The Cross-pollination Between Athens and Jerusalem
Thomas J. Carmody

[1] Terry Lindvall, "The Humor and Humility of the Christian Mind," in *From the Outrageous to the Scandalous: Re-imagining Christian Thinking and Scholarship in an Age of Tribalism and Ideological Resentment*, eds. Robert H. Woods Jr. and Mark Allan Steiner (Integratio Press, 2025), 54.

[2] George M. Marsden, "Mere Christian Scholarship," in *From the Outrageous to the Scandalous: Re-imagining Christian Thinking and Scholarship in an Age of Tribalism and Ideological Resentment*, eds. Robert H. Woods Jr. and Mark Allan Steiner (Integratio Press, 2025), 15–18.

[3] Madeleine L'Engle, *Walking on Water: Reflections on Faith and Art* (Wheaton, IL: Harold Shaw, 1980), 121–122.

[4] A collect is a liturgical prayer that gathers the petitions of the people into a single prayer. These prayers are usually composted of five parts; the address, the acknowledgement, the petition, the aspiration, and the pleading and are often prayed at specific times in the liturgy of the Christian year. See C. Frederick Barbee and Paul F. M. Zahl, *The Collects of Thomas Cranmer* (Grand Rapids, MI: Wm. B. Eerdmans,1999), x. See also Marcus Fabius Quintilian, *Quintilian on the Teaching of Speaking and Writing, Translations from Book One, Two, and Ten of Institutio Oratoria*, ed. and trans. James J. Murphy (Carbondale, IL: Southern Illinois University Press, 1987), 129.

[5] Anglican Church of North America, *The Book of Common Prayer and the Administration of the Sacraments with the Other Rites and Ceremonies of the Church According to the use of the Anglican Church in North America Together with the New Coverdale Psalter* (Seoul, South Korea: Asia Printing Co., 2019), 598.

[6] Aristotle, *The Rhetoric of Aristotle*, trans. Lane Cooper (New York: Appleton-Century Croft 1932), 7–9. See also Lindvall, "The Humor and Humility of the Christian Mind."

[7] Mortimer J. Adler and Charles Van Doren, *How to Read a Book* (New York: Simon and Schuster, 1972), 48–50.

[8] George M. Marsden, *The Outrageous Idea of Christian Scholarship* (New York: Oxford University Press, 1997), 108–109, and Mark A. Noll, *The Scandal of the Evangelical Mind* (Grand Rapids, MI: Wm. B. Eerdmans, 1994), 6–7.

[9] Jessica Booth, "Anxiety Statistics and Facts," *Forbes Health*, accessed May 22, 2025, http://www.forbes.com/health/mind/anxiety-statistics/.

[10] L'Engle, *Walking on Water*, 121.

Chapter 14
Bad Timing: Cultural Redefinitions of "Intellect" at the Beginning of American Evangelicalism
Mark A. E. Williams

[1] As a working reference, I would think of the Enlightenment as running from about 1600 to about 1800, and Modernism running from about 1800 to about 1945. In this essay, we are thinking primarily about evangelical and Catholic replies to their cultures in those time frames.

[2] Paul A. Soukup, SJ, "A Catholic University: A Religiously Oriented Approach to Teaching and Research," in *From the Outrageous to the Scandalous: Re-imagining Christian Thinking and Scholarship in an Age of Tribalism and Ideological Resentment*, eds. Robert H. Woods Jr. and Mark Allan Steiner (Integratio Press, 2025), 73–78.

[3] The sketch provided here is partial and certainly there were substantive debates in Catholic education, from early monastic training schools all the way up through university debates in the era of Scholasticism and beyond, about the powers and facets of the human soul. In other words, there was no indisputable single view of the human soul, of course, but the facets outlined here would have been met with broad recognition and endorsement in the premodern world.

[4] The Greek equivalent would be *pistis*, translated as conviction, confidence, trust, faith.

[5] Aristotle would mark these as *logos* (considered reason), *pathos* (disciplined emotion), and *ēthos* (proven authority).

[6] The history of evangelicalism is tricky, and I am aware that there are reasons—perhaps some good ones—for pushing the beginning of the movement back to the opening of the Reformation itself. But

evangelical Christianity in America has been shaped as much, and arguably more, by the American revivalist traditions than the 1521 Diet of Worms. In the 1790s, America's Second Great Awakening was on low simmer during the tumultuous early days after the new Constitution had replaced the failed Articles of Confederation. It was arguably the Cane Ridge revival of 1801 which served as the trebuchet of the Second Great Awakening, and that revival event became, in many ways, a defining template of American evangelical faith.

[7] Roger Bacon was a Franciscan friar, as was Louis Receveur, who anticipated contemporary environmental concerns by two centuries. Gregor Mendel, considered the father of genetics, was an Augustinian priest. Maria Agnesi became the first woman to serve as a university professor of mathematics when, in 1750, Pope Benedict XIV appointed her to that position at the university of Bologna; she later founded a hospice mission, working with local nuns to serve the poor and dying. Giovanni Cassini, the first person to calculate the size of the solar system (and for whom the Cassini space probe is named), was a famously devout Catholic, educated by Jesuits in the 1600s. Georges Lemaître, who first presented the Big Bang, was a Jesuit priest. John MacEnery was an Irish priest famed for his archaeological work in Palaeolithic remains in England. And the list goes on and on. Whatever its limitations, Catholic education was at the center of the scientific revolution.

[8] Mark A. Noll, *The Scandal of the Evangelical Mind* (Grand Rapids, MI: Wm. B. Eerdmans, 1994), 239–264.

[9] Noll, *Scandal*, 294.

Chapter 15
Lessons from Chautauqua for the Future of Christian Higher Education
John R. Terrill

[1] John H. Vincent, *The Chautauqua Movement* (Chautauqua, NY: Chautauqua Press, 1886), 2.

[2] George M. Marsden, *The Outrageous Idea of Christian Scholarship*, 2nd ed. (New York: Oxford University Press, 2024), 139.

[3] Jon Schmitz, *CHAUTAUQWhat? A Short History of a Place and an Idea* (Chautauqua, NY: Chautauqua Institution, 2024), 4.

[4] Vincent, *Chautauqua Movement*, 25.

[5] Vincent, *Chautauqua Movement*, 25.

[6] Vincent, *Chautauqua Movement*, 4–5.

[7] Vincent, *Chautauqua Movement*, v.

[8] Vincent, *Chautauqua Movement*, vi.

[9] Kate F. Kimball, "Bishop Vincent and His Work," *The Chautauquan*, June 1912, 46.

[10] Douglas N. Harris, Bradley Birzer, Carol, Graham, Mona Hanna, Frederick M. Hess, Gary Hoover, Ariel Kalil, Anna Lembke, Joseph Romm, Patrick Sharkey, Heidi Shierholz, Kiron Skinner, Michael Strain, Scott Winship, Anjana Nair, and Emilia Nordgren, *State of the Nation Report 2025*, https://stateofnation.org.

[11] Marsden, *Outrageous Idea*, 1.

[12] C. John Sommerville, *The Decline of the Secular University* (New York: Oxford University Press, 2006), 4.

[13] Marsden, *Outrageous Idea*, 2–3.

[14] Marsden, *Outrageous Idea*, 6.

[15] Daniel K. Williams, "The Religious Reason Why Academia Is Liberal," May 28, 2025, https://open.substack.com/pub/danielkwilliams/p/the-religious-reason-why-academia?utm_campaign=post&utm_medium=webdanielkwilliams.substack.com.

[16] Marsden, *Outrageous Idea*, 14.

[17] Marsden, *Outrageous Idea*, 14.

[18] Mark A. Noll, *The Scandal of the Evangelical Mind*, 2nd ed. (Grand Rapids: Wm. B. Eerdmans Publishing, 2022), 112.

[19] Willams, "The Religious Reason Why Academia Is Liberal."

[20] Sommerville, *The Decline of the Secular University*, 16.

[21] Marsden, *Outrageous Idea*, 15.

[22] Marsden, *Outrageous Idea*, 17.

[23] Marsden, *Outrageous Idea*, 119.

[24] Marsden, *Outrageous Idea*, 19.

[25] Marsden, *Outrageous Idea*, 25.

[26] Jeffrey Simpson, *Chautauqua: An American Utopia* (New York: Harry N. Abrams, 1999), 48. One can access the entire CLSC book list from 1878 to 2024 at https://www.chq.org/wp-content/uploads/2024/06/CLSC_Historic_Booklist_2024_060624.pdf.

[27] Vincent, *The Chautauqua Movement*, 169.

[28] Simpson, *Chautauqua*, 55.

[29] Rebecca Richmond, *Invitation to Chautauqua* (Chautauqua, NY: Chautauqua Institution, 1953), 10.

[30] James M. Houston and Bruce Hindmarsh, *For Christ and His Kingdom* (Vancouver: Regent College Publishing, 2013).

[31] Houston and Hindmarsh, *For Christ*, 32.

[32] Jaroslav Pelikan, *The Christian Intellectual* (New York: Harper & Row, 1965), 127.

[33] Noll, *Scandal*, 262.

[34] Marsden, *Outrageous Idea*, 88.

[35] Wendell Berry, *Home Economics* (San Francisco: North Point Press, 1987), 76.

[36] Berry, *Home Economics*, 77.

[37] Berry, *Home Economics*, 77.

[38] Marsden, *Outrageous Idea*, 126.

[39] Vincent, *Chautauqua Movement*, 175.

[40] Richard P. Heitzenrater, *A Short History of Chautauqua and the Suffrage Issue* (Chautauqua, NY: Oliver Archives Center, 2020), 4.

[41] Shirley A. Mullen, *Claiming the Courageous Middle: Daring to Live and Work Together for a More Hopeful Future* (Grand Rapids, MI: Baker Academic, 2024), 70.

[42] Richmond, *Invitation to Chautauqua*, 40.

[43] Simpson, *Chautauqua*, 37.

[44] Vincent, *Chautauqua Movement*, 30.

[45] Vincent, *Chautauqua Movement*, 30–31.

[46] Vincent, *Chautauqua Movement*, 89.

[47] James Davison Hunter, *Democracy and Solidarity: On the Cultural Roots of America's Political Crisis* (New Haven, CT: Yale University Press, 2024), 319.

[48] Vincent, *Chautauqua Movement*, 6.

[49] Dennis D. Cali, "A Sacramental View of Life in the Academy: Integration of Faith and Field," in *Professing Christ: Christian Tradition and Faith-Learning Integration in Public Universities*, ed. Jonathan Pettigrew and Robert H. Woods Jr. (Pasco, WA: Integratio Press, 2022), 33.

[50] Alexander Schmemann, *For the Life of the World* (Crestwood, NY: St. Vladimir's Seminary Press, 1973), 14.

[51] Marsden, *Outrageous Idea*, 105.

[52] Gregg Okesson, *A Public Missiology: How Local Churches Witness to a Complex World* (Grand Rapids, MI: Baker Academic, 2020), 2–3.

[53] Okesson, *Public Missiology*, 118.

[54] Okesson, *Public Missiology*, 111.

[55] Okesson, *Public Missiology*, 46.

[56] James Davison Hunter, *To Change the World: The Irony, Tragedy, and Possibility of Christianity in the Late Modern World* (New York: Oxford University Press, 2010), 263.

[57] Emily Raymond and Edward Everett Hale, *About Chautauqua: As an Idea, As a Power, and As a Place* (Toledo, OH: Blade Printing & Paper Co., 1884), 59.

Chapter 16
Leo Tolstoy's School for Peasant Children
Lance Croy

[1] Paul A. Soukup, SJ, "A Catholic University: A Religiously Oriented Approach to Teaching and Research," in *From the Outrageous to the Scandalous: Re-imagining Christian Thinking and Scholarship in an*

Age of Tribalism and Ideological Resentment, eds. Robert H. Woods Jr. and Mark Allan Steiner (Integratio Press, 2025), 73–78.

[2] Leo Tolstoy, *The Long Exile: And Other Stories* (New York: T. Y. Crowell, 1899), 286.

[3] Eugene Matusov, "Lev Tolstoy, A Founder of Democratic Education," *Integrative Psychological and Behavioral Science* 58, no. 4 (2024).

[4] Tolstoy, *The Long Exile*, 171.

[5] Tolstoy, *The Long Exile*, 240.

[6] Leo Tolstoy, *Tolstoy on Education*, trans. and ed. Edward J. Hughes (Chicago: University of Chicago Press, 1967), 55.

[7] Tolstoy, *Tolstoy on Education*, 55.

[8] Tolstoy, *The Long Exile*, 236.

[9] Tolstoy, *The Long Exile*, 209.

[10] Tolstoy, *The Long Exile*, 195.

[11] Susanne Langer, *Feeling and Form: A Theory of Art* (New York: Scribner, 1953).

[12] Tolstoy, *The Long Exile*, 286.

[13] John Piper and D. A. Carson, *The Pastor as Scholar and The Scholar as Pastor* (Wheaton, IL: Crossway, 2011), 82.

[14] Piper and Carson, *The Pastor as Scholar*, 76.

[15] Tolstoy, *The Long Exile*, 251–52.

Section Two: Reimagining the University and Christian Higher Education

Chapter 17

Reimagining the University: Substantive Truth as the Path to Pluralism

Jonathan Pettigrew

[1] Clifford G. Christians, "Substantive Truth in an Intellectual Pluralism Setting," in *From the Outrageous to the Scandalous: Re-imagining Christian Thinking and Scholarship in an Age of Tribalism and Ideological Resentment*, eds. Robert H. Woods Jr. and Mark Allan Steiner (Integratio Press, 2025), 69–71.

Chapter 18

Professor or Poulterer? Cultivating Religious Higher Education in the Postmodern Turn

Craig E. Mattson and *Desiree C. Duff*

[1] This work was originally published by Craig E. Mattson and Desiree C. Duff as "Professor or Poulterer? Cultivating Religious Higher Education in the Postmodern Turn" in *Christian Scholar's Review* 33, no. 3 (2004): 333–344. Reprinted by permission. All rights reserved.

[2] C. S. Lewis, *The Abolition of Man* (New York: MacMillan, 1947), 32–33.

[3] Marion Montgomery, *Liberal Arts and Community: The Feeding of the Larger Body* (Baton Rouge, LA: Louisiana State University Press, 1990), 31.

[4] Frank H. T. Rhodes, *The Creation of the Future: The Role of the American University* (Ithaca, NY: Cornell University Press, 2001), 44. Rhodes acknowledges the inevitability of pragmatization in university education: "Indeed, there are some who lament the growing presence of professional studies within the university, claiming they dilute 'purer' scholarship. But," he adds, "it is too late now. We are what we are, and there is no realistic possibility of going back, even if we wished to do so" (32).

[5] James Neuchterlein, "Evangelical and Catholic Together?" *First Things* 116 (October 2001): 8–9, http://www.firstthings.com/ftissues/ft0110/opinion/thistime.html.

[6] We use the term "reformational" instead of "Reformed" to align with a Christ-transforming-culture worldview rather than with a particular denomination.

[7] Jean-François Lyotard, *The Postmodern Condition: A Report on Knowledge*, trans. Geoff Bennington and Brian Massumi (Minneapolis: University of Minnesota Press, 1984), 48.

[8] Lyotard, *Postmodern Condition*, 48.

[9] Lyotard, *Postmodern Condition*, 48.

[10] Lyotard, *Postmodern Condition*, 48–49.

[11] Lyotard, *Postmodern Condition*, 48.

[12] Lyotard, *Postmodern Condition*, 51.

[13] Lyotard, *Postmodern Condition*, 49.

[14] Lyotard, *Postmodern Condition*, 48.

[15] Lyotard, *Postmodern Condition*, 13.

[16] Lyotard, *Postmodern Condition*, 51.

[17] Lyotard, *Postmodern Condition*, 51.

[18] Lyotard, *Postmodern Condition*, xxiv.

[19] Lyotard, *Postmodern Condition*, 50, 51, 53. Note also, as Davyd J. Greenwood and Morten Levin argue in their essay, "Reconstructing the Relationships between Universities and Society through Action Research," that the freedom of the university has for some time now been a chimera. "The autopoetic role of the faculty in setting much of the research agenda is largely a fantasy" (*Handbook of Qualitative Research*, 2nd ed., eds. Norman K. Denzin and Yvonna S. Lincoln [Thousand Oaks, CA: Sage, 2000], 89). Academic research, funded by tax benefits and directed to the ends of national defence or corporate aggrandizement, has become "a fascinating blend of two apparently contradictory principles: external control and internal autonomy" (Greenwood and Levin, "Reconstructing the Relationships," 89). The concerns of governmental and corporate sponsors (external controllers) embraced by elitist peer review boards (internal controllers) necessitate a preoccupation in graduate education with tracking a way through the political morass of obtaining funding. Inevitably, "for businesses and the government, funding university research is mainly a practical proposition, not an act of charity or commitment to the life of the mind" (Greenwood and Levin, "Reconstructing the Relationships," 91).

[20] Lyotard, *Postmodern Condition*, 5.

[21] Lyotard, *Postmodern Condition*, 48. It should, perhaps, be added that not all of Lyotard's predictions were wholly right in this connection. He argued that "experimentation in discourse, institutions, and values" improving "curriculum, student supervision and testing, and pedagogy" would die off, because such innovation would be "regarded as having little or no operational value" (Lyotard, *Postmodern Condition*, 50). But he failed to anticipate what Rhodes describes as "the remarkable level of scores of professional services, from surgery to retailing, the quality and value of hundreds of products, from fruit to computers to freeway design and automobile safety, [which] reflect the benefits of this growth in university professionalism" (Lyotard, *Postmodern Condition*, 32). We grant Rhodes' point (and share his gratitude) that federal and corporate preoccupation with performativity may have helped to transform education to redirect research to productive technological development, but we are concerned in this essay about the elements traditionally supplied by the liberal arts education which make meaningful our partaking and enjoyment of the items on Rhodes' list.

[22] James Tunstead Burtchaell, *The Dying of the Light: The Disengagement of Colleges and Universities from their Christian Churches* (Grand Rapids, MI: Wm. B. Eerdmans, 1998), 839.

[23] Burtchaell, *Dying of the Light*, 839.

[24] Dallas Willard, *The Spirit of Disciplines: Understanding How God Changes Lives* (San Francisco: HarperCollins, 1988), 15.

[25] Burtchaell, *Dying of the Light*, 840.

[26] For reasons Lyotard makes clear, it is generally difficult in the non-religious Academy to identify either a single "point" or an overacting "all." But a utilitarian denaturing of education could eventually have effects that are recognizably devastating even from a wholly secular point of view. In the morning hours of Western civilization, Archimedes, it is said, put a geometrical theorem on his gravestone. Instead of a record of his inventions, thus earning the mockery of utilitarians ever since. But as Michael Polanyi explains, it was unfortunate that the Greeks did not share the great geometer's valuing of theoretical beauty over technical savvy. Only an appreciation for such elegance could have preserved Archimedean mathematics from the demise it suffered after his death. Educators across the disciplines would do well to attend to the Polanyian fear that disregarding theoretical elegance to privilege pragmatic sophistication could "bury modern mathematics in an oblivion more complete and lasting than that which enveloped Greek mathematics twenty-two centuries ago" (*Personal Knowledge: Towards a Post-Critical Philosophy* [Chicago: University of Chicago Press, 1962], 192–193).

[27] Richard John Neuhaus, "While We're at It," *First Things* 100 (February 2000): 77–92; http://www. firstthings.com/ftissues/ ft0002/public.html.

[28] Alan Wolfe, "The Opening of the Evangelical Mind," *The Atlantic Monthly* 286 (October 2000): 4, http://www.theatlantic.com/issues/ 2000/10/wolfe.htm.

[29] Mark A. Noll, *The Scandal of the Evangelical Mind* (Grand Rapids, Ml: Wm. B. Eerdmans, 1994), 77–81.

[30] J. I. Packer, *The Quest for Godliness* (Wheaton, IL: Crossway, 1990), 12.

[31] Leland Ryken, *Worldly Saints* (Grand Rapids, MI: Zondervan, 1986), 157.

[32] Brutchaell, *Dying of the Light*, 840.

[33] Everett Rogers, *A History of Communications Study: A Biographical Approach* (New York: Free Press, 1994), 203.

[34] Recall, for example, the by-now-infamous ""hypodermic' model," which conceives media influence in terms of a "power to 'inject' a repressive ideology directly into the consciousness of the masses" (David Morley, *Television, Audiences and Cultural Studies* [London: Routledge, 1992], 45). Media-effects scholar Paul Lazarsfield renovated this model, creating "the era of limited media-effects" (Rogers, 288), which assumed "a linear process from a sender, by way of a channel, in the form of a message, to a receiver, to achieve some kind of effect, whether intended or unintended" (Denis McQuail, *Mass Communication Theory: An Introduction*, 2nd ed. [London: Sage, 1987], 43). Two movements that helped to breathe life into the media-effects model of research were cultivation analysis and "uses and gratification" research. The first, which is still advocated today (Nancy Signorielli and Michael Morgan, eds. *Cultivation Analysis: New Directions in Media Effects Research* [Newbury Park, CA: Sage, 1990], 10), tries to ascertain if those who spend more time watching television are more likely to perceive the real world in ways that reflect the most common and repetitive messages and lessons of the television world, compared with people who watch less television but are otherwise comparable in important demographic characteristics" (Signorielli and Morgan, *Cultivation Analysis*, 16). "Uses and gratification" research argues that mass audiences, so far from being passive imbibers of media messages, are actually highly selective of which messages to attend to. Audiences dole out their attention to messages that are perceived in some way pleasurable or profitable (Jay G. Blumler and Denis McQuail, *Television in Politics: Its Uses and Influence* [London: Faber, 1968], 11). But the essential transmissiveness remains.

[35] James Carey, *Communication as Culture, Media and Popular Culture*, ed. David Thorburn (Boston: Unwin Hyman, 1989), 15.

[36] Carey, *Communication as Culture*, 16.

[37] Carey, *Communication as Culture*, 18.

[38] Carey, *Communication as Culture*, 18.

[39] Quentin Schultze, *Communicating for Life: Christian Stewardship in Community and Media* (Grand Rapids, MI: Baker, 2000), 54.

[40] Carey, *Communication as Culture*, 18.

[41] Walker Percy, *The Message in the Bottle* (New York: Noonday, 1975), 150–158. Thomas Merton has also dealt with this subject in his essay "Symbolism" in *Love and Living*, eds. Naomi Burton Stone and Roderick P. Hart (New York: Bantam, 1979).

[42] Percy Miller has connected this notion usefully with the Puritan tradition in his essay "The Rhetoric of Sensation," in which he details how Locke's psychology influenced the preaching of Jonathan Edwards. Words were understood by Edwards to make possible the eruption in the audience's mind of the same ideas that are in the rhetor's mind (*Errand into the Wilderness* [Cambridge, MA: Belknap Press, 1956], 181).

[43] Walker Percy's *Lost in the Cosmos* implies that whether teaching involves signs or symbols has immense ethical import. The contrast between a student's relationship to a transmissive or a ritual pedagogy could potentially be as striking as the change in relationship between Helen Keller and Anne Sullivan before and after the incident at the pump when the child finally figured out that "w-a-t-e-r" was not simply a sign pointing to water, but a name that *meant* water ([New York: Picador, 1983], 98–99).

[44] Hans Georg Gadamer, *Truth and Method*, 2nd rev. ed., trans. Joel Weinsheimer and Donald G. Marshall (New York: Continuum, 2002), 292. Roger Lundin, who pointed us to this passage, explains further, "According to Gadamer, human understanding is most fruitfully conceived as a form of dialogue in which the horizon of our prejudices is fused with that of the other's as we both gaze upon the object or

truth in question" (*The Culture of Interpretation: Christian Paith and the Postmodern World* [Grand Rapids, MI: Eerdmans, 1993], 223).

[45] Gadamer, *Truth and Method*, 16.

[46] Gadamer, *Truth and Method*, 15.

[47] Michael Polanyi, *Personal Knowledge: Towards a Post-Critical Philosophy* (Chicago: University of Chicago, 1962), 196.

[48] Another way to cast this recognition of the power of forgetfulness would be to say that ritual pedagogy is as much hermeneutic as it is epistemic. In making this distinction, we appropriate the work of Richard Rorty (*Philosophy and the Mirror of Nature* [Princeton, NJ: Princeton, 1979], 315–356). Epistemic instruction is preoccupied with creating a knowledge cache in the student's mind. A hermeneutic emphasis, on the other hand, would be less concerned with the transference of information than with the cultivation of meaning. Practically speaking, a hermeneutic emphasis in ritual pedagogy offers rationale for the supplementary materials teachers already use, especially when these materials are as much imaginative as informative. Cartoons, movie clips, improvisational drama—these need not be considered frivolous attention-getters made unfortunately necessary by the shortcomings of an MTV generation. Instead, such materials enable something like the "re-description" Rorty is so fond of, though not necessarily in his anti-realist usage of the word. They are oblique generators of gist. Along these same lines, a conversation with Professor Bob Rice at Trinity Christian College suggested, contrarily, that education in lower-level courses may need to be more epistemic than hermeneutic in the sense that students need to have a working vocabulary and conceptual base before they can explore the meanings that help create a culture or a worldview. His comments were also helpful for our ensuing discussion of the implications of inductive logic in the classroom.

[49] Sandra Moriarty, "Abduction: A Theory of Visual Interpretation," *Communication Theory* 6, no. 2 (May 1996): 178. Our first contact with abductive logic, a term usually associated with Charles S. Peirce, though Polanyi deals with the concept as well, was in literature on the young field of visual rhetoric. To elaborate on what we have drawn from Moriarty, we should add that she exegetes the Peircean "criterion of interpretability" as "a two-step function that involves both translation and extension, a process that leads to an infinite chain of signification" (Moriarty, "Abduction," 178). This makes abduction sound linear, but actually, as Moriarty explains, "Interpretation means that every interpretant, besides translating the immediate object or the content of the sign, also increases our understanding of it in new ways" (Moriarty, "Abduction," 178.). So the movement in abductive thinking is a tacking, back and forth between translation and extension, between interpretation and heurism. Our understanding of a ritual pedagogy also finds enrichment in James Jasinksi's description of "conceptually oriented" rhetorical criticism, which "proceeds through the constant interaction of careful reading and rigorous conceptual reflection" ("The Status of Theory and Method in Rhetorical Criticism," *Western Journal of Speech and Communication* 65, no. 3 [Summer 20011]: 256).

[50] Polanyi's description of the artistic process might also be appropriated for describing the educational process: "a constant invention of means for expressing [the teacher's] aims, coupled with readjustment of his aims in the light of his means" (Michael Polanyi and Harry Prosch, *Meaning* [Chicago: University of Chicago Press, 1975], 99).

[51] David Naugle has identified the tendencies of worldview thinking to be disconnected from anything but philosophic systems (*Worldview* [Grand Rapids, MI: Wm. B. Eerdmans, 2002], 336–337).

[52] Michael Polanyi, *Study of Man* (Chicago: University of Chicago Press, 1959), 95.

[53] Montgomery, *Liberal Arts and Community*, 34.

[54] Charles Colson, "Backyard Apologetics," *Touchstone: A journal of Mere Christianity* 12, no. 6 (November, December 1999): http://www.touchstonemag.com/docs/issues/ 12.6docs/ 12-6pg41.html. We are also grateful for a conversation with Professor Aron Reppman at Trinity Christian College that pointed out the integrality of this insight for reformational thought.

Chapter 19
Christian Scholarship Thirty Years On
A. Chase Mitchell

[1] George M. Marsden, *The Outrageous Idea of Christian Scholarship* (New York: Oxford University Press, 1997), 5.

[2] George M. Marsden, *The Outrageous Idea of Christian Scholarship*, 2nd ed. (New York: Oxford University Press, 2024).

[3] Marsden, *Outrageous Idea*, xiv.

[4] Rhonda Hustedt Jacobsen, "Intellectual Pilgrimage: Christians in the Contemporary Academy," *Christian Scholar's Review*, Christ Animated Learning Blog, May 22, 2025, para. 1, https://christianschol-ars.com/intellectual-pilgrimage-christians-in-the-contemporary-academy-2/.

[5] Jacobsen, "Intellectual Pilgrimage," para. 3.

[6] Jacobsen, "Intellectual Pilgrimage," para. 2.

[7] Marsden, *Outrageous Idea*, 134.

[8] Marsden, *Outrageous Idea*, xiv.

[9] Marsden, *Outrageous Idea*, 134.

Chapter 20
A Sacramental View of Communication and
Media Studies in the Digital Age
Dennis D. Cali

[1] Mother Teresa of Calcutta, in *Where There is Love, There is God: Her Path to Closer Union with God and Greater Love for Others*, ed. Brian Kolodiejchuk (New York: Doubleday, 2010).

[2] Abraham Joshua Heschel, *God in Search of Man: A Philosophy of Judaism* (New York: Harper and Row, 1955), 74.

[3] Mark A. Noll, "The Scandal of the Evangelical Mind: Then and Now," in *From the Outrageous to the Scandalous: Re-imagining Christian Thinking and Scholarship in an Age of Tribalism and Ideological Resentment*, ed. Robert H. Woods Jr. and Mark Allan Steiner (Integratio Press, 2025), 10, 12.

[4] George M. Marsden, "Mere Christian Scholarship," in *From the Outrageous to the Scandalous: Re-imagining Christian Thinking and Scholarship in an Age of Tribalism and Ideological Resentment*, ed. Robert H. Woods Jr. and Mark Allan Steiner (Integratio Press, 2025), 17.

[5] Albert Borgmann, *Technology And the Character Of Contemporary Life: A Philosophical Inquiry* (Chicago: University of Chicago Press, 1984), 76; and Pope Francis, Laudato Si, May 24, 2015, https://www.vatican.va/content/francesco/en/encyclicals/documents/papa-francesco_20150524_enciclica-lauda-to-si.html, and paraphrased here by David E. DeCosse and Brian Patrick Green, Santa Clara University Markula Center for Applied Ethics, https://www.scu.edu/media/ethics-center/environmental-ethics/en-cyclical-handout.pdf.

[6] Jacques Ellul, *The Technological Society*, trans. John Wilkinson (New York: Vintage Books, 1964), 28.

[7] Chiara Lubich, "Love for Our Neighbour and the New Commandment," in Conversation with the Women Focolorine International School of Grottaferreta, November 16, 1965, in Pasquale Foresi, *The Incarnation of the Light* (Welwyn Grden City, Herfordshire, UK: New City Publishing House, 2022), 105–112.

[8] Martin Heidegger, *Being and Time*, trans. John Macquarrie and Edward Robinson (New York: Harper and Row, 1962).

Chapter 21
Merging Faith and Intellectual Pursuits in
Christ-centered Universities
Donna M. Elkins

[1] Richard J. Mouw, *Called to the Life of the Mind: Some Advice for Evangelical Scholars* (Grand Rapids, MI: Wm. B. Eerdmans, 2014), 70–71.

[2] Mouw, *Called to the Life*, 71.

[3] George M. Marsden, *The Outrageous Idea of Christian Scholarship*, 2nd ed. (New York: Oxford University Press, 2024), 49.

[4] Marsden, *Outrageous Idea*, 3.

[5] Ann M. Garrido, *Redeeming Administration: 12 Spiritual Habits for Catholic Leaders in Parishes, Schools, Religious Communities, and Other Institutions* (Notre Dame, IN: Ave Maria Press, 2013), 4.

[6] Garrido, *Redeeming Administration*, 68–69.

[7] Garrido, *Redeeming Administration*, 172.

[8] Sandra Petronio, "Translational Research Endeavors and the Practices of Communication Privacy Management," *Journal of Applied Communication Research* 35, no. 3 (August 2007): 219.

Chapter 22
Between Technology and Tyranny:
Twin Threats for Christian Higher Education
David Dockery

[1] Mark A. Noll, "The Scandal of the Evangelical Mind: Then and Now," in *From the Outrageous to the Scandalous: Re-imagining Christian Thinking and Scholarship in an Age of Tribalism and Ideological Resentment*, eds. Robert H. Woods Jr. and Mark Allan Steiner (Integratio Press, 2025), 11.

[2] Noll, "Then and Now."

[3] Aristotle, *Nicomachean Ethics*, trans. H. Rackham, vol. 19 of *The Loeb Classical Library*, 23 vols. (Cambridge, MA: Harvard University Press, 1934), http://www.perseus.tufts.edu/hopper/text?doc=Perseus:text:1999.01.0054.

[4] Hans-Georg Gadamer, *Truth and Method*, trans. Joel Weinsheimer and Donald G. Marshall (London: Bloomsbury Academic, 2013), 772.

[5] David Roochnik, *Plato's Republic*, The Great Courses, 2005, audiobook, https://www.audible.com/pd/Platos-Republic-Audiobook/B00DG67A0S.

Chapter 23
Communication Challenges for Christian Higher Education
Reid Vance

[1] George M. Marsden, *The Outrageous Idea of Christian Scholarship* (New York: Oxford University Press, 1997).

[2] George M. Marsden, "Mere Christian Scholarship," in *From the Outrageous to the Scandalous: Re-imagining Christian Thinking and Scholarship in an Age of Tribalism and Ideological Resentment*, eds. Robert H. Woods Jr. and Mark Allan Steiner (Integratio Press, 2025), 15–18.

[3] Marsden, *Outrageous Idea*, 104.

[4] Marsden, *Outrageous Idea*, 104.

[5] Marsden, "Mere Christian Scholarship," 16 emphasis added.

[6] Marsden, "Mere Christian Scholarship," 16.

[7] Baskin-Robbins, "About us," *Baskin-Robbins*, April 20, 2025, https://www.baskinrobbins.com/en/about-us.

[8] Council for Christian Colleges and Universities, "About," *Council for Christian Colleges and Universities*, April 20, 2025, https://www.cccu.org/about.

[9] Council for Christian Colleges and Universities, "About."

[10] Alexander W. Astin, Helen S. Astin, and Jennifer A. Lindholm, *Cultivating the Spirit: How College Can Enhance Students' Inner Lives* (San Francisco: Jossey-Bass, 2011).

[11] Marsden, *Outrageous Idea*, 110.

[12] Marsden, "Mere Christian Scholarship," 17.

[13] Marsden, "Mere Christian Scholarship," 18.

[14] Marsden, "Mere Christian Scholarship," 18.

Chapter 24
The Catholic University: Preserving the Mission
Amidst Contemporary Pressures
Kathleen M. Edelmayer

[1] *Land O' Lakes Statement: The Idea of the Catholic University*, 1967, https://cushwa.nd.edu/assets/245340/landolakesstatement.pdf and United States's Conference of Catholic Bishops, *Application for Ex Corde Ecclesia for the United States*, 1999, https://www.usccb.org/committees/catholic-education/application-ex-corde-ecclesiae-united-states#:~:text=On%20August%2015%2C%201990%2C%20Pope,education%20entitled%20Ex%20corde%20Ecclesiae.&text=The%20Apostolic%20Constitution%20described%20the,to%20help%20fulfill%20its%20vision.

[2] John Paul II, *Fides et Ratio*, 1998 and *Ex Corde Ecclesia*, 1999.

[3] Association of Catholic Colleges and Universities, https://www.accunet.org/data.html.

[4] Paul A. Soukup, SJ, "A Catholic University: A Religiously Oriented Approach to Teaching and Research," in *From the Outrageous to the Scandalous: Re-imagining Christian Thinking and Scholarship in an Age of Tribalism and Ideological Resentment*, eds. Robert H. Woods Jr. and Mark Allan Steiner (Integratio Press, 2025), 73–78.

[5] Soukup, SJ, "A Catholic University," 76.

[6] Association of Franciscan College and Universities, "Characteristics of Franciscan Higher Education," https://franciscancollegesuniversities.org/about-us/characteristics-of-franciscan-higher-education/.

[7] William J. Short, OFM, *A Franciscan Language for the 21st Century* (Berkeley, CA: Franciscan School of Theology, 2003), 6.

[8] Association of Franciscan Colleges and Universities, "Members," https://franciscancollegesuniversities.org/members/.

[9] "Notre Dame's Theology Department Ranked Best in the World," *University of Notre Dame College of Arts and Letters*, April 8, 2025, https://al.nd.edu/news/latest-news/notre-dames-theology-department-ranked-best-in-the-world/#:~:text=The%20University%20of%20Notre%20Dame,1%20distinction.

[10] Jack Dunn, "Boston College Ranked 10th Worldwide in Theology, Divinity, and Religious Studies," *BC News*, March 2023, https://www.bc.edu/bc-web/bcnews/faith-religion/theology/bc-in-top-10-worldwide-for-theological-studies.html.

[11] Mark A. Noll, "The Scandal of the Evangelical Mind: Then and Now," in *From the Outrageous to the Scandalous: Re-imagining Christian Thinking and Scholarship in an Age of Tribalism and Ideological Resentment*, eds. Robert H. Woods Jr. and Mark Allan Steiner (Integratio Press, 2025), 9–13.

[12] Noll, "Then and Now," 11.

[13] Dennis Sadowski, "Catholic Colleges Cut Humanities Programs, Citing Student Interest in Other Fields," *National Catholic Reporter*, March 24, 2023, https://www.ncronline.org/news/catholic-colleges-cut-humanities-programs-citing-student-interest-other-fields; Karl Winter, "St. Norbert College Laying off 27 Faculty Members, Discontinuing 15 Majors," NBC 26 News Northeast Wisconsin, March 13, 2025, https://www.nbc26.com/news/local-news/in-your-neighborhood/de-pere/st-norbert-college-laying-off-27-faculty-members-discontinuing-15-majors.

[14] Craig Trainor, "Dear Colleague Letter," United States' Department of Education Office for Civil Rights, February 14, 2025, https://www.ed.gov/media/document/dear-colleague-letter-sffa-v-harvard-109506.pdf.

[15] Charles J. Russo, "Is a Faith-Based Charter School a Threat to Religious Freedom, or a Necessity to Uphold it?" *University of Dayton Magazine*, May 2, 2025, https://udayton.edu/magazine/2025/05/faith-based-charter-schools.php

[16] Massimo Faggioli, "Catholic Universities in the Crosshairs? Trump's Attack on Higher Education Extends Beyond the Ivies," *Commonweal*, March 11, 2025, https://www.commonwealmagazine.org/education-catholic-universities-trump-faggioli-georgetown-DEI.

[17] Massimo Faggioli, *Theology & Catholic Higher Education: Beyond our Identity Crisis* (Maryknoll, NY: Orbis, 2024).

[18] Faggioli, *Theology & Catholic Higher Education*, 6.

[19] Mark A. Noll, *The Scandal of the Evangelical Mind*, 2nd ed. (Grand Rapids, MI: Wm. B. Eerdmans, 2022), 114.

[20] Faggioli, *Theology & Catholic Higher Education*, 10.

[21] Cardinal Newman Society, "Recommended Colleges," https://cardinalnewmansociety.org/college/.

[22] Maria Benevento, "Letter Signed by More than 1,500 Accuses Pope Francis of the 'Canonical Delict of Heresy,'" *National Catholic Reporter*, May 1, 2019, https://www.ncronline.org/news/quick-reads/letter-signed-more-1500-accuses-pope-francis-canonical-derelict-heresy.

[23] William M. Treanor, "Letter from Dean and Executive Vice President of Georgetown Law to Edwin R. Martin Jr., Interim United States Attorney," *Washington Post*, March 6, 2025, https://www.washingtonpost.com/documents/06480bde-06ed-419f-841e-762c8198b508.pdf.

[24] Faggioli, *Theology & Catholic Higher Education*, 151–152.

[25] Sadowski, "Catholic Colleges Cut Humanities Programs."

[26] Association of Catholic Colleges and Universities, https://www.accunet.org/about.html.

[27] Faggioli, *Theology & Catholic Higher Education*, 10.

Chapter 25
Christians' Progress Through the Academy:
The Need to Journey Together
Elaine V. Fung and *Brandon Knight*

[1] John Bunyan, *The Pilgrim's Progress* (Oxford: Clarendon Press, 1879).

[2] George M. Marsden, *The Outrageous Idea of Christian Scholarship* (New York: Oxford University Press, 1998), 101.

[3] Pew Research Center, "Men, Women and Social Connections," *Pew Research Center*, January 16, 2025, https://www.pewresearch.org/social-trends/2025/01/16/men-women-and-social-connections/, para. 2.

[4] Johanna Alonso, "The New Plague on Campus: Loneliness," *Inside Higher Ed*, November 8, 2023, https://www.insidehighered.com/news/students/physical-mental-health/2023/11/08/new-epidemic-gripping-college-campuses-loneliness.

[5] Pew, "Men, Women and Social Connections," paras. 4, 8.

[6] Nicholas Burk and Amy Pearson, "Encouraging Student Sense of Belonging through Instructor Face Support," *Journal of Communication Pedagogy* 6 (2022): 214–30.

[7] Linda W. Rutland Gillison, "Community-Building in Honors Education," in *Teaching and Learning in Honors*, ed. Cheryl L. Fuiks and Larry Clark (Lincoln, NE: National Collegiate Honors Council, 2000), 33.

[8] Mary Page James and Dan Witters, "Daily Loneliness Afflicts One in Five in U.S.," *Gallup*, October 15, 2024, https://news.gallup.com/poll/651881/daily-loneliness-afflicts-one-five.aspx, para. 1.

[9] James and Witters, "Daily Loneliness," para. 5.

[10] James and Witters, "Daily Loneliness," para. 8.

[11] Marina Galioto, Francesca Pedone, Apostolos Vantarakis, Paula Tavares, and Antonino Bianco, "The Use of Social Networks in Institutional Communication at University: A Prospective Pattern for Enhancing the Sense of Belonging among Students," *Frontiers in Communication* 10 (2025): 2.

[12] Burk and Pearson, "Encouraging Student Sense of Belonging," 215.

[13] Alonso, "The New Plague on Campus."

[14] Quentin Schultze, *Communicating with Grace and Virtue: Learning to Listen, Speak, Text and Interact as a Christian* (Grand Rapids, MI: Baker Academic, 2020), 87.

[15] James and Witters, "Daily Loneliness," paras. 12–15.

[16] Galioto, et al., "The Use of Social Networks," 6.

[17] James and Witters, "Daily Loneliness."

[18] Schultze, *Communicating with Grace*, 87.

[19] Dietrich Bonhoffer, *Life Together: The Classic Exploration of Faith in Community* (New York: Harper & Row, 1954), 10.

[20] Bonhoffer, *Life Together*, 13.

[21] Bonhoffer, *Life Together*, 29.

[22] Bonhoffer, *Life Together*, 15.

[23] Barna Group, "New Research: Belief in Jesus Rises, Fueled by Younger Adults," *Barna*, April 7, 2025, https://www.barna.com/research/belief-in-jesus-rises/, para. 2.

[24] Barna Group, "New Research," para. 12.

[25] Barna Group, "New Research," para. 14.

[26] Greg Spencer, "An Outrageous Scandal: Three Rs for the Future of Christian Education," in *From the Outrageous to the Scandalous: Re-imagining Christian Thinking and Scholarship in an Age of Tribalism and Ideological Resentment*, eds. Robert H. Woods Jr. and Mark Allan Steiner (Integratio Press, 2025), 45–52.

[27] Marsden, *Outrageous Idea*, 102.

[28] Kristos Logos Paideia Honor Society, "Our Mission Statement," *The Christianity & Communication Studies Network*, https://www.theccsn.com/kristos-logos-paideia-honor-society/, para. 2.

[29] Marsden, *Outrageous Idea*, 105.

[30] Ronald C. Arnett, *Dialogic Education: Conversation about Ideas and Between Persons* (Carbondale, IL: Southern Illinois University Press, 1993), 37.

[31] Nancy Stanlick, "Creating an Honors Community: A Virtue Ethics Approach," *Journal of the National Collegiate Honors Council* 7, no. 1 (2006): 75–92.

Section Three: Communication, Pedagogy,
and Intellectual Formation

Chapter 26

The Unlikely Intellectual: How Reuben "Uncle Bud" Robinson's
Rhetorical Invention Challenges Noll's Scandal

Abram J. Book

[1] Mark A. Noll, *The Scandal of the Evangelical Mind* (Grand Rapids, MI: Wm. B. Eerdmans Publishing Co, 1994), 109.

[2] Noll, *Scandal*, 123.

[3] Noll, *Scandal*, 249.

[4] Steven D. Cooley, "The Pressure of Reality and the Sound of Holiness: Developments in the Methodist/Holiness Poetic, 1870–1950," *Methodist History* 59, no. 3 (April 2021): 174.

[5] Noll, *Scandal*, 125.

[6] Cooley, "The Pressure of Reality,"174.

[7] Darius L. Salter, *The Demise of the American Holiness Movement: An Historical, Theological, Biblical, and Cultural Exploration* (Wilmore, KY: FirstFruits Press, 2020), 6.

[8] Stan Ingersol, *Nazarene Roots: Pastors, Prophets, Revivalists, Reformers* (Kansas City, MO: Beacon Hill Press, 2009).

[9] Bud Robinson, *My Life's Story* (Jawbone Digital Publishers, n.d.), www.jawbonedigital.com.

[10] John Lakin Brasher, *Glimpses: Some Personal Glimpses of Holiness Preachers Whom I Have Known, and with Whom I Have Labored in Evangelism, Who Have Answered to their Names in the Roll Call of the Skies* (Cincinnati, OH: The Revivalist Press, 1954), 42.

[11] Noll, *Scandal*, 120.

[12] Noll, *Scandal*, 116.

[13] Salter, *Demise*, 61.

[14] Abram Book, "Southern Folk Preaching: Suggesting the Existence of a Genre through Comparison of the Sermons of 'Uncle Bud' Robinson and Fred Craddock," *Artifact Analysis* 1, no. 3 (2022): 1–26.

[15] Bud Robinson, *Religion, Philosophy, and Fun* (Kansas City, MO: Beacon Hill Press, 1942), 34.

[16] William A. Welch Jr., "The Welch Family Robinson: A California Pastorale" (unpublished manuscript, 1998), 6.

[17] John Lawrence Brasher, *The Sanctified South: John Lakin Brasher and the Holiness Movement* (Chicago: University of Illinois Press, 1994), 94.

[18] Cited in Cooley, "The Pressure of Reality," 1.

[19] Robinson, *Religion, Philosophy, and Fun*, 32.

[20] Abram Book, "Southern Folk Preaching," 3–4.

[21] Angela Duckworth, *Grit: The Power of Passion and Perseverance* (New York: Scribner, 2018), 8.

[22] Joe Gorman, *Resilience* (Kansas City, MO: The Foundry Publishing, 2023), 16, 18.

[23] Abram Book, "Give Me a Backbone as Big as a Sawlog: An Analysis of the Preaching of 'Uncle Bud' Robinson—the Will Rogers of the Holiness Movement," *Kentucky Journal of Communication* 40, no. 2 (September 1, 2021): 29–49.

[24] Bud Robinson, *My Hospital Experience* (Louisville, KY: The Herald Press, n.d.), 8.

[25] Mark A. Noll, *Jesus Christ and the Life of the Mind* (Grand Rapids, MI: Wm. B. Eerdmans Publishing Co, 2011), 44.

[26] Bud Robinson, "Booker T. Washington, As I Saw Him," *Pentecostal Advocate* (April 29, 1909): 2.

[27] Booker T. Washington, "1907 Letter from Booker T. Washington Regarding a Speech He Gave at Vanderbilt University," *Samford University Library, Special Collection Department*, accessed May 12, 2025, https://digitalcollections.samford.edu/Documents/Detail/1907-letter-from-booker-t.-washington-regarding-a-speech-he-gave-at-vanderbilt-university/54916.

[28] Robinson, "Booker T. Washington," 2.

Chapter 27
Jest the Facts
Lance Croy

[1] Christopher Ben Simpson, *The Truth Is the Way: Kierkegaard's Theologia Viatorum* (Eugene, OR: Wipf and Stock, 2011), 13–15.

[2] Thomas C. Oden, *Parables of Kierkegaard* (Princeton, NJ: Princeton University Press, 1978).

[3] Søren Kierkegaard, *Provocations: Spiritual Writings of Kierkegaard*, ed. Charles E. Moore (Farmington, PA: The Bruderhof Foundation, 2002), 54.

[4] Søren Kierkegaard, *Works of Love*, trans. Howard V. Hong and Edna H. Hong (Princeton, NJ: Princeton University Press, 1995), 157.

[5] Søren Kierkegaard, *Fear and Trembling and The Sickness Unto Death*, trans. Walter Lowrie (New Jersey: Princeton University Press), 176.

[6] Søren Kierkegaard, *For Self-Examination and Judge For Yourselves!* trans. Walter Lowrie (New Jersey: Princeton University Press, 1944), 51–55.

[7] Søren Kierkegaard, *Either/Or Volume I*, trans. David F. Swenson and Lillian Marvin Swenson (Princeton, New Jersey: Princeton University Press, 1961), 30.

[8] Benson P. Fraser, *Hide and Seek: The Sacred Art of Indirect Communication* (Eugene, OR: Cascade, 2020), 81.

[9] Kierkegaard, *Works of Love*.

[10] Kierkegaard, *Purity of Heart is to Will One Thing: Spiritual Preparation for the Office of Confession*, trans. Douglas V. Steere (New York: Harper & Rowe, 1948).

Chapter 28
Dorothy Sayers: The Gospel and The Power of Indirect Communication
Kim Okesson

[1] Humphrey Carpenter, *The Inklings: C. S. Lewis, J. R. R. Tolkien, Charles Williams and their Friends* (Boston, MA: Houghton Mifflin, 1979), 189.

[2] Michael Cart, *Confessions of a Book Reviewer: The Best of Cart Blanche* (Chicago: ALA Editions, 2018), 12.

[3] Cart, *Confessions*, 12.

[4] Laura Simmons, *Creed without Chaos: Exploring Theology in the Writings of Dorothy L. Sayers* (Grand Rapids, MI: Baker Academic, 2005), 17.

[5] Simmons, *Creed without Chaos*, 17.

[6] Simmons, *Creed without Chaos*, 18.

[7] Barbara Reynolds, *Dorothy Sayers: Her Life and Soul, A Biography* (New York: St. Martin's Press, 1993), 1–97.

[8] Reynolds, *Dorothy Sayers*, 13.

[9] Reynolds, *Dorothy Sayers*, 18.

[10] Reynolds, *Dorothy Sayers*, 22.

[11] Reynolds, *Dorothy Sayers*, 27.

[12] Reynolds, *Dorothy Sayers*, 97.

[13] Simmons, *Creed without Chaos*, 19.

[14] Simmons, *Creed without Chaos*, 12.

[15] Simmons, *Creed without Chaos*, 17.

[16] Simmons, *Creed without Chaos*, 19.

[17] James Beitler III, *Seasoned Speech: Rhetoric in the Life of the Church* (Downers Grove, IL: InterVarsity Press Academic, 2019), 62.

[18] Beitler III, *Seasoned Speech*, 62.

[19] Beitler III, *Seasoned Speech*, 62.

[20] Beitler III, *Seasoned Speech*, 65.

[21] Beitler III, *Seasoned Speech*, 68.

[22] Beitler III, *Seasoned Speech*, 68.

[23] Fred Craddock, *Overhearing the Gospel: Preaching and Teaching the Faith to Persons Who Have Heard It All Before* (Nashville, TN: Abingdon Press, 2002).

[24] Craddock, *Overhearing the Gospel*, 15.

[25] Craddock, *Overhearing the Gospel*, 9.

[26] Choan-Seng Song, *In the Beginning were Stories, Not Texts: Story Theology* (Eugene, OR: Cascade Books, 2011).

[27] Song, *In the Beginning*, 18.

[28] William Harrison, "Loving the Creation, Loving the Creator; Dorothy L. Sayers's Theology of Work," *Anglican Theological Review* 86, no. 2 (2004): 239–257.

[29] Reynolds, *Dorothy Sayers*, 310.

[30] Harrison, "Loving the Creation," 253.

[31] Beitler III, *Seasoned Speech*, 83.

[32] Beitler III, *Seasoned Speech*, 83.

[33] Beitler III, *Seasoned Speech*, 83.

[34] Beitler III, *Seasoned Speech*, 83.

[35] Song, *In the Beginning*, 18.

[36] Simmons, *Creed without Chaos*, 46.

[37] Simmons, *Creed without Chaos*, 47.

[38] Simmons, *Creed without Chaos*, 48.

[39] Simmons, *Creed without Chaos*, 48.

[40] Simmons, *Creed without Chaos*, 50.

[41] Simmons, *Creed without Chaos*, 51.

[42] Simmons, *Creed without Chaos*, 51.

[43] Simmons, *Creed without Chaos*, 52.

[44] Simmons, *Creed without Chaos*, 53.

[45] Simmons, *Creed without Chaos*, 65.

[46] Simmons, *Creed without Chaos*, 49.

[47] Walter Hooper, ed., *The Collected Letters of C. S. Lewis. Volume 2: Books, Broadcasts, and War, 1931–1949* (San Francisco: HarperOne, 2004).

[48] Simmons, *Creed without Chaos*, 56.

[49] Dorothy Sayers, *The Whimsical Christian: 18 Essays.* (New York, NY: MacMillan Press, 1978), 41.

[50] Simmons, *Creed without Chaos*, 55.

[51] Simmons, *Creed without Chaos*, 56.

[52] Simmons, *Creed without Chaos*, 67.

[53] Beitler III, *Seasoned Speech*, 82.

[54] Beitler III, *Seasoned Speech*, 82.

[55] Simmons, *Creed without Chaos*, 145.

[56] Simmons, *Creed without Chaos*, 148.

[57] Nancy M. P. Tischler, *Dorothy L. Sayers: A Pilgrim Soul* (Atlanta, GA: John Knox Press, 1980), 61.

[58] Tischler, *Dorothy L. Sayers*, 21.

[59] Tischler, *Dorothy L. Sayers*, 15

[60] Tischler, *Dorothy L. Sayers*, 61.

[61] Tischler, *Dorothy L. Sayers*, 62.

[62] Harrison, "Loving the Creation," 240.

[63] Harrison, "Loving the Creation," 257.

[64] Christine Fletcher, *The Artist and the Trinity: Dorothy Sayers' Theology of Work* (Eugene, OR: Pickwick, 2013), xvii.

[65] James Nordlinger, "Sing It, Dorothy," *National Review* 67, no. 6 (2015): 27–28.

[66] Nordlinger, "Sing It," 28.

[67] Tischler, *Dorothy L. Sayers*, 62.

[68] Rosemary Erickson Johnsen, "Dorothy L. Sayers and Virginia Woolf: Perspectives on the Woman Intellectual in the Late 1930s," *Virginia Woolf Miscellany*, no. 87 (2015): 23–26.

[69] Simmons, *Creed without Chaos*, 12.

Chapter 29
All Truth is Still God's Truth:
Christian Scholars Modeling Reality
Nick Pertler

[1] Mark A. Noll, *The Scandal of the Evangelical Mind*, 1st ed. (1994) and 2nd ed. (2022) (Grand Rapids, MI: Wm. B. Eerdmans).

[2] George M. Marsden, *The Outrageous Idea of Christian Scholarship*, original ed. (1997) and updated ed. (2024) (New York: Oxford University Press).

[3] H. Richard Niebuhr, *Christ and Culture* (New York: Harper and Row, 1951).

[4] Niebuhr, *Christ and Culture*, 33.

[5] Niebuhr, *Christ and Culture*, 37.

[6] Niebuhr, *Christ and Culture*, 191.

[7] Niebuhr, *Christ and Culture*, 194.

[8] Niebuhr, *Christ and Culture*, 195.

[9] Niebuhr, *Christ and Culture*, 208.

[10] Augustine, *On Christian Doctrine*, trans. D. W. Robertson, Jr. (New York: Macmillan, 1958), 2.18.28.

[11] James J. Murphy, "The Metarhetorics of Plato, Augustine, and McLuhan: A Pointing Essay," *Philosophy & Rhetoric* 4, no. 4 (1971): 204.

[12] Augustine, *On Christian Doctrine*, 4.5.7–4.6.10.

[13] Murphy, "Metarhetorics," 205.

[14] Gerald A. Press, "Doctrina in Augustine's *De doctrina christiana*," *Philosophy & Rhetoric* 17, no. 2 (1984): 114.

[15] Press, "Doctrina," 115.

[16] Arthur Holmes, *All Truth Is God's Truth* (Grand Rapids, MI: Wm. B. Eerdmans, 1977).

[17] Holmes, *All Truth*, 12.

[18] George M. Marsden, *The Outrageous Idea of Christian Scholarship*, 2nd ed. (New York: Oxford University Press, 2024), 71.

[19] Robert Wuthnow, "The Scandal of the Evangelical Mind: A Symposium," *First Things*, no. 51 (March 1995): 41.

[20] Marsden, *Outrageous Idea*, 76.

[21] Marsden, *Outrageous Idea*, 138.

[22] Mark A. Noll, *The Scandal of the Evangelical Mind*, 2nd ed. (Grand Rapids, MI: Wm. B. Eerdmans, 2022), 18.

[23] C. S. Lewis, "Christianity and Culture," in *Christian Reflections*, ed. Walter Hooper (Grand Rapids, MI: Wm. B. Eerdmans, 1967), 28.

[27] Lewis, "Christianity and Culture," 27.

Chapter 30
Christianity and Communication:
Faith-inflected Scholarly and Pedagogical Praxis
Janie Marie Harden Fritz

[1] James Davison Hunter, *Culture Wars: The Struggle to Define America* (New York: Basic Books, 1991).

[2] Charles Colson and Richard John Neuhaus, eds. *Evangelicals and Catholic Togethers: Toward a Common Mission* (Nashville: Thomas Nelson, 1995). See Mark Noll's chapter in that volume, which bears as its epigraph a quote from a 1983 book review by J. I. Packer, in which Packer offered a personal observation about changes in the relationship between evangelicals and Roman Catholics: "Things are not as they were!" Mark A. Noll, "The History of an Encounter: Roman Catholics and Protestant Evangelicals," in *Evangelicals and Catholics Together: Toward a Common Mission*, ed. Charles Colson and Richard John Neuhaus (Nashville: Thomas Nelson), 81–114. See also Timothy George and Thomas G. Guarino, eds., *Evangelicals and Catholics Together at Twenty: Vital Statements on Contested Topics* (Grand Rapids, MI: Brazos, 2015).

[3] Alasdair MacIntyre, *After Virtue: A Study in Moral Theory*, 3rd ed. (Notre Dame, IN: University of Notre Dame Press, 2007).

Chapter 31
Reimagining Evangelical Communication:
John Wesley's Three Rules as an Antidote to Mark Noll's
Scandal of the Evangelical Mind
Abram J. Book

[1] Vinson Synan, *The Holiness-Pentecostal Tradition: Charismatic Movements in the Twentieth Century*, 2nd ed. (Grand Rapids, MI: Wm. B. Eerdmans, 1997), 1.

[2] David Bennett, *John Wesley: The Man, His Mission and His Message* (Capalaba, Queensland, Australia: Rhiza Press, 2015), 12.

[3] Kenneth Latourette, *A History of Christianity: Reformation to the Present*, vol. 2 (San Francisco: Harper & Row, 1975), 1023–1029.

[4] Mark A. Noll, *The Scandal of the Evangelical Mind* (Grand Rapids, MI: Wm. B. Eerdmans, 1994), 4.

[5] Noll, *Scandal*, 4.

[6] The United Methodist Church, "The General Rules of the Methodist Church," *UMC.org*, 2016, accessed January 23, 2024, https://www.umc.org/en/content/the-general-rules-of-the-methodist-church, under the section "First: By doing no harm."

[7] The United Methodist Church, "The General Rules," under the section "Secondly: By doing good."

[8] The United Methodist Church, "The General Rules," under the section "Thirdly: By attending upon all the ordinances of God."

[9] John Wesley, *Advice to the People Called Methodists*, 2nd ed. (1746), 7, accessed March 26, 2025, https://archive.org/details/bim_eighteenth-century_advice-to-the-people-cal_wesley-john_1746/mode/2up.

[10] John Wesley, *An Earnest Appeal to Men of Reason and Religion*, 6th ed. (Bristol: William Pine, 1765), https://wesleyscholar.com/wp-content/uploads/2018/09/Earnest-Appeal-Men-of-Reason-Religion-6th-ed-1765.pdf

[11] David Hempton, *Methodism: Empire of the Spirit* (New Haven, CT: Yale University Press, 2005), 58.

[12] Richard P. Heitzenrater, "John Wesley's Principles and Practice of Preaching," *Methodist History* 37, no. 2 (January 1999): 89–106.

[13] Gregory S. Neal, "Wesleyan Theology: The Sacraments as Means of Grace," *Grace Incarnate*, last modified 1996, https://revneal.org/Writings/Writings/WesMean.htm.

[14] Scott M. Peck, *The Road Less Traveled: A New Psychology of Love, Traditional Values and Spiritual Growth* (New York: Random House, 2012), 116.

[15] Richard Foster, *Celebration of Discipline: The Path to Spiritual Growth*, 20th Anniversary ed. (San Francisco: HarperCollins, 1998), 176–177.

[16] Thomas Oden, "Do Not Rashly Tear Asunder," *First Things: A Monthly Journal of Religion & Public Life*, no. 222 (April 2012): 40–44.

[17] Elizabeth W. McLaughlin, "John Wesley (1703–1791): Bearing Witness Through Divine Gift, Sacred Choice, and Embodied Action," in *Words and Witnesses: Communication Studies in Christian Thought from Athanasius to Desmond Tutu*, eds. Robert H. Woods Jr. and Naaman K. Wood (Peabody, MA: Hendrickson Publishers, 2018), 131.

Chapter 32
Communication Standpoint Theory and Animal Theology:
Applying George Marsden and Quentin Schultze
Terri Lynn Cornwell

[1] George M. Marsden, *The Outrageous Idea of Christian Scholarship*, 2nd ed. (New York: Oxford University Press, 2024), 73.

[2] Marden, *Outrageous Idea*, 99. Furthermore, notes Marsden, embracing Christian theism "at least provides grounds for supporting the moral intuitions that many academics share" (101).

[3] Quentin Schultze, "Five Root Assumptions for Communication Scholarship," in *From the Outrageous to the Scandalous: Re-imagining Christian Thinking and Scholarship in an Age of Tribalism and Ideological Resentment*, eds. Robert H. Woods Jr. and Mark Allan Steiner (Integratio Press, 2025), 31–35. Schultze's other three assumptions are: Understanding as the primary goal of communication; storytelling as the most potent form of human expression; and excellence in scholarship, teaching, and overall communication.

[4] Barbara A. Allen, *Animals in Religion* (London, UK: Reaktion Books, 2016), 183.

[5] Allen, *Animals in Religion*, 7.

[6] David Clough, "The Bible and Animal Theology," in *The Oxford Handbook of the Bible and Ecology*, eds. Hilary Marlow and Mark Harris (Oxford University Press, 2022), 401–12.

[7] Clough, "The Bible."

[8] Clough, "The Bible."

[9] Ken Stone, "'All These Look to You': Reading Psalm 104 with Animals in the Anthropocene Epoch," *Interpretation: A Journal of Bible and Theology* 73, no. 3 (2019): 236–247.

[10] John R. Schneider, "Not One Shall Fall to the Ground," *Christianity Today* (April 2023): 39.

[11] Genevieve R. Cox, Paula FireMoon, Michael P. Anastario, Adriann Ricker, Ramey Escarcega-Growing Thunder, Julie A. Baldwin, and Elizabeth Rink, "Indigenous Standpoint Theory as a Theoretical Framework for Decolonizing Social Science Health Research with American Indian Communities," *AlterNative (Nga Pae Maramatanga (Organ))* 17, no. 4 (December 2021): 460–468.

[12] Em Griffin, Andrew Ledbetter, and Glenn Sparks, "Feminist Standpoint Theory," in *A First Look at Communication Theory*, 11th ed. (New York: McGraw Hill, 2023), 387.

[13] Mark Bekoff, *The Emotional Lives of Animals* (Novato, CA: New World Library, 2007).

[14] Belinda Recio, *When Animals Rescue* (New York: Skyhorse Publishing, 2020).

[15] Temple Grandin and Catherine Johnson, *Animals in Translation—Using the Mysteries of Autism to Decode Animal Behavior* (New York: Scribner, 2005).

Chapter 33
Rethinking the Role of Dialogue in Persuasive Risk Communication: Introducing Normatively Responsible Instructional Advocacy
Timothy L. Sellnow and *Deanna D. Sellnow*

[1] George M. Marsden, *The Outrageous Idea of Christian Scholarship*, 2nd ed. (New York: Oxford University Press, 2024), 116.

[2] Marsden, *Outrageous Idea*, 113.

[3] Sana Loue, "Community Health Advocacy," *Journal of Epidemiology & Community Health* 60, no. 6 (May 2006): 458–63.

[4] Fulvio Scognamiglio, Allessandro Sancino, Francesca Caló, Carol Jacklin-Jarvis, and Jame Rees, "The Public Sector and Co-creation in Turbulent Times: A Systematic Literature Review on Robust Governance in the COVID-19 Emergency," *Public Administration* 101, no. 1 (March 2023): 53–70.

[5] Marsden, *Outrageous Idea*, 116.

[6] Marsden, *Outrageous Idea*, 113.

[7] Marsden, *Outrageous Idea*.

[8] Timothy L. Sellnow and Deanna D. Sellnow, *Before Crisis: The Practice of Effective Risk Communication* (Solana Beach, CA: Cognella, 2024), 147.

[9] Scognamiglio et al., "The Public Sector," 53–70.

[10] Marsden, *Outrageous Idea*, 52–53.

[11] Marsden, *Outrageous Idea*, 113.

[12] David Kolb, *Experiential Learning: Experience as the Source of Learning and Development* (Hoboken, NJ: Pearson, 2014), 44.

[13] Sellnow and Sellnow, *Before Crisis*, 79–93.

[14] Marsden, *Outrageous Idea*.

[15] Daniel J. O'Keefe, "Normatively Responsible Advocacy: Some Provocations from Persuasion Effects Research," in *Pondering on Problems of Argumentation: Twenty Essays of Theoretical Issues*, eds. Frans H. van Eermeren and Bart Garssen (Netherlands: Springer, 2009), 79.

16 Michael L. Kent, "Dialogic Theory in Public Relations," in *Public Relations Theory III: In the Age of Publics*, eds. Carl H. Botan and Erich J. Sommerfeldt (New York: Routledge, 2023), 133–150.

17 Sellnow and Sellnow, *Before Crisis*, 29–33.

18 Marsden, *Outrageous Idea*.

19 O'Keefe, "Normatively Responsible Advocacy," 79–90.

Chapter 34
Art in Action: The Metaphor and the Image on the Move in Evangelistic Thought and Practice
Gillette Elvgren

1 Nicholas Wolterstorff, "Listening to the Call," in *From the Outrageous to the Scandalous: Re-imagining Christian Thinking and Scholarship in an Age of Tribalism and Ideological Resentment*, eds. Robert H. Woods Jr. and Mark Allan Steiner (Integratio Press, 2025), 19–29.

2 Nicholas. Wolterstorff, *Art in Action: Towards a Christian Aesthetic* (Grand Rapids, MI: Wm. B. Eerdman's, 1987).

3 Aristotle, *Poetics*, trans. S. W. Butcher (New York: Dover, 1997), chapters 6–19.

4 Christopher West, "Art and the New Evangelization: How Beauty Will Save the World," *Discovery*, April 24, 2018, https://media.ascensionpress.com/2018/04/24/art-and-the-new-evangelization-how-beauty-will-save-the-world/.

5 C. S. Lewis, *The Weight of Glory and Other Addresses* (New York: HarperOne, 2001), 25.

6 Lewis, *Weight of Glory*, 25.

7 Flannery O'Connor, "The Nature and Aim of Fiction," in *Mystery and Manners* (New York: Noonday Press, 1999), 82.

8 William C. Spohn, "Sovereign Beauty: Johnathan Edwards and the Nature of True Virtue," in *Theological Studies* 42, no. 3 (1981): 394–414.

9 Kenneth Burke, *A Grammar of Motives* (Berkeley, CA: University of California Press, 1969), 447.

10 William Shakespeare, *Hamlet*, ed. Barbara A. Mowat and Paul Werstine (New York: Washington Square Press, 1992), act 3, sc. 2.

11 Paul Pastor, "Treasures of Darkness," *Ekstasis* 9 (2022): 8–13, https://www.ekstasismagazine.com/blog/2022/treasures-of-darkness

12 Gerald Manley Hopkins, *Gerald Manley Hopkins: The Major Works*, ed. Catherine Phillips (Oxford: Oxford University Press, 1986), 128.

13 Nicholas Wolterstorff, "Art and Aesthetics," presentation at Biola University, Center for Christian Thought, February 13, 2012, https://cct.biola.edu/people/nicholas-wolterstorff/.

14 Pete Hammond, "Mind the Gap between the Church and Marketplace Ministry," *Lausanne Committee for World Evangelization*, Paper on Marketplace Ministry presented in Pattaya, Thailand, September 29, 2004, https://www.theologyofwork.org/lausanne-committee-for-world-evangelization-occasional-paper-on-marketplace//#mind-the-gap-foundations-for-marketplace-ministry.

15 Wolterstorff, "Art and Aesthetics."

16 Nicholas Wolterstorff, "Art and Aesthetics," *YouTube video*, February 2012, https://www.youtube.com/watch?v=eMTbI-OGHUY.

Chapter 35
Spiritual Growth in a Digital Age
Kim Okesson

1 Sherry Turkle, *Reclaiming Conversation: The Power of Talk in a Digital Age* (New York: Penguin Books, 2016); Sherry Turkle, *Alone Together: Why We Expect More from Technology and Less from Each Other* (New York: Basic Books, 2017); Quentin Schultze, *Habits of the High-Tech Heart: Living Virtuously in the Information Age* (Grand Rapids, MI: Baker, 2002); Larry Rosen, *iDisorder: Understanding Our Obsession with Technology and Overcoming Its Hold on Us* (New York: St. Martin's, 2012); Jonathan Haidt, *The Anxious Generation: How the Great Rewiring of Childhood is Causing an Epidemic of Mental Illness* (New York: Penguin, 2024).

2 Eugene Peterson, *A Long Obedience in the Same Direction: Discipleship in an Instant Society* (Downers Grove, IL: Intervarsity, 1980).

Chapter 36
Counter-cultural Christians in a World of High-speed Communication
Kevin Schut

[1] Steam, "Best of 2024," July 25, 2025, https://store.steampowered.com/sale/bestof2024.

[2] Oskar Stålberg, *Townscaper* (Raw Fury, 2021); Pounce Light, Tiny Glade (Pounce Light, 2024).

[3] Toukana Interactive, *Dorfromantik* (Toukana Interactive, 2022).

[4] Dogubomb, *Blue Prince* (Raw Fury, 2025).

[5] Jacques Ellul, *The Presence of the Kingdom*, trans. Olive Wyon (New York: Seabury, 1967), 42.

[6] Ellul, *Presence*, 59–60.

[7] James K. A. Smith, *You are What You Love: The Spiritual Power of Habit* (Grand Rapids, MI: Brazos, 2016).

[8] Bill Strom, *The Relationship Project: Moving from "You and Me" to "We"* (Kansas City, MO: The Foundry Publishing, 2014).

[9] Quentin Schultze, *Habits of the High Tech Heart: Living Virtuously in the Information Age*, upd. and exp. (Pasco, WA: Integratio Press, 2024).

[10] Walter J. Ong, *Orality and Literacy: The Technologizing of the Word* (London, England: Routledge, 1988).

[11] Neil Postman, *Amusing Ourselves to Death: Public Discourse in the Age of Show Business* (New York: Penguin, 1986).

[12] Robert H. Woods Jr. and Paul D. Patton, *Everyday Sabbath: How to Lead Your Dance with Media and Technology in Mindful and Sacred Ways* (Eugene, OR: Cascade Books, 2021).

Section Four: Personal and Vocational Reflections

Chapter 37
The Christian Professor in the Twenty-first Century
Geraldine E. Forsberg

[1] George M. Marsden, *The Soul of the American University: From Protestant Establishment to Established Nonbelief* (New York: Oxford University Press, 1994).

[2] George M. Marsden, *The Outrageous Idea of Christian Scholarship*, original ed. (1997) and updated ed. (2024) (New York: Oxford University Press).

[3] Mark A. Noll, *The Scandal of the Evangelical Mind* (Grand Rapids, MI: Wm B. Eerdmans, 1994).

[4] Charles Malik, *The Two Tasks* (Westchester, IL: Cornerstone Books, 1980), 26.

[5] Calvin L. Troup, "A Framework for Biblical Integration in Communication," in *From the Outrageous to the Scandalous: Re-imagining Christian Thinking and Scholarship in an Age of Tribalism and Ideological Resentment*, eds. Robert H. Woods Jr. and Mark Allan Steiner (Integratio Press, 2025), 59–67.

[6] Troup, "A Framework for Biblical Integration," 60.

[7] Charles Malik, *A Christian Critique of the University* (Downers Grove, IL: Intervarsity, 1982), 10, quoting Malik in the Foreword by John North.

[8] Charles Malik, "Foreword," in *A Christian Critique of the University*, 10–11.

[9] Jonathan Pettigrew and Robert H. Woods Jr., eds. *Professing Christ: Christian Tradition and Faith-learning Integration in Public Universities* (Pasco, WA: Integratio Press, 2022).

[10] Rick Hove and Heather Holleman, *A Grander Story* (Orlando, FL: Cru Press, 2017).

[11] Kelly K. Monroe, ed. *Finding God at Harvard: Spiritual Journeys of Thinking Christians* (Grand Rapids, MI: Zondervan, 1996).

[12] Jonathan Rauch, *The Constitution of Knowledge: A Defense of Truth* (Washington D.C.: Brookings Institution Press, 2021), as quoted by George Marsden at the unconference, George M. Marsden, "Mere Christian Scholarship," in *From the Outrageous to the Scandalous: Re-imagining Christian Thinking and Scholarship in an Age of Tribalism and Ideological Resentment*, eds. Robert H. Woods Jr. and Mark Allan Steiner (Integratio Press, 2025), 15–18.

[13] Julien Benda, *The Treason of the Intellectuals*, trans. Richard Aldington (New Brunswick, NJ: Transaction Publishers, 2007).

[14] Julien Benda, *The Treason of the Intellectuals*, trans. David Broder (London, UK: Eris Press, 2021), 29.

[15] Jacques Ellul, *Propaganda: The Formation of Men's Attitudes*, trans. Konrad Kellen and Jean Lerner (New York: Random House, 1965).

[16] Konrad Kellen, "Foreword," in *Propaganda* by Jacques Ellul, vi.

[17] Malcome Muggeridge, *Christ and the Media* (Grand Rapids, MI: Wm. B. Eerdmans, 1977), 24.

[18] Jacques Ellul, *Jesus and Marx: From Gospel to Ideology*, trans. Joyce Main Hanks (Grand Rapids, MI: Wm. B. Eerdmans, 1988).

[19] Ellul, *Jesus and Marx*, 24–25.

[20] Marsden, "Mere Christian Scholarship."

[21] Terry Lindvall, "The Humor and Humility of the Christian Mind," in *From the Outrageous to the Scandalous: Re-imagining Christian Thinking and Scholarship in an Age of Tribalism and Ideological Resentment*, eds. Robert H. Woods Jr. and Mark Allan Steiner (Integratio Press, 2025), 53–58.

[22] Marsden, "Mere Christian Scholarship," 18.

[23] Vishal Mangalwadi, *The Book that Made Your World: How the Bible Created the Soul of Western Civilization* (Nashville, TN: Thomas Nelson, 2011).

[24] Vishal Mangalwadi, *This Book Changed Everything: The Bible's Amazing Impact on Our World* (Pasadena, CA: Sought After Media, 2019).

[25] Neil Postman, *The End of Education: Redefining the Value of School* (New York: Vintage Books, 1995).

[26] Paul A. Soukup, SJ, "A Catholic University: A Religiously Oriented Approach to Teaching and Research," in *From the Outrageous to the Scandalous: Re-imagining Christian Thinking and Scholarship in an Age of Tribalism and Ideological Resentment*, eds. Robert H. Woods Jr. and Mark Allan Steiner (Integratio Press, 2025), 73–78.

[27] Soukup, SJ, "A Catholic University."

[28] Charles Malik, *The Two Tasks*, address delivered at the dedication of the Billy Graham Center, Wheaton, IL, 1980 (PDF), https://charlesmalikinstitute.org/wp-content/uploads/The-Two-Tasks-green.pdf, 9.

[29] Soukup, SJ, "A Catholic University."

Chapter 38
Reflections on Christ-centered, Holy Spirit-inspired Learning in an Age of Propaganda and Polarization
William J. Brown

[1] See Lifechangers, https://lifechangers.org/about-us/

[2] Joel Carpenter, "Reawakening Evangelical Intellectual Life: A Christian Scholar's Review," *Christian Scholar's Review* 51, no. 2 (Winter 2022): 127–151.

[3] Amos Yong and Dale M. Coulter, *The Holy Spirit and Higher Education: Renewing the Christian University* (Waco, TX: Baylor University Press, 2023).

[4] Milton Rokeach, *The Nature of Human Values* (New York: Free Press, 1973), 7, 28.

[5] George M. Marsden, *The Soul of the American University Revisited: From Protestant to Postsecular* (New York: Oxford University Press, 2021), 6–7.

[6] Carpenter, "Reawakening Evangelical Intellectual Life," 151.

[7] Alexander Solzhenitsyn, "Live not by Lies," *Index on Censorship* 33, no. 2 (2004): 203–7.

[8] Esther Ng, "Truth, Being True, and Theological Education," *Integrating Theology, Church, and Ministry in a Chinese Seminary* (2024): 43.

[9] George M, Marsden, *The Outrageous Idea of Christian Scholarship*, 2nd ed. (New York: Oxford University Press, 2024), xiv.

[10] Anthony R. Pratkanis and Elliot Aronson, *Age of Propaganda*, revised ed. (New York: Henry Holt and Company, 2001), 10–16, 103–118.

[11] Grace Panetta, "The White House is Set to Launch a $1.5 billion Ad Campaign to Win Over Vaccine Skeptics, Report Says," *Business Insider* (March 15, 2021), https://www.businessinsider.com/white-house-launch-1-billion-ad-blitz-covid-vaccines-report-2021-3?op=1

[12] Pratkanis and Aronson, *Age of Propaganda*, 11.

[13] Joel Laennec, *Public Healthcare Communication During the COVID-19 Pandemic* (PhD diss., Regent University, 2023).

[14] Peter R. Breggin and Ginger Ross Breggin, *COVID-19 and the Global Predators* (Ithaca, NY: Lake Edge Press, 2021), iii.

[15] Breggin and Breggin, *COVID-19*, v.

[16] H. Andaç Demirtaş-Madran, "Accepting Restrictions and Compliance with Recommended Preventive Behaviors for COVID-19: A Discussion Based on the Key Approaches and Current Research on Fear Appeals," *Frontiers in Psychology* 12 (2021): 558437.

[17] Robert F. Kennedy Jr., *A Letter to Liberals: Censorship and COVID: An Attack in Science and American Ideals* (New York: Skyhorse Publishing, 2022), 23–26.

[18] Breggin and Breggin, *COVID-19*, Introduction.

[19] Sharyl Attkisson, *Follow the Science: How Big Pharma Misleads, Obscures, and Prevails* (New York: HarperCollins Books, 2024), ix–xv.

[20] Naomi Wolf, *Facing the Beast: Courage, Faith, and Resistance in a New Dark Age* (White River Junction, VT: Chelsea Green Publishing), 1–12.

[21] Kennedy Jr., *A Letter to Liberals*, 31–41.

[22] William J. Brown, Joel Laennec, Matt Mattingly, and Mary M. Myers, "Freedom of Speech and Media Censorship: Ethical Implications of Three Contemporary Case Studies" (paper presented at the 95th Annual Convention of the Southern States Communication Association, Norfolk, VA, April 2–6, 2025), 5–14.

[23] Pratkanis and Aronson, *Age of Propaganda*, 1.

[24] Josh A. Goldstein and Girish Sastry, "The Coming Age of AI-Powered Propaganda," *Foreign Affairs* 7 (2023).

[25] William P. Eveland Jr and Kathryn E. Cooper, "An Integrated Model of Communication Influence on Beliefs," *Proceedings of the National Academy of Sciences* 110, no. supplement 3 (2013): 14088–14095; Nicole Martins, Andrew J. Weaver, and Teresa Lynch, "What the Public 'Knows' about Media Effects Research: The Influence of News Frames on Perceived Credibility and Belief Change," *Journal of Communication* 68, no. 1 (2018): 98–119.

[26] John Demuyakor, "The Propaganda Model in the Digital Age: A Review of Literature on the Effects of Social Media on News Production," *Shanlax International Journal of Arts, Science and Humanities* 8, no. 4 (2021): 17.

[27] Samuel L. Perry, "American Religion in the Era of Increasing Polarization," *Annual Review of Sociology* 48, no. 1 (2022): 87–107.

[28] Amos Yong and Dale Coulter, *The Holy Spirit and Higher Education: Renewing the Christian University* (Waco, TX: Baylor University Press, 2023).

[29] Timothy Larsen, "'The Idea of a Spirit-Infused College': A Response to Dale M. Coulter and Amos Yong," *Christian Scholar's Review* 53, no. 1 (2023): 93–95.

[30] Yong and Coulter, *The Holy Spirit*, 155.

[31] Mark A. Noll, *The Scandal of the Evangelical Mind*, 1st ed. (1994) and 2nd ed. (2022) (Grand Rapids, MI: Wm. B. Eerdmans).

[32] Kenneth Ubani, "Perspectives in Character and Skill Development: The Example of Apprenticeship in Visual Art," *International Journal of Academia* 1, no. 1 (May 2016): 197–208.

[33] Uschi Backes-Gellner and Patrick Lehnert, "The Contribution of Vocational Education and Training to Innovation and Growth" (Zurich, Switzerland: University of Zurich, 2021), *Oxford Research Encyclopedias: Economics and Finance*, https://www.zora.uzh.ch/id/eprint/204924/.

Chapter 39
Long Walks of Teaching and Faith
Douglas Kelley

[1] Mark A. Noll, "The Scandal of the Evangelical Mind: Then and Now," in *From the Outrageous to the Scandalous: Re-imagining Christian Thinking and Scholarship in an Age of Tribalism and Ideological Resentment*, eds. Robert H. Woods Jr. and Mark Allan Steiner (Integratio Press, 2025), 9–13.

[2] Parker Palmer, *The Courage to Teach: Exploring the Inner Landscape of the Teacher's Life* (San Francisco: Jossey-Bass, 1998).

[3] Mark A. Noll, *The Scandal of the Evangelical Mind* (Grand Rapids, MI: Wm. B. Eerdmans, 1994), 247.

[4] Martin Buber, *Between Man and Man: The Realms in The Human Dialogue: Perspectives on Communication*, eds. Floyd W. Matson and Ashley Montagu (New York: Free Press, 1967), 133.

[5] Douglas L. Kelley, *Just Relationships: Living Out Social Justice as Mentor, Family, Friend, and Lover* (New York: Routledge, 2017).

[6] George M. Marsden, "Mere Christian Scholarship," in *From the Outrageous to the Scandalous: Re-imagining Christian Thinking and Scholarship in an Age of Tribalism and Ideological Resentment*, eds. Robert H. Woods Jr. and Mark Allan Steiner (Integratio Press, 2025), 15–18.

[7] Palmer, *Courage to Teach*, 10.

Chapter 40
Christian Pedagogy: Formation vs. Indoctrination
Rick Olsen and *Julie Morgan*

[1] George M. Marsden, "Mere Christian Scholarship," in *From the Outrageous to the Scandalous: Re-imagining Christian Thinking and Scholarship in an Age of Tribalism and Ideological Resentment*, eds. Robert H. Woods Jr. and Mark Allan Steiner (Integratio Press, 2025), 15–18.

[2] John Piper offers several apologetics for the integration of critical thinking in the Protestant and Evangelical expressions of faith including the following: John Piper, *Think: The Life of the Mind and the Love of God* (Wheaton, IL: Crossway, 2011).

[3] One of the most seductive barriers to ongoing formation is certainty. As people of faith, we are often called to "know that we know, that we know," yet we are also called to walk by faith, not by sight (see 2 Cor 5:7). Peter Enns offers a wonderful exploration of this paradox. See Peter Enns, *The Sin of Certainty: Why God Desires Our Trust More Than Our "Correct" Beliefs* (San Francisco: HarperOne, 2017).

[4] Terry Lindvall, "The Humor and Humility of the Christian Mind," in *From the Outrageous to the Scandalous: Re-imagining Christian Thinking and Scholarship in an Age of Tribalism and Ideological Resentment*, eds. Robert H. Woods Jr. and Mark Allan Steiner (Integratio Press, 2025), 53–58.

[5] Marsden, "Mere Christian Scholarship," 16.

[6] Coordinated Management of Meaning is a theory that offers rich application to counselors and other practitioners of intentional communication and personal growth. To learn more consider: W. Barnett Pearce and Vernon E. Cronen, *Communication, Action, and Meaning: The Creation of Social Realities* (New York: Praeger, 1980).

[7] Greg Spencer, "An Outrageous Scandal: Three Rs for the Future of Christian Education," in *From the Outrageous to the Scandalous: Re-imagining Christian Thinking and Scholarship in an Age of Tribalism and Ideological Resentment*, eds. Robert H. Woods Jr. and Mark Allan Steiner (Integratio Press, 2025), 45–52.

[8] Spencer, "An Outrageous Scandal," 52.

Chapter 41
A Scandal of Evangelical Pedagogy:
An Outrageous Idea of Christian Teaching
Adam Sonstroem

[1] Mark A. Noll, *The Scandal of the Evangelical Mind*, 1st ed. (Grand Rapids, MI: Wm. B. Eerdmans, 1994) and 2nd ed. (Grand Rapids, MI: Wm. B. Eerdmans, 2022); George M. Marsden, *The Outrageous Idea of Christian Scholarship*, original ed. (New York: Oxford University Press, 1997) and updated ed. (New York: Oxford University Press, 2024).

Chapter 42
The Call to Folly: Creating a
Breakthrough in Teaching and Learning
David Enns

[1] George M. Marsden, "Mere Christian Scholarship," in *From the Outrageous to the Scandalous: Re-imagining Christian Thinking and Scholarship in an Age of Tribalism and Ideological Resentment*, eds. Robert H. Woods Jr. and Mark Allan Steiner (Integratio Press, 2025), 15–18.

[2] Terry Lindvall, "The Humor and Humility of the Christian Mind," in *From the Outrageous to the Scandalous: Re-imagining Christian Thinking and Scholarship in an Age of Tribalism and Ideological Resentment*, eds. Robert H. Woods Jr. and Mark Allan Steiner (Integratio Press, 2025), 53–58.

[3] Marsden, "Mere Christian Scholarship."

[4] Mark A. Noll, "The Scandal of the Evangelical Mind: Then and Now," in *From the Outrageous to the Scandalous: Re-imagining Christian Thinking and Scholarship in an Age of Tribalism and Ideological Resentment*, eds. Robert H. Woods Jr. and Mark Allan Steiner (Integratio Press, 2025), 9–13.

[5] Lindvall, "The Humor and Humility."

Chapter 43
Remember Who You Are: Confession, Memory, and the Formation of Ethos
Annalee R. Ward

[1] George M. Marsden, *The Outrageous Idea of Christian Scholarship* (New York: Oxford University Press, 1997), 4.

[2] James K. A. Smith, *You Are What You Love: The Spiritual Power of Habit* (Grand Rapids, MI: Brazos Press, 2016).

[3] Marcus Fabius Quintilianus, *Institutio Oratoria*, trans. John Selby Watson, ed. Lee Honeycutt (Ames, IA: Iowa State University, 2006), book XII, chapter 1, section 1.

[4] Lucius Annaeus Seneca, *Moral Letters to Lucilius*, trans. Richard M. Gummere (Cambridge, MA: Harvard University Press, 1917), letter VI.

[5] Aristotle, *Nicomachean Ethics*, trans. Marin Ostwald (Indianapolis, IN: Bobbs-Merrill, 1962).

[6] Alasdair C. MacIntyre, *After Virtue: A Study in Moral Theory*, 2nd ed (Notre Dame, IN: University of Notre Dame Press, 1984).

[7] Charles Duhigg, *The Power of Habit: Why We Do What We Do in Life and Business* (New York, NY: Random House, 2012).

[8] Saint Augustine, *Confessions*, trans. Garry Wills, Penguin Classics Deluxe Edition (New York: Penguin Books, 2006), book 10, 209–254.

[9] Gary Wills, "The Book of Memory," in *Augustine's Confessions: Critical Essays*, ed. William E. Mann, *Critical Essays on the Classics* (Lanham, MD: Rowman and Littlefield, 2006), 195.

[10] Richard J. Mouw, *Restless Faith: Holding Evangelical Beliefs in a World of Contested Labels* (Grand Rapids, MI: Brazos Press, 2019), 155.

Chapter 44
A Ticket to the Big Game: How Lesslie Newbigin, Michael Polanyi, and George Marsden Gave Me Plausibility during Perilous Doctoral Research and Post-pandemic Teaching
Michael A. Longinow

[1] G. K. Chesterton, *Orthodoxy* (San Francisco: Ignatius Press: 1908/1995), 90–91.

[2] Mark A. Noll, *The Scandal of the Evangelical Mind* (Grand Rapids, MI: Wm. B. Eerdmans, 1994), 3–4.

[3] Avihu Zakai, "The Rise of Modern Science and the Decline of Theology as the 'Queen of the Sciences' in the Early Modern Era," *Reformation & Renaissance Review* 9 no. 2 (2015): 125–152; Mike Higton, *A Theology of Higher Education* (New York: Oxford University Press, 2012), 1–2; Mary K. Tillman, "The Tension between Intellectual and Moral Education in the Thought of John Henry Newman," *Thought: Fordham University Quarterly* 60 no. 3 (1985): 322–334.

[4] Jesse J. Thomas, "From Joy to Joy: C. S. Lewis and The Numinous," *Journal of Interdisciplinary Studies* 12, nos.1–2 (2000): 109–124; George M. Marsden, *The Soul of the American University: From Protestant Establishment to Established Nonbelief* (New York: Oxford University Press, 1994), 369–375; George M. Marsden, "Introduction," in *The Secularization of the Academy*, ed. George Marsden and Bradley Longfield (New York: Oxford University Press, 1992), 3–7.

[5] Frederick Rudolph, *The American College and University: A History* (Athens, GA: University of Georgia Press, 1990), 481–482; Laurence Veysey, *The Emergence of the American University* (Chicago: The University of Chicago Press, 1965), 133–134.

[6] Denise Daniels, Caleb Henry, and Bradley J. Murg, "The Future of Christian Higher Education: A Political Economy Analysis," *Journal of Markets & Morality* 22 no. 2 (2022); Michael T. Falder, *Advancement's Role in Enhancing Financial Viability at Christian Colleges* (PhD diss., Regent University, 2021).

[7] Meg L. DuMez, *Mission, Money and Motivation: A Case Study of Traditional and Adult Undergraduate Programs at a Christian College* (PhD diss, Azusa Pacific University, 2018); Richard H. Johnson, *A Case Study of One Small Christian College overcoming Decline and Implementing an Institutional Turnaround* (PhD diss., Abilene Christian University, 2021).

[8] Colleen Flaherty, "Presidents Weigh in on the Public Confidence Crisis," *Inside Higher Ed* (March 6, 2025); Hilary A. Edwards, *Navigating the Unprecedented: A Study on How Senior Administrators in Higher Education Learned and Made Decisions during the COVID-19 Pandemic* (PhD diss., University of Maryland, 2024); Xinqiao Liu and Jingxuan Wang, "Depression, Anxiety, and Student Satisfaction with University Life Among College Students: A Cross-Lagged Study," *Humanities and Social Sciences Communications* 11, no. 1172 (2024): 1–11.

[9] George Barna, "Doubt & Faith: Top Reasons People Question Christianity," *Barna Group*, March 1, 2023, https://www.barna.com/research/doubt-faith/; Patricia Wittberg, "Generational Change in Religion and Religious Practice: A Review Essay," *Review of Religious Research* 63, no. 3 (2021): 461–482.

[10] Phil Davignon, "Factors Influencing College Choice and Satisfaction Among Students at Christian Colleges and Universities," *Religion & Education* 43, no. 1 (2015): 77–94; Todd C. Ream and Perry L. Glanzner, *The Idea of a Christian College: A Re-examination for Today's University* (Eugene, OR: Cascade Books, 2013).

[11] Arthur F. Holmes, "What About Student Integration?" *Journal of Research on Christian Education* 3, no.1 (2009): 3–5; Arthur F. Holmes, "The Methodology of Christian Philosophy," *The Journal of Religion* 42, no. 3 (1962): 215–216; Jessica Daniels, "Christian Education as Sacred Liminal Space," *Christian Scholars Review* 51, no. 2 (2022): 189–200.

[12] Beverly Johson-Miller and Robert W. Pazmino, "Christian Education Foundations: Retrospects and Prospects," *Christian Education Journal: Research on Education Ministry* 17, no. 3 (2020): 1–17; Morne Diedricks, "Calvin's Use of the Scholastic Method from his Vision of the Church as Mother and School," *The Expository Times* 136, no. 7 (2025): 296–308; Gary D. Hyrne, *Cultivating Advanced Education for Christian Faculty in Higher Education Institutions: A Phenomenological Study* (PhD diss., Liberty University, 2025).

[13] Lesslie Newbigin, *The Gospel in a Pluralist Society* (Grand Rapids, MI: Wm. B. Eerdmans, 1989); Robin Gill, "Berger's Plausibility Structures: A Response to Professor Cairns," *Scottish Journal of Theology* 27, no. 2 (1974): 198–207.

[14] Bob Woodward and Carl Bernstein, *All the President's Men* (New York: Simon & Schuster, 1974); Alan J. Pakula, director, *All the President's Men* [Film], Warner Brothers, 1976.

[15] Alexandra Juhasz, "Forgetting ACT UP," *Quarterly Journal of Speech* 98, no.1 (2012): 69–74.; Craig Gingrich-Philbrook, "ACT UP as a Structure of Feeling," *Quarterly Journal of Speech* 98, no. 1 (2012) 81–88.

[16] Jim Euchner, "The Medium is the Message," *Research-Technology Management* 59, no. 5 (2016): 9–11; Kenneth E. Boulding, "The Medium and the Message," *The Canadian Journal of Economics and Political Science* 31, no. 2 (1965): 268–273; Marshall McLuhan, *Understanding Media: The Extensions of Man* (New York: McGraw-Hill, 1964), 4–8.

[17] Richard Gelwick, *The Way of Discovery: An Introduction to the Thought of Michael Polanyi* (New York: Oxford University Press, 1977); Michael M. Polanyi, *The Tacit Dimension* (Chicago: University of Chicago Press, 1966), xiii–xiv.

[18] Peter Berger, *The Sacred Canopy: Elements of a Sociological Theory of Religion* (New York: Doubleday, 1967).

[19] Michel Foucault, *Madness and Civilization* (New York: Vintage Books, 1998); Richard Rorty, *Philosophy and the Mirror of Nature* (Princeton, NJ: Princeton University Press, 1981); Friedrich Nietzsche, *Beyond Good and Evil: Prelude to a Philosophy of the Future*, trans. Walter Kaufmann (New York: Vintage Books, 1886/1966); Paulo Freire, *Pedagogy of the Oppressed*, trans. M. B. Ramos (New York: Continuum, 1970/1993); Kenneth A. Bruffee, "Social Construction, Language, and the Authority of Knowledge: A Bibliographical Essay," *College English* 48, no. 8 (1986): 773–790.

[20] Michael M. Polanyi, *Meaning* (Chicago: University of Chicago Press, 1975).

[21] Walter J. Ong, "Communications Media and the State of Theology," *CrossCurrents* 19, no. 4 (1969): 462–480; Walter J. Ong, *Orality and Literacy: The Technologizing of the Word* (London: Methuen, 1982);

Rishi Raj Bahl, *Outsourcing our Memory 2.0: Using Walter Ong's Orality/Literacy Studies to Recognize Technologies Effects on Memory* (PhD. Diss., Duquesne University, 2017).

[22] Philip Gorski and Jeffrey Guhin, "The Ongoing Plausibility of Peter Berger: Sociological Thoughts on the Sacred Canopy at Fifty," *Journal of the American Academy of Religion* 85, no. 4 (2017): 1118, 1131.

[23] Martin Buber, *I and Thou*, trans. Walter Gregor Smith (New York: Simon & Schuster, 1984; originally published 1937); Oren O. Soffer, "The Competing Ideals of Objectivity and Dialogue in American journalism," *Journalism* 10, no. 4 (2009); Ronald C. Arnett, *Communication and Community: Implications of Martin Buber's Dialogue* (Carbondale, IL: Southern Illinois University Press, 1986).

[24] Lesslie Newbigin, *The Gospel in a Pluralist Society* (Grand Rapids, MI: Wm. B. Eerdmans, 1989), 8–9.

[25] Kenneth Collins, "Why the Holiness Movement is Dead," *Asbury Theological Journal* 54, no. 2 (1999): 1–10; Andrew C. Thompson, "From Societies to Society: The Shift from Holiness to Justice in the Wesleyan Tradition," *Methodist Review* 3 (2011); Joy L. Arroyo, "John Wesley's Empowered Regimen: Cultivating Health and Sanctification," *Wesley and Methodist Studies* 13, no. 2 (2021): 154–174.

[26] George M. Marsden, *The Outrageous Idea of Christian Scholarship*, 2nd ed. (New York: Oxford University Press, 2024), 49–66.

[27] Helen Lefkowitz, *Campus Life: Undergraduate Cultures from the End of the Eighteenth Century to the Present* (Chicago: University of Chicago Press, 1988); Jeffrey M. Stuber, "Class, Culture and Participation in the Collegiate Extra-curriculum," *Sociological Forum* 24, no. 4 (2009): 877–900; Julian Woodward, "The Extra-Curriculum as an Educational Institution," *Bulletin of the American Association of University Professors (1915–1955)* 31, no. 3 (1945): 383–391; Michael S. Hevel and Heidi A. Jaeckle, "Trends in the Historiography of American College Student Life: Populations, Organizations and Behavior," in *Rethinking Campus Life: Historical Studies in Education*, eds. Christiane A. Ogren and Marc A. VanOverbeke (Cham, Switzerland: Palgrave Macmillan); Jonathan A. Powers, "Unmute Yourself: Attentive to God's Presence: Reflections on the Asbury Outpouring," *Liturgy* 38, no. 4 (2023), 11–14; Alexa Groen, *Effect of Extra-Curricular Activities on Students' Spiritual Growth* (Master's thesis, Dordt College, 2017).

[28] Gregory D. Richardson, "Faith and Learning in Higher Education: Merging the Bible with Discipline Specific Content," *Journal of Research on Christian Education* 28, no. 1 (2019): 51–70; Daisy Savarirajan and Su Fong, "Bridging Bible and Biology: The Impact of Faith Integration on the Spiritual Growth of Students in Christian Higher Education," *Journal of Instructional Research* 8, no. 1 (2019): 5–16; Ken Bradley, "The Faith/Learning Integration Movement in Christian Higher Education: Slogan or Substance?" *Journal of Research on Christian Education* 3, no. 1 (1994): 13–33; Elizabeth Sinclair Powell, Theresa Tisdale, Michelle Willingham, Joy Bustrum, and Claire Allan, "Faith Development in Graduating Christian College Seniors," *Christian Higher Education* 11, no. 3 (2012): 177–191.

[29] Mark A. Yarhouse, "Sexual Identity Development: The Influence of Valuative Frameworks on Identity Synthesis," *Psychotherapy: Theory, Research, Practice, Training* 38, no. 3 (2001): 331–341; Mark A. Yarhouse, Stephen P. Stratton and Heather L. Brooke, "Listening to Sexual Minorities on Christian College Campuses," *Journal of Psychology and Theology* 37, no. 2 (2009): 96–113; Stanton L. Jones and Mark A. Yarhouse, "A Longitudinal Study of Attempted Religiously Mediated Sexual Orientation Change," *Journal of Sex & Marital Therapy* 37, no. 5 (2011): 404–427.

Chapter 45
Not That Kind of Horn Guy: An Auto-ethnographic Reflection on Faith Leading the Way and Intellect Bringing the Assist
David Enns

[1] Mark A. Noll, *The Scandal of the Evangelical Mind*, 1st ed. (Grand Rapids, MI: Wm. B. Eerdmans, 1994) and 2nd ed. (Grand Rapids, MI: Wm. B. Eerdmans, 2022); George M. Marsden, *The Outrageous Idea of Christian Scholarship*, original ed. (New York: Oxford University Press, 1997) and updated ed. (New York: Oxford University Press, 2024).

[2] David Enns, "Dave the Horn Guy," website, 2025, https://www.davethehornguy.com.

[3] Enns, "Dave the Horn Guy."

[4] Nicholas Wolterstorff applies the concept of code-switching to the context of faith and public life. The term originates in sociolinguistics, where John Gumperz used it to describe shifts in language style depending on social context. See Nicholas Wolterstorff, "Listening to the Call," in *From the Outrageous*

to the Scandalous: Re-imagining Christian Thinking and Scholarship in an Age of Tribalism and Ideological Resentment, eds. Robert H. Woods Jr. and Mark Allan Steiner (Integratio Press, 2025), 19–29 and John J. Gumperz, *Discourse Strategies* (Cambridge: Cambridge University Press, 1982).

[5] George M. Marsden, "Mere Christian Scholarship," in *From the Outrageous to the Scandalous: Re-imagining Christian Thinking and Scholarship in an Age of Tribalism and Ideological Resentment*, eds. Robert H. Woods Jr. and Mark Allan Steiner (Integratio Press, 2025), 15–18.

[6] Mark A. Noll, "The Scandal of the Evangelical Mind: Then and Now," in *From the Outrageous to the Scandalous: Re-imagining Christian Thinking and Scholarship in an Age of Tribalism and Ideological Resentment*, eds. Robert H. Woods Jr. and Mark Allan Steiner (Integratio Press, 2025), 9–13.

[7] Noll, "Then and Now."

[8] Wolterstorff, "Listening to the Call."

[9] Marsden, "Mere Christian Scholarship."

[10] Wolterstorff, "Listening to the Call."

Chapter 46
Producing "Procedural Rationality"
Robert Stephen Reid

[1] George M. Marsden, *The Outrageous Idea of Christian Scholarship* (New York: Oxford University Press, 1997), 1.

[2] During the twentieth century a "largely voluntary and commendable disestablishment of religion has led to the virtual establishment of nonbelief," Marsden, *Outrageous Idea*, 6.

[3] For a more textured understanding of what is entailed for Christian scholars to commit to a "procedural rationality" of basic rules of evidence and argument in order to be welcome to reintroduces normative religious concerns as possible in scholarship see George M. Marsden, *The Soul of the American University* (New York: Oxford University Press, 1994), 431. This book's postscript is the source of the argument found in *The Outrageous Idea* book.

[4] Robert S. Reid "When Words Were a Power Loosed: Audience Expectation and Finished Narrative Technique in the Gospel of Mark," *The Quarterly Journal of Speech* 80 (1994): 427–47. I subsequently published an edited version of that thesis commentary that demonstrated how Mark's rhetoric was structured to call forth a faith response from hearers in Robert S. Reid, *Preaching Mark* (St. Louis: Chalice Press, 1999).

[5] Martin J. Medhurst, "Introduction," *Rhetoric & Public Address* 7, no. 4 (Winter, 2004): 446. Essay authors were James Arnt Aune (Judaism), Randall L Bytwek (Calvinist), John Angus Campbell (Episcopal), Michael W Casey (Church of Christ), James Farrell (Catholic), Michael P. Graves (Friends), Robert Hariman (Presbyterian), Susan Schultz Huxman & Gerald Biesecker-Mast (Mennonite), Martin Medhurst ([former] Pentecostal), David Proctor (Methodist), Robert S. Reid (Baptist), Dale Sullivan (Lutheran).

[6] Robert S. Reid, "Being Baptist," *Rhetoric & Public Address* 7, no. 4 (Winter, 2004): 597.

[7] Martin J. Medhurst, "Religion and Scholarship: A Pluralistic Conversation," *The Journal of Communication and Religion* 27, no. 1, (2004).

[8] Medhurst, "Religion and Scholarship," 40–47.

[9] Medhurst, "Religion and Scholarship," 115.

[10] Martin J. Medhurst, "Religious Rhetoric and the Ethos of Democracy: A Case Study of the 2000 Presidential Campaign" in *The Ethos of Rhetoric*, ed., Michael J. Hyde (Columbia: University of South Carolina Press, 2004), 114–135.

[11] Medhurst, "Religion and Scholarship," 40.

[12] Robert S. Reid, "A Rhetoric of Contemporary Christian Discourse," *The Journal of Communication and Religion* 31, no. 2 (November 2008): 109–142.

[13] I have summarized the significant academic shift away from systematic to narrative theology that took place in the third quarter of the twentieth century in Robert S. Reid, *The Four Voices of Preaching: Communicating Faith in a Connected World* (Pasco, WA: Integratio Press, 2024), 96–98. For a more extended exploration see David Tracy, *Blessed Rage for Order: The New Pluralism in Theology* (San Francisco: Harper and Row, 1988); Hans W. Frei, *Theology & Narrative: Selected Essays*, eds. George Hunsinger and William C. Placher (New York: Oxford University Press, 1993); cf. Walter R. Fisher, *Human Communication as Narration: Toward a Philosophy of Reason, Value, and Action* (Columbia: University of South Carolina Press, 1989).

[14] Robert S. Reid, "A Rhetoric of Contemporary Christian Discourse," *The Journal of Communication and Religion* 31 (Fall 2008): 109.

[15] Reid, "A Rhetoric of Contemporary Christian Discourse," 114.

[16] Reid, "A Rhetoric of Contemporary Christian Discourse," 137.

[17] Robert S. Reid, "Solzhenitsyn's Christian Civilization Rhetoric: The Other 'Prophetic' Speech 30 Years Late," in *And the Word Became Flesh: Studies in Scripture, Communication, and History in Memory of Michael W. Casey*, eds. Thomas H. Olbricht and David Fleer (Eugene, OR: Pickwick Publishers, 2009), 231–46.

[18] Ronald Berman, ed. *Solzhenitsyn at Harvard: The Address, Twelve Early Responses, and Six Later Reflections* (Washington, D.C.: Ethics and Public Policy, 1980).

[19] James Reston, "A Russian at Harvard," The New York Times, June 11, 1978; reprinted in Berman, *Solzhenitsyn at Harvard*, 37.

[20] Michael Hyde, "Introduction: Rhetorically, We Dwell," in *The Ethos of Rhetoric*, ed. Michael Hyde (Columbia: University of South Carolina Press, 2004), xiii.

[21] Martin Marty, "On Hearing Solzhenitsyn in Context," *World Literature Today* 53, no. 4 (1979): 579.

[22] Marsden, *Outrageous Idea*, 6.

[23] Mark A. Noll, "Foreword," in *Professing Christ: Christian Tradition and Faith-learning in Public Universities*, eds. Jonathan Pettigrew and Robert H. Woods Jr. (Pasco, WA: Integratio Press, 2022).

[24] Noll, "Foreword," xxvii. Understandably, the majority of personal testimonies found in the *Professing Christ* volume tell the author's story in terms of finding ways to express a Christian identity institutionally and educationally in the classrooms of public universities. The question of how their faith commitment is a critical theory factor in their scholarship is more diffuse. A notable exception is how Dennis D. Cali allows his sacramental perspective to find explicit expression in published efforts in mass communication literature. See his essay "A Sacramental View of Life in the Academy," especially 39–42; Clifford G. Christians also speaks to this issue more directly as one who has service was conducted in a research university; Christians, "Recovering Truth: Ideas as Vocation," 161–169.

[25] David Tracy, *Plurality and Ambiguity: Hermeneutics, Religion, Hope* (New York, NY: Harper & Row, 1987).

[26] Stephen H. Webb, "Reviving the Rhetorical Heritage of Protestant Theology" in *A Companion to Rhetoric and Rhetorical Criticism*, eds. Walter Jost and Wendy Olmsted (Malden, MA: Blackwell, 2004), 409–424.

[27] Charles Taylor, *The Ethics of Authenticity* (Cambridge: Harvard University Press, 1991); Charles Taylor, *A Secular Age* (Cambridge: Belknap Press of Harvard University, 2007). This provision of an "ethic of" is commensurate with the third resource of the proposal of "A Rhetoric of Contemporary Christian Discourse" I made.

Chapter 47
Horns and Holy Nudges: A Faith-led Journey Beyond the Classroom
David Enns

[1] George M. Marsden, *The Outrageous Idea of Christian Scholarship*, original ed. (1997) and updated ed. (2024) (New York: Oxford University Press).

[2] Mark A. Noll, *The Scandal of the Evangelical Mind*, 1st ed. (1994) and 2nd ed. (2022) (Grand Rapids, MI: Wm. B. Eerdmans).

[3] Marsden, *Outrageous Idea*.

[4] Richard J. Mouw, "The Christian Mind: Humility and 'World Viewing,'" in *From the Outrageous to the Scandalous: Re-imagining Christian Thinking and Scholarship in an Age of Tribalism and Ideological Resentment*, eds. Robert H. Woods Jr. and Mark Allan Steiner (Integratio Press, 2025), 37–43.

[5] Noll, *Scandal*.

[6] Richard J. Mouw, *Uncommon Decency: Christian Civility in an Uncivil World* (Downers Grove, IL: InterVarsity, 2011).

[7] Mouw, "The Christian Mind."

Chapter 48
The Rabbit Room: An Outrageous Perspective
of Christian Communication
Kate Mead

[1] George M. Marsden, *The Outrageous Idea of Christian Scholarship*, original ed. (1997) and updated ed. (2024) (New York: Oxford University Press).

[2] George M. Marsden, *The Outrageous Idea of Christian Scholarship* (New York: Oxford University, 1997), 64.

[3] Marsden, *Outrageous Idea*, 65.

[4] Marsden, *Outrageous Idea*, 70–72.

[5] Kate E. Mead, *Culture-Building Through Online Communication: A Case Study on the Rabbit Room Nonprofit Organization* (PhD diss., Liberty University, 2022).

[6] "About Us," The Rabbit Room, accessed May 19, 2025, https://www.rabbitroom.com/about-us.

[7] Peter L. Berger and Thomas Luckmann, *The Social Construction of Reality: A Treatise in the Sociology of Knowledge* (New York: Anchor Books, 1966); Ernest G. Bormann, "Fantasy and Rhetorical Vision: The Rhetorical Criticism of Social Reality," *Quarterly Journal of Speech* 58, no. 4 (1972): 396–407; James W. Carey, *Communication as Culture: Essays on Media and Society* (Boston: Unwin Hyman, 1988).

[8] Eric W. Rothenbuhler, "Revising Communication Research for Working on Community," in *Communication and Community*, eds. Gregory J. Shepherd and Eric W. Rothenbuhler (New York: Routledge, 2000).

[9] Rothenbuhler, "Revising Communication Research," 139.

[10] Rothenbuhler, "Revising Communication Research," 140.

[11] Marsden, *Outrageous Idea*, 92.

[12] Marsden, *Outrageous Idea*, 77.

Chapter 49
I Have a Vision
John R. Peck

[1] This unpublished piece is from the heart and mind of Reverend John R. Peck, 1978. It was recited by Paul D. Patton during the unconference on November 18, 2024, in New Orleans, Louisiana, on the campus of New Orleans Baptist Theological Seminary just prior to our keynote presentation by Calvin L. Troup, President, Geneva College.

Section Five: The Church, Public Witness, and Evangelical Identity

Chapter 50
The Rise of Managerialism in the Evangelical Mind:
A Historical, Theological, and Organizational Analysis
R. Tyler Spradley

[1] Mark A. Noll, *The Scandal of the Evangelical Mind* (Grand Rapids, MI: Wm. B. Eerdmans, 1994), 3–24.

[2] George M. Marsden, *Understanding Fundamentalism and Evangelicalism* (Grand Rapids, MI: Wm. B. Eerdmans, 1991), 36–62.

[3] Neil Postman, *Amusing Ourselves to Death: Public Discourse in the Age of Show Business* (New York: Penguin Books, 1985), 87–108.

[4] Marva Dawn, *Reaching Out Without Dumbing Down: A Theology of Worship for the Turn-of-the Century Culture* (Grand Rapids, MI: Wm. B. Eerdmans, 1995), 76–94.

[5] David F. Wells, *No Place for Truth: Or Whatever Happened to Evangelical Theology?* (Grand Rapids, MI: Wm. B. Eerdmans, 1994), 95–136.

[6] Carl R. Trueman, *Reformed or Deformed? A Theological Critique of Contemporary Evangelicalism* (Wheaton, IL: Crossway, 2010), 45–67.

[7] Irenaeus, "Against Heresies," in *The Ante-Nicene Fathers*, eds. Alexander Roberts and James Donaldson, vol. 1 (Grand Rapids, MI: Wm. B. Eerdmans, 1990), 309–567. Originally published ca. 180.

8 John Calvin, *Institutes of the Christian Religion*, ed. John T. McNeill, trans. Ford Lewis Battles (Philadelphia: Westminster, 1960), 1:241–255. Originally published 1559.

9 Jonathan Edwards, *A Treatise Concerning Religious Affections* (New Haven, CT: Yale University Press, 1959), 266–291. Originally published 1746.

10 Peter F. Drucker, *Managing the Non-Profit Organization: Principles and Practices* (New York: HarperCollins, 1990), 45–67.

11 Stanley A. Deetz, *Democracy in an Age of Corporate Colonization: Developments in Communication and the Politics of Everyday Life* (Albany, NY: SUNY Press, 1992), 17.

12 Bill Hybels and Lynne Hybels, *Rediscovering Church: The Story and Vision of Willow Creek Community Church* (Grand Rapids, MI: Zondervan, 1995), 123–145.

13 Rick Warren, *The Purpose Driven Church: Growth Without Compromising Your Message and Mission* (Grand Rapids, MI: Zondervan, 1995), 95–120.

14 Mara Einstein, *Brands of Faith: Marketing Religion in a Commercial Age* (New York: Routledge, 2008), 101–123.

15 Mary Jo Hatch, *Organization Theory: Modern, Symbolic, and Postmodern Perspectives*, 4th ed. (Oxford: Oxford University Press, 2018), 56–78.

16 Richard R. Osmer, *Practical Theology: An Introduction* (Grand Rapids, MI: Wm. B. Eerdmans, 2008), 134–156.

17 Einstein, *Brands of Faith*, 45–67.

18 Phillip Luke Sinitiere, *Salvation with a Smile: Joel Osteen, Lakewood Church, and American Christianity* (New York: NYU Press, 2015), 88–110.

19 Wells, *No Place for Truth*, 214–236.

20 Mats Alvesson, *The Triumph of Emptiness: Consumption, Higher Education, and Work Organization* (Oxford: Oxford University Press, 2013), 45.

21 Frederick W. Taylor, *The Principles of Scientific Management* (New York: Harper & Brothers, 1911), 29–56.

22 Neil Postman, *Technopoly: The Surrender of Culture to Technology* (New York: Knopf, 1992), 51–71.

23 Wanda J. Orlikowski, "Sociomaterial Practices: Exploring Technology at Work," *Organization Studies* 28, no. 9 (September 2007): 1435–1448, https://doi.org/10.1177/0170840607081138; François Cooren, "Communication Theory at the Center: Ventriloquism and the Communicative Constitution of Reality," *Journal of Communication* 62, no. 1 (2012): 1–20, https://doi.org/10.1111/j.1460-2466.2011.01622.x.

24 Orlikowski, "Sociomaterial Practices."

25 Einstein, *Brands of Faith*, 145–167.

26 François Cooren, *Action and Agency in Dialogue: Passion, Incarnation, and Ventriloquism* (Amsterdam: John Benjamins Publishing, 2010), 45.

27 François Cooren, "Communication as Ventriloquism," in *The Routledge Handbook of Organizational Communication*, eds. Gail T. Fairhurst and François Cooren (New York: Routledge, 2015), 34–47.

28 Dawn, *Reaching Out*, 112–134; Einstein, *Brands of Faith*, 189–210; John E. Sanders, "Spiritual Leadership in the Digital Age: Navigating Technology and Faith," *Journal of Religious Leadership* 18, no. 2 (Fall 2019): 105–128.

29 James Davison Hunter, *To Change the World: The Irony, Tragedy, and Possibility of Christianity in the Late Modern World* (Oxford: Oxford University Press, 2010), 205–227.

30 Barna Group, "The State of the Bible 2018: Six Trends for the Church," *Barna Research*, https://www.barna.com/research/state-of-the-bible-2018/.

31 Scott Thumma and Dave Travis, *Beyond Megachurch Myths: What We Can Learn from America's Largest Churches* (San Francisco: Jossey-Bass, 2007), 45–67.

32 Karl E. Weick and Karleen H. Roberts, "Collective Mind in Organizations: Heedful Interrelating on Flight Decks," *Administrative Science Quarterly* 38, no. 3 (September 1993): 357–381, https://doi.org/10.2307/2393372.

33 Weick and Roberts, "Collective Mind," 360–365.

34 Trueman, *Reformed or Deformed*, 89–112.

35 Hybels and Hybels, *Rediscovering Church*, 167–189; Greg L. Hawkins and Cally Parkinson, *Reveal: Where Are You?* (South Barrington, IL: Willow Creek Association, 2007), 34–56.

36 Karl E. Weick, *Making Sense of the Organization* (Oxford: Blackwell Publishing, 2001), 89–114.

[37] Mats Alvesson and Hugh Willmott, "Identity Regulation as Organizational Control: Producing the Appropriate Individual," *Journal of Management Studies* 39, no. 5 (July 2002): 619–644, https://doi.org/10.1111/1467-6486.00305.

[38] Dawn, *Reaching Out*, 156–178.

[39] Tanya Riches and Tom Wagner, *The Hillsong Movement Examined: You Call Me Out Upon the Waters* (Cham, Switzerland: Palgrave Macmillan, 2017), 67–89.

[40] Sanders, "Spiritual Leadership," 115–120.

[41] Pew Research Center, "Religion in America 2020: The Impact of Virtual Worship," *Pew Research Center*, https://www.pewresearch.org/religion/2020/08/07/.

[42] Weick and Roberts, "Collective Mind," 368–372.

[43] Wells, *No Place for Truth*, 287–310.

[44] Stewart R. Clegg, *The Sociology of Power and Authority in Organizations* (London: Routledge, 2013), 112–134.

[45] Gerardo Marti and Gladys Ganiel, *The Deconstructed Church: Understanding Emerging Christianity* (Oxford: Oxford University Press, 2014), 78–100.

[46] Thumma and Travis, *Beyond Megachurch Myths*, 89–112.

[47] Weick and Roberts, "Collective Mind," 374–378.

[48] Osmer, *Practical Theology*, 178–200.

[49] Cooren, "Communication as Ventriloquism," 39–42.

[50] Weick and Roberts, "Collective Mind," 357–381; Deetz, *Democracy in an Age*, 17.

[51] Weick and Roberts, "Collective Mind," 365–370; Weick, *Making Sense*, 134–156.

[52] Deetz, *Democracy in an Age*, 45–67.

[53] Noll, *Scandal*, 245–67.

[54] Dawn, *Reaching Out*, 200–22.

[55] Alvesson, *Triumph of Emptiness*, 78–100.

[56] Timothy Keller, *Center Church: Doing Balanced, Gospel-Centered Ministry in Your City* (Grand Rapids, MI: Zondervan, 2012), 145–167.

[57] Barna Group, "Trends in Worship 2019: The Rise of Liturgical Practices," *Barna Research*, https://www.barna.com/research/worship-trends-2019/.

[58] Weick and Roberts, "Collective Mind," 372–376.

[59] David Goodhew, *Church Growth in Britain: 1980 to the Present* (London: Routledge, 2017), 89–112.

[60] Barbara Czarniawska, *Cyberfactories: How News Agencies Produce News* (Cheltenham, UK: Edward Elgar Publishing, 2011), 67–89.

[61] Leadership Network, "The State of Church Leadership: Trends in Trust and Longevity," *Leadership Network*, https://leadnet.org/research/state-of-church-leadership-2020/.

[62] Osmer, *Practical Theology*, 212–234.

[63] Alvesson and Willmott, "Identity Regulation," 630–638.

[64] Navigators, "Discipleship Impact Report 2018," *The Navigators*, https://www.navigators.org/research/discipleship-impact-2018/.

[65] Noll, *Scandal*, 3–24; Marsden, *Understanding Fundamentalism*, 36–62.

Chapter 51
The Christian Mind to Serve the Church: Thinking Pastorally about the Contemporary Value of Noll and Marsden
Mark Allan Steiner

[1] Jerry Bridges, *Respectable Sins: Confronting the Sins We Tolerate* (Colorado Springs, CO: Navpress, 2007).

[2] Ronald Sider, *The Scandal of the Evangelical Conscience: Why Are Christians Living Just Like the Rest of the World?* (Grand Rapids, MI: Baker, 2005).

[3] Mark A. Noll, *The Scandal of the Evangelical Mind*, 1st ed. (1994) and 2nd ed. (2022) (Grand Rapids, MI: Wm. B. Eerdmans).

[4] William Deresiewicz, *Excellent Sheep: The Miseducation of the American Elite and the Way to a Meaningful Life* (New York: Free Press, 2014).

[5] For an example of an accessible yet effective approach to the basics of biblical exegesis and hermeneutics, see Gordon D. Fee and Douglas Stuart, *How to Read the Bible for All Its Worth*, 3rd ed. (Grand Rapids, MI: Zondervan, 2003).

Chapter 52
How Scholars Can Serve the Church
Brian D. Mattson

[1] Mark A. Noll, *The Scandal of the Evangelical Mind* (Grand Rapids, MI: Wm. B. Eerdmans, 1994), 3–27.

[2] Noll, *Scandal*, 10–12. See also Jacques Ellul, *The Subversion of Christianity* (Eugene, OR: Wipf & Stock, 1986), 19–51.

[3] Michael Wittmer exposes this kind of thought as a form of remnant Gnosticism that has crept into Christian churches and theological teaching in Michael E. Wittmer, *Heaven is a Place on Earth: Why Everything I Do Matters to God* (Grand Rapids, MI: Zondervan, 2004).

[4] Barbara Blodgett, "Practicing Curiosity," *Reflective Practice: Formation and Supervision in Ministry* 38 (2018): 39–47.

[5] Blodgett, "Practicing Curiosity," 40.

[6] James K. A. Smith, *On the Road with Saint Augustine: Real-World Spirituality for Restless Hearts* (Grand Rapids, MI: Brazos Press, 2019), 143.

[7] Smith, *On the Road with Saint Augustine*, 144.

[8] Norma Cook Everist, "The Practice of Collegiality," *Currents in Theology and Mission* 38, no. 5 (October 2011): 354.

[9] Everist, "The Practice of Collegiality," 355.

[10] Amos Yong, "Foreword," in *Habits of Hope: Educational Practices for a Weary World*, eds. Todd C. Beam, Jerry Pattengale, and Christopher J. Devers (Downers Grove, IL: IVP Academic, 2024), x.

Chapter 53
Exposi-story Preaching
John R. Katsion

[1] Mark A. Noll, *The Scandal of the Evangelical Mind*, 2nd ed. (Grand Rapids, MI: Wm. B. Eerdmans, 2022), 247.

[2] Noll, *Scandal*, 253.

[3] Jo Ann Davidson, "Biblical Narratives: Their Beauty and Truth," *Andrews University Seminary Studies* 49, no. 1 (2011): 155.

[4] BibleProject, "Writing Styles of the Bible & Why They're Important to Understand," YouTube video, 5:47, June 22, 2017, https://www.youtube.com/watch?v=oUXJ8Owes8E.

[5] Matthew Henry, "Commentary on Matthew 13," *Matthew Henry Commentaries*, accessed June 7, 2025, https://www.blueletterbible.org/Comm/mhc/Mat/Mat_013.cfm?a=942003.

[6] Stephen Spiewak, "Parables of Jesus: A Guide to Parables in the Bible, What They Are and Why Jesus Used Them," May 1, 2025, https://hallow.com/blog/parables-of-jesus/#how-many.

[7] Jonathan H. Westover, "The Power of Storytelling: How Our Brains Are Wired for Narratives," Human Capital Innovations, May 1, 2025, https://www.innovativehumancapital.com/article/the-power-of-storytelling-how-our-brains-are-wired-for-narratives.

[8] Uri Hasson, Asif A. Ghazanfar, Bruno Galantucci, Simon Garrod, and Christian Keysers, "Brain-to-Brain Coupling: A Mechanism for Creating and Sharing a Social World," *Trends in Cognitive Sciences* 16, no. 2 (2012): 114–21.

[9] Matt Johnson, "How Two Brains Synchronize in Conversation," *Psychology Today*, May 2024, accessed June 7, 2025, https://www.psychologytoday.com/us/blog/mind-brain-and-value/202405/how-two-brains-synchronize-in-conversation.

[10] NeuroLeadership Institute, "The Neuroscience of Storytelling," June 17, 2021, https://neuroleadership.com/your-brain-at-work/the-neuroscience-of-storytelling/.

[11] Chip Heath and Dan Heath, *Made to Stick: Why Some Ideas Survive and Others Die* (New York: Random House, 2007).

[12] NeuroLeadership Institute, "The Neuroscience of Storytelling."

[13] Walter Fisher, "Narration as Human Communication Paradigm: The Case of Public Moral Argument," *Communication Monographs* 51 (1984): 277. Reprinted in *Readings in Rhetorical Criticism* ed. Carl R. Burgchardt (State College, PA: Strata Publishing, 1995).

[14] Haddon W. Robinson, *Biblical Preaching: The Development and Delivery of Expository Messages* (Grand Rapids, MI: Baker Academic, 2001), 20.

[15] Robinson, *Biblical Preaching*, 20.

[16] September C. Fawkes, "Writing the Right Details," My Story Doctor, accessed June 7, 2025, https://mystorydoctor.com/writing-the-right-details/.

[17] C. S. Lewis, *The Last Battle* (London: Harper Collins, 2015), 172.

Chapter 54
The Role of Christian Magazines in Christian Scholarship
Ken Waters

[1] Mark A. Noll, "The Scandal of the Evangelical Mind: Then and Now," in *From the Outrageous to the Scandalous: Re-imagining Christian Thinking and Scholarship in an Age of Tribalism and Ideological Resentment*, eds. Robert H. Woods Jr. and Mark Allan Steiner (Integratio Press, 2025), 9–13.

[2] Noll, "Then and Now," 12.

[3] Ken Waters, *Words That Shape Us: How America's Most Influential Evangelical Magazines Craft the Narrative of Christian Culture* (Pasco, WA: Integratio Press, 2025).

[4] I am not talking here about radio talk shows that fuse Christian ideals with conservative political ideology, as is common among the nation's hundreds of Christian radio stations.

[5] Quentin Schultze, *Christianity and the Mass Media in America* (East Lansing, MI: Michigan State University Press, 2003), 100.

[6] Schultze, *Christianity and Mass Media*, 101.

[7] Schultze, *Christianity and Mass Media*, 101.

[8] Richard Hofstadter, *The American Political Tradition: And the Men Who Made It* (New York: Vintage Books, 1989), 185.

[9] Hofstadter, *The American Political Tradition*, 185.

[10] Mark Galli, "Trump Should Be Removed from Office," *Christianity Today*, December 19, 2019, https://www.christianitytoday.com/2019/12/trump-should-be-removed-from-office/. It is worth noting that the publication also criticized, but fell just short of advocating conviction, when President Bill Clinton was impeached for lying about his alleged affair with intern Monica Lewinsky. See, Editorial, "The Prodigal Who Didn't Come Home," *Christianity Today*, October 5, 1998, https://www.christianitytoday.com/1998/10/prodigal-who-didnt-come-home/.

[11] Quint Forgey, "Trump Lashes Out after Christian Magazine Calls for His Removal," *Politico*, December 20, 2019, https://www.politico.com/news/2019/12/20/trump-attacks-christian-magazine-impeachment-088591; see also, Bill Chappell, "Calling Trump 'Morally Lost,' *Christianity Today* Editor Calls For His Removal," NPR, December 20, 2019, https://www.npr.org/2019/12/20/790130632/christianity-today-editor-discusses-calling-for-trumps-impeachment.

[12] When another publication revealed damaging allegations against a pastor, church, or Christian organization, *Christianity Today* did not hesitate to follow up with its after-the-fact reporting.

[13] Daniel Silliman, "Ravi Zacharias's Ministry Investigates Claims of Sexual Misconduct at Spas," *Christianity Today*, September 29, 2020, https://www.christianitytoday.com/news/2020/september/ravi-zacharias-sexual-harassment-rzim-spa-massage-investiga.html.

[14] The editors, "Why We Report Bad News About Leaders," *Christianity Today*, September 29, 2020, https://www.christianitytoday.com/ct/2020/september-web-only/editors-note-ravi-zacharias-investigation.html.

[15] Daniel Silliman, "Sexual Harassment Went Unchecked at *Christianity Today*," *Christianity Today*, March 15, 2022, https://www.christianitytoday.com/news/2022/march/sexual-harassment-ct-guidepost-assessment-galli-olawoye.html.

[16] Timothy Dalrymple, "We Fell Short in Protecting Our Employees," *Christianity Today*, March 15, 2022, https://www.christianitytoday.com/ct/2022/march-web-only/we-fell-short-in-protecting-our-employees-editorial.html. Dalrymple's explanation contains a link to a PDF copy of the entire report conducted by Guidepost Solutions.

[17] Marvin Olasky, *Telling the Truth: How to Revitalize Christian Journalism* (Wheaton, IL: Crossway Books, 1996), 33.

[18] Olasky, *Telling the Truth*, 25.

[19] Mark A. Kellner, "Marvin Olasky Preaches Journalism through the Lens of Scripture, Faith," *Deseret News*, September 18, 2014, https://www.deseret.com/2014/9/18/20548678/marvin-olasky-preaches-journalism-through-the-lens-of-scripture-faith.

[20] Jack Shafer, "Who Said It First?" Slate, August 30, 2010, https://slate.com/news-and-politics/2010/08/on-the-trail-of-the-question-who-first-said-or-wrote-that-journalism-is-the-first-rough-draft-of-history.html.

Chapter 55
Techne and Testimony:
The Mandate for Christian Scholars in a Digital Age
Franklin Nii Amankwah Yartey

[1] Mark A. Noll, *The Scandal of the Evangelical Mind*, 1st ed. (1994) and 2nd ed. (2022) (Grand Rapids, MI: Wm. B. Eerdmans).

[2] Mark A. Noll, "The Scandal of the Evangelical Mind: Then and Now," in *From the Outrageous to the Scandalous: Re-imagining Christian Thinking and Scholarship in an Age of Tribalism and Ideological Resentment*, eds. Robert H. Woods Jr. and Mark Allan Steiner (Integratio Press, 2025), 9–13.

[3] "Nourishing the Spiritually Thirsty," Patristic Nectar Publications, updated 2024, https://patristic-nectar.org/.

[4] Tom Nichols, *The Death of Expertise: The Campaign against Established Knowledge and Why it Matters* (Oxford: Oxford University Press, 2024).

[5] Nichols, *Death of Expertise*, xiii.

[6] Nichols, *Death of Expertise*, 21.

[7] Nichols, *Death of Expertise*, 111.

[8] St. Mary's Greek Orthodox Church, "Technology, Orthodoxy, and Parenting," 2023, https://stmarysgoc.org/technology-orthodoxy-and-parenting/#:~:text=Fr.%20Tim%20Sas-,Towards,-an%20Orthodox%20Understanding.

[9] Meg Bowles, Catherine Burns, Jenifer Hixson, Sarah Austin Jenness, and Kate Tellers, *How to Tell a Story: The Essential Guide to Memorable Storytelling from The Moth* (New York: Random House, 2022); Brant Pinvidic, *The 3-Minute Rule: Say Less to Get More from any Pitch or Presentation* (New York: Penguin Random House, 2019).

[10] Esau McCaulley, "Author. Professor. Public Theologian," *EsauMcCaulley.com*, https://esaumccaulley.com/.

[11] Tish Harrison Warren, "Anglican Priest and Author," *TishHarrisonWarren.com*, https://tishharrisonwarren.com/.

[12] Truth Unites, "About Gavin Ortlund," *TruthUnites.org*, https://truthunites.org/about-gavin-ortlund/.

[13] Jeremy M. Norman, "Exploring the History of Information and Media through Timelines," *HistoryofInformation.com*, https://www.historyofinformation.com/detail.php?id=3219.

[14] Maximos Constas, "'Attend to Thyself:' Attentiveness and Digital Culture," in "Hesychasm: Theology and Praxis from Late Byzantium to Modernity," eds. Tikhon A. Pino and Mihail Mitrea, *Theologia Orthodoxa* 67, no. 2 (Dec. 2022): 365–375.

[15] Holy Post Media, *Holy Post Media YouTube Channel*, https://www.youtube.com/@HolyPostMedia.

[16] Gavin Ortlund, *Truth Unites YouTube* Channel, https://www.youtube.com/@TruthUnites.

[17] Father Justin, *Notes From Sinai*, Father Justin's Blog, https://www.fatherjustinsblog.info/; Marha Groves, "An Icon? He'll Leave that Image for Others," *Los Angeles Times*, March 2, 2019, https://www.latimes.com/archives/la-xpm-2007-feb-20-me-gettymonk20-story.html.

[18] Patristic Nectar Publications, *Patristic Nectar*, YouTube, https://www.youtube.com/@PatristicNectarFilms.

[19] Esau McCaulley (@esaumccaulley), "The internet is a wasteland. I got this comment in reply to this photo. Y'all the book is not even out yet. 😭)," *X* (formerly Twitter), October 16, 2024, https://x.com/esaumccaulley/status/1846646270129328500/photo/2.

[20] Tish Warren (@Tish_H_Warren), "1,000s of refugees (many women & children) woke up today under the threat of religious persecution or other extreme forms of violence. Pres. Trump's executive order keeps them in danger. They are legally seeking asylum, which is a human right. Learn more: https://worldrelief.org/stand-in-the-gap, *X* (formerly Twitter), January 30, 2025, https://x.com/Tish_H_Warren/status/1885128113777942982.

[21] Truth Unites, "About Gavin Ortlund—Truth Unites," March 26, 2025, https://truthunites.org/about-gavin-ortlund/.

[22] Noll, *Scandal*.

[23] Charles Habib Malik, "The Two Tasks," *Journal of the Evangelical Theological Society* 23, no. 4 (December 1980): 295.

[24] C. Thi Nguyen, "Echo Chambers and Epistemic Bubbles," *Episteme* 17, no. 2 (2020): 141–161.

Chapter 56
Reflections on Pragmatics and Excellent Communication
Isaiah Lin

[1] Nicholas Wolterstorff, "Listening to the Call," in *From the Outrageous to the Scandalous: Re-imagining Christian Thinking and Scholarship in an Age of Tribalism and Ideological Resentment*, eds. Robert H. Woods Jr. and Mark Allan Steiner (Integratio Press, 2025), 19–29; Quentin Schultze, "Five Root Assumptions for Communication Scholarship," in *From the Outrageous to the Scandalous: Re-imagining Christian Thinking and Scholarship in an Age of Tribalism and Ideological Resentment*, eds. Robert H. Woods Jr. and Mark Allan Steiner (Integratio Press, 2025), 31–35.

[2] Wolterstorff, "Listening to the Call," 25.

[3] See H. P. Grice, "Logic and Conversation," in *Syntax and Semantics*, Vol. 3: Speech Acts, eds. Peter Cole and Jerry L. Morgan (New York: Academic Press, 1975), 41–58.

Chapter 57
Cross-fertilizing the Evangelical Mind in the Current Media Age
Joshua D. Hill

[1] Mark A. Noll, *The Scandal of the Evangelical Mind* (Grand Rapids, MI: Wm. B. Eerdmans, 1994), 20–21.

[2] By the language of separate "spheres," I am thinking of the "montages of publics" pragmatically defined as spheres of shared discourse around specific problems from Gerard Hauser, *Vernacular Voices: The Rhetoric of Publics and Public Spheres* (Columbia, SC: University of South Carolina Press, 1999), 30–33. It is famously difficult, now more than ever, to define "evangelical" or chart the exact boundaries of its American public sphere, its world public sphere, or the smaller spheres within it, but I do lean on David W. Bebbington's definition as a stable grounding concept, as developed in "The Nature of Evangelical Religion," in *Evangelicals: Who They Have Been, Are Now, and Could Be*, eds. Mark A. Noll, David W. Bebbington, and George M. Marsden (Grand Rapids, MI: Wm. B. Eerdmans, 2019), but see the full discussion of the term in the rest of that book. I also recognize the caveat that some evangelicals have accrued additional identity markers and values (such as creationism, particular views of inspiration, specific perspectives on abortion and other social issues, specific perspectives on the nation of Israel, and so forth).

[3] Mark A. Noll, "The Scandal of the Evangelical Mind: Then and Now," in *From the Outrageous to the Scandalous: Re-imagining Christian Thinking and Scholarship in an Age of Tribalism and Ideological Resentment*, eds. Robert H. Woods Jr. and Mark Allan Steiner (Integratio Press, 2025), 9–13.

[4] Noll, "Then and Now," 12.

[5] One of Bebbington's well-known characteristics of Evangelicalism along with "conversionism," "activism," and "biblicism"—in Bebbington, "Nature of Evangelical Religion," 34.

[6] Noll, *Scandal*, 48. The specific concept I am drawing attention to is what Noll says about the Pietists, who "had rediscovered the truth that Christianity is a life as well as a set of beliefs" and rebuilt habits and institutions for mission work, lay activism, and "acts of social compassion." And then, Noll says, the Pietists went too far, moving away from objective grounds and toward a religion prioritizing "feeling." My assertion here is that to a non-scholarly audience that may not understand or value the words of objective truth and scholarly distinctions, we must rediscover the life of the mind that brings scholarship into practical and local visibility as a "way of life." Scholarly truths must the communicated incarnationally.

[7] Noll, "Then and Now," 12.

[8] Noll, "Then and Now," 12.

[9] Candy Gunther Brown, *The Word in the World: Evangelical Writing, Publishing, and Reading in America, 1789–1880* (Chapel Hill, NC: University of North Carolina Press, 2004); Susan O'Brien, "Eighteenth Century Publishing Networks in the First Years of Transatlantic Evangelicalism," 34 and David W. Bebbington, "Evangelicalism in its Settings: The British and American Movements since 1940," in *Evangelicalism: Comparative Studies of Popular Protestantism in North America, the British Isles, and Beyond*, eds. Mark A. Noll, David W. Bebbington, and George A. Rawlyk (New York: Oxford University Press, 1994), 379–80; George Tsakiridis, "Populism, Evangelicalism, and Technology: Applying Intellectual Virtue to a Familiar Trinitarian Formula," in *Engaging Populism: Democracy and the Intellectual Virtues*, eds. G. R. Peterson, M. C. Berhow, and George Tsakiridis (London: Palgrave Macmillan, 2022), 67.

[10] Nicholas Carr, *The Shallows: What the Internet is Doing to our Brains* (New York: W. W. Norton, 2010), 63–65, 73–76, 102–108.

[11] Brad Edwards, "The Empty Ecstasy of Digital Crowds," *The Dispatch*, May 18, 2025, https://thedispatch.com/newsletter/dispatch-faith/christianity-social-media-meaning-church/

[12] Noll, *Scandal*, 106.

[13] Betty Skinner, *Daws: The Story of Dawson Trotman, Founder of the Navigators* (Grand Rapids, MI: Zondervan, 1974). A suggestion in the parallel conundrum of public science communication put forth by Evan D. Morris is that institutions of higher education add "public communication" to the traditional three areas of "publication, teaching, and service" so that innovative public science communication can be incentivized. See Morris, "Scientists Need to Explain Themselves," *The Dispatch*, May 27, 2025, https://thedispatch.com/article/scientists-communication-social-media-academia-funding/.

[14] Walter Ong, *The Presence of the Word: Some Prolegomena for Cultural and Religious History* (New Haven, CT: Yale University Press, 1967).

[15] Summarized from Walter Ong, *Presence of the Word*, as well as his *Orality and Literacy: The Technologizing of the Word* (London: Methuen, 1982). See also Elizabeth Eisenstein, *The Printing Revolution in Early Modern Europe*, 2nd ed. (Cambridge, UK: Cambridge University Press, 2012).

[16] Ong, *Presence of the Word*, 77.

[17] Ong, *Presence of the Word*, 256–57.

[18] Bradley Jersak, "Transcending the Tribalism of the Culture Wars Spectrum," in *Cultivating New Post-Secular Political Space*, ed. Roger Haydon Mitchell (London: Routledge, 2019); Matthew Fisher, Joshua Knobe, Brent Strickland, and Frank Keil, "The Tribalism of Truth," *Scientific American* 318, no. 2 (2018): 50–53.

[19] Ronald C. Arnett notes this effect of the survivor mentality in his "Existential Homelessness: A Contemporary Case for Dialogue," in *The Reach of Dialogue: Confirmation, Voice, and Community*, eds. R. Anderson, K. N. Cissna, and R. C. Arnett (Cresskill, NJ: Hampton, 1994), 229–45, quoted on 232–33.

[20] For one study since COVID-19, see Johanna Bard Richlin and Anthony Reinemer, "COVID-19 and Evangelical Christianity: Growing Distrust and Faith Among White Rural Americans," *Journal for the Anthropology of North America* 28, no. 1 (2025), https://doi.org/10.1002/nad.70002

[21] Noll, "Then and Now," 12.

[22] "Introduction," *Evangelicalism: Comparative Studies of Popular Protestantism in North America, the British Isles, and Beyond*, ed. Mark A. Noll, David W. Bebbington, and George A. Rawlyk (New York: Oxford University Press, 1994), 6, 9.

[23] George M. Marsden, "The Evangelical Denomination," in *Evangelicals: Who They Have Been, Are Now, and Could Be*, eds. Mark A. Noll, David W. Bebbington, and George M. Marsden (Grand Rapids, MI: Wm. B. Eerdmans, 2019), 21–22.

[24] Edith L. Blumhofer, "Transatlantic Currents in North Atlantic Pentecostalism," in *Evangelicalism: Comparative Studies of Popular Protestantism in North America, the British Isles, and Beyond*, eds. Mark A. Noll, David W. Bebbington, and George A. Rawlyk (New York: Oxford University Press, 1994), 357.

[25] Blumhofer, "Transatlantic Currents," 357.

[26] Noll, "Then and Now."

[27] Molly Worthen, "Idols of the Trump Era," in *Evangelicals: Who They Have Been, Are Now, and*

Could Be, eds. Mark A. Noll, David W. Bebbington, and George M. Marsden (Grand Rapids, MI: Wm. B. Eerdmans, 2019), 260–61.

[28] Worthen, "Idols of the Trump Era," 260-261.

[29] Morris, "Scientists Need to Explain Themselves."

[30] Joshua D. Hill, *The Return of Participatory Scriptural Hermeneutics in Evangelicalism: An Augustinian Philosophy of Communication* (PhD diss., Duquesne University, 2016), 357–58. https://dsc.duq.edu/etd/38/.

[31] Bruce Olson, *Bruchko* (Lake Mary, FL: Charisma House, 2006), 151–52.

[32] George Patterson and Richard Scoggins, *Church Multiplication Guide: The Miracle of Church Reproduction*, rev. ed. (Pasadena, CA: William Carey Library, 2002), 74–75.

[33] Ong, *Orality and Literacy*, 57; Karl Kroeber, *Retelling / Rereading: The Fate of Storytelling in Modern Times* (New Brunswick, NJ: Rutgers University Press, 1992).

[34] Carr, *Shallows*, 91, quoting Cory Doctorow.

Chapter 58
Toward a Rhetorical Evangelical Mind
Ben Voth

[1] Mark A. Noll, *The Scandal of the Evangelical Mind*, 1st ed. (Grand Rapids, MI: Wm. B. Eerdmans, 1994) and 2nd ed. (Grand Rapids, MI: Wm. B. Eerdmans, 2022); George M. Marsden, *The Outrageous Idea of Christian Scholarship*, original ed. (New York: Oxford University Press, 1997) and updated ed. (New York: Oxford University Press, 2024).

[2] Mark A. Noll, *The Scandal of the Evangelical Mind*, 2nd ed. (Grand Rapids, MI: Wm. B. Eerdmans, 2022).

[3] See Tom Holland, *Dominion: How the Christian Revolution Remade the World* (New York: Basic Books, 2019); Edward O. Wilson, *The Social Conquest of Earth* (New York: Liveright, 2012); Bart D. Ehrman, *The Triumph of Christianity: How a Forbidden Religion Swept the World* (New York: Simon and Schuster, 2018).

[4] William Barrett, *Irrational Man: A Study in Existential Philosophy* (New York: Doubleday, 1958).

[5] Jürgen Habermas, *Time of Transitions* (Cambridge, UK: Polity, 2006), 150–151.

[6] Habermas, *Time of Transitions*, 150–151.

[7] Thomas Gregersen, "A Misquote About Habermas and Christianity (Updated)," *Habermas Forum*, 2009, https://www.habermasforum.dk/news-139/a-misquote-about-habermas-and-christianity-updated.

[8] Theology Matters, "Habermas on Christianity and Liberalism," *YouTube video*, 1:03:48, posted October 16, 2024, https://www.youtube.com/watch?v=SjfBqMlr4rk.

[9] Ben Voth, "Secular Mythology: The Scopes Monkey Trial," *American Thinker*, July 15, 2025, https://www.americanthinker.com/articles/2025/07/secular_mythology_the_scopes_monkey_trial.html.

[10] Ben Voth, "Jesus and Academia," *American Thinker*, April 18, 2025, https://www.americanthinker.com/articles/2025/04/jesus_and_academia.html.

[11] Jim Denison, "One of Americas Greatest Scientists is a Committed Christian," *Faithwire*, May 28, 2020, https://www.faithwire.com/2020/05/28/one-of-americas-greatest-scientists-is-a-committed-christian-the-urgency-and-privilege-of-loving-god-with-all-our-mind/.

[12] Ansley Quiros, "Still Scandalized—Another Noll Review," *Patheos*, October 2024, https://www.patheos.com/blogs/anxiousbench/2024/10/still-scandalized-another-noll-review/.

[13] Noll, *Scandal*, 2.

[14] Noll, *Scandal*, 14.

[15] Noll, *Scandal*, 10.

[16] Peter Wehner, "NIH Director: We Need an Investigation into the Wuhan Lab-Leak Theory," *The Atlantic*, June 2021, https://www.theatlantic.com/ideas/archive/2021/06/francis-collins-nih/619065/.

[17] Allysia Finlay, "What Was Anthony Fauci's Top Aide Hiding?" *Wall Street Journal*, May 26, 2024, https://www.wsj.com/opinion/what-was-anthony-faucis-top-aide-hiding-investigation-0d890911.

[18] Dimitri A. Christakis and Phil B. Fontanarosa, "Notice of Retraction: Walach H, et al. 'Experimental Assessment of Carbon Dioxide Content in Inhaled Air with or without Face Masks in Healthy Children: A Randomized Clinical Trial,'" *JAMA Pediatrics*, July 16, 2021, https://doi.org/10.1001/jamapediatrics.2021.3252.

[19] Jingyi Xiao, Eunice Y. C. Shiu, Huizhi Gao, Jessica Y. Wong, Min W. Fong, Sukhyun Ryu, and Benjamin J. Cowling, "Nonpharmaceutical Measures for Pandemic Influenza in Nonhealthcare Settings—Personal Protective and Environmental Measures," *Emerging Infectious Diseases* 26, no. 5 (May 2020): 967–75.

[20] KFF News, "Morning Briefing," KFF News, June 3, 2024, https://kffhealthnews.org/morning-breakout/science-didnt-support-6-feet-apart-pandemic-guideline-fauci-concedes/.

[21] Ben Voth, "Free Trade has Failed to Reform China," *Real Clear Markets*, May 28, 2025, https://www.realclearmarkets.com/2025/05/29/making_a_case_that_free_trade_has_failed_to_fix_china_1113110.html.

[22] Paul Wehner, "An Interview with Dr. Francis Collins," *Trinity Forum*, June 2, 2021, https://ttf.org/an-interview-with-dr-francis-collins/.

[23] Henry Ward Beecher, quoted in *Forty Thousand Quotations: Prose and Poetical*, comp. Charles Noel Douglas (New York: Halcyon House, 1917; repr., Bartleby.com, 2012).

[24] Thomas S. Kuhn and Ian Hacking, *The Structure of Scientific Revolutions*, 4th ed. (Chicago: The University of Chicago Press, 2012), 80.

[25] "BART Workers Fired Due to COVID Vaccine Mandate Get 1 Million Each Federal Jury Decides," KGO TV-ABC 7 News, October 25, 2024, https://abc7.com/post/bart-workers-fired-due-covid-vaccine-mandate-get-1-million-each-federal-jury-decides/15469448/; "Covid News: Pfizer Applies to F.D.A. for Two-Shot Vaccine for Children Under 5," *New York Times*, February 4, 2022, https://www.nytimes.com/live/2022/02/01/world/covid-19-cases-vaccine; Google Artificial Intelligence, "Examples of Lawsuits Won Regarding COVID Restrictions," *Google*, July 28, 2025, https://www.google.com/search?q=examples+of+lawsuits+won+regarding+covid+restrictions&client=safari&sa=N&sca_esv=2b9a61f20e275e74&rls=en&udm=50&aep=1&ntc=1&ved=2ahUKEwiqg4aSxOCOAxVSmmoFH-flzLhk4FBDYnw56BAgDEAM&biw=1054&bih=621&dpr=2&mstk=AUtExfAsQfplOGzjmU7XYR-plGalAGtQb27IlCj8SL6XzrfLYczo3TSgzinghSi2haHzRuKdhx0asUIO0gQ8WPQdSfVaWUcbJO7Gx-C1RcrO9w4zsUQywlCJtHbBj3cDHBzWs39dNFpQMVyLh5FksozExp5GDrsiyIpCtfGSUR1iDqOymF-dwFIAT7OSw8e0G1El78YYGjMGF44nzGBiYktn7Tu-eikKRz5iXjOH1YR-4e87ikAXhqrYf4ryI7q4Q&c-suir=1.

[26] Steven Dutch, "Falsifiable Rule," *EBSCO Research Starters: Religion and Philosophy*, 2023, https://www.ebsco.com/research-starters/religion-and-philosophy/falsifiability-rule#:~:text=The%20Falsifiability%20rule%2C%20proposed%20by,existing%20methods%20to%20test%20them.

[27] The point here is not to make a point defended by Paul Feyerabend. The point is to operationalize the point of Thomas Kuhn's work focusing from a history of science of perspective on how revolutions in science tend to take place.

[28] Ben Voth, *James Farmer Jr. The Great Debater* (Lanham, MD: Lexington Books, 2017).

[29] For those who make the exact opposite claim that "Christians are closed minded," I would urge reading the following books I have written on this matter: Ben Voth, *The Rhetoric of Genocide: Death as a Text* (Lanham, MD: Lexington Books, 2014), with special emphasis on "Chapter 6: Christianity as Critical Theory;" Ben Voth, *Debate as Global Pedagogy: Rwanda Rising* (Lanham, MD: Lexington Books, 2021), with special emphasis upon the conclusion of Chapter 1, pp. 14–16, where I utilize C. S. Lewis's content in his book *The Screwtape Letters* (London: Geoffrey Bles, 1942) to explain Christianity's preference for argument as a rhetorical form over the competitive rhetorical form of propaganda.

[30] The disagreement many Christians expressed during and in the aftermath of COVID-19 is consistent with the dialectic drive of science Kuhn documents in his work. This observation does not require any rhetorical resort to Feyerbend's argument. This dialectic drive goes back to Popper's observation that science and its conclusions are inherently "falsifiable."

[31] Within the study of Christianity, knowledge acquisition is continually freighted with the risk we will see ourselves as gods. This is a primary factor in why the Ten Commandments begin with warnings about idolatry.

[32] "Global: Recorded executions hit their highest figure since 2015," *Amnesty International*, April 8, 2025, https://www.amnesty.org/en/latest/news/2025/04/global-recorded-executions-hit-their-highest-figure-since-2015/#:~:text=China%20remained%20the%20world's%20leading,death%20penalty%20was%20used%20extensively.

[33] Hannah Arendt, "Hannah Arendt from an Interview," *New York Review of Books*, October 26, 1978, https://www.nybooks.com/articles/1978/10/26/hannah-arendt-from-an-interview/.

Chapter 59
The Scandal of *The Evangelical Imagination*
Abram J. Book

[1] Mark A. Noll, "The Scandal of the Evangelical Mind: Then and Now," in *From the Outrageous to the Scandalous: Re-imagining Christian Thinking and Scholarship in an Age of Tribalism and Ideological Resentment*, eds. Robert H. Woods Jr. and Mark Allan Steiner (Integratio Press, 2025), 9–13.

[2] Mark A. Noll, *The Scandal of the Evangelical Mind* (Grand Rapids, MI: Wm. B. Eerdmans, 1994), 12.

[3] Karen Swallow Prior, *The Evangelical Imagination: How Stories, Images & Metaphors Created a Culture in Crisis* (Grand Rapids, MI: Brazos Press, 2023).

[4] Prior, *Evangelical Imagination*, 3.

[5] Prior, *Evangelical Imagination*, 181.

[6] Prior, *Evangelical Imagination*, 7–9.

[7] Prior, *Evangelical Imagination*, 77.

[8] Prior, *Evangelical Imagination*, 91–92.

[9] Prior, *Evangelical Imagination*, 85.

[10] Prior, *Evangelical Imagination*, 53–76.

[11] Mark A. Noll, *Jesus Christ and the Life of the Mind* (Grand Rapids, MI: Wm. B. Eerdmans, 2011), 22.

[12] Prior, *Evangelical Imagination*, 228.

Chapter 60
We Should Talk: G. K. Chesterton and Lesslie Newbigin
Respond to George Marsden and Mark Noll
Michael A. Longinow

[1] Dena Counts, Carley Dodd, J. D. Wallace, and Joe Cardot, "Tumult in Higher Education: An Open Systems Perspective of Faculty Reactions to Organizational Change in Universities," *Christian Higher Education* 21, no. 4 (2022): 244–263; Michelle E. Shelton, *Christian Higher Education Faculty's Perceptions of Occupational Stress, Job Demands, and Job Resources as Predictors of Job Burnout* (PhD diss., George Fox University, 2020); David M. Compton, "Faculty Attitudes and Interest in Conducting Research at a Teaching Institution," *Creative Education* 13, no. 7 (2022); Neil Selwyn, *Should Robots Replace Teachers? AI and the Future of Education (Digital Futures)* (New York: Polity, 2019).

[2] Douglas Belkin, "Why Americans Have Lost Faith in the Value of College: Three generations of 'College for All' in the U.S. has Left Most Families Looking for Alternatives," *Wall Street Journal*, January 19, 2024, https://www.wsj.com/us-news/education/why-americans-have-lost-faith-in-the-value-of-college-b6b635f2; Robert Bozick and Stefanie DeLuca, "Not making the Transition to College: School, Work and Opportunities in the Lives of American youth," *Social Science Research* 40, no. 4 (2011): 1249–1262; Linda Lee, *Success without College: Why your Child May Not Have to Go to College Right Now—And May Not Have to Go at All* (New York: Broadway Books, 2001); Michael B. Horn and Bob Moesta, "Not every student should go to college and that's OK," *Education Week*, March 10, 2020, https://www.edweek.org/teaching-learning/opinion-not-every-student-should-go-to-college-and-thats-ok/2020/03; Britany Freelin and Jeremy Staff, "Uncertain Adolescent Educational expectations and college Matriculation in the wake of the Great Recession," *Sociological Quarterly* 62, no. 4 (2020): 734–762; Matthew Smith, "Christian universities need a reset," *The Gospel Coalition*, February 28, 2022, https://www.thegospelcoalition.org/article/christian-universities-reset/; Joel Robbins, "Continuity thinking and the problem of Christian culture: Belief, time and the anthropology of Christianity," *Current Anthropology* 48, no.1 (2007): 5–38.

[3] Emily Vogels, Monica Anderson, Margaret Porteus, Chris Baronavski, Sara Atske, Colleen McClain, Brooke Auxier, Andrew Perrin, and Meera Ramshankar, "Americans and 'Cancel Culture:' Where Some See Calls for Accountability, Others See Censorship, Punishment," *Pew Research Center*, July 19, 2021, https://www.pewresearch.org/internet/2021/05/19/americans-and-cancel-culture-where-some-see-calls-for-accountability-others-see-censorship-punishment/; Vasilios N. Makrides, "Orthodox Christianity in the Context of Postcolonial Studies," in *Politics, Society and Culture in an Orthodox Theology in a Global Age*, eds. Hans-Peter Grosshans and Pantelis Kalaitzidis (Leiden: Brill, 2022), 338–67.

[4] Mark A. Noll, *The Scandal of the Evangelical Mind* (Grand Rapids, MI: Wm. B. Eerdmans, 1994), 17.

[5] Noll, *Scandal*, 16–17.

[6] Roger E. Olsen, review of "The Scandal of the Evangelical Mind, with a New Preface and Afterword," *The Christian Scholars Review* (February 16, 2023), https://christianscholars.com/book-review-the-scandal-of-the-evangelical-mind-with-a-new-preface-and-afterword/.

[7] Mark A. Noll, *The Scandal of the Evangelical Mind*, 2nd ed. (Grand Rapids, MI: Wm. B. Eerdmans, 2022), 257; Carl Trueman, *The Real Scandal of the Evangelical Mind* (Chicago: Moody Publishers, 2011).

[8] Mark A. Noll, "The Evangelical Mind Today," *First Things: A Monthly Journal of Religion & Public Life*, October 1, 2004, https://firstthings.com/the-evangelical-mind-today/.

[9] Noll, *Scandal*, 18.

[10] Nathan Tilley, "The Reply of the Evangelical Mind: Responding to Mark Noll's Scandal" (undergraduate honors thesis, Duke University, 2019).

[11] David Bundy," Locating the Scandal of the Evangelical Mind," *Wesleyan Theological Journal* 32, no.1 (1997): 157–160.

[12] Charles F. H. Henry, *The Uneasy Conscience of American Fundamentalism* (Grand Rapids, MI: Eerdmans-Lightning Source (1947/2003); Michael A. Longinow, "Carl F. H. Henry (1913–2003): Indicting Evangelical Inaction on Social Problems," in *Words and Witnesses: Communication Studies in Christian Thought from Athanasius to Desmond Tutu*, eds. Robert H. Woods Jr. and Nathan Wood (Peabody, MA: Hendrickson, 2018), 267–268; Henry, *Confessions of a Theologian: An Autobiography* (Waco, TX: Word Publishing), 112–113.

[13] Richard J. Mouw, "The Evangelical Conscience, Still Uneasy 70 years Later," *The Gospel Coalition*, November 4, 2016, https://www.thegospelcoalition.org/article/the-evangelical-conscience-still-uneasy-70-years-later/.

[14] Rachel Ivie, "Playing the Con Game of Academe," *Nature* (2009); Nick Butler, "Academics at Play: Why the 'Publication Game' is More than a Metaphor," *Management Learning* 51, no. 4 (2024); Allison Lee and Erica McWilliam, "What Game are We In? Living with Academic Development," *International Journal of Academic Development* 13, no.1 (2006): 67–77.

[15] Frederick Rudolph, *The American College & University: A History* (Athens, GA: University of Georgia Press, 1962/1990), 2–7.

[16] Avihu Zakai, "The Rise of Modern Science and the Decline of Theology as the Queen of the Sciences in the Early Modern Era," *Reformation & Renaissance* Review 9, no. 2 (2007): 125–152.

[17] Darryl G. Hart, "Faith and Learning in the Age of the University," in *The Soul of the American University*, eds. George M. Marsden and Bradley J. Longfield (New York: Oxford University Press, 1992), 108.

[18] Timothy L. Smith, *Revivalism & Social Reform: American Protestantism on the Eve of the Civil War* (Baltimore, MD: Johns Hopkins University Press, 1957/1980): 34–35

[19] Frank L. McVey, *A University is a Place, a Spirit: Addresses and Articles* (Lexington, KY: University of Kentucky Press).

[20] William David Hart, "Humanism and Education" in *Educating Humanists: The Challenge of Sustaining Communities in the Contemporary Era*, ed. William David Hart (Cham, Switzerland: Palgrave Macmillan, 2022), 1–16; Warren Shipton, Youssry Guirguis, and Nol Tudu, "Humanism and Christianity: Shared Values?" *Journal of Adventist Mission Studies* 16, no. 2 (2020): 1–25.

[21] Michael S. McPherson and Morton Owen Schapiro, "Tenure Issues in Higher Education," *Journal of Economic Perspectives* 13, no. 1 (1999): 85–98; Robert P. Lowman, "The Changing Role of Tenure at the American Research University," *The Psychologist-Manager Journal* 13, no. 4 (2010): 258–269.

[22] Stanley Hauerwas, "The Christian Difference: Surviving Postmodernism," *Cultural Values* 3, no. 2 (1999): 164–181; Richard J. Edlin, "Keeping the Faith: The Christian Scholar in the Academy in a Postmodern World," *Christian Higher Education* 8, no. 3 (2009): 203–224; Patrick Otto and Lani M. Malcolm, "The Postmodern Paradox: How the Christian Scholar has Both Declined and Thrived as a Result of Postmodernism's Influence in Higher Education," *International Christian Community of Teacher Educators Journal* 9, no. 1 (2014).

[23] Robert Kantra, "Undenominational Satire: Chesterton and Lewis Revisited," *Religion & Literature* 24, no. 1 (1992): 33–34.

[24] G. K. Chesterton, *Orthodoxy* (San Francisco: Ignatius Press: 1908/1995), 18–19.

[25] James Carey, "The Roots of Modern Media Analysis: Lewis Mumford and Marshall McLuhan," in *James Carey: A Critical Reader*, eds. Eve Stryker Munson and Catherine A. Warren (Minneapolis: University of Minnesota Press, 1980), 34.

[26] C. S. Lewis, *The Problem of Pain: How Human Suffering Raises Almost Intolerable Intellectual Problems* (New York: Macmillan, 1962/1978), 93, 95.

[27] Benjamin Fischer and Philip C. Derbesy, "An Alternate Reading of Influence in the Work of C. S. Lewis and G. K. Chesterton," *Religion and the Arts* 19, no. 4 (2015): 389–410.

[28] Chesterton, *Orthodoxy*, 18.

[29] Noll, *Scandal*, 15–16.

[30] Noll, *Scandal*, 253.

[31] Reinhold Niebuhr, *Moral Man and Immoral Society: A Study in Ethics and Politics* (Philadelphia: Westminster John Knox Press, 1932/2013); Joseph E. Rhodes, *Reinhold Niebuhr's Ethics of Rhetoric* (PhD diss., Louisiana State University, 2012); Kevin Carnahan, "Reading Reinhold Niebuhr against Himself Again: On Theological Language and Divine Action," *International Journal of Systematic Theology* 18, no. 2 (2016): 191–209; Brother Lawrence, *The Practice of the Presence of God* (New Kensington: Whitaker House, 1692/1982), 24–25.

[32] Lawrence Cremin, *The Genius of American Education*, The Horace Mann Lectures (Pittsburgh: University of Pittsburgh Press, 1965), 3–7; Timothy L. Smith, *Revivalism & Social Reform: American Protestantism on the Eve of the Civil War* (Baltimore, MD: The Johns Hopkins University Press, 1957/1980), 51.

[33] Nathan O. Hatch, *The Democratization of American Christianity* (New Haven, CT: Yale University Press, 1989), 126–127; David P. Nord, "Systematic Benevolence: Religious Publishing and the Marketplace in Early Nineteenth-Century America," in *Communication & Change in American Religious History*, ed. Leonard I. Sweet (Grand Rapids: Wm. B. Eerdmans, 1993), 239–248; Harry S. Stout, "Religion, Communications, and the Career of George Whitefield," in *Communication & Change in American Religious History*, ed. Leonard I. Sweet (Grand Rapids, MI: Wm. B. Eerdmans, 1993), 117–122.

[34] Hatch, *Democratization*, 5.

[35] Charles Hambrick-Stowe, "The Spirit of the Old Writers: Print Media, The Great Awakening, and Continuity in New England," in *Communication & Change in American Religious History*, ed. Leonard I. Sweet (Grand Rapids: Wm. B. Eerdmans, 1993), 126–132; Hatch, *Democratization*, 73–76.

[36] Ilsup Ahn, *Position and Responsibility: Jurgen Habermas, Reinhold Niebuhr, and the Co-Reconstruction of the Positional Imperative* (Eugene, OR: Pickwick Publications, 2009), 2–3; Stanley Fish, "Interpretive Communities," in *Literary Theory: An Anthology*, eds. Julie Rivkin and Michael Ryan (Malden, MA: Blackwell, 1998/2004), 217–218.

[37] James K. A. Smith, *How (Not) to Be Secular: Reading Charles Taylor* (Grand Rapids, MI: Wm. B. Eerdmans, 2014), 2–5.

[38] Lesslie Newbigin, *The Gospel in a Pluralist Society* (Grand Rapids, MI: Wm. B. Eerdmans, 1989), 11.

[39] Barry H. Corey, *Love Kindness: Discover the Power of a Forgotten Christian Virtue* (Carol Stream, IL: Tyndale Publishers, 2016), 8–9.

Chapter 61
Developing the Ethos to be Outrageous and Scandalous:
Preparing for the Inspiration to Change the World
Stephen D. Perry

[1] See David R. Dewberry and Kate Zittlow Rogness, "Rhetorics of Female and Trans-Women's Breasted Bodies in the context of the First Amendment," paper presented to the Freedom of Speech Division of the Southern States Communication Association Conference, Norfolk, VA (April 4, 2025); Loretta Lees, "The Urgency of Properly Engaged Dialogue in Urban Research in the Context of the New Landscape of 'Shitification,'" *Dialogues in Urban Research* 2, no. 1 (2024): 59–62; Jonathan Stephen Carter and Caddie Alford, "A Cesspool of Toxicity, Hatred, and Discrimination: Twitter, Free Speech Absolutism, and Adoxastic Enshittification," paper presented to the Freedom of Speech Division of the Southern States Communication Association Conference, Norfolk, VA (April 4, 2025).

[2] George M. Marsden, "Mere Christian Scholarship," in *From the Outrageous to the Scandalous: Re-imagining Christian Thinking and Scholarship in an Age of Tribalism and Ideological Resentment*, eds. Robert H. Woods Jr. and Mark Allan Steiner (Integratio Press, 2025), 15–18; Greg Spencer, "An Outrageous Scandal: Three Rs for the Future of Christian Education," in *From the Outrageous to the Scandalous: Re-imagining Christian Thinking and Scholarship in an Age of Tribalism and Ideological Resentment*, eds. Robert H. Woods Jr. and Mark Allan Steiner (Integratio Press, 2025), 45–52.

[3] Stephen D. Perry and Ray L. Carroll, "Subgenre Radio Formats: The Case of Music-Intensive Religious Stations," *Journal of Radio Studies* 3 (1995): 41–58.

[4] Stephen D. Perry and Arnold S. Wolfe, "Testifications: Fan Response to a Contemporary Christian Music Artist's Death," in *Religion and Popular Culture: Studies on the Interaction of Worldviews*, eds. Daniel A. Stout and Judith M. Buddenbaum (Ames, IA: Iowa State University Press, 2001), 251–267.

[5] Stephen D. Perry, "Religious Broadcasting in Australia: Improved Prospects Develop in an Expanding Marketplace," *Journal of Mediated Communication* 10, no. 1 (1995): 55–69.

[6] Seow Ting Lee, "Peace Journalism. Principles and Structural Limitations in the News Coverage of Three Conflicts," *Mass Communication and Society* 13 (2010): 361–384.

[7] Stephen D. Perry, "Doing Harm in War Reporting: An Ethical Call for Properly Contextualizing Loss of Life," *Selected Proceedings of the 2015 Ethics in Media and Culture Conference*, Virginia Beach, VA, Regent University, 2015, https://www.researchgate.net/publication/352107143_Doing_Harm_in_War_Reporting_An_Ethical_Call_for_Properly_Contextualizing_Loss_of_Life.

[8] Barbara Hall, Lyla Oliver, and Alex Cooley, "Spartan Figures," *Madam Secretary*, season 2, episode 3, directed by David Semel, aired October 18, 2015, on CBS. Produced by Morgan Freeman and David Semel.

[9] Stephen D. Perry, "Value Consistency in Peace Journalism: Opposing Structural and Cultural Violence through Prodding for Positive Peace," *Journal of Broadcasting and Electronic Media* 66 (2022): 623–646.

[10] Courtney Lawton and Brenda Wawa, "Hybridizing Just War Theory and Peace Journalism to Report Violent Conflicts," *Journalism and Mass Communication Quarterly* 101, no. 1 (2024): 5–25.

[11] Mahmood Mamdini, "A Brief History of Genocide," *Transition: An International Review* 10, no. 3 (2001): 26–47.

[12] Stephen D. Perry, "From Fourth Estate to Jubilee: How Journalists Should Approach Their Craft from a New Paradigm," webinar presented to the Christianity and Communication Studies Network, https://vimeo.com/1071254342 (March 31, 2025).

[13] Stephen D. Perry, "A Renewal of Journalistic Credibility through the Ancient Religious Tradition of Jubilee," *A Future for the News: What's Wrong with Mainstream News Media in America and How to Fix It*, ed. Jim A. Kuypers (Rowman & Littlefield, 2024), 87–106.

Chapter 62
Theorizing the Supernatural:
Exploring Spiritual Interaction through Social Science
Jonathan Pettigrew

[1] Pamela J. Shoemaker, James William Tankard, and Dominic L. Lasorsa, *How to Build Social Science Theories* (Thousand Oaks, CA: Sage, 2004).

[2] Francis MacNutt, *Deliverance from Evil Spirits: A Practical Manual* (Grand Rapids, MI: Chosen Books, 2009).

Chapter 63
Book Review of Beyond Equality:
Women Leaders in Higher Education
Elizabeth B. Jones

[1] Savanah N. Landerholm, *Beyond Equality: Women Leaders in Higher Education* (Minneapolis: Fortress Press, 2024).

[2] Landerholm, *Beyond Equality*, 8.

[3] Landerholm, *Beyond Equality*, xiii.

[4] Landerholm, *Beyond Equality*, 1.

[5] Landerholm, *Beyond Equality*, 8.

[6] Landerholm, *Beyond Equality*, 39.

[7] Landerholm, *Beyond Equality*, 49.

[8] Landerholm, *Beyond Equality*, 70.

[9] Landerholm, *Beyond Equality*, 70.

[10] Landerholm, *Beyond Equality*, 97.

[11] Landerholm, *Beyond Equality*, 7.

[12] Landerholm, *Beyond Equality*, 1, 99.

Afterword
Communicating Scholars
Kenneth R. Chase

[1] In his new "Foreword" to the 2022 printing of *Scandal*, Noll identifies "white evangelicals" as tending to dismiss the results of "modern learning"; Mark A. Noll, *The Scandal of the Evangelical Mind*, 2nd ed. (Grand Rapids, MI: Wm. B. Eerdmans, 2022), 8.

[2] George M. Marsden, "Response to Reviewers" *Christian Scholar's Review* 54, no. 3 (2025): 34.

[3] Mark A. Noll, "The Scandal of the Evangelical Mind: Then and Now," in *From the Outrageous to the Scandalous: Re-imagining Christian Thinking and Scholarship in an Age of Tribalism and Ideological Resentment*, eds. Robert H. Woods Jr. and Mark Allan Steiner (Integratio Press, 2025), 9–13.

[4] Noll, "Then and Now," 12.

[5] George M. Marsden, *The Outrageous Idea of Christian Scholarship*, 2nd ed. (New York: Oxford University Press, 2024).

[6] Marsden, *Outrageous Idea*, 135.

[7] Nicholas Wolterstorff, "Listening to the Call," in *From the Outrageous to the Scandalous: Re-imagining Christian Thinking and Scholarship in an Age of Tribalism and Ideological Resentment*, eds. Robert H. Woods Jr. and Mark Allan Steiner (Integratio Press, 2025), 55.

[8] Mark Allan Steiner, "The Christian Mind to Serve the Church: Thinking Pastorally about the Contemporary Value of Noll and Marsden" in *From the Outrageous to the Scandalous: Re-imagining Christian Thinking and Scholarship in an Age of Tribalism and Ideological Resentment*, eds. Robert H. Woods Jr. and Mark Allan Steiner (Integratio Press, 2025), 333.

[9] Richard J. Mouw, "The Christian Mind: Humility and 'World Viewing,'" in *From the Outrageous to the Scandalous: Re-imagining Christian Thinking and Scholarship in an Age of Tribalism and Ideological Resentment*, eds. Robert H. Woods Jr. and Mark Allan Steiner (Integratio Press, 2025), 40.

[10] Noll, *Scandal*, 8.

[11] For the connection between rhetoric and subjectivity that, building on Foucault, challenges the notion of a self (or, we may say, a mind) as capable of sufficient self-presence to function as an intellectual and moral vantage point for truth claims, see, e.g., Bradford Vivian, *Being Made Strange: Rhetoric Beyond Representation* (Albany, NY: State University of New York Press, 2004), 51–54; Gerald Posselt and Andreas Hetzel, "Rhetoric as Critique: Towards a Rhetorical Philosophy," *Theory, Culture & Society* 40, no. 3 (May 2023): 41–61.

[12] For a recent review of the term "ideograph" in rhetorical scholarship, see Ragan Fox, "Refining McGee's Ideograph: Celebrating 45 Years of Ideographic Criticism," *Western Journal of Communication* 89, no. 2 (2025): 278–297; for "god terms," see the classic essay by Richard M. Weaver, "Ultimate Terms in Contemporary Rhetoric" in *The Ethics of Rhetoric* (Chicago: Henry Regnery Company, 1953), 211–232.

[13] Terry Lindvall, "The Humor and Humility of the Christian Mind," in *From the Outrageous to the Scandalous: Re-imagining Christian Thinking and Scholarship in an Age of Tribalism and Ideological Resentment*, eds. Robert H. Woods Jr. and Mark Allan Steiner (Integratio Press, 2025), 53–58.

[14] Willie James Jennings, *After Whiteness: An Education in Belonging* (Grand Rapids, MI: Wm. B. Eerdmans, 2020), 6. Also see *The Christian Imagination: Theology and the Origins of Race* (New Haven, CT: Yale University Press, 2010).

[15] Jennings, *After Whiteness*, 9.

[16] Jennings, *After Whiteness*, 120, 13–14.

[17] Willie James Jennings, "Race and the Educated Imagination: Outlining a Pedagogy of Belonging," *Religious Education* 112, no. 1 (2016): 63.

[18] Jennings, "Race and the Educated Imagination," 63.

[19] George M. Marsden, "Mere Christian Scholarship," in *From the Outrageous to the Scandalous: Re-imagining Christian Thinking and Scholarship in an Age of Tribalism and Ideological Resentment*, eds. Robert H. Woods Jr. and Mark Allan Steiner (Integratio Press, 2025), 17, quoting Noll, *Scandal*, 181.

[20] Greg Spencer, "An Outrageous Scandal: Three Rs for the Future of Christian Education," in *From the Outrageous to the Scandalous: Re-imagining Christian Thinking and Scholarship in an Age of Tribalism*

and Ideological Resentment, eds. Robert H. Woods Jr. and Mark Allan Steiner (Integratio Press, 2025), 45–52.

[21] Lindvall, "The Humor and Humility."

[22] Wolterstorff, "Listening to the Call."

[23] Mouw, "The Christian Mind," 42.

[24] Mark Fackler and Robert Fortner, "Learning, Teaching, and the Christian Mind: A Dialogue," in *From the Outrageous to the Scandalous: Re-imagining Christian Thinking and Scholarship in an Age of Tribalism and Ideological Resentment*, eds. Robert H. Woods Jr. and Mark Allan Steiner (Integratio Press, 2025), 79–86.

[25] Paul A. Soukup, SJ, "A Catholic University: A Religiously Oriented Approach to Teaching and Research," in *From the Outrageous to the Scandalous: Re-imagining Christian Thinking and Scholarship in an Age of Tribalism and Ideological Resentment*, eds. Robert H. Woods Jr. and Mark Allan Steiner (Integratio Press, 2025), 73–78.

[26] Quentin Schultze, "Five Root Assumptions for Communication Scholarship," in *From the Outrageous to the Scandalous: Re-imagining Christian Thinking and Scholarship in an Age of Tribalism and Ideological Resentment*, eds. Robert H. Woods Jr. and Mark Allan Steiner (Integratio Press, 2025), 31–35.

[27] See, e.g., Quentin Schultze, "Jacques Ellul: Communicating Wisely with Hospitable Resistance in a Technological World," in *Words and Witnesses: Communication Studies in Christian Thought from Athanasius to Desmond Tutu*, eds. Robert H. Woods Jr. and Naaman K. Wood (Peabody, MA: Hendrickson Publishers, 2018), 252–258; Calvin L. Troup, "Balking at progress: Present Hope from Ellul's Technological Trilogy," *Explorations in Media Ecology* 15, nos. 3–4 (2016): 261–74; Paul A. Soukup, "Ritual and Movement as Communication Media," *Journal of Communication and Religion* 11, no. 2 (1988): 9–17; Clifford G. Christians and Jay M. Van Hook, eds. *Jacques Ellul: Interpretive Essays* (Urbana, IL: University of Illinois Press, 1981).

[28] For this summary of Ellul, and his view of ends and means, I rely on Jacques Ellul, *Presence in the Modern World*, trans. Lisa Richmond (Eugene, OR: Cascade Books, 2016), 39–62. As one of his first books, this provides the seed insights of his later, more famous works; also see Schultze, "Jacques Ellul."

[29] Ellul, *Presence*, 51.

Index

www.ingramcontent.com/pod-product-compliance
Lightning Source LLC
Chambersburg PA
CBHW081651120626
46550CB00010B/2857